44 Days Backpacking in China: The Middle Kingdom in the 21st Century, with the United States, Europe and the Fate of the World in Its Looking Glass

44 Days Backpacking in China: The Middle Kingdom in the 21st Century, with the United States, Europe and the Fate of the World in Its Looking Glass

A Personal Conversation with China's Peoples, Their Histories, Regions, Economies, Cultures, Work, Foods and Future

Jeff J. Brown

44 Days

Published by 44 Days Publishing

Library of Congress Cataloguing-in-Publication Data
Brown, Jeff J.
44 Days Backpacking in China : The Middle Kingdom in the 21st Century, with the United States, Europe and the Fate of the World in Its Looking Glass / Jeff J. Brown
p. cm.
Includes index.
Summary: "An intimate social, cultural and political look into historical and modern China, while comparing these observations to the history and current trends of the United States and Europe."-Provided by publisher.

ISBN-13: 978-1484939994
ISBN-10: 1484939999

1. China-United States-Europe-Anecdotes-History-Current Events. I. Title.
LCCN: 2013909214

Cover design by Roland Chen and Chara L. Brown

All photographs and visual aids by Jeff J. Brown, unless otherwise noted

Book cover photographs:
Upper left: Guizhou, Chishui, at the incomparable 76 meter tall Shizhangdong Waterfall
Upper right: Gansu, at the Tibetan village of Qiqing, with Lao Pu
Lower left: Gansu, White Dragon River with the nomadic Tibetan couple, Mr. and Mrs. Hong Bei
Lower right: Gansu, looking at the Qilian Mountains, from the July 1st Glacier, with Mr. Ye Zhihua in front

Note: some Chinese family names of people met are changed to avoid confusion.

Printed by Create Space
First Edition

Ebook is available at www.44days.net

Typesetting services by BOOKOW.COM

For my father, who is a great writer
and wouldn't play the game to get published!

Contents

Part I

Prologue

Rules of the Road: The Future

"Consider the past and you shall know the future."
Chinese proverb

"As for the future, your task is not to foresee it, but to enable it."
Antoine de Saint-Exupery

"We have come too far, we have sacrificed too much, to disdain the future now."
John F. Kennedy

PROLOGUE

Welcome aboard China's 21st Century Express!

The genesis of *44 Days* comes about from an interesting alignment of life experiences. Leaving the US in 2010 to return to China after a fourteen year absence, I read several books in succession: *Guns, Germs and Steel* and *Collapse: How Societies Choose to Fail or Succeed*, by Jared Diamond; *The Collapse of Complex Societies*, by Joseph Tainter; Martin Jacques' *When China Rules the World*; Ma Jian's *Red Dust*; *Chinese Lessons*, by John Pomfret, *The Tyranny of Good Intensions*, by Paul Craig Roberts and Lawrence Stratton, and then I translated from French into English *Tibet, the Last Cry*, by Eric Meyer and Laurent Zylberman. I encourage you to read them all. It's like getting honorary degrees in history, political science and sociology. This scholarly and riveting reading was followed up with hundreds of hours of research that I undertook on my own. It gained me a deeper understanding of the world's current events and just how interconnected every region of the globe is. Putting it all together and being back in China, I just had to hit the roads of this country's hinterland. I wanted to meet its salt of the Earth people face to face, to put China's past, present and future into perspective, and how it all relates to my native country, the United States, and my ancestral home, Europe. Through it all, my views of the world have evolved and matured beyond my upbringing and what is commonly called the *Washington consensus* - the official narrative, the status quo. And Beijing, Tokyo, Paris or London for that matter. This will bring inspiration, joy or consternation to your heart, depending on where you are in life's journey on Planet Earth.

I am writing *44 Days* because China matters to its people and everyone else on Planet Earth. The West, principally the United States and Europe equally matters. How these three centers of power interrelate in the 21st century is and will be critical to humanity's survival. *44 Days* is also about my generation's legacy to the future, which is of great interest and concern to me. What kind of society and planetary environment will my children and grandchildren live in, as they approach the 22nd century? Because of world history over the last 500 years, the West will play a key role in this scenario. With China's exponential transformation since the 1980s, it too will share an equal part, as each side writes and rewrites this century's headlines. George Orwell wrote in *1984*, "He who controls the past controls the future. He who controls the present controls the past." As events unfold, which version will most of Earth's citizens be accepting as the truth?

44 Days in Western China will be a great exploratory adventure for you to travel vicariously. I am excited to share the stunning natural beauty, fascinating cultures and amazing peoples spanning this continent wide country. It will also be a unique opportunity to take China's temperature and check its pulse, so to speak, and compare it to the health of the West, with a keen eye on past and current events, while looking to the future. I will meet and talk with hundreds of Chinese across five provinces, covering thousands of kilometers on buses, trains and on foot; trekking through wilderness, big cities, rural towns and tiny hamlets.

I have unique perspectives to do so. I was born, raised and got a public school education through college, in the heartland of the United States. In graduate school, I traveled to Brazil in hopes of seeking my fortune (1978 - I learned Portuguese fluently). Thereafter, I was a volunteer in the Peace Corps in Tunisia (1980-82) then in Africa and Middle East for eight years (1982-90), where I learned Arabic and French fluently, married a French woman and became a dual national *world* citizen; then seven years in China (1990-97, learning Mandarin fluently and becoming a father of two children); then in Normandy, France (1997-2001), returned to the USA (2001-2010) and now back in China (2010-present). Through it all, I worked in corporate management and business ownership for 28 years and teaching seven. All of these itinerations have brought me into contact with thousands of individuals from every walk of life: princes, paupers, politicos, populists, tin pot tyrants, worldly saints and humble citizens - originals all, and most just trying to survive and be happy. They have taught me, and continue to help me hone my skills at observing, seeing the big picture, as well as the nuances and details of daily life that paint the portrait of a country, its people, their culture and where they are headed. Yes, a jaundiced eye is useful when necessary, but I am not a hopeless cynic, nor a misanthrope. I love humanity in its panoply of colors and characters, warts and all… Today, this cultural curiosity and keen eye is becoming paramount in China. We can all hold our collective breath when the most important tectonic shift of the 21st century arrives: the West and the rest of the world will be playing second fiddle to the world's new Number One economic superpower, the People's Republic of China. It will be just as transformative to how the world does business as the last great continental change in the planet's pecking order: when the US became the biggest economy after WWII, as Europeans watched their 500 years of colonial, resource-rich real estate devolve into independence for tens of countries in the developing world.

Starting half a millennium ago, rapacious, expansionist and extractive policies first emanated out of Western Europe, then across America to Japan, forging the Industrial Age, and today, this economic model of infinite growth and limitless resources still dominates the world, including China. Conducting their world affairs nowadays, Britain and France seem to have forgotten they no longer control one-third of the world's lands, or that since WWII, their hubristic hegemony has been passed on to America, with its macho Monroe Doctrine, multiple preemptive interventions and overweening *US exceptionalism.*[1] While China stages the greatest bi-millennial comeback humankind has ever witnessed, the behavior of the United States, with Europe playing sidekick (still trying to relive the salad days of world domination), is provocative and not very encouraging. China has been taking the long view for 2,500 years and is watching and waiting. Historically for the Chinese, spheres of external influence emanated out from their self-perceived center of the world, like concentric circles, with waning interaction the greater the distance; the Americas, Africa and Europe were the furthest.[2] But all that changed 150 years ago, when Europe came barging into the Forbidden City, and on through to today, with the United States militarily ensconced in China's first-sphere neighboring countries, and is now brazenly bringing more than half of its entire naval fleet to cruise up and down the Middle Kingdom's beaches.[3] All of this does not bode well for stability in an ever greater interdependent world, especially with an ascendant, self-assured China, whose leaders and central government I smilingly call *Baba Beijing* (爸爸北京= Father Beijing). They too have a streak of vainglory and love to jerk the chains of nationalism, when they need to shore up support for their flagship Communist Party. What will China do? History tells us that the Chinese have never had a lasting expansionist policy outside their perceived national boundaries (Tibet and Xinjiang excepted), and only recently has Baba Beijing been looking to the exterior in a big way. Like Europe of old (and America, and Rome and on and on…), China is now in search of badly needed natural resources and commodities, and is on the prowl in every inhabited continent on Earth, especially Africa, making deals and sometimes overbearingly, friends too. Hopefully, this long history of taking care of China's internal wellbeing and territorial integrity will take precedence, at the expense of international conquest, as it moves to the top of the world's 21st century economic ladder.

The one period of history that could cause an unpleasant casting change is China's self-perceived *century of humiliation.* This was from the 1840s-1940s, when the Qing Dynasty and post-1912 Republic were weak and vulnerable. Britain, France and other industrial powers camped out in China's big cities and plied (the then) one-fourth of the world's people with imported opium. China hit its national nadir when the Japanese conquered Manchuria and coastal China, in their bid to rule the world, alongside Hitler and Mussolini. This 100 years of shame still rankles in the local press and is part and parcel of Chinese text- and reference books: *Never Forget-Never Again!* Thus to this day, it is very much in the socio-political consciousness of the people, from the poorest peasants to the princes of power and politics. In plain and simple terms, 20% of the world's citizens have a huge, historical chip on their collective shoulder, which should concern us all.[4]

With the US moving its naval fleet to China's (as well as Russia's eastern) shores, preparing to install anti-missile shields in Japan (against both of the just mentioned) and pressing Australia, the Philippines, Singapore and Vietnam to allow American military bases on their soil, all in an ostentatious effort to flaunt its hard power directly in China's face - the fate of the world literally hangs in the balance. If Baba Beijing does get out of historical character, decides to avenge their dark century and lashes out at the West, the consequences could be unthinkably dire, and the gates of a Hobbesian Hades might be unleashed on the four corners of the planet. It could very well happen, with Russia likely aligning itself with China. And then there are Brazil, India and the other acronymed BRICS countries. They will undoubtedly be forced to choose sides. Which way will they align themselves? The one great historical fulcrum that holds hypnotic sway over all these scenarios, is Baba Beijing's *Heavenly Mandate* (天命 - tianming). In a nutshell, from the point of view of the Chinese people, it means, *OK Baba, you can govern as long as you keep the country together, you know, keep us proud, protect us, make sure we can feed and shelter ourselves - and just don't muck it up too badly while you're at it!*

Ever since China was unified by Emperor Qin Shihuang (秦始皇) in 221 BC, this Heavenly Mandate has been and still is to assure peace, prosperity and the people's wellbeing, while maintaining the territorial integrity of the empire. The Heavenly Mandate continues to color and will forever trump everything Baba Beijing does, *vis à vis* the United States, Europe, Africa and its immediate Asian neighbors. China's almost genetic encoding and fealty to this ancient, celestial chronicle of its leaders, peoples, the ebb and flow of its borders and its relations with the outside world, is central to any rational understanding of what will happen across our planet in the years to come. To ignore it is to possibly risk catastrophe.

That is why *44 Days* has such an important story to tell you about the past, present and future: the Middle Kingdom in the 21st century, with the United States, Europe and the fate of the world in its looking glass, as Baba Beijing leads its citizens surging into our third millennium. China is changing so rapidly and its peoples evolving equally dramatically; it is essential for humanity's survival to understand and put into perspective all of these head spinning and vitally critical developments. This voyage and all of China's staggering scenic wonders, eclectic cultures and getting eye to eye with the country's many peoples are the extra icing on your cake. On the day China officially takes its place at the head of the world's economic table, a lot is at stake for you, me and our children. I'll be here at ground zero when it happens, watchfully observing and interacting up close with the country, its regions and peoples. Until then, all aboard China's 21st Century Express and bon voyage… or as we say in Mandarin,

走吧!

(*Zouba!!* = Let's go!!)

Jeff J. Brown, China

1- The Week the World Stood Still: The Cuban Missile Crisis and Ownership of the World, *chomsky.info/articles/20121015.htm.*

2- *Martin Jacques'* When China Rules the World: The End of the Western World and the Birth of a New Global Order: Second Edition, *2012, does a nice job of describing the importance of China's historical perceptions of the outside world.*

3- *It is being euphemistically called* The Pivot*:* *www.telegraph.co.uk/news/worldnews/northamerica/usa/9307583/US-to-move-the-majority-of-its-naval-fleet-to-Asia.html.*

4- *A great companion book for* 44 Days, *to read about the history of China and its interactions with the outside world during the last 400 years is,* The Search for Modern China, 3rd Edition (2012), *by Jonathan Spence.*

Author's note: as a service to print book readers of *44 Days*, please go to www.44days.net, where you will find a complete list of all the hyperlinks, chapter by chapter.

For all print and ebook readers, there you will also find many supplemental maps and other information that can be referred to while reading *44 Days*.

Part II

Beijing

Rules of the Road: Travel

"Travel brings power and love back into your life."
Rumi (13th century)

"Only he who has traveled the road knows where the holes are deep."
Chinese proverb

"To travel is worth any cost or sacrifice."
Elizabeth Gilbert

Chapter 1: Beijing

Doing it the hard way. I almost don't make the train from Beijing to Yinchuan. The whole kit and caboodle of this summer journey flashes before my eyes, or how to bluff your way onto a train in China, whilst breaking all the rules.

You never know in China. You just never know...

The first panic button of the day is when I stand in line outside the Beijing Train Station (BTS) to have my ticket verified. When I bought my ticket, I forgot that they print your passport number and name on it. That way, the police can verify the ticketholder's identification. Small town train stations here don't give a hoot and you can just walk in. At the very least in big cities, a controller will check to make sure you have a valid ticket to get through the front doors. But here in Beijing, the hub of Chinese bureaucracy and the birthplace of Mandarin culture, you can't even get near the front doors of the BTS without first having your ticket *and* your ID scrutinized. For citizens, they each have to present their *shenfenzheng* (身份证), or national identification card. We *dabizi* (大鼻子= big noses, or foreigners) have to flash our passports.

I must digress a little here. When I bought my first three tickets, I had to go to work and couldn't go to the ticket office. And to compound the snafu even further, my passport had been languishing at the visa renewal office for three weeks and counting. No passport, no ticket purchases. Why not just wait until I get my passport, you might ask? The problem is supply and demand. Tickets cannot be bought until *ten days before* departure date and let me tell you, you've got about a New York City nanosecond to get the kind of seat you want, or any seat at all for that matter, when all the thousands of ticket windows open after midnight on your appointed day.[1] Just like me, millions of customers are standing in line each day, at umpteen ticket offices all across the country, and it is first come first served. And when I say millions, I am not padding the numbers. Every day in China, the long distance rail lines haul an average of 5,000,000 bodies. Multiply that by 365 days and you get the staggering rail traffic of 1,825,000,000 rides per year. So, on the tenth day before my first three departures, I had no passport and I had to work. Out of desperation, I asked a Chinese friend of mine to go buy my tickets. To make matters worse, my friend sent a young female employee. So, my first three tickets not only have a Chinese name on them and not the usual foreigner's passport number, but they have a young girl's name to boot. When I get to the BTS control station, the young lady turns a wry eye and cocks her head like a dog does when they're trying to figure something out. She asks me who this Miss Meng is and I tell her she is one of my employees who bought it for me, since I had to work.[2] Big mistake Jeff. But what else could I say, that my dog ate my passport that day and later regurgitated it whole? She retorts authoritatively that I am breaking official government security rules, stiff arms my ticket and passport back at me and barks,

"您不去了!" (*Nin BU qu le!* = You are NOT going!)

Gulp... Harking back to the dynastic days of powerful mandarins, you can tell she has been waiting a good long while to announce her version of a legalistic death sentence. She is salivating, just savoring this moment to drop her vocal gavel on the head of this poor *laowai* (老外= old outsider, an affectionate term for foreigners of any race). So, I sheepishly tuck my tail between my legs and bow out gracefully. Admittedly I have a scared stare on my face, as I quickly figure out what to do next. Is my whole travel adventure and *44 Days* going down the tubes, in a badly botched Beijing breech birth? Jeesh, an old travel hand like me and I can't even leave my home town? What a humiliation. But, first things first: I melt into the massive crowd and get out Ms. Mandarin's focus, which is the long line directly in front of her.

Luckily this is China and there are thousands of passengers trying to get into the station. I count 12 lines, half of which are on my side of the station. Then, like a thief in the day, I take off my hat and hunch over, so Miss Smarty Britches can't see me standing in *another* line about three columns over. To be safe, I should probably start over on the other side of the station, but am counting on all the hubbub around me to keep this beautiful bureaucratic babe from noticing my half-hearted Houdini act. Years of experience have taught me that now is *not* the time to divulge that I can speak their language, no, not one darn word, umm, character, as is the case for Chinese. This time I get a young man and to firmly establish my total ignorance of the amazing Chinese language, I do not even give the guy a chance to second-guess me, and I blurt out in a big Oklahoma drawl,

"Howdy. How are you doing today, siiiiiirr?"

No hound dog face on this one. He takes one look at the young lass's name on the ticket and screws his eyes on my passport photo. Then he gives my face a long penetrating look, one of those Western Oklahoma, 10km deep gas-well-drilled-looks. He doesn't flinch a whisker. Now it is my turn to give him the happy puppy, tilted head *where is my dog bone?* visage. Then, he kind of shakes his head and I do not know if he is disgusted or simply amused, but he hands my ticket back. I honestly think it is my grey hair, which was hidden under my hat in the first line. The Confucian culture of respect for elders still runs very deep in Chinese (and Asian) culture, 2,500 years after his death. But, I'm only half way home baby, because he cleverly does *not* give it his almighty little red stamp. Yikes. He is passing off this little pain in the neck called *me* to the next controller. He may respect his elders, but he sure as heck is not going to get his bureaucratic butt burned for a white skinned boy like me. But I decide to push the envelope, just a little. I hand him back the ticket, almost slipping up and starting to speak Chinese, but save myself and mime the action of stamping my magic pass to freedom. However, he just shrugs me off and waves me inside the phalanx of control check points that stand guard outside BTS's main entrance. Don't look a gift horse in the mouth Jeff, you're already skating on thin, hot summer ice. But who cares man, I am on the inside. Oh, yeah! I tell myself that if the English-only Oklahoma hound dog routine can work once, it can dance a second reel and jig further on down the line.

The original BTS is nothing like the ultra-chic bullet train terminals recently constructed in China, such as Beijing South and Tianjin. The BTS was built back when China and the Soviet Union were chummy, post-WWII buddies, battling the evil forces of capitalism and the wanton West. So, several of the modern historical buildings in Beijing are in this unmistakable Stalinist Soviet style, including the BTS. Stalinist architecture's influence can especially be felt in smaller communities all across provincial China, where its blueprint was extensively adopted in the years after China's 1949 independence. Yes, it is old fashioned. But like Art Deco, there is an architectural timelessness and nostalgia that is evoked, a wistful, goose-bumpy feeling that flows over you when entering an edifice like the BTS. Considering it's almost an historical monument, it is kept in remarkably good condition, in spite of millions of passengers who pass in and out of here every year.

There is no air conditioning in Waiting Room #4 and it is lunchtime. So, the hundreds of passengers waiting for train K1177 to Yinchuan, Ningxia are in a desultory, fatalistic mood, as they buy instant noodles at five RMB a pop (€0.60/$0.80), from a couple of ambulatory hawkers. It's steamy in Waiting Room #4: the body heat of a thousand ticket holders mixes with dozens of noodle bowls full of boiling water and noodles. Like in many train and bus stations across China, piping hot water is freshly offered out of six old fashioned faucets marked, *Drinking Water* (开水= *kaishui*). The air is as dead calm as a vampire's coffin and the morning coolness has already long left all our hearts. Sweat is dripping down my temples and running off my forehead. About the only finishing touch missing is a few flies buzzing around my head, swooping in for a salty drink off my exposed body parts. I guess this dog day of summer has even filled them with apathy, or maybe they have found tastier morsels out on a streetside pile of garbage. At 12:30, the announcer mercifully calls on this sea of sweltering humanity to start boarding the train. Waves of black-haired heads bobble up and down, cerebral corks in a Chinese sea, negotiating all their hundreds of bags and suitcases - rolling, hoisted, dragged and otherwise. Like many of my fellow passengers, I have two bags. One is a run of the mill, soft shell, student's day pack. In it I carry everything I have of value and of importance. It is my fail safe bag, if the other one gets stolen, what would I want to keep on going? It weighs up to 6kg when full. The second one is a bigger rolling backpack, with two small wheels and a retractable top handle that can be pulled out to roll on the ground, weighing 12kg. I pull my rolling backpack with the masses, trying not to run over people's feet. Everybody is so sapped from the July heat that we shuffle along, a mute funeral dirge. Whatever collective enthusiasm we should have for finally starting our individual journeys has been sucked out of our steamy souls.

Jeez Louise, there is one final ticket control up ahead. There are so many fellow travelers in front of me that I can't tell if they are checking IDs or not. Out of habit, people are unconsciously holding both their tickets and *shenfenzheng* in their encumbered hands, so it's hard to say. A couple of young guys from Yinchuan are curiously asking me questions, since I'm one of only three foreigners in this flotilla of flesh. One of the foreigners is an Ivy League type doing his *semester overseas so I can put it on my CV* shtick and the other one, hmm… I'm not so sure. He appears to be the 50 year-old son of Allen Ginsburg and some lost Haight-Ashbury flower child. Where does this guy come from? Given our generational proximity, we eye each other nonchalantly and opt for simple eye contact. Foreign travelers do that sometimes when they first see each other so far away from home. We can also get kind of territorial,

"What are you doing here?"

"Hey, this is my foreigner's gig, pal. You must be on the wrong train, bub. Can't you go to Xi'an instead?"

Not to mention, one of my goals on this trip is to ramp up my Chinese language, and my ritual to do so is total immersion. Having just started my trip, I'm seeking Chinese brethren to chat with, not fellow *waiguoren* (外国人= foreigners). The line keeps oozing and undulating towards the platform turnstiles. It's the moment of truth. Drumroll please… Alright! All she is doing is punching the tickets and *not* checking IDs. I'm in baby, home free. Western China here I come.

1- Since my return home, I have since signed up to buy train tickets online: www.12306.cn. As I write this though, the website is in Chinese only. Another one, www.51766.com, can switch to English.

2- If I had had my passport, I could have given it to my friend when buying my ticket. For purchasing, they will usually accept photocopies of passports. Further on in smaller cities, where big city bureaucratic obsessions slack off considerably, I even see copies of shenfenzheng being bandied about while waiting in line. If every local government practiced Mandarin bureaucracy as avidly as Baba Beijing does, this country would grind to a halt before you could say, Ni hao.

CHAPTER 2: BEIJING - YINCHUAN

Parts of the train ride are worthy of an Indiana Jones chase scene. From coastal mountains to Inner Mongolian Loess highlands to 1km above sea level in the Gobi desert; plus frightening thoughts on China's coal produced electricity vis-à-vis the US - then a mysterious tap on the shoulder.

I board the K1177 train, find my sleeper berth and settle in. It doesn't take too long after leaving Beijing that we enter the Yanshan Mountains (燕山= Swallow Mountains) in northern Hebei (河北). This province and its mountains encircle the north, west and south of the Beijing/Tianjin coastal plain, which sits at only 30 MASL (meters above sea level). These mountains figure prominently in Imperial Chinese history, as they were often used as a refuge by the royal court to get away from Beijing's insufferable summer weather. Beijing today is fine example of that logic. The air is coffin calm, sticky, sweaty and jungle hot, much like the American Midwest in full summer climatic oppression. For Europeans, there is no place to compare, really, since its maritime climate is so moderated by all the surrounding waters.

Highways seek the path of least resistance because they are so wide and they have to blast out large swaths of whatever gets in the way. A train track though only needs a few meters of berth to plow thousands of kilometers forward. So, we are winding along the bottom of sheer cliffed narrow gorges, the kind that are rarely seen when driving by car, which I did so many times around Beijing back in 90s. The day trips were breathtaking. Back then, even the main roads and highways were incredibly primitive, and there were a fraction of the cars that there are today, so the wilderness of this mountain terrain and the deplorable condition of the roads made for especially memorable outings.

The Yan Mountains are deceptively beautiful. They average only 500 to 800m tall, but they are incredibly rugged and jagged. They resemble gigantic limestone and granite crystals that have been savagely carved by eons of senseless lightning. They are not unlike the hallucinogenic planet- and moonscape peaks that still supercharge my imagination, those fanciful ones portrayed on umpteen *Yes* album covers. Leaving the confines of Beijing, the train ride quickly feels like some wild getaway from an army of mythical, marauding Myrmidons, as we serpentine along the narrowest of gorges. The sense of excitement is heightened by the illusionary, stroboscopic effect of suddenly shooting through numerous pitch black tunnels of varying length and back out into the bright, sunny summer day. These two hours of mountain track are worthy of a film set for a high-speed chase in the next Indiana Jones thriller… I am channeling Harrison Ford,

"Where's my bull whip, six-shooter and broad-brimmed felt Fedora hat when I need them the most? Well, this here floppy cloth camping hat of mine will do in a fix. Pry open one of these sealed train windows. I'm ready to climb up on top and go for a RIDE!"

Naturally, the end of this fantasy film set is a bit of a letdown. We break on through to the other side (thanks Jim Morrison and the Doors) of these coastal mountains and onto an agriculture flatland, about 300 MASL. It looks like it is shaping up to be a good corn crop for China this year, at least in this neck of the woods. There is still a lot of wet season summer rains to wait for, but so far so good. We should always hope for a favorable Chinese harvest. Why? Because China's insatiable thirst for grain can drive up world prices in a heartbeat, and hence your grocery bill in a big way, if its billion plus hungry citizens have to start importing cereals. Except for soybeans, of which China is now the world's biggest importer, Baba Beijing maintains a maniacal policy of self-sufficiency for grain production, which causes tremendous demands on the available farmland.[1] Throughout this journey, I will see what happens in a country that has about 10% of world's arable land, but feeds twice this percentage in terms of world population. It is awe inspiring. By contrast, the United States has over 17% of the world's arable land to feed only 4.5% of humanity. Proportionally speaking, if China was as blessed as the US in terms of arable land for its people, the country would be 75% tillable soil.

My place on this train is an ultra-rare soft sleeper, with a private locking cabin and only four beds. Even buying the ticket ten days in advance, my friend who got it on my behalf was very lucky. They usually sell out so fast that the best one can hope for is to get a hard sleeper, which are open bays and have six beds each. I start talking to my cabin mate who tells me we are going north via Inner Mongolia. And now I see we are stopping in Zhangjiakou (张家口), which sits at 400 MASL and is in the far northwest corner of Hebei. Around here, Hebei's mountains can reach over 2,000 meters, with the tallest peak being Mount Xiaowutai (小五台), with an altitude of 2,882m. My berth pal, Mr. Zeng, is in his twenties and works for the Yili dairy company (伊利). You may have read about the Hohot (Inner Mongolia) milk wars, involving this company and another one, Mengniu (蒙牛): dirty tricks, sabotaged products, black flag Internet rumors, scurrilous headlines. About the only crime not committed is murder and the way they are going after each other, who knows? Mengniu's CEO is actually a turncoat progeny of Yili, so bad blood runs deep between these fiercely feuding competitors. These two groups only know one way to approach each other: fists flying. It's the kind of romantically sanitized story on capitalism that the financial press just has an orgasm over, the externalized costs to society and Mother Earth be doomed. I am polite enough not to bring up that illustrious part of his company's history, nor wax poetic about Inner Mongolian business practices. Both companies got caught up in the tainted milk melamine scandal in 2008, where children died and 300,000 got seriously sick. These two companies only suffered from a huge loss in sales and the two mutually loathing bosses publically humiliated themselves with much publicized apologies. But at Hebei-based Sanlu (三鹿) company, their tainted infant milk formula actually killed and hospitalized kids. Twenty-one Sanlu executives, milk producers and traders were sentenced, which were upheld on appeal. The punishment ranges from two death sentences to long jail terms. *Ouch.* At least heads roll here, quite often actually, compared to America, where corporate lawlessness and criminality have been business as usual for the last 15 years…[2]

The K1177 rolls on. The lay of the land is starting to change fast, now that we have passed through Hebei's coastal mountains. Cruising at a leisurely 100-120kph, we spend the next hour or so in a Loess region. In the Loess (黄土= *huangtu* = yellow soil), the effects of humanity on the face of the Earth are more than manifest. What used to be tall hills are now low level, flat mesas. Thousands of years of agricultural abuse have caused massive erosion, as farmers have terraced the slopes, creating huge ravines and gullies. As the ravines grow wider, the farmers push higher and higher up the hillsides, terracing their way towards the sky, as millions of cubic meters of tillable soil are washed into the ravine beds below, eventually flowing into the Yellow River and the Bohai Sea, off the coast of Tianjin. So the Loess terrain ends up as kilometers of truncated, human created mesas, terraced hillsides and ever changing, ever growing ravines and gullies. It is a testament to the Earth's amazing resilience that after millennia of overuse and incessant abuse, this land is still able to help feed one-fifth of the world's population.

Corn production quickly gives way to soft white summer wheat, which is scaling up these stressed-out staircase plots. I can even see some fruit trees and as it gets dryer every klick (kilometer) we move west, I spy some almond trees and other semiarid crops, even what looks like a test orchard of olive trees. They may be something else, but it gives a good idea of how rapidly this train is approaching the desert. It seems as if every klick represents a change in topography and climate. After an hour or so of this Loess geography, the land suddenly flattens out into an infinite plain and the agriculture becomes more and more a monoculture of soft white wheat. Soft wheat does not work for Western breads and pasta, but is the backbone of China's fresh (hand pulled) noodle, cracker and cookie industries. The US, Canada, EU and Russia grow more hard red winter wheat, which is ideal for bread, with its higher gluten content. The gluten helps hold the bread in place after it has fermented and risen, but is unwanted in cookies and crackers. Otherwise, they would be chewy, instead of crunchy and crispy. There is a completely different kind of wheat for Italian style pasta, called semolina, which is especially high in protein and nutrients. The science of wheat is staggering in its depth and complexities. Modern flour mills pour over the lab analyses of wheat purchases as assiduously as Sotheby's scrutinizes a rare piece of Song Dynasty artwork.

The Sun is slowly setting on the left side of this northwest bound train and mountain ranges can be seen off in the distance. In the foreground, falling from hazy, leaden, gun metal clouds, are bands of rain illuminated in grey white sheets. On this part of the planet, rain is akin to a benediction. Much, if not all of the production around me is obviously being sustained by irrigation. We are not far from the Yellow River and its seasonally dry tributaries, and I keep asking myself, how long can Mother Earth keep giving more than is being given back, century after century? The other feature of this ever growing desert landscape is the kilometers and kilometers of power lines that crisscross this relatively unpopulated land from horizon to horizon. Hundreds and hundreds of towering pylons, connected with four full sets of high voltage cables seem to go to nowhere. Can you imagine this being done in America or any other expansive country, in such a low population density area? We are talking about billions of dollars or euros in infrastructure development here and whether or not it makes a profit is immaterial. In China, the only goal is to provide every nook and cranny of the country with electricity,

"What about that feasibility and environmental impact studies, Mr. Geng?"

"And did we do a depreciation and profit analysis on our capital investment, Ms. Zhai?"

"And what about that return on investment chart, going out 30 years, Mr. Cheng?"

This all goes out right the window, because none of that matters in Baba Beijing's model of planned, regulated and subsidized state capitalism. They will probably be happy to just get back most of their capital investment over 40-50 years. Baba Beijing is totally focused, obsessed even, on fulfilling its Heavenly Mandate. Thus, it is expanding the world's biggest middle class to the furthest regions of the country and making sure the needs of the poorest and most isolated are met. What is really frightening is what is connected to the *end* of these power lines. They have to start somewhere, right? Try coal fired, CO_2 and sulfur coughing, particulate matter dispersing, horribly polluting, multi-megawatt power plants. In Europe or the US, if a power plant gets built, it's a big deal, since one costs around €/$1 billion to get online. Not exactly chump change and its installation, profitability, environmental impact and feasibility studies are forever in the public's crosshairs. So, how many coal fired electrical power plants does China build? Like *two a week.*[3] Back in 2006, the movie *An Inconvenient Truth* stated that China was adding *one per week* to the national grid. I seriously doubt that this prodigious pace has diminished much, given that China's annual growth has been 10% since the 80s, and as I can see here, there is a lot of inland territory that needs electrical service in such a huge country. In fact, on this train ride, I see several of these power plants, with their skyscraper tall, slender smoke stacks, usually two to three of them side by side, one for each furnace, painted with red and white rugby shirt stripes, and looking like forlorn covers of Pink Floyd albums. Attached to each one of these units is a couple of big cooling towers, which are used to condense the steam back to water for reinjecting into the coal burning furnaces. Adding water to the coal firing process increases the fuel efficiency. However, even the most efficient coal power plant can only convert about 44% of the coal's energy into electricity production. The rest, 56%, is lost as heat that goes into the environment, along with all the greenhouse gases and dust. What's really scary to think is that there is *another* megawatt plant behind that mountain ridge here, *another* one over the horizon there and on and on. This is the reason that China burns more coal than the US, Europe and Japan *combined.* It also has the world's largest proven coal reserves, most of it the soft, low quality, high sulfur kind. Yikes.

When the Earth's biosphere collapses later this century, as humanity follows its biblically inspired limitless expansion and the strip mining of the air, water and land, our grandchildren will look back and read their history books. They will forlornly discuss that when the world really, *really* demanded leadership, vision and courage, George W. Bush sat on the Kyoto Treaty for eight years, refusing to implement it and Barack Obama did W. even one better: he just abrogated the whole thing and threw it in the garbage, by refusing to attend future meetings,

"*There, that takes care of that,*" as Obama brushes off his hands over the treaty filled dust bin. "*FIRE* (the finance/insurance/real estate sector) *said no and that's who I work for...*"

That window of opportunity is lost forever and has let China, India, Brazil, Australia, Russia and all the countries with any industrial capacity off the hook to keep on sullying our paper-thin atmosphere and rapidly acidifying oceans. The world still reflexively looks to America for leadership. If the USA had taken a bold lead, we might have had a chance to save our planet as we know it, but it is not to be. Our grandchildren and even our children are going to live in a radically reconfigured way of life, just being thankful for keeping humanity in sustainable mode, much less *prospering* and having *continual growth* as we know it today. So go on China, keep on building two huge, filthy, stinking coal fired power plants a week. Nobody gives a rat's rear end. Actually, China is doing way more than the US to mitigate global warming, but it is a case of one step forward and two steps back. China is now the world's biggest producer of carbon dioxide. You would be too if you were building one to two megawatt coal fired power plants a week, touted the planet's largest automobile and manufacturing industries. In spite of all this, China is also the world's leader in building more costly, but more efficient and cleaner coal fired power plants.[4] The Chinese are also adding scrubbers to some of their plants to reduce sulfur and particulate emissions. And they have a few plants where they are sequestering some of the CO_2 emissions underground. But at the end of day, China is still going to be pumping astronomical quantities of greenhouse gases and particulate matter into the atmosphere. Along with America's unsustainable, profligate lifestyle, where 4.5% of humanity gluttonously consumes 25% of the Earth's resources, this is the stuff that is bringing our planet's ecosystem to its metaphorical knees. Conversely, China also has in a few short years become the global leader in solar power and wind power. How are they able to do this? Baba Beijing is using its unique *planned +regulated +subsidized* state capitalist system to chew up America's bogus *free* markets, which viewed from China, are working swimmingly for the 1%, but few others.

And what do you know, speak of the devil, I actually get to meet someone in the solar power industry, right here on the train. During this 19-hour train ride, I have to eat something and with eighteen cars packed to the rafters with passengers, you can forget about arriving to the restaurant car and sitting at your own table, all by your little lonesome self. Misanthropes need not apply. In any case, giving my Mandarin a booster shot is one of my big goals on this trip, so dining with three strangers is right up my alley. They are ecstatic to have a *dabizi* (foreigner) sit with them and eagerly accept when I ask if I can join. After all, I am only one of three foreigners I saw boarding this packed-to the-gills train. One gentleman is a farmer in Yinchuan (Mr. Leng, who I text in Yinchuan to go out and eat together, but he never answers back - oh well), one a young soldier who has been in the PLA for five years and is transferring from Beijing to a new post in the hinterland (and who would gladly blow my head off if given the order) and the third, Mr. Xu, is a guy in his 30s who works for MEMC, an American solar power outfit. He is proudly sporting his corporate logo-laden polo shirt and baseball cap, just like in the US, which turns out to be a great conversation starter. Xu has traveled to the US and is very happy to tell me about his visit to the MEMC headquarters in Missouri. He is enjoying getting to talk to a foreigner (albeit in Chinese) about his industry, his work (marketing) and how much Baba Beijing is supporting solar energy via policy, regulation and subsidies. In spite of all the recent doomsday predictions about China's solar panel industry collapsing (the Western press has been predicting China's imminent economic ruin for 30 years now), he is very upbeat about his job and his sector's future.[5]

One of the dishes I get is especially delicious and a Yinchuan specialty. It is recommended by my table mates and is called *shaguo tuji* (砂锅土鸡= sand pot native chicken). Sort of a Chinese-tasting version of the French *coq au vin*, this one has big broad, flat noodles, kind of like the Shanxi *daoxiao* noodles (刀削= sliced), chunks of cut up black skinned and black boned chicken and diced vegetables, all in a yummy consommé broth.[6] I will definitely be ordering this one again when I get to Yinchuan.

Later, outside of Wuhai, the train passes a massive solar power station and we see other solar power plants of varying size along the way. These impressive Sun driven electrical power plants will continue to be a part of the local topography as I travel in Ningxia (宁夏= Peaceful Summer) and Gansu (甘肃= Sweet Su). I also see on this train ride, along a number of mountain ridges, large scale wind power farms, which in spite of their incongruence with any natural landscape, still manage to enchant me. Their towering, futuristic, white tentacle look and the graceful, almost imperceptible movement of their three and four blade propellers is hypnotic and almost extraterrestrial - they just fascinate me. I too will see many wind farms on the rest of my trip, even as far south as Dali in Yunnan. Thus, this is the picture of China frantically trying to electrify its continent scaled country for its many citizens: via history-setting production of coal fired plants, alongside unprecedented world leading initiatives in renewable energy. It really saddens me to see all this. Just think how China would have responded if W. Bush, Obama and America's Washington elite, who are bought and paid for by FIRE, would show true world leadership and vision?

The Sun finally gives us its long, languorous *hasta manaña*, as I recall that tonight is a full Moon. The land commences to flatten out into eternal darkness, with fading mountain ranges hanging like blackened cutouts along the distant horizons. Silhouettes of power station smokestacks and low level, one to four story mud and brick buildings, in interspersed villages can be seen along the way. I finish writing my first chapter for this trip, fueled by the excitement of barely making my way onto this train K1177 and the giddiness of starting such an ambitious journey. I made the right call treating myself to a 50g jar of Nescafé Espresso instant coffee. For the first time in my life, I'm sleepless on a train ride, which like planes, usually knocks me out like Nembutal. My three berth mates are much less restive than me and have been sleeping soundly all night. Luckily, other than the occasional snort and grunt, none of them are big snorers. The train is well air conditioned, but I wish I could just fling open the sealed windows and suck in the cool, high altitude Gobi desert air. Working on a new chapter, I finally and fitfully fall asleep around three o'clock. An hour later I awake with a start. Under the dome of the crystal clear sky and the luminous full Moon, the whole landscape reeling before me looks other-worldly and with a haunting, surreal beauty. Not far from the train track is running, klick after klick, an impressive mountain chain jutting out of what is now obviously a desert landscape. I could be in Oman, Morocco or central Algeria. My feelings are flooded with nostalgia, as I think back to those ten years of my life in that other part of the world, to what Shakespeare called, *the salad days*. I only sleep for a total of two hours and awake at daybreak. What were once brick and modern structures are now more and more low lying mud and adobe structures. Off in the near distance I surprisingly see the silver shimmer of shallow lakes and ponds, cascading off to the horizons. There is clearly a lot of irrigated agriculture around here, and in spots it looks like real wetlands, almost like oases are making an appearance.

I look at K1177's path on Google maps. After Zhangjiakou, Hebei (张家口河北 @ 400 MASL), we pierce the heart of Inner Mongolia (内蒙), stopping at Ulanchaab (乌兰察市) for 35 minutes to fill up with diesel. Can you imagine how many liters of fuel a train like this burns, especially climbing over a klick in vertical ascent?; Hohot (呼和活特), which is Inner Mongolia's 'capital @1,500 MASL), then Baotou (包头), Wuhai (乌海) and finally crossing into Ningxia and its capital, 1,100 MASL Yinchuan (银川= Silver River). From Ulanchaab on, we are faithfully following the Yellow River valley and the parallel national highway G6, which goes to Tibet.[7] This would explain all the irrigated agriculture I am seeing and it belies all the stories we hear about the Yellow River regularly drying up. Is it the result of good rains, Baba Beijing pulling a rabbit out of the hat or doomsday rumors? We finally get to Yinchuan at 08:30 the next day, a 19-hour journey. Just out of curiosity, I ask the train attendants when this K1177 train was built. They tell me 2011, but I find this hard to believe. It looks much more well-worn than that. But then I mull over that every train in China runs daily and is packed like sardines 24/7. So, maybe they are right and it is just showing its expected wear and tear. I amble off the train and lazily bring up the rear of the crowd. It is hard to believe that we just filled to capacity eighteen diesel driven train cars. I start to curve my way around with the still sleepy passengers, towards the escalators taking us to the underpass and the main Yinchuan train station, when I suddenly get a can't-be-mistaken tap on my shoulder. I wonder who this could be?

1- *Baba Beijing wants to go for gross tonnage for their grain production, so decided to concentrate their efforts on corn, rice and wheat. The weight of one liter of soybeans is about the same as corn, rice and wheat, but a farmer can only get one-half the tonnage per hectare of soybeans, compared to grains. Thus, China became the world's top soybean importer starting in 2004.*

2- *Ron Unz at the American Conservative nails it on the head, comparing China's milk scandal to America's Vioxx mega-scandal that should have been:*
www.ronunz.org/2012/04/18/chinese-melamine-and-american-vioxx/

3- *news.bbc.co.uk/2/hi/asia-pacific/6769743.stm*

4- *www.nytimes.com/2009/05/11/world/asia/11coal.html?_r=0*

5- *Saudi Arabia just stepped up to the solar energy plate in a big, multibillion way:*
www.renewableenergyworld.com/rea/news/article/2013/01/
saudi-arabia-set-to-expand-solar-energy-development-buys-stake-in-utility-acwa-power

6- *This famous black chicken is called wuji (乌鸡). It is supposed to cure all kinds of ailments. Critters and body parts that would shock a lot of Westerners are on sale in broth shops, including bull penis, turtle, frog, salamander and on and on. Each one is believed to be a cure for this ailment or that. This is unfortunately why these ancient old superstitions are helping to denude the world's landscape of endangered species.*

7- *Great article on driving the G6: www.economist.com/news/china/*
21568755-china-building-motorway-across-tibetan-plateau-some-reaching-lhasa-road

Figure 1: The sublime Stalinist architecture of Beijing Train Station's main entry hall. It's like walking into a time machine on a movie set. Photo by Steve Evans.

Figure 2: Beijing Train Station Waiting Room #4. The beautiful, ceiling-high glass walls on two sides provide solar warmth in the freezing winter. But in summer, this turns it into a sweltering greenhouse. Photo by Steve Evans.

Figure 3: Still in great shape after all these years. This Beijing Train Station platform is a ubiquitous scene being replayed thousands of times a day across China. All aboard! Photo by Steve Evans.

Part III

Ningxia

Rules of the Road: Criticism

"Never criticize a man until you've walked two moons in his moccasins."
Native American proverb

"Criticism may not be agreeable, but it is necessary. It fulfills the same function as pain in the human body. It calls attention to an unhealthy state of things."
Winston Churchill

"A gem is not polished without rubbing, nor a man perfected without trials."
Chinese proverb

Chapter 3: Yinchuan

Mr. Mysterious, Xixia Tombs, Helanshan Rock Carvings and the Baisikou Twin Pagodas. Wow! What a great first day on the ground...

His name is Steve Evans. He hails from Cambridge, England. And after spending 24 hours with him, I convincingly believe that he has traveled to all the world's 196 countries, except Libya, of all places. And while I had a good laugh at his expense in Chapter 1, that he resembles the pride of Allen Ginsburg's loins, I know as an English gentleman, he will undoubtedly enjoy a chuckle with me and probably admit my comparison has an element of truth to it. The English are world masters at satire and the savage insult. But, unless it involves football and/or too much alcohol, they know it is all in good fun and are just as gracious in receiving a verbal volley as they are in lovingly giving one.

Steve is what I would call a professional traveler. He obviously has the means to not work. Some people would cruise around town, feign running an unneeded business, doing drugs or realizing some passionate hobby. Steve's passion is clearly crawling over as many square meters of Planet Earth as possible. Married for 17 years (best as I can estimate) to a career woman and both deciding not to have children, he has the rest of his life to see Planet Earth. He started traveling when he was 19. This trip will last six months, including isolated nether regions of far eastern Russia, where he has already traveled several times. On this trip, he wants to *fill holes* on the Russian Federation's map where he has not trekked, then he will go south through China to try to end up in Nepal. On another recent journey, he traveled over much of Afghanistan for several weeks (he avoided Helmud), hitchhiking, backpacking and taking local buses. He stays in low cost lodgings, has camping equipment when needed and bums around using the transportation of the locals. Steve just doesn't land in the capital, plant his flag, put a notch in his journeyman's gun and move on. He makes it a point to visit every region of every country he travels to. From his stories, and he is a very good storyteller indeed, I can see he really hits the ground and gets out all over wherever he may be at the time. How committed is he to the cause? Well, in this day of worldwide 3G and GPS, Steve refuses to carry a mobile phone and relies on his wits, the Queen's English, a sense of humor and a dog-eared copy of Lonely Planet (LP) for whichever country he happens to be in. We end up spending our first day in Yinchuan together and share a hotel room for one night, in the interest of economy. He is probably ecstatic to have a traveling companion who can chatter away and read Chinese, I find him fascinating and erudite and convince myself that I have many days to speak nothing but Chinese, starting tomorrow.

Today is serendipitous the way things fall into place. At the train station, we find the local bus that takes us near the Ningxia Museum, where according to LP, a hostel is opening up (really just a hotel) and voilà, there it is. We are just about ready to spend the money to rent an expensive taxi to go to the Xixia Tombs (西夏王陵= Western Summer Royal Tombs), because the guy in the hotel says Bus #2 runs too infrequently. We step outside and Bus #2 pulls up at our feet at the stop right outside the hotel. We change buses and the connecting bus immediately pulls up. We reach the terminus and there is a taxi waiting to take us to the tombs for the price indicated in LP. We take a chance and not pay the driver to wait for us and when we leave Xixia, a taxi is begging for customers to avoid going back to Yinchuan empty seated. He's hungry, so we strike up a deal to take us to the Helanshan Rock Carvings (贺兰山岩画= Congratulatory Orchids), the Baisikou Twin Pagodas (拜寺口双塔= Worshiping Temple Pass), and back to Yinchuan. We eat dinner and drink beer like princes for ¥15 apiece (€1.90/$2.38). Today is one of those days when everything and I mean *everything* just clicks. And we have a lot of space to move around and get it right. Yinchuan is one of those new cities in underpopulated areas of the world where illusions of grandeur must infect the minds of city planners when they lay out the streets and boulevards. Yinchuan has many four, six, and if you include the bike lanes, up to eight lane boulevards for a China-tiny berg of only a little over one million people. Parts of the two main east-west axes, Beijing and Helanshan Streets are *ten* lanes wide. These massive bands of nearly empty asphalt give the impression that Yinchuan is desperately deserted.

The Xixia Tombs are just outside the southwest corner of Yinchuan's ring road. These people were from the Middle Ages and being a proud and prosperous people, they refused to pay homage to the ascendant Mongols. So, naturally, as humans are wont to do, the latter exterminated the former. Examples have to be made, right? Their tombs look like gigantic adobe beehives and they are mainly what we have left to tell their story. There is also a nice museum to visit as well. What is most uncanny about the whole place are the art motifs. We could be in Guatemala or southern Mexico: truncated pyramids, big fat, huge breasted gargoyles and masks with fangs, terracotta pottery, etc. It is another powerful reminder of how closely our origins are related, the further back we go in human history. Native American cultural icons really seem to have roots in ancient China. I will see them everywhere during the rest of *44 Days*.

The other pleasant surprises today are the paucity of fellow humans wherever we go. And the weather – I love it hot. The piercing, tufted white cumulus clouds, contrasting against a spectacular, azure sky, really stand out at a pleasing 1,000 MASL. When I look back on the breadth of this journey, this first day ranks as one of hottest. At this elevation, the Sun's rays on a clear day are penetrating. The lack of air movement also augments the effects of Sol's power. It is on days like this we can really appreciate that in just one minute, the Sun's radiation that hits the Earth provides all the energy needs that humanity is currently using during one year. Yet, get out your calculators: only *0.05%* of humanity's energy needs are being met by solar power. It just does not add up.

The Helanshan Rock Carvings are a UNESCO World Heritage Culture Site, and deservedly so. At 6,000 years of age, Helanshan (means Helan Mountains) is older than the ones on Algeria's Tassili Plateau (3,000 years old), but younger than France's Lascaux Caves (15,000 years old). All of these numbers are inlaid in the path leading up to the entrance and if you research them, it is easy to find widely differing estimates, depending on the source. But they are all old, very old, to be sure. The park is very well laid out. There is again such an incredibly small number of visitors, Chinese or otherwise (I see no foreigners the whole day, except us), which is really a nice change of pace. This very young range is in stark contrast to the ancient, glacier rounded, tectonic torn mountains seen all around the world in places like the Eastern US, Central France and elsewhere. The Helan Mountains are pushed over on their sides 30-45°, like the geologically famous Arbuckle Mountains in Oklahoma. However, the Arbuckles are 1.4 billion years old and have suffered the abuse of numerous glacier sheets flowing back and forth over them, as well as eons of tectonic plate movement, grinding their once towering peaks down into glorified, big hills. The Helan Mountains were formed at the same time as the Himalayas, just 50 million years ago, when the Indian subcontinent started plunging north into Asia, and is continuing to do so today. We are treated to some memorable souvenirs. My Zeiss binoculars are fabulous for studying the rock carvings up close, like a macro lens from five to ten meters away. There is a very nice 35m tall waterfall, cascading down from the river coming out of the mountains above. Coming from Jiangsu, a grandmother, mom and her little prince son, replete with a cheesy Broadway show parasol, ask me to take their picture, and I'm happy to oblige. We also get to see a herd of endangered mountain goats called Bharal. We get a really good look at them up the mountainside through my binoculars. My crystal clear 8 x 56's are paying double down today. We chuckle at the signs posted around the park and which are hilarious in Chinglish,[1]

DO NOT TERRIFY THE CRAVEN BHARAL

Well, OK, if you say so. And I was soooo looking forward to doing just that. Drat, you ruined my day! On our way out, a group of grade schoolers is excited to show us some river frogs they caught in the calm pools of the two converging mountain streams. They are also very proud to practice on us what little English they know. I admonish them to not take the frogs with them. But I'm not sure if my conservationist pleas will have much of an effect. Chinese school groups are hard to miss. They usually have a de rigueur uniform of sky blue gym pants and jacket, white collared shirt, with a red and yellow scout scarf around the neck, and a matching baseball cap of these two bright colors. One thing is for sure: it is easy to see a Chinese school group coming from far away. Final stop is the Baisikou Twin Pagodas, which offer a rare glimpse of Xixia architecture, built by this people 1038-1227 AD. For the first time in my life in China, we are the only two visitors in the *whole* park. Other than us, it is absolutely deserted. What an amazing feeling of privilege and isolation. These 13- and 14-story high, medieval, stucco monsters are impressive on this mountainside, since there is nothing else within 5km of them.

1- *There are books and websites that extol the mirth of Chinglish: en.wikipedia.org/wiki/Chinglish*

Chapter 4: Yinchuan – Next Day

Unceremoniously kicked out of my hotel, then on to Western Film Studios, Suyukou National Park; meeting the Hui and Ouigher minorities and a very flirtatious Muslim girl to boot.

Steve is moving on to Lanzhou, so I need to change to a single room. The lady who is on duty this morning is acting really squirrely about the whole room switch and I can't quite pin down why. It isn't until we get out of the room that it all comes to fruition. At the reception counter, when we settle up on the old room's account, I give her back the key and it is time to put a fresh deposit on my new room. She tells me in fact I no longer have one and need to go someplace else to stay. I come to find out that right across the street is a big provincial meeting at the Ministry of Environmental Protection. She is siding with giving my room to a local person who might be able to return the favor at a later date. I can't say that I blame her, but I am miffed at the moment that I might waste time looking for another hotel.

Ah, but Sister Serendipity quickly makes a counterplay in my favor. A taxi driver evidently sees me gesticulating at the hotel attendant of her now not-so-enchanting establishment (I admit it, I give her a frigging piece of my mind). He is patiently waiting for me to come outside. Upon exiting, I explain my travel destinations and we negotiate an excellent 200 yuan (€25/$32) fare for the day. Not only that, but he says not to worry about a hotel, as he has lots of contacts in the business. It will be no problem finding a room for the 98 kuai I was to pay at Miss Demon Tail's now-on-my-list-of-hellholes (like the Chinese, I use RMB, kuai, yuan and ¥ interchangeably for China's currency, the *renminbi*= 人民币). My driver, Wei Hongwei (魏宏伟) is 33 years old, Han Chinese and married, the proud father of a 10 year-old daughter. His wife works at the most expensive hotel in Yinchuan, starting at ¥800 (€100/$127) a night. I can and do start to call him Xiao Wei (小魏= Little Wei), because I am his elder. He used to manage a restaurant, but couldn't stand all the pressure and long hours, so three years ago he started his new career as a taxi man. Wei says that it was the right move, because now his attitude about life is much more sanguine and he has time to be a good father and husband. Xiao Wei comes across as a thoughtful and caring man, for whom relations and friendships are paramount.

We stop for gas, *literally*. I know something is up when he opens his car *hood* to fill up. Xiao Wei says that most of the cars in Yinchuan run on natural gas. This is because Ningxia is a producer of natural gas, not to mention being rich in a number of other underground resources, such as coal, oil, gypsum and barite. He also talks about there being a fleet of new battery powered electric cars driving around and I express to him my curiosity and desire to see them while in Yinchuan.

First stop is Western Film Studios (镇北堡西部影城), where the award winning *Red Sorghum* (1988) was filmed and which helped make this place world famous overnight. It is about thirteen klicks (kilometers) north of Yinchuan. Since Red Sorghum, many great Chinese films that you may have seen were filmed here. It is still a working studio and big production films are shot here each year. Western Film Studios is kind of like a Chinese Universal Studios, with an oriental blend of Williamsburg, Virginia or Louisbourg, Nova Scotia thrown in for good measure, but much more hands on and proactive. And that is what makes it so entertaining. There are two huge sets, one for the Ming Dynasty and one for stories that take place in the Qing, plus odd ones for more modern plots. There are thousands of people here and I kid you not, I am the only foreigner on the set. The Chinese tourists can relate to the many sign boards showing outtakes from all the well-known Chinese films shot here. I have seen Red Sorghum (and the flicks that did well in the West), but other than a vague notion of the titles, none of the others mean much to me. Still, I am having as much fun watching the Chinese enjoying themselves, as I am seeing all the sets and props. It is a pleasure to see so many locals having such an animated and lighthearted time. It's very hands on, so guests get to sit in chairs, handle the props, or stand in room sets where their favorite actor or actress played a role. They can act out a favorite movie scene with their friends, which many of the Chinese tourists do. Given the history behind it, the set for the Cultural Revolution is a perverse blast, with its manacled statue sporting a huge dunce cap, mock WWII vintage rifles and tourists taking turns sporting humiliation and confession placards around their necks, just like in the bad old days. Portrayed is Mao's cherubic, snickering face, looking positively impish, with angelic, red rays of light beaming out from his head, like the old imperial flag of Japan. To each side of Mao are propaganda signs that say,

"Maliciously criticize rightists and firmly crack down on counterrevolutionaries!"

"Suppress spy infections like Ren Xiaode!"

"Long live the people's communes!"

"Long live the Great Helmsman Chairman Mao!"

Maliciously criticize, crack down and suppress - the Red Guards surely did just that. Trust me, you would not have wanted to be whoever this poor sap Ren Xiaode was. He may not have lived to tell the story. I also get a kick out of a horror movie set (some blockbuster called Dahuaxiyou= 大话西游), that is a haunted house and sports a huge half human, half witch black widow hanging overhead, with a Dantesque chamber of bloody, cut up body parts. There are just tons of different sets, so there is something for everyone. For every kind of Ming and Qing movie plot imaginable, there are streets and squares full of period piece façades, which replicate shops, houses, offices, restaurants and inns. Many are three dimensional, so scenes can be filmed inside as well. There are also actors dressed up in costumes playing various roles, camels to ride, theme related midway games to waste your money on, and of course all kinds of trinkets, souvenirs and junk to load up all the cars in the jam-packed parking lot. I am just as guilty as the locals and take my fair share of kitschy photos. Xiao Wei helps me out in a big way in this department, taking pictures of me in front of several well-known sets, like Moon Gate (月门= Yuemen). Say cheese.[1] Since Western Film Studios is open for movie making, different parts are shut down to the public for shootings. The fact that it is a real working studio just lends to the credibility and excitement of the visit. A highly recommended stop the next time you happen to be passing through Yinchuan.

Upon leaving, we spot something I have never seen before and that is the start of a mountain range. They have to start somewhere, right? In this instance, it is graphic and dramatic because the Helan Range (贺兰山= Helanshan) starts out from a vast desert plain, with nothing around it for several klicks. Looking like the tail of some mythical geological monster, the range starts out from the level of the plain, only centimeters wide and tall, and slowly extends itself, growing to meters, then hundreds and thousands of meters wide and tall, rapidly becoming this spectacular, jagged and etched chain of mountains. I have never seen anything quite like it. From a kilometer away that is our view and with my binocs, I can easily fantasize a gargantuan serpent crawling up from the bowels of Hades, ever growing and ever more powerful, as it slithers and rampages across the desert.

Next stop is Suyukou National Park (苏峪口公园). The Suyukou Mountains are in the same region as the Helan range, but much more verdant, with a lot more varied flora and fauna. The concrete steps are very well laid out, so I opt to walk up and then down, instead of taking the chair lift. Xiao Wei thinks I'm nuts. At the top where the lift station is, the GPS apps on my trusty Galaxy Tab P-1000 measure the altitude at 2,136m (I use Google's altimeter as well as an Android app, since one is often picking up satellite readings better than the other, depending on location). The base of the mountains is at 1,921m, thus, so I get in a 205m vertical ascent today, a 70-story skyscraper's worth. Yinchuan sits at 1,078m, so these rugged, etched, pine and scrub-covered desert mountains look very beautiful on the horizon. Once up to the top, there are numerous trails and paths to take. I luckily take one that ends at the most spectacular suspended walking bridge I have ever seen. Unfortunately, it is closed. There are pictures on a big signboard showing dignitaries walking across and touting it as China's best walking bridge, and as I scan its 250m wide expanse, hovering hundreds of meters over a spectacular, precipitous canyon, I'd say it's a pretty safe brag to claim. Acrophobes beware. It is narrow, with slatted planks to walk on, and other than a respectably high wire mesh on each side, you are literally hanging as high as a skyscraper in midair. I also suspect there are some serious enough safety issues that it had to be shut down. For the posted 30 yuan (€3.80/$4.80) ticket price, it would be a memorable round trip trek, that's for sure. On the way back down, there are Chinese packed around three to four tables, playing card games. They have a nice spot, under garden tents and the guy renting them the space has beverages and snacks. Everybody is having a grand old time.

Back in Yinchuan Xiao Wei finds me a nice room only 1.5km from the train station. It is run by Turkic speaking Muslim Ouigher (魏格) and only costs ¥80/night (€10/$13), so I save 20 kuai over Ms. Demon Tail's place. The Ouigher are from Xinjiang and spread out all over China, with their trademark being Halal noodle and beef restaurants just about everywhere. You cannot travel in the hinterlands of China without living on their big bowls of fresh, spicy, hand pulled noodles. Ouigher do not look oriental, unless there has been some cross marriage with the Han. They look very Middle Easterner. The men wear the knitted Muslim *taqiyah* skullcaps and the women are usually in a fully covering head scarf, leaving only the face exposed, much like a nun in a proper habit. Division of the sexes in public places is de rigueur and alcohol is never served in their restaurants, although commercial considerations triumph if they own a grocery store, and beer is normally available.

Right around the corner there are several Hui restaurants, China's largest minority. The Hui (回) are Muslims too and Ningxia has a huge number of them, which helps explain all the mosques in Yinchuan. The Hui emigrated from the surrounding regions about 1,000 years ago, assimilated the Chinese language and kept the rest. There is a whole range in looks, from 100% Turkish looking to 100% Chinese in appearance, but they give themselves away by being bigger boned and heavier set than the Han, especially the women. You can also distinguish many of the women and even young girls, as they wear colorful, old fashioned head scarves that Doris Day wore two generations ago, playing opposite Rock Hudson or Jimmy Stewart. Like the Ouigher, the face is left exposed, but the rest of the head is fully covered. I have a nice dinner and talk quite a bit with the Hui mom and pop restaurant owners and their 19 year-old daughter, Miss Hang. She is a surprisingly brazen young flirt and the longer she sits at my table chatting me up, the more and more mom and dad start to hang around the table. It is pretty funny actually and I get to speak a lot of Chinese with all three of them, but I can see the parents are less than amused. I eat a great Hui meal. The main dish is *xihongshi jidan banmian* (西红柿鸡蛋拌面). This is a lovely dish of tossed noodles with diced tomatoes and silky strands of whipped eggs, flash fried in a tasty soy sauce and sesame butter concoction. My side dish is *yancaisi* (盐菜丝), which is a Hui dish of shredded salty vegetables, mainly turnips, radishes, garlic, bell peppers and the like, with some exotic Chinese mushrooms thrown in for good measure. This is a cold dish and its salty, tangy flavor goes great with my icy beer. Throw in a couple of big bottles of brew and the whole thing sets me back for the onerous sum of ¥22 (€2.80/$3.50). While Ouigher restaurants never serve beer, the Hui, being much more assimilated into the local culture are happy to offer it to their customers. They may not drink it, but they sell it. And to think I could go to McDonald's or Kentucky Fried Chicken instead. What a pity… It begins to rain and all the customers scurry for cover, as the tables and served food are brought inside. This is a good cue to break up my conversation with young flirt Miss Hang, and I can now sit and work on my book.

Back at the hotel, my room is very near the reception, so it is noisier than I would like. But I am so wound up from all the excitement surrounding the trip and how well it is going, that I'm not sure I will sleep that well anyway, which in fact turns out to be true. One thing I keep thinking about is that Xiao Wei is Han and he gave my business to a minority family. The Han have a generalized, but somewhat well-deserved reputation for being boorish, patronizing and discriminatory against the minority population, when they move into their territory. I can only guess that Wei is the exception to the rule or has something else up his silk sleeve. Anyway, I pegged him early on as a really decent sort and it is refreshing to see.

晚安 (*wan'an* = good night).

1- *The Chinese actually say* eggplant, *to get people to smile for a photo (茄子= qiezi).*

Chapter 5: Yinchuan – Last Day

Museums with unambiguous messages, Chinese journalism at its worse, electric cars of the future present and an unsettling, iconoclastic analysis comparing Chinese capitalism to FIRE's version.

Next morning in my hotel room, I hit the *Panic in Detroit* button. After getting out of the shower, I am lounging on the bed, drip drying and checking stuff out on my Galaxy. I do not notice that the shower has softened up the sizable scab on my liquid nitrogen torched index finger.[1] Hidden from my view, it is bleeding all over the bed sheet. Nice bright red, oxygen rich, arterial blood. Why the panic? It is not because of the blood, which fascinates me, but it is because of blood on the sheets in a Chinese hotel that is freaking me out. In China, if you get body secretions on hotel linens, all *bloody* heck breaks loose, and it's *peichang* (赔偿= compensation) baby, time to shell out big bucks for the supposedly horrific inconvenience of having to specially handle the *tainted* cloth and wash it separately.

How costly you might ask? Well, our first winter here since moving back in 2010, we went snow skiing and stayed at a resort hotel. My daughter Chara brought two friends and one of them had a menstrual accident. It was the morning of our departure and in China they always inspect the rooms before you can leave, so you can get back your deposit. There was way too much blood to try to rinse out the sheets, so we were caught *red* handed. While everybody else was waiting in the car, here I was arguing with the big boss at the reception, accompanied by about thirty locals watching the show. Nothing like having a public forum about bloody sheets, the terrible danger the workers were being put through, having to roll up the sheet and heaven forbid, do a load of wash in cold water. For dramatic effect, the manager called down a couple of the maids, who were screaming and yelling about my bloody sheets, for the well entertained and ever growing crowd in the reception area. He wanted 600 RMB (€75/$95) and I was saying that my 100 yuan (€13/$16) deposit was more than enough. He was even citing laws governing hotels and to be quite honest, it's probably true. When I started to leave with my 100 kuai deposit left on the counter, he even began to call the police, and I don't think he was bluffing. After all, at this point the deck was pretty stacked against me, like fifty to one, with the kangaroo court reception full of looky loos, the screaming, sneering, victimized maids and a car full of people waiting for me outside, who keep sticking their heads through the front door, with impatient looks on their faces. Mr. Big Boss and I haggled toward the golden mean: ¥100-600, ¥200-500, ¥300-400, and when he settled for only 300 yuan, I considered it quite a victory, under the circumstances. I noticed the three red ¥100 Mao Zedong bills went straight into the manager's front shirt pocket, where I half suspect is as close as they got to the hotel cash register. Or maybe he kept ¥200 and gave the two irate maids 50 kuai each. As I was leaving, I flashed back to the 90s and recalled a similar situation with my wife. We were in some provincial backwater and the housekeepers were chasing us down the hall and into the reception, waving and shaking the menstrual stained sheets for all the world to see. It was like a Cultural Revolution public struggle session, with a heavy dose of shame and humiliation to hit their marks, combined with a public, hands-on mammalian physiology class. I had to pay a wad of money that time too...

Anyway, now back in Yinchuan, here I go again. My rosy red blood is still wet and hasn't had time to set, so I am able to get it all rinsed out. I hear them talking when they go to check the room and when they ask why the bed is wet, I explain that I sat down on the bed wet after getting out of the shower, which in fact is not a lie. They are mumbling to each other in Turkic (they are Ouigher, after all), as I am waiting for my taxi, but absent of any *bodily secretions*, I am going to win this round. Third time's the charm.

This is my last morning in Yinchuan before departing to Zhongwei at lunchtime. I go back to one of the Hui restaurants around the corner and fill up on a big bamboo steamer pan full of spinach and egg *baozi* (包子= steamed dumplings) and get some boiled water to make myself a cup of coffee from my jar of Nescafé. I ask the owner for a small dish of soy sauce, which most Chinese would never do; they would ask for dark vinegar. For the Chinese, putting soy sauce on a dish is akin to Westerners pouring catsup on veggies and meat. So it makes us *laowai* (foreigner) really gauche when we ask for it. The owner politely does not act surprised and refrains from putting on a scene, which is usually the case: asking me loudly and in shock two to three times, so all my neighbors can hear, if I could possibly be asking for something so culinarily outrageous. No, this wizened old Hui gentleman has probably seen it all and maintains a gentlemanly, reserved composure, which I appreciate. And the soy sauce he brings out is really something else. It has the consistency and color of the La Brea Tar Pits. I don't think I have ever seen a soy sauce so viscous. It has a rich, smokey flavor and a pleasant, slightly bitter taste that just goes great with the morning dumplings. Ol' Mr. Hui may be giving me a slight wink of the, *this is my special reserve eye*, as he sets the dish of soy sauce down on the table, but I cannot be for sure.

I call Xiao Wei to come pick me up. He is all excited about something he wants to show me, that I absolutely must see before leaving Yinchuan. But first, the museum. Wei knows I want to go to the Ningxia Provincial Museum, but pulls up in front of another strange looking building with the feel of *museum* written all over it, but looking like a huge square, green crystal. Xiao Wei tells me it's the brand new Ningxia Geology Museum and would I like to go see it? You bet. Given Ningxia's abundant mineral riches, this new paean to Planet Earth is expertly and aesthetically well done. More than just a rock hound's wet dream, it is really an eclectic science museum covering from the Big Bang to the newest technologies in green energy, with whole sections on evolution and the geological time periods in between. No mamby pamby elitist equivocation here, just the facts ma'am. Yes, one display explains, we are all related to a single species of origin about 3,500,000,000 years ago. Another diorama shows humans' ancient ancestors portrayed as extremely hirsute bipeds (modestly covered with loin cloths, but braless). And they steal a page right from Neil Shubin, with a diorama showing a fish in the sea, a Shubin-looking Tiktaalik halfway out of the water and a horned toad-looking reptile up on land.[2] So nice to see science portrayed in such a matter of fact way, absent of all spurious and illegitimate controversy. We still have enough time to see the Provincial Museum, which is also free to enter. The Chinese must just love to poke fun at creation myths. This museum also extensively covers Homo speciation and even has a series of bronze statues depicting our early ancestors as knuckle crawling ape quadrupeds, with future species slowly evolving into bipeds and becoming less and less hirsute. Just the facts, ma'am...

Wei and I have a really strange experience before leaving. A shortish, obese and heavily sweating young man, with a very expensive, gunslinger's Canon 35mm camera approaches us and asks to take our picture. As a *waiguoren* (foreigner), I am used to being asked to have my picture taken with the locals. I have no idea what they plan to do later with my mug standing next to them, but it's one of those rituals that I take in stride. But this guy is different. Mr. Peng Zhaozhi wants us to pose for a shot and not just any shot. He wants Wei and me to act like we are looking at and pointing towards an exhibit in the museum. We ask why and he explains he is a journalist and needs a picture for his newspapers, Xinhuawang (新华网) and Xinhua Meiri Dianxun (新华每日电讯). Xinhua is the government's press organ and these are their online venues. Well, why not? So very rotund Peng takes a few shots of us gamely pointing at some non-descript poster on the wall (we happen to be in the section about Mao Zedong and his pre-independence exploits), trying to look like we are mulling over the weightiest of metaphysical Communist theory conundrums. Peng's sweat glands are so profuse that he has to wipe his impressive camera with a handkerchief when he gets finished. Poor guy. So naturally, I expect him to now get out his notepad to ask us our names and find out a little background on us, to give the picture some social color and humanity to complete the article. That's what journalists do, right? No, Peng can't be bothered. All he wants is the photo. So we say our goodbyes. But later, I realize this is one picture I can see what happens to it. I get on Xinhua's website and search his name and filter for July. He is obviously the agency's photojournalist in Yinchuan, as he is getting about ten or so photos online each month. But apparently, our vapid attempt to exhibit philosophical political ruminations was wholly transparent, as our photo did *not* make it online.

After learning that many of Yinchuan's cars run on natural gas, Wei casually mentioned yesterday that Yinchuan started to roll out electric cars three months ago. They are starting with twenty-eight e-taxis and have built two *filling* stations.

Needlessly to say, my curiosity is more than piqued and it is something I just have to see. This is his big surprise he wants to show me. We pull up to the battery station at a good time, as an electric taxi is about to *fill 'er up*. But instead of plugging in, he just swaps out the batteries in the back of his car. The station is owned by China's national electric company, the State Grid. Here is how it works: There are four batteries, each weighing 65kg. There is a bank of around forty batteries connected to the grid that take only two hours to fully charge. Each charge keeps a taxi going around town for 80-90km; they are designed to go 100km, so they've got some R&D to reach this goal. Two station employees come bouncing out of their little office, one notes the kilometers driven while the other notes the printed stock number of each returning battery and locates and logs four fully charged ones in the bank. How do you effortlessly and quickly swap out 260kg of batteries, so this driver can get back on the streets and start collecting fares again? They have an electric pan lift with little steel ball rollers built in the surface and each green (naturally) battery has a grip handle on its end, where it is exposed when you open the back hatch. With a little pull, once the battery hits the rollers, they become essentially weightless, and it takes only five minutes to change out the four batteries. Pretty impressive. And off the fully charged taxi goes, silently and cleanly. Next to the battery station is a full-fledged filling station with 600 volt/200 amp *pumps*. I see a city bus and a fleet of about twenty cars, including Chevrolets. This is phase two of an ambitious program to electrify China's motor fleet.

Baba Beijing is not messing around. They are already building the infrastructure to put five million electric cars on China's streets by 2020. The central government is offering a ¥60,000 (€7,500/$9,500) direct subsidy for the Chinese to buy e-cars and Beijing City just offered its citizens a matching grant of the same amount. Every other major metropolitan center on down to little burgs the size of Yinchuan is getting in on the action. This is a country that in just twenty short years - one generation, has installed thousands of klicks of urban subway lines, 9,300km of 300kph bullet train lines, put hundreds of thousands of city and interurban buses on tens of thousands of kilometers of streets and four lane highways, all for the betterment of China's poor, working and middle classes.[3] Let's not forget that for the jet set, China has also built one of the world's largest airline industries in the same time period. How is China able to do this, you might ask? Like its electric power generating plants and renewable energy sectors, China's markets and banks are not free at all. The heavy hand of government intervention and regulation, long term planning and the willingness to subsidize industries that benefit the country's poor and exploding middle class are beating and will continue to whip the West's supposedly free markets, every step of the 21st century.

It is vexing to watch, because it appears that the West, especially the US and its diminishing list of international allies, will finally put two and two together when it's too late, and China and its growing list of acolytes will be there to fill the breech, as the Middle Kingdom assumes the mantle of the world's reigning economic superpower. It must be said that the US royally deserves to fall hard, with its printing presses cranking out trillions of fiat dollars to keep afloat insolvent too-big-to-fail banks. This paper money is also being used to finance eight hundred or so military installations around the world and these are being used to conduct war in more and more countries, in a last ditch effort to force a *Bellum Americana* on a growing list of mostly poor and defenseless Muslim countries. What is so easy to see after spending five years in France and nine years in the US, most of those being a business owner, and now living in China, is that America's version of libertarian, robber baron, FIRE capitalism is not working for anybody but these thieves. Europe still has a sense of humanity, but is being brow beaten by these same crooks to succumb to the banksters' world order. Look no further than Greece, Italy, Spain, Ireland, etc.

From 1880 to 1930, the United States went through an eerily similar cycle of economic plundering, massive vacuum cleaning of the country's natural and human resources into the pockets of the 1%, the concomitant populist revolts by the 99%, rampant government corruption, along with the expected wars and international incursions. It was called the Gilded Age. A careful reading of the final century of Imperial Rome shows the same scenario: the 1% unscathed, the 99% being overtaxed and paid in coins with higher and higher levels of lead, instead of silver and gold. This diluted money was used to pay for *surges* of military expansion, to maintain internal order and increasingly desperate attempts to repulse barbarian tribes along the borders. In desperation, many citizens began defecting to join the barbarian invaders, the Western Empire collapsed and the Eastern Empire was subsumed by German tribes. When the plundering of America begins to deliver less and less marginal returns, its 1%, many who carry passports from Belize, Costa Rica and the Bahamas, will bring down the United States in the same fashion they did in 1929, mark my word. Back then, they had no other place to go. Now they can hop on their jets, carpetbag in their newly adopted countries, and they'll do exactly that. They couldn't care less about United States or its people (nor the planet and the fate of humanity for that matter). Please spare me the ideological mumbo jumbo and zip the worthless whining about how unfair it is that China is not playing by America's rules, nor bowing to Firemen's protestations. Which capitalist system is benefitting the greatest percentage of its citizens, especially the poor, working and middle classes? China's state version or the United States' jungle one? Riding on bullet trains and partaking in China's infrastructural development everywhere I go, I know the answer empirically. I am living it and am deeply disappointed in my native and ancestral homes. Just the facts ma'am...

1- *Two weeks before taking off, I gave my very popular liquid nitrogen show to all the students where I teach. Unfortunately, I really badly burned the first digit of my right index finger - a serious 3rd degree eyesore. It took weeks to heal and to this day, I have lost sensation in this finger. I'll be more careful next time.*

2- Your Inner Fish, *by Neil Shubin is a fascinating and informative lay person's voyage of our human bodies' origins, going back billions of years. With lots of drawings, it is easy to understand. He is the paleontologist famous for discovering the Tiktaalik fossil, the half-water, half-land link that anti-evolutionists said would never be found. Oops.*

3- *Baba Beijing will install a planned 20,000km of bullet train lines by 2030. One can now take a bullet train from Beijing to Guangzhou (2,300km), and soon to Urumuqi in far Western China (3,172km), but not from LA to San Francisco (614km), nor New York to Boston (345km). As an American, this is just embarrassing and sad...*

Chapter 6: Zhongwei - Shapotou

Riding on the back of a Vespa to my farm house room and its bucolic calm, before the tourist madness on the Yellow River.

I did not buy my train ticket from Yinchuan to Zhongwei (中卫) the day they were available for sale, so I got a *no seat* ticket. When you buy an SRO (standing room only) ticket, you pay the same price as hard seats (which truth be told, are padded these days; they are just more narrow than the soft seats). Then you take your chances dog fighting with the hoi polloi to get an unclaimed seat. In the charge of the heavy brigade onto the train, I just assume that empty seats are a pipe dream and plant myself on my tripod folding seat in the area where people wash their hands. When a train steward comes by, she tells me there are empty seats in Car #2; I am in Car #8. No sooner do I enter Car #7 that I find an empty seat anyway, which is a surprise to me. I suspect some of it has to do with fact that this is only a two-hour ride and leaves several times a day. Zhongwei here I come. One entertaining thing, although it can border on being irritating at times, is all the stuff the stewards are flogging for sale up and down the aisle. They move through the train, selling belts, credit card sleeves, battery powered, handheld body massage gloves, toys, puzzles - it's like an extended, live infomercial at the Barnum & Bailey Circus. This is obviously for their personal profit and a way to supplement their more than likely meager income as train employees. It is fun to watch them hustle the crowd and flog their wares, especially toys to the kids.

After getting to Zhongwei, I take a motorized surrey (I kid you not, just like in the musical *Oklahoma*, it really has a fringe on top) to China Unicom, to pay my mobile bill. This month it is especially important, since I expanded my plan to 2GB, as I am using my 3G Galaxy so much. While China has over one billion mobile phones in service and a wireless network covering the four corners of the country, it is hardly seamless. While not as balkanized as the bad old days in the 80s, when the pioneering US had cell phones that only worked in their small cellular areas (hence the name), the back office and administration in China leave much to be desired. At the Zhongwei China Unicom service store, they can pull up my account on their screens, but cannot let me pay or make any changes. While there, I discover they have my wife's and daughter's names, passport and phone numbers switched. But in security conscious China under Baba Beijing's omnipresent eye, they tell me I have to go back to the original Beijing store where I bought the SIM cards and show them all three passports. There they can check our ID photocopies on file and then and only then, can we get the records corrected. So, all I can do today is buy charge up cards, 50 kuai each to pay my bill, so I need twelve of them. I then have to input on my Galaxy two long numbers on each card, in order to pay my account. This takes about 15 minutes. I find this same system of balkanization in banking later, when I'm in Gansu. Bank of China is one of the biggest banks on the planet, yet going into a branch outside of my hometown Beijing is like being at a competitor's. I have to pay a 1% fee to transfer money from my savings to my debit card account, at *my own* bank. Later towards the end of this journey, I say to heck with that, get a hotel room in Guizhou with a computer and transfer online my own money between my own accounts for *free*. Jeez Louise. I guess they are trying to encourage online banking, but how many millions of rural Chinese don't have PCs at home? Bank of China does not allow mobile phone banking, so it's either a face to face visit or a computer.

Zhongwei is a nice town, but Shapotou is where the action is, so I immediately take a city bus there. I have to tip my hat to my surrey driver. He kindly waits for me to pay my phone bill and then takes me to the Shapotou bus stop. The bus has just taken off and is coming our way and he flags down the bus to get the driver to stop in the middle of the street, so I can get on. Nice touch. Everywhere I go these parts, the cost to ride the city bus is only one to two yuan (€0.13-€0.26/$0.16-$0.32).

Like the metro in Beijing, which is also only ¥2, I suspect they are being subsidized to make them affordable for the 99%. I have no idea what to expect, because Shapotou is a well-known tourist mecca, but my first impression riding out there is how much water there is here in the middle of a desert. We drive along a huge, wide irrigation canal filled to the max, which is sustaining wetland rice, wheat, barley, vegetable and fruit production. Knowing the mighty Yellow River is not far away, I am again scratching my head about all these stories that the Yellow River is drying up. Definitely not the case this far up stream. There are stone markers along the canal with its name, *Meili* (美丽= Beautiful). After the relative peace and quiet in Yinchuan, Shapotou is a three-ring circus of crass tourism. The place is teeming with thousands of local tourists and other than an elderly Aussie couple, I am the only *dabizi* in the area. It is remarkable to look at all the license plates in the parking lot. It is not unlike seeing all the cars at a major tourist attraction in the US or Europe: a quick survey shows that people are coming from the four corners of the country, and like I just said, there isn't a black-plated foreigner's car to be found, which are easy to distinguish from the Chinese's blue tags. Once inside the visitor's center and meeting the people behind the information desk, there is a lot of pressure as a foreigner to stay at the very expensive tourist hotel right outside the park complex, but I know with all these Chinese tourists thronging the place, there has to be more options. I just flat out tell the manager of the visitor's center that I am not your typical tourist and I cannot stay in such an expensive hotel. He kind of tells me under his breath, like we are not supposed to be privy to such priceless information,

"Well, there are some farm houses to stay at, but you know, *waiguoren* really are supposed to spend their money at the expensive hotel."

Not for me, Daddy-O, please give me farmer Ting's phone number so I can confirm a room. I dial it up and we agree on the phone for a discount to 80 yuan a night (€10/$13, discounted from ¥100). I am flattered when he shows up and his jaw drops when he sees I am a *laowai*. My Chinese is reaching enough fluency that he did not know until he arrived that I am not Chinese. My mastery of Mandarin's four tones leaves a lot to be desired, but that is true for about a half a billion Chinese, so I am in good company. Language fluency aside, he refuses to take me, saying it is against the law for him to accept foreigners. Farmer Ting takes off like a scaredy cat. I think the visitor's center employees are a little embarrassed and I can see them making phone calls. They tell me to wait for a few minutes. Fifteen minutes while away. I kind of forget about the whole drama and am working on *44 Days*, when I get a fast tap on the shoulder and a young and atypically plump women asks me to come with her. I ask her name and she just says *Gao*. Ms. Gao is in her early 20s and by Chinese standards is truly exotic. Olive skinned, rotund, with a sizable bust and sporting big round gypsy eyes, she looks more like a colorful character from the pages of a Victor Hugo novel. She comes across as almost the archetypal anti-Han. Then I remember we are in Hui country and assume she can't be bothered with the Doris Day head scarf get up. I get a big smile on my face along with a silent, jolly chuckle when Gao points to her vehicle and says that we will be going to her farm on *this* - a sporty white Vespa scooter. Gao is not petite, neither am I, nor my rolling backpack, and Vespas are not very big, so I am sure we will have to make two trips. Not at all, Gao tells me confidently, grabbing my rolling back pack, slinging it in front between her legs and telling me to hop on the back. I see she can barely get her foot to touch the pedal on the right, but what the heck, I am sure she has done this before. She goes tearing off and I grab onto her shoulders to keep from falling off. Since other farmers apparently don't take foreigners and I'm the only one in a sea of locals, needless to say, Gao and I stick out like a sore thumb.

"Look, a *waiguoren*."

"See Gao with an old foreigner!"

"Hey Gao, who is that?"

I can overhear them shouting out and see them pointing and waving to us as we pass. The whole scene is a hoot for me and Gao seems to be taking it in her stride. She luckily has the good sense to keep her hands on the handlebars, not wave to anybody and mostly keeps her eyes on the road, although I can see her turning her head and smiling to them. Her farm is only 3km from Shapotou. We agree to the discounted price of 80 yuan (€10/$13), instead of 100 and she takes me to Room 2 of two. It is cavernous and has a huge raised traditional Chinese bed that can comfortably sleep four. It is already later in the afternoon, so Shapotou will have to wait until tomorrow. Gao suggests I take a rest until dinner and I'm happy to oblige her. Gao's farm is the anti-universe of Shapotou. Absolute calm and quiet rule the day here, and what a welcome ambiance after the seething madness at the visitor's center and the thousands of tourists crawling over each other outside the main park entrance. Towards dinner time, I go sit under the big shaded veranda, where the dining tables are. A young man, Mr. Zhang and his female cohort are alternately taking care of a two year-old boy named Tonghao, and busily preparing dinner for us. Gao has disappeared for the time being; probably out looking for other customers.

I order off the menu a dish with eggs and the young woman walks off to another farm home about one hundred meters away and comes back with a sack full of just laid eggs. Talk about farm fresh. Mr. Zhang is a good cook; the food is well prepared, seasoned and very tasty. Nothing fancy or noteworthy, just a good mixture of veggies, meat and tofu. Tonghao is anywhere and everywhere, keeping us all on our toes. He can tell I'm different and for the longest time just looks at me in amazement when I asked him questions in Chinese. But we become buddies and by the end of the evening, Tonghao is talking to me. As I look around my surroundings, I see walnut trees already bearing fruit, sunflowers, vegetables of all kinds, apricot and peach trees and ornamental flowers along some of the plot borders. Yellow River irrigation water has this place teeming with life, fecund and fertile. It is breathtakingly calm. The only sound is the almost imperceptible hum of an aquarium pump. I go to investigate and see that Gao has a big, deep bathtub sized holding tank with a few large, plump carp getting a constant flow of fresh irrigation water. Any thought of doing star gazing with my binoculars is a moot point. After the first brilliantly lucid day in Yinchuan, it has been and continues to be overcast. I'm not complaining. At over 1,000 MASL, it is keeping the days in the upper 20s to 30° max, which is making for very comfortable weather to walk and hike in. As I fall asleep, I can hear that Gao's hustling has paid off. A car pulls up to Room 1 and a group of people noisily pile out, as they make their way inside. The last sign of life I hear is a farm dog balefully howling at the rising gibbous moon. I sleep the sonorous dreams of cool, dry, high altitude, country fresh air.

Chapter 7: Shapotou

Disneyland along the Yellow River and atop Gobi Desert sand dunes. I'm adopted by a Chinese family for the day. Also, I relish putting a little local harpy in her place.

At Gao's farmhouse, I wake up to the pastoral tranquility of two or three roosters competing for airtime in the nearby farms. This peace and calm is all I will have for the rest of the day, after running the tourist gauntlet of Shapotou. We have to wait a couple of hours before starting out, as these first few days of overcast skies bear desert fruit and we get a nice downpour to cool things off even more. When you don't want rain, the desert is a good place to be, since it usually does not last very long. While waiting, Gao and company invite me to breakfast, along with the late arriving group in Room 1. They are Mr. Wu and Mrs. Yang, along with their teenage son, Jianzhi and Mr. Wu's parents, who are retired farmers. Mr. Wu and Ms. Yang are your typical 21st century Chinese middle class family: the peasant parents have survived the double insanity and social cannibalism of the 50s' Great Leap Forward and the 60-70s' Cultural Revolution, and their children's generation is driving a new family van (Chinese Chery brand), owns a nice apartment and has nice white collar jobs, in their case, the pharmaceutical and insurance industries, respectively. But I can tell that Wu and Yang grew up in poverty: they are real skinflints. When we go to park his car at Shapotou, he tries really hard to not pay the ¥5 (€0.60/$80) fee and lies through his front teeth, telling the attendant,

"You'll see, I'll be coming back out in just a few minutes, after I drop off all these people."

This of course, even though he is going with his family to the park for the day. And he gets away with it. All that for five kuai. But I have to be indulgent, since they are graciously inviting me to spend the day with them and be an adopted member of the family. And they prove to be really generous and convivial with me, from start to finish.

Shapotou (沙坡头= Sandy Hilltop) is like a gigantic desert amusement park and its midway is the Yellow River (黄河= Huanghe). Similar to any amusement park, there are set pieces, set rides and set activities. It is not unlike going to Disneyland - just add a huge, historically famous river in the middle of it, surround it by towering sand dunes and voilà. If striking out on your own and exploring in solitude a cozy corner of our Pale Blue Dot is your absolute requirement, then don't go to Shapotou. It is a barking human zoo. Would I bring my family here? Probably not. Do I plan on coming back for Day 2? Hmm… I might come back and hang out at Ms. Gao's farm to chillax in the high altitude desert air. As for today, it is fascinating to be here with all the thousands of Chinese who are taking the summer vacation of their lives. People are having fun and are very excited to be at Shapotou. So, from a standpoint of living the local culture, you cannot ask for more. Thus all told, it is a grand slam success and something I really enjoy doing. First step is everybody puts on a life preserver and goes upstream on the Yellow River, about two klicks in an outboard motor boat. I grew up water skiing, so it brings back a lot of fun memories for me. It is easy to see that the level of excitement is very high among the Chinese and that this is a special treat for them. It is a smoothly run and highly coordinated operation. Thousands of people are being transported each day in these ski boats and each one can only hold about ten passengers. Once we disembark at the other dock upstream, we are looking at a big sand dune bank that flanks the river's coastline through this area. Momma Yang and son Jianzhi elect to climb up the steep sand embankment and the rest of us take the big enclosed escalator, like the ones on Hong Kong Island. Once up top, the massive river valley is incredibly photogenic. To the north are sand dunes. To the west are towering craggy cliff faces where the Yellow River has, over thousands of years, carved an arcing, curved gouge out of the Earth's face. Unfortunately, further east, back towards Zhongwei, are the silhouettes of several low-tech factory chimneys, belching out gray-white plumes of smoke, wafting hundreds of meters towards the sky. Ah, the sweet smell of progress, jobs and production of goods. Across the river to the south is a large land reclamation project, consisting of expansive plots of bamboo and reed looking stands, with deciduous trees along their periphery. This area is one of many where the Chinese have said,

"*No more desertification!*"

They are putting a lot of human, financial and natural resources in keeping the Gobi dunes from hopping the river to the south. The dunes have obviously made it right up to the north shore of the Yellow River at Shapotou, after all, I'm standing on one, which makes for good tourism. From this breathtaking top-of-the-sand-dune view, we have several options to go back down. There is a chair lift, one can slide down sitting in a big lens-shaped bowl, or the coolest way is to ride a two stage zip line, hanging and flying all the way across the Yellow River and then from the south bank, taking another zip ride back across the river and down to the dock level. I really want to do the zip line, but there is a 90kg limit, so it's no go for me this time (although I make up for it later in Lanzhou). But first we take a shuttle on this north side of the park and arrive at a huge zone with sand dunes. Here we can walk around, ride camels, take a few laps in a dune buggy, eat and drink, etc. I think the real reason we are coming over here is so that Jianzhi can drive a dune buggy. He has the time of his life, tearing around a few laps on the dunes, acting out the Chinese equivalent of his *Mad Max* video game fantasies. I sit with Grandma and Grandpa, as they smile over today's events. I opt to not bring up unpleasant memories, but as I see their joyful faces, I cannot help but wonder how they juxtapose this wonderful summer vacation with watching neighbors, friends and family starving like skeletal dogs during the Great Leap Forward and likely being victims, possibly separated for years, persecuted, physically and psychologically tortured during the Cultural Revolution. At least they survived. They are alive to see a better China, a more hopeful China.[1] Jianzhi knows only this 21st century China of gadgets, conveniences and comfort. Do the grandparents ever tell him about what it was like when they grew up as destitute peasants before 1949 and thirty years of living Hades thereafter? Just like American students get a totally whitewashed history of their people's extermination of the Indians, among many other Orwellian Memory Hole travesties, Jianzhi gets a much-sanitized version of modern Chinese history; the official interpretation being heavily vetted by Baba Beijing.[2]

Jianzhi takes the zip line down and the rest of us use the chairlift, to meet back at the dune dock. Getting back to the entrance is more than memorable, as we float back downstream. But it is not on a big house boat that holds a hundred passengers. No, we ride on real traditional rafts. Each one holds four passengers plus the oarsman. How big is one of these rafts? About 2m on each side, which for five adults means we are precariously perched and immobilized, back to back, for the slow ride back downstream to the entrance. How are they kept afloat, you might ask? Well, when I say traditional, these babies are the real McWang. The frame is made of tree branches, lattice wood and reeds. And how do we stay afloat? Each raft is kept buoyant by having around ten whole body sheep skins that are treated to be waterproofed and are tied off at the ends of the legs and neck. Thereafter, they are inflated to a very taunt level and strapped to the bottom of the raft. They look like comic book versions of pigs, without the heads. So, four of us adults pile onto this bubbly, bouncy affair and our folded-up knees keep our feet right to the edge of the raft. We are sitting just centimeters above the Yellow River. We are entrusting our camera equipment, binoculars, back packs and our lives to our boatswain, who is going to get us back home with a little plastic paddle, the sole expression of modernity on this ancient form of river transport. We are buffeted by motorboat wakes and rock and roll on the Yellow River's surface, as the waves splash up to our feet, but we make it back safely. Many of the big waves are caused by larger, specially rigged motor boats that transport six to eight of these empty rafts back upstream to the dune dock. One of my boat mates is the CEO of Xuehua (雪花= Snow Flower) Beer Company. It is a popular brand out west and over the course of this journey, I regularly partake in his company's finest. He is a real hoot and we talk and joke the whole way back.

Back at the farm, we all have a family meal together with Gao and company, in her big home dining room. Afterwards, the Wu-Yang family takes off for Yinchuan, a three hour drive, where Mr. Wu will stay for his pharmaceutical job and the rest of the family will take a train to Shijiazhuang (石家庄) in Hebei, their ancestral home. So it is just me holding down the fort until 01:19, when my overnight train leaves for Lanzhou. Gao and I start asking each other questions about our lives and families. I am naturally very curious about this semi-exotic and quite young and successful businesswoman. Xiao Gao

(小高), whom I can call by this form of affection now, given our age difference and the fact that we have become friends is 24, married to a man who is a pilot for the motor boats we took this morning and Tonghao is their two year old son. In fact, Xiao Gao owns the four farm houses I see around us. All told, she has a total of eight guest rooms, four big and four small ones. She also has a train of six camels (which I remember seeing yesterday evening, ambling into the place) given to her by her father. Her father died and she inherited the old farm, saw an opportunity in Shapotou to do more than just grow watermelons and tree fruit, and two years ago converted the homestead to tourism. It has grown so much that she now has the two full time employees, Mr. Zhang and his female partner. My curiosity gets the best of me and I ask her if she is Han or Hui. She nonchalantly tells me she is Han Chinese and acts surprised by the question, replying that,

"Didn't you notice we just had pork for lunch?"

Oh yeah. Duh... She maybe got some economic development loan to launch her business, although I forget to ask. In any case, even without foreign customers, she is clearly doing very well for herself and her family. I suggest she try to tap into the *laowai* clientele that is being herded into the expensive hotel. I ask if she has a PC and get the nod I am looking for. I explain to her that I am going to put an ad on the Lonely Planet website to tell all the readers about her farm and what a great place it is to stay. But, she gets all distressed, throws her hands up and says she can only speak Chinese. I ponder this quandary for a minute and think of a way to use translation on the web. So, in the ad, I put her email and mobile phone number, explaining that she will be using it to communicate. She has never seen it, so I show her how to translate back and forth, using China's Google equivalent, Baidu. Gao is a very smart lady and catches on quickly. She seems really excited about the opportunity.

About this time, her husband gets home and it's time for my last farm cooked family meal. After finishing, there are still about six hours until my early morning departure. Gao says she needs a break and invites to show me around her local town, Zhongwei, until it is time for me to go to the station after midnight. How can I say no? I need to settle the bill and she tells me it is 100 yuan. I tell her that is not possible, but that is all she will take for the two nights and all the food I was served. I guess it is her way of expressing her gratitude for my interest in helping her. I feel humbled by her generosity. There is now a brand new Nissan family van parked outside Room 1 and she tells me to hop in. It has a yellow and red student driver sticker in the rear window, so this is obviously Xiao Gao's newest acquisition. No sooner do we leave the confines of the farm that she starts to unburden her heart of all that is ailing her: she's exhausted, has no freedom, can't leave anywhere because she's built up this big operation, has to constantly worry about finding clients day in and day out, and once on the farm, answering to their every need, etc.

First, I am terribly honored that she has chosen this *dabizi* for succor and advice. I had earlier told her about my varied career, so I think she trusts me. I try to offer some suggestions. She's obviously successful, so why can't she cut back a little on the hours, even if it means making less money? After all, her husband has a good job too. She explains that her father was married twice, so with him being gone, she really has two families to take care of, with a total of six brothers and sisters between the two mothers. I do not know what all these siblings are doing for the good of the country, but clearly she feels a huge burden to take care of her two mothers. Being only 24 years old means her father died quite young. She is apparently the big sister, which would represent a huge responsibility on her part. She got the farm, so that must be what her father wanted. I can see that one of the biggest headaches for her is to go out and hustle for customers every day, but her response tells me she is not yet ready to relinquish to an employee what she considers a key part of the business. I also suggest she can go in the other direction and build the business up so big that she *can* afford to hire a full time manager. She mulls this over as a possible plan.

Gao parks her car in front of the Gao Temple (no relation, just a common Chinese family name), in the center of Zhongwei. We are greeted by Ms. Feng and it is explained to me that she and Gao were classmates all through school, since both their fathers were neighbors. Feng is pleasant. She is a cosmetology teacher in Yinchuan, where I just visited, and is back for summer vacation. We make a quick tour of this central city park, which has scuds of citizens making good use of the really clear, cool evening air, dancing, singing, playing musical instruments, cards, mahjong, snacking, picnicking, practicing taichi and the like. We exit Gao Park, walk around the Drum Tower, which has tens of insect-eating bats navigating in and out of the many spot lights illuminating it. Ms. Feng refuses to believe they are bats and insists they are birds. I know better, but don't push the point. Xiao Gao has called another school friend, Ms. Tang, who is a yoga instructor. The four of us now walk through a huge public square that is just pullulating with humanity, mostly just standing, sitting, snacking and talking. On a big outdoor screen is playing a Chinese action film, where throngs of people are enjoying its high tech shootout and wild chase scene. I can't help but notice that Gao stops and says a warm hello to several people as we make our way through the crowd. She clearly knows a lot of people, or better yet, a lot of people know her. I suggest going to a café or tea house and lo and behold, on the other side of the square is a trendy, hip looking place where young people hang out. We settle into comfy, cushioned seats and a private table; I'm on one side and the three of them are on the other, so they can have eye contact and a chance to chat with this strange creature from so far away.

Ms. Tang quickly starts to irritate me. In front of all four of us, she keeps teasing my new friend Xiao Gao about her weight, and it is being done in a fairly vicious fashion. She is grabbing Gao's arms, pinching her chubbiness, hooting like a shallow harpy, and to really rub it in, is comparing Gao to her tiny, petite, ironing board-breasted frame. Gao is clearly embarrassed as Yang keeps grabbing, poking and comparing the two of them. Xiao Gao says to me while this continues that in fact, she has lost a lot of weight and used to be much heavier. To point out the success of Gao already being married (in China, where especially in more rural areas like this, the pressure to get married sooner than later can be quite intense), I ask Feng and Tang why they aren't married. Well whining, we just can't find any good men, they commiserate with me. Now Feng is as nice as can be, but Tang, how could any halfway decent guy stand to be around this insecure, miserable wretch? About another minute of this blatant bullying and I politely but firmly lay into this little twat,

"Please stop talking about Gao like that. She gave birth to a child two years ago. She is a mother of a young child. She probably nursed her baby - how long did you nurse Tonghao, Gao? Six months? See Yang, Gao nursed her baby for half a year. Gao is married and has the responsibilities of being a wife. She has a very successful business and all the pressure that comes with managing it. And in any case, Gao was born the way she is, just as you were born the way you are. Please don't ever bully Gao again like that, OK?"

I have no idea what Gao is thinking, as she keeps looking back and forth at me talking and the expression on Tang's face, but Tang actually says *OK* when I finish, and poor Feng is just keeping her head down and ducking for cover. We manage to keep the conversation going for another twenty minutes, but the hour is getting late. It is about 22:00 when we say goodbye to Gao's two compadres (I now have a hard time calling Tang her *friend*) and we get back to the car. Gao kindly offers to take me to her stepmother's house to rest until it is time to go to the station, but there is no way I can take her up on her offer. Gao has already been more than gracious with her time and her money. Heck, when I go to pay the café bill, she already discreetly instructed the servers to refuse my money and picked up the tab herself. I ask her to please take me to the train station and I will rest there. Gao refuses to let me off in front of the station, parks her car, goes with me inside the station and asks the three ladies attending (who seem to know her) to take good care of me and wake me up if I fall asleep before the train takes off at 01:19. We say our goodbyes and it's off to Lanzhou, the capital of Gansu.

1-*For a terrific and chilling look into the mass psychosis that was the Cultural Revolution, John Pomfret's* Chinese Lessons - Five Classmates and the Story of the New China *(2006), shares the intimate and revealing personal testimonies of several survivors.*

2- *Jianzhi and a billion other Chinese don't have any choice with Baba Beijing's heavy handed censorship, but* you do. *Howard Zinn's instant classic,* A People's History of the United States (2003) *is essential, critical reading for anyone on the planet who has a desire to understand the viewpoint of the 99%: women, workers, laborers, miners, blacks, Indian, Latinos, etc. There is a student version,* A Young People's History of the United States, *an oral history, à la Studs Terkel, called* Voices of a People's History of the United States *(book and DVD), plus a documentary,* The People Speak *(2010). Get smart!*

Figure 4: How fast will you be traveling? Every train in China displays its maximum cruising speed. This is the K1177 from Beijing to Yinchuan.

Figure 5: Yinchuan: the uncanny, Mesoamerican looking gargoyles of the Xixia Dynasty in the 11th century. You walk under this lovely lady to get inside the Xixia Tombs Museum. Photo by Steve Evans.

Figure 6: Yinchuan: two Xixia Tomb gargoyles. These could be swapped with those at Pre-Columbian cultural sites in Central and South America and it would be hard to tell the difference.

Figure 7: Yinchuan: one of the stone pagodas at Baisikou. This pair is in immaculate condition and very striking, due to its isolation on a lonely mountainside. Photo by Steve Evans.

Figure 8: Yinchuan: sometimes, the hike is pretty steep! This arduous pathway rewards intrepid visitors with the rare rock artwork of the UNESCO Helan Rock Carvings. Photo by Steve Evans.

Figure 9: Yinchuan: the Baisikou Twin Pagodas near the Helan Mountain Range and Tengger Desert. Yours truly is in midfield studying one of the pagodas with my trusty Zeiss binoculars. Photo by Steve Evans.

Figure 10: The public kangaroo court movie set for the Cultural Revolution at Western Film Studios, Yinchuan. Notice the statue on the left of a victim with a dunce cap and his hands manacled behind his back. This was a life and death situation for millions and brutally real. I don a humiliation signboard so that my driver Xiao Wei can take my picture!

Figure 11: The Yinchuan charging station with two attendants operating the articulated pan lift. Customers can swap four big batteries and be on their way in a matter of minutes. The future is now in China.

Figure 12: Yinchuan: the very flirtatious Muslim Hui young lady, Misss Hang.

Figure 13: And who is keeping a watchful eye on us, but her ever vigilant, restaurant owning Hui mom! Notice her beautiful tribal headdress. Moms are moms around the world…

Figure 14: Yinchuan: China has a large Muslim population, around 23 million and growing, bigger than many Islamic countries. The two cultures are inextricably intertwined. Here a large mosque at sunset can be seen a Chinese sign displaying part of its name - Great Muslim. Photo by Steve Evans.

Figure 15: Spectacular view of the timeless Yellow River, from atop the sand dunes overlooking Shapotou. The distant main park entrance is behind the low lying footbridge spanning the river.

Figure 16: Shapotou: this is our mode of transportation on the Yellow River. With five adults and all our gear, it is a hilarious blast bobbing up and down together in the water.

Part IV

Gansu

Rules of the Road: Knowledge

"The wise man does not hang his knowledge on a hook."
Spanish proverb

"Knowledge that is not used is abused."
Cree proverb

"When you cease to strive to understand, then you will know without understanding."
Chinese proverb

CHAPTER 8: ZHONGWEI - LANZHOU

Welcome to Lanzhou where first, I witness a real live torture chamber chair up close and personal, and then check under the hood of China's 21st century bureaucracy. Does it get my seal of approval?

Zhongwei is a really nice town, but the train station is in dire need of a facelift. I have over three hours till departure to Lanzhou, the capital of Gansu Province and the gateway to all of its cultural and geological treasures to the west. Once inside, Xiao Gao insists that I sit close to the three lady station attendants and she promises they will wake me up if I fall asleep. But the Zhongwei train station is not at all conducive to R&R. Maybe Gao knew something that I didn't by sitting me in the opposite corner of the toilets, because the heavy haze of unflushed urine hangs all through the waiting room air. And like so many public waiting areas, every two seats has an arm rest anchored in between, so anybody taller than a good sized dwarf can't stretch out their legs.

I suddenly remember that one of my last minute pre-journey purchases is one of those inflatable neck pillows so commonly seen being used by airline passengers. If I have to sit in a urine stenched hall, I'm going to at least make the most of it. I briefly live a Mr. Bean skit, coveting the pillow with self-satisfying relish. I grandiosely unfurl it for the whole waiting room to see, inflate it, making a spectacle of myself as I do. In my new role as *Zhongwei Mr. Bean*, I am in my own little self-indulgent world. At this ungodly hour, there is only a handful of other people, and like me, they are all trying to make closing their eyes a meaningful experience. The three lady attendants have their backs turned towards me and are not offering any interest in my solitary vanity. Even with my legs draped over an armrest, it is just not working. One guy has found the sole place where the armrest is missing and he is stretched out, a lizard lounging in the Sun. Other than the three lady musketeers, who are having the midnight gabfest of their lives and appear to have forgotten their pledge to Xiao Gao, the rest of us who are waiting it out all seem to be playing our parts in a B-movie horror flick, as catatonic zombies.

The train's arrival cannot happen soon enough. No lady musketeer reveille necessary for this train bird. I am up on two feet at the first sound of the incoming train's horn. We all sleepwalk on board and I can only rejoice that I have a reserved hard sleeper, which I employ to immediate effect. But my night's sleep is fitful and unsatisfying. When we arrive to Lanzhou, I am as groggy and unsteady on my feet as a rum soaked sailor making the most of his port of call. In fact, I am so fuzzy headed that I get all the way outside the train station, when I realize I left my Mr. Bean's pride and joy on the train. Oh, the horror of it all. What a tragic slight to my materialistic ego. But not to worry, it should be a simple matter of going back out to the train and recuperating my dearly mislaid pillow, right? As a souvenir, I always take a photo of the plaque fixed to each train car, showing its provenance, line number and destination, and I remember that the terminus for my train number is in fact Lanzhou, so it can't be that hard can it? *Well...* I decide that if I tell them it's just a pillow, they will not take my quest seriously, so in the interest of science, I tell them it is a *doctor's prescribed* model to support my injured neck. As I say this, I act out to the turnstile attendant, grabbing the back of my neck and showing pangs of anguish on my forlorn face. That and flashing my punched ticket gets me back into the main waiting hall, where I ask the first person I see in blue how to proceed. She takes me to the station Gongan (公安= Public Security) bureau. There, the police officer on duty asks me to go with him to inquire at the station's traffic control center, where there is a big, color electronic board showing all the rail lines entering and disembarking at the station. The control center manager tells him to call such and such, so, we go back to the Gongan bureau and he makes the call.

It is while we are waiting for this station manager to arrive that I start focusing a little on what is in this bureau, which is not very big and has a low ceiling, since it's housed under a big staircase. Not more than two meters in front of me, I spy a slightly bizarre piece of furniture. What I thought was just a chair, is in fact not your run of the mill variety. We can politely say, like Americans euphemistically call it, that it's for *enhanced interrogation*. The rest of the world is not afraid to use the word: this is a chair for *torturing* people. It's like a big and tallish high chair that infants sit in to eat at the table with the grownups. It even has an oversized, Formica covered table top where you would normally put Junior's food. But, anchored into it via the thick tubular cast iron frame which makes up the chair, are two stainless steel manacles to immobilize the victim's arms at thc wrist. It is easy to see why they have the nice smooth, extra big table top: the easier to wipe up all the blood and spittle while they bash your face and brains in. The chair itself is held down at the base of the legs with thick, heavy, round, cast iron weights, much like you would put on hand barbells. These are obviously there as ballast to keep the chair from tipping over as they continue to pummel your body. And of course no torture chair would be complete without two suitably sized, adjustable manacles to immobilize the victim's legs at the ankles. Jeesh. And to top it off, hanging on one of the back legs are six stainless steel rings about 10cm in diameter, with adjustable clamp openings, undoubtedly to clasp and screw down onto the victim's various body parts, to maximize the pain and suffering. It's a real Guantanamo special, a torture machine that Torquemada would definitely see the value in for extracting worthless confessions and false information. China has surely exported torture equipment like this to the USA and the many countries where America houses its black (torture) prisons in Europe, Africa, the Middle East and elsewhere. No wonder America and Europe have a trade deficit with China. I *so* want to take a photo of this infernal machine, but am never left alone long enough to get the chance. Drat…

The train station manager shows up, snappily dressed in coat and tie and proudly sporting a nice sized Communist party pin on his navy blue lapel. After inquiring about my nationality, he tells me that foreigners may think the Chinese don't want to help when they have a problem, but he is here to prove otherwise.[1] Oooooooookaaaay... I must say that up to now, everybody involved in this bureaucratic adventure is proving to be exceptionally charming, torture chair notwithstanding. I flash back to the bad old days in the nineties and smile at how much the Chinese have evolved, alongside their one generation of record breaking and meteoric economic growth. Back then, I would have probably never made it back inside the train station and if I did, would have more than likely been met with total indifference or yelled and screamed at in front of the entire world to see, Cultural Revolution struggle session style, for being so stupid for having left my pillow on the train in the first place.

Ever-so-charming Mr. Party Man hops on his walkie-talkie and in a few minutes, a nice, junior flunky appears and asks me to come with him. Warm, hearty handshakes are exchanged with the smiling Train Station Commie Man and Sgt. Torture Chamber Teng. Other than the disappointment of not stealing a photo of the W. Bush-Obama high chair, up to now, so far, so good. My new aide-de-camp, Mr. Junior Good Guy and I start to mill about the station, as he inquires about the train. I ask him why we just don't go out on the platform where the train let me off, and he explains that the train has already been moved to another area of the station, I would assume to be cleaned and prepped for tomorrow. We finally leave the station and go about a hundred meters down a side street. There we stand in front of a big entrance where lots of men and women in blue are entering and exiting. The sign over the doors says it's the employee center for the train company. Junior is asking several people who are hurriedly fanning through the doors in both directions, showing each one my punched ticket. Then, a guy who looks and acts like he knows what he is talking about, spends a minute or two chatting with my escort. Something is not adding up. I mean this is the Lanzhou train station, not some megadrome in Beijing or Shanghai. How far away could the side track be where my train is parked anyway? Well, as it turns out, far away, really far away. Like Xining (西宁) far away, the capital of Qinghai (青海), a three hour train ride from here. Mr. Expert holds his palms out and turned up, saying with a look of animated exasperation,

"*Meiyou banfa!*" (没有办法!= There's nothing we can do)

Junior All Smiles tells me sheepishly that my train is managed by another company, and they thought it ended in Lanzhou, but in fact it has just started its journey to cross over the provincial boundary and on into neighboring Qinghai. I had no idea that China has diversified its state train company, even if it may only nominally be by employee groups. I'm so sorry, Mr. Bean. Will you ever forgive me? Where's Teddy for consolation? More heartfelt handshakes all around, really sincere thanks on my part for trying so hard to help me, and tender goodbyes in the name of international cooperation. Still, why they couldn't suss out the train situation faster is a bit of a mystery to me. I mean what about that big, electronic traffic control board we saw when I first asked? No big deal. The whole adventure took less than an hour and I still have a long, full day to explore Lanzhou, before my overnight train to Dunhuang, at the western end of Gansu. Experiencing the torture chair and the nice demeanor of the Chinese bureaucrats, to compare to the dog-eat-dog China of the nineties, made it all worthwhile. Come on Mr. Bean, shake it off and pillow or no pillow and let's do Lanzhou in a day.

1- *This gentleman's comment is very revealing. Even after 30 years of liberalization and phenomenal socio-economic progress, Chinese Communist Party members still to this day have an air of defensiveness about them, a manifest chip on their shoulders, when it comes to foreigners. This is of course inculcated into them through an endless number of publications and meetings. PLA soldiers whom I meet, CCP members all, are usually taciturn with* outsiders, *and given their lower rank, this is understandable. But, I have met many PLA officers at banquets over the years, who, given their more secure status and probable higher education, can be quite loquacious, especially after four or five rounds of alcohol. They, along with the hundreds of CCP government workers I have met, mostly exhibit this sense of insecurity or unease with* dabizi. *Don't throw stones in glass houses. Whether it is the US, France, Islam, Christianity or any other place where dogmas pervade, there are billions who are steadfast in their certitudes that,* all things great are my belief system and my belief system is all things wonderful. *And each group has the ideologically pure publications, propaganda and meetings to prove it too. Fundamentalism, nationalism and ideology are the flip sides of God, Country and Party, a poisonous, pernicious cocktail that has and is bringing nothing but misery to the world.*

Chapter 9: Lanzhou

Strange day in unloved, under-appreciated Lanzhou - Lonely Planet sends me on a wild goose chase that turns out to be a lot of fun, and mucking up Google maps sends me to two museums, not one.

Lanzhou may be a provincial capital, but after spending a day here, I can see why it is not at the top of people's lists for tourism. At the same time, if one digs a little deeper here and takes the time, then Lanzhou surely has a lot more to offer than meets the eye. I just don't have that time.[1] In any case, it is historically the gateway between eastern and western China along the Silk Road. Lanzhou is the eastern trail head of the strategically and commercially essential Hexi Corridor (河西走廊= *Hexi Zoulang*), the western end being Dunhuang, my next stop. The Hexi Corridor is one of the most celebrated stretches on the Silk Road route, kind of like the section of Route 66 that runs through Oklahoma, in the United States. Iconic is a good word that comes to mind... Thus, Lanzhou is one of those ancient *all roads lead to* kind of a place. So, I find myself passing through Lanzhou to get where I want to go, one way or the other.

The first thing that strikes me as I exit the train station area and go out on the streets is how little Lanzhou seems affected by China's generation-long economic boom. Walking along the big boulevard out front, it feels like I'm in 1990's Beijing. Of course Lanzhou has benefitted from the country's rapid development. What I'm seeing is just indicative of how very far behind Lanzhou was, compared to the coastal regions, when the economic tidal wave took off thirty years ago. Gansu is infamous all over China for a being one of the poorest provinces in the country, second to only Guizhou (which I visit in a big way at the end of this trip). It's not Gansu's fault, nor Lanzhou's. Baba Beijing just neglected the interior of the country for years while it pumped money into the *blue* or coastal provinces. Now in the last ten years or so, Baba Beijing, sensing impatience and increasing, simmering envy among the people out here, has started to prime the development pump in the *yellow* or interior provinces such as Gansu. But the 20-year late start is manifest, compared to the one generation lead the eastern provinces were accorded. And that is what I see here: about a one generation difference with the coastal zones. So, no surprise, the train station looks incredibly outdated, with its kitsch faux metallic diamonds on the facade and the colored glass panes. It looks like a throwback to the 1980s, as does the whole city. Lanzhou is also hexed by its geography. About 20km long, it is packed in a narrow, walled canyon, with the Yellow River roaring down the middle of it. This thin passage runs east to west and the prevailing winds are north/south. Thus, Lanzhou finds itself in an atmospheric trench, so the air pollution can build up and infamously languish for days on end. It's one of those place Beijingers can cite when the air thickens back home,

"*You think this is bad, heck we could be living in* LANZHOU*!*"

Some consolation. Today, I am lucky, as the air is actually fairly clear, with decent visibility for several klicks across and up and down the river front. First, a hot, spicy bowl of beef noodles to start my day. I also order a couple of hard boiled eggs that have had their shells slightly cracked and have been marinated in a tea and spice broth. Muslim noodles are the best, but lacking in protein, so I frequently order and egg or two as a cheap nutritional insurance policy. I'm doing a lot of walking and climbing on this trip and need to keep myself healthy. The whole breakfast costs ¥9 (€1.10/$1.40). A large group of Ouighers, who are Muslim, enter the restaurant, the men going to one table and the colorfully head-scarfed women to another. I'm between their two tables, so I'm not sure what I'm arbitrating here.

A friendly traffic cop gets me heading in the right direction for the White Temple, which is in the western part of town. Friendly fellow passengers, overhearing me ask the bus driver if this is the right one going there, keep a watchful eye out and voluntarily tell me where to get off. Very neighborly of them. Remembering that Lanzhou is in a narrow gorge along the Yellow River, the climb up to the top of White Temple is quite a good workout. With the river elevation being around 1,400 MASL, the air is quite thin here. At the top of White Temple, my GPS shows the elevation is 1,632 MASL, so it's a more than a 200m vertical climb, which is like scaling the steps of a 65-story tower. I decide to take the chair lift down, since it goes all the way across the river to drop you off on the opposite bank. From where I am, the quickest way to get to the chair lift station is to ride a zip line (飞行挂索= *feixing guasuo*) across a deep ravine, so now is my chance to make up for not being able to ride the one in Shapotou. It's a lot of fun hanging in the air and flying along at a good rate, with the ground many meters below your feet. This one is not quite flat enough at the terminus and to mitigate this problem, they have installed a huge, vertical shock absorbing pad that you plow into, rugby style, while the attendant grabs onto you at the same time as you come in over the platform, to help slow you down. Yee-Ha. To be honest, White Temple is very unexceptional and to compound its ordinariness, there is a lot of construction going on. At the temple, I have a nice chat with a group of Buddhist nuns, in their robes and with cue ball smooth heads. Along the way to the lift, I walk with a truck driver from Qinghai, who complains about how difficult his job is and the fact that he is constantly pushed to drive long hours, way beyond the legal norms, whatever *that* means in free-wheeling, rule breaking China. The same thing is happening to US drivers as a result of deregulation, so join the WTO treadmill, Mr. Qinghai Driver. We are all the Chinese 99% now. At least you are probably ascending to the middle class through your toil, instead of falling out of it, by the millions, like in the US.

The chair lift affords excellent views of Lanzhou up and down the gorge, as well as the very fast moving Yellow River. We fly alongside the Zhongshan (Dr. Sun Yat-Sen) Bridge.[2] It is historically significant, in that this military looking, steel trussed span was the first to be built across the Yellow River, in 1909. Either the water is shallow or the drop in elevation is precipitous, because the flow of the river is impressively fast and powerful. It is also 250 meters wide, which just adds to its allure. When the current runs into a bridge support, it crashes into it violently, non-stop. It is easy to become slightly hypnotized by the water's rapid, sine wave movement. After the chair lift ride from the top of White Temple, I'm now on the opposite bank and start what turns out to be a wild goose chase. Lonely Planet gets it way wrong for the whereabouts of the Water Wheel Park, saying it is just to the west of the White Temple entrance. I am now on the other side of the Yellow River, so I have a really good view of the temple across the way, and for the life of me, as I gaze across the river to the other bank, I cannot see anything remotely looking like a water wheel, big or small. Before crossing the Zhongshan Bridge back over, I scan the other bank with my razor sharp Zeiss binoculars to be sure, but see nothing round and moving.

I start asking around and everybody tells me that I'm on the right side of the river and it's to the east, the opposite direction stated in Lonely Planet. So, I start walking along the river cornice and end up strolling through a really nice city park, with lots of shade trees, well maintained flower gardens and huge topiaries of elephants, penguins and the like. The park is very well kept, clean and a real pleasure to be in. Many people are out and enjoying the expansive shade everywhere, as the afternoon is proving to be a hot one. Vendors are selling all kinds of beverages and food and I help myself to a freshly roasted ear of corn being sold by a young Ouigher man. Not a lot of *waiguoren* roll through here and he peppers me with questions and beams with pride at his neighboring competitors for landing my business. They all chatter away in Turkic about *the event of the day*, as I say goodbye. Since the Lonely Planet says the water wheels are next to the White Temple entrance, I figure they got the side of the river wrong and they would be just ahead. I keep asking people and they keep shaking and waving their arms east: it's not far, they tell me, I only have 500m to go. Yeah, sure. We have all been there, you know, keep going, it's just around the corner, you're not far.

Along the way, I hear music and singing coming from a gazebo and go to have a look. An attractive woman with shoulder length, wavy, brunette hair and in her thirties is singing with a microphone, whose sound is emanating from a small battery powered amplifier hidden inside a big, blue reusable cloth shopping bag. She sings quite well, can carry a note and has good clarity to her voice. She is accompanied by two older gentlemen. One is playing the Chinese miniature version of the upright bass, the two-stringed Erhu *(二胡)*, and the other is squeezing away on his European style accordion. I sit down in the much appreciated, cool gazebo shade to take it all in. This is not just some public fling for them. They are taking their little trio quite seriously, stopping in mid-refrain to discuss a particular bar of music or who should start playing when.

It's like being a fly on the wall of some outdoor studio recording session. Then they finally hash out the details and play the complete number. The singer has the printed lyrics and her accompanists are keeping time reading from sheet music poised on a musician's stand. I am woefully ignorant of Chinese musical genres, but the song they are playing seems to be of the classical variety. She takes the final refrain to an extended, climactic high. One other (Chinese) tourist and I, who is also photographing them, applaud. These musicians are obviously playing for the love of music, not for an audience. I thank them for their performance and as I get up to leave, the pretty singer sticks the microphone in my hand and implores me to sing a tune. Surprised, unprepared and totally ungifted for the occasion, I speak into the mic,

"*Wo bu hui chang ger, xiexie*" (我不会唱歌儿，谢谢= I don't know how to sing, thank you).

Two or three more arm gesticulations from the shade seeking passersby, each accompanied by a rote *it's just about 500 more meters*, and I finally see the water wheels. The problem is I'm on a raised concrete boardwalk about one story above the cornice, where the park and its entrance are, which in turn is about one story above the Yellow River. Checking the time, I still want to go to the provincial museum, the reproduced water wheels are actually well positioned to photograph, there is no park entrance anywhere to be seen, and the mid-afternoon Sun is bearing down with all its fusional might - so I snap a couple of pics and move on. Lonely Planet only got the Water Wheel Park's location off by the wrong side of the river, the wrong direction and 3km. It makes me wonder if anybody even carrying one of their business cards has even been near this place. Or, did they just use Google and got a botched translation off the web, which is not hard to do. After all, Chinese has got to be one of the most wickedly difficult languages on Planet Earth to translate and interpret accurately. It could also be the lazy efforts of a locally hired journalist, who just doesn't care. I'm not sure what's going on. I stop off for my *second* bowl of noodles of the day. My favorite way to order Chinese dishes is to survey what the other customers are eating, finding one that looks scrumptious, pointing to it and telling the server,

"Umm... I'll take one of... *those*."

Doing just that, I also order a dish of pickled bean sprouts and a hardboiled egg. It's a busy place and I am soon joined by a Han tablemate who happens to order the same dish. The server, whose thick Ouigher accent reached my ears as, *laomian* (old noodles), is, according to my new Chinese buddy, *liangmian* (凉面= cool noodles). The circle is closed when our bowls arrive and they are in fact slightly cooler than room temperature. This being the second hottest day of the trip (the first visiting the Xixia Tombs in Yinchuan), I made a fortuitous choice. Two neighboring Chinese college co-eds spend their entire time furtively looking over at me, giggling and making whispering comments to each other.

Time to go see the Gansu Provincial Museum. In Chinese, I input, *Gansu Lanzhou Museum* in Google maps and what do you know, it is only 1.5km away. With still plenty of time before my overnight train to Dunhuang, I decide to make it a post lunch stroll, in spite of the heat. I finally get to the location and no typically gargantuan museum edifice is to be found. I ask around and get pointed to a little Chinese temple-fronted building that calls itself the *Lanzhou Municipal Museum*. Ouch. Putting the name, *Lanzhou* in my map search gave me a bum steer. I will not make that mistake again. As long as I am here, I might as well go in. Like most provincial museums, this one is free to enter. It is a fairly modest affair, done in the style of a traditional Chinese house, the famed *siheyuan* (四合院= four enclosed court), with an open courtyard, two side wings and a back wing of rooms. The Lanzhou Municipal Museum has three long exhibition halls. Only the one on the right is open and a fair number of people are milling in and out.

They are here to admire the work of an apparently popular Gansu calligrapher who has quite a display of various styles to show off, and is also here in person, Mr. Yao Wenyuan (姚文渊), from Jiayuguan, where I will visit later in *44 Days*. Local and regional calligraphers can be veritable rock stars in China. He has books for sale and blank sheets of thick, mulberry calligraphy paper, along with his quiver of brushes and inks, to write impromptu dedications for his adoring fans, much like an author at book signings. I cannot read 90% of the works, since they are intentionally written in highly stylized fashion, so there is not much for me to understand, but it is easy to see the patience and perseverance that must go into each project. I see a pair of red, embossed banners, with large, vibrant characters that really catch my eye and photograph them. Apparently, his *chef d'oeuvre* is a long, horizontal banner 10m in length and 50cm tall. The story/poem is written in fairly small characters, so it is composed of hundreds of them. For a work of such magnitude, one has to appreciate the skill that goes into having all these characters perfectly lined up in precise rows and columns. The fact that the author has maintained a consistent writing style, drawing each character flawlessly and in their own inimitable style, over such a large and expansive piece is especially impressive. I don't know how many scrolls of mulberry paper ended up in the recycle bin, but he at least got it right one time, which in the art world is all you need. I mull over meeting the artist on the way out, but he is actually quite popular and has book buying fans waiting for his signature. I'm not in a position to buy a tome, so leave him in peace.

I google the right name this time and can see that the big, provincial museum is quite a ways to the west, up the river valley. Time is starting to matter and the better part of expediency tells me now is not the time to learn Lanzhou's bus system more intimately. I hail a taxi and drive quite a ways up the narrow city gorge for only ¥11 (€1.40/$1.80). My friendly Ouigher driver drops me off in front of the huge, imposing edifice. Now this is more like it. No sooner do I get out that I see a sign in the thick, glass plated guard's station that says, *Zhouyi Xiuxi* (周一休息= Closed Mondays). Now I know why it looks so deserted. Ah, yes most museums are closed on Mondays. On this journey, I am doing well keeping up with the dates, since I want to stay on schedule. But for the most part, me being able to tell you what day of the week it is has more or less gone by the wayside, and today this inattention to temporal detail has bitten my butt. But not a problem. I take the bus back to the train station, find a noodle house for an early dinner and an always needed electrical outlet to recharge my Galaxy Tab and external battery. I make sure to choose a non-Ouigher restaurant, so I can savor a couple of big, frosty beers with my meal. I anxiously board the train for far Western Gansu and the sand dunes of Dunhuang. So far, this journey has been a dream come true and I've barely started. How long will my traveler's luck hold out?

1- Based on this chapter as a rough draft on my blog, a laowai Lanzhou handyman responded with a comprehensive list of places to visit here, most of them not found in the Lonely Planet or other tour guides. Like many places, there is more in Lanzhou than meets the eye. His personal favorite *list is posted on 44days.net. I will have it tucked in my suitcase next journey out.*

2- Dr. Sun is a towering figure in modern Chinese history and equally revered and claimed as a native son by both mainland China and Taiwan. To be honest, he was a frustratingly ineffectual leader. But he did actively play a part in bringing down the Qing Dynasty and for the first time in China's history, led in the creation of a republican form of government. Most importantly, his idealism and visionary dream for a unified China, free of colonialism and the humiliation of nationwide opium addiction, all at the hands of Western (and later Japanese) powers, planted the seeds for China's eventual political and economic independence in 1949.

Chapter 10: Dunhuang

Adopted by another Chinese family, to the Mogao Caves. And why not: this UNESCO World Heritage Site is selling all kinds of ivory statues and jewelry. Go figure…

In Yinchuan, I was adopted by the taxi driver Xiao Wei. In Zhongwei, Xiao Gao took me under her wing and in Shapotou, the Wu-Yang family did the same. In Dunhuang, my newest adoption is starting on the train as soon as we board. I am chatting with my hard sleeper berth mates and we immediately start talking about accommodations in Dunhuang (敦煌= Sincere Brilliance). One woman, Ms. Chen, lives there and makes a couple of calls to hotels she knows and gets me a room reservation for 120 yuan (€15/$19) a night. A very nice gesture, as she is proffering to help me on her own volition. Overhearing all this is an extroverted and talkative young woman. She is with her teenage son and younger sister, who, being quiet as a door mouse, is the antithesis of her animated older sibling. Her name is Ms. Zhou (as in Zhou Enlai) and they come from Hangzhou. They liked Dunhuang so much after coming last year, that they are making a repeat trip, which is an encouraging sign. Ms. Zhou has a local contact, Mr. Cai and texts him to confirm the lodging, including me. Again, another nice, voluntary gesture. Ms. Chen graciously calls *her* hotel back and cancels my reservation. There is naturally a little face losing here, but she takes the reservation change gracefully.

By the time we get to Dunhuang early the next morning, it is all set. I'm now an unofficial member of the Zhou family. I say goodbye to Ms. Chen. She is in fact returning from a month in Paris for an archeological exchange with the French, since she works at the Mogao Caves research center that takes care of the place. Cool job to say the least and I will later learn more fascinating historical insights about why she went to France on behalf of the Mogao Caves. Zhou's friend, Cai meets us at the train station and drives us to a really cool hostel in an oasis garden (we go out and pick fresh apricots off the trees) called Charley Johng's (a clever permutation of *Zhang*). And at only ¥30 (€3.80/$4.80) a night, I like the price too. After getting settled in, who do I see sitting there busily writing in his journal, but Steve Evans from my Yinchuan visit, who has crisscrossed every country on Planet Earth, except Libya. We exchange hellos and catch up on our whereabouts the last few days. He has done the sights at Dunhuang and is leaving tomorrow for Golmud, Qinghai. The Zhou family (now including me) leaves for an early lunch. We are joined by an interesting young man from Nanjing, who has adopted the western name of Danny. Married and with a five year old daughter, he is the only Chinese person I have met so far (and who I will meet on the whole trip) who is traveling solo. A rare bird indeed. When I inquire about his work, I get a very oblique,

"I have some investments."

Hmm... I know that in the 90s, by force of the status quo back then, I would have assuredly gotten a much different reply.

You have to like the laid back pace in Dunhuang. The public buses nominally have stops to pick up and let off people. But the drivers will stop wherever you are standing along the street. This gives the town a real quaint, small town feel. We go to a very nice, covered food court in the center of town, where we eat the local specialty, yellow noodles (黄面= *huangmian*). The classic dish actually has horse or donkey meat in it, but the gang in tow orders all the bowls without it. The sauce really is yellow and has a rich meat broth taste. I suspect the yellow color comes from sesame oil and saffron, which I can taste and smell. To show my appreciation, I try to pay for everybody's lunch, but Ms. Zhou has already beaten me to the punch. Not only that, but she will not even let me pay for my own bowl. This kind of generosity to strangers was unheard of when we lived here in the 90s. Back then, most Chinese were doing everything possible to separate us *laowai* from our money and possessions, no matter how little the amount or mundane the object.

Danny joins us to go see the Mogao Caves. They are really impressive and have been impeccably restored numerous times, after centuries of neglect. It is a UNESCO World Heritage site and well protected. All cameras must be checked in before entering. No one can just walk around and explore. You must go with a group and its guide. I am not about to torture the other twenty Chinese in my group with a bad English translation, so I push the envelope on my Mandarin and go on the tour with the guide only speaking Chinese. Any thought of getting with a *foreign* group is out of the question, since the only *dabizi* I see today are the six to eight who are staying at the hostel, and they are not here. In any case, the guide has a headset microphone and small, amplified speaker, so everybody can hear. I will be honest: my head is spinning from trying to digest the rapidly spoken Chinese for one hour. Not to mention the obscure subject matter of 1,000 year-old carvings, statues and esoteric Buddhism. Still, I'm understanding about half, which is enough. The guide even takes me aside and tells me he is *trying* to slow down for my benefit. But in all my years of world travel, this is just not a natural thing for people to do and can only be maintained over time with much practice and attention to the conversation at hand. With my countless encounters across the planet in several languages, I can proudly say I can keep it up when speaking with people all day long. It is either that or not communicate effectively. Not the case today for my benefit. He is firing away on all vocal cylinders, although I appreciate that his heart is in the right place.

There are well over 400 Mogao Caves, some Herculean in size and some as small as tiny rooms. Each one is numbered and has a lock and key steel door blocking the entrance. The cave openings are all on the front of a big cliff face and there are two stories of them, over and under. There are the requisite caves to visit, the big ones that everyone wants to see. Most of the time, we wait outside for another group to get out, but some are so big and so popular that two or three groups may be inside at one time. Surprisingly, the headset system works really well and having other groups together in one big cave is not a distraction. The guides can talk in a low voice with the little speaker attached to them, so it is not echoing all over the place. The Mogao Caves are stunning in their size and number. They are also immaculate and in pristine condition. As much as I like them, I slightly favor the Yungang Caves (云冈石窟) in Shanxi. True, Mogao was started 100 years before Yungang, in the 4th century. But many of them were built as late as the 14th century, and Yungang's were almost all built around the 5th century. Also, Mogao has been restored and re-restored up to five times, as recently as the Qing dynasty and even during the Republican period, from 1917-1949. The Yungang Caves have mostly remained in their original 5th century state and thus are not as perfect looking as Mogao. Unfortunately, Yungang suffered significantly during the Cultural Revolution. I ask our guide if the Red Guards depredated Mogao. Did Zhou Enlai (周恩来), Mao Zedong's right hand man, go behind the Great Helmsman's back, give a call and rally the troops to save the place, like he did for so many other historical and cultural sites around China? He replies that there were two political factions in Dunhuang during the Revolution, and luckily, the less foaming-at-the-mouth rabid Red Guard faction was stronger. Whew.

The Mogao Caves have an infamous archaeological story to tell and it involves a French sinologist and explorer, Paul Pelliot and a Jewish subject of the British Empire, Auriel Stein. A secret multilingual library was discovered at Mogao in 1900 by the temple guardian and abbot, Wang Yuanlu. Today, it is known as Cave 17. It was sealed up around the year 1000. No one knows why. Dunhuang's dry climate and the cave's constant, cool temperatures kept the trove in perfect, hermetic condition for almost a millennium. Wang was restoring a bigger cave and found a crack in the entryway wall, which had been buried under a patina of stucco mud, and this proved to be the library's door. Inside were around 25,000 5th -11th century manuscripts, including the world's *oldest printed book*. The vast majority of these Buddhist texts are in Chinese, but are also in several other regional languages used at the time. You can just imagine what all of this represents in cultural and monetary terms. You cannot even put a price on it.

Mr. Pelliot was not the first *waiguoren* sniffing around at Mogao's footsteps. Auriel Stein, a British archaeologist, had a three-month head start and managed to walk away with the world's oldest book and about 13,000 of the texts, for the *staggering* sum of £130 (which actually equals about £11,000 today, but still...). But, Pelliot was an accomplished sinologist. He was well versed in China's history, culture and could read and speak the language flawlessly. Thus, he spent two weeks perusing through a thousand texts a day and knew what to look for. The fact that he was born with a Hollywoodesque photographic memory was also a huge asset for his endeavors. So, even though he *only* got 10,000 of these treasured documents (for the princely sum of £90), his collection was of much better quality, both historically and monetarily. He was able to cherry pick through the remaining collection and get one version of each document. Stein, who was illiterate in Chinese and only spoke the Queen's English, got many duplicate copies of the same texts. Pelliot got *la crème de la crème* of the library, as the French say. Pelliot was being paid by his government for the expedition and he dutifully shipped the collection off to the Musée Guimet and the Biblioteque Nationale in Paris. Stein was being financed by England and India, so he divvied up his trove and shipped it off to London and Delhi (London got the world's oldest book). As a result, Paris and London together have the greatest repository of medieval Buddhist manuscripts on the face of the Earth. On his way back to France, Pelliot showed Beijing authorities a sample or two from the collection and in a panic, they telegraphed Dunhuang and requisitioned what was left in Cave 17. This modest collection is now housed at the National Library in Beijing. But Wang was clever little bugger and managed to hide some of the manuscripts inside some of the statues in other caves around Mogao. After Beijing got what they thought was the rest, Yuanlu sold what he had absconded with, to two better-late-than-never archaeologists, a Russian and a Japanese. The former got 200 manuscripts and the latter 600, which are still enough to organize a small museum around.

The Chinese now paint Mr. Paul Pelliot as a rapacious, money grubbing, landlubbing corsair. Stein, being a museum archaeologist, apparently escapes China's calumny. After all, our dear Paul was just an explorer and adventurer. Poor abbot Wang Yuanlu is depicted as a bit of a well-meaning dupe, who only wanted a little money to pay the costs of refurbishing the caves, which his superiors, local and provincial governments never had any to send. Pelliot is so infamous in China that Danny, from our group, left Mogao with a book in Chinese on Mr. Pelliot and he told me it is all about what a dastardly SOB he was and such an outrage to Chinese sensibilities and identity. But here is how I look at it. Thanks to Pelliot and Stein, the planet does have all these priceless cultural documents in perfect condition for the whole world to see, admire and research. In fact, the collections are being digitalized and are already available online. I remember meeting Ms. Chen on the train yesterday and today. She just spent a month in Paris for her work at the Mogao Caves Research Center. Want to guess what she was studying back in Paris? Neither Pelliot nor Stein made a *sous* or a shilling off their exploits, and dutifully sent everything they *absconded with* back to their respective national, meaning taxpayers' museums. They were both adventurers to be sure, but they were educated gentlemen who were doing a noble, professional job at what their governments asked them to do. What with the utter chaos, madness and self-destruction that was China during the first eighty years of the 20th century, who knows what would have happened to these unique collections had they ended up staying in-country? Chiang Kai-Shek (蔣介石= Jiang Jiashi or 蔣中正= Jiang Zhongzheng) is probably the biggest criminal gangster in history to ever run *two* countries (China and then Taiwan). He would have been happy to sell them off to the Japanese to pad his billion dollar overseas accounts. Not to mention venal, iniquitous local officials, people starving during the Great Leap Forward, then the frenzied psychosis of the Cultural Revolution - who knows? The only reason Beijing even learned about the true value of Cave 17 is because Pelliot innocently showed a sample manuscript to them on his way home. In fact, local Mogao authorities contacted their fellow bureaucrats in Lanzhou to tell them about the discovery, well *before* Stein and Pelliot arrived on the scene. And what was their response? They didn't have the money in their budget to send transport to go pick up the collection. It was never their intention, but we have Stein and Pelliot to thank for keeping 90% of this cultural treasure trove intact. Otherwise, there is a really good chance it would have been disbursed all over kingdom come into private collections, sold by looters and unscrupulous authorities, or very possibly destroyed in post-independence China. In any case, a fascinating international cultural adventure story…

The one jarring experience at Mogao Caves that is really throwing me for a loop is the museum store. Of course we are going to get walked through the museum store on the way out. This is a rite of passage all over the world. But serious, shocked cognitive dissonance overwhelms my brain and sense of propriety when I see a whole long display counter full of *ivory* carved amulets, statues, jewelry and the like. I thought the sale of ivory was banned period. But apparently it's not. In 2008, China and Japan bought 108 tons *legally* through an *approved* CITES sale (Convention on International Trade in Endangered Species of Wild Fauna and Flora - based in Washington, DC). Can you imagine how many dead elephants it takes to get 108,000 kilograms of ivory? Just as fish in the sea are being mined, the catches are getting smaller and the average size is growing ever more diminutive - the same trend is happening in elephants. Based on the most recent survey, the average weight of ivory tusks decreased one-half to one kilogram per year, from 1970 to 1990. They dropped in average weight from 12kg each to a featherweight 3kg. At the 3kg level, 6kg per elephant, the haul of ivory that China and Japan bought and which I am looking at in these glass cases represents *18,000* slaughtered pachyderms.[1] Right here at Mogao Caves, a *United Nations World Cultural Heritage Site*. Can you believe it? The bitter irony of all this is beyond reproach. When was the last time a UNESCO representative came to visit? They were probably spared the commercial ignominy of being flogged with souvenirs on the way out. What a strange way to end my visit. I leave speechless and shaking my head.

1-library.sandiegozoo.org/factsheets/african_elephant/african_elephant.htm

Chapter 11: Dunhuang – Next Day

Adopted by a group of fellow teachers, sunset atop a towering sand dune, overlooking an oasis and a wild and wooly return home through a dungeon-dark, Dunhuang camel labyrinth.

Back at Charley Johng's oasis hostel, Cai brings the Zhou family a big batch of the local version of cool noodles, like I ate in Lanzhou. Instead of being wheat-based noodles, these are made from rice flour. You can tell because rice noodles become almost translucent once they are cooked. Whether wheat or rice based, this slightly chilled dish is really refreshing when it is hot outside. The Dunhuang noodle has a really unique shape. They are broad, about 2cm wide and close to 1cm thick. In spite of their hefty volume, they still easily snap off in small chunks, when picked up with chopsticks, as rice flour noodles are wont to do. That's because rice flour contains no gluten. Gluten is what makes it possible for bread and rolls to rise with fermentation and keep their shape. Wheat gluten is like structural *glue* and girders for baked goods. Wheat flour is around 12% protein. Rice flour only contains half as much. Some varieties of rice are *glutinous* because they have higher levels of a starch called amylopectin, whose molecules are in the form of branching chains, so they snag and stick together.[1] But unlike gluten, starch has low tensile strength and cannot hold its stretch. The molecule chains easily break apart when stressed. So, trying to hold onto these fat, slippery-as-snot rice noodle pieces with chopsticks and get them into your mouth is a mean feat, let me tell you. As with most Chinese noodle dishes, these are very spicy, with a healthy dose of red pepper. Just what the doctor ordered for lunch. Having been here last year, the Zhou family has a little different schedule than my first time visit. So, as I go off to meet different people at Charley's, well more than half who are Chinese, my honorary adoption passes to a group of seven just graduated school teachers, from Fujian and Henan. Needless to say, there is an immediate affinity amongst us fellow members of the guild. Nanjing Danny joins us to make a group of nine and it's time to start our adventure to go climb a towering sand dune and watch the sunset. It is a rite of passage when coming to Dunhuang.

Andy, a second generation, German speaking Swiss of Lebanese heritage (and who can't speak a word of Arabic) tells us it is not necessary to pay the ridiculous sum of ¥120 (€15/$19) to go through the Dunhuang Desert Park, where there are throngs of people, camels, concessions and the like. All we need to do is go about 500 meters to the east of the park's fence line, until we get to a huge, open land, Buddhist cemetery, and start climbing dunes there. He tells us there are guards looking for people to sneak in at the northeast corner of the park, but if we go far enough east, they won't bother us. Or so we hope. Our expedition of nine takes off. Using Andy's map that he drew in my notebook, we attempt to get east of the park without arousing too much attention. We get chased off by camel herders and park employees on the first couple of attempts and then it is third time the charm. We do an end around further away to angle over towards the southeast, heading towards the outside of the unfenced property line of the dune park. Using my trusty binoculars, I can see where the fence ends at the northeast corner of the park. As we approach, I start to go further east, since as a well-traveled *waiguoren*, experience tells me I want no trouble with the park police. Danny is a daredevil and takes off much closer to the fence corner, I guess not wanting to be outdone by an old China hand like me. So, three others split off with him and attack a smaller dune. Poor guy, he forgets that he asked me to carry his camera in my backpack, so he ends up going without it till the next morning.

Respecting Confucian traditions as the eldest of the group, I end up being chosen the *ascent* leader of our group of five; I ambitiously choose one of the tallest dunes around us (you know me). Luckily I am in really good shape for the mission. We slowly work our way up right along a sharply beveled dune ridge. It makes the dune we are on into the shape of a giant tetrahedron. At first, we are kings and queens on the mountain. But quickly, we start taking more numerous and longer stops as we ascend. The first stops are after every thirty, then twenty steps up, with five big inhalations before moving on. It is an incredibly arduous and long haul up to the summit, much more physically taxing than I ever imagined. My teaching cohorts exhort me ever upward and I need all the moral support I can get,

"*Jiayou Jiefu, jiayou!*" (加油杰富，加油! = Go Jeff, go! Literally, Add oil Jeff, add oil!)

Our energy dissipates as we waddle up the ridge, like hunched over sumo wrestlers. During the last 20 to 30 meters we are taking five leg trembling, wobbly steps, followed by ten to fifteen big breaths. The last ten meters seem to take an eternity and we will ourselves up, all yelling out the steps in unison,

"*YI! ER! SAN! SI!*" (一! 二! 三! 四!= ONE! TWO! THREE! FOUR!)

Sinking each step to above our ankles, as we have been the whole way, in the quicksand dune ridge. *Finally*. We make it to the peak and collectively collapse in a human pile at the top. Soaking wet with sweat, exhausted and heaving for oxygen like wounded animals, we ceremoniously plant our symbolic flag. I am not going to lie: I am gassed. Kinetic efficiency walking in deep sand must approach zero and the dune we climbed is a big one. Each lift of the foot out of the above-the-ankle-deep sand feels like trudging up a steep hillside made of wet concrete. My comrades are especially impressed with my feat, not only because of my age, but because I habitually walk around, hike and climb with my backpack, which always weighs around 6kg. I could make it lighter, but I intentionally carry it this way to give my upper body a great daily workout. And Danny's forgotten, big Canon SLR camera that I am toting just makes it even more daunting. With this ascent, I almost regret – almost - carrying my full pack. But I made it. Knowing that we were coming to watch a desert sunset, I have my camera tripod in my backpack, which I normally use to mount my binocs. I'm not about to dare using Danny's expensive gear, but my jolly band members all have pocket cameras. We mount one on the tripod and take a well-deserved group souvenir photo of our exploits. We scream and razz Danny's band across the distance to the west. Their mini dune can't hold a candle to the behemoth we conquered. We also give hearty, self-satisfying raspberries to the mountains of teeming flesh further on, who paid a ton of money to do the same thing we are doing, but under much less peaceful and adventurous conditions. Heck, I can see in my binoculars they even have a staircase built into their dune to ascend and then they can use sand bowls to slide effortlessly to the bottom. Wussies one and all. We spend a few minutes admiring the spectacular view overlooking Dunhuang to the northwest and the slowly setting Sun, falling behind the rows of dunes to the west and north of us. This dune desert is halted at Dunhuang, which from our vantage point, we can see is a real oasis: green and luxuriant vegetation across its table flat terrain. To the northeast, stretching off to the darkening horizon as far as the eye can see, is nothing but a flat scree rock desert plain. Not a place I'd like to get lost in. Right below us to the north is a massive Buddhist cemetery, the one Andy was telling us about. It is an incredible sight to scan across from this height, but it is getting too dark to go down that way to rummage through it. Gotta start heading back, which will be in the dark. We descend down a long dune ridge to join Danny's group and they decide to go back through the paid park area. I grew up with notions of trespassing. In spite of their insistent pleas, I elect to return by myself by circumnavigating the property line and not flaunting our escapades in the faces of the park authorities. I watch them through my binocs over the next hour, as they disappear towards the *main entrance* of the park to go back to the hostel. My oh my, they are a cheeky bunch. The recklessness of youth.

I walk back along the eastern periphery of the cemetery and take photos of some tombs. Luckily, Andy later gives me the pictures he took of its expanse, which are really outstanding. I wend my way back through a strange annex of Dunhuang and can see that this is where they house the hundreds of camels for rent in the park. Enough dogs are barking and howling from the barns that I pick up a hefty stone in one hand and nice pointed stick in the other, just in case I get attacked, which has happened enough times in my life, to make me leery and want to be prepared. I don't carry a heavy backpack just for my health and get out my flashlight to combat the now pitch black surroundings. Since this place is for animals to sleep and not for people, the streets are very narrow and not well laid out. I have a really good sense of direction, but this is an oasis and I quickly get lost in tall palm trees, house-high hedges and tall barns (camels are, after all tall) that are built on these snake-thin, ramshackle streets. It gets so dark and the range of my flashlight is so limited that I get the great idea to use my laser pointer, the one I use to help people locate stars when I am showing them the night sky. It has a range of 3km, which is overkill here, but it immediately helps me identify the passable trails from the culs-de-sac. Camel trains are being brought back in after a day's work and are not accustomed to seeing tourists walking through here. They and their herders all panic when they come upon me or when I turn a corner and walk into one of them. Commotion ensues as the camels stop, back up and turn away when they sense me, and the herders are trying to calm them down, as they make out my silhouette. None of us living creatures is comfortable in the melees. I say hello to each herder, in any case and apologize. All of them are nice enough not to yell at me for turning their camel train into momentary chaos.

By now, it is after 22:00 and I'm getting a little concerned about making my way through this camel labyrinth. Not to mention, I'm flat out haggard and weak from the hike to and up the dune, and have not eaten since lunch. My body has long since finished off its muscle glycogen reserves and I'm now burning body fat for energy. I already finished off my thermos of tea at the top of the dune and with all the sweat I've lost, am really dehydrated. It is all starting to catch up with me, alone here in the pitch black, ensconced in a maze full of dense vegetation, and dogs barking at me like mad with every barn I walk by. I give up the stone and settle for just the sharp stick for anti-canine protection. Would I bash its skull in with the rock or would I stab its face and neck with the stick? I choose the stick. My hand on the stick would be further away from the dog's muzzle full of, well, *canine* teeth. It's lighter anyway. I keep creeping forward, using the laser to avoid any blind alleys and culs-de-sac. Just to be safe, I crank up the compass on my Galaxy, to make sure I keep heading in a northwesterly direction. Eureka. I finally break through and get to the street that has a wall along the east side of Dunhuang. Civilization. Humanity. People. I stop at a hostel (which I now recall seeing when we came to Dunhuang from the train station) and have a much, much deserved ice cold beer. I'm just too shagged to eat, but the beer serves as a rapid source of energy and hydration. Dunhuang is not small, I'm on its eastern edge and my hostel is, you guessed it, on the *far* west side of town. So, time to make my way back. Street lights and paved streets seem like a luxury now. I get back to the hostel around 23:30. Three of the very young workers at the hostel are playing a drinking card game and are seriously bombed out of their minds. Each round of cards lost means that player has to drink all three glasses of beer. They are too drunk to eat their dinner and by now, I need to get something in my stomach. They offer me what they have as drinking snacks: salt brine peanuts, soaked in the shell, raw onions, bell peppers and sunflower seeds in the shell. Not my dream meal, but it is calories, which is what I need.

I'm too wound up to sleep and from my bed, I hear my gang of teachers getting back after 01:00. The next morning, they tell me they went out to eat, but there are not many restaurants in small Chinese towns that stay open that late. I'm dubious of their story. I suspect they may have spent the evening in the offices of the dune park, negotiating their *peichang* (compensation), for having walked onto their property and trying to exit with all the paying customers. They could be seen for hundreds of meters crossing the park all by themselves. If I could observe them from afar with my binoculars, then it only makes sense the park guards were just as attentive. Of course, under the circumstances, it would be a huge loss of face for Danny and the teachers to admit any problems, so I will never know. But I will always wonder.

1- To complete the picture, long grain rice and wheat contain less amylopectin and more amylose, whose molecular chains are in single strands, not complex chains. Hence, this type of starch is much less sticky.

Chapter 12: Dunhuang – Last Day

A long trek visiting two little seen national parks near the Xinjiang border: the deeply historical Yumenguan and the surreal, extraterrestrial Yadan.

After yesterday's amazing climb up a huge sand dune to watch the sunset over oasis Dunhuang, and the precarious return back to the hostel through a hostile camel town, my seven teacher friends and I rent a family van to go see the Yumenguan (玉门关= Jade Gate Pass) and Yadan (雅丹= Elegant Red) national parks, near the border with Xinjiang. Xinjiang is the Turkic speaking, predominately Muslim province that makes up the northwest corner of China. In fact, Danny is going there today and the Zhou family is doing their own thing around Dunhuang, so we are a gang of eight teachers on this adventure. We end up going over 200km out one way and then back, so we cover a lot of ground. Yumenguan is part of the earliest Great Wall, being over 2,100 years old, from the Han Dynasty. Through here was a key feeder route of the western Silk Road, the start of the Hexi Corridor, all of which eventually converges towards Lanzhou. The actual Yumenguan Fort is nothing to shout about and is fenced off. So, we can only look at it from about 50m away. It just looks like a huge hollowed out, sandstone, rectangular cube with openings for gates on all four sides. The walls were built to last, being several meters thick. The fact that it is over two millennia old and still standing is impressive enough. We see a remaining section of the Great Wall and it is thankfully unrestored. It is incredibly modest, about 2m high and not more than 1m thick. And the most amazing feature? It is constructed entirely of layers of reed and bamboo-woven mats, sandwiched between layers of good old fashioned mud. And parts of it are still standing, since before Jesus Christ. What is so striking to consider is that this was an adequate defense against the weapons of their day, that is, spears, clubs and arrows. Then, looking at the Great Walls built around Beijing during the Qing and Ming dynasties (the last 600 years or so), which are massive in scope and scale, and it is easy to see the incessant, ever escalating technology in our means of slaughtering each other. And in the 21st century with killer drones, Hellfire missiles, depleted uranium bullets, bunker busters, cluster bombs, landmines and white phosphorus, all raining down on defenseless civilians? Did I forget the threat of annihilation from nuclear weapons? My oh my, how times have changed...

The poor driver has to deal with a flat tire on the way to Yadan NP. We fellow teachers, spanning two continents and two very different perspectives on pedagogy, share our snacks, cut up and clown around taking pictures of each other, only a few klicks from the Xinjiang border. My Chinese counterparts are infatuated with the idea of jumping up like cheerleaders and being photographed midair. In fact, over the course of the trip, I am seeing that this pose is all the rage among Chinese tourists, going viral across the country. I've got to come up with something original now. The Western world's reputation is at stake here. I crack everybody up by lying in the middle of this deserted, desert road, spread eagle, like I'm passed out or have been hit by a car. They love it! We finally get to Yadan. Think of surreal, science fiction art, portraying extraterrestrial, lost worlds and you have some idea about what the Yadan rock formations look like. What used to be a 400km^2 lake only 12,000 years ago, slowly dried up, leaving these fantastic, hallucinogenic, anthropomorphized rock statues, one to ten plus meters high. What makes Yadan so special is the huge land area the formations cover. It would be a really spectacular place to shoot a futuristic or strange exoplanet movie, à la *Alien*, *Star Wars* and *Star Trek*.

It has been a long, gratifying day with my new teacher friends. We have had a wonderful day together. With the flat tire to boot, we get back to Dunhuang at 22:30. It takes some arm-twisting, but we convince hippy-haired, John Lennon spectacled, groovy dude Charley, the hostel owner, to cook us a simple, late dinner. I am meeting all kinds of interesting characters at places like this hostel. A young American is working on a TV deal, using his website as a platform. His Hollywood pitch is, *Traveling Asia on $15-20 a day*. When I ask him how he rounds the square peg in the hole of the 180 yuan (€23/$29) ticket to Mogao, not to mention the ¥240 (€30/$38) each teacher spent for the day at Yumenguan and Yadan National Parks, his flippant answer is,

"I don't need to go to Mogao, I've already seen tons of caves, and I've already seen the Great Wall anyway."

I find this ideological rigidness stultifying and nihilistic. So, I'm going to sit with my thumb up my backside in a 30 kuai (€3.80/$4.80) a night hostel and eat Ramen noodles three times a day, so I can meet my ideological quotient? And that is exactly what this guy is doing. He is hiding in the hostel and hanging, just like a starving peasant, just so his square peg can be forced into his round purity hole. Sad to say, he'll probably get his TV deal. Steve Evans talked about two guys who are competing against each other (go figure, an American and a Frenchman) to travel completely around the world, over land and across seas and oceans, using only their body power to do so, i.e., walking and rowing. Naturally, building a boat to row across the Atlantic is not cheap, nor is walking across the entire breadth of Russia. Thus, they have sponsors. Even young Mr. Hollywood Ideologue explained that he has been traveling for over 18 months on other people's money. He also said there are two guys competing for a book and TV deal, as the first person to travel *and* extensively tour (whatever that means) every country on the planet. One is a former British Columbian marijuana grower who is using his substantial cash reserves to finance his odyssey. And his fierce, globetrotting competitor? Another French guy! What is it about these *Français*, anyway? France just isn't beautiful and big enough for them? In any case, all this is food for thought, as I dream about my travels into the future.

CHAPTER 13: JIAYUGUAN

I'm frankly underwhelmed by this iconic, photogenic fort; a traveling bee farm, nonsensical post-revolutionary Communist statues, another great local noodle dish... And this dabizi finally breaks the culture barrier - my first Chinese hostel.

Time to say goodbye to Dunhuang, with its Mogao Caves, ivory for sale jewelry, dunescape sunsets and two amazing national parks, Yumenguan and Yadan, Jiayuguan (嘉峪关= Glorious Valley Pass) is only about a three hour bus ride from Dunhuang, on the main highway that heads southeast back to Lanzhou, and runs the length of Gansu Province. It is one-fourth of the distance across this elongated, barbell shaped province. Jiayuguan is a pleasant enough, small, modern, clean Chinese city of zero tourist value. No, you go to Jiayuguan to see its iconic, Ming Dynasty (300 to 700 years ago) fort. Yes, it is iconic, having been used on countless posters and in innumerable tourist brochures. But I'm underwhelmed. The setting is very pretty and the fort has a natural moat around it comprised of lush wetland marshes. The weather is nice, cool and lightly overcast. I'm sitting at a fresh 1,632 MASL. The air is crystal clear. Couldn't ask for a nicer day, really. But, I'm still blasé. And for ¥120 (€15/$19) no less. To make matters worse, there are a lot of repairs going on all over the fort, so scaffolding is everywhere I turn. Late in the afternoon, there is a kitschy show with acrobats and martial artists, and actors dressed up in plastic, faux Ming military uniforms, doing an uninspired rendition from a dance scene in *All that Jazz*. As is too often the case in China, the music can't be turned up loud enough. Just like the hilarious, heavy metal hair band Spinal Tap, they always seem to find *11* on a volume dial that only goes up to 10. The performing troupe has two tall banks of loudspeakers and they are totally fuzzed out from overuse and abuse.

There is in fact another section of Jiayuguan that flanks this main fort, and that is the Great Wall that extends from either side of it. But quite frankly, what I have seen so far does not inspire me to be curious enough to go check it out. I see a scale model of the surroundings and the two extending walls, as I walk back towards the entrance. I use that model vicariously to call it a day. My decision is vindicated when I get back home and look at the pictures Steve Evans so graciously let me copy to take a look at. I see rebuilt, newish guard towers and a wall technologically between Yumenguan, from the Song Dynasty, 2,100 years ago and the Qing Dynasty walls (the last 300 years) around Beijing.

But at Jiayuguan, I finally bag big game. Wow, my first big tour group of foreigners. Around twenty, who sounds like Dutch, are prowling Jiayuguan's high walls. So far on this journey, Steve Evans and that Ivy League dude I saw at the Beijing Train Station excepted, I have seen the one same elderly couple from Australia ("G'DAY!" with the bush hat, big beer belly hidden under an untucked tropical shirt, khaki shorts, knee socks, high top hiking boots - iconic) at Zhongwei and the White Temple in Lanzhou (amazing we run into each other in two places so far away) and about eight foreigners at the Dunhuang hostel. These are the sum total of non-oriental foreigners I have seen to date on this voyage. Where are they, China's billion dollar international tourist industry? I can merely guess they only hit the top sites, like Beijing, Shanghai, Xi'an and the like. But their numbers out this far are statistically zero, in a tsunami of Chinese travelers. I'm sure there are some Koreans (I met a couple of groovy Korean dudes on the train to Dunhuang - we had a hoot comparing all our Samsung mobile gear), and I think I heard a couple of guys speaking Japanese. But I'm not going to spend my vacation practicing Asian phrenology.

Back in Jiayuguan town, I do something very few foreigners can contemplate doing: staying at a Chinese hostel, or *zhaodaisuo* (招待所). I have seen on reservation websites where hotels are designated *Chinese only*, but until today, had never been confronted with the practice. My Fujian teaching friends from Dunhuang texted me the names of a couple of these Chinese hostels, both close to the Jiayuguan train station. Just knowing where to go gives me the added courage to try. I walk into one of them. The woman at the desk, a Mrs. Guan, takes one look at my big nose and says,

"You can't stay here, foreigners have to stay at the tourist hotel."

I tell her my story: Beijing teacher, not a short term visitor, and to appeal to her practical, maternal side, I tell her that as a teacher, I don't have a lot of money and cannot afford the expensive tourist hotel. I can see that Mrs. Guan is sympathetic. This goes on and on, back and forth for ten minutes, and she keeps telling me that she does not want to get in trouble with the *paichusuo* (派出所), or neighborhood police station. We are at a stalemate. I appreciate that she is just doing her job and wants to stay out of trouble. No one wants to get on the wrong side of their local *paichusuo*. They can move mountains in a time of need and if you get on their wrong side, they can turn your life into a living Hades. And what can I say? She is being extremely charming about it and I can tell she really wants me to stay there. She just feels that her hands are tied. The whole problem is my passport. She can't read a word of it: it might as well be from planet Zenon. The fact that I have a much cherished *Z*, or residential visa to show off means nothing to her. Then suddenly, I remember: I have the death ray gun to blow all of her arguments (really worries) out of the galaxy. I dig into my money purse that I keep hanging around my neck and hidden inside my shirt, unzip one of the little pockets and pull out my *residence permit*. Not only is it in Chinese, but guess who issues said residence permit? Why, the local *paichusuo* where one lives. And on it, what is big and round and fat and red and sticks out like a sore thumb for all the world to see? My local *paichusuo's* official stamp, that's what. Now that she has something she can read and wrap her brain around, I suggest she call her local police, tell them what I have and see what they say. I have no idea what to expect, but how can they refuse a document issued and stamped by their very own homologs in Beijing? Now if this were the 1990's, it would definitely be a whole different horror show on the big screen of my life in China. But, let's see what happens 20 years later... She is on the phone for a few minutes. I can hear her describing my residence permit and the all-important death ray gun red chop. She hangs up, comes back into the reception area all smiles and says,

"OK, you can stay!"

I think she is just as happy as I am. We almost make it a celebration. And for the rest of my trip? I think I'm on to something here. After checking in, I walk down the long boulevard from the train station to go to the Bank of China at a big main square. One of the coolest things I've ever seen is a large sized transport truck with open sides parked at a big street corner. But this guy is not selling toys, vegetables or junk electronics. No, he is selling honey and his bees are with him, living and traveling in their mobile hives on the huge truck bed. He has a honey and comb separator, filter, jars - the works, to sell to the public. What a novel idea. I suspect he stays in one place long enough for the bees to get oriented to come in at night. At that point, I suspect he battens down the hatches and moves on to the next place. Sort of a Johnny Appleseed, but this guy might be called Peng the Pollinator.

And then there before me, shall we say, is a huge, indescribable statue in the middle of a roundabout that counts for the town's main commercial square. Oblique, dense, unfathomable and unless you go up to the base of this monster and read what it is about, totally baffling. Even after reading the artist's vision, it's still towering gobbledygook. Thirty-nine meters tall and made of stainless steel, this is an interprovincial cooperation with the Shaanxi Sculpture Design Institute and made by a sculpture factory in Xi'an, Shaanxi's provincial capital and the location of the famous terracotta soldiers. For the enlightened, in this gigantic, silver tuning fork monster can be seen the Great Wall, the Weijin Tombs, modern farming and defense patrols, as it depicts a huge vertically positioned sword, pointing straight to the sky. These esoteric, revolutionary statues are everywhere in China: tall, small, metal, stone, tiled, and plastic in every color of the rainbow, in most towns all across the country. They are invariably a hangover from the 80s, when after the Cultural Revolution finally petered out with the death of the Great Helmsman, there was this flurry of pent up artistic expression that just burst out all over the place. However, there was a catch, a *big* catch: all the controls and mechanisms to censor and *maintain revolutionary purity* were still firmly in place and did not really ebb until well into the 90s (this kind of ideological censorship and control is still very much in place, but it is more flexible and open then back then). All public art was forced to hew to the litmus test standards of the Communist Party, which resulted in these baffling geometric, curvilinear, block or abstract works of imponderable *what-the-hey*. All these bizarre, absurd, and yes, I think we can say in retrospect, ridiculous statues (at least from the point of view of Western aesthetics) that grace millions of town squares and intersections all over rural China are still standing, to confuse and amuse us.

I go to a neighborhood noodle place and get a big plate of *chaocuoyu* (炒搓鱼= fried rubbed fish). Not unlike florid French menus, as is often the case with Chinese dish names, the names can be very misleading. This dish contains no fish. But, the dish has what the Chinese call fish sauce (鱼露= *yulu*),which is a coulis of cut up fish parts reduced for hours over low heat, down to this famous, syrup-thick, chocolate colored sauce. Chinese fish sauce is way too overpowering to use more than sparingly, so the main sauce is gravy thick and brown, from beef. Swimming in this rich sauce are scrumptious little worm shaped noodles that look like big, fat maggots. Hence the name *rubbed*, since the chef pushes and rolls them off a big mass of soft, fresh dough stock with his fingers or more likely, his thumb. The noodles are heavily laden with whatever fresh veggies the chef found in the fridge. It's all flash fried in a flaming wok and umm-umm - *out of this world.*

As I walk back to the hostel, I look up and bam - I feel like I have been bonked on the head with a Looney Tunes cartoon sized mallet. Off in the distance are the snow-crested peaks of the Qilian Mountain Range. I now realize that the overcast sky has cleared up to grace the pinkish red sunset. The mountains are stunningly beautiful and I just stand there for a good five minutes and gawk at them. That's where I'm going tomorrow. Time to head back to my boundary busting, culture bending Chinese hostel room, which is costing me a whopping ¥40 (€5/$6). I could share a room for only ¥25 (€3/$4), but decide to splurge. Not to mention I have a pair of binoculars to take care of. I admire all the wet bed sheets hanging on the barely lit, stair balustrades, as we wend our way up to the third floor. The walls have a nice, grimy, gray prison patina that I will soon not forget. The hall floors radiate a blackish, truck stop, oil-stained parking lot. Savor the moment Brown, suck in the memories. My first *zhaodaisuo*. So, *this* is where China's salt of the Earth stays. As I learn on the rest of trip, the interior decor and lighting may leave a lot to be desired, and some turn out to incredibly nice. But, they all have what we want, bottom line: a firm bed with clean sheets and hot water 24/7. None of that was usually on offer back in the 90s, even in the ripoff tourist hotels, so putting things in perspective, it's just what the doctor ordered. Tomorrow, the July First Glacier, 4,300m up in the majestic Qilian mountains.

Chapter 14: July 1st Glacier

Reflecting on life in China during the Wild West 90s. Climbing the sublime July 1st Glacier at 4,300 MASL in the majestic Qilian Mountains. Plus, how I paid less than a bus load of Chinese for a tour package. Oh yeah, they were bummed!

The Jiayuguan Fort was a bit of an aside to the main attraction of coming to this part of Gansu: the July First Glacier (七一冰川= *Qiyi Bingquan*), about 130km southwest of Jiayuguan Town. No one I talk to seems to know about the Luhua (绿化= Green Change) train station talked about in the Lonely Planet. They keep telling me the train to Jingtieshan (镜铁山= Mirror Iron Mountain) leaves right outside my Chinese hostel door, which is situated just in front of the main Jiayuguan train station. So, I can only assume that the 08:00 departure time indicated in LP is from my next door station. After all, how many train stations can a little city like Jiayuguan have? Two, exactly. I luckily get to the station at 06:30 and as usual there are long lines to buy tickets. When five million passengers a day take interurban trains, activity around ticket windows is intense, from the moment they open till the second they close. In bigger cities they can be open 24 hours a day. Even here in puny Jiayuguan, the windows are open from 06:00 till midnight, seven days a week.

This is so much nicer than in the 90s. Back then, bus and train ticket offices kept bankers' hours and there would maybe be two or three windows open out of ten or twenty. They'd randomly and cruelly open and close the windows for unknown lengths of time. Another favorite game of sadism was to post a sign on the glass, *Will open at such and such a time*, only to see that hour pass, leaving all the customers stranded in line. Then another one would suddenly open further to the side and like hyena packs, the mobs would rush over, pushing, clawing, scratching and railing the whole way. The train employees were just messing with the public and getting their sociopathic jollies by watching all the chaos and suffering. There were no lines. It was just rabid masses of elbows, knees and screaming heads crushing and stomping on each other, in a funnel shape in front of the window. Not as many people traveled back in those days. But still, in a country of a billion souls, buying a train ticket, any ticket, was fiendishly ferocious. Everywhere people had to queue up, pushing matches and fistfights between traveling families and groups were not uncommon. These were actually great moments to take advantage of the confusion and make a big push to the front of the ticket window line, proving the veracity of Charles Darwin's natural selection and adaptation.

Those were the buckaroo days, a cowboy frontier in China, to be sure. I spent seven years of my life in that surreal, Wild West, gold rush world. I'm still nostalgic about them, in a twisted, demented way. It's like an ex-smoker reminiscing about the pleasure of their three-pack-a-day habit, knowing it was killing them. Living here in China back then really was like having an incurable drug habit, with its claws deeply embedded into your soul. You knew it was bad for you, but you just could not get enough of it. Every day was a thrill ride, a mentally bruising video game, an exhausting body rush. You changed and became socially feral. Still warped from the psychotic perversities of the Cultural Revolution, the Chinese were afflicted with PTSD (posttraumatic stress disorder) on a national scale, treating each other like animals, so it was adapt or die. When we finally moved to France, it was like going through extended detox. It took months to rearrange my brain and pull out of the reptilian mindset that was necessary to survive on a day-to-day basis in 90s China.

I get to the window a little bit before 07:00, thinking I have a good hour till departure and the lady says,

"The train leaves at seven, you'd better run!"

And run I do, sprinting as fast as I can and making it into the car as the massive diesel engine pushes down on the accelerator to slowly pull away. Luckily it's a small, provincial train station. I'm scratching my head as to how the train schedule could be an hour off, when about fifteen minutes after departing, we stop at, of course, Luhua Station, which is situated in the northwest part of Jiayuguan. And from there, it does leave at 08:00. I really count myself lucky, since this is the one daily train that goes to Jingtieshan, which is the gateway to the July First Glacier. And at only ¥5.50 (€0.70/$0.90) for the beautiful climb into the Qilian mountain range, I can't bicker about cost. Jiayuguan is 1,600 MASL and Jingtieshan sits at 2,600 MASL so over the course of the three-hour train ride, we climb one kilometer in elevation. The story of how this relatively accessible glacier got its mundane name is predictably banal. Back in the day when post-WWII China and the USSR were kissing Communist cousins, a joint Sino-Soviet geological survey team discovered the glacier on, that's right, a July 1st. How creative! This just mentioned ticket price is the only one listed in last year's Lonely Planet that I can find, which is less expensive today than when it was published. What with inflation and a burgeoning Chinese tourist industry, price rises are to be expected. Yet this one has dropped from ¥10 to ¥5.50, almost half the price. Of course there is no way a train can run for three hours, climbing a klick in altitude, burning up a carload of diesel and still be profitable, even at ten kuai. What this suggests is the local government is doing everything in its power to keep Jingtieshan happy or populated or both. With a subsidy this ridiculous, it will be interesting to see what the town is like.

When we get there, the train station literally sits in the shadows of the iron ore complex, as the mixture of (mainly) mine workers and tourist glacier hounds bounds off the train, into a big, open area, resembling a parking lot. Quite a few of the train passengers have on full body blue mining company uniforms, and I can see the insignia of the Jingtieshan Iron Ore Company above their front pockets. There are numerous buses and shuttles, big and small, to take all the mine workers to their respective posts, along with two big vans marked, *July First Glacier Tours*, only in Chinese, which gives you some idea of how few foreigners come up here. And all the taxis that are mentioned in Lonely Planet to take me up there? They do not exist. So it looks like these two vans are it. There are around thirty glacier seekers, all Chinese except yours truly, their token *laowai*. It all happens pretty fast. Some of the Chinese ask if I want to join them, the driver says hop on board and we are off, thirteen in total. Being the only Chinese speaking white boy on the bus, I get pumped with about a hundred questions during the incredibly scenic drive, climbing up into the massive Qilian Range, to the glacier's base camp. Even though the questions are repetitive and predictable, it is great practice for me, as my group is made up of tourists from Guangdong, Sichuan and Shaanxi. Even though they are all speaking Mandarin, the lingua franca of China, their accents are strikingly different, which really keeps me on my toes. It's sort of like talking with groups from the Bronx in New York, Mobile, Alabama and the barrios of Los Angeles at the same time.

The glacier's base camp is at 3,800 meters. So, today is a 1km climb from Jiayuguan to Jingtieshan and now another 1.2km from Jingtieshan to the glacier's base camp. The bus driver buys entry tickets to the park for everybody, including me, which I find a little unusual. As he hands me my ticket, he tells me it is a *package deal*, for a total of ¥240 (€30/$38), which I find kind of pricy. The ticket is ¥101 (€13/$16), not the ¥51 indicated in Lonely Planet. This is actually the student/child price. I'm the only person from whom he is asking money, which has got me scratching my head, and I find the ¥139 (€17/$22) bus fare for only a half an hour drive each way for a total of thirteen paying passengers to be way over the top. At this point, I just keep my mouth shut, because I really want to see a glacier up close. In all my travels, I've seen a number of them from a distance, but I've never hiked up to one. At base camp, three hikers buy bags of oxygen. They look like a big blue, over inflated camping pillow, with a rubber hose sticking out at one end and a stopcock to control the flow of gas, as it is being inhaled. Pretty clever idea if you ask me and at ¥30 (€3.80/$4.80) a pillow, it must a good money maker, I'm sure. A tall tank of oxygen is not that expensive. Back in the 90s, they would have just filled it up with air and sold it as pure oxygen. Who knows today? After everybody on the bus buys snacks, drinks and oxygen pillows, we all pile back on and drive about 2km to a parking area, where it is time to start our 5km long trek, over which we will make a rapid vertical climb of 500 meters up to the glacier, perched at 4,300 MASL. While this may not sound like much, it is the equivalent of climbing a 150-story skyscraper, or one and half Empire State Buildings. And to climb one and a half Empire State Buildings at 4km above sea level? Well... We'll see. The driver says to be back around 15:00, so that gives us almost five hours to make the 10km round trip loop and spend some time at the glacier.

It does not take long to see that out of the thirteen of us on the bus, most are not going to make it to the summit. At

3km above sea level, the air's oxygen content (and air pressure for that matter) are already only 70% of what they are on the beach. And at 4,000 meters, it drops to 60%, so getting to the top today means breathing air that has almost one-half the oxygen compared to Beijing. After a couple of klicks, there are three of us out front and one of these two men, whom I later learn is an artist from Guangdong, Ye Zhihua (we are still staying in touch), is the second oldest person in the group, after me. It feels good that the two oldest guys in our group are heading the pack. On the way up, I feel very safe filling up my water bottle with glacier melt water, since herd animals are non-existent and I see no animal spoor anywhere. I drink down a liter and fill my bottle full. Wow! What an incredibly refreshing taste. I start to pull away about half way up and make it to the summit, enjoying a few minutes of alpine solitude. Ye Zhihua shows up next. Mr. Third Place makes it, as do his son and Ye's daughter, both preteens. She is having fun cavorting and clowning up the mountain with someone her own age, rather than with her very fit and artistic dad. Then, another younger couple makes it to the top. And that's it. The others, including all the oxygen pillow breathers, will enjoy the pristine mountain air and view of the July 1st Glacier from further below. Many people struggle with hypoxia, so the numbers who made it all the way to the top are not surprising.

The glacier itself is as majestic and sublime as you would expect. We climb up to its tail end, where it terminates and is melting at 4,300m, but it does extend up to 5,150m in altitude, covering 5km². It is easy to see the incredible power of erosion that glaciers have, as they flow down the face of a mountain over the millennia. There are tons and tons of rock along the bottom of the glacier, suspended in the ice, several meters deep, which have been sucked up with its century-slow, grinding movement,. Unfortunately, human caused global warming is having predictably onerous effects on its wellbeing. Just in the last few years, it has receded 50m up the mountain side, its 78m thickness is starting to thin and its melt water volume has increased a breathtaking 50%. Will it be here for my grandchildren to see? Count me doubtful. With my binoculars, I can easily observe three scientists who have set out various instruments along the length of the glacier's tail. They have a campsite all set up towards the bottom. When the sky does clear, they must have an awe inspiring night sky to do star gazing. If they don't have a good telescope in their camp, they are really missing out. It's time to head back. Before leaving the glacier, I quaff my water bottle and slake my thirst, refilling it before continuing my descent. I am taking this liter of crystal clear, glacier spring water as a souvenir to be savored over the next day or two. What do you call the tree line when there are no trees? These mountains are covered with meadow grass, brilliantly colored flowers in every direction and scrub brush, but nary a tree. How does *plant line* sound? The plant line starts when I'm only about 200m down the trail from the start of the glacier melt runoff, which rapidly turns into a raging torrent of water just a couple of hundred meters further below. There seems to be nothing much for animals to eat at this elevation, wild or domesticated, although that does not exclude any nocturnal creatures. Marmots can been seen in even the most barren of mountain ecosystems, but not one can be observed poking its squirrel-like head out from behind some rocks here.

I actually end up being the last person to get back to the bus, as I stop to take a number of photos on the way down. I briefly consider staying the night at base camp, in order to do some star gazing, but decide against it, due to the fact that I do not have the warm clothing to stay out at night and secondly, the sky continues to be full of fluffy, broken clouds. On the way back to Jingtieshan in the bus, I am chitchatting with my neighbors and just have to find out what my Chinese brethren are paying for today's tour, compared to what I consider to be my pricy ¥240. What I learn is that they all prepaid their tours through the *zhaodaisuo* where they are staying in Jiayuguan. And get a load of this: They all paid ¥260 to ¥280, even more than this old *waiguoren*. The extra money is the commission their hotels added to the tour cost. Like a rare, great wine, I savor this amazing occurrence:

"I, Jeff J. Brown, just paid less money for the same service than all my Chinese brethren. This will go down in all of China expats' story telling annals as one of the greatest of exploits! It briefly assuages my long afflicted soul, for the thousands of times I've paid more for the same service or product as the locals have."

As we enter Jingtieshan, it is starting to sink in among the passengers. All the Chinese passengers are looking at me, a few are whispering in each other's ears, I'm staring back at them and we are all thinking the same thing: This can't be right. What the heck is going on here? Now *they know how it feels...* On the way back to Jingtieshan, we have a long and impressive look at the Qilian mountain range, which is located in Gansu's narrow handle between the two bulging barbells at either end. The Qilians are just as impressive as the Rockies or the Alps, but the chain is 800km long, compared to the

1,200km long Alps and the continent long Rockies. Even though this is the desert, many of the tallest peaks are permanently covered in thick snow. It seems like every mountain range has a defining characteristic as to how the peaks are shaped and the Qilians are marked by a large number of small, craggy points on top, almost like the teeth on an irregular saw blade. As I scan the skyline, one peak juts out over the others. This must be Gansu's tallest peak, the eponymous Qilian Peak topping out at 5,547m. This is 900m taller than the tallest peak in the Rockies and 700m taller than that of the Alps. This is not even the range's tallest peak. There are two that top out at 5,800m, further south in Qinghai. So, while it is not the longest of mountain ranges, it does pack a spectacular altitude punch. Qilian Peak is a strange looking apex. On top is a tall, cliff-faced butte that shoots straight up. And then, like a big wedding cake, two or three progressively smaller ones are stacked, one on top of the other. And then to crown it off, a long, narrow butte is perched on the very top, shaped much like the United Nations building in New York. All in all, a most impressive mountain peak... Funny enough, it is barren, in spite of its superior height, compared to all the snow covered crags on each side. I can only assume this is due to its really unusual shape and how the generally northwest winds hit it.

CHAPTER 15: JINGTIESHAN

A journey into the Twilight Zone of 50s Chinese Communism. Right here, right now! Part I

Our July 1st Glacier tour bus gets back to the Jingtieshan Mine parking lot right outside the train station. The station hangs under the shadow of a huge pile of rust colored iron ore that has been extracted from the mountain looming just behind it. It is starting to rain and the one daily train is returning to Jiayuguan in just a few minutes. I have a decision to make, or to coin the title of The Clash's smash hit, *Should I Stay or Should I Go?* I open up my Lonely Planet PDF file on Gansu and check out the section on stuff to do around Jingtieshan, besides the glacier. Lemme see... There is a really cheap *zhaodaisuo* where I can sleep in Jingtieshan Town. Being right on the border with Tibetan Gansu to the south, there is an enchanting Tibetan village in the mountains above, called Qiqing, as well as a nearby village whose name in English means Swan Lake (天鹅湖= Tian'e Hu). There are cheap taxis to take me there and it's all doable in one day, whereupon I can take this same said afternoon train back to Jiayuguan tomorrow afternoon. It all sounds like an absolutely charming adventure in the nearby Kingdom of Tibet. Assessing the situation, OK, no taxis materialized this morning when arriving to go see the glacier, but hey, maybe it was just an aberration or a slow day. I mean surely a big mining town must have a taxi or three trolling the pavement in search of fares, right? Currently, I am only having warm, fuzzy feelings of cheap lodging and quaint Tibetan culture, just waiting to greet me with open arms up there in the snow-capped Qilian Mountains. I take the bait and decide to stay. Jingtieshan Town is three or so klicks long. Looking upstream, it wends its way up the valley and is cut in half by a suicide-for-kayakers torrent its entire length. It's a really pretty view, but there are no taxis. All I is see is load after load of long buses, full of blue clad mine workers being brought to the station at the end of the workday, for them to hop on the train to Jiayuguan.

Do they really ride the train six hours a day to work, here and back? Or since it is Friday afternoon, are they going back down to Jiayuguan for the weekend? I would assume the latter, but then I remember the train was full of workers this morning to come here. Maybe they share the wealth by rotating shifts. In any case, this confirms my earlier supposition about the low ticket cost of only ¥5.50: the three-hour, 1km ascent is certainly heavily subsidized to help the workers get to the mine and back. After ten or so minutes of watching all these mine workers going home and seeing no taxis whatsoever, I start talking to some of the bus drivers. They all tell me the same thing: Jingtieshan has no taxis and they all dismissively look at me a little cross eyed for asking such a ridiculous question,

"*What do you mean taxis here, are you out of your wig* laowai?"

When traveling, I use my trusty triple confirmation method: if three people tell me the same thing, I can assume it's probably true. In this case, it is about five of them, so I think I can take this fact to the bank: there *are* no taxis in Jingtieshan. And it just keeps getting weirder. As I'm standing there about to decide to start walking into town, I notice that in addition to all the big buses bringing mine employees to the train station, cars are also pulling up to drop off people, office types or managers, although the blue mining company uniform seems *de rigueur* for every sentient biped here. Finally, as one driver is letting off a couple of blue clad workers with briefcases, I snag him and ask if he could please take me to the *zhaodaisuo*, so I can rent a room for the night. He tells me to hop on in. Mr. Qiang is a married man in his 30s from Lanzhou, with a young daughter and a wife who also works at the mine. From all I've seen, this is a true company town, so where else would she work? He's very happy here. He and his wife like the steady work, the pristine, high altitude air, being so close to wild nature and far away from what he considers is his grungy, crowded hometown. He also thinks their daughter has a better, more wholesome life, culturally eons from the intrigues and temptations of big city life. It couldn't have been better said than by countless other people I've met around the world, who make the decision to pull away from the superficialities and materialism of modern civilization, to stake out a new beginning in the countryside or a small town. Qiang kind of chuckles as I inquire about Jingtieshan's celebrated hostel, telling me he's been working at the mine for seven years and has never heard of a *zhaodaisuo* in Jingtieshan. When I ask Qiang about the taxis, he smiles and tells me there are no taxis, just company buses and company cars. I am already wondering what's going on: in ten minutes I learn there are no taxis and no hostel. He tells me there is only one place to stay in this here town, you guessed it - the *company* hotel. And it just keeps getting more and more back to the past… As we drive on, I ask him where there is a store, so I can buy some snacks, and you are catching on, there *are* no stores and he's right. I see nothing but mining company buildings, all abandoned and derelict; all of the work units in the mining complex looking completely run down and sitting in corroded silence, the same rusty red color as the ore being extracted from the mountains above. The odd blue uniformed mine worker is milling about solo or at most, with just one other *tongshi* (同事), or comrade. A couple of men ride by on their antique, rusted out Flying Pigeon bicycles, the standard model during the Mao years. Then suddenly, I get it: these are not workers, they are zombies lost in a time warp. They've been walking and riding for years on end, lost to time, lost to reality. Their faces are expressionless, dead. I have to ask,

"And is there a place where I can get dinner tonight?"

At this point, I start to hear the 1960's most memorable, hair raising, gooseflesh tingling four-note theme song ever dreamed up – *The Twilight Zone* - and I can see Rod Serling's TV portrait floating in front of me on top of the dashboard, like a hologram bobblehead saying,

"Some people say that Communism faded into oblivion in the twentieth century, where entire towns depended on their state owned companies for their every need. Some people say that all ended when the Berlin Wall came tumbling down. But, they'd be wrong.

There is a fifth dimension beyond that which is known to man. It is a dimension as vast as space and as timeless as infinity. It is the middle ground between light and shadow, between science and superstition, and it lies between the pit of man's fears and the summit of his knowledge. This is the dimension of imagination. It is an area which we call 'The Twilight Zone'…

Jeff, will you ever escape the 1950s zombies of the Jingtieshan Iron Ore Mine?"

Gulp! What have I gotten myself into? Mr. Serling's TV jingle culminates in its climatic crescendo of flat- and minor-note horns, bassoons and oboes, and his doppelganger visage and voice fade through the windshield. We suddenly lurch right into a huge company complex – The Communist Party Headquarters. *It is 1954, the year of my birth.* We drive past the huge edifice that is the Communist Party main bureau, make a couple of quick lefts and rights, go well off the main road towards the back of the compound and stop in front of the *Jingtieshan People's Iron Ore Mine Hotel.* I say goodbye to Mr. Qiang, the nice company man who brought me here. In a court of law, I'm beginning to think he's what they call an accomplice. He jerkily gesticulates with his hand towards the front door, as if to convince me to walk the plank. All's that's missing is the blindfold and a pack of saber-poking ne'er-do-well land pirates chanting,

"*Jump, jump, JUMP...*"

Menacing Disney film orchestration cascades in the background. Mr. Company Driver smiles diabolically, with just the hint of a sneer, and shakes his head as he roars off and out of the vacant complex.

The Party headquarters are totally deserted. The buildings in the whole compound are covered in standard issue, revolutionary, vapid, beige and yellow tile. A patina of grey black soot seems to cover every exposed surface. I push open one of the squeaky glass hotel doors. It is festooned with a semi-opaque, lime green wind curtain, the kind with the long strips of thick plastic hanging from above, only here, it feels like setting the stage for entering a time-warped haunted house. What's next? The sound of clanking skeleton bones and wind swept howls? The reception area is tastelessly modeled after Stalinist era interior design, but with local characteristics: gaudy, tacky chrome and colored-glass chandeliers, pompously oversized and overstuffed *faux* leather sofas and a garish winding staircase made of chrome, plastic and tile that turns upstairs to a floor of rooms. There is no reception desk. One isn't needed in a proletarian People's hotel. I must be the only creature in the building who can fog a mirror. I walk down the ground floor hallway as my footsteps echo in the timeless silence. I almost make it to the end when two old zombie women appear out of nowhere, chanting in drab monotone,

"*Meiyou, meiyou*!" (没有, 没有!= There are none, there are none! - rooms that is.)

They wave their brooms in somber unison, advancing towards me in metronome fashion with their redundant chant, symbolically sweeping me out the front door. As they brush me towards the exit, I see room after empty room, some perfectly arranged, some having been slept in, some with garbage strewn on the floors, and they haven't been cleaned in 58 years. Other than the echo of my feet walking on the tile hall floor, the Jingtieshan People's Iron Ore Mine Hotel is uninhabited. Why, there is not a single proletarian comrade around to comfort me and inspire my ardor for country and party, as we march fearlessly on our way to great industrial victories, crushing the yellow capitalist running dogs in spiritually polluted Western Europe and America. The last wisp of broom brushes my backside as I amble outside, wondering what to do. I work my way further back into the complex. Besides the Party Bureau's main building out front, there are three other big edifices, all covered in the same pallid tile. The walls of the buildings are lined with glass covered presentation displays, where great soldiers of the revolution are shown emulating selfless sacrifice and their undying love for The Great Helmsman Mao Zedong, Country and Party. They are pictured receiving medals, certificates and ribbons. In the background of each photo, the golden hammer and sickle is prominently displayed on Communist crimson. We don't know it yet, but in four years, our iron ore will be of great strategic value, when China launches the Great Leap Forward, and we rapidly bury the West with our vastly superior industrial capacity and peasant powered savoir-faire.

One of the buildings is the Workers' Dormitory, another is the Workers' Mess Hall and the third is the Workers' Recreation Center. Knowing already that this is the only place to sleep in Jingtieshan, I stand there staring at the three deserted buildings, the propaganda posters and over my shoulder, at the hotel that doesn't want me. I start to seriously think about finding someplace to sleep outside for the night, when suddenly, a young woman ambles out of the dormitory. Is she another 1954 workers' zombie? I introduce myself to this very surprised and pleasant young lady. She has a look on her face like the citizens meeting the tin man alien in the 1951 classic sci-fi movie, *The Day the Earth Stood Still*. She incredulously asks me why I am here. I explain my predicament. She looks at me half unbelievingly: surely I must have misunderstood the hotel zombies. She asks me to follow her back into the hotel. While I wait sitting on one of the elephantine reception sofas, the two zombie sweepers try to persuade her that the hotel is full and it is impossible to find a spare bed in the hotel's echoing, lifeless, ghostly air. But great Gaia, this young thing doesn't take their answer as gospel truth, disappears for about five minutes and comes back with another youngish woman. They go inside a hotel room that has been converted into the hotel office and *de facto* reception desk. They are both in there for quite some time. I induce myself to admire the awful, kitsch plastic and glass, insipid tile and Naugahyde decor. The zombie sweepers have crawled back into their funereal cracks in the dingy, grey walls. I savor my solitude with a bit of a smirk on my face. Heck, this is kind of fun! Finally, the kind woman who rescued me outside, my Ms. Iron Mine Nightingale comes out and approaches me with a troubled look on her face. My fate is in her hands. The envelope, please?

Chapter 16: Jingtieshan - Continued

A journey into the Twilight Zone of 50s Chinese Communism. Right here, right now! Part II.

Ms. Iron Mine Nightingale, my savior who found me lost outside and got me this far from sleeping on the street, comes out of her comrade's hotel room office and approaches me across the kitschy reception area. She looks at me sheepishly and explains that the reason the hotel is *full* is because tomorrow, the iron ore company is having a *huge* workers' meeting and the hotel staff are overwhelmed with all the preparations (yeah, sure honey). But since I am here and it is a *difficult situation* for everyone involved, the hotel manager has gotten special administrative approval from the Party Bureau to permit me to stay in this magnificent hotel for one night only. And even though it is a *luxury proletarian* hotel, the Party Bureau has also authorized me to pay only ¥80 (€10/$13), instead of the usual room price of ¥120 (€15/$19). Will this be acceptable to me? Hmm…

And then it suddenly dawns on me who this young lady is. Ms. Iron Mine Nightingale is an acolyte, a paradigm, an avatar of Lei Feng, Mao Zedong's 1950's self-sacrificing superhero and super-patriot, showing me how merciful, hospitable and generous the Revolution is, even when the visitor is a gutless, yellow-bellied, lackey whore for capitalism - like me. *In spite of the shame and oppressive guilt I should be feeling for my unrepentant origins, this angel of Communist perfection is going to take care of me… She will now forever be called* Ms. Iron Mine Nightingale-Comrade Lei Fengette *in my heart.*

I don't have a lot of room to negotiate here. It's either this or sleeping under the canopy of a tree on the sidewalk somewhere. So, I graciously accept the terms and manifestly express my thanks for her kind efforts. She asks me to follow her into the hotel office. Seated there is the young manager, gloriously decked out in her Jingtieshan People's Iron Ore Mine Hotel uniform. It has big, gaudy, gold braided Colonel Muammar Gaddafi shoulder epaulettes, and down the front, large, embossed brass gold buttons. It is all decked out on a royal blue US Marines dress jacket. Ten-hut! Large red, gold and blue insignias of the iron ore company proudly blaze away on each upper arm. Clearly, a person of high ranking in the Communist Party hierarchy, who commands my deepest veneration. Due to the sartorial pomp of her audacious, official company uniform, I christen her Ms. Epaulettes–Comrade Gaddafi Shoulder Pads.

Luckily, Lei Fengette is here to assist her well dressed, worthy comrade in undertaking this most arduous and solemn of administrative duties: registering a running dog foreign devil in this finest example of proletarian hospitality. Ms. Epaulettes asks Lei Fengette how to proceed and she coyly suggests that it might be a good idea to ask for my passport. My capitalist passport would be way beyond the administrative capacities of Ms. Epaulettes, so I proudly present my Chinese residence permit that, even though it is in the national language of the People's Republic of China, is still more than she can absorb. So, Comrade Lei walks her through the whole process and shows her where the lines on my permit correspond to the lines in her registry book. After this nearly insurmountable bureaucratic conundrum is vanquished, there is the Gordian knot of trying to provide me with dinner tonight and breakfast tomorrow morning, since there is only the Workers' Mess Hall and I am definitely not a member of the Chinese proletariat. Comrade Lei Fengette applies her ever-sharp Occam's razor and mildly suggests to the imminently qualified hotel manager that maybe I could buy some People's food vouchers. What a marvelous solution. My angel Ms. Nightingale is quite something. So, Comrade Epaulettes uses her steel honed revolutionary genius to find a book of food vouchers in the desk drawer and places them in front of her esteemed self. I can see her mind fiercely cogitating, as sharp and as powerful as a Kodiak bear trap. She is unsure of how many to sell me and looks up over her shoulder, where savior Lei is standing behind her, to offer ideologically pure counsel. Fengette wisely and humbly reminds her qualified comrade that dinner is worth eight yuan and breakfast two.

The genius of the Chinese Communist revolution is that the book of food vouchers is printed so that there are exactly *ten* per page, that is, just the right number for one breakfast *and* one dinner, since lunch would be served in the field at the mines. How logical and intellectually superior the Communist revolution is. But these vouchers are worthless as they are, because they have not been baptized by the omnipotent red stamp, which is in the possession of, you know who, Ms. Gaddafi Shoulder Pads. This is her moment of regal, revolutionary rectitude: all those years of studying the Thoughts of Mao Zedong, all those sleepless nights sweating over countless Party propaganda circulars and tracts, memorizing them in the faint light of her Lei Feng worker's candle, fighting off the frigid temperatures in her communal dorm room next door. It all finally culminates in this most solemn of tasks. She slowly and respectfully opens her top desk drawer, savoring this unforgettable moment in her Communist career: she is about to chop ten food vouchers for a visiting and however odious member of the running dog capitalist road class. She is not going to rush this, oh no-no... She purposefully and slowly searches for her all-powerful administrative saber and finally finds it towards the back of the big drawer. She takes an equally long time locating the ink bowl. Obviously, this most delicate of tasks doesn't happen every day. She languorously unfurls the ink bowl cover and fondly gazes at its contents. All of her power and credibility reside in this flat, cup-shaped container, and the Party stamp that neatly fits in it. Comrade Epaulettes could stamp up to four food vouchers at one time, by chopping four corners simultaneously. But not on your life, that would go too fast, and this is an historical moment in the annals of the Jingtieshan People's Iron Ore Mining Company, the hotel and the local Communist Party. Making sure not to chop more than one food voucher at a time, she meticulously stamps all ten vouchers, one by one, restocking the face of the stamp with bright red, gooey ink every other voucher. Then she ceremoniously tears off the sheet of ten food vouchers and with great admiration and veneration for the role she is playing, tells me,

"It's my duty, I am a person for the revolutionary cause, just like a screw for a machine."

I cannot thank Comrade Gaddafi Shoulder Pads enough, verily touched am I to play an important role in such a momentous occasion. I think we all three struggle to keep our eyes dry, so moving is this unprecedented experience. But a bed on which to rest my weary body and a pillow on which to lay my tired head must be found, to consummate all this international cooperation. The noise, the veritable din of all the hundreds of fraternal comrades who are not here in this vacuous, echo chamber of a hotel is deafening. The sound of our six feet walking up the winding colored glass, chrome and tile Stalinist staircase travels infinitely into the void. What an honor to get a room on the *top* floor of this hotel - the second floor. Maybe if I'm lucky, I'll have a view overlooking a work unit, industriously hammering and hewing the machines that will soon reduce my corrupt and venal civilization to the ash heap of history and shame. And just to think, I am going to get a ringside seat tonight, right outside my hotel window. It's going to be a challenge, but maybe, just maybe, there might be one bed left unoccupied in the hotel, yes, that would be Room 205, the standard model with three beds. Revolutionaries rarely like to be left alone. We'll just open the door to take a peek inside. My joy borders on ecstasy when I see that there is not just *one* unused bed, but all *three* are vacant. I strongly sense this room has not been broached since the hotel's grand opening in 1954, but my lady comrades for the cause insist that my two roommates are surely out using their spare time advancing the cause of the Great Helmsman and the unbreakable forces of Communism. I can't wait to meet these shining beacons of inspiration and rectitude. My female hosts, having fulfilled their proletarian mission of the day, and full of well-deserved self-admiration, are ready to say their goodbyes. Warm and heartfelt thank yous and vigorous, tender handshakes crown a most eventful hotel check-in. I never see these two ladies again. Are they real? Did they really exist today, or are they ghost zombies? I will go to my grave always wondering.

Finally, I get to relax a little and lap up the luxury of this crown jewel of the iron ore company. It's been a long day and I worked up a good sweat hiking the 10km and climbing up 500 vertical meters to the July 1st Glacier. Time for a well-earned hot shower and if there's one thing I just love about luxury hotels in China, that's the piping hot, 24 hour a day availability of shower water. I get my shower kit ready and then I suddenly notice that there *is* no shower in Room 205. In fact, there is no sink, no toilet, no mirror, no chairs and no table: just three ultra-luxurious, rock hard, paper-thin mattresses on single beds. No time for lying around or watching TV here. We are in Jingtieshan to make China more perfect than it already is, roll up our sleeves and put our backs into the causes of justice and liberation. Jeez Louise, what an embarrassment of riches. These three beds are all mine. Not to worry. Like a good soldier of the cause, I'll just saunter my way down the hall to the communal showers. It could be dicey, what with all the hundreds of comrades who are not here. How long will I have to wait in line? Well, as it turns out, not long at all, because this sumptuous Jingtieshan People's Iron Ore Mining Company Hotel doesn't *have* any showers. What a relief. One less guilty bourgeois luxury to worry about.

No problem, I can just clean up and shave using the hot water pouring forth from one of the three sinks installed to serve the hygiene needs of the entire second floor and all its screws in the machines of the revolution. Luckily, I don't have to wait to use a sink, since all of the comrades who are not here are not using them. Hey, that's funny, there *is* no hot water. Darn, I'm too late. All my fellow comrades who are not here have used it all up. But that's OK, this isn't the first, and surely won't be the last time that I clean up and shave using a thermos full of boiled water. Suddenly, I hear voices down the hall approaching and two hotel zombiettes enter the bathroom, each carrying and pretending to sword fight with wet mops. The pair of wrinkled, broom sweeping zombies who brushed me out the front door on the ground floor were much older. These two on the second floor are playful, twenty-something ladies; revolutionary water sprites, enjoying the briefest of reposes from the ardors of ineluctable world domination. And such a long day of struggle it has been, tending to the hundreds of comrades who never made it. That is what is making this water fight all the more spiritually fulfilling. After their mirth has subsided somewhat, I kindly ask these youthful zombies where I can find a thermos of hot water. And I am about to mark history here,

This paean of Communist bliss has no *kaishui* (开水), no *boiled water*!

It takes me a minute or two for the magnitude of what I was just told to sink in... Over nine years and two generations apart, from famine to fat, from thistle needles to salad days, from the most destitute and humble of hosts to the inner gates of philistine, five star luxury, and I have *never, ever* been refused a thermos of boiled water in the Middle Kingdom. In China, it is tantamount to saying, well, we have hotel rooms, but there are no beds; you have to sleep on the concrete floor and crap in the corner (which is about what I get one night, later in Guizhou, but at least I had boiled water). Around this country, it is beyond the limits of imagination and propriety, beyond the palest of the pale to not have thermos bottles full of hot water readily available. And these two little aqua squirts just did it. Thanks girls for setting a land speed, cultural, historical and social *faux pas* record... As long as I'm there in the People's restrooms, I take advantage of the one Turkish toilet out of three that actually has a door with both its hinges attached and can close. Now, time for an early dinner.

If the hotel is the Twilight Zone, then like the 2010 movie *Inception*, the mess hall is a Twilight Zone within a Twilight Zone. A scattering of burned out zombie employees mechanically goes through the motions of having a comradely dinner together. All eyes are on a big, low definition television that was built when Lucille Ball was a black and white weekly sensation in 50's America. I ceremoniously and respectfully remove my sheet of ten food vouchers from my billfold, making my way to the cafeteria window. Not too many lackey whore foreign devils must eat here. They are all staring at me, while catching furtive glances at the nearly dead TV; you would think that my ears have been replaced by my left and right buttocks, the way they are gawking at me and so slack jawed... At the window, I ostentatiously tear off a rectangle of eight food vouchers, the equivalent of eight kuai (€1.00/$1.30), and ceremoniously hand them to the chef behind the big glass display, through a slot underneath, that is just high enough for a plate of food to be delivered. The kitchen in back of him is cavernous and set up to feed hundreds of the faithful at a time, not the handful of blank-faced zombies with whom I'm dining. There is a huge table behind him, with bowls and bowls of different fresh veggies and fungi, along with some plates of fresh meats. He asks me what I want to eat for dinner. I get it, we diners, zombies or not, get to pick out the ingredients and comrade chef here stir fries them up. Pretty classy for a proletarian paradise, if you ask me. I pick some mushrooms, cauliflower, hot peppers and sliced pork. He tells me to go sit down. *Ja wohl, mein Herr.* I intentionally sit facing away from the droning TV, so all of the zombie diners are actually looking towards me, as they vacuously stare at the loud screen, mindlessly masticating their food. I say hello to all of them collectively, so they know that I speak at least a modicum of Mandarin. Upon hearing me, their faces make various, shocked contortions,

"*How can this be?*" They seem to be saying.

They don't know it, but now they are in the Twilight Zone too with a real live *dabizi*. The furniture has a wonderful Alice in Wonderland effect, as the chairs are all way too short, so the table top level is almost at shoulder height. I'm in a parallel universe for sure. In addition to the huge kitchen where I ordered my dinner, I am facing another gargantuan one that has a chef with nothing to do. It looks like it has not been cleaned since the day it opened in 1954. This reposing chef is using chopsticks, mechanically working dinner into his pie hole, eyes glued fixedly to the propaganda being regurgitated from the boob tube. He almost imperceptibly nods to me, acknowledging my existence. Between masticating their mouthfuls, they try so hard to discretely mumble to one another about me. Amazingly, I do not get the twenty standard questions from any of them, almost a first in China in similar situations. I can only assume that zombies cannot communicate with me across the time warp of 58 years. Comrade Chef brings out my dish and it is big enough to feed a work unit. For ¥8.00, this truly is a Communist paradise. For the first time I notice both he and his un-utilized partner are the only ones not wearing company blue uniforms, but are actually in chef's whites, replete with floppy French toques. Snazzy, and dare I say, counterrevolutionary. My freshly stir-fried dish is actually out of this world and I astonishingly finish the whole thing. I can only assume traveling across 58 years through the fabric of space-time builds up a powerful hunger. The communal gut filling bowl of white rice and vegetable consommé to finish the meal, which are being offered in the corner of the hall need not apply here. I thank the chef profusely for the excellent dinner and say to everyone,

"*Mingtian jian*!" (明天见!= See you tomorrow!)

At this point, social protocol is just too overbearing and most of the zombies, mouths full of chewed up stir fry and eyes transfixed on the badly colored TV screen, mumble something akin to an audible goodbye. As I amble out the door, I ponder what my two remaining food vouchers will render for breakfast… I don't know how long it has been playing, but once outside, I notice for the first time propaganda blaring over loud speakers. It takes me a minute or two, but I finally locate two megaphone-shaped public announcement speakers perched high on top of the four story workers' dormitory. It is from this building that my guardian angel, Ms. Iron Mine Nightingale appeared and who kept me off the streets tonight. As I stroll around the ghostly complex and explore, martial music is blasting away, then Chinese opera, then some pithy interviews between a Party apparatchik and an acolyte of Lei Feng, answering all the weighty social, political and cultural questions with revolutionary precision. Iron ore workers can never get enough of Communist indoctrination, er... education. What used to surely be thousands of workers is now reduced to these few wandering zombies who I see aimlessly meandering about solo and in pairs, with no perceptible goal in mind. They look more like extras in the background of an eerie movie set. The main actors, director and the production crew have all gone home and they forgot to tell these poor saps to quit walking back and forth across the empty stage.

I have to remind myself the reason I decided to stay here for the night is to go to the enchanting Tibetan mountain village of Qiqing tomorrow morning. Since there are no taxis as advertised, I need to figure out how to get there. A little bit of panic sets in as I ponder the possibility of not being able to go, and spending all day tomorrow in this workers' ghost town, until the train returns to Jiayuguan tomorrow evening. Oh joy. As these peripatetic zombies wander by me, I begin to ask them about going to Qiqing. I notice that in addition to the Stalinist looking company logo on their blue uniforms, each one has their own unique embroidered employee number just below it. Using my three person confirmation rule, I ask four or five of them and consistently get the key words: *bus, little, yellow, nine o'clock and main road.* Being such a late departure, I opt to explore Jingtieshan in the morning.

Entering my abode for the night, I push my way through all the comrades who are not in the hotel reception area and on the staircase to my *sans*-boiled-water Room 205, where I soak up my communion with the spirit of Chinese Communism. The treacle of babbling, megaphone propaganda mercifully turns off as the sunset fades into darkness. Will I leave this Twilight Zone tomorrow morning, or am I stuck here for eternity, as the Jingtieshan People's Iron Ore Mine's token, zombie *waiguoren*?

Chapter 17:
Qiqing

A parting shot on time warped Jingtieshan and its mysterious mining operation; visiting the Tibetan Qiqing village is another Lonely Planet letdown, but I end up exploring a Tibetan mud hut ghost town and get an invitation to visit an old woman's Tibetan home. In other words, making something out of a nothing visit.

The next morning, before leaving for Qiqing, it's time for a revolutionary breakfast at the Jingtieshan Mining Company People's Mess Hall. The *Inception* dream within a dream continues, as I don't think the Iron Ore Mine restaurant zombies ever leave their places: still here, still masticating the same stir fry, and still glued to the larger than life Lucille Ball boob tube. Having seen me now for the second time in twelve hours, when I sit at my Alice in Wonderland table facing them, a few of them actually respond back when I say good morning. Now that's what I call progress. My ¥2 (€0.25/$0.30) in food vouchers gets me the typical blue collar Chinese first meal of the day: rice porridge (粥= *zhou*). Ugh, all the taste of chewed up notebook paper and one of my least favorite Chinese dishes. There is also an assortment of pickled cabbage, root vegetables (carrots, turnips, etc.) mixed with hydrated mushrooms that traditionally are added to the *zhou* to give it some desperately needed flavor (healthy and good with beer, but really, at six o'clock in the morning?), plus soya milk (sorry, blech) and hard-boiled eggs (yeah!). Other than eggs, breakfast is the least favorite meal of the day for me in China, unless I go to a good Muslim noodle shop. A big bowl of piping hot, capsicum charged, hand pulled Xinjiang, Turkic-blessed beef noodles - now *that's* the way to kick start a traveler's body and brain. Spicy noodles are also a depth charge usually guaranteed to blow out your bowels, before starting a long day on the road or trail. Knowing I'm not going to get much out of this à la carte proletarian menu selection except the eggs, I ask for three of them. The white smocked, white toqued chef hesitates, takes my two remaining meal tickets and asks for a cash supplement of two whole RMB (€0.25/$0.30). One yuan per egg… What a deal.

I leave the Jingtieshan People's Iron Ore Mine Hotel with a sense of elation and liberation. What a bizarro and amazing time machine *that* place is. It is not even 07:00 yet and the purported small, yellow bus on the main road is a full two hours off. I set out to explore the town. Before even leaving the Party Bureau compound, I peek into the workers' large recreation hall and can see that it is chockablock full of exercise equipment, weight machines, gym mats and the like, all on the inevitable descent towards complete entropy. The whole interior and its contents are covered with a thick patina of dust and soot. None of it has been touched for at least a decade, if not longer. Twilight Zone or no, the Arrow of Time is remorseless in its forward trajectory. A storage yard with huge pieces of rusted, blackened machine parts, conveyor belts, boiler tanks and the like gives the impression of a post-nuclear war set from a *Transformers* flick. Right next to it are several pallets of empty, green beer bottles, stacked high up against a warehouse wall. I sure wasn't offered one last night. And right next to it, above the warehouse's double wide, double high door is the Chinese Communist revolution's most celebrated mantra, barely visible after decades of neglect,

毛泽东万岁! - *Mao Zedong Wansui!* = Long Live Mao Zedong! (literally, Mao Zedong 10,000 Years Old)

Retro-relics of the Great Leap Forward, (1958-61) and the Cultural Revolution (1966-76), both which nearly destroyed the country, are getting harder and harder to locate in their original, unrestored state. I visually savor this faded find, like a tomb raider plundering a sarcophage of its priceless mummies, laden with gold and jewels. I go out on the main street and start to study all the various work units that dot the desolate landscape. Juxtaposed with all this degradation in each yard are large blackboards that are freshly and immaculately rendered in multicolored chalk, with lines of text and quite homey drawings of flowers, faces, symbols and the like. They are exhorting the mine workers to achieve ever greater levels of productivity, safety and quality control. People have recently spent hours decorating these big chalk boards and for whom? Where are they? The whole place looks as forlorn as the rusted out hulls of all the nineteenth and twentieth century steamships beached along the Skeleton Coast in Namibia. I continue on my way. The few mine workers I do see, none of whom are doing any labor and are just milling around on the main road, keep pointing me towards the train station downstream, so I keep wending my way in that direction. Head-high weeds choke all the gardens and plots of small trees planted along the raging river that is roaring towards Jiayuguan, more than a kilometer in elevation below us. The place really does have a post-nuclear war vibe, some industrial *Planet of the Apes*. Like Charleston Heston's character seeing the top of the Statue of Liberty sticking out of a long ago deserted beach, am I going to come upon the half buried torso of Mao Zedong, or maybe Confucius, protruding from a pile of iron ore?

A really weird scene is a steel bin about 50cm deep and 2.5m square, planted alongside the main road. Inside this big hopper, which could hold several tons of rock, is a dainty little pile of ochre colored ore rock that could easily fit in a handheld dustpan. Its diminutive size looks Wonderland weird in the bottom of this gargantuan steel container. Attached to the bin is a large sign asking all the workers to leave here any ore found in their pockets and uniforms. This laughable pile of rubble makes me speculate about why they are keeping the old Jingtieshan mine open: maybe it is in reality a rare earth mineral mine and the iron ore shtick is just a cover. It doesn't take many tons of rare earth ore to be worth hundreds of thousands of euros or dollars and China has the largest and most diversified proven reserves on the planet. And with all the dilapidated, deserted dormitories, decrepit production units and crumbling conveyor belts (I even spot an abandoned, cavernous, indoor Olympic swimming pool), there *is* some kind of mining going on in Jingtieshan. The occasional oversized dump truck comes roaring out of the mountains, filled to the brim with ore and they are building two new huge processing silos over the conveyor belt that leads towards the train station, to replace the three defunct ones right next to them. All these many abandoned work units are supposed to process iron ore, which goes through the multiple refining steps of crushing, milling, screening, magnetic separation, washing, desulfurization and pelleting, before it can be transformed into steel. These various processing units are obviously not working, so what are these occasional truckloads carrying as they go careening down the switchbacks? That tiny pile of rocks in the bin wouldn't be worth a one one-hundredth of a red cent if were iron ore, but it would be worth some serious cash if it were *rare earth ore*. That hypothesis is looking less and less absurd, the more I see on my stroll down the river valley. The Jingtieshan Rare Earth Mining Company would surely garner the attention of China's adversarial intelligence agencies (like, every country on the Planet Earth that has one), with their nosy, high resolution satellites. *Iron Ore* makes for nice, soporific camouflage.

I get to the parking lot outside the train station right before 09:00 and voilà, what do I see, but a little yellow bus waiting to take off for Qiqing (祁清= Vast Clear). It's only ¥6 (€0.75/$0.95) to drive all the way there. To Jingtieshan's belated credit, towards the outskirts of town, I can see a small grocery store and one small restaurant. Cases and cases of beer are stacked to the ceiling, filling the entire front window of the store. In this most berserk of socio-historical fifth dimensions, at least the zombies have their priorities straight. *Mao Zedong Wansui*. Or something like that... Further out of town I see the offices and administrative buildings for a brand new mine, proudly sporting the Jingtieshan Company's corporate blue color. Undoubtedly, many of those snazzy buses at the train station drop off employees and miners here. Mine and abandon, slash and burn and move up the valley for more promising ore reserves, iron or rare earth.

I can hardly believe that I survived the historical time warp of Jingtieshan's Twilight Zone, for what Qiqing ends up being. I have no idea what Lonely Planet is basing their recommendation on to visit here, but either they never came, or they are regurgitating decades old information. As a place to visit, Qiqing is a royal disappointment. According to the driver and my fellow passengers, the village being touted in LP was abandoned about 10 years ago and is a further 15-20km up the road. The *New Qiqing*, and apparently other smaller hamlets in between, were all consolidated over the last decade right here. Maybe all these once semi-nomadic Tibetan Qiqingers are better off living here. For example, as I start to explore the place, I walk by a nice medical clinic cum mini-hospital right in town. And just next door is the omnipresent and obligatory Gongan police station. And there is of course the convenience of numerous stores and restaurants. All of the homes are lined up like townhouses on one side, with all the businesses lined up opposite them. But why the abandonment and consolidation of all the valley's hamlets to create this New Qiqing? Much of the agitation for more freedom and independence among Tibetans takes place outside modern Tibet, right here in the historical regions of the Kingdom, that are today in the Chinese provinces of Qinghai, Gansu and Sichuan. Could it be that the Han authorities want them all close together and nearby, so they can keep an eye on them? Did something happen ten years ago in this valley that gave Baba Beijing pause for concern, panic even? I dare not ask and even if I did, I would surely get an uncomfortable, paranoid non-answer. Asking questions like this is risky, as the locals can easily assume you are a *laowai* spy for Baba Beijing. This valley is so remote that there could have been an uprising and it would have been easy to keep the news from spreading. Cut off the only cul-de-sac road coming in and out, shut down the mobile phone towers and lay siege to the place. It would have been easy pickings for the well trained, Myrmidon soldiers of the PLA. And then I recall we went through a road barricade control point on the way up here from Jingtieshan, manned by gun toting army types, from Han China into Tibetan country. Hmm…

This is all an intriguing aside to the voyager's conundrum of the day. If I did not speak Chinese, my time in this New Qiqing would be, in almost anyone's travel log, a busted day. If one is a non-Mandarin speaker, there is absolutely nothing to do or buy here. And that enchanting sister village mentioned in LP called Swan Lake? Well, it is not even in this valley. The locals tell me it's on the other side of the Qilian Range and quite far away. So much for doing them both in one short day and in one of those phantom taxis lauded in LP. Clearly, Lonely Planet has not been up here for years. Otherwise, I can't imagine them recommending voyagers to take the time and effort to visit.

Since I have all day before the bus returns back to the Jingtieshan train station, I am very tempted to hitchhike up to the old abandoned Qiqing, the one that is probably described in LP. But the townsfolk convince me there is nothing left to see. They all tell me it's an abandoned ghost town. The driver is nice enough to let me keep my rolling backpack locked up for the day in the bus, so this frees me up considerably to move around and explore the surroundings. I have hours to kill and my own personal Lonely Planet to create about this modern Qiqing. While the New Qiqing is unfortunately soulless, the broad valley here and the surrounding, 5,000m snow graced Qilian Mountains are very picturesque. We are at a lofty 2,850 MASL and the sky is translucently clear, so it actually feels really hot outside. At this altitude, when the sky is blue, it is an unforgettable azure that takes on a whole new holistic dimension.

The view coming into town looked really pretty, so I hike the 500m to the edge of town. As I approach the town limits, I begin to wander through an abandoned mud and stucco hamlet. This is where a group of the Tibetan town folk lived just a decade ago. It is strange traipsing through ghost towns and they are such eerie places for a reason: they allow your imagination to run wild about how the place got in this apocalyptic situation in the first place. All kinds of questions and scenarios flood your mind and none of them can be very positive, given the state of the surroundings. The detritus of modern society is scattered everywhere. I'm starting to see a pattern here, as I pass a monstrous pile of broken, green beer bottles. Bottles of soy sauce, vinegar and other condiments are sitting in dust and cobweb encrusted window sills, with varying levels of their original contents still there. Shoes, clothes, sheep horns, animal bones, sun bleached livestock skulls, weather worn CDs and broken DVDs, empty and broken bottles of hard liquor, old medicine bottles and piles of no longer needed tender and firewood are everywhere. It is almost as if they hurriedly grabbed what they could, loaded up the pack mules and fled, leaving behind a nightmarish, post-neutron bomb scene. Most of the houses are empty or nearly so, but one is almost knee deep in moth eaten mining uniforms and another is full of piles of plain white newspaper stock, of all things. To print out Party propaganda tracts? One thing left behind has great symbolic importance: it is one of those outdoor public announcement speakers that the local Communist Party likes to use to blare out propaganda before and after work, like what I heard in Jingtieshan last night. Are they still getting their daily dose in the new village? The more I explore, the more I get the feeling that the Tibetan uprising hypothesis is credible. This mud hamlet was abandoned in a hurry. Most of the roofs are falling in, but a few look like they were installed more recently, being constructed of modern tile. The only sound is my feet crunching over what will be fossil remains unearthed by paleontologists, a million years from now. I start to ask myself,

"What was the last person walking out of here thinking or saying to themselves, as they peered over their shoulder?"

When I walk through a backyard and come around the corner into an obviously occupied front courtyard, in the confines of a high outer wall. Yikes, I'm *trespassing*. Everything about the place oozes Tibetan culture, starting with a magnificent, quilted wind curtain hanging over the front door, embroidered with a large, multicolored, round mandala on its face. I freeze for a few minutes, not sure what to do, but now I know there are holdouts, resisters, the last of the last, the diehards. Or, is this family the pariahs, the unwanted? I am so tempted to knock on the door, but what the heck would I say? Pizza delivery? It just does not feel right. A big ol' white boy pounding on their door might scare the bejeezuz out them and elicit an unwanted reaction. For all I know, they could sic a Baskerville beast of a Tibetan mastiff on me. I opt for the traveler's MASD: mutually assured social discretion and tiptoe out the back way, from whence I entered. I continue on, come to the end of the village and turn back up a tall-tree lined dirt road that leads back to the new town. I notice three parked cars and a couple of small motorbikes outside what are probably an equal number of still lived in houses. So, it is not just the town loon who is holding out, there are several hangers on. Why are they still here? Are these the riffraff no one wants for neighbors? Are these the agitators the Communist Party wants to ostracize? Surely a house, any abode in town, would be better than this phantom existence. Then again, the New Qiqing has all the charm of a Plasticine Potemkin façade, so maybe we can chalk it up to well-grounded nostalgia and good old fashioned stubbornness

By this time, I am being accompanied by some ground foraging hens and we are all instinctively seeking shaded ground, under the towering trees, away from the blistering sunlight. I spot a young woman with a child, and they are helping a very old, crumpled up woman, slowly working her way across the deserted road. Her two female companions are serving as human crutches. The young woman is carrying the old lady's two walking canes in her free hand, as she leans in to keep her from falling down. Curious, I catch up, say hello and ask if they are three generations of ladies: grandmother, daughter and granddaughter. No, no, no, she is just our neighbor and we are helping her back home after a house visit. We sit down together in the shade outside of what must be the old woman's house. The mother relents and lets me take a picture of her five year old daughter, named Cairen Zhuoma (才人卓玛). The vast majority of Han people's names are three characters long, with some being just two. But like this little girl, many Tibetan names contain four. Also, Zhuoma is a very common Tibetan name and means, *Outstanding Agate*, Cairen means *Talented Person*. Agate is an important gemstone in Tibetan culture, as it is used to make prayer beads and rosaries. The beads can be beautifully etched and carved and are called *dzi* in Tibetan, which means *clarity* or *splendor*. In traditional Tibetan medicine, agate also imparts important healing properties, as it can calm a mind cluttered with unnecessary claptrap that is vain or trivial. Thus, an agate rosary is a twofer: the *dzi* lend medicinal powers and the act of chanting mantras offers a suffering soul the soothing sagacity of Buddha. I will see several Tibetan agate rosaries being carried by the faithful, before I leave the Plateau during *44 Days*.

I start to talk to the wizened and weathered old woman and amazingly, she lets me take her photo. The afternoon is a hot one, and at almost 3km above sea level, the Sun is pitiless. I recall this as I study the old woman's textured, bronze face, with its infinite layers of wrinkles and canyon-like creases. A poster child for sunscreen use? I don't think so. I offer to the mother to send the photos to her mobile phone, which she excitedly accepts. However I later learn that most people in this part of China only have 1G phones and can send messages, but with no attachments. In any case, it is a nice thought. Finally rested from the arduous trek across the dirt road, the old lady suddenly perks up and invites me into her home for a cup of water. Wow! What an honor, to be invited by Tibetans in their home. Of course I accept! Her name is Lao Pu (老浦= Old Mrs. Pu); I never learn her first name), she won't give me her exact age and actually does not even seem certain of it, but tells me she is over eighty. She looks like she could be a hundred. Lao Pu has five children and nine grandchildren. She likes her cigarettes and smokes a couple while I am here. But it looks to me like she is just puffing and not inhaling. She understands my Mandarin very well, but hers is heavy going and the mother, who I now know to be Mrs. Wang, helps decipher her answers. Lao Pu's next-door neighbor, a woman of about seventy, joins us and I share my glass of boiled water with them, as we curiously exchange our stories. They are giving me the standard twenty questions and I am happily dishing them back. Each round of questions and answers allows us to share our lives. Lao Pu is a widow and has lived in this old mud hamlet every day of her life. She has never traveled further than Lanzhou, Gansu's capital. She got no formal education and is very proud that her children and grandchildren have more opportunities than she could ever dream of. She's been through a lot in life and it shows on her shamanic face. It is easy to hear in the tone of her voice that she is proud to be a survivor, to have made it through so much for so long.

Lao Pu's house is a modest affair. It is composed of only two rooms, with the small living room where we are sitting and a bedroom in the back, with a traditional, huge and almost waist high bed that can sleep four or more. The ceilings are quite low. I suspect this is to keep as much heat as possible during the long subzero winter months, as close to body level as possible. She has electricity and graciously lets me charge up my Galaxy Tab while we chat. The kitchen is tiny - no bigger than a closet sized room and just big enough to house a small two burner, gas bottle stove. It is situated between where we are and the bedroom in the back and comprises one wall of the short hallway connecting the two. The kitchen door is a sepia colored curtain impregnated with decades of cooking oil and steam. I can just make out the white countertop gas stove, but cannot see if there is a sink with a spigot or not. I doubt it. That leaves no room for a toilet, so her bathroom is surely an outhouse in the back, which I saw a few of during my amblings through the ghost town. Lao Pu's heat is supplied by a low level potbellied stove that is installed between us. She uses a small electric heater in the bedroom to stave off frostbite. At this altitude, the tree cover is so sparse; she must use coal for fuel, although I did see quite a few piles and stacks of small caliber wood around the abandoned houses. I just don't see enough forest at this altitude to support wood as a form of heating. Can you imagine the winter temperatures up here? There are a couple of uncovered, cooked dishes on top of the stove and in this summer heat, they both look like they are in desperate need of a refrigerator, which she does not have. My gut is a worldwide tested catalytic converter, but even for me, I'd think twice before eating from them, if they were offered. Fortunately, this does not happen.

As I am chatting with Lao Pu, her neighbor, Momma Mrs. Geng and young Cairen Zhuoma, I finally get to the question of why they are still here in this nearly abandoned old mud village. Mrs. Geng confirms there are still four families living here and talks about her family situation. Her husband is a truck driver and she is at home to take care of Zhuoma, who will be going to first grade next year. The abandoned village school is as moribund as the rest of this mud hamlet, so, why don't they have a new house? Is it a lack of money, or are they staying put to care for Lao Pu? She goes on to explain that in order to move, there needs to be a house available for them, and they are all taken, none are left for them. After several glasses of boiled water and more chitchat about the weather and climate here, it's time to move on. I sincerely thank Lao Pu and Mrs. Geng for their humble, Spartan hospitality. I feel truly honored to be invited into their Tibetan home and count myself fortunate for the eye opening experience.

Later in the day, I show the photos of my Tibetan friends to a family who owns a restaurant in town, where I have a late lunch. They immediately recognize all of them by name. They explain that all of Lao Pu's children moved away and she doesn't have the support to move. Given her age and status as a widow, I can see her not wanting to move from where she has lived all her life. But I never get a clear answer from anybody about Mrs. Geng's situation and my confusion is further fueled when I see two new houses on the main street (the only street in fact) that have started construction, and for now are just roofless, cinderblock walls. Are these their homes? All the other town's houses are finished and occupied. This would suggest that the problem might be a question of having enough money, and these restaurant owners are not going to divulge something that personal about Geng and Pu. Before leaving, I tell the restaurant owner I feel bad not living up to my promise to send Mrs. Geng the photos I took. He has a 3G phone, so I send him the pictures I took with Lao Pu's gang and he promises me he will get them sent to them.

I leave New Qiqing with more questions than answers to some juicy socio-political meanderings about what happened in this valley a decade ago and where the holdouts in the nearby mud hamlet fit into the picture. Being able to visit with four Tibetan ladies across three generations, in their humble abode, made for a very gratifying cultural experience and saved what would otherwise have been an extremely lackluster day. The little yellow bus cranks up its engine. It's time to head back to Jiayuguan and hopefully catch an overnight train back to Lanzhou, with a quick bus connection to Xiahe and its sublime Labrang Temples. And most incredibly, that is exactly what happens, just like clockwork. Well synchronized, on-time connections are now being almost taken for granted on this journey, and were totally unimaginable when living here in the nineties. Back then, I'd probably still be trying to get from Beijing to Ningxia, the first leg of my trip. And that is no exaggeration. Another sign that China is coming of age: while standing in line to buy my train ticket from Jingtieshan to Jiayuguan, the man queuing ahead of me asks me my nationality and a couple of other questions, and then loudly and gaily insists on buying my train ticket, making sure all the people standing in line behind me take notice. He will not take no for an answer and is clearly chuffed with himself. I know it only costs ¥5.50 (€0.70/$0.85), but this kind of spontaneous generosity would have been unthinkable in the nineties, and it happens again and again during the voyage, these small tokens of friendship and cooperation. Ah yes, *friendship and cooperation*, that takes me back. This frequently flagellated, hopelessly hollow, *ganbei*-banquet-bandied slogan from the 90s is *finally* starting to bear fruit.[1] It only took a generation.

1- Ganbei = 干杯, *is how you say* cheers *when making a drinking toast and it literally means,* dry glass, *or* bottoms up, *to quote David Lee Roth and Van Halen.*

Chapter 18: Jiayuguan - Lanzhou

Standing-room-only train-ticket Class 101: how to get from the vertical position to the horizontal without having a sleeper berth ticket; the honest low down on China's hundreds of millions of itinerant workers.

On the train from Jingtieshan to Jiayuguan, I run into the three Fujian just-graduated teachers, with whom I climbed the huge sand dune at sunset in Dunhuang. We have a nice chat about the glacier hike and I tease them for not yet emailing me the group picture we took at the dune's summit. To be safe, I get one of their email addresses (called *QQ* in China). But it is all wasted worrying, as flashing forward into the future a couple of weeks, I receive our great souvenir. In fact, I am staying in regular touch with one of them, Zhu Biying. In her emails and SMS, she goes by the flattering handle *Meng* (梦= Dream). With 51 students all by herself in the classroom, compared to my 26 kids with two fulltime assistants, my hat goes off to her for surviving in such difficult teaching conditions. Chinese teachers' salaries are structured to encourage this size of class. They are actually paid *per student*, so it is in their best interest to have as many learners as possible in the classroom, seated to the rafters. I have seen in many classrooms in China where there are 60-75 students packed eyeballs to elbows, seated on long benches, hunched along narrow communal tables, all chaotically chanting in cascading unison their characters and math problems. Like clockwork, I arrive at the Jiayuguan train station, stand in a short line, get my overnight ticket to Lanzhou, and feel like I can safely say goodbye to the ghost of Rod Serling and Jingtieshan's Twilight Zone, at least for the time being.

Before leaving, I have a bowl of *guanguan jiaozi* (罐罐饺子). Man, this baby is a true culinary grand slam. It is a crock pot full of diced meat, tofu noodles, chunks of fermented tofu (the variety that looks like baby Swiss cheese), some cabbage, sea kelp, rice noodles and scrambled egg; and all this in a steaming clear broth and sitting on top of a bed of meat and vegetable dumplings. Add a healing spoonful of ground red peppers, preserved in capsicum soaked peanut oil and wowzer: absolutely out of this world. Personally, I think the chef uses this dish to clean out the ice box and pantry, so if this is eating leftovers, I'm first in line. As is usually the case, I hit a home run: if I see a good dish someone else is eating, and they are not keeling over with violent cramps or retching over their shoulder, I say to myself,

"*OK, it passes the food poisoning and disgust thresholds, so guess what you're having for lunch, Jeff?*"

Time to catch my train to Lanzhou. But, buying an overnight ticket on the spur of the moment has its share of hazards. I am forced to take a standing room only ticket (SRO), which in Chinese is, *wu zuowei* (无座位). And never having done this on a long, overnight ride, I will just have to *take it as it comes* (thanks, Jim, for another great line from a Doors' song). This evening is becoming very serendipitous for me. In the teeming sea of flesh that is the waiting room for the train to Lanzhou, I happen to get a seat literally next to the boarding turnstile. It is close to take off time and some impatient soul just liberated this spot to start to preemptively get at the head of the line. Other than having my feet resting in a nearly dried out pool of fly paper sticky cola drink, I'm pretty chuffed at my momentary real estate conquest. Maybe it's just punishment for not planning ahead, but in seeing all the tickets-in-hand around me, it looks like all the poor suckers who buy SRO tickets get sent to Car #13. And yes, in China, it is a very unlucky number. Unlucky to the point that many buildings will skip this floor number, especially in Southern China. Like *fengshui* (风水= wind water), that ancient metaphysical art of designing a home and its contents for maximum positive energy and to avoid negative, evil forces, the Chinese take numerology very seriously. *Si* means *four* (四), but also *death* (死). Thus, hotels will also have floors and rooms with no number four in them, so you climb from floor number 12 to 15 and the room numbers skip from 239 to 250. As they announce the boarding, I can see the two guys ahead of me also have Car #13 tickets, and once past the turnstile, they start tearing off down the platform towards our lucky number. I'm no fool - if they are running, it must be for a good reason, so rolling backpack bouncing in tow, I'm hot on their trail. Monkey see monkey do is not a bad mantra when you are traveling by the seat of your pants. They are the first ones inside and they immediately claim the spot between Cars #12 and #13. It is a place where, when the passage door between the two cars is opened, it closes up a little cubby area, making it almost like a private box. Well, two can play this game, so I sprint to the same spot between Cars #13 and #14, crashing my rolling backpack against the aisle seats as I go. I toss my gear in my new found little fiefdom and close the passage door behind me. At this point I'm the first one here who is even in this car. But not for long. What a cool idea. I start to test out different positions to put my packs, when an attendant raps on the glass above me and tells me to go take a seat. Well, OK, if you say so. I follow suit, but by this time, all the aisle and window seats are taken by the boarding hordes, so a middle seat will have to do. I am bigger and especially broader than most Chinese, so it is a very tight fit. My lateral seat mates show that great Chinese, Confucian stoicism, the western equivalent of the stiff upper lip, at the discomfort of me being between them. The Chinese are well practiced at these situations. They get a lot of opportunities like this in public situations, living in a very crowded country with a big chunk of the human race squeezed inside its borders. The Chinese have a very vivid way of describing their oft tested oriental stoicism, *chiku* (吃苦), which means to *eat bitterness*. Car #13 is 100% SRO, so the seats are first come, first served, just like the bad old days. Now I will know for future SRO train rides. I guess those two guys I chased after boarding the train prefer their little private rolling apartment to the mass of pressed flesh that ends up squeezed into most hard seat cars. Can't say that I blame them actually. I later see that the train attendant lets them stay there, once the train takes off.

It is amazing to see some of the characters using ground public transportation in this part of the world. Hardened, somber men and women, they frequently live a solitary life, but can be seen also be seen with a travel buddy. At night, like the Great Depression Hoovervilles and today's Bushobamavilles sprouted up all over America, they congregate for friendship and protection from a society that guiltily hates them for their tenacious adaptation and survival. As they roam from one place to the next, they are seemingly diminutive, lugging hay bale sized nylon bags with everything they own under the Sun, on their well-worn, muscle hewn backs. Their daily exposure to the elements from living on the streets makes them look wizened well beyond their years. These are the several hundred million internal migrants, China's itinerant, floating population (= *liudong renkou*) of manual laborers, street sweepers, recyclers and wandering trinket sellers. They are the WD-40 for this country's white-hot economy. Like America's and Europe's immigrant populations, China's economy would rapidly grind to a screeching halt in their absence. While coming from the four corners of the Republic, there are higher percentages from the poorest provinces: Guizhou, Gansu, Yunnan and Tibet, all of which I visit on this journey, if historical Greater Tibet is included.

They are so despised in the urban popular imagination (not unlike the pariahs in India) and seriously feared by the Princes of Power. Why? They are mostly invisible in our daily lives. We *see* them everywhere in our routine space, along China's arteries of public transportation: street corners, sidewalks, metro stations and pedestrian bridges, but we don't *recognize* them. However, if social or political unrest should ensue, they would be like camouflaged animals stepping out in the light of day. We would then suddenly take notice of them. Since they all live hundreds and thousands of klicks away from their homes, other than what they are carrying in those huge, color-stripped nylon suitcase bags, they have absolutely nothing to lose. Being made invisible by society at large, being looked down upon and treated like the dregs of the economy, clearly makes them dried tender for any unrest that might ignite. Knowing this, Baba Beijing nervously frets over them like a bottle of nitroglycerin and keeps meticulous tabs on the flow and concentration of their whereabouts. No Chinese citizen can buy a train or interurban bus ticket without their national ID (*shenfenzheng*) being entered into the station's database. A fiber optic cable here, a DSL connection there and Baba Beijing can maintain an up-to-date national map of their concentrations. Americans can't chortle at China's authoritarian world view. They are rapidly moving closer to this country's police state system, much, much faster than China is moving towards attempts at western style democracy. In the US, no fewer than 16 intelligence agencies track the moves and lives of its citizens, just as assiduously as Orwellian China, and probably even better, through bank transactions, credit cards, emails, text messages, phone calls, you name it.[1]

I have no idea what is going on, but as soon after taking off, I see a bunch of passengers holding their tickets out, almost in supplication, to a train attendant sitting inside a stainless steel cage in the corner of our Car #13. It looks like the mobile poker chip cages that tellers sit inside of in casinos. Like I say, monkey see, monkey do, and in complete and total ignorance of what I hope to achieve here, get in line with all the other bipedal simians in tow. Through the metal bars, I smilingly slide my ticket to this apparent power broker. He turns my ticket over and scrawls the numeral 9 with his black gel pen. The Chinese like to write with a super fine 0.3mm pen, not the 0.5-0.7mm variety most Westerners prefer. His 9 is written the same way most Chinese writes this number, seemingly backwards to the Westerner's version, almost a modified Arabic style. As I stare at it, I can immediately hear that hair raising, drug drenched song by the Beatles on their White Album, *Number 9*. Is this exchange a cross-cultural paean to that slab of unhinged psychedelica, or what? Helter Skelter, baby. I sit back down and proudly show this mysterious cipher to my neighbor, a Han gentleman, Mr. Xiang, telling him others are lining up and doing the same thing, then quickly put my ticket back in my billfold for safe keeping. He is a stately, erudite looking gentleman and dressed to the *nines*, who definitely seems to be below his social station in this salt of the Earth Car #13, and is probably a last minute ticket buyer like me. So, pulled by the currents of popular conformity, he too goes, patiently wading his way through China's unwashed hoi polloi, and gets a number scratched on his ticket. By this time, his is Number 15. I ask this not so young Chinese man how this is going to help us, or what does it all mean, and I break out into a big guffaw when he replies,

"*Wo ZHEN bu zhidao*!" (我真不知道!= I REALLY have no idea!)

Luckily, I at least have a seat. The aisles are packed like pixels with vertical travelers. The thought of swimming and sleeping in this moving ocean of humanity all night barely enters the ranks of edifying experiences. With people getting up and moving around, I manage to get an aisle seat, but with all the passengers packed in said aisle, calmly and patiently vying for a small plot to plant their standing feet, there is no joy here for any of us kindred souls. The next time any person tells me how badly the Chinese behave towards each other, I present prima facie evidence to the contrary in Car Number Unlucky 13. There is no pushing, no shoving, nary an unkind word, in social conditions that would test the most humble of cultures. It is true, in the nineties, the Chinese treated each other like crazed, caged animals who hadn't seen a bowl of food in a few sunsets. We would be in prime fisticuffs territory right about now. Not to mention that reserved seats weren't worth the paper the tickets were printed on, what with all the Party apparatchiks and tin pot chest bangers with uniforms, badges, red cards and all sorts of other paraphernalia from the gallows of officialdom, throwing their small town, toady weight around. Twenty years ago, it would be total chaos right about now, but it isn't. In fact, it is downright civil under the circumstances.

While my head is strategically sandwiched between the armpits of two bystanders, who are struggling to remain upright with the rolling, rollicking train, I try to tell myself it could be worse, much worse. But it is hard to overcome the ennui. I so much want to close my eyes, but based on all my experience, now is not the time to let my guard down. With so many epicanthal (hooded oriental) eyes as witnesses, the chances of anybody stealing anything is indeed slim, but a coordinated diversionary ploy is not out of the realm of possibilities. That's what good street thieves do, working in teams, is to create distractions, then move in for the haul and slither away in all the confusion. This is especially true during the many small town stops we make along the way. During that two or three minutes of mayhem, people are piling on and off the train, in and out of the cars with their massive baggage and belongings, so it quickly gets chaotic. I can secure my money pouch with passport and Galaxy P-1000 inside my shirt. But protecting my 1988 made-in-West Germany, $4,000 replacement Zeiss binoculars is enough to keep me edgy and slightly grouchy at having to fight off sleep. I put on my headphones and crank up the 32GB and 5,500 songs of eclectic music on my trusty old Ibiza Rhapsody MP3 player to keep me company. One of my main goals on this journey is to take my Mandarin to the next level, which I am doing, going for days without speaking either of my national languages. But the passengers all seated around me apparently are *not* proud owners of any high value possessions, as they are all sound asleep. And there is only so much I can say to the two armpits starting me in the face. I really feel I have exhausted my cultural avenues here and deserve the treat of a Western musical cocoon for a few hours. Setting my Ibiza on random song play to keep me on my toes, I start out with a killer power pop hit by the Shoes, then Material Issue, then Bill Lloyd and the Shins. It is going to be a good night. I whip out the Galaxy and begin swyping out my next chapter of *44 Days*, to stave off sleep. After a half an hour, I see out of the corner of my eye a chain of hand-to-arm taps and signals working its way up the aisle towards me and it finally reaches my level. One of the neighboring armpits forcefully shakes my shoulder, knowing that I've musically shut out the world around me. I look up and now see the two train attendants behind the monkey bars, furiously waving me in their direction. I guess #9 means something after all. I wend my way through all the standing citizens doing cavalry and one of the attendants asks for my ticket,

"*Ni shi jiu hao ma*?" (你是九号码?= Are you number nine?)

"*You Betsy kind Siiiiiirr! Just let me stick my ticket-filled hand far enough into your stainless steel garrison for you to verify the same said, what do you think about that idea?*"

He verifies his backward, Arabic-Beatles-Chinese #9 and passes it to his partner in crime, who is holding what looks like a portable credit card terminal. They do some quick calculations on a piece of scrap paper and one of them says,

"For 72 more yuan, you can have a hard sleeper the rest of the way to Lanzhou. You want it or not?"

My head is still ringing with rock and roll and half asleep, so at first, it doesn't register and I ask him to repeat what he said. Others around me lend a verbal helping hand and then it dawns on me what he is really offering. Just to be safe, I ask what time we arrive to Lanzhou. Seven thirty, six more hours. I glance back at my seat and the guy sitting next to me has crumpled over on his side, fast asleep and now taking up both our places. Mr. and Mr. Armpits are watching me like cock headed dogs, longing for a chewy treat, waiting for my verdict's hammer to fall... Do I really have to tell you what my decision is? I mean come on, I can be the traveling ascetic as much as the next trooper, but this one definitely belongs in the no-brainer bracket. The cage attendant presses a few buttons on his handheld, mobile terminal, a new supplemental ticket spits out, my 72 RMB (€9/$11.50) enter the steel cage, the freshly minted hard sleeper ticket gets passed back to me in exchange, and off I go. My berth is in Car #1, all the way to the other end of the train, but under the circumstances, I am more than happy to oblige. In fact, it almost feels like a run to freedom. I push, pull, drag, slide, carry over my head like a coolie porter and sometimes just bull my rolling backpack through car after car, each one being SRO from one end to the other. Car 12, Car 11, Car 10, Car 9 and finally, daylight. The start of the sleeper cars. A really aggressive train attendant cum bouncer, who is relishing his little turf of authority, is blocking the door and carefully checks my two tickets, the original SRO and the new sleeper one. I guess I can appreciate his gruff demeanor. I am sure that every Huang, He and Han on the train is trying every trick in the book to get in the sleeper section for free. There must be some method to the madness, but I walk through two hard sleeper cars that are nearly empty and unused. I'm not sure what's going on. Car #1 is only half full. But now is not the time to question the ticketing algorithms in the train company's software, nor their profitability model. I am ready to rest my weary head. Hard sleeper berths in China are three bunks high and I get a middle one for the first time in my life. I am so used to the upper berth and can climb in and out quite easily, but for some reason, I find the height of the middle bed devilishly vexing and I struggle every time to negotiate my entry and exit. But hey, don't get me wrong, I'm not complaining. All the pent up desire for badly needed and postponed sleep is taken out on my hard mattress, as I place my binoculars under the provided bed pillow. I conk out immediately for a good night's sleep, as train K9662 rolls and rumbles through this desert, along the Hexi Corridor, which served as the final stretch of the medieval Silk Road into Lanzhou.

The highlight of my first visit to Lanzhou was getting a close look at the Gongan torture chair and China's 21st century service economy, flying through the air on a zip line and going on a wild goose chase in search of water wheels and museums. This time, poor Lanzhou gets a much shorter shrift. I promise, Dear Lanzhou, the next time I come back, I will do this Silk Road weigh station the proper justice it deserves, to prove all those discerning travel guides wrong. I roll out of the train station and take a taxi straight to the bus station. I tell you, there is no rest for the weary. In my just awakened fog, I fail to notice that my Ouigher driver didn't turn on his meter. I know this song and dance by heart and start whinging in his unreceptive ear. A good verbal jousting match and a case of principled indignation will wake me up. He plaintively retorts, with mock sincerity,

"Oh, I'm an honest man, I would never try to rip you off!"

Yeah, sure pal, give me a break. And he also is a really lousy, jerky driver, which just adds to the morning's fun. With all my world travels, I don't get easily overworked about bad or even dangerous drivers, but he's just plain awful behind the wheel. When we get to the Lanzhou South Bus Station, he does exactly the expected, hitting me up for ¥20 (€2.50/$3.20).

If I hadn't started my verbal assault, he would probably be asking this *dabizi* for fifty. I'm sure he is envisioning a quickly paid-for carton of local cigarettes for his tobacco stained fingers and teeth. Based on my earlier taxi ride to the big Lanzhou provincial museum, I offer ten kuai, probably a little low. After a minute of berating him for trying to rip me off and me commiserating on the shoulder of a bus station attendant, who helpfully bends down to stare at the driver for a few seconds through the passenger's side window, Mr. Petty Thief settles for ¥15 (€1.90/$2.40), which is probably about right. I can hear him moaning and complaining to no one in particular, as he drives off, so 15 RMB must not be too much.

1- *www.fas.org/irp/official.html*

CHAPTER 19: LANZHOU - XIAHE

An important chapter and primer on China's astoundingly beautiful river valleys.

Up to now, Ningxia, and its Yinchuan and Shapotou, and Western and Central Gansu, with Dunhuang, Jiayuguan and Lanzhou, I have been firmly in desert country. Now that I'm going to Xiahe, in Southern Gansu, I have no idea what to expect. The three plus hour bus ride from Lanzhou to Xiahe is *spectacularly* scenic. And being seriously behind on my chapters, due to trying to write on a phone pad, I can take you into the future and tell you that every bus trip on this 44 day journey is incredibly memorable. In fact, several of them rank as highlights of the trip. These many amazing river valleys do have some commonalities. The simple rule is that for any human occupation that populates the place, they take whatever the valley, its waters, arable land, walls and mountains will give them. And this has been going on for thousands of years. Leaving the vastness of the Gobi Desert, I am now entering China's great western expanse of the Land of Valleys. This will continue for the rest of the trip, until I leave Guiyang, Guizhou, to return home, so a clear understanding of this region's topography is critical to following the rest of *44 Days*. From now on, over the course of a day traveling, by bus or train, the route wends and winds, as it interconnects several interlaced valleys along the way. These Chinese valley treks often remind me of that great 1966 sci-fi movie classic, *The Fantastic Voyage*, where a submarine full of scientists is miniaturized and they course through one part of a human body's organs to another. Except in this case, it is different geologies, localized climates and cultures, and therefore different agricultural productions, local manufacturing systems and architectures. Driving through a Chinese valley often resembles flying on the back of a dragon in full flight. When the wings are horizontal and the dragon is gliding, it's like the valley walls or mountains flatten out, as usually does the valley floor too. The river broadens, deepens and its current slows to a crawl. Sometimes, these wide, flat or slightly oscillating floors can be several kilometers across, and as you can imagine, the agricultural production can take your breath away, given its intensive nature.

Steep, even ridiculously pitched mountain walls are no impediment to crop production. If there is any topsoil there, Chinese farmers are going to push terraced agriculture up the heights, until there is not enough soil to get at least a modicum of a crop. Some of these terraces are no bigger than a twin bed, but there you will find fifteen or twenty corn plants reaching for the sky. And don't forget, hardy farmers (men, women and children) are scaling on foot up there on a regular basis, tilling, planting, tending to, weeding, hauling fertilizer and (usually too much) insecticide, and if necessary, water up on their backs when the rains don't come; then harvesting and hauling down all the grain and fodder at the end of the growing season - by hand. All of this for a basket full of eared corn and a few bags of corn fodder. But multiplied billions of times, one can begin to appreciate why China can keep confounding Western prognosticators and pundits and remain mostly self-sufficient in cereal production, on stressed out, eroded soil that has been worked and overworked for thousands of years. However, China long ago threw in the towel on trying to be self-sufficient in soybean production and starting early in the 21st century, became the world's largest importer of this high protein, tofu and soya milk making product. Soybean use in China is a great barometer of overall economic development in China. In 1995, the Republic was self-sufficient, producing 14 million tons of this amazingly versatile, yellow bean. Today, it is still only producing 15 million tons, but is consuming about 75 million tons, the rest being imported and for better or for worse, transforming the agricultural landscape in the US, Brazil and Argentina. All of this is ironic, given that the soybean was first domesticated for agriculture production in eastern China 3,000 years ago.

I have not been below 1,100 MASL since arriving in Yinchuan, Ningxia. And projecting into the future, I spend most of the rest of *44 Days* at +2,000m, much of it at 3,000m. In China's valleys, at the lower reaches of these elevations, expansive corn, colza (rapeseed) and soft summer wheat production are predominant in the Northern provinces I visit, Ningxia and Gansu, and going south, the wheat is replaced with rice. Go higher up in altitude (2,500m) and barley and potatoes start to predominate. Over 3,000m and you are in Tibetan country, where they grow a high altitude crop called *qingke* (青稞= Alpine barley), as well as potatoes and fava beans. In Yunnan and Guizhou, where it seems it is 2,000 MASL everywhere you turn, the flat lands are wall to wall rice, corn and lots and lots of tobacco. Any place that cannot sustain these crops, but still has some topsoil, Yunnan and Guizhou farmers plant sweet potatoes, no matter how small the patch of land or steep the incline. Baba Beijing is really pushing potato production as a rice substitute, and parts of Yunnan and Guizhou look like one gigantic sweet potato plantation. Hillsides in these provinces can look like huge, green waterfalls of sweet potatoes, clinging to the near vertical pitch.

Where valley soil cannot sustain a crop, next on the economic totem pole are fruit trees: apples, plums, apricots, peaches, some grapes, walnuts, bamboo (I have since quit using disposable chopsticks - what a tragic waste of valuable farm land) and *huajiao*, the Sichuan pepper kernel condiment that make your mouth go numb. If the soil is so poor that fruit trees won't bear, next on the economic check list is pastoral animal production: yaks, some cattle, along with lots of sheep, goats and horses grazing on natural grasslands or on managed and often paddocked pastures, with western style barbed wire and sheep fencing. This animal production include pigs and chickens, of which most farms will have a sty and a coop, unless they are Muslim, in which case you can scrub the hog and throw in a milking yak. You can also include vegetable gardens, which most farm houses have, with popular crops being fava beans and potatoes, as well as your typical summer veggies such as tomatoes, peas, onions, carrots and the like. When *none* of the above will produce, and using the dragon wings analogy, this is usually when they are in the vertical position and the walls of the valley narrow into a gorge or canyon; it draws up, gets very shallow and becomes a raging, angry, lethal, fast moving torrent of froth and cascades. These awe inspiring rivers are everywhere you turn, and are mesmerizing and breathtakingly beautiful. Villages are often found in these harrowing straits, seemingly glued to the cliff sides and planting vegetable gardens where they can capture some top soil around their homes. In these spectacular, violent, water filled gorges, they will mine gravel for road and concrete production, since nothing will grow here anyway. Like I said, the human populations will take whatever these valleys will give them, in the clearly defined economic pecking order just described. Thus, China's long, interconnected, sinuous and often rapidly ascending valleys rhythmically narrow and flatten, just like the wings of a flying dragon, flapping wide and open, then closing up and narrowing to near closure. This ebb and flow of the many valleys I traverse during this journey, like riding some Herculean, cosmic roller coaster, is one of the indescribable pleasures of the whole trip, something I never expected.

Culturally, Ningxia and many parts of Eastern Gansu are predominately Muslim. Western Gansu trends towards Chinese Buddhism (or at least an absence of the Tibetan version). Southern Gansu and Western Sichuan are historically and still very much spiritually Tibetan Buddhism. Going south from Sichuan into Yunnan and Guizhou, the culture goes back to being Chinese Buddhism, spread across a number of internationally celebrated minority races, such as the Hui and Ouigher (both Muslim), Yi, Naxi, Bai and Mosuo (all with various locally infused versions of Buddhism and local gods, with this last one being matrilineal). Did I forget to mention that uncontroversial, obscure ethnic group called the Tibetans?

There is one other common point that all these valley cultures possess, regardless of how wild or unpopulated they might be: mobile phone towers. As I discovered in Qiqing, trying to send Lao Pu and Mrs. Geng photos to their phone, it might only be 1G, but there are not many places where a call or text message cannot be dispatched across these hinterlands. It is impressive how saturated Baba Beijing has covered China for its one billion plus mobile phones. Like all the coal fired electrical power generators going in, these decisions are as much political as they are economic: to improve the lives of one billion mostly poor, working class and farming citizens who are impatient join China's 300 million who are solidly in the middle class, and who are living the Chinese Dream. Baba Beijing can never forget the Heavenly Mandate, so there is also the weight of helping assure social and political stability on the leaders' collective shoulders… The downside to these amazingly beautiful and informative valley treks is sometimes, taking buses and trains in China can be less than relaxing and not always comfortable. But, knowing that each leg is going to provide me with many hours of stupendous scenery, natural beauty, local culture and architecture, it makes it all worthwhile.

Chapter 20: Xiahe

The drive into Xiahe and tussling with a Tara Tibetan Torquemada; the august Tibetan Labrang temple complex and thoughts and observations on Tibet and Tibetan culture: shall we just say it is a text of Tibetan tirades and tautologies, and call it a chapter?

The bus drive from Lanzhou to Xiahe has an interesting travel twist, starting when I wake up at the Lanzhou train station. Steve Evans, the amazing world traveler who has toured every country on Earth except Libya and who I met in Yinchuan, showed off his large, stainless steel thermos. I was somewhat surprised that he expressed a certain amount of pride in devoting its large volume to the very valuable and limited space in his backpack, as well as lauding it usefulness. I thought nothing of it till this morning, when I got off the train in Lanzhou. I had a can of beer in my backpack that I bought at the Jiayuguan train station, to celebrate my wonderful hike to the July 1st Glacier and to ponder the surreal two days I spent in Jingtieshan and Qiqing. By the time I got on board, the can's pull tab had somehow gotten pried loose and it had lost about a quarter of its contents in my backpack. Great. I will have to wait for the yeast and hops smell to dissipate over the next day or two. Until then, I will be walking around smelling like a brewery. I finished what was left of my beer, toasting the mountains and their people above, and thought nothing more about it. But it was an unfortunate ruse to an even bigger unknown problem. When I wake up in Lanzhou, my bed is soaking wet, as are the contents of my backpack, which for security reasons on trains I always put behind my pillow, where I keep my binoculars. Come to discover that my expensive, ¥96 (€12/$15), one liter *unbreakable* plastic water bottle is in fact very breakable and all my precious July 1st Glacier water is lost. Everything is soaked, including the notebook used for writing this book. Luckily, I use a gel pen and after several days of drying, it is still legible. Thus one of my first purchases in Xiahe is a nice 1.2 liter stainless steel thermos. Now I understand what Steve was telling me. It serves me brilliantly the rest of the trip, and I will never journey without one again.

Going south from Lanzhou means saying goodbye to the Yellow River, but I am blessed with equally resplendent waterways every step of the way. What an enchanting first bus ride to start this leg of the trip, my first foray into the Land of Valleys. It only takes three and a half hours, but it could easily be extended into a long weekend of slow driving and a natural, cultural, culinary and agricultural feast. These two long valleys between Lanzhou and Xiahe would be a great way to spend a few days driving a car. You could kick back, stopping, relaxing, eating, visiting and taking one gorgeous picture after another beauteous photo, then staying the night in cute, rural village homes. To put things in perspective, it would be much like taking a driving tour through the Loire or Rhone valleys in France or Napa and Shenandoah in the US. It is an incredibly rich and bountiful area. Not a square centimeter goes to waste. These river-graced valleys are a terraced-to-the-sky, multicolored tapestry of wheat (beige by now), barley (aquamarine), colza (bright yellow) fruit trees (red, green and yellow), pulses (purple and white flowers), vegetables (like your garden) and grapes (grown on wood trellises). It is stunning to see all this agricultural production in a relatively dry area. This route just exudes timeless culture, with quaint, colorful, picturesque villages nestled among small plots and terraced agriculture. And being a transition zone between Islam and Buddhism, there are dueling minarets and pagodas everywhere you turn, often side by side. From Lanzhou to Xiahe, the proportion of Muslim minarets vs. Buddhist temple stupas paints an accurate picture of which kind of people live in the area. South of Lanzhou, the skyline is dominated by the minarets of Islam. About half way to Xiahe, the ratio is 50:50. As we approach Xiahe, the preponderance of Tibetan temples with their towering white, gold topped stupas populate the countryside. Many personal residences have miniature stupas, as well as tall banner poles too. These slender poles are for the most part bare all the way up to the top. Some though, have multicolored silk bands wrapped on part of the pole, especially towards the top, where there sits a basket or often a pointed tip. Inside the basket, it is overflowing with hanging strips of white (to dirty-white) silk cloth or bundles of barley, with the grain heads sticking out. The total drive is 254km: south out of Lanzhou on the highway G75 (G stands for the national 4-6 lane highways and usually with paid tolls), then west on the S2 (S roads are provincial level 2-laners) to Linxia, then southwest on the S213 and S312 into Xiahe, climbing up in elevation all the way. This is the rainy season, so both rivers are fast paced and powerful. And as they should be. Lanzhou and the Yellow River sit at about 1,450 MASL and Xiahe at 3,100m. So, we are ascending upstream over 1.5km in just three and a half hours. Driving up into this dramatic fall in topography is what helps make these two rivers look so impressive and dramatic. The rivers are as follows,

From Lanzhou to Linxia (临夏= Lookout over Summer), we track the Tao River (洮河= Cleansing River, which is a Yellow River tributary).

From Linxia to Xiahe (夏河= Summer River), we follow the Daxia River (⊠夏河= Big Summer River, which feeds into the Tao).

I think we can take it that *summer* is a big theme in these parts. As it should be. At this altitude, the summer weather is just cool to warm week after week. The days are gorgeous, the sky radiant. Even though there are many Muslims living here, the architecture is pure Chinese, with the *siheyuan* (四合院), open air central courtyard homes dominating the landscape. The roofs are in the classic sine wave tiled style, with the dragon tails coiled at the ends of each gable. The farmers are harvesting all their crops by hand, backs bowed to the soil, with the ancient scythe and sickle. It is probably some early season white summer wheat (it could even be a late maturing winter wheat at this altitude). Being China, they don't have large areas in these valleys to install modern grain silos. So, they store their grain on the harvested plants, bundling them in vertical stands called shocks, just like in 18th and 19th century western paintings of rural countryside. In these two valleys, they make really unique wheat shocks. They are about one to 1.5m tall and they look just like big Caribbean voodoo poppet dolls, the ones they stick needles in. Or, they resemble giant, straw colored mushrooms. Either way, when there is a whole terrace of them, neatly and geometrically arranged like statues, it is really eye catching and unique. The whole drive from Lanzhou to Xiahe is one of the most memorable and scenic I have ever been on, regardless of the continent traveled. One dream for my China bucket list is to come back here and repeat this journey on bicycle, making it a slow motion, one-week culture feast.

We arrive at Xiahe and the journey is going really well. Everybody is, for the most part so helpful and courteous, that I almost forget that I'm bound to eventually come across a first class jerk, the kind that I used to deal with as a daily part of my routine, every hour of the day, in the 90s. And it happens in Xiahe, Gansu, home of the celebrated Labrang Tibetan Temples. Lonely Planet lists three youth hostels, all very close to each other and not far from the temple complex. As I have alluded to, one of my main goals on this journey is to really take my Chinese to the next level, and I'm succeeding by speaking nothing but Mandarin for days on end. So, I choose the Tara Guesthouse rather than the Overseas Tibetan Hotel, because LP says the guy who runs the Overseas place speaks flawless English, which is definitely not good for my Mandarin. I go inside the Tara and a Tibetan guy behind the desk warmly shakes my hand, smiling from ear to ear and says no problem, they have dorm beds for ¥30 (€3.75/$4.75) a night - just what the doctor ordered. Please wait until my colleague gets off the phone and we'll get you fixed right up. I mentally start calling the guy on the phone Big Boss Kahuna, as he talks on and on for close to 10 minutes, speaking excellent Mandarin the whole time to his interlocutor, and I bide my time until he gets off. We even make a few smiling glances to each other, signaling his frustration at not being able to get off the phone. When he finally gets off the phone, I tell him I understand they have dorm beds available and I'd like to stay for two nights. He pretends not to understand my Chinese, which I fully understand, since I also pretend I don't understand when people speak to me in English. It is naturally in my interests to keep the conversation in the Chinese column. I did not learn to speak fluent Portuguese, Arabic, French and Mandarin by speaking English with the locals.

So, fair is fair. It's a game I've played a thousand times learning languages. He responds back in English and I respond back in Chinese, which is fine with me; we both get to practice our respective foreign languages. I've experienced this kind of inter-linguistic tango and give and take since 1976, when I started to learn my first foreign language, Portuguese (well, not counting Latin for three years in high school). But this guy's self-esteem is not up to the task. His little ego is wounded because I am answering back to his English in Mandarin; he is taking it as a personal insult and as a slap to his authority as the manager of this hostel. After two or three exchanges, I'm even keeled, just like I always am with my students in class, maintaining a calm tone of voice. But he is already starting to act chippy and I can just see the bitch fit brewing between his ears. I am surprised when he asks me to fill out the exact same full-page registration form, like they used to make us fill in back in the nineties, with fifteen or twenty inane questions to feed the paranoia of any authoritarian government. Because he is getting so tetchy, I try to lighten up the situation with a little humor, so I say, admiring the paper in my hands,

"Cool, I haven't seen this form since the 1990s."

Almost anybody would laugh about it too. I understand this is Tibetan country and the atmosphere is continually tense in many areas, with monks and nuns self-immolating in protest of the Han's heavy hand of control on the area since the large scale, bloody riots in March, 2008. Then Xiahe was one of the first places the riots spread from Tibet proper and into the rest of historical Tibet. I also understand this security form is being given to me because Baba Beijing scapegoats foreigners for all that ails The Land of Snow. By now, he is just itching to make me pay for my perceived insolence and he finds his pretext in my passport. My original passport when I arrived to Beijing in 2010 expired in the interim, and with it went my original entrance stamp, August 11th, 2010. Many times I have checked into hotels, explained about the expired passport, giving them the date of entrance and they dutifully write it in the requisite box. But that is all he needs as an excuse to refuse my registration to stay at his hostel. Which is fine. I respect the linguistic lines that are being drawn in the sand and it is, after all, his place and his prerogative. Not a problem, there are two more hostels. To get to the Red Rock, I need to turn left and the Overseas my third choice, is immediately next door to the right on the way out. I turn left and head to the Red Rock, which is about 350m away. I no sooner get one foot in the door that the woman attendant looks me over and says,

"*Mei you, mei you!*" (没有没有!)

As in, there are no rooms. The whole scene has echoes of Jingtieshan's Twilight Zone Communism, just really bizarre. I didn't say a word and she is already ushering me out the door. I could be lost, need to use the bathroom or make a phone call, and she already has me marked before I get my second foot past the threshold. Hmm... All of my suspicions about how microscopic Big Boss Kahuna's self-worth equals is confirmed when I walk into his next door neighbor's place, the Overseas, and guess who is standing in front of the counter, but Little Man Boy himself, with a big, self-satisfied grin on his face. Of course registration is no problem, says the grinning lady behind the Overseas reception counter. But sorry Charlie, we have no ¥30 dorm beds left. However, we do have a single room with your name written all over it for only ¥200 (€25/$32) a night; just fill out the registration form right here. I say thanks but no thanks and leave, with Big Boss Kahuna himself smiling from ear to ear. So, all I do is walk down the street, check into a Chinese hotel, with no formalities, no form to fill; I just show her my residence permit and she fills out a simple receipt.

While I cannot prove it, I am certain Big Boss Kahuna saw me turn left when I exited the Tara, so he knew I was heading to the Red Rock. He called, explained the situation and gave her my description. Thus when their attendant saw me enter, I got a very forced and rushed refusal before I could even get through the door. It just does not add up. The Tara has plenty of dorm beds and the best real estate on the main street's corner, where everybody is hanging out. The Red Rock is off on a back street, hard to find, is as dead as a sarcophage when I walk in, yet has no rooms of any kind? I might be able to rationalize what happened in the Red Rock as just the fluke of a grumpy old lady who is in a bad mood. But when I see Big Boss Kahuna himself gloating, as I walk into his next door competition, with the clearly contrived attempt to rip me off, he went way over the line. Big Boss would be perfect as a Red Guard Torquemada, during the Cultural Revolution, torturing, publicly beating and psychologically destroying countless lives, families and communities. Sorry Mr. Kahuna, but you are about two generations too late for your dream job. I came to Xiahe to see one of the greatest Tibetan temple complexes on the face of the Earth. So I shrug off what just happened, smile at my good fortune to still exist in this life and to be healthy, happy and free.

And no Tibetan Torquemada is going to keep me from trying some great local dishes. I find a nice little hole-in-the-wall

Ouigher place. Clusters of customers are grouped at their respective tables: three monks at one, Chinese tourists at another and a few of the younger, local talent spread out at other tables, all showing off and using their tech gear of laptops and smartphones. A Babel of Turkic, Mandarin and Tibetan quietly fills the air. I would be happy to sit with any of them, but the taciturn Ouigher manager (come to think of it, Ouigher restaurant workers always seem taciturn) steers me to the just vacated, last empty table in the house. It's a hopping place for this time of the morning. As an early lunch, I try and love two great regional plates. My noodle dish of choice is *mianpian* (面片= noodle pieces). The noodles are a blend of wheat and rice flour and each piece is a thin square, of about 2cm. They are stewed in a rich, beef and onion broth. I add some dried, ground hot pepper from the condiment trough on the table. The pepper looks and kicks like blackish, blood-red gunpowder. Just what the doctor ordered. While not in every restaurant, these condiment trays are pretty cool, kind of like a culinary control panel. There are usually four compartments: salt, red pepper, MSG and *huajiao* (花椒= flower pepper). I use the first two and avoid that last pair. I know I am eating MSG in most every restaurant meal served and many people love the numbing sensation and aromatic kick of Sichuan's most famous spice, *huajiao*. I can take *huajiao* in small doses, but don't like the fact that it kills your taste buds to the point where the food begins to lose its flavor. Because of their size and thinness, mianpian are frustratingly difficult to negotiate with chopsticks. Mr. Taciturn sees me struggling somewhat and offers me a spoon. I scan the other tables. No one else is using one, so I push my manual dexterity envelope to the limit and finish off the bowl.

I still have most of the day to explore the Labrang temple complex (拉布朗寺), and I call it a complex, because it is composed of numerous buildings and is spread out in several spots. It is a very special place, indeed. Labrang can easily count as temple visiting in the Tibetan motherland, which is blocked to us evil laowai *agents provocateurs* right now, and I later learn, blocked to even Tibetans living outside Tibet. Labrang will be my crowning Tibetan cultural experience on this journey. This place is considered one of the six great temples of the Gelug school of Tibetan Buddhism, the famed Yellow Hat followers. Further on in *44 Days*, I know I will get big doses of Tibetan culture, as I continue my travels across Western Sichuan, which like Xiahe, is historically a part of Greater Tibet.

Hotel taken care of, I take off to explore Labrang. During my first temple visit, two things happen. First, I almost take a step back when at the temple altar I see *three* photos, not the usual two. In Chinese Tibetan temples, there are two portrait photos commonly seen. One is of the Beijing-appointed 11th *Panchen Lama* (Great Scholar), Mr. Gyaltsen Norbu. In China, he is officially the face of the Tibetan faith. The rest of the world considers him a rank pretender and recognizes Mr. Gedhun Choekyi as the true leader. At the age of 5, this Gedhun disappeared just days after his selection was announced in 1995, arrested by Han authorities. No joke, he has never been seen again. I wonder if Baba Beijing knows where he is? It is a big, dark secret. While it is doubtful that Baba Beijing would kill him, it is assumed he is living under very tight house arrest somewhere in the nation's capital. The official government line is he is living and studying quietly somewhere in China. So, since Gedhun Choekyi has been disappeared, one of the portraits commonly seen in Tibetan temples is that of Beijing's favorite son, Gyaltsen Norbu, although I'm sure the vast majority of monks and Tibetans hold their noses and symbolically spit on the ground at being forced to having it hung on the wall. The second photo seen everywhere is of Choekyi Gyaltsen, who was the Panchen Lama from 1938-1989. His round, cherubic face is unmistakable. And then there is of course Tenzin Gyatso, the 14th Dalai Lama and the one living in India in exile since 1959. This is the man that all the world leaders meet and for Baba Beijing, he is the most reviled Tibetan to walk on the face of the Earth. The relationship between the Dalai Lama and the Panchen Lama is a difficult one to explain. For me, a good analogy is that the Dalai Lama is like the president in a parliamentarian form of government, and the Panchen Lama is like the Prime Minister. The president handles foreign policy, provides leadership, vision and stays above the domestic fray. The prime minister is like the managing director, who rolls up their shirt sleeves and gets their hands dirty running the government on a daily basis.

So, shock of shocks when I see a photo of the *exiled Dalai Lama* hanging in the first Labrang temple I visit. Given how hated and feared he is by the Han, it is truly remarkable that his portrait is here, right next to Norbu's and Choekyi's. I'm not sure what is going on. Monks in Tibet can be persecuted if just caught with a photo of Tenzin Gyatso and here he is for all the world to see. I'm not sure if some monk hung it up in protest or if the local authorities are allowing it as a pressure release valve. In any case, it is incendiary and the only time I see the Dalai Lama's image on the rest of the trip. Xiahe is definitely on Baba Beijing's radar. The very same Baba Beijing-appointed Gyaltsen Norbu came here to Xiahe two years ago, on an official visit. He was all of 21 years old. Xiahe has a history of violent, anti-Beijing backlashes, but comparatively speaking, it was probably too much to risk trying to send Mr. Norbu to Lhasa, the Mecca of Tibet.[1] Other than being on a political map in Gansu, Xiahe is part and parcel in ancient Tibet and today is at the same level of importance spiritually, as Tibet proper. Other than the shock of seeing the Dalai Lama's poster image, the second interesting thing at Labrang is a little boy monk, about eight years old, tears off the entire stub of my ticket, when I enter the aforementioned temple. I don't think anything about it, until I get to the next one and the vermillion robed monk asks to see my ticket,

"Oh, you can't come in, you've used all your ticket up."

He explains how fingernail sized pieces of the ticket end are supposed to be torn off with each visit, even though there are no serrations in the paper.

"Really?" (真的= *zhende*?)

I explain what his young smart Alec compadre did and he reluctantly lets me through. At this hour, all the other places except one are not being controlled anyway. At this last one, the huge school temple where the monks go to study, the old geezer is just *not* letting me in. About that time, one last big group of Chinese tourists rolls up, and I take advantage of the aged monk's failing eyesight and sneak in and out with them. Thereafter, I continue to crawl up, over, around, in and out of Labrang's many buildings. It is getting dark and I'm now almost the last one here, staying well after all the marauding Chinese tour groups have long gone.

Architecture aside, and Labrang is an incredibly photogenic place, I leave with three other, more cerebral souvenirs. One is listening to some monks practicing on their super vibrato bass long horns, called the *dungchen* in Tibetan. They look like bassoons with a severe overdose of steroids. And they sound equally as amped up too. Their sound is unmistakable. Their blast is so resonating and powerful that they can be heard echoing for many hundreds of meters, even hidden behind enclosed temple doors. Second is where I come upon a temple that has a sign out front, saying it is closed to the public for four days, and to drive home the message, the sign on the entrance has a small black flag attached to it. Is this some kind of funeral or wake? More likely, they are performing some kind of exorcism. For Tibetans, black unsurprisingly represents evil, negativity and hate. Bodhisattvas, those Buddha looking beings so often seen in temple paintings, who represent enlightenment, can be portrayed with black rays emanating from their bodies, as they purge all the impure, materialistic evils from themselves. Thus, this black flag could represent evil that needs to be exorcised. In any case, very beautiful choral singing is coming from inside the temple. Trying to split hairs and not disrespect their four-day closure, I just quietly slip inside the outer front doors and sit down to listen. I am still a good twenty meters from the temple entrance, but a large group is singing (I'd say, fifty carolers) and it is quite loud, pouring out of the big front doors towards me. Thinking I will only sit for a minute or two, I end up listening for more than a quarter of an hour. They never stop singing and I am beginning to think this may go on for ninety-six hours, with monks taking turns at relay. I try to record some of it, but realize my Galaxy app is voice activated to recognize a particular language. I don't even bother to check if Tibetan temple singing is one of the choices. I need to download an app that just records sound, not spoken word, which I do when I get back to my hotel. This is brought home again about a half an hour later, in the pale light of a diminishing sunset, after crawling through as many of the temple buildings I can find. On the way back into town from Labrang, I explore the Tibetan neighborhood where all the monks live. I see some similarities between it and the Tibetan village, Qiqing, I visited in central Gansu earlier this week. First, both neighborhoods eschew a square layout of the houses, preferring a long, single row instead. The Labrang village has two very long streets, running from the town's main street to the temple complex. Qiqing is the same. All the town's houses are in a long, single row extending along one side of the road. Even the abandoned mud village in Qiqing is only three long rows. Old Qiqing apparently couldn't do one long row, because they built the town at a bend in the valley. But rectangles and squares are not part of the equation. This is of course the exact opposite of Han Chinese perspectives. One look at a Beijing map, with its ancient and modern concentric squares and rectangles says it all. Other ancient cities with their very concentric geometric layouts are no different, such as Pingyao, Shanxi; Xi'an, Shaanxi and Kaifeng, Henan.

The other observation, which I see again and again during my travels in Greater Tibet, is the juxtaposition of frenetic building and rebuilding on top of and beside ongoing decay and decomposition. It is almost as if Tibetans live out the cycle of life: birth, growth, maturity, aging, decrepitude, death and decay, in their homes and neighborhoods. Ditto the temples: ancient art and edifices can be falling apart, with maniacal construction and renewal, going hand in hand alongside. This all seems to evoke a powerful cultural and philosophical statement by the Tibetans, living and praying in an architectural circle of life. Not only in their daily lives, but their homes and edifices are also a constantly turning wheel of temporal and metaphysical existence. As I walk along the inner row of houses, I come upon one with the courtyard full of what sounds like maybe twenty or so young monks chanting together. Nothing musical here at all and I'm not sure I can even detect a repetitive cadence, but it is indeed captivating, almost hypnotic, which I guess is the point. Against all hope, I try to record it with my voice app and leave with only the memory of their prayer logged in my grey matter.

I go back to Mr. Taciturn's Ouigher noodle shop for dinner. He actually falls out of character when he sees me back and breaks a smile, just barely. For dinner I order *ganbanmian* (干版面= dry version noodles). Wow, what a great meal. The noodles are 100% wheat based and look just like Italian spaghetti, but these are hand pulled and cut fresh right in the kitchen. It is just incredible how uniform they are in diameter. The sauce is full of diced tomatoes and thinly sliced zucchini squash. The chef has thrown in a healthy dose of onions, leeks, red and green bell pepper with garlic. I could be in Naples or Florence. Yummy. Put that one on your list. Being a Ouigher restaurant, no beer is served. I spot the *Tibetan Cafe* on the way back to my hotel. It is upstairs and has huge glass windows overlooking the main Renmin East Street below. There are a few crimson tuniqued monks sitting two tables away, drinking tea. They continue to peek over at me and whisper. Normally, I'd go and introduce myself, but it's been a long and eventful day and I stay put. I call it a night. Walking back to the hotel, I reflect on how magnificent Labrang really is. Just the scale of the complex, the massively thick earth and brick walls, the spectacular temple façades with their rainbow colored painting and needlework tapestries; the nearly garish luxury of the temple interiors, all the sounds of singing, chanting, the musical instruments heard behind walls in the background and observing the lives of the monks who live and work here, is all unforgettable. The modern political history of Xiahe being a hotbed of Tibetan resistance offers further sociopolitical intrigue. And to top it all off, the drive from Lanzhou to Xiahe combines stunning natural and cultural beauty.

1- The most recent deadly riots occurred in 2008:
www.nytimes.com/2008/03/16/world/asia/16tibet.html?pagewanted=all&_r=0.
Nonviolent protests are still ongoing:
ntdtv.org/en/news/china/2013-02-12/tibetans-in-xiahe-china-say-no-new-year-celebrations.html

CHAPTER 21: LANGMUSI

Deeper into the heart of the Tibetan world with a world class hike up a sacred, magical valley - The Great Namo Gorge in Langmusi, on the Gansu/Sichuan border.

Before leaving Xiahe, I can't resist and go back to the Ouigher restaurant for a classic bowl of Xinjiang style Muslim beef noodles. When Mr. Taciturn, the owner sees me for a *third* time in two days, he almost hugs me, the good friends we have now become. I've got a long day on a rural bus ahead of me to get to Langmusi, so I add a couple of hard boiled eggs to my breakfast. In China, they are called *tea leaf eggs* (茶叶蛋= *chayedan*). They are boiled in a marinade of spices, soy sauce and tea leaves. They are then left in this marinade until eaten. Oftentimes the shells get cracked up in the process and the cooked egg white inside the shell absorbs the marinade and takes on a dark hue. Very tasty. Getting around Xiahe is a breeze because of a unique system developed by the local taxis. If you are in a hurry, it is very practical too, because the main thoroughfare, Renmin Street, is quite long. On Renmin Street, you simply flag a taxi. As long as there is one seat left, they stop for you. You get in, hand the driver the handsome sum of ¥1.00 (€0.13/$0.16). They take off, driving slowly up the street. Where you want to stop, you just stay,

"Please stop the car here." (请停车这儿= *Qing ting che zher*)

They pull over, you get out and the taxi keeps going up Renmin Street keeping the car full, until they get to the end of town. There they turn around, coming the other way to complete the circuit. They keep doing that all day. For only one kuai, I see lots of Xiahe citizens using this service to only go just two or three hundred meters, to save time. I counted six taxis making this round. I suspect they do very well financially with this communal arrangement. At the Xiahe bus station, I meet a young London woman traveling around China on her own for six weeks. In her twenties and not speaking a word of Chinese, my hat is off to her. She must surely make quite an impression on the locals here. Not only is she traveling solo as a linguistically handicapped female, but she is about 1.85m tall, and is of African descent, in a country where overt prejudice against black people is palpable. In China's historical perception of the world order, it is the center of the universe (hence *Middle* Kingdom) and ever further concentric circles of influence away from the mother lode represent less and less civilized peoples. For the Chinese, Africa and its dark races are the most distant sphere of influence, the end of the world, so to speak. In a country whose people are so openly racist against dark skinned people, not being able to understand what the locals are saying might be the best self-defense. I meet briefly only one other solo female traveler on this trip, probably Dutch or Scandinavian. The antithesis of the English woman, she is very blond and petite; it looks like her backpack is going to topple her over. But in both cases, I really admire them for their sense of adventure. The one great advantage for women traveling solo in China is the chances of being sexually assaulted or raped by the local population might be low compared to other places on the planet. I suspect if a Chinese man got caught doing such a thing, that justice without much due process would be quick and severe, with a large caliber slug of lead in the back of the head. For something that severe to happen to a foreign woman would be such a huge loss of face for the authorities. They would surely be put in a position to set a very firm example. But it can happen. Foreign women are not totally immune. Upon my return to Beijing, I do learn that a French high schooler was in fact dated raped by a Chinese man last year, a victim of Rohypnol. Unfortunately, she did not report it, even though they were outside in public where her spiked drink was given. Had she done so, the rapist may very well have been identified by the CCTV cameras that are so ubiquitous these days - he drove her to a fleabag hotel to rape her. Out of fear of having to tell her parents, she refused to do so. It's really unfortunate, because he may still be on the streets as a result.

One thing is for sure, the concept of traveling by oneself is definitely not in the mentality of the Chinese. Other than Danny from Nanjing, whom I met in Dunhuang, I have seen thousands of local tourists and they have at least one traveling partner, and usually several. Even these independent traveling groups are well within the minority, as most Chinese, at least these days, like to travel in organized tour package groups. This will undoubtedly evolve, as the Chinese become more experienced and confident in their travels. On the ride down from Xiahe to Langmusi, two Europeans sit behind me, and I remember seeing them in the Tara Hostel reception, when I had my tussle with the Tibetan Torquemada. I can't help but think what they wonder happened at the Tara. I take them for northern Europeans, maybe Dutch. I can see that these two European compadres are reading out of a very dog eared copy of the Lonely Planet. I have been speaking so much Chinese the last two weeks that a chance to have some Western companionship might be nice. Speaking some French or English would be a pleasant change of pace. We introduce ourselves to each other. They are Rafal Cebulko (he tells me his family name means *Onion*) and Marta (I never get her family name), college students from Poland. Rafal has been studying Mandarin three years and plans to continue his studies in Shanghai next year. For not living in China, Rafal is making good progress with his Chinese studies. Like me, he takes his language learning seriously and devotes a lot of time to it. Marta is also in the linguistics department and is considering going to France to study and learn French. Once we get to Langmusi, we decide to bunk together.

Leaving Xiahe on the G213 means starting to head south, after the first couple of weeks of heading in an east-west tack. It also means leaving a Ouigher/Hui Muslim presence and moving fully into the world of Tibetan culture, as Western Sichuan is historically part of what was once Greater Tibet. Luqu County is about 80km out of Xiahe, after going through the fairly nightmarish industrial town of Hezuo. Luqu is a broad valley that is almost a high altitude plain. Starting here, many of the traditional Chinese *siheyuan,* open courtyard houses, have an exterior anteroom made of glass or Plexiglas, just like a greenhouse, usually on the south side. This transparent add-on is an excellent solar heat collection system, which they are using to dry laundry. During the clear sky winters, when the 3,000 MASL temperatures are well below zero, these attached solariums must be a godsend to help warm their homes.

We finally arrive to Langmusi. It doesn't have all the flash and pizazz in the Lonely Planet guide as some other sites where I have been and will be visiting. But in retrospect, it will end up being one of the best places where I spend time on this amazing six-week journey. If you like Tibetan culture and sublime, wild places to hike and explore, all for a pittance, then throw a dart at the map of China until it lands on the twin provincial town of Langmusi (郎木寺= Bright Wood Temple). Langmusi really does straddle two provinces: Gansu is on the north bank of the White Dragon River (白龙河), where I just spent an unforgettable week. Sichuan is on the south side, so today represents my first steps in this province during this journey. Langmusi's streets are all dirt and with the seasonal rains that this region is getting, they have turned into a thick soup of mud and sludge. It is definitely not a town that is seeking the tourist trade, which just adds to its charm. I can imagine this is what the streets of frontier towns looked like in North America in the 19th century.

It is lunch time, so the Sara hostel recommended by Lonely Planet is closed, and we don't even get to another LP listed hostel called Nomads, before finding a nice Chinese *zhaodaisuo* (of which there are several along the main street), with three beds to a room, which fits our situation perfectly. Right as we go upstairs, there is an old faded poster of Mao Zedong, dressed in his requisite, revolutionary grey, self-named jacket. He is intently gazing out at the proletarian masses: his unified people. Like Jesus, Jefferson or France's Marianne, how icons are portrayed by the princes of power and as a result of faddish, popular tastes, is a really fascinating point of history to look at. National, cultural and religious icons all go through cycles and trends: sagacious, macho, effeminate, stern, erudite, cherubic and on and on. This portrayal of The Great Helmsman is decidedly avuncular and tenderhearted. Our room window looks out over the mudslide known as Langmusi Main Street. Our hostel is on the Sichuan side. Behind the row of buildings across the street is the White Dragon River. The *White Dragon River*. What an enchanting name, one that evokes all kinds of romantic, mystical images and legends. This is a 100% Tibetan town, full of monks, residential neighborhoods, two monasteries, some nice temples and shrines, all sitting at an oxygen-starved 3,272 MASL.

Over the next two days I discover that Langmusi has some of the best hiking I have ever experienced on this fair planet, and I have done a lot of trekking in some pretty spectacular places on every continent except Australia and the Antarctic. So, this compliment is truly sincere. There are two major hiking areas around Langmusi and being a bi-provincial twin city, naturally there is one on each side of the river. It is still early enough in the day to have a quick lunch, get in one of the two hikes today and the second one tomorrow. Quite by coincidence, I'd like to opt for the Sichuan trail today and Rafal and Marta want to attack the Gansu side. We will flip trails tomorrow and can compare notes. Befitting a twin city, each side has a monastery, so Langmusi is a wonderful place to see how Tibetan monks live on a day to day basis. They are everywhere, from young elementary aged boys to cane and crutch dependent genarians, waddling along with crooked backs. Most of the monks live in a cluster of houses surrounding the Kerti Gompa Monastery, on the Sichuan side, and are fully integrated into Langmusi's daily town and commercial life. Unlike Qiqing and Xiahe, these Langmusi Tibetan houses are not constructed in one long row, but seem built in a haphazard arc fashion. It probably has more to do with geography than choice, since the town is situated in a bit of a bowl and on the Gansu side, Langmusi runs up against a fabulous looking, sheer butte cliff face. Like the two aforementioned Tibetan towns I've visited, there is this amazing juxtaposing of frenetic building and rebuilding on top of and next to decay and ruin. The wheel of life never stops turning in the lives of Tibetans, be it praying in a yak butter-candle-lit temple, chanting in a hypnotic trance, or adding an extension to their humble abodes. A novel way they secure the roofs here is to simply lay down the roofing material, such as wood, metal or slate rock and then strategically putting medium sized rocks on top of them, to keep the roofs from blowing away. This would never last in places I've lived, like Oklahoma and Normandy, where strong winds are a part of the fabric of daily life, but it obviously gets the job done here. While making my way through the neighborhood, some excited little boys call me over to show off lots of frogs and some fish living in the town's large, open and less than salubrious looking cistern. It is really touching as we talk about their big discovery. Obviously, they have more fun games to play outside in nature than big city video games like Myst and Minecraft. They make me nostalgic for when I grew up as a kid their age, spending most of my free time exploring outdoors. Since they are not in monks' tunics and having seen many other youngsters in vermillion robes, I get the impression young Buddhist followers start their training around eight to ten years of age – definitely before puberty.

There were open trench sewers in the Xiahe neighborhoods where the monks live, and here the outhouses are perched right over the White Dragon River and its small tributaries that course through the town. Xiahe is in the process of installing an underground sewage system, but in Langmusi, as I'm sure in countless other Tibetan mountain villages, they are still clinging to social practices which have served them well since antiquity: the idea that these high altitude, fast moving and seemingly infinite, snow-melt and rainy-season replenished rivers will keep carrying all their refuse, excrement and the detritus of daily life, thousands of klicks away and thousands of meters below, to distant oceans and seas, never to be seen again. But rising population pressures and a newer, more modern 21st century paradigm, with much greater expectations, not to mention a rapidly transforming Tibetan plateau landscape due to anthropogenic global warming, is making this ancient system of faith in Mother Nature and gravity untenable. Piles of garbage, tattered clothing, rotten food, plastic and glass bottles dot the banks of the White Dragon River in town, waiting for the next cloud burst to raise the river's water level and carry it all to the lowlands and oceans below. Two boys bring a wheel barrow of household rubbish to the river and unceremoniously jettison it into the river. Several plastic items are stuck in the bottom of the wheelbarrow and they are having a grand old time trying to shake them out, while leaving it hanging over the rushing waters. When will this pre-modern system of waste and refuse disposal rupture and come to an end?

If anybody thinks I'm picking on the Tibetans, it is not exclusively their problem. In many Han and (other) minority villages that dot these breathtakingly beautiful mountain valleys and gorges, it doesn't take a hydrology engineer to see where all the toilet (public outhouses, really) runoff is heading, unless they have figured out a way to suspend Newton's laws, given that these odious, malodorous platforms are perched not far above the raging cascades below. This is not a Tibetan, Han nor minority problem. This is a rural development issue. Yes, Baba Beijing is spending billions to provide infrastructure for a sustainable way of life in the countryside. I can attest to the thousands of kilometers of roads, highways, bridges, train tracks, and even in the poorest villages, I have seen decent to very good housing in the hinterlands. None of this was the case just a short generation ago. Most rural hamlets were shockingly poor and medieval. When we lived here in the nineties, much of the raw sewage in China's big cities, Beijing, Shanghai and Guangzhou included, was unceremoniously dumped directly into local rivers and seas. I will never forget swimming at the beach in Qingdao (home of the famous, German inspired beer), and realized after ten minutes or so that that wasn't brown algae floating in the water, but human feces. And this was Qingdao's public beach.

It is not just a Chinese problem, it is a developmental priority conundrum. Make money and create jobs first, then ask consequential, costly questions later, usually years or generations too late. I recall staying in Penang, Malaysia during the same time period, in a real touristy, beach resort area. No one could swim at the same said sandy beaches, because there was so much heavy metal and sulfuric acid runoff from microchip and computer hard drive factories in the hills above. A creek running down to the beaches below was a tar black flow of toxic death, as the breathtaking acid-stenched plume bloomed like an ebony flower from Hades into the bay's waters. This was Malaysia, in the 1990's. I couldn't believe it. Unfortunately, this money and jobs first, unlimited extraction philosophy that the human race has zealously followed for the last 500 years, Planet Earth be doomed, has more than caught up with our Pale Blue Dot, multiplied seven billion times. I guess it is asking too much of any people, the Chinese included, to see what their population needs to crawl out of the pre-industrial age, look back over the last 500 years, seeing how Europe then North America and Japan became manufacturing and trade juggernauts, at the expense of everyone and everything in their wake, somehow have a crystal ball and say with omniscient sagacity,

"*You know, we're going to take a different path and do it the* right *way.*"

Even though Baba Beijing takes a very long term view of the future (unlike America's post 1980-next quarterly stock bonus reports), they are at heart a very conservative lot (in the classical sense, not the American political one). Furthermore, they have the weight of Mao's visionary madness during the 50s' Great Leap Forward and the 60s-70s' societal cannibalism of the Cultural Revolution, haunting them over their shoulders, alongside their leadership commitment to upholding China's 2,200 year old Heavenly Mandate. It's just too much to ask for them to do otherwise: best to just stick to a proven script and don't rock the historical boat. And so it goes. Thus, in rural China, it is one village after another in isolated, sublime, beautiful river valleys, taking care of all their waste the old fashioned, Dark Ages way. Maybe in another generation or three...

After exploring the residential neighborhood surrounding the Kerti Gompa monastery, I wend my way to a beautiful, open, flower filled meadow that ushers you into the Great Namo Gorge. Different groups of young boys, 10 to15 years of age, are relaxing in the meadow grass, adorned in their vermilion and gold monks' tunics. One group of boys is sitting on a rise, looking down across the meadow's busy activities, making comments and grinning and snickering like Cheshire cats. Another group of about ten or so are playing Tibetan versions of King of the Hill, Leap Frog and just general rough housing and wrestling. This is an activity I also saw a lot of in the Xiahe neighborhood: Tibetan boys love to wrestle, play fight and rough house all the time. It may be a way to release energy, after spending hours relatively immobilized during prayers and tantric lessons. Adult monks are also taking advantage of the beautiful weather, sitting and walking in various group sizes. Near the Namo Creek's banks, below the mouth of the gorge, are several tents being occupied by migrant Tibetan shepherding families, who are grazing their flocks of sheep, goats and herds of yaks on the nearby hillsides. They are mingling, chatting and eating with the monks from town. All in all, out of the 700 monks who belong to the Kerti Gompa, about 100 are enjoying the meadow's tranquility.

Namo Great Gorge is sacred to Tibetans. There are several caves which they enter, offer votives, chant and pray. The first cave is believed to be inhabited by a holy fairy (like an angel) and a number of people, especially women, are congregating around its shrine outside the cave mouth. The shrine has that classic Tibetan look of a huge number of tree branches of various lengths propped up together in vertical fashion, shaped in a big round or square fagot of wood, supported by a surrounding stone plinth. Atop these poles of varying length are multicolored flags, most of them all with the same prayers of supplication in Tibetan and containing a mythical winged horse in the center, known as the *wind horse*. The women are wearing gypsy style Tibetan dresses: thick, black skirts with different hues of full-length leggings, cloth sandals, along with brightly colored smocks, blouses and a rainbow of head turbans. They approach the shrine, circle it, chanting, singing forlornly and then kneel down on all fours to pray. They repeat this sequence several times: getting up, circling and kneeling on all fours, etc., before finally going into the Fairy Cave. Once inside, I can hear them continuing to sing and chant, sometimes together and other times it becomes a bit of a cacophony of voices, echoing out of the small entrance. Once inside the cave, it sounds like they are almost in a trance. Tibetans also throw votive papers at the base of these shrines or inside the cave. These papers can also be burned as an offering. About 5cm square, they again have the wind horse printed on them, but are too small for text, so the horse is adorned with Buddhist fresco designs all around it. This results in the Namo Creek being covered with these votive paper squares all over the ground outside the cave.

Very few people, locals or tourists, venture more than 500m up this splendid gorge, with its scintillating, crystal waters cascading down from the mountains above. It doesn't take long before I am all alone, where at the top of this first leg is a big meadow that veers up and to the right (southwest). The weather is splendid, with warm, but not hot temperatures and a brilliant blue sky behind moving banks of tufted, cumulus clouds. I push on in total isolation and solitude. The gorge is banked on both sides by beveled to sheer cliffs, hundreds of meters high. Wildflowers with yellow, mauve, white and red blooms are everywhere. Mountainsides off into the horizon are covered with conifers and spruce. After a couple of more klicks, the gorge branches off into a fork, with the creek continuing southwest. Due west is a broad flat, fast rising meadow that scales up a treeless mountain. I want to continue along the banks of Namo Creek, so before leaving, I survey the other mountain meadow with my trusty Zeiss. The mountainside has a good two hundred yaks grazing on its lush grass and about half way down I see a shepherd's tent. Outside of it is a Tibetan monk in his vermilion tunic taking care of his camp. If I had another day, it would be fascinating to hike up there and say hello, but he is probably enjoying the metaphysical advantages of his high altitude solitude. Langmusi sits at 3,272m and my Galaxy's GPS indicates this second meadow is already at 3,446m. The shepherd is about 200m above me. I suspect this herd is communal, belonging to the Kerti Gompa monastery monks, and they take turns tending to them. I sit there pondering this monk's isolated existence, while the Sun breaks through the clouds and onto my face.

What a joyous occasion, to be in this magnificent, tranquil gorge and only one monk within kilometers of me. I feel so privileged to be here. Back in Beijing, twenty million souls are suffering through stifling heat, humidity, snarled traffic jams and intermittent air pollution. I savor a cup of hot tea from my thermos and notice a group of 3mm long black ants on the ground between my legs. Each one has a tiny larva in its jaws, dancing in place, sunning them or airing them out, which I've never seen ants do before. Some ants raid other species' nests, capture their larvae and bring them home to raise as slaves. Maybe this is their victory dance. Then the most amazing thing happens: my Galaxy phone starts ringing. I kid you not. Here I am in the bottom of this incredibly deep gorge cum valley and my phone is getting a signal. From where I have *no* idea. The signal must be bouncing off the clouds. And to make it even more memorable, it's an international call from my wife Florence, who is vacationing in Normandy, France, with our younger daughter, Chara. We talk for about ten minutes. What a bizarre occurrence in the middle of Tibetan nowhere.

Time to move on, with only a few more hours of daylight left. By this time, I've given up trying to keep my sandaled feet dry. There are just too many places where the only way to navigate the Namo Creek is to walk in it. This gorge must be teeming with livestock, as there are yak and sheep footprints, with their manure everywhere, and tufts of black yak hair are caught in the branches of needled acacia bushes. I get further and further from civilization and decide to turn back to Langmusi when it hits 18:00. That gives me two hours until dusk, which should be plenty of time to return to Langmusi, since I took my time, shooting all my photos and exploring the flora on the way up. I see a narrow switchback in the creek's course a few hundred meters up and decide to go through it before turning around. At this point, Namo Creek is more like a brook and I would give anything to hike up to its source, but I have to start back. I check my GPS tracker and altitude. I have broken the 3.5km mark, hitting 3,510 MASL and have hiked 5.4km one way. As the Sun falls behind the western range of mountains, the temperature starts to drop precipitously, which at this altitude, is not surprising. For the first time on this trip, I get out and put on my Saudi *shamagh*, the big red and white cotton, hounds tooth square cloth that Arab men fashion into a headdress. It is incredibly handy in so many travel situations and now it is keeping my head comfy and warm.

In the hundreds of meters of jagged, vertical cliffsides, there are numerous caves. One is fairly big and quite accessible, but being solo, I stick to my route back home. While the flora in China is rich and varied, the lack of fauna and fowl is a sad reminder of the devastation wreaked upon wild animals and birds during those mad years of revolutionary excess from the 1950s-1970s. Compared to many hikes taken around the world, in such a rich valley, there would be tons of birds to observe, especially being the middle of the rainy season. But even crows are almost non-existent. I'm afraid they have been hunted for food in the worst of times and I would not be surprised if they still are. Without any legal controls, that is how we humans evolved as predators and it is just what we do. Ditto seeing any other animals. Insects, much less lizards, snakes, turtles, amphibians and small mammals should be abundant with all the water, trees, bushes and flowering plants. But there is nothing of the sort. Well, almost nothing. I keep seeing these big holes in the ground, which look like they have been dug by animals, but since I haven't spotted anything all day, I assume whatever they are, they must be nocturnal, or at least crepuscular. And then as I come back into the second meadow at the valley's fork, I suddenly see movement in my peripheral vision. Most marmots are on the small side, but this one is a beast. It's as big as a medium sized dog and looks like a huge land beaver, with its flat, twitching tail and very big, black eyes. Marmots are members of the squirrel family, but don't live in trees. He is wary of me and keeps about 20m between us. I take a step forward, he takes one back. I study it for quite some time with my binocs, before moving on.

I see a little hillock pointing towards the monk's tent off in the distance and decide to scale it for one last look. The hillock looks strange, being without any grass, as if it has been worn down by excessive all-terrain vehicle use. The hill is full of holes and it suddenly occurs to me that it is a *colony* of marmots. Just as I reach the top, what do I see but one of these mammoth marmots charging straight at me in a full run. I'm thinking, don't tell me, it's going to defend its territory. Yikes! It all happens so fast that I really don't have time to react, when just as it gets less than a couple of meters in front of me, it quickly veers right and plunges into one of the colony entrances. Whew. After that adrenalin rush, I get to the bottom of the hillock on the other side and see a yak's hoof, with about 20cm of its leg still attached. The protruding bone shank is broken or bitten off and not clean cut, which is ominous. It is still fresh enough to smell putrid and I'm asking myself, what killed this yak? Wolves, carnivorous marmots or what? It is getting close to dusk now and I'm wondering just how brave that monk is up there all by himself.

Before getting back to the first meadow, two young, funky dressed non-monks surprise me as they are heading upstream. I talk to Cidu, the elder of the two, a Tibetan shepherd who lives in a tent up in the stratospheric highlands above. He tells me they still have a three-hour climb and that he lives at close to 5,000 MASL, another one and half klicks towards the sky. Given the late hour, this is all the more impressive, since both of them are carrying a hefty haul of food supplies bought in town, both on their backs and in handheld bags. Nervous and fast talking, Cidu reminds me of the Mad Hatter in Alice in Wonderland, Tibetan style. I am pleasantly surprised when he invites me to join them and stay the night up at their camp. But when he sees my wet pants, drenched feet and sandals, and no coat, he recommends I come up tomorrow, otherwise I'll freeze to death. As rapidly as the temperature is dropping at this elevation with the setting Sun, I believe him. We exchange phone numbers and I'm all excited by the cultural opportunities. Wait until Rafal and Marta hear about this. On my way out of the gorge, another local man is sporting a big backpack full of supplies to take back to his tent home somewhere in the heights of the livestock covered mountains. I can't help but notice he is wearing a pair of knee high rubber boots to wade in the mystical Namo Creek waters. What a great idea.

"Hey sir, did you buy those boots in Langmusi?"

"Sure did."

"And how much would a pair of such fine, fair boots like that set me back?"

He never really stops walking the whole time; living at over 4,000m and dusk settling in fast, he's a man on a mission.

"Fifty yuan!" he cries out over his shoulder, as he disappears into the crepuscular grey of near darkness.

Little do I know now that this information will spell the difference between success and failure for tomorrow's White Dragon adventure. I get back right at darkness. A 12km hike with a 238m vertical ascent. That's like climbing up and down a 75-story skyscraper that's sitting 3km above sea level. Not a bad day's walk. No sooner do I get back to the hotel, all excited to tell Rafal and Marta about the invitation to spend the night with Cidu, that it starts to rain. It is a shower that feels like it is not just an early evening cloudburst, and so it goes, it keeps coming down. Communicating by text messages, Cidu is getting inviter's remorse. He texts me a photo of himself standing in a dashing, spread-armed pose, with a white shawl blowing in the wind over his shoulders like wings, as he grins broadly, with the famous Potala Temple in Lhasa in the background. Finally, Cidu gets cold feet and his invitation never pans out. Who knows, maybe his parents put the kibosh on his enthusiastic idea, or maybe he is loath to hike back down in the rain tomorrow. I can only speculate. But who would dream that I will be invited for lunch into the tent of some Tibetan nomads on the White Dragon River, as compensation?

Figure 17: Dunhuang's open air, covered market. Markets, be they Tesco, Costco or rural barter, are one of civilization's great cultural constants all over the world.

Figure 18: You are never far from someone wanting to prepare you hot, tasty snacks. A Dunhuang market Han lady offers all kinds of meat, veggie, mushroom and tofu shish kebabs, fried and served piping hot, with hot red pepper and mixed spices. Delicious and only ¥10!

Figure 19: This Buddhist cemetery outside Dunhuang is eerily spectacular, butted up against the massive sand dunes, fading into grey with the slowly fading sunset. Photo by Andy, the Lebanese Swiss.

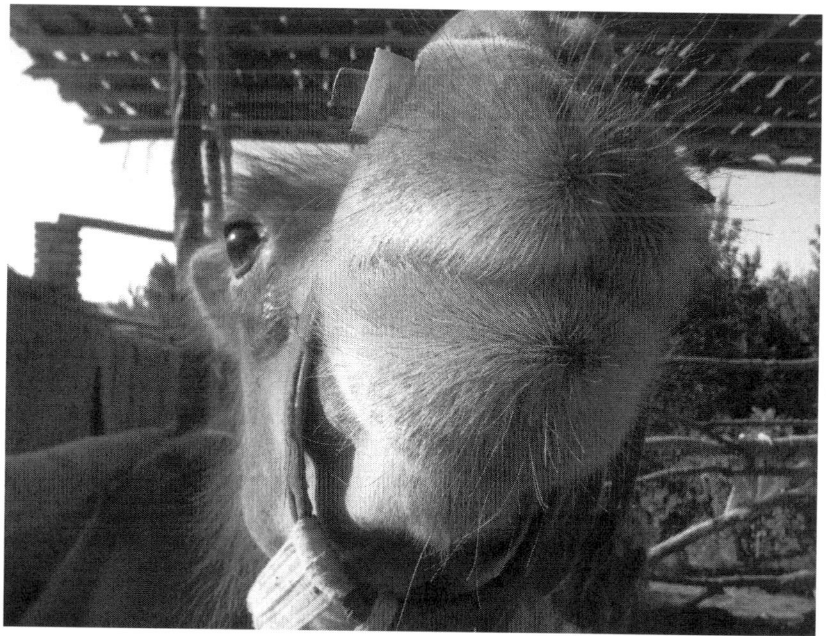

Figure 20: Hundreds of camels and their operators work at the Dunhuang Desert Park. The large, plastic-capped metal spike piercing the camel's nostrils is used to attach a bridle. Photo by Andy, the Lebanese Swiss.

Figure 21: Team Jeff's victory shot atop the massive sand dune we climbed to watch the sunset, overlooking the oasis town of Dunhuang. The Chinese love to flash the peace/victory symbol in photos. Photo by Zhu "Meng" Biying.

Figure 22: Jiayuguan Fort choreographed dance routine, with actors in plastic Ming Dynasty armor and the fort's high mud walls in the background. The audience applause is muted at best.

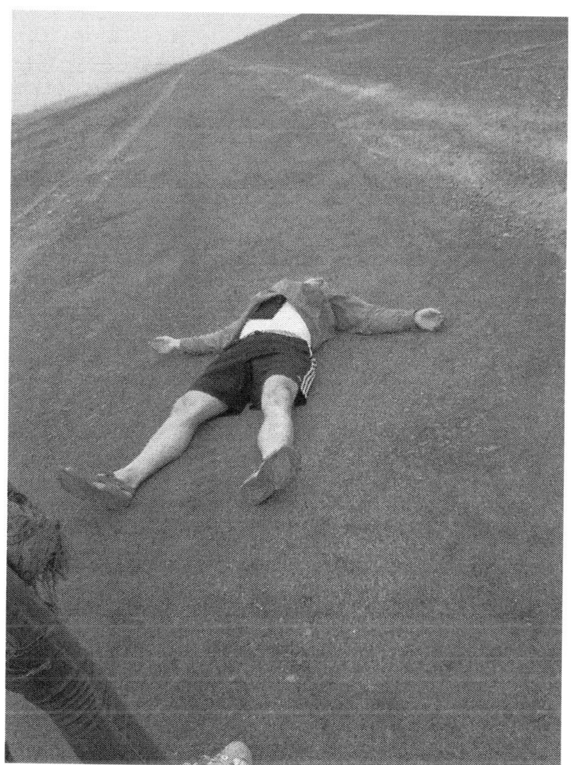

Figure 23: Dunhuang: while changing a flat tire on the way to Yadan National Park, I act like I am passed out in middle of the highway. My fellow teachers love it and go berserk!

Figure 24: Dunhuang Yadan National Park: the bottom of a prehistoric dried up lake, surreal and extraterrestrial. Two people on the far left give you some idea of its scale: it goes on for many kilometers. Photo by www.geolocations.ws

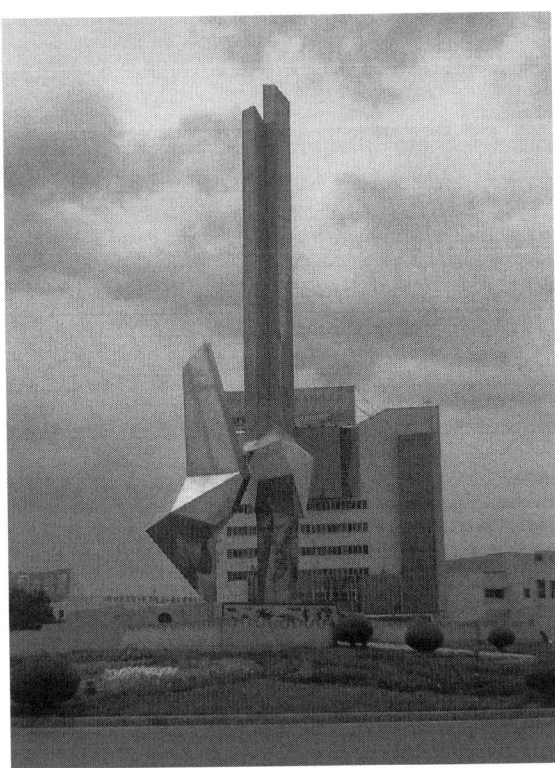

Figure 25: Millions of absurdly abstract, ideologically pure, post Cultural Revolution statues dot China's cities and towns. What is this 39 meter Jiayuguan monster telling us?

Figure 26: Dunhuang Yumenguan National Park: this 2 meter high, mud thatched wall was the height of defensive technology from marauding invaders using spears and arrows, 2,100 years ago during the Han Dynasty. The Great Wall's size increased dramatically over the centuries, as military technology advanced.

Figure 27: A traveling beekeeper with a truck full of hives, parked on a busy intersection in Jiayuguan to sell his wares.

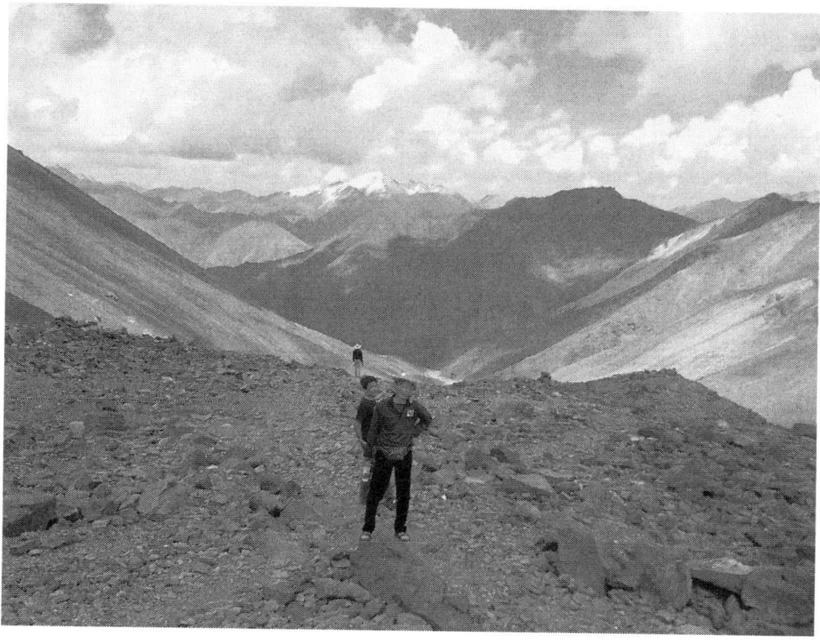

Figure 28: The challenging trail leading to the July 1st Glacier, with the Qilian Mountains behind. The Guangdong artist, Mr. Ye Zhihua is in the foreground.

Figure 29: Unfortunately, with global warming, the awe inspiring July 1st Glacier is receding rapidly back up the mountain.

Figure 30: Abandoned and derelict buildings at the Jingtieshan Iron Ore Mining Company, with an ideologically pure statue in an overgrown roadside park. Jingtieshan turns out to be a really bizarre time warp.

Figure 31: The train from Jiayuguan Luhua. Every rail car in China has a plaque telling you its route number, where it starts and its final destination. The Lv is not a misspelling, in Pinyin it is pronounced Lu.

Figure 32: Given the bad roads and horrible conditions, it is a testament to the steely skills of China's long-distance bus drivers that there are few accidents. This yellow junker takes me from Jingtieshan to Qiqing and back.

Figure 33: Qiqing: Old Tibetan Lao Pu, taking a breather outside her house before inviting me in for a cup of hot water and some fascinating conversation.

Figure 34: Overlooking the nearly abandoned mud village of Qiqing, with the ever impressive Qilian Mountains behind.

Figure 35: Qiqing: inside Lao Pu's humble Tibetan abode, with her elderly neighbor. I never get a clear answer as to why they are still living in the abandoned mud village below the new town.

Figure 36: Lanzhou and the mighty Yellow River from my gondola lift down from the Buddhist White Temple. The temple entrance and the 1909 Sun Yat-Sen Bridge, are mid view. In the foreground, the imprint of Islam on Western China is everywhere.

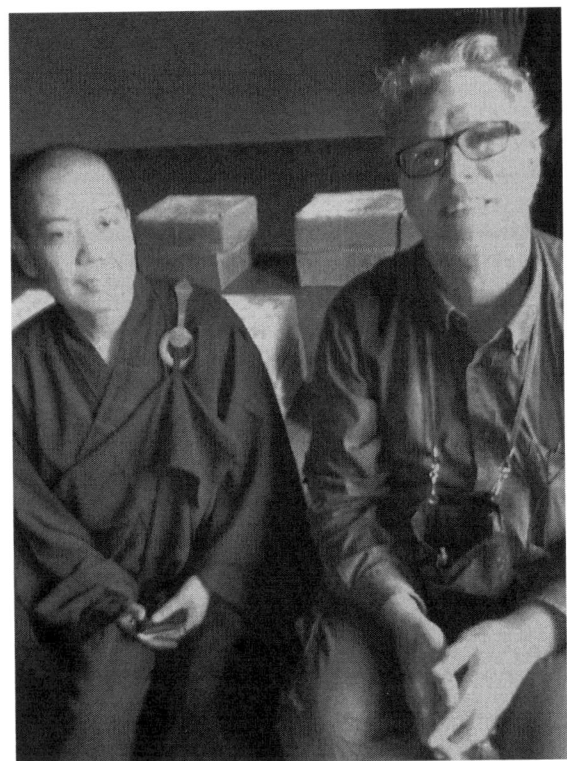

Figure 37: Inside Lanzhou's White Temple with a Buddhist nun. She is ecstatic to receive this photo on her mobile phone.

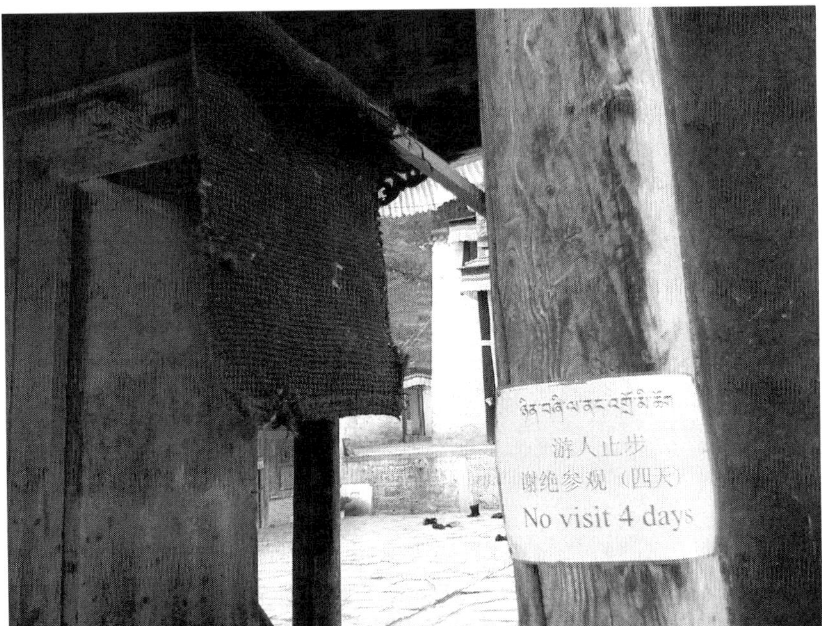

Figure 38: Xiahe Labrang Temples: a black flag ceremony in the big temple where a chorus of monks is singing for 96 straight hours.

Figure 39: Xiahe Labrang Temples: great view of the general layout and architecture of this most majestic of Tibetan Buddhist complexes.

Figure 40: Xiahe Labrang Temples: a solitary Tibetan monk meditating and making a walking circuit around one of the temples.

Figure 41: Xiahe Labrang Temples: magnificent silk portico with protective gods is to ward off women and foreigners, or so says the sign by the door.

Figure 42: Xiahe Labrang Temples: one of many beautiful cloth and silk façades that house the covered entryways and atriums.

Figure 43: Inside one of Labrang's majestic temples are large festival masks, worn over the heads of monks for dance and drama.

Figure 44: A couple of elderly Tibetan ladies chatting at the Labrang Temples in Xiahe.

Figure 45: Xiahe: Muslim cook preparing a bowl of freshly hand pulled, hot spicy beef noodles. It is hard to get tired of this dish!

Figure 46: Xiahe: three Tibetan women and a child relax and watch the world go by.

Figure 47: A Xiahe shoe cobbler, set up on the town's sidewalk. There are many different kinds of craftsmen who work in China's towns on public property.

Figure 48: Langmusi: outside the Serti Gompa Temple, Tibetan faithful are coming with armfuls of fresh cedar branches to burn in stupa-shaped ovens that dot the path. The smell of incense wafting through the air is intoxicating.

Figure 49: Langmusi, White Dragon River: Tibetan Hong Bei and his wife, outside their tent home.

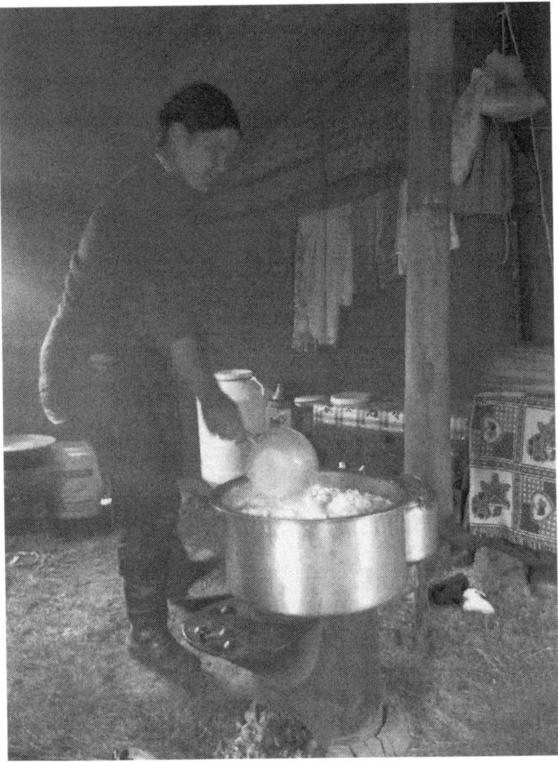

Figure 50: Langmusi, White Dragon River: Tibetan Hong Bei's wife cooking a huge casserole of clabbered milk on a potbellied stove, using yak dung for fuel.

Author note: Readers may notice that the hikes in Langmusi are not correct in their Gansu and Sichuan Parts. This is because on my first day in Langmusi, I arrive from Gansu, hike on the Sichuan side up the Great Namo Gorge, wake up the next morning, hike up to the source of the White Dragon River on the Gansu side, and then the following morning, officially leave Gansu and go south into Sichuan. As a result, Chapters 21 and 22 are not in their correct provincal book parts, nor are their corresponding photos.

Part V

Sichuan

Rules of the Road: Dissent

"I do this real moron thing, and it's called thinking. And apparently I'm not a very good American because I like to form my own opinions."
George Carlin

"I'd rather die for speaking out, than to live and be silent."
Fan Zhongyan (1036)

"Criticism of the state is all right, but don't forget the nation is you."
German proverb

Chapter 22: Langmusi – Next Day

Langmusi hits the jackpot again with another world class hike, deep into the Tibetan wilds and the source of the magical White Dragon River - oh yeah, I lose both big toenails in the process.

Yesterday's world class hike was in the spectacular Great Namo Gorge, resplendent with towering cliff buttes and livestock clinging to verdant pastoral slopes, which arch to the tops of spruce and pine covered mountains. These animals are shepherded by a vermillion tuniqued Tibetan monk, who can cast his gaze, overlooking meadow flowers in every direction and with colors to make a rainbow blush. Finally, this sublime, Renoir landscape painting is graced by a sacred, babbling mountain brook at 3.5km above sea level. So, who would think today's trek could rival it? *Nahhhh*, just can't happen, or so I thought... Upon awaking, Rafal, Marta and I discuss our options. All we can see out our hostel window is it is still raining more often than not. But the three of us are determined to get our hikes underway, regardless. The main street below looks like a prehistoric flood scene, as monks and civilians trudge and labor in the thick muck that is serving as Langmusi's thoroughfare. Time to get out see what we can do, so we say our goodbyes and take off in different directions on the main street. To test out my sandals, I decide to go check out some really intriguing revolutionary *dazibao* that are plastered on a big factory wall on the outskirts of town, and which caught my eye when our bus rolled into town yesterday. *Dazibao* (大字报= big word report) are the ubiquitous banners and sayings hanging and painted everywhere in China as public service announcements, and to exhort the masses to hew to whatever Baba Beijing is fretting over at the time.[1] On this factory wall, it says in eight huge white characters on a Tibetan vermillion colored background,

"Lacking oxygen does not mean lacking vitality – we are not afraid of hardship, we just bear our suffering."

Wow, what a great *dazibao*. Definitely not an admonition you would find in New York or Paris. It is easy to see that this particular call to arms is just one of several permutations over the years. Older, faded out and painted over characters can be seen on the same wall, like some sociopolitical palimpsest. This is often true about *dazibao* wherever traveling in China. New concerns, new campaigns, new *dazibao*. Testing out my footwear in these conditions is a smart idea. The factory is only a half a kilometer away. But the slog through the mostly ankle deep main street proves to be a veritable disaster. By the time I get back to the hostel, my sandals are each embalmed in about 1kg of muck wrapped around my feet. It takes me quite some time to extricate my earth-leaden sandals from my feet, pry and scrape off the epoxy-like mud from all of the above, and then laboriously soak and scrub my sandals to grant them their freedom. I don't know how they are going to dry out. The way it keeps raining, I will be leaving Langmusi tomorrow wearing cold damp footwear. More bad news about my saunter through the sludge: where the straps on my sandals lay across my skin, there are bloody scratches and abrasions. Not the best condition for my feet to start out today's trek.

Time to buy some sailor's rubber boots like I saw that two legged mountain goat of a Tibetan wearing last night. I run into Rafal and Marta coming down the street, of course, sporting brand new, knee high rubber boots, sloshing through the mountains of muck with impunity. I gawk at their miraculous purchase: I'll take a pair of those in any style or color, thank you. As they take off on the Great Namo Gorge trek that I took yesterday, they point me the right direction. I tippy toe, jump and pirouette as gracefully as I can from least muddy spot to least mucky hole in my soaking wet, clean sandals. The last thing I want to do is scrub and scrape them again. Once inside the general store, the next big hurdle is hoping I can find some rubber boots that will fit me. I slip on the pair of gym socks I packed for the trip and ask to try on the biggest pair they have, size 44. Amazingly, even with my canoe wide feet, I can *just* get them on. It is a snug fit and I count myself lucky. Time to attack the Langmusi hike on the Gansu side.

Not to be outdone by their contemporaries on the Sichuan side of the White Dragon River, the Gansu side of town also has a sister monastery, called the Serti Gompa. Smaller and 335 years younger than the built-in-1413 Kerti Gompa on the Sichuan side, it is sparkling white and covered in gold leaf that glistens against the gun metal gray, high altitude sky. Lots of Tibetan tourists are walking around with fronds of fresh, evergreen cedar branches, to burn as offerings in small, stupa shaped ovens that are typically found outside Tibetan temples. When they toss a bundle of cedar leaves in one, the whole area smells incredibly delicious. I go into the main Serti Gompa Temple. The morning sermon and catechism are in full swing. The temple could easily sit a thousand, but only about a hundred monks are being beseeched and berated to follow the spiritual path. Like in other temples, the head priest seems to amplify his physical presence with suitable body armor. Put them on a steed, hand them a slashing saber and they could pass for Samurai warriors. Or maybe a silver screen Obi Wan Kenobi? I am convinced that Buddhist head priests, who almost always sport polished, clean shaven heads, must use yak butter to bring their craniums to a golden sheen. Depending on your point of view, their glowing bald heads in the faint halo of the yak butter candles that barely illuminate Buddhist temples, give them either a saintly or demonic mien. This head priest is festooned with broad, golden yellow sashes and a front bodice that would make a Sioux chief grin with envy. Using the girth of his outsized and regally embroidered vermillion tunic to maximum effect, he waves his hands with authority at each turn of his erect body. He paces up and down the temple's central passageway, arms mostly held out to the sides of his body, as if making a pronouncement, or pleading in gentle supplication. Like all good preachers, this priest has a wonderful, lilting cadence to his delivery, in steady, hypnotic and metronomic stanzas. Changing from the pleadings of reason to the earnest exhortations of portending doom, there is only one path to righteousness, and the consequences of not doing so are dire indeed. Some of his younger flock seem unfazed by the mystical and metaphysical supplications of the moment, but he keeps his lambs on their toes by regularly asking them to respond to his calls with the appropriate chanted response. The assistant priest, seated lotus style on his red upholstered cubic dais, helps the chanters keep time by rhythmically clapping a hand sized cymbal. Some of the monks' voices are astonishing in their range and power, from bottom of the gut bass to sonorous tenor. Even though these chants come across as chaotic, it is much too hypnotic to be that haphazard. Most of the adherents are in rapt, respectful attention, but like in every congregation, there is a fair number who are acting out their eastern interpretation of Tom Sawyer and Huckleberry Finn. Seated together in clots of two to six, they continue their outdoor horse play, wrestling, jousting, locking arms, surreptitiously sending text messages, gabbing and joking *sotto voce*. They try to maximize their advantage by strategically sitting behind the many multicolored, drape covered support columns, or stationing themselves at oblique angles to the head priest's peripheral vision. Showing their practical knowledge of using angles and columns for maximum shenanigans, I'm sure they would all pass a planar geometry exam with flying colors.

Time to move on. I have to ask four or five different people before I am confident that I'm on the right path: to trek up in the mountains to the source of this very same said White Dragon River. Rafal and Marta were somewhat nonplussed about their trek here yesterday, so I have no idea what to expect. No one can tell me with any precision how far it is up there, nor how high is the source's elevation. I guess I will just have to find out for myself. As I am leaving town I walk past a couple of households that have slaughtered a yak this morning along the banks of the White Dragon River. They are well advanced in the process, with it already being skinned and two quarters sectioned off. It is really a bizarre contrast, seeing all this red and white spread out over the green summer grass. It stops raining and the first two klicks lull me into a sense of entitlement, as it is flat and paved with concrete. As the pavement peters out, there is a tent with a work site to repair the road, or possibly extend the pavement. A Tibetan man comes out and excitedly waves me to come his way. I'm all smiles with my new boots, as they sink into ankle deep ooze, while I make my way towards his tent. Bang Kao (帮考) could pass for a full blooded Native American or a Roma from the hinterlands of Southeastern Europe. He looks incredibly exotic. He is very excited to tell me about his buddy who has a restaurant about five kilometers up the road, called the Gongquhu (贡去乎). To be sure, I ask him to write it down in Chinese in my notebook, along with his name and his friend's name. Bang Kao is almost bursting with overjoyed excitement, saying to me,

"Just tell him I sent you and he'll set you right up."

Jeez Louise, this guy could be a successful nightclub punt in New York City. But, who knows? Having a name to drop never hurts and all I can do is hope that this restaurant up in the mountains is surely overlooking the little babbling brook that starts the White Dragon River on its great journey to the lowlands and beyond. My sense of languor is short lived, as after a couple more bends, the pitch of the road begins to track upwards and I am frequently slipping and sliding, as I try to get a grip in the slimy mud. For cheapo rubber boots, they actually have a pretty good traction, especially given the difficult conditions. I round another bend and I cannot believe my eyes. Awesome, a flock of about a dozen vultures is having a carrion banquet about 50 meters ahead. For many Tibetans, these huge winged beasts are the conveyors of souls to the afterlife. Priests will take the cadaver of the faithful to designated funeral areas in the mountains, dismember the corpse, crack open the skull and expose all the intestines. The body is then left for these birds to eat the brain, organs and entrails, and then over the ensuing days, pick the skeleton clean, only to leave the bones laying there to return to the Earth in the decades to come. While most non Tibetans are viscerally ill at ease vis-à-vis this burial method, no one can argue about its sublime symbolism: a faithful loved one's bodily remains are transported thousands of meters above, toward the diaphanous, azure heavens, where they are scattered over the peaks and valleys of sky-scraping Greater Tibet, the Land of Snow, the Top of the World. The soul moves onto a new life, a new creation is born on the face of the Earth, while the body returns back to the planet's dust. The cycle of life is completed one more time, with a new day, a new beginning. My Rolls Royce of binoculars are paying off like a rigged slot machine. I spend some time observing them and slowly creeping step by step, get a little closer. The vultures are encircling their fetid feast, busily at work. Having gotten their momentary fill, two or three of them individually take flight, only to land a hundred or so meters away across the road, overlooking the stink fest. They sit alone to digest their meal and keep a leery eye on my presence. The remaining gourmands are savagely tearing at whatever carcass constitutes their pleasure. Like the needles of a high speed industrial sewing machine, their bald, corrugated heads bob up and down, as their powerful beaks try to pick and pull whatever bodily remains lay at their clawed feet. It is time to break up this merry band of soul transporters, as their feast is between me and the headwaters of the White Dragon River. I slowly walk towards the glutting flock and they fly off one by one, until the last two or three reluctantly depart in unison. They act very put out by the interruption. I try to take pictures of them as they make their getaway; their wingspan is all of two meters, maybe more. I walk down to their harvest table to see what is whetting their appetite and the strong stench of dead fish slaps me in the face. I see the blackened remains of a sheep, with really only the skeleton and skin remaining. It sure looks like thin pickings for all the frenetic activity they were devoting just now. With this meager offering, I'd say these hungry birds could use a soul transporting Tibetan funeral about right now. I think back at what might be the leftover remains of the slaughtered yak in Langmusi as an alternative. But that Tibetan family will efficiently use everything in that animal's body down to the muzzle.

The climb up into the mountains is incessant. The nearly 100% humidity in the air is robbing it of its already attenuated oxygen levels and I really have to concentrate on deep breathing to keep from getting gassed. I have no idea how far or how high I have to hike today, so I need to be careful. Huge chunks of topsoil, some the size of boulders, dot the rocky shoals along the White Dragon, broken off from the banks higher up from all the rain we've had. These stranded green and black islands of valuable farmland will continue their journey downstream, slowly broken down to dust with each succeeding cloudburst. The soil here in the valley is ebony dark and must be very rich. I can see a building off in the distance and assume it must be Bang Kao's famous mountain restaurant. Alright, a warm meal, maybe some tasty Tibetan barbecue, a roof over my head and some hot tea to warm my tired, oxygen starved muscles and brain. But Bang Kao's restaurant is a mountain mirage. This once glorious farmhouse is completely dilapidated and falling apart. It hasn't been occupied for years. When was the last time Bang Kao ventured up here?

I see a Tibetan shepherd working around his tent and having nothing to lose at this point, show him the names Bang Kao wrote in my notebook and ask him what he thinks. He does not recognize any of the names, but tells me if I'm hungry, I am welcome to eat in his tent. Just to make sure there are no hard feelings, I ask him how much it will cost. He tells me I can pay whatever I like. I try to get him to give me a price, but I get the same reply. Well, OK... The tent is about five meters square and tall enough to stand in along the central ridge. This Tibetan shepherd's name is Hong Bei (红北= Red North) and his wife is busy doing her housekeeping, or tent keeping, as it were. She has a big, transparent glass mug of tea on the floor and it is full of berries, flowers and herbs. She also has a clear jar, with large rock sugar crystals in it. Before I leave, she will have emptied it out, chewing and sucking on the entire contents. Are Tibetans diabetes resistant, or what? The tent is neat and orderly, like any house would be, and like an efficiency apartment, it's all kind of together in one room. Hong Bei and I sit on their ground level mattress/bed. Patriarchal roles are clearly set out: the woman of the house does all the work here and the men watch. Across from our bed cum sofa is the tender box full of dried out yak manure, which she continually adds to the low, flat, potbellied stove in the center of the tent. A flue pipe carries the smoke outside through the top of the tent. Given the number of times she replenishes the stove, manure has a very low caloric content compared to even a soft wood like pine. Now I can see why Tibetans have to make large mounds of the stuff as fire fuel to make it through the winter. The other half of the tent is given over to food storage and preparation. Hong Bei's wife can only speak Tibetan, but he speaks good Mandarin. He asks if I like *mian* (面) and taking this as noodles, or possibly bread; it sounds good to me. My food order makes it the three meters across the tent and the missus sets to work. She pulls out a handleless teacup and fills it about half full of yak butter, which she stores in a larder. Using her index finger and keeping it shaped like a fish hook, she pumps her digit up and down rapidly until the contents are nice and soft. She even stops long enough to show me the contents. I smile encouragingly, having no idea what finished product I will be served. In the meantime, Hong Bei and I chat. He is 39 years old and they have two children who are going to a trade school college in Hezuo, Gansu, halfway from here to Xiahe. Their children are 20 and 21 years of age, so Hong Bei and his wife were probably no older than 17 or 18 when they got married. Like most of the many nomad tents I see on the Tibetan Plateau, they have a small cylinder motorcycle to get into town and to even use to herd their animals across the mountainsides, as a mechanized substitute for a horse. They also have a half meter square solar panel to charge a tractor battery for a light bulb at night and to play a radio for news and entertainment, but no TV. They have a tent neighbor right next door, with a woman busily buzzing around it. She has the identical setup: tent, motorbike and solar panel. Hong Bei tells me he and his wife have forty head of yak up on the slopes. Since the husband next door is absent, I suspect they combine forces and graze and paddock their herds together. Given their tents' proximity, they are probably related. I have a lot of questions I'd like to ask, but don't know how far to push it, and I sure don't want to offend them. I am gracious for their hospitality. Remembering the bloody shank of yak hoof I found yesterday in the Great Namo Gorge, I ask a tantalizing question,

"Are there wolves out there?"

"Oh, yes, for sure."

I'm skeptical, given that everywhere I go, the fauna and fowl are pretty much expunged from the face of Chinese soil. Maybe he is talking about feral dogs, which are a serious problem wherever livestock are grazed. However, I later learn there is in fact a Tibetan wolf, which looks like the gray European wolf, but has shorter legs. This may explain the chewed off yak shank I found, after all. Anyway, he confirms they bring their herd into a paddock every night, for safe keeping. The missus (I decide to err on the side of propriety and not ask her name) now pours what looks like a real dark flour into the softened yak butter. Hong Bei confirms that it is from *qingke*, or Alpine barley, which is the national grain of Tibet, given that no other common cereal will grow at this altitude (corn, sorghum, wheat or rice). With the dark barley flour now added to the softened yak butter, she continues to gouge her index finger in the tea cup like a dough hook on a bread machine. After these two ingredients are mixed together, she next adds an equal quantity of granulated sugar and keeps furiously manipulating the concoction with her jabbing finger. A few more minutes of this kneading and voilà, it's ready. The mixture looks like dark, caramel colored pizza dough, but thicker and heavier. She ceremoniously hands me my bowl of *mian*, while Hong Bei pours me a tall glass of boiling water. He tells me this dish is called *suiyou chamian.*[2] *You* (油) means fat or oil and *mian* means all things grain and noodles, so good enough for me. As I dig out a small dob of the stuff and pop it into my mouth. I can see why Hong Bei's counsel to eat this Tibetan bread with hot water is such good advice: without it, it's almost impossible to eat. It is so rich, so heavy and so dense that the hot water helps liquefy it just enough to get it down my gullet. Otherwise, the blob would probably just lodge in my throat. My gosh, is it filling. After only finishing half of it, I feel like I just had third helpings at a Thanksgiving dinner. Amazing stuff. And all it is, is about one-third each yak butter, barley flour and sugar. Meanwhile, the missus has been getting out some yak yoghurt and again, she adds a healthy dose of sugar. It only amounts to about a half a cup, but I feel so distended that I can only finish about half of it too. And for dessert? *Voilà Monsieur*, half of a fresh apple. I ask if I can take pictures and Hong Bei generously accepts. I ask if his wife can take our picture together and she happily agrees. And then most surprisingly, Hong Bei suggests that he take a picture with his wife and me. They switch places and she sits near me and we get a good photo. The pictures are very nice and I suggest sending him copies when I return to Beijing. I ask him to write his address in my notebook and he does one better. He goes to a drawer by the bed and pulls out a thick envelope that was mailed to him. He is expecting me to copy it down. I can read Chinese quite adequately and easily write it on a computer or cell phone by transcribing pinyin to Chinese, but handwriting it? I labor and gnash my teeth doing it. I then get the great idea to just take a picture of the envelope. Presto. Before leaving, the missus puts a huge, institutional sized cooking pot on top of the potbellied stove, into which she ladles clabbered yak milk from a large, 25 liter plastic jerry can. She fills it right to the brim and stokes the fire with a few more chunks of yak manure. I can guess she is going to boil down this lumpy dairy stew to make some kind of cheese, or maybe the yoghurt I just ate.

It is time to relaunch my hike to the magical source of the White Dragon River. I give Hong Bei ten yuan for my meal with reassurances that I will send the photos next month (I do, but they get returned). They both seem very pleased with my visit and I am too. This lunch, meeting and talking to Hong Bei and watching his wife's life in the tent is a rewarding experience in itself and is giving me a rare opportunity to get a taste of nomadic Tibetan culture and ways. Hong Bei points up at the rapid incline, as the mudslide for a road quickly disappears over the rise. He tells me it is only two klicks to the source and an easy climb up. Well, that shouldn't be too hard, should it? Wrong on all counts. But I am blissfully ignorant of all that for now. Across the road is a nice modern tent with about ten Chinese tourists in a circle eating lunch, and I'm sure it's different to what I just ate. They were brought up in a small bus and are going to ride horses up to the river source. Chinese City Slickers. I wonder which ones are playing the parts of Billy Crystal and Jack Palance?

Up to now, the rain has been intermittent and drizzly, but now it is starting to come down pretty fiercely. At the same time, the pitch of the road is becoming really precipitous and all the slipping and sliding is making my ascent that much more inefficient and laborious. From here on out, I am having to stop every so often and take hyper-breaths to keep my brain and muscles oxygenated. My rubber boots are also starting to show their newness. My feet are chafing at their barely adequate size and my big toenails are really painful as they push and slam against the inside of the shoes. After twenty more minutes up the steep slope, I have to put on my rain poncho. I am already pretty wet and have been avoiding putting it on, since I know I will sweat like a galley slave under it, with all the calories I'm burning every step of the way. I am so gassed that when I re-depart, I get about a kilometer further up the mountain, when I suddenly realize I left my Zeiss binoculars back on the rock where I put on my poncho. Holy mackerel. How negligent can I get? Bought in 1988, been to tens of countries, seen countless galaxies, globular and open clusters, nebulae and planets; fish, fowl, fauna, flora and fungi of every hue and shape; peoples, cultures, the surface of the Earth in all its magnificence, a $4,000 replacement cost for the Made in (West) Germany version; those binoculars that I swore the only way I could justify buying them ($1,000 in 1988) was to never lose them - and I just left them on a roadside rock in the rain for any passerby to help themselves to? *Jeez Louise*! Adrenaline shoots through my veins like a turbocharged drug. I try to run, but the road is as slippery as a trough full of entrails and after 300m, I can only walk as fast as my pituitary gland's hormones will push my brain and body. Also the pounding of my big toenails is really starting to come to full force, and I realize it is ten times worse going downhill. I have got to get there before the Chinese Billy Crystal and Jack Palance beat me to them. Gosh, I feel like such a fool. But that's what happens at high altitude and getting gassed: hypoxia is like being drunk or stoned and you don't even realize it is happening. What an incredible blessing, all the rain has made this road virtually unusable. A different day, and no telling how many minibuses full of tourists would have driven by that binocular-laden rock by now. Bend after bend and the rain is making the whole ordeal more and more ominous. I am trying to remember landmarks, but my adrenaline stressed, oxygen starved brain is blowing fuses left and right. Finally, finally, a couple of hundred meters up ahead, I can see an unnatural black shape on top of a big sandstone rock. Hallelujah. Made it. Saved. Almost a fool no more. Whew. Now, let's get to the top of that sacred mountain and the White Dragon source. The ascent is relentless and I just added two kilometers to my itinerary, to boot. Bravo, Jeff, way to go…

There are nomads' tents and large herds of yak, sheep and goats, with some cattle and horses, dotting the mountainside across the expansive river valley. Many hundreds of animals are seen along the way. I have only spotted one sheep dog, it was far away from the flocks and I wonder how they protect their animals at night, from feral dogs, wolves, or whatever. Like Hong Bei, I can only assume they bring them in every night to be penned up, but no fence is going to stop canines, so what do they do, take turns keeping all night vigils? As I am climbing, I get a great view of a camp slightly below my level across the valley and see people outside. Way too far for the naked eye, I take back out my Zeiss, giving them a ceremonial kiss and caress for my carelessness. There are plumes of smoke billowing out of two of the five big tents, so I can just picture Hong Bei's tent interior to know what's inside. A couple of smaller tents serve some other purpose. Two women are simultaneously milking yaks, with their seated, hunched backs turned toward me. Both are donning huge pink head dresses, piled up high. One is wearing a full length grey tunic and the other one's is brown. Like everywhere in the world, laundry is hanging out – here on the tent wires. With this weather, it is going to take a while for it to all dry. A too-curious ewe wanders close to the camp and Mrs. Grey Milkmaid wearily unfolds her doubled over body, leaving her stool next to her cud chewing yak. She picks up a stone, lumbers towards the anxious ewe and heaves the rock towards the miscreant. She then waves her arms over her head as if saying,

"*Get on back out there, eat mountain grass, fatten up for the winter and get ready for the breeding season like you are supposed to.*"

The ewe nobly complies. Mrs. Grey Milkmaid goes back, folds herself up under her milk laden yak and gets back to pulling and squirting. Another kilometer up the demonic, greasy-slick ascent and I see a shepherd riding by on his horse. It is incredible how much Tibetans look like Native Americans, and I ponder what is called the *Tibet-Pueblo Connection* – the idea that ancient Tibetans made the great migration of humanity across the Bering Straits over the last several tens of thousands years.[3] Other than the surroundings, I could be in Comanche Country right now. The Tibetan is riding at a trot, rocking forward and back in his saddle, oblivious to the precipitation. Bare chested in all his magnificence, he is singing a chant to the heavens and it just augments his Indian allure. We wave and smile at each other, the briefest of connections between the past and the present. How much longer can Tibetan nomads sustain this way of life into the future, as China continues to inexorably advance into the 21st century?

A further 1km of slipping and sliding two steps forward and one back and still no sign of any river source, which shoots down Hong Bei's sunny estimation. Little do I know that I haven't even arrived at the really challenging part of the day's trek yet. My real adventure has not even begun. Out of the mist a man with a heavy grain sack over his shoulders signals to me. His long, shaggy hair sprouting from under his hat and his sparse, very long, stringy salt and pepper beard remind me of the woodcut old men on the front of Jethro Tull's *Stand Up* album. He looks almost elfin. Without saying a word, he motions towards my back and volunteers to pull my rain poncho over my backpack, which I cannot do by myself. We smile from ear to ear at each other, I thank my Tibetan gnome warmly and extend my hand, which he shakes brotherly by our thumbs (I have noticed when I do shake hands around here, they like to do so in hooked thumb fashion). We hardly say a word to each other, but it is a very touching moment, the two of us out here in the harsh, rainy conditions of the White Dragon Mountains, him proffering his help and us recognizing each other.

The road, as it were, finally ends and I begin to walk along and back and forth across the river, making my way ever upward. The cloud line is not far above my head and with the increasing altitude, the temperature is starting to drop rapidly. There is another klick of this slow going river walk, but at least it is mostly rocks and rushing water, and not like the wall of mud below. There are some really treacherous stretches, where the narrow trail is cut into the mountainside and many meters above the river bed. With the rain, it is as scary as all get out, because one slip and it would be the hospital or the morgue. I cling like crazy to the bushes and grass on the mountain face, sometimes inching forward one small step at a time, to make sure I don't go tumbling down below on my left. The White Dragon River begins to dig into the soil now. It is no longer on a rocky bed, but carving a huge, deep gash in the fertile, black dirt. I look up to the horizon and about 2km away, I can see what looks like a mountain pass. Dime to a dollar that's where the river source is. But at this point, 2,000 meters might as well be twenty thousand. I am now pushing myself on raw willpower and whatever adrenaline my body can muster. I am cold, drenched wet with sweat and fatigued down to my bone marrow. Not a good combination.

I am now walking up a huge expanse of mountain meadow. But in several areas it is just as dangerous as the riverbed portion I just survived, if not even more treacherous. There are tens of narrow, slick cattle trails all pointing to the pass above, but sections are quite steep, pitched towards the river gash to the left. Trip and fall here and it is going to be a long, neck breaking tumble down the steep incline, before crashing into what is now a very deep scar of a ravine for a river. The rain is making this hike a frighteningly memorable one. I am dripping wet from all the sweat and it is only because of my rain poncho that I'm not freezing to death. It's getting so cold and I'm getting shiverish from my soaking wet shirt, that I wrap my Saudi shamagh around my head, Palestinian fashion, leaving only my eyes exposed. The cloud line is breaking over the pass and is now just above my head. A handful of Tibetan nomad tents are set up right below the pass. I am walking through a herd of yaks peacefully grazing on the lush, rain soaked wild pasture. They reluctantly disburse if I get too close to them. I look back and see the City Slickers on their horses, gaining on me coming up the trail, which just motivates and pushes me forward in exhaustion: they will *not* beat me to the source. About 500m from the top, the river ravine starts to branch out into a whole series of smaller and smaller gullies. I have to move left and right to weave through them to keep pushing upwards. The pasture surface is as soft and soggy as a bog. I am so utterly spent, so cold, so wet, in so much in pain with my big toes, which by now are throbbing miserably, that several times I come to one of the lower gullies and say to my oxygen starved, semi-hallucinating self,

"Well, aren't all these gullies the source of the White Dragon River? Don't they all slowly fill up with seeping water to create the cascading torrent just a kilometer down the mountain?"

But I can see it. I can see the gully above all the other gullies just as the mountain pass disappears into the mist of clouds. Self-pride gets the best of me. I have come too far to cut corners now. *I will not be denied.* Finally, *finally*, I make it to the top. The source of the magical White Dragon River is a flat, muddy patch about five meters square. About ten meters above the source is a thermal spring creating a small pond, whose waters are giving off profuse amounts of steam, even in the now howling, mountain pass winds. Just beyond it, on the other side of the pass, another huge valley drops off rapidly with a flank of mountain tops disappearing into the cloud mist. I can only imagine what it looks like up here on a clear, azure day. With the Tibetan tents dotting one side, yak herds scattered on the other, the river valley cascading to the horizon below me and the rapidly coursing underside of clouds rushing just above my head, the scene is unforgettable. I think about where I started out and what I am accomplishing. I get a big smile on my face when the City Slickers finally pass me after I have started my descent back. They look at me like I'm crazy. Today, maybe they are right. But I did it. I scaled the source of the White Dragon River on foot, in the most challenging, slippery, rain soaked conditions. I check my altitude before leaving, 3,815 MASL which is 543 meters above Langmusi. I climbed over a 0.5km of vertical ascent. That's about 155 stories or 1.5 Empire State Buildings, at close to four kilometers above Beijing. I also set my tracker and clock 11km to get back. So, the round trip to the source is 22km. I have to add two more for my misplaced Zeiss, so my trek today is a robust 24km. The verdant, emerald vistas all the way up and down, with the narrow White Dragon River rushing at the bottom of its steep valley, which is dotted with Tibetan tent homes, sheep and yaks, and beyond all this, cascading mountain ranges fading into the horizon, are vivid images that will forever be branded into my memory.

Outside Langmusi, I see a huge flock of big, tall, Dorset looking sheep covering the far mountainside. On the near side of the road, I can see about fifteen ewes that are separated from the flock. They are up on a very steep ridge, when suddenly, I see a shepherd pop out of some bushes and scale this incredibly pitched bank like a mountain goat, *deus ex machina*. Anybody else would be on all fours, hanging on for dear life trying to get to the top. It has been raining all day and that grass covered near-cliff must be as slippery as duck innards. I just have to stop to watch this amazing performance in athletic skill. The shepherd has a walking stick for support, but their hands never touch the ground and this gravity-defying acrobat stays upright the whole time. The shepherd gets above the lost group and drives them down the embankment, and seems to have an easier time getting down to the road that the errant sheep. Just incredible. Now I understand why I see so few sheep dogs. Tibetans do it one better. I start walking towards Langmusi again and this Spiderman shepherd comes walking up fast behind me. My shock of shocks is when I see this person is a diminutive young woman. Like me with my *shamagh*, her face is completely covered up with a long scarf (black and white stripes to my red and white checks), but she is much better prepared for the weather. She has a full body rain suit that sports a hood with a stiff bill over the eyes, to keep the water from running in her face. She obviously came to talk, but being Tibetan, I'm not sure if we can communicate. I say hello in Mandarin and she responds back with no problem. Being younger means she has learned Chinese at school. She tells me she is the shepherdess for this flock of over two hundred magnificent sheep. I can see her tents off on the other side of river, up the mountainside. She is probably just old enough to be married, but not yet with children. I congratulate her on her climbing and shepherding skills and with her nearly covered face, I only have her soft voice and chocolate black, Tibetan eyes to go on, to sense that she seems genuinely flattered. We talk for another couple of minutes, I wish her luck and move on. As I pass by Hong Bei's place, I can see a good sized herd of yak being brought into the paddocks for the night. The total number of head is about 150, so his next-door neighbor's herd must be quite big, unless they are tending a communal group of animals, which is quite possible. When I get back to the hotel and pull off my day saving rubber boots, I can see I sacrificed my big toe nails for the bragging rights. They are both as loose as a goose and suppurating blood serum. Yikes. I put tincture of iodine on them and they turn ochre dark, as the black fluid saturates all the freshly damaged tissue underneath the nails, burning like flaming irons in the fire. Looks like I get a special souvenir for my trek after all.

1- *One of the most frequented blogs I have ever written, with thousands of page views, it can now be found on www.44days.net:* 21st Century Dazibao. *It has even been incorporated into school curricula for middle and high schools back in the US.*

2- *I was not about to ruin the atmosphere in Hong Bei's tent home by asking a* Tibetan *to give me a quick lesson in Chinese characters. But best as I can tell, this is (穗油茶面), which means* grain-spike oil tea flour. *It is possible that the brown powder she started with was a mixture of Alpine barley flour and ground tea leaves, and could help explain why it was so expansive in the stomach.*

3- *tibettalk.wordpress.com/2007/11/01/linkssimilarities-between-tibetan-and-native-american-groups/.*

Chapter 23: Langmusi - Songpan

The saintly bus ride from Langmusi to Songpan - a great town to crash in after yesterday's 24km climbing feat. Also, up close and personal with Tibetan rosary beads, a trendy new development in Sichuan tourism, a primer on Tibetan/Han relations and thoughts on Chinese cooking mojo.

There is only one morning bus from Langmusi, south to Songpan (松潘) and my two Polish friends, Rafal and Marta and I continue to travel there together. After 17 days journeying across northern and western China, I finally descend into the belly of the beast, the great and mighty province of Sichuan, famous for its spicy foods, pandas, thick Chinese accents and its favorite son: the physically diminutive, political powerhouse who changed the course of human history, Deng Xiaoping.

You can pretty much cut modern-drawn Sichuan in half, from north to south and make two very different provinces in the process. The western half is in the ancient kingdom of Tibet and is part and parcel of the 3,000m plateau that is Tibet itself. Mountains reach over 6,000m and you might as well be in Tibet as far as the local culture, architecture and language are concerned, because well, you are. Baba Beijing drew these 20th century Sichuanese boundaries after invading and taking over Tibet in 1950, just one year after the Republic's independence. And in 1997, they changed them yet again. Historical Tibet used to be comprised of three regions, Amdo is essentially all of the modern province of Qinghai to the north, and the southern side of the Qilian mountains in Gansu, where I visited the July 1st Glacier, Jingtieshan (where I went back to 1954 with mining company, Communist zombies) and the Tibetan village of Qiqing (visiting Old Lao Pu's home). The second region is U-Tsang, which is where the western two thirds of modern Tibet is situated. The third region is Kham, which is the eastern third of modern Tibet, plus the western half of Sichuan. The Tibetan plateaued western half of Sichuan couldn't be more different than the eastern half, which is iconic and classic China: the Han majority and their Chinese style of Buddhism. The valleys of Eastern Sichuan are only about 500m above sea level, so the descent off the three-kilometer Tibetan Plateau is precipitous indeed, and only a few hours away by bus. Lowland eastern Sichuan is archetypically subtropical China: humid, sweaty, smoggy, teeming with humanity, multicolored flora and blanketed with rice, corn and tobacco production, alongside post-WWII-technology factories gracing the skyline with rainbow colored plumes of noxious smoke and fumes.

In the 90s, I visited postcard perfect Emeishan and Leshan outside Chengdu, Sichuan's provincial capital. The mountain peak of Emeishan erupts out of the lush lowlands, reaches the same height as the Tibetan Plateau and is one of China's four sacred Buddhist peaks. Leshan, in a valley below, touts its 71m tall, Tang Dynasty Buddha. Carved during the 9th century into a cliff face, it is the largest image of Buddha in the world, as it towers over the confluence of three rivers: the Min, Dadu and Qingyi, whose Tibetan headwaters I explore further on in Sichuan. This 1990s journey gave me a taste of Han Sichuan. Thus, I planned *44 Days* to stay in the western Tibetan zone as much as possible.

Sichuan got a political *provincectomy* in 1997, which must have taken some amazing negotiating to bring to fruition. Chongqing (重庆) is the famous *Chung King* and is emblematic as the soul of Han Sichuan. Chongqing is a colossus of a city, sitting astride the Yangtze River, where it is fed by one of its great tributaries, the Jialing River. It is one of the world's great megalopolises, with over 32 million inhabitants. This is seven million more souls than the entire state of *Texas*. With Chongqing's daily floating population of millions of migrant workers on top of these seven million more than Texas - go on, throw in New York City to the comparative total as well. Chongqing, this standard bearer of all things Sichuanese, was hived off of the provincial map in 1997 and made into its own *city-province*, like Shanghai and Tianjin. Given that

Sichuan still has almost 90 million citizens, even without Chongqing, I guess the now truncated province could afford to be magnanimous.

And as it seems like everywhere in China, in this age of Chinese Twitter (微博= *Weibo*), Google (百度= *Baidu*), emails (邮件= *youjian*, or QQ) and text messaging (短信= *duanxin*), a juicy political scandal is always just around the corner for all to gape at, like a sordid, Chinese soap opera. In March 2012, the former provincial leader of Chongqing, Bo Xilai (薄熙来), who was poised to ascend to the highest ranks of China's Communist Party leadership, was suddenly and ingloriously deposed and has disappeared from public view. *Uber*-charismatic and a rousing firebrand for the little people, he has been piled high with criminal charges and a much mediatized show trial. Bo is an oriental doppelganger of Louisiana's depression-era governor, Huey "Kingfish" Long. But poor Kingfish was unlucky enough to be a rabblerousing populist in trigger happy America and got his guts shot out on the Bayou State's capitol steps. Even more salacious, Bo's wife, Gu Kailai (谷开来) was convicted in August, 2012 for murdering (by poison in November, 2011) a high flying British businessman and purported MI6 stringer, Neil Heywood. Heywood proved the validity of the Peter Principle perfectly, overreaching the limits of his natural talents, and Gu got a suspended death sentence. But the woman who showed up at her televised sentencing looked like a last-minute, desperately chosen double who was hustled off the sidewalk outside the courthouse.[1] That got the hundreds of millions of Weibo and QQ accounts in China erupting like a volcano for days on end. Gu (or at least one of her doubles - there were apparently at least two) was prominently splashed all over the tightly controlled and carefully orchestrated Chinese media, during her equally controlled and orchestrated show trial. Since the trial, Gu and Bo have been disappeared by Baba Beijing. Man-of-the-people Bo and his conniving sidekick wife will probably serve Kabuki prison sentences, and still be as rich as Midas when they walk free. Such are the never boring shenanigans that are epidemic among China's business elite and political princes of power. Meanwhile, Baba Beijing finds it more and more difficult to play whack-a-mole, trying to control the message and suppress embarrassing information in the face of a billion people tirelessly working their fingers on their mobile phones and keyboards.

But, other than being in Sichuan, I digress. I am traveling from Langmusi to Songpan, almost due south. No comfy, interurban, air-conditioned, seat-belted bus this one. No, we are going down market in the transportation department today to a smaller, mid-sized junk heap, packed to the gills with standing room only passengers and piled high with those huge, multicolored, striped nylon suitcases that you see all over the developing world. This is one of those days where a seat, any seat, is a blessing. Rafal, Marta and I get to the bus early in Langmusi and so we are blessed indeed. During today's jaunt, we only descend 500m from Langmusi to plateau-hugging Songpan, which sits at 2,800m, so we are just hanging onto the side of the Tibetan highlands. Of course at this altitude, you can just imagine the staggering beauty of the surroundings, as we drive for hours along the periphery of one of the world's highest table tops: Tibet, the Roof of the World, the Land of Snow.

Along the way, an antique, wrinkle-faced, tattooed Tibetan woman, in her full crimson colored regalia and rainbow colored bodice is standing sandwiched right up to me by my aisle seat. She is trying her best to keep her grand- or great granddaughter from getting whipsawed by the floating sea of upright bodies and moving baggage that are being rocked and rolled, as we swerve, dodge and snake our way along this mostly bad and bouncy, yet boundlessly beautiful plateau road. This grandma is finding spiritual solace in her chain of 108 Tibetan prayer beads, or rosary, which in Tibetan is called a *mala*. The quirky number of 108 is traditionally explained with two reasons. First, each bead represents one of the 108 human passions. Secondly, the extra eight are to make up for absentmindedness and miscounting. This surplus therefore assures that a full 100 mantras are said each go-around. Grandma is clutching the *mala* in her left hand and moving the beads with her thumb, while harboring her petite scion as best as she can in her right arm. She is not very tall and I can just overhear a breathless, audible hum. It's her mumbling *sotto voce* Buddhists mantras, as she works her way through her *mala*. My face is just centimeters from her beads and their seamless clacking, as her withered, agile and bony hand rests atop her sagging chest. I'm so close I might as well be a macro lens. There are brightly colored intermediate beads and what look like randomly chosen amulets on her rosary, spaced out at irregular intervals. I suspect that each amulet can tell quite a story. Tibetan *malas* are usually made of sandalwood, seeds or agate, and like hers, can be a mixture of different materials. In Tibetan, the beads are called *dzi*. Really pricey rosaries have *dzi* that are individually carved by hand. Attached to the *mala* are two protruding leather extensions, each with ten movable, sliding silver grommets. This is called the *sumeri*. The *sumeri* holds its place on the *mala* where the ring of beads is tied together. This is done with three bigger *dzi* and marks the start and finish of each round of rosary mantras. These three anchor beads are a reminder of Buddhism's Three Jewels, they being *sangha* (community), *dharma* (the path to righteousness) and Buddha himself. To top it all off, the hidden string that holds all the *dzi* together like a necklace, represents Buddha's powers of penetration. Each time Grandma makes a round of the 108 *dzi*, she stealthily reaches over with her thumb and index finger, without ever having to look, and moves one grommet to the other end of the *sumeri*, to keep count. In all of this amazing commotion and jostling, she is in a trance, another reality. These beads are fused to her body, to her very soul. Ten plus ten equals twenty grommets on the *sumeri*, so I suspect she tries to get around the *mala* that many times each day. With all the interruptions of people getting on and off the bus at frequent stops and having to spend so much time consoling her little granddaughter, she only gets around it three or four times before they get off in the middle of nowhere, at a desolate, windswept Tibetan hamlet outside of Langmusi.

People are getting on and off and a young guy takes the seat next to me that just emptied. Zhong is a 27 year-old Tibetan, from Lhasa who moved here seven years ago. He has that ruddy red, sun drenched, Native American complexion so common among Tibetans on the plateau. He is a driver for this bus's company and is going into Songpan to work. He is married and has a boy and a girl. He explains to me that Baba Beijing allows Tibetans to have more than one child, since they are a minority. Mom stays home and takes care of the kids. Zhong asks if I'm going to Tibet on this trip and I explain that foreigners are not allowed to go. He is really surprised and asks why, so I tell him the truth: Baba Beijing blames overseas people for all the problems in Tibet, including the recent rash of monks self-immolating. I tell him the official version is that the Han are blameless and it's all *our* fault. Zhong seems genuinely shocked at this and acts rather upset. Not at me, but at Baba Beijing and the Han authorities. He tells me that it is not at all like that. The problem *up there* is too many Han are moving in and the PLA is installed to protect them…

Why, anybody in their right mind would have to concur with Baba Beijing that the mere thought of a white boy like me walking down the streets of Lhasa is what is causing all those monks and nuns to pour yak butter over themselves and self-immolate. It has nothing, absolutely nothing to do with the tens of thousands of Han soldiers laying siege in Tibet, nor the machine gun nests outside temples and shrines. There's no need to mention all the PLA troops, dressed in civilian clothes, guarding the interiors of the temples and the armored personnel carriers cruising the streets 24 hours a day, full of SWAT teams armed to the teeth and covered head to toe in full body anti-riot gear. This is all just totally immaterial to what is ailing the Tibetans.[2] *OK, OK, I confess, it's all my fault. My mere existence is to blame for the powder keg called Tibet. How can I even sleep with all those deaths on my conscience?*

With Tibet's seemingly endless supply of fresh water, timber, minerals, recently discovered petroleum, while making up much of the Himalayas and sharing strategically important borders with India, that other Asian colossus to the south, I am afraid this is a predicament for Zhong and his people that is not going to go away any time soon - if ever.[3] The Chinese are never leaving Tibet. It is too ingrained in the Han national consciousness about millennia of the Heavenly Mandate. One key tenet of the Mandate is that the reigning central power is obligated to keep the country unified - at any cost. Sad to say, but long term, I think the Tibetans can see their future in what happened to Native Americans at the hands of rapacious Europeans and Americans, unless they and the Han can come up with some mutual accommodation.

Frequent stops at plateau hamlets afford me the chance to study these big and blackened bread loaf shaped objects that are dotting the ground wherever a few people's houses congregate. I slowly realize they are huge open-air piles of stored yak, cattle and horse manure, to use as fuel for their fires. I did not see any of these storage piles around Hong Bei's tent at White Dragon River, but they must have the same thing nearby. The piles are about two to three meters long, just over a meter high and 2 meters wide. This means the animal herders go out all over the treeless plateau to collect cow patties to burn in their potbellied stoves, to survive what must be some of the world's most brutal, bone-desiccating, windswept winters. Edifying work, I'm sure, but it sure beats freezing to death. Thousands of yaks, goats and sheep are scattered across the rolling plateau pasture, which in this rainy season is the color of deep-mined emeralds. Silvery, shimmering rivulets and brooks of pure plateau water course and coil everywhere, almost making for a seasonal wetland. The livestock are being tended to by nomadic Tibetans, whose tents dot the landscape; they resemble onyx and alabaster jewels on a magnificent, malachite tapestry. Some herders are walking, some are on horseback and others are using their small motorbikes. The landscape is adorned with protruding ridges of erosion-rounded, grass covered knolls and granite-faced buttes that sporadically undulate in chains, jutting 100 to 500m above the plateau pastureland. This breathtaking highland scenery extends from horizon to horizon under a broken sheet of low lying, slate grey, stratocumulus clouds. The lack of people up here, the solace, the eerie chime of the incessant light wind, the naked beauty and absolute calm outside the walls of this bus are deafening in their isolation. This is a country with 1.3 billion people? You gotta be kidding.

Now that she has gotten off, I miss my old Tibetan grandmother's presence, the chants and the hypnotic cadence of her prayer beads. My entire body is aching from yesterday's arduous, 24km jaunt to the source of the White Dragon River and the nails on my big toes are bloody, suppurating and throbbing with pain. Not only the distance, but I made a vertical ascent of 550m up and slid and sloshed in the muck 550m back down, so my hypoxic brain and body are really feeling the effects. Along the way, using my Galaxy's altimeter, I notice we hit a pass that tops out at 3,850 MASL, only 35m higher than the mind blowingly majestic pass at yesterday's White Dragon River source. After two hours on the road, we actually have to change buses in Zoige (若尔盖= Ruo'ergai). Inside the bus station, Tibetan monks are trying to cut in line while I buy Zoige-Songpan tickets for Rafal, Marta and me. I have to get a little feisty and mouthy, doing the stiff arm and body block treatment, to keep my place. Jeesh, this is a Tibetan village. If I let every noble, vermillion robed Tibetan monk get ahead of me, the sky funeral vultures I saw on the White Dragon hike would have time to pick my carcass bones clean, as I die here standing in line. A young, non-Chinese speaking English woman is in front of me and I have to do her policing too, since she can't speak a word to these local line leapers. She looks a little unnerved and frightened by all the commotion. If I follow her lead, the vultures would have us both for lunch. When she finally gets to the window, I brace my arm around either side of her body like a cage barricade to keep all the red robes from piling in line. As she is getting her ticket and change, I ask her to exit to the right when she is finished, so I can coordinate my manoeuver to secure my place at the window. Yeah, *victory*! This is just like the old days were everywhere in China. Now, in metropolitan areas around the country, line standing is much, much more respected.

There is only one seat on the 10:00 bus, so I go ahead and take it. Rafal and Marta get tickets for the next bus at 13:00. We agree to meet up in Songpan and decide on Emma's Kitchen Hostel for a room, so they will know where to find me. I have been in contact with Emma by text messages, so the room is secure. I send one more SMS to let her know we need enough beds for three. Songpan is a one street town full of stores, restaurants and hostels. This commercial street is the main highway that continues on to Chengdu, Sichuan's capital. Being so close to ancient Tibet, I don't know what the racial makeup of this plateau-hugging berg was a generation ago, but it is definitely full of Han Chinese today, all here seeking the Eldorado of tourism. The first thing that strikes you is how *cute* Songpan is. Through a very coordinated effort, all the establishments have the same model of store sign. It is about two meters long, one meter tall and made of stained wood, almost to a burled walnut color. They all hang side by side above each place and have the Chinese name and English equivalent below the Chinese. I must say, yes it is touristy, but it really makes the street look smart and attractive. I actually like it, if for no other reason than it is so unusual in China and the real wood, stained signboards look very natural and *national park*, so to speak.

Some of the translations are predictably hilarious. We call it *Chinglish* here. *Shredded Pig Intestines in Noodles Restaurant*, *Cow Penis Soup Broth Specialty*, *Mountain Tourist Happy Local Cloud*, or other such hilarity is regularly seen, and I will continue to see them in the other places I visit in Sichuan. Given the uniformity of the signs and their ubiquity, it is clear that the Sichuan government has inaugurated a big campaign to make the province tourist friendly and attractive, albeit with some real guffaws in the translation department. I commend their efforts, but you have to wonder if the owners of the Pig Intestines and Cow Penis places have *ever* wondered why *no* foreigners ever eat there and always go next door. Heck, I might go to the Cow Penis place one day just to see what one looks like.

After yesterday's mud, muck and rain soaked trek, my clothes look like they've been kept for a week at the bottom of a compost pit. I'm desperate to get them washed. At Emma's place, I unfurl them and we agree on a price of ¥13 (€1.60/$2.00) for a good sized load. Given their nearly stiff, crud encrusted state, I cannot complain. According to LP, there is good hiking around Songpan, but my body and oxygen starved brain need a rest. I start writing away on my Galaxy Tab when Rafal and Marta arrive. I continue to write a chapter in *44 Days* while they take a walk around the hills surrounding Songpan. Upon their return, we walk around the town and I am tempted to buy a hunk of dried yak meat, which is hanging on hooks and along lines strung in the stores all up and down the street. It seems that every body part of the yak is used to make jerky, including bull testicles, reproductive organs and every possible shape and size of meat parts imaginable. I get one that looks like a huge, reddish colored turkey leg. Unfortunately, later on during the trip I keep seeing maggots crawling around my rolling suitcase and I'm thinking they came from someone else's bag in the usually crammed bus luggage holds. It isn't until I finally pull out this air dried hunk of yak meat that I discover it is hollow on the inside and has become a traveling maggot nest, with hundreds of the little white larvae swimming inside! Yummy… Needless to say, I don't bring this Songpan souvenir back to Beijing as a culinary delicacy for my family.

Dinner is a set of outstanding Sichuanese dishes. I choose sautéed yak meat tossed with onions and bamboo shoots, with a side of *youcai* in a white garlic sauce. *Youcai* (油菜) is a luscious, deep green veggie from the rapeseed family that is like a cross between spinach and broccoli. With a full stomach and a couple of beers to help me unwind, it's time for a good night's sleep – my aching body and brain are more than ready. Here in Sichuan, the cooks know how to add just a little of the numbing pepper, called *majiao* (麻椒= numb pepper) or *huajiao* (花椒= flower pepper). It is all the rage in faraway places like Beijing, to use it way too much in quantity and way too often in too many dishes where it shouldn't be. It kills the taste buds on your tongue and just puts your lips and mouth to sleep. Either you like it or you don't. I can pass. *Huajiao* was almost unheard of back in the 90s or would only be sparingly found in a few Sichuan inspired dishes. My only theory is that back in the bad old days, it was frightfully expensive and not widely cultivated, since the land was surely plowed up to grow more nutritious crops for the hungry during the 50s' Great Leap Forward, when tens of millions of Chinese starved and died. Central agricultural planning took years to fade away after Deng Xiaoping's launch of *get rich* liberalization policies, starting around 1980. Changing over from the badly needed nutrition of grain crops and fruit orchards to *huajiao* is symbolic of China's economic and political transformation over the last 30 years, including all the egregious excesses. Now, *huajiao* almost seems like an overkilling status symbol at wannabe restaurants,

"Look, we can put your mouth to sleep with tons of what used to be expensive huajiao."

I usually forget to request that it not be added and end up digging out the little dark spheres, which are like oversized black peppercorns. In any case, I find it counterproductive to ask Chinese chefs to make special requests. No MSG, not too much red pepper or oil, no salt, no *huajiao* and the like. It just seems to knock the culinary mojo, their kitchen moxy right out of them. They seem to get self-conscious, timid and afraid they might offend. The results are predictably depressing for the palate. It comes out tasting like a microwaved, out-of-date can of American Chung King Chop Suey. Yuk. Better to just let them do their *thaaaaang baaaaby*, stir in and stir fry their stove top magic over that high shooting, flaming fire, tossing and turning all the ingredients half way up to the ceiling with their rapidly gesticulating, oscillating wok and bringing out your dish freshly made and piping hot. Umm, umm, umm. Have you ever been in a traditional country Chinese restaurant kitchen? There can be tens of little bowls of this and that, green, red, yellow, brown, white, black; powders, seeds, liquids, animal, vegetable, mineral; chopped up, whole chunks, pieces, morsels, stems, twigs, buds, fresh, desiccated: pinches of *who knows what the heck that is?*, and all sorts of other concoctions that go into each dish. And while there are similarities within regional cuisines (Beijing, Shanghai, Sichuan, Hunan, Guangdong, etc.), each chef has their culinary quiver of secret recipes, using all these goodies to make their kitchen their very own. Start putting demands on their creative cooking souls - don't do this, don't add that, and they end up adding *none* of the above.

The next morning, it is time to say goodbye to Rafal and Marta. I'm going north to the famous Jiuzhaigou World Heritage Nature Park and they are heading south to Chengdu, to see the aforementioned world famous sights that I saw back in the 90s: Leshan and Emeishan. Keeping up with people met during travels is always very satisfying. Upon my return to Beijing, Rafal and I are staying in touch. He has realized his dream and is studying Chinese in Shanghai. Knowing that his dedication to learning Chinese is along the same levels as my intense language learning rituals, I'm sure he will make great strides in his fluency. With three days of English to rest my brain, it is time to get back into intense, full immersion Chinese. I'm going off circuit again. Bring on that thick, fat, slurry Sichuan accent, people, I'm ready for ya'll!

If you think the West is not below such crude, manipulative antics as this, check out all the purported Osama Bin Laden tapes released by the US government. Nor will we ever know if the person supposedly assassinated by Obama's CIA kill squad was really Bin Laden, as no independent laboratory was allowed to test the victim's DNA and the body was conviently buried at sea. , ,

2- *Ref:* Tibet, the Cry, *by Eric Meyer and Laurence Zylberman,*
www.blacksmithbooks.com and www.amazon.com.

3- *Ibid.*

Chapter 24: Songpan - Jiuzhaigou

Bus etiquette, traveling warrior stories and rules of the road in China - how to take control of a bus. Plus, the stunningly beautiful, giant roller coaster bus ride into Jiuzhaigou, with its crass tourism as penny stock hustle, plus must have Chinese dishes to fall back on when time is short.

Every bus and train ride offers some humorous or fascinating glimpse into the day to day life of Chinese society. This morning's ride from Songpan, north to Jiuzhaigou, proves to be no different. A guy gets on our small, fifteen-passenger bus with a 25kg nylon feed sack hanging down vertically from his extended arm. Nothing unusual about this. Everything, including the kitchen sink gets transported on these small feeder buses. But this sack is barely full, like it has something about the size of a grapefruit in the bottom of it. Then it starts moving, and then it starts meowing. He's got a kitten inside. During the whole trip, he tries to take it out and hold it inside his jacket, next to his chest. But anybody who knows cats understands that maybe one in a hundred can tolerate riding around in a vehicle, much less one that is as busy as a Sunday morning market. So, it is clawing him like crazy every time he takes it out, but outside the sack it doesn't meow. Then, he has enough of getting scratched and gouged to the point of drawing blood by the kitten's hard-to-hold paws, and he puts it back in the sack, where it starts howling with meows, filling up the whole bus. The poor guy obviously really wants this kitten and is dearly attached to it. He is trying so hard to treat it well, showing perfect aplomb, but it is a no win situation. Luckily for the rest of us bipedal passengers, he gets off at one of the first stops outside of Songpan. He is not dressed in monk's digs, but he may be transporting it to a monk friend. Cats are very popular pets in Tibetan monasteries... Weird stories like this happen on every bus or train, one cultural vignette after another. When you live in a country with 1,300,000,000 citizens, a whole lot of them are colorful characters.

Buying bus seats, even reserved ones from a ticket office machine always seem like a crapshoot. Today, I am on the front row, which in China is really riding in first class among equals. Yesterday, my seat was on the back row. Chinese buses have tractor duty suspensions, to survive the rugged hinterland roads and the lay of the land and chaotic traffic is such that there is a lot of bobbing, weaving, swerving and sudden stops. Most of these mountain and valley roads are tortuous and serpentine, climbing up and down like a roller coaster. That is why on any rural bus worth its salt, they have a hook hanging somewhere inside with a bunch of grocery store produce plastic bags, for those ill at ease. Predictably, some don't get a bag soon enough. If the road reputation precedes it, the attendant will go around and proffer the bags when passengers get on. But people still miss or get caught off guard. Some of them try to blow their chow out the window. Bad idea. It usually backfires - for the blower, the bus and for any passengers sitting behind them who have window seats. These buses can get stuffy with all the collective humanity on board, especially if it is standing room only, so the windows are often open. Eight hours in one of these passenger buses is a workout, even seated down the whole time. Many times during *44 Days*, I finish with a day's worth of buses and feel like I've been riding a stiff legged horse nonstop. I am often much sorer than after a long, arduous hike. You just get the heck beaten out of you. But, hey, it's exercise. And the wild countryside, the valleys, the mountains, the raging torrents and cascades, the quaint villages, spectacular agricultural and delicious roadside meals? It makes it all worth it.

Today, I am sitting next to a young, very Native American looking Tibetan who can somehow manage to read a book through all the hubbub. The book is in Tibetan, which is the first time I see someone reading a tome in this language in public. Then he whips out a cigarette to start to smoke. Time to take control of the bus. Smoking is infrequently a problem on the big 50 passenger interurban buses. They are nice, with air conditioning, often seat belts, reclining seats, television and trash cans up and down the aisle. So, the expectations are much higher. When someone does light up, the sharply dressed, uniformed attendant is more inclined to take action. But in these smaller rural buses, all bets are off and I have to do the attendant's job for them, although I always do try to enlist their support, with mixed results. Reason number one for doing this is I find smoking so disagreeable on public transportation. And the biggest problem is, if one starts sucking away, very rapidly the whole bus turns into a fog of smoke and stench. On trains, it's a lost cause in China trying to do anything about it. Even if you get someone to put out their butt when they are sitting in the train car with you, they can just join the group of addicts who are standing between each two cars, chain smoking. Since the doors between cars on Chinese trains are open 24/7, unless you are sitting in the very first car, the smoke just builds up the further back you sit. And even in the front car, there are a dozen guys piled in the very first boarding area, sucking away. But, at least you limit to the damage to *only* a dozen lost causes. But on buses, I don't mess around. I take control of the bus. I get up and politely ask the person to stop. Usually they don't and just give me a dog end eating smile, like they don't understand. Step two is I tell them I am waiting there in front of them until they put it out,

"Come on…well…I'm waiting…I'm waiting…"

That works about half the time. The other half of the time, I have to embarrass them in front of all the passengers. I talk to them about *rules*, which must be followed,

"We have old people and children on the bus who shouldn't have to breathe your smoke. You need to be respectful of their health."

There are *always* kids and genarians on these buses. If they still won't listen to reason, I have to start getting more personal. I talk about *Old China* and that now we are living in the *New China*, and in the New China, we don't smoke on buses. Are they still sitting there with the fag hanging out of their mouth, or trying to sheepishly hide it under their seat? If so, I ratchet it up a notch. I start talking about *culture* and *education* and appeal to their sense of national pride,

"Surely you must have gone to school, right? You got an education, right? You can read and write? See the signs inside the bus? I know China is country with *culture*..."

Usually by this time, they realize I mean business and the butt is long put out. Everybody on the bus is of course thoroughly enjoying the show, this white boy *dabizi* sparring with a local. The miscreant is just too embarrassed to keep it up and they snuff it out. They have, as we say, lost face. After all, what I am asking is totally reasonable, not to mention all the no smoking signs staring them in the face. So, they don't have much of a leg to stand on. If all else fails, or if they try to light up again, and a few do, I drop the S-bomb,

"I can't believe you are soooooo SELFISH!" (我不能相信你怎么自私自利!= *Wo bu neng xiangxin ni zenme ZISI ZILI!*)

In public, in front of a bus full of fellow citizens, the accusation of selfishness is tantamount to being really asocial, which in very conformist, Confucian Chinese culture is really out in left field. No one has kept smoking at this point. And almost always, no one else tries. It is also complicated by the fact that 90% of the drivers smoke. If I had this nerve racking, dangerous, largely thankless job, I'd probably smoke too. Some respect the rule and wait until the requisite pee 'n' smoke stop every two hours, but most don't. What can I say? They are working. But just the smell of it in the confines of the bus gets all the addicts twitching away. Many of the drivers, seeing and hearing one of my on-board challenges, coaxing or shaming a passenger, actually quit smoking or cut way back thereafter. Out here in the countryside, I think the only males over eighteen who do not smoke are either already dead or are in the hospital dying from emphysema, heart disease and cancer. It is incredibly ubiquitous in the hinterland. Want to conquer China? Just take away their nicotine fix. They'll beg for mercy. Oh, and by the way, my Tibetan reading partner put out his cigarette. And he did try a second time - it never even got close to his lips!

I leave Songpan with a certain amount of trepidation, because all I hear about Jiuzhaigou (九寨沟= Nine Camp Gulley) is not exactly inspiring: too commercialized, too crowded, too hectic and ridiculously expensive. Wow. What an infamous reputation. Lonely Planet even offers pointers and strategies on how to avoid all of Jiuzhaigou's pitfalls, the ticket price excepted, which is unavoidable. So, why am I flagellating myself by going? Well, it is a UNESCO World Heritage Site.

These places are limited in number and usually merit this exceptional moniker (the only one I visit on this trip that doesn't is Lijiang in Yunnan - more on that later). Also, I'm a teacher, all around scientist, amateur evolutionary biologist and geologist. The description of Jiuzhaigou's earthly origins and formation, the flora and fauna and the nearly mythical layout of the place - what can I say, it all just draws me like a June bug to a naked 200 amp light bulb on a sultry, semi-tropical night. And I guess it is for these reasons as well, that millions of people have gone there since it opened in 1984, and continue to do so.

This bus ride is especially exciting, or harrowing, depending on your point of view. Barf bags are a hot item on this leg, I can tell you. It is only about 130km, but with all the stops, twists and turns, it takes over two hours. One bus leaves Songpan each morning and comes back late in the afternoon. From Songpan, starting out at 2,800 MASL, we descend north towards the 2,000 MASL valley floor of the same said river. Forty klicks out of Songpan, we pass the big airport (Huanglong) that serves the park and shuttles in the thousands of tourists who visit each day. I find it strange they would build the park's airport almost 90km away, but they obviously have their reasons. And when I say thousands, I mean it. All told, there are close to forty flights a day coming into this isolated, remote airport. And they are all landing to go see Jiuzhaigou Park. To those forty airplanes chock-o-block full of impatient Chinese tourists, you can add our humble little bus of twenty land lubbers, bringing up the rear... This bus ride is exceptionally beautiful and given the fierce *scenic valley* competition on this journey, that's saying something. Starting north from Songpan, the valley has intense Tibetan agriculture: along with the iridescent, verdigris terraces of Alpine barley, there are fava beans, vegetables and some kind of root crop that looks like turnips, giant radishes or the like. Higher up on the steep slopes are yaks and goats. The day and weather are just outstanding. A piercing, Tibetan azure sky, broken with numerous, cotton ball cumulus clouds. The temperature is a little on the cool side. Most of the 800m drop in elevation occurs in the last hour before the park. This is where you literally fall off the Tibetan Plateau in a hurry.

On the way down, the valley rapidly narrows into an Alpine forest, covered with tall conifers towering over a lower canopy of cypress and deciduous trees. We could be in the upper reaches of the Rockies or the Alps. Right at the cusp before the big drop from the Tibetan Plateau, we pass the Jiabo Ancient City, which even has a Holiday Inn *and* an Intercontinental. It is not in the Lonely Planet and I cannot even find it on the web, so I don't know what to say, except that it looks like a kitschy, pseudo-cultural tourist town and theme park. Given that millions of Chinese have tons of disposable income to burn on tourism, and thousands of them pass this way every day, coming and leaving, I'm sure it's going great guns. Holiday Inn and Intercontinental are not down market, much less Chinese hostels, so I'm sure it is high dollar. The backdrop to Jiabo is well worth looking at. It is the Ganhaizi Wetlands, a marsh that extends for several klicks on both sides of the road. All of this wetland water feeds into the river that crashes down to the Jiuzhaigou valley below. *Crashing* is not hyperbole. A river falling the better part of 800 meters in less than 20km (take out all the twists, turns and switchbacks, and that 800m drop is in just five klicks), is bound to impress, and this one surely does. I don't see any kayakers on this river and for very good reason. It has *death* and *suicide* unofficially written all over it. There are some sections where I can envision a manic-depressive daredevil kayaker, who is off their meds, might have a go at it, ready to play either Hercules or Lucretia, depending on their mood. But, how would they stop before the impending death trap at the next turn and how would they exit the raging, roiling torrent with their body and boat intact? I don't even see anybody along its banks trying to fish either. If you fall in, it would be a quick, grizzly and mangled end, for sure. The locals are obviously leery of these killer cascades and I'm sure they have a few sobering, empirical *scare the living bejeezuz out of you* horror tales to keep their kids at a safe distance. The waters are so violent, fast moving and torrential, that it is hypnotizing just watching them - from a safe distance. The dramatic drop down into the Jiuzhaigou valley is such that the local road authorities have even taken to numbering the switchbacks as you descend. So as you go careening around each hairpin turn, there is a big traffic sign that blares out,

Jiuzhaigou the Fifth Turn

Jiuzhaigou the Sixth Turn

Et cetera. There are nine numbered switchbacks and a total of eleven in all. I have no idea why they petered out and did not put a signboard on the last two at the bottom. Ran out of budget maybe? The driver is doing a great job, keeping the bus in low gear and below 40kph. If he passes 45kph, an alarm buzzer goes off under the dashboard, which is a great safety feature. It must measure the incline, since it does not go off when he is driving at faster speeds on flatter land. After the series of switchbacks and 16km from Jiuzhaigou, the valley's slant calms down somewhat, as we go through a unique ecosystem between the Alpine forest above and the the Jiuzhai River valley below. Through here, the Alpine forest gives way to deciduous scrub, walnut, wild chestnut and acacia trees. In the lower canopy are brightly colored, variegated sumacs. This is the flowering red berry bush found all over the forest floors of eastern United States and made famous as a high-in-vitamin C infusion, commonly brewed by Native Americans. There is another low lying tree with large, magnificent bouquets of white flowers. I know my trees back home and can identify many of them in my travels, but this one escapes me. A couple of guys get off about 5km from the park. They got on board with a big bundle of 3cm diameter PVC pipes, which are about 4m long. It is quite comical to see them trying to negotiate carrying them around all the passengers and baggage inside the sardine packed bus and out the door. In the spirit of cooperation, people duck and lean over as needed, keeping their cool. Jiuzhaigou is a long, east-west, serpentine valley floor that goes on for many kilometers. With the tourist traffic that flows in and out of here, you can imagine how it is built up. Like Songpan, all the street signs, shop signs and even much of the façade architecture are coordinated in style and color. Very cute and eye catching, I must say. *Dazibao*, those ubiquitous, long, propaganda and public announcement banners are strung everywhere and tell the story,

Tourism is the foundation of our success!

Customers come first!

Tourism is for the benefit of all the people!

Service is paramount!

They are *everywhere*, with big, white or gold characters on the standard red background, in the hopes of keeping the locals in line. Too bad it does not work out that way. This place just reeks of *hustle and jive* the moment you get off the bus. From the taxi drivers to the hostels, from the restaurants to the shops, Jiuzhaigou immediately rubs me the wrong way. Maybe not pricy by Swiss or Japanese standards, but everything is two or three times more expensive than Gansu and Ningxia, and everywhere else I visit through the rest of my journey. The attitude of the *service* people is snarky and capricious. All the youth hostels and Chinese hotels are demanding ¥240-300 (€30-38/$38-48) for a cubby hole room with a bed squished inside. Dorm rooms are non-existent, a warm bottle of beer costs ten kuai (€1.25/$1.60) at the supermarket and they try to get more than that at the restaurants. Food is pricey, taxis wouldn't know what a meter looks like if you hit the drivers over the head with one. You get the picture. Anybody who has done some traveling has been to lots of places like this. It is a penny stock hustle from the get-go.

I haggle with a street punt for a hotel room at 180 RMB (€23/$29). He takes me there and it is kinda sorta – no - not even a hotel, in the middle of a four or five story building - this is nothing but a concrete shell and in full construction mode. Unbelievable. Construction materials are piled up in the big corridor leading to the *reception area*, which also looks like the backside of a bombed out movie set. There is one lone naked bulb in the corridor and another dangling from the unpainted, concrete ceiling inside. It is just a bare, cement shell. The lady asks for a 100 yuan (€13/$16) key deposit and we barter for ¥60 (€7.50/$9.50). Since getting off the bus, I am already as chippy and nasty as the Tara Torquemada back in Xiahe, and now in this concrete crater, I'm in a thoroughly foul mood. Before starting my journey, I had scheduled two days in Jiuzhaigou, but it is still early enough in the morning that I have plenty of time to see the park today. I make an executive decision on the spot to leave for Chengdu first thing next day. I look around this wrecking ball of a construction site and ask,

"I'm leaving very early tomorrow morning. Will there be somebody here to give me back my key deposit?"

"Sure, sure, sure. No problem."

We'll see, but I'm doubtful. She has a son who is acts severely autistic, poor little guy. During this whole charade, he is positively unhinged, screaming like a crazed banshee at that the top of his lungs, from inside his shell, crying profusely and hitting and slapping at his mom. It is going to be a long night. Do I need to even tell you what my room looks like? While not as bad as the Twilight Zone Jingtieshan People's Iron Ore Mine Hotel time warp, this place is a real close second. I have to pull the desk away from the wall to find the sole electrical plug in the room, in order to charge my Galaxy. The room looks like it was finished out by a band of ADHD teenagers badly in need of their Ritalin.

It's time for an early lunch and then off to the park. Just leaving my so called hotel feels like escaping from the bowels of Hades. When I am in a rush, there are two great Sichuanese dishes and one Guangdong one I can order, without even perusing the menu, and which are almost always available anywhere in China. Call these my *in a pinch* plates. Spicy shredded pork (鱼香肉丝= *yuxiang rousi*, or fragrant fish shredded meat) is a classic dish from this neck of the woods that you can faithfully count on time and time again. It does not really have fish in it, but fish sauce is added for flavor. This dish's pork can be in long shoestring strips or in small, thinly sliced pieces. It is served with whatever veggies the chef has at their disposal, but onions and garlic are *de rigueur*. Green, red and yellow bell peppers are a popular choice. Of course, it is going to pack quite a capsicum punch, with maybe a touch of *huajiao* (numbing pepper) added for good measure. The Chinese veggie dish that never goes south on you is eggplant. Unless you order it, eggplant is usually not too spicy. In any case, a bowl of neutron bomb-hot pepper, powdered, dried, paste or in peanut oil, is never far away for this or any other dish that you want to napalm. *Hongkao qiezi* (红烧茄子= red grilled eggplant) is sliced or diced eggplant that has been grilled first, so the outside looks and tastes like it has been roasted over an open fire. Then, the chef takes it and quickly stir fries it in a red pepper soy sauce concoction. It usually does not have a lot of other veggies added to the dish, but it will almost always be served with chopped up spring onion shoots and finely diced, grilled garlic. If the kitchen does not have eggplant, just substitute it by saying,

Hongkao shucai (红烧蔬菜).

Shucai means *vegetable*, so whatever greens tickle the chef's fancy (or whatever they need to get rid of), the same sauce will be made with another vegetable. Sex it up and in your mind call it *le legume du jour*... Another great one is 番茄炒蛋 (*fanqie chaodan*= foreign eggplant stir fried egg). This is a classic Chinese dish of southern origin. It is basically a scrambled eggs-and-diced-tomato omelet, with chopped fresh scallions or chives thrown in, all slowly stir fried, so it comes out with a thicker sauce than other quick fried dishes. Students of Chinese will be quick to notice that the word for *eggplant* and *tomato* have the same character (茄-*qie*). Tomatoes are an introduced food, so they are *foreign* eggplants. The only drawback to *fanqie chaodan* is they usually do add a little sugar. But the sweeter version is more common the further south you go, towards Guangdong. Up north in Beijing, I often do not taste the sugar much at all. This dish also affords your palate a break from the scorching hot peppers that so many Chinese dishes have, as it almost never has any added, unless you ask for it. For the calorie needy, white rice (白饭= *baifan*) or fried rice (炒饭= *chaofan*) can be ordered as a gut filler. In Sichuan, white rice is a great deal if you are hungry. They usually bring out a big communal tub of it, and for one ridiculously low price, you serve yourself to as much as you want. Up north, you pay for each bowl of white rice ordered, although it is only 1-3 RMB (€0.13-0.38/$0.16-0.48) a bowl. In Sichuan, you have absolutely *no* excuse to leave the restaurant hungry... Belly full? Check. One point two liter stainless steel thermos full of hot tea? Check. Galaxy Tab has a good charge? Roger that. It's time to go find out what all the hullabaloo and hype are surrounding this famous World Heritage Park, Jiuzhaigou.

Chapter 25: Jiuzhaigou

How many people get to stroll around one of the most overrun-with-humanity, swarming-and-teeming-with-bipeds-like-a-termite-colony World Heritage Sites on the face of the planet - all alone? Well, at least one – me!

Leaving my construction site hotel and going into Jiuzhaigou World Heritage Nature Park is like going from the fat to the fire. First, my gastrointestinal tract has finally succumbed to the superior force of introduced bacteria and I've got a medium level dose of traveler's diarrhea. With so many years living and working around the world, my guts are practically food poisoning proof, but eventually on a long trip like this, I'm bound to get hit once or twice with the runs. I gave up years ago trying to play Sherlock Holmes about whatever I ate, whichever dish it was that gave it to me - I have no idea and almost never do. I believe it is just the accumulation of road wear and tear and the slow buildup of strange microbial flora that finally overwhelms the usual microbes in my gut. I'm not flushing my brains down the can - yet, but I am going to have to add *toilets* to my radar scanner as I hike around the rest of the day. I take a half-finished roll of toilet paper from my so-called hotel room. Over the years and across the continents, I've been caught more than a few times without it and have resorted to all kinds of creative solutions to that *ad hoc* problem.

The other hot coal in my spiritual britches is trying to find a taxi driver who is not over-the-top obnoxious and venal. None of them will use the meter, so in these cases, I take my time and ask several drivers how much the fare is, so I know I am only going to get ripped off as much as the next tourist and not a *mao* more, by golly.[1] Fair is fair. The taxi driver I pick is not venal; he is merely as oily as a basket of leftover French fries at a Norman beach picnic. In tourist traps like Jiuzhaigou, that is about the best you can hope for. Buying the ticket to my now favorite place in the whole wide world, *Outta Here*, or since I am feeling metaphorical, *St. Elsewhere*, gives me such a sense of relief and perspective. I can now concentrate on dedicating the rest of my day in the park, knowing I'll be on the long distance bus to Chengdu, Sichuan's megalopolis capital, at 07:00 tomorrow. I never like to have to categorize a travel visit as *hit and run*, but Jiuzhaigou is fertile soil to cultivate the term and I'm not going to stick around and help this garden grow. The taxi driver actually turns out to be halfway decent. We both know the score: money. He gets mine. He charges me twenty yuan (€2.50/$3.20) to go several klicks down the road, wait less than five minutes while I buy the bus ticket and then take me 500m back up the road to the park entrance. For such a famous, frequented place, the entrance to the officially named Jiuzhaigou Valley Scenic and Historic Interest Area is not just unassuming, but bordering on imperceptible. A couple of pointing fingers get me to the ticket office. Since I'm here after the morning rush hour, I don't even have to wait much in line. The ticket office's size attests to how many people pass through the park each day. There are enough ticket windows here to cover the mobs at an oversold Lollapalooza concert.

Three hundred and ten RMB. I let that outrageous entrance fee wash over me like the park's one hundred plus lakes. I cascade across all the travels I have taken to more than eighty-five countries, all the parks, tickets, stamps and such, and I just cannot come up with any place that tops this handsome sum. A quick calculation in my head and we're talking half a Benjamin ($49), or close to 40 Euzies (€39) to leave this ticket office and turn left. The ticket given is so big and ostentatious that it would make a menu at a fancy Parisian restaurant blush with envy. Where is the Pink Panther's Inspector Clouseau when you need him? He could have a grand old time with a menu this size, ordering his meal in a trying-too-hard, down market faux French restaurant. Of course, I get the psychology of it: after burning a big hole in your pocket 310 times, it is to suppress the buyer's remorse that is boiling up inside them as they walk by the wall of ATM machines on their way to the turnstiles. At least I was able pay for my ticket with my (Chinese Union Pay brand) bank card. Otherwise, with the many thousands of Chinese tourists who mob this place each day, they would need a Brink's armored car parked right out front 24/7, just to keep the ATM machines filled with adequate funds. As usual, I don't see enough *dabizi* to count off the fingers on one hand during my whole time here. Up to now, I'm still not getting the real Jiuzhaigou experience, with its pullulating masses crawling over the place like a swarm of pheromone crazed termites. I was not here when the madhouse opened to bedlam first thing this morning. I enter through the deserted turnstiles and walk into the huge roundabout receiving area where the buses pull in. This is where we now empty-pocketed tourists start our Jiuzhaigou adventure, and there is only a family of four and me. Where is everybody? Trust me, I don't have to wait long to find out the answer to *that* stupid question.

If you have a strong sense of direction to keep your bearings, like I do, the map of Jiuzhaigou is frustrating to say the least. The park's three valleys are connected together in a perfect Y shape, but here's the problem: the bottom of the Y is pointing north, so it's an upside down wishbone. Thus the maps are oriented with north facing down to the bottom of the page and the top of the park is due south, which is geographically correct. This reminds me of those wonderful world maps put out by the Southies that flip the globe upside down, where Australia and the Southern Hemisphere are on top. It is just a wonderful effect and a powerful reminder of how much we arrogant colonialists in the northern hemisphere just assume that any map you pick up will have north oriented towards the top of the page. Even though I know the map is upside down for my brainwashed head, I still have to constantly be reminding myself of the inversion all day.

What makes Jiuzhaigou so special and deserving of the World Heritage moniker? That would be its extremely unique topography. From the entrance at the bottom of the Y to the fork is about 15km of road and each branch of the Y is another 15 klicks or so of road. Thus, the whole park is around 30km long. As just mentioned, the ascent from bottom starts at 2,000 MASL and climbs up to 3,000m at the top of each road in the Y. That's one klick up in thirty, which is a 3% climb. The topography is actually much steeper than that of course, since the road switches back and forth so much. Essentially, we drove off the Tibetan Plateau this morning into the Jiuzhaigou river valley and we can climb back up to the terminus of each fork in the neighboring Min Mountains. From these two high points, within the confines of the park, you can look up and see mountain peaks that are 4,500m tall. This description is nothing to get excited about and could portray a number of parks in the European Alps or American Rockies. But what sets Jiuzhaigou apart is how it was formed during repeated Ice Ages that sat on top of this part of the world over the last 2.5 million years. During these Ice Age periods, the world's oceans were up to 120m lower than they are today. And where was all that H_2O? Right here, on top of us and it was a sheet of ice up to 4km thick, at times covering 30% of the Earth's surface. I look up in the greyish, partly cloudy sky and try to imagine a behemoth of a continent-wide iceberg as tall as where single engine airplanes plot their flight plans, on top of me. Nah, can't really do it. Like light years and nanometers, it is truly beyond the scope of human proportions. Of course, each time an Ice Age finished, the ice sheet melted and flowed down into the oceans, filling it back up. You can just envision the erosion caused by the movement of cubic kilometers of ice and water falling towards the seas. One cubic kilometer of water weighs a billion tons. Doing quick math with the park's 720km^2 and 4km thick glaciers, that is about three trillion tons of ice working its way up the Jiuzhaigou valley and back down into the oceans - seven times over the last 750,000 years alone. This does not even include tectonic plates and earthquakes, which largely contributed to the formation of the Alps, Rockies, Andes and the nearby Himalayas. Even this description does not particularly distinguish Jiuzhaigou from these aforementioned mountain regions. What is amazing about this place is how the glaciers carved the rock up the valleys in a stair step fashion, over and over, and not in a more or less straight, sloping line, like most of these just mentioned mountain ranges, which makes for great for snow skiing. Alpine skiing cannot work at Jiuzhaigou, with the dozens of flat areas full of shallow lakes and all the near vertical drop-offs connecting them, which is where the park's many waterfalls are.

Instead, we are dazzled with over a hundred iridescent wetland lakes and thirty sublime waterfalls interspersed along the three valleys that make up the Y shape of the park. And since the valley entrance is a cul-de-sac trapped in the Min Mountains, its evolutionary development is quite isolated. Thus, it is home to hundreds of rare species of flora, as well as fauna, such as the giant panda, lesser panda, golden monkey and antelope. Not only was Jiuzhaigou geologically isolated, but it was almost unknown to the outside world before 1975. Justly crowned a UNESCO World Heritage Site in 1992, it has gone from total obscurity to having to shut the gates each day when the maximum allowed 12,000th person shells out 310 kuai to bring up the rear; this daily limit is ostensibly to avoid the inevitable ecological degradation from turning the park into a human anthill every day. I don't know how well *that* is working out, what with a year round average of 7,000 visitors per day, or over 2.5 million per year.

Once inside the park, the waters' colors border on something out of a J.R.R. Tolkien fantasyland. The lakes are surreal and extraterrestrial, with an infinite spectrum of blues, greens, yellows, browns, whites and reds, frequently found in same lake, like a psychedelic patch quilt for sale in a Haight-Ashbury hippy dippy cooperative. This impressionist painter's palate of colors is caused by thousands of years of fallen tree branches, bushes, flowers and autumn leaves that have collected and decomposed on the undisturbed bottoms, leaching all their rainbow of chemical compounds into the limpid, gossamer waters. The white, cottony look on the bottom of many parts of the lakes is due to the high levels of calcium carbonate in these waters, which precipitates over the millennia from the karst rock formations, and which make up much of the geological formation below the surface. Karst rocks are full of so much calcium, because they are the fossils of dead ocean creatures from the sea beds dredged up thousands of meters above sea level by glaciers, tectonic plates and earthquakes, over millions and millions of years. It was finding sea bed fossils at the top of the Andes Mountains, 10km above the bottom of the Pacific Ocean, which helped Charles Darwin develop the ineluctable science of evolution and natural selection. And to top it all off at Jiuzhaigou, fallen, massively girthed, primeval forest tree trunks are piled helter skelter in all the lakes, eerily suspended in the shallow waters and seeming to defy gravity, like Leviathan pick-up sticks.

Then there are the waterfalls that transcend all human imagination. Tens of meters tall and hundreds of meters wide, they grace the park's atmosphere with a constant, hushed roar. But not over the din of bus after bus of sardine packed tourists, engines screaming and decelerating up and down the steep roads, belching blackened diesel soot all the way. At every site where this conveyor belt of vehicles regurgitates thousands of bipeds, the howl of humanity dominates the ambiance. As just mentioned, it is not a very big park by international standards, only 720km^2. But like Egypt's ninety million inhabitants, who are almost all living eyebrows to elbows on the razor thin strip of the Nile River, 99% of the tourists here are on these three valley roads, all stopping at the same famous twenty sites. Of course, the same can be said for many popular parks in the US and Europe as well. How few visitors venture off the loop of road the runs through California's Yosemite National Park is just one example. It's just that the population base is so huge in China.

Don't get me wrong, these masses of Chinese tourists are incredibly indulgent of each other, given the teeming lines, packs, knots, swarms and incessant movement of people swirling around each other. This civility would have been unimaginable twenty years ago. Of course back then, it was unthinkable that up to 12,000 Chinese a day would have the financial resources to spend a wad in travel expenses to come here. But if they could have, there would have been fisticuffs, shouting matches, pushing and shoving all day long - guaranteed. Not only has China's economy exploded but the Chinese people's social evolution has been just as dramatic. I would challenge Americans and Europeans to be in the same environment, stuffed to the gills on narrow wooden boardwalks and undulating series of outdoor stairs (many of which would not pass Western public safety codes), with mobs of total strangers, and keep their cool the way the Chinese are doing today. I'm truly impressed at what I am experiencing. Jiuzhaigou has become the Chinese's iconic Yellowstone Park and a must place to notch on their traveler's guns. And when they get someplace, the Chinese want to be photographed in front of the said famous place, with that place identified in the picture if at all possible. That is why you will see the Chinese patiently wait their turn, as family after group after tour sets up in front of a building, large stone stele with the place's name carved into it or a natural backdrop, to have their picture taken. Westerns do too, but here it is a social epidemic of joyous proportions. After two generations of personal deprivation, suffering and national socio-political suicide, the Chinese want to be able to offer testimony to their friends and family: see, look, I have been here. They also can't get enough being pictured with *laowai*. Any foreigner traveling in the hinterlands of China (by that I mean outside of the ten biggest cities) can expect frequent requests from total strangers to mug with them while a photo is taken. Foreign children and teenage girls almost need casting agents and personal assistants, Hollywood style. The requests are non-stop for them and the further you get out into the interior, the more the requests pile up. I never say no and why would I begrudge them? They love it and I am happy for them. It is also a great way to meet people and chat in Chinese. I also, *ex post facto*, stay in contact via email with some of these shutter bugs and exchanged pictures, which is a lot of fun.

I thought that the bus from the main entrance of the park would go all the way to the top of one of the forks in the Y and I could then work my way down. But, no, it dumps you off at the central junction where the three valleys meet, at a place called Nuorilang (诺日朗). And the scene stops me in my tracks. This football field sized staging area is one giant parking lot cum bus terminal and about half the day's human allotment must be here. Ridiculously long lines are queued up to take buses to the two upper valleys. So needless to say, I am in good and bountiful company. Badly maintained and running on the dirtiest diesel fuel refined on the planet - otherwise known as black cloud Chinese buses - are taxiing in and out like planes at Heathrow on Christmas Eve. I just got here and there is no way I'm going to spend half my afternoon standing in line to go further up. This is as far as I advance. But the fact of the matter is, many people, the most determined, fanatical and it must be said, superficial in their yearnings, visit the sites on the three park roads in one day. The majority of them get here when it opens at 07:00, rapidly hitting the hot spots in the two upper forks and then work their way back down the main valley, Shuzheng (树正沟) to the main entrance. And yes, there is a good chunk who spend a second night in an overpriced hotel or *zhaodaisuo* in town and shell out another 310 RMB for a second day, emulating social insects and their mass cooperative behavior.

Time to explore: over the next half day, I wade through cascading waves of *Homo sapiens* and visit the top sites around Nuorilang: Mirror Lake, Pearl Shoals, Pearl Waterfall, Golden Bell Lake, Peacock River and Five Flower (Colorful) Lake, all up towards the right half of the Y in the Rizegou Valley (日则沟). The grey skies begin to release intermittent light showers. If you think platoons of Chinese, bumping and bobbing into each other is fun sport, just add ten thousand umbrellas to the commotion and craziness. Oh joy. My diarrhea is flaring up every hour or so. Luckily, being such a high traffic place, there are frequently spaced toilets and rest stops everywhere I go. But it is weakening me more than I want to admit. Partly to exercise my upper body and abdominals and partly because I carry my binoculars, a large thermos of hot tea and other such trappings of the modern age, the backpack that I walk with weighs in at 5-6kg. But today, I pay the price for trying to stay physically fit. As the rain is sprinkling down, I am getting dizzy and light headed from losing all my body's electrolytes from the diarrhea. I suddenly slip on a set of three wood steps along the boardwalk and go crashing to the ground. It is more surprising than painful, and luckily, falling into the ascending steps reduces the distance I fall, so that helps. But, I realize just how weak I am when I try to get myself back on my feet and really struggle against the weight of my backpack jostling back and forth, as I shakily right myself. I need to be careful and stop to buy a package of Haochidian brand (好吃点= Good Eating Snacks), almond flavored crackers for some energy. For only ¥5 (€0.60/$0.80), they are one of my favorite energy snacks in China, kind of a cross between a low sugar cookie and a cracker. I finish off my 1.1 liter steel thermos of hot tea and against my environmental promise to not purchase beverages in plastic bottles, get a big bottle of mineral water. Right now, that principal is going out the window. I need to make it back to base camp and that fall was a wakeup call to just how weak I am today.

After a 15-minute sit with hundreds of other Chinese occupying the same rest stop, I make my way further on. But I don't get very far heading up the Rizegou Valley. All of a sudden I see lines of tourists coming back towards me heading to the Nuorilang bus terminal, and another few hundred meters further on explains why: the park closes at 17:00 (LP says 18:00) and a burly, overweight Chinese park attendant is pushing everybody towards the Mirror Lake parking lot. He is actually very nice about it. People stop in droves to take their pictures in front of named steles and mountains behind the glassy waters of the lakes. Mr. Park Bouncer even graciously takes pictures of groups of tourists, so no one is left out. There is a kind of passive resistance to his herding and the hundreds of people in front of him are dragging out the inevitable departure for as long as possible. But as soon we get within earshot of the Mirror Lake parking lot, we can all hear one of the most obnoxious declarations announced in the daily lives of all Chinese:

"KUAI YI DI'ER!" (快一点儿! = HURRY UP!)

You hear it everywhere you go in China and it is usually said with a snarling, menacing and insulting growl. It grates on my nerves and ears every time I hear it, because it is usually lashed out like a punishment or pain to be administered. The driver in the parking lot across the bridge cutting back over Mirror Lake can be heard from a half a klick away and like a tightly wound metronome, he relentlessly and repetitively keeps shouting it out at the top of his lungs. Like obedient human cattle, the hundreds of tourists in my coalescing clot of humanity make their way to the head of the bridge. I stop to rest for a few minutes before heading across. Every time the driver ruins his voice screeching his mantra, I get more and more gnarly and truculent. It is so insulting and demeaning. These thousands of mutual strangers have patiently tolerated, even embraced each other in the most trying of public circumstances, paid a pretty penny to do so and now we are being treated like stupid sheep who can't find their way forward across a footbridge, the only way out. Well, that's not really true… I see that what they have done is take two long sticks and crossed them over the boardwalk going back to the Pearl Waterfall. They have hung a bogus yellow safety sign over it, saying that there is construction going on and to not enter.

I impetuously and impulsively construct my own little rebellion: OK, I'll hide out and explore the park until sunset and then walk out. And the fifteen klicks to walk back to the main park entrance? After many days hiking and the 24km monster hike to the White Dragon River source in Langmusi, I say under my breath, *piece of cake* and assuage myself that the park entrance from Nuorilang is 500m downhill, not like the 500 meters of vertical ascent I hiked at White Dragon. It'll be a late night, but what the heck and what an adventure. All I have to look forward to when I get back is my construction site hotel and that poor autistic boy, whose trapped soul is caged inside his screaming rictus of emotional agony. And that cursed driver keeps barking like an arrogant pimp working the street corner outside a big city convention. It is so undignified… That's it, I can't take it anymore, I'm outta here. I'm going to make a statement. Exit stage left. The cut off to the parking lot is hidden from all the crowds behind me, being below a little rise in the boardwalk, and I cannot even see the buses, nor the vocal ogre ruining what has been a satisfying social outing and experience with the Chinese. He and his bus are completely hidden behind a thick copse of trees. Thus, from the parking lot across the bridge over Mirror Lake, he and the tourists who are already ignominiously herded over there can be eliminated as a threat to foiling my conspiracy of freedom and tranquility. I walk back up a few meters on the boardwalk so I can see the approaching throngs of soon-to-be corralled sheep. They are still stopping and taking pictures, so I have to act fast and wait for a break in the procession. With so many people coming my way, I will only have a few seconds to make my break… I wait until there is a lag in the clot of people coming towards me. Now Jeff – *go*! I turn around, sprint to the crossing and hurriedly wiggle my way through the two sticks blocking the boardwalk. My plan is almost undone by my big backpack. I can't get through with it on, so I rip it off and pull it behind me as I crouch through. The bogus safety sign gets dislodged, but I can't be concerned. I run around a bend along the path and out of sight of the oncoming crowds. I'm suddenly all alone on the forested boardwalk. I made it. Freedom. Solitude. And it's *all mine*.

My weakened state is completely masked by the massive adrenaline rush coursing through my veins and pounding arteries. I go about 100m away from the parking lot turnoff and back towards Pearl Waterfalls and just sit for about a quarter of an hour, waiting to see what happens. Is any burly bouncer going to come this way? If they do, well, at least I tried. In any case, I need to conjure up a good excuse for staying back, and being beaten down with dehydration from the diarrhea, I have a plausible story to recount: I have the runs (*laduzi*= 拉肚子), got really weak, went into the forest to sleep for a while and after I woke up, all the buses had left. Hmm… not bad… I think it will fly. The demonic, droning driver finally shuts up. I can just see patches of his bus through all the trees, as his human cattle car takes off down the main road. The last air-choking bus from the upper valleys passes and finally fades into the distance. And then silence. Total silence. Total calm. Total isolation. I am all alone in one of the busiest, most celebrated and spectacular natural settings on Planet Earth. For the next four hours, I trace my steps back to Nuorilang, living, really feeling the philosophy of that great Simon and Garfunkel song, *Feeling Groovy*,

Slow down, you move too fast, you've got to make the moment last
Just kickin' down the cobble-stones, lookin' for fun and feelin' groovy

Feeling groovy

Hello lamp-post, what cha knowing, I've come to watch your flowers growin'
Ain't cha got no rhymes for me, do-it-do-do, feelin' groovy

Feeling groovy

I've got no deeds to do, no promises to keep
I'm dappled and drowsy and ready to sleep
Let the morning time drop all its petals on me

Life I love you, all is groovy

Don't laugh: in the youth of my generation, it was way cool to say *groovy* every chance we could get. *Bookends*, the album containing this ode to joy, was the first vinyl LP record I owned. I can still recite this song verbatim from deep memory... The cascading roar of the waterfalls and water coursing between the connected lakes is Mother Earth rhythmically respiring a giant *Om Mani Padme Hum* Tibetan mantra. Birds start to come out. *Everywhere*. This primeval forest is starting to come alive in these few crepuscular hours before sunset. All the critters here are surely well adapted to the daily exodus of humanity and have to pack a day of foraging, eating, mating and frolicking into a brief, late afternoon. Leaves start to rustle: forest mice and lizards start to come out, some of which I can spot. Up in the trees, several species of shrike birds furiously feed on moths and other flying insects, or pick crawling ones off the leaves and branches. The ground tit bird likes to forage and mostly runs and darts along the ground. I take out my trusty binocs, the preferred model for bird watchers around the world, and spend close a half an hour at different points along my way back to Pearl Waterfall and Pearl Shoal, just stopping and studying these amazing creatures, the remaining ancestors of the dinosaurs. In the forest I lie flat on the now deserted boardwalk and look up through the tree canopy to spy on all the activity. I take copious notes on each species and hopefully one day will find a good book on birds of China, or a helpful ornithologist and be able to identify all of them. Having the unique and awe inspiring Pearl Waterfall *all* to myself is an experience I will never forget. At 310m wide and 28m tall, it rages with the force of Greek gods and goddesses, an earthly and watery Mt. Olympus. Ditto the Pearl Shoals. I just sit there in the middle of this shimmering, shallow-surfaced cascade, all 200m of its length, before it crashes over the Pearl Waterfall, and savor the experience of watching the sky slowly turn to dusk.

I am thirsty as all get out and fill my empty thermos with ice-cold water from this expansive cataract. There is a risk of giardia, but I'm desperate to keep my weakened body hydrated. I can always go to the pharmacy and get some metronidazole or better yet, tinidazole and kill it off, which I've done tens of time in all my travels.[2] Mirror Lake now exudes a tranquility and spiritual resonance that is totally lost in the throngs of the thousands who show up here every day of the year. This is how Jiuzhaigou is meant to be experienced. Cut off from the rest of humanity, this is the way the Tibetan and Qiang people have lived, prayed and meditated here for thousands of years. I make my way north on the road out of Nuorilang and amble peripatetically past the famous sites along the way: Nuorilang Waterfall, Rhinoceros, Shuzheng and Tiger Lakes, Shuzheng Falls, Wolong, Shuanglong and Reed Lakes. I take peopleless, humanity-free pictures along the way. As the Sun is lost to darkness, it is about 21:30 and I still have several klicks till the entrance. It is mercifully downhill all the way. Fireflies start to dance an aerial ballet and chaotically escort me on the way below. The chances are small, but I pick up a nice, hefty walking stick, just in case I cross paths with a mammal that feels threatened by my existence. I also take out my little flashlight, ready to use, just in case.

I'm out of food and water. But my fatigue and exhaustion from a day's worth of diarrhea and a lot of hiking are masked by all the adrenalin and endorphins coursing through every one of my body's fibers. I am buzzing, droning with joy and exaltation. I simply cannot wipe the smile off my face. I know that I am living an experience that very few people, other than the native villagers who live inside the park, ever get the chance to do. And a handful of those inhabitants are out driving around, enjoying the solitude as much as I am. A few pass me, their headlights shining on my obviously white, *waiguoren* face, as I look back over my shoulder. I refuse to wave anybody down. I decide that if anyone stops and offers me a ride, I'll take it. But, I don't want to ruin one of the most perfect traveling experiences of my life by negotiating how much it will cost me to be taken to the entrance. I figure if they stop and offer, it will be out of kindness and goodwill and that is where I want it to stay.

After about five klicks, a husband and wife stop and offer me a ride to the main park village below. I'm too knackered at this point to engage in much conversation, but push myself. They picked me up out of cross cultural curiosity and I feel an obligation to indulge their inquiries. I tell them my bogus story about falling asleep in the forest, waking up alone, and almost start to believe it myself. I thank them as I get out. I'm not far from the entrance now, but almost immediately, a small Toyota pickup truck stops and picks me up. In the darkness, he is young guy who works in the park and is out for a nice evening drive. Telling him my spiel, he talks to the police unit guarding the park entrance. They scan me over slowly in the glare of the pickup's headlights, looking dumbfounded and incredulous. Dressed in military fatigues, one of them goes back to the guard station and makes a phone call, undoubtedly to a higher authority. I can't imagine too many *laowai* trying to get out of here in the middle of the night, but they wave me on through. Handshakes and profuse thank yous to everyone present and I walk out onto the main street and trek the two klicks back to where my hole-in-the-wall is.

First, I've got to get some nutrition in my calorie starved, empty gut. I've had quite a day. It is approaching the witching hour, but restaurants are still open. There's money to be made in this hardcore tourist town, 24/7. I get a big plate of braised tomatoes with scrambled eggs (番茄炒蛋= *fanqie chaodan*) and drink two big bottles of beer. Just what the doctor ordered. The mom and pop owners, with their son and daughter-in-law sit down at the table next to me for an end of the day family dinner. They have the cutest little pigtailed daughter, about two years old, who looks like a plump, oriental baby Cameron Diaz. They slap her hands and head repetitively during the whole meal. You can just see the fulmination and fear behind her cherubic little face. Unfortunately, *spare the rod and spoil the child* is still very much a part of Chinese child raising culture. She keeps looking over at me, searching for some solace, but any intervention on this foreigner's part would likely be counterproductive in the long run. She'll probably grow up to be a psychopathic Fortune 500 CEO and be very successful pillaging her workers and plundering Planet Earth, getting even with her upbringing every step of the way. This little Miss Cameron *Dian* might be the future of the 21st century, staring me in the face.

The hotel reception area is empty of human presence, so I head straight to my gawd awful black hole of a room. As I fall asleep, sated with life, I ponder the great debate: is Jiuzhaigou China's crown jewel of national parks or an ecotourism Frankenstein? Depending on your point of view and cultural background, I've seen them both today.

1- *The* mao (毛) *is a subunit for the Chinese yuan. To make things even more confusing, it is also called a* jiao (角). *It is the same thing as a dime in the US, i.e., 1/10 of a yuan. There used to be the* fen (分)*, which is the same thing as a penny in the US or centime in Europe, i.e., 1/100 of a yuan. You still end up with fens in your pocket, whether you like it or not, and even run across the occasional two fen and five fen coins. Officially no longer in use, fens will probably continue to float around in cash drawers and purses for years to come. America and Europe should follow China's lead and get rid of the penny/centime.*

2- *Upon my return to Beijing, I knew I had giardia and took two 2-gram courses of tinidazole, 10 days apart to get rid of it. If you do any traveling outside the 34 OECD countries, chances are good you will get a bout of it. You can go months and not realize you have it. The symptoms can be very subtle, but I've become an expert at detecting them - I've caught it over 30 times. The other frustrating aspect of giardia is it is devilishly difficult to detect under a microscope in a stool sample, so most of the time the results from the lab inevitably come back negative, even if you have intestines full of this pesky, waterborne amoeba. In Europe and the US, these drugs require a prescription and I have to be forceful with the doctor about getting a script, even though they are staring at a false negative lab result. A recount of my overseas exploits usually does the trick. Elsewhere in the world, China included, I can just buy what I need at my neighborhood pharmacy, without the Rx. Now that's market liberalization.*

Chapter 26: Jiuzhaigou - Chengdu

Playing the part of a plundering pirate to avenge my dump hotel, highways for rollerblading giants, the politics of earthquakes and another provincial Chinese megalopolis, ho-hum.

I'm still tingling and meditating like a transcendent Buddhist monk, thanks to the breathtaking, once in a lifetime experience I had yesterday, having Jiuzhaigou Park all by my lonesome, and pulling off the amazing nighttime hike back out. But before I leave, I relish the opportunity to give my crappy, crass, overpriced, should never have opened yet, hole in the ground, farce of a construction site *hotel*, a well-deserved riposte. The desk attendant and the street punt assured me last night, *guaranteed* that someone would be here in the morning to give me back my key deposit of ¥60. They wanted one hundred, but I refused - and as it turns out, quite presciently. No one is there of course. Even the hotel help won't stay here. The only ones who sleep in this concrete shell are principled adventurers who resist tourist trap schemes as much as possible, Jiuzhaigou style. I'm not happy. It's 05:30, this whole town is an overpriced rip off and here we go again. I step around the back of the counter to see if just by idealistic chance they left my money attached to a paper clip or something, and all I see are a bunch of room keys haphazardly scattered all over the place. Hmm... My instantaneous reaction is to just take my key with me, quid pro quo for the 60 kuai they stole from me. But I'm feeling really indignant right about now, with a liver full of revenge and a head swimming with spite. I'm also heaving with instructorial rage: I want to give these jokers a *laowai* lesson. I furtively scoop up *all* the keys I can find, toss them into my backpack and saunter out onto the nearly empty street. When the coast is clear, I check my booty: seven nice keys, with large, custom imprinted tags on them, beseeching the finder to please call their number if found. *Not this time, suckers.* Even nicer, they and the keys are attached together by real nice, heavy duty, spring loaded fobs, which will come in handy back in Beijing for years to come. I feel the rush of pirate illegitimacy flow through my veins. Color me a corsair, broad brush me a Barbary pirate. I flash back to the baby Chinese Cameron Diaz-future-Leona Hemsley-Imelda Marcos last night and for a few brief moments, vicariously feel the insensate power of a Fireman, destroying lives and Mother Nature for the bottom line. To quote Arlo Guthrie in the song, *Alice's Restaurant*, I'm feeling like,

"I got blood 'n guts 'n veins in my teeth!"

I at least try to atone and be as environmentally sensitive as a vengeful thief can. I remove the keys and tags, toss them into a recycling bin, and pocket the nice fobs for future use. I am not going to take their little racket sitting down and repeat that oft abused mantra that excuses all kinds of reckless, selfish behavior: *gotta break some eggs, baby, if you wanna make an omelet*. My traveler's diarrhea has passed, but I want to up the ante and make sure I get a full gut flush to clean out whatever was ailing me: I start my day at a grungy hole in the wall noodle shop, you know the kind, the cook hasn't changed his apron since he reached puberty and when you walk across the floor, there is that kind of sickening, sticky-tacky sound each time you lift your feet off the floor,

"Give me the biggest, baddest bowl of pulled noodles you got pal. Do I want it spicy? Oh yeah, the Sichuan special - extra on-fire please... And gimme a couple of hardboiled eggs while yer at it there buddy, that oughta do the trick."

As usual, another duh-leesh dish... Now it's St. Elsewhere, here I come. Long distance buses in China are now a pure pleasure to ride in: lots of them going every which way, cheap, comfortable, clean, air conditioned, we stop every two hours for a potty/smoking break and around noon, have lunch at a nice country-style, open air, roadside kitchen. I often get to meet some very interesting locals this way and if they are not talkative or I need a break, I crank up my Rhapsody Ibiza

32GB MP3 player and rock and roll my soul down the road. If the route is smooth enough, I get out my trusty Galaxy Tab and swype a chapter in *44 Days*.

As usual, the countryside is postcard picturesque and always culturally interesting. The nine-hour ride from Jiuzhaigou has its moments, as we continue to slide off the Tibetan Plateau and descend into swampy, sultry, subtropical Chengdu. We double back down through Songpan and from there it is all new territory for me. It is south of Songpan that I am first amazed, then shocked and eventually numbed to the point of banality at the extensiveness, audacity and cost of all the transportation infrastructure China is pushing forward. One to four kilometer long, four-lane tunnels are a dime a dozen. To traverse some of the most rugged territory on Earth, entire freeways, hundreds of kilometers' worth, are being built on towering, massive, concrete pedestals. To get from precipitous valley peak to the next, many of these four-lane concrete supports are as tall as sky scrapers and almost as big in girth. It's as if a master race of giants is building a roller blading park and wants a nice smooth, level mountain ride the whole way. At first I am gape jawed by the magnitude of these engineering marvels and I wear out the camera app on my Galaxy Tab. But for much of the rest of the trip through to Kunming in Yunnan, they are everywhere and I slowly calm down. Cynics might call these freakish freeways mere billion buck follies. But you have to understand that China is planning for the 21st century and the need to move around one-fifth of the world's souls, along with all the merchandise and materials they need for a middle class standard of living. In any case, they are all toll roads, so the government is getting back the cost of construction over the long haul; toll fees here are not cheap, being in line with the US and Europe.

In spite of the high cost, at least these elevated highways should at least theoretically have less of an environmental impact than dynamiting all the valley rises and laying the roads on the ground. At least I'd like to think so. On the Trans-Tibet railway, they did the same thing with the train track, for the expressed purpose of not disturbing the migration of local wildlife, especially the movement of wild yaks (*Bos grunniens*) and Tibetan antelopes (*Pantholops hodgsonii*), the latter also being called Chiru, or Zanglingyang (藏羚羊) in Chinese. This last species has been on CITES's endangered species list since 1979. Being so close to the Plateau, it is very possible that there are these species, as well as others that are being kept in mind during all this road construction. Where are some American Bison, when you need a few million of them?

But all these engineering marvels cannot change a human society completely in only one or two generations. We get about halfway into a long tunnel and traffic stops in its tracks. What is supposed to be a four-lane tunnel has been shunted into two for repairs. And predictably, some impatient driver lurches his vehicle into the oncoming lane to try to pass, getting a few meters ahead at the most and then having nowhere else to go into the oncoming lane of traffic. Now the whole kit and caboodle is chaos defined, with a thousand horns blaring, a thousand drivers and passengers getting out, standing and walking around to see what's going on, screaming, yelling, fists shaking, hands signing and all lighting up cigarettes. Pride is being impugned, egos are raging, tempers are boiling over - and this human Gordian knot is all echoing inside a tunnel so long you can't see the light at either end. Oh joy… Another day in paradise. This is not one of Chinese society's prouder 21st century moments, although this happened constantly on any and all roads in China in the 90s and still happens too much in big cities, albeit less than a generation ago. Road snafus were different back then. Beijing had 50,000 vehicles and 10,000,000 bikes. Just imagine New York, Paris or London, their streets filled with this many two wheelers and almost no cars, and you will have a feel for what it was like. Today, Beijing has five million vehicles and many fewer bicycles in use. In any case, no matter the country, give someone a gun, a vehicle or other symbol of power and control, and they can easily transform themselves for the worse, much worse, especially testosterone-on-the brain men. The tunnel's ventilation fans are not running, apparently because of all the repairs, but the overhead lights are on. Luckily, everybody has the good sense to finally turn off their motors. We might not have been so fortunate in 90s, just from a lack of experienced on the part of the driving public. After a good half hour of this cacophony and social madness, some traffic cops finally come trudging up on foot between the two snarled lanes of mayhem and slowly get all the pig headed, chest beating hicks (and yes they are all men) to calmly back down and finagle their cars and trucks back and forth, to eventually get the two lanes of traffic flowing again.

My question as to why traffic is being reduced to two lanes is answered when I begin to notice big billboards commemorating *Wenchuan 5.12* (汶川5.12). This is the name of the epicenter and the date honoring the sacrifice of everyone concerned from an earthquake that hit this region in 2008. Earthquakes in China are something akin to tornadoes in the Eastern US or floods in Bangladesh. They just kind of go together. By historical standards, Wenchuan was a biggie and still stands as the world's 20th worst quake of all time. What made it so devastating was not just that it topped out at Richter 8.0, but the epicenter was very shallow, only 20km below the Earth's surface.[1] It rumbled for two minutes, starting just northwest of Chengdu and cascading its death and destruction along a major fault line, the Longmenshan, for over 300km to the northeast. The nature of that fault line and its topography were destined to ensure the macabre: around the epicenter, the Tibetan Plateau lifted 3.5m straight up, sheared 3.5m north to south and lunged east onto the Sichuan Plain a staggering 4.8m – all at the same time. Even 300km away, up the fault line to the northeast, these three spatial movements each measured around two meters. Imagine lifting your house 2m straight up, half of it 2m to the north, the other half 2m to the south, and the whole property 2m to the east, all within 120 seconds, like a gigantic knight moving on a geological chessboard. Talk about redoing the kitchen and adding on a sunroom in the back.

The grim reaper had a hay day: 69,000 dead, 18,000 missing, 375,000 injured and 5-10 million left homeless. Homeless numbers caused by earthquakes tend to have large range estimations in China, depending on the source, since it is so difficult to cover so much ground with statisticians and there are so many people affected. Still, this pales in comparison to the world's second all-time biggest quake, Tangshan, outside of Beijing in 1976: a quarter of a million officially dead; nor the fifth biggest, the Indian Ocean Boxing Day rumbler that laid waste to 300,000 kindred souls in 2004.[2] In any event - a bad day in Sichuan all around if you ask me.

Natural disasters in China are political dynamite. The whole legitimacy of how the government and leadership respond can sustain or delegitimize a regime. Americans over the last generation have succumbed to the Tea Party treacle of, *Let the markets work their miracles*; the shameful, criminal aftermath of Hurricane Katrina was thus a guaranteed outcome. That will not fly here. Chinese leaders, be they emperors or the Communist Party's top governing body, the State Council, are thin skinned and painfully aware of their legacy in the annals of history books and their solemn duty to honor the Heavenly Mandate. How imperative is the Heavenly Mandate? In the 1400s, Ming Dynasty China's great explorer, Zheng He (郑和), who was an imposing 195cm tall, Hui Muslim eunuch - go figure, made seven voyages as far as the east coast of Africa, the Red Sea and Indonesia, a full 87 years *earlier* than Columbus's 1492 voyage to the New World. Zheng's flotillas included hundreds of ships. Several Chinese historical records, including the official Ming dynasty chronicle (明史= *mingshi*), indicate that the largest ones (treasure ships) had nine masts, weighed 1,500 tons, were more than 120m long, and could carry over 1,000 passengers each.[3] By contrast, Columbus' Santa Maria, a sturdy European ship of its day, was a diminutive 20m long and its pint sized 150 tons was leading a mighty armada of *two smaller* vessels. Columbus' boats may have been diminutive yachts by today's standards, but given their rapacious, extractive economic priorities, Columbus' Europeans changed the course of human events. Zheng He's leaders merely changed the course of Chinese history. Pondering these historical tendencies and the balance of the 21st century, this is some serious food for thought.

In the 15th century, with their invention of gunpowder, China already had proven-on-the-battlefield cannons, rocket-propelled arrows, bombs, and the triple barrel pole gun to fight against Europe's knights in shining armor. Europeans had access to gunpowder since the 14th century, transported back from China on the Silk Road, but were slow to lose their love affair with chivalry, pikemen and longbows. Two or three battles with China's salt peter powered armory would have undoubtedly changed the course of world history. The Chinese could have taken over the world. But the emperors of that day pulled the plug on all the potential wealth and conquest, and concentrated their efforts on successfully carrying out their Heavenly Mandate back home. Granted, the European colonial powers were exhausting their local natural resources and were on the prowl for fresh supplies, and continent scaled China was still able to prosper without so many imported commodities. But this is again an important and extraordinary testament to how different China's leaders' priorities are, compared to the ravenous, expansionist nature of European-American people. A quick glance at current events and this is still true today.

The bar has been raised even further since Mao Zedong found eternal retirement in his massive mausoleum at Tiananmen in Beijing (where he himself vicariously gazes over the whole affair via his huge, cherubic portrait hanging on the square's namesake gate). Mao was a man of amazing vision and a charismatic revolutionary, but as history has amply demonstrated, people who possess these qualities are often not the best day-to-day practitioners of statecraft (Fidel Castro being an exception). Hundreds of millions of Chinese suffered through two of the modern world's most catastrophic and cataclysmic social engineering projects ever attempted, the Great Leap Forward in the 50s and the Cultural Revolution in the 60s and 70s. Who knows how long this second madness would have continued, if not for Mao's death? The remaining leadership could finally pull the plug on the revolution's sociopolitical debauchery. As a result of these insane terrors, Chinese leaders post-Mao now have these twin millstones of historical misery weighing on their legacies as keepers of the Mandate, while playing the role of Oriental Herculeses, holding up the planet.

No Chinese leader worth their soy sauce would be caught dead pulling a George W. Bush, a scared little boy in Air Force One flying over the decimation and devastation of New Orleans and the Gulf after Hurricane Katrina, while looking out the plane's window, a detached, unfeeling psychopath. The definition of a psychopath is someone who knowingly causes pain, suffering and death, yet feels no emotions or remorse for the victims. Most political leaders and CEOs are psychopaths - they have to be. This is not controversial. Psychopaths by nature must compartmentalize their behavior to keep doing what they do best. Stalin was a doting, loving parent, as I'm sure Goldman Sachs' Blankfein and Obama are too. Stalin never witnessed the suffering he caused, nor do CEOs and politicians. They just sign orders, edicts, contracts and pass laws. All of us are prone to these same, self-protecting mental mechanisms. Myriad atrocities go on around us, but we shut them out, so that life can go on.

At least since Mao, every flood, earthquake or major accident is responded to post haste, literally boots on the ground (PLA troops) within hours and lots and lots of TV and print space are given over to local and provincial leaders, and as soon as they can get there, name brand Communist Party leaders arriving on the scene, surveying the damage, commiserating with the survivors and the bereaved. Given that many of Baba Beijing's top leadership are trained engineers, they can also talk shop and sound intelligent in front of the cameras about the practical needs and the next steps to take. Contrast this to George W. Bush exclaiming with an impish, college fraternity boy grin, while endorsing his incompetent party hack of a man to head the Federal Emergency Management Agency (FEMA), to take care of the Katrina disaster,

"You're doing a heck of job, Brownie!"

You remember that imminently qualified party hack, Michael D. "Brownie" Brown, who honed his disaster management skills as Judges and Stewards Commissioner for the International Arabian Horse Association – egad, as a native American, it's shameful and embarrassing. In the United States, this is now accepted as good governance, the height of care, concern and expertise. After Katrina, Firemen turned the hyenas of disaster capitalism loose to scavenge all the misery and suffering. Washington's Lords of the Loot sat back and fruitlessly waited for all those thousands of charities to fill the breech in New Orleans, services that used to be filled by effective government. The coalition government in the UK is waltzing through the same phony charade, slowly regressing back to Dickens' 19th century debtor's prisons and private charities as statecraft. Now compare Katrina to Wenchuan: Baba Beijing's response? They sent Sichuan thousands of soldiers, relief agents, trains and truckloads of medical supplies, equipment, shelters *and* to kick things off for a start, a cool one billion yuan (€125 million/$160 million. And as I can see all around me, Baba Beijing is still pumping billions more to get this region back to normal. Emperor Qin is looking over Baba's right shoulders and Mao's ghost is perched on their left.

But Wenchuan almost got the best of the Party's State Council. Seven thousand schools were destroyed during the earthquake and many schools are boarding schools in China, especially in the interior. Proud rural parents send their children to better institutions in larger cities, where they must reside, due to the long distances to get there. Wenchuan struck at 01:00 and thousands of children died in their sleep, the ultimate nightmare. The outrage was that so many died unnecessarily, due to the shoddy, illegal construction of the school buildings, which is a common refrain among the Chinese. I have some personal perspective on the shady side of construction. I remember working on the Cimarron Turnpike when I was going to Oklahoma State University back in the early 70s. Every week, we'd see the state highway inspector go into the road contractor chief foreman's office. The common understanding among all of us workers, including even our crew boss, was that he was paying a visit to pack his pocket with some filthy lucre, to make sure he did not pay too close attention to the wet concrete samples being brought into his state lab for QC inspection. OK, so society had to live with a few precocious pot holes and cracks in the cement. But innocent children just living their and their families' Chinese Dream for a brighter and better future and, being crushed like bugs in their beds? Not the same thing. Like any modern government, when the magnitude of the schoolhouse disasters could not be contained, the Communist Party leadership geared into well-oiled PR action. Hands were held and people were allowed to vent - *locally*. Important heads dutifully nodded and promises were made to investigate the scandal. The many thousands of bereaved parents were granted permission to circumvent the national one-child per family law, in order to have a second baby. But organized demonstrations and spontaneous protests were quickly quashed and Baba Beijing went into to high gear to suppress the spread of the details in the country's tightly orchestrated press. The use of cell phones, text messaging, email and the like were not nearly as widespread and sophisticated when Wenchuan struck. Still, the egregiousness of the scandal could not keep all this indignation from rapidly becoming common knowledge around the country. China already has the world's largest number of mobile phone users (over one billion) and only 1G (which most of rural China has, not 3G) is needed for scurrilous, sensational text messages to multiply by the millions in a matter of hours. But as long as the government could contain the outrage at the level of the afflicted, nobody in Beijing, Shanghai or Guangzhou is going to grab a banner and protest something that happened over 1,500 km away. This is especially true of an inland province, which all the coastal provincial citizens disdain and turn up their noses to in the first place. Modern communication did create a new vernacular for the Chinese language. Mobile phones were buzzing with the derisive *tofu-dregs schoolhouses* (豆腐渣校舍= *doufuzha jiaoshe*). This is a double insult to not only the corrupt quality of Chinese construction, but also how widespread the problem is. This is because everybody and their dead dog in China can make fermented tofu and the process always leaves a good quantity of watery dregs, which look and feel weak and mushy.

More and more scandals and corrupt practices are becoming nationally noticed, thanks to an ever savvier Chinese public armed with ten hot digits on hand held screens. Chinese is an incredibly efficient language and it only takes a few characters, sometimes only one, to speak volumes. The powers that be are learning to become politically and socially agile, very quickly: 21st century damage control, 24/7. Throughout the annals of history, the more things change, the more they stay the same. The expediency and money to be skimmed off of corrupt construction projects is a mercury vapor light for swarms of hungry parasites: they just can't keep from diving head first into that deep, dirty pot of money at the center of it all. Case in point: right behind where I work in Beijing is a huge three-story apartment complex going up. I've been watching for weeks in dumbfounded disappointment at how shoddily they are constructed. They will surely come crashing down like a house of cheap cards with the first Richter 6-7 quake. Many children will be asleep in those apartments every night at 01:00. The more things change…

We arrive at Chengdu late in the afternoon. I came here in the 90s and for *44 Days*, did not leave a big, oft air-polluted, oppressively hot and humid city of twenty million to take a vacation in a big, much polluted, sticky-hot, steam engine city of fourteen million. Yes, Chengdu, in the heartland of China, is famous for its fabulous ancient culture and traditional teahouses, but I have Tibetan tofu to fry. I buy a bus ticket for Kangding (康定= peaceful stability), back up on top of the Plateau, get a ¥50 (€6/$8) room in a serviceable *zhaodaisuo* right across the street, tuck into a some delicious Sichuan dishes and suck down a couple of well-deserved Panda brand brewskies. Oh, and another wonderful Chengduan cultural tradition that we can all pull up a chair for: being a shirt soaking, semi-tropical locale, beer is always served just this side of freezing. Ahhhhhhh………….. Cheers!

1- *To compare, the April 2011 Fukishima, Japan earthquake that brought down the Daiichi nuclear reactor was a 7.1 trembler. It is easy to forget that the Richter scale is logarithmic. Therefore, each* 0.1 *increase in measurement equals a* 102.92% *increase in earthquake strength. Thus, each whole number increase equals* 10 times *more earthquake power, two Richter numbers is* 100 times *stronger, etc.*

2- *Unofficially three times that many died in Tangshan, but Mao was still six weeks away from dying and public relations damage control was in high gear, vis-à-vis the shutout western world. All international aid was refused and who could blame China's puppet masters at the time? Their cultural revolutionary grim reaper of another sort was harvesting millions of tortured, imprisoned, beaten, raped, and killed citizens. And if you and your family were not personally effected by the insanity, he was happily ripping communities asunder, psychologically and physically destroying the health and wellbeing of an entire generation of Chinese- one-fourth of the world's people at the time... Oh, the joys of social engineering and planned political chaos.*

3- Ref: When China Rules the World: The End of the Western World and the Birth of a New Global Order, by Martin Jacques, www.martinjacques.com.

CHAPTER 27: CHENGDU - TAGONG

A modern day traveler's version of invading Tibet, on the road to Tagong; whiskey lunches, lepers and murderers beside a symbolic bridge; riding in a taxi with Han carpetbaggers, a PLA soldier, Granny T and her brood of Tibetan farmers; and more thoughts on Tibetan-Chinese relations into the 21st century.

Leaving pullulating, steamy Chengdu and heading back up to the Land of Snow is a great way to start the day. Back up to over 3km above sea level, back up to the remoteness, the isolation and the naked beauty of the Tibetan Plateau, where the air is so pure, so evanescent and the sky as translucent as Waterford crystal. Back to an emptiness which defies belief that so many of the planet's humans live in this colossal country. You don't just get on a motorized escalator and saunter effortlessly to Roof of the World. You've got to fight your way up and my samurai warrior today is an engaging and friendly Han Chengduan named Peng. His sword is of the round, dull kind - a loosey-goosey steering wheel; the war saddle a well-worn driver's seat; his stirrups are a worn clutch, bad brakes and a sticky accelerator pedal; his reigns are a cranky, grinding stick shift and his mighty steed is a long-ago, fully depreciated rust bucket of a bus that holds about twenty restless souls. Every upward and onwards Prince Peng.

Today's drive is empirical evidence as to why invading Tibet over the ages has happened only six times, since its inception as a modern kingdom in the 7th century: it's darn difficult to even get up here by bus on a *how-did-they-ever-build-that* road, never mind armies on foot carrying, supplies and weapons across deadly rivers and sheer valley walls. The readily accessible gates of Jerusalem have changed hands over forty times in its long history and surely will again. But Tibet is the tallest plateau on Earth and a very inhospitable place for the uninitiated. Each incursion is fascinating in its own right. The first assault was undertaken by 30,000 Mongol soldiers to wrest control of the kingdom and Genghis Khan's ever efficient statecraft that he created (he died in 1227) managed to stay there the longest so far, from 1236-1354. As in other areas the Khans conquered, religious freedom was assured and the locals were mostly left alone, as long as they paid their taxes and humble fealty to the Mongol state.[1]

From 1717-20, the nomadic steppe Zunghar people came down from the Turim Basin, in what is now Xinjiang and had fun terrorizing and slaughtering the locals in Lhasa. The reason was good old fashioned sectarian violence: they didn't like their brand of Tibetan Buddhism. Off with their heads! But like the Americans claiming victory in Afghanistan by nominally hanging on to the capital, Kabul, these swarthy sword swingers only had control of Lhasa and its surrounding narrow, east-west Yarlung Tsangpo River/Lhasa River Valley. Tibet is huge: the historical Kingdom of Tibet is 4,000,000km^2, about the size of the Eastern United States or Western Europe. You want to control a country this size, you have to be ready to put boots on the ground, which is what Genghis Khan's offspring did.

Tibet's southern border is the Earth's most Herculean Great Wall ever created - the Himalayas. The Nepalese Gurkhas managed to come down from these mountains to briefly occupy one Tibetan city, Shigatse, in 1791. While they were lousy occupiers, they proved their martial prowess by sacking and destroying the regal and fortress-like Tashilhunpo Monastery, which was then the seat of the Panchen Lamas (the spiritual leaders of Tibet). While the Gurkhas proved it is not militarily impregnable, Tashilhunpo is to this day one of the four great Gelugpa Buddhist Temples on the Plateau.

During the Sino-Sikh War, British Punjabis invaded in 1841, took over a few towns, but didn't last the winter. Like Hitler (1941), Napoleon (1812) and the Swedish psychopathic bloodmeister, King Charles XII before them (1708), who all gambled everything on the harsh realities of Siberia's winter weather, these Indians lost their fingers and toes to frostbite, were reduced to burning their gun stocks to stay warm and slowly starved to death. So much for the genius of military logistics and planning ahead, not to mention gift-wrapped Chinese schadenfreude with a ribbon on top.

The Chinese Qing Dynasty managed to rule Amdo and Kham (modern day Qinghai and Western Sichuan, respectively) in fits and starts during the 18th to 19th centuries, but the main prize, what is now modern day Tibet, was pretty much left to its own devices during that time. Thus, the Qing invasion was qualified at best. However, all was not well in Tibet at the time, with political and religious infighting, unforgiving feudal overlords, pandemic illiteracy, serfdom, slavery, extreme poverty, infrastructure and development straight out of the Middle Ages. When they marched into Tibet in 1950, this less than egalitarian, medieval way of life was a perfect context for the Communists to look like benevolent, modernizing saviors, and in many respects, they were.

Then, it was not until 1904, when the very British-named Colonel Francis Younghusband entered Lhasa, back before the days of modern WTO corporate colonialism, to force a trade treaty with the Top of the World. For the first time ever, a Chinese government (the Qing Dynasty) claimed sovereignty over Tibet and asked that the treaty go through them, although two treaties were signed, one Tibetan and one Chinese. But that first shot across the bow of Tibet's modern history and its dreams of independence would come back to haunt them 46 years later, as England and Russia solidified Han claims of sovereignty by signing a 1907 treaty with Baba Beijing, which recognized China's suzerainty over the Land of Snow.

Except for the medieval Mongols, none of these invaders controlled much of Tibet's territory, mostly just pockets, areas of influence and cities. But Mao Zedong knew his Chinese history well, especially when it concerned threats to the Heavenly Mandate, and all of Tibet's invasions fell into this category. They were surely not lost on the strategically minded Helmsman, when he decided to gobble up Tibet. It took the 20th century contrivances of trains and vehicles to finally make for a geographic equalizer, to be able to fully control the four corners of the Tibetan kingdom: from the long and strategically critical southern border with India, Nepal and Bhutan, to anchoring Xinjiang with Tibet's northern flank and unifying all of historical Tibet to the northeast in Qinghai and east to Sichuan. It was with these modes of modernity that Mao was able to make his move, to greatly expand the country's borders. He had already done the impossible by truly reunifying historical China for the first time in hundreds of years, thus fulfilling that part of his Heavenly Mandate. The Communists had already entered Muslim Xinjiang to the north of Tibet, in 1949 and Mao could not appear vacillating or weak.[2] It was time for his *pièce de resistance*: to make the newly minted People's Republic of China into a continent scaled behemoth, and that meant absorbing Buddhist Tibet. Between these two non-Chinese territories, Mao could increase the size of his country by *a third*. Pull off a feat like that and you've got the Heavenly Mandate on steroids. Not to mention becoming the third largest country in the world in land area, after only the USSR/Russia and Canada and just besting China's capitalist arch nemesis, the USA.[3]

Voilà, in October, 1950, one year after he stood atop Tiananmen Gate, waving to a million just liberated Beijingers, the Tibetan Plateau was flooded with four divisions - 40,000 of the finest from the People's *Liberation* Army, all battle hardened, revolutionarily inspired soldiers. This was 10,000 more troops than the Khans used to control the region 700 years earlier. They only had to get as far as Chamdo, just across the border from Sichuan and 1,000km from Lhasa, for the Tibetan leadership to experience their very own Sino-version of *Shock and Awe* and accept the obvious: they signed away their freedom in 1951 with the ignimonius *Seventeen Point Agreement*... All of this is fascinating history and food for thought, as our bus makes it out of Chengdu and heads towards to Tibetan Plateau. The Sichuan Plain is resplendent in wall to wall corn, rice and tobacco, with quaint, neatly manicured villages and hamlets dotting the landscape, as they fade into the humidity filled haze. The national G5 highway leaving Chengdu is a modern four-lane affair and we are moving fast to the southwest. Like yesterday's look at fabulous tunnels and skyways, on this toll road we go through a 4km tunnel, several 2km ones and across tens of elevated bridges. Impressive. About 100km out of Chengdu, we suddenly turn off due west at Ya'an (雅安= elegant peace) onto a two lane road that rapidly narrows. This is the G318, as it sinews into a river engorged valley towards the Tibetan Plateau. The section of the G318 from Tianquan (天全) to Luding (泸定) is the first valley, with the Qingyi River (青衣江) and from Luding to Kangding is the second. The second section is actually composed of numerous interconnecting valleys and river tributaries that feed into each other, as we ascend to the top of the Tibetan Plateau. The bridges and switchbacks are usually where we cross from one valley into another.

You don't climb almost three klicks in a very short time without getting to marvel at the Earth, its geography in full splendor and its crust totally exposed. This rapid rise from the Sichuan Plain below to the Tibetan Plateau on top is the massive wall of earth's crust that caused so much devastation and misery during the 2008 Wenchuan earthquake. It truly defies the scope of human scale that this gigantic cliff rise could move as much as it did, when this rumbler hit the area. As we start to work our way in and up, maybe I could envision it happening in a localized area. But a nearly 3km high gash that is 300km long doing that? The geological power of our planet loses me now and I'm feeling *swiftly* Lilliputian, as this plateau valley absorbs our tiny bus. The Qingyi River is impressive and majestic. The water is moving at a good clip, but is deep enough not to cause any cascades. I am looking at water from the glaciers of the Himalayas, as it eventually works its way down to the Yangtze River basin below, and further east, emptying into the waters of the Pacific Ocean. The agriculture starts at water's edge with fruit trees, rice and vegetables of all kinds, terracing up the valley walls, with deciduous forest trees above all this activity, up to the mountain tops. Villages, some quite big, hang onto the valley walls, occupying flattened areas just above the river shores. Every square centimeter of level land is producing something to eat. We cross the river at Daduhe (大渡河= Big Ferry River). This is where Emperor Kangxi built a bridge in 1706 linking Tibet to China. The Han Chinese still use, even today, this connection between the two territories as an arrow in their quiver of political unification. Further on, we pass a leprosy hospital, outside Ya'an. It is situated 5km away from the four lane G5 toll road, so they are not taking any chances, if not with the vastly overblown infectiousness of this ancient disease, then surely with the people's exaggerated fears. We also drive by a place called Sharengang (杀人岗= Murderer's Ridge). What happened here and who was involved? Undoubtedly, a great local yarn of a story can be found in this fanciful name.

At a fork where the Qingyi is being fed by a smaller river, we leave its broad river bed, to follow this tributary, lurching onto a seriously bad road, and the bus becomes a bucking bull rodeo ride. The sudden change in topography is dramatic; it is like entering a completely new biome. This deep, narrow valley has the feel of a Spielberg movie, a *Lost World*, a cinematic leap in time to another era. Am I in the rain forests of Africa, on Avatar's Pandora or in China? The walls are lush with tropical vegetation. Huge, thick jungle vines, towering bamboo forests with trunks as thick as your leg, banana trees and many other plants and bushes I have never seen before blanket the ever more precipitous walls, as this river draws in its width and shallows out into a roaring, violent, churning mass of energy. The local population lives in a series of hamlets that are ensconced in all the lush vegetation. They laugh mockingly at Newton's Law of Gravity and seem glued with sticky tack to the rugged cliff faces, almost suspended over the raging torrent below. I shudder to think what would happen to the people if an earthquake ever struck this sublime, surreal valley. At least death would come quickly. No one could last more than a few seconds in this kamikaze cascade, before being bludgeoned to death, ragdoll style, and dismembered to pieces against the numerous boulders that dot the river, a veritable Greek mythology obstacle course.

Ho hum, I'm getting spoiled on this journey. Just another mighty, massive mountain river crashing down from above. Everyone else is non plussed, as I'm sure they have taken this route a hundred times to go to Chengdu for shopping, doctor appointments, visiting relatives, stamping administrative paperwork and the like. I'm just taking it all in, with a subtle smile of satisfaction on my face, as we cross these raging rivers back and forth. Several times midway on the bridges or at switchbacks, the views of the valleys are simply magnificent. Hanging there, sometimes 100 to 200m above the roiling waters below, as we cross each bridge or switchback, we can look up and down the valley, and can fully appreciate the scale and magnitude of the amazing topography going up to the Tibetan Plateau, from river to mountaintop.

Why are there not more local hydroelectric stations on these powerful rivers? Even further downstream, where the Qingyi River was deep and wide, I did not see any electricity production. China is the world's largest producer of hydropower and derives 16% of its electrical demand from rivers. Currently, the country has 150 gigawatts of river power, with plans to expand this to 700GW. But apparently they prefer the grandiose kind, like the Three Gorges Dam and eschew smaller units to serve the people locally. It may be a question of efficiencies or scale of hydroelectric production, though later on during the journey, I will see one river in Guizhou with a series of small hydroelectric plants. Another shocker is the number of bicycling tourists who have been on this road since we started up the G318. Tens and tens of them, all Chinese, or at least Asian, pedaling and pumping away towards the top. They are in it for the long haul, with plenty of gear in saddle bags, front and back. There are a good number of women and they all look to be in their 20s-30s. They are traveling in small groups for a memorable summer vacation. They've got good mountain bikes, with three to four front gears and six to eight in the back, to tackle the severest of inclines, which they need on this road. They all wisely wear helmets, and most are sporting sunglasses and elastic biker face masks to help filter out all the dust on this narrow passage, giving them the look of roving bandits in training. Strangely, I see no toe straps on the pedals and some of them are even pumping away wearing flip-flops. The road is antediluvian, the traffic deadly and insane, yet here they are, two-wheeled ants weaving in and out of the way of all the buses, trucks and cars, and we are all just trying to get on and off the Plateau in one piece. The views are right out of National Geographic magazine or a Discovery explorer program, so I suspect the G318 is a popular launching point for touring bicyclists to ascend to the Plateau and spend time up there taking it all in slowly, while pitching tents at night. Not a bad summer in my books.

As usual, at lunchtime, we stop at an open air roadside restaurant in one of these cliff hugging bergs. Today's eatery is a communal collective of local cooks offering their protean selection of specially prepared dishes. One is selling spicy, stewed peeled potatoes. Others are hawking cooked veggies of all kinds, luscious varieties of meat dishes, stews, noodles, tofu products in their usual, every-which-way consistency and shape, alien looking mushrooms and the like. Still have a hole in your leg? A huge wooden barrel of sticky Sichuan white rice is available to all the diners in unlimited quantities. We are already at 1,500 MASL, so the weather is idyllic and in this narrow, harrowing valley, the sun is shining above, but not directly on us. The hamlet where we stop to eat has a narrow sidewalk with a country style open air food court full dining tables. Others are selling drinks in plastic bottles, grilled corn on the cob roasted on an open fire wok, along with fresh picked fruit for dessert. Juicy, tree ripe peaches, plums and pears are in season. Below us can be heard the roar of the raging river rushing ever downward. What more could you ask for?

During these stops, there is a sudden influx of diners, and being lunchtime, there can be other buses also converging onto the same food court. Thus, misanthropes struggle, since it is common to share group tables with total strangers. For my new found tablemate, this utopian lunch setting is not quite good enough, as it turns out. No sooner do we sit down that Mr. Jiang pulls out a bottle of whiskey from his coat pocket, cracks the seal, pours himself a half a glass of late morning reveille, smiles and offers me one. I politely decline, we start chatting and he downs round one over the course of about 27 seconds. With that eyebrow raising warm up, Mr. Jiang pours another stout one and starts tucking into his lunch, as I do. I'm going mainstream traditional today and get a big bowl of the spicy new potatoes along with a dish of stir fried sliced pork and spring onions in a white garlic sauce (*xiangsuanjiang* = 香蒜酱). I like the juxtaposition of our meals: my blue collar meat and potatoes to Jiang's whiskey as liquid lunch. Classic.

Mr. Jiang is a real local country boy and his thick Sichuan accent is off the charts, so beyond the twenty regular questions, we struggle to communicate, although he understands my Mandarin inflected Chinese no problem. Speakers of foreign languages learn to do a lot of polite, earnest nodding about right now, asking questions with newly heard words, sitting back and seeing what returns. Mr. Jiang finishes rock gut round two before getting through his first dish. Round three is set and ready to go. This guy is good, really good. And it's only 11:30. By the time we finish eating, and these roadside lunches are not very long, since the bus driver is always anxious to get back into the chaos and get home, Mr. Hard Core has just polished dry a 375ml bottle of you-can-barely-call-it Chinese whiskey. Wow… I suspect he will sleep well the rest of the trip, but I watch him and he never does. He does however, make a beeline out of the bus when we stop two hours later, and races to the toilets to take a leak.

The last half of this ever climbing, ever winding ascent to the top gets quite hair raising at times. The G318 has no shoulder and long sections of it turn into muck and rubble. It is here where I start to experience, and will continue to do so until I leave Sichuan, one rock slide after another, frustrating and at times stopping road traffic in its tracks, as we circumnavigate around all the road repair. Not only that, but there is often just a scanty guard rail along the river side of all this serpentining mess. The sheer drop to the valley floor is so deep in some places that we cannot even see the speeding river below us. Death would be assured to all if we slip or veer off this narrow strip of busted, bomb holed, blocked and cracked concrete. Not for the superstitious, nor the faint of heart. Hats off to Prince Peng. He never drives faster than 30 to 35kph, does an incredible job of navigating and negotiating all this entropy, keeps his cool and manages to get us safely up onto the Plateau in one piece, after almost eight hours of driving. Warrior Peng and I shake hands and I thank him for his outstanding service, with heartfelt sincerity. And to think he'll turn around and make the descent tomorrow, only to start the cycle over the day after tomorrow.

There is no bus all the way to Tagong. It's so isolated that it does not get that level of service. The terminus for today's bus is at Kangding. Kangding is a happening place, as it is perched on the edge of the Tibetan Plateau at 2,600m and is at a crossroad that connects it to Yunnan to the south, Tibet proper to the west, Qinghai to the north and of course Chengdu and Sichuan back to the east. Kangding is a pleasant enough Tibetan town, with a large Han Chinese presence. Essentially one very long main street, it is bustling with street buskers and vendors, restaurants and tens of stores selling all the household goods and accoutrements that China produces for export around the world. Tibetans are famous for their silver and gold jewelry. While I walk around sucking in through my nostrils the incredibly rare air of the Plateau, I watch a silversmith working an impressive ingot of the metal about as big as my index finger. A Tibetan woman anxiously looks on, as he straddles a small anvil, heats up, hammers and kneads her glittering bullion with various hand tools of the trade. Wish I could stick around to see what she is envisioning and what he is going to concoct, but Tagong awaits me. It is hard to believe we still have another kilometer of vertical ascent to get up there. What an amazing part of Planet Earth. I ask around and learn there are small buses, family vans really, that drive all over the Plateau where the larger lines can't afford to go. I make it to the downtown intersection where these vehicles congregate to fill up and take off for the four cardinal points on a compass. Of course as I start meeting drivers, they see my big wide eyes and nose and naturally assume I am prepared to pay for the ride like a taxi, all by myself (包车= *baoche*, guaranteed car). Talking to them, I quickly learn the word for *carpool* (拼车= *pinche*) and they are all surprised I'm prepared to press the flesh with their Tibetan brethren. Heck yeah. I hook up with a Tibetan named Zhaxi, who lives in Tagong (塔公= pagoda public) and is making his last trip of the day, over a hundred klicks to the north. We wait around as he barks and calls out in Chinese and Tibetan,

"Tagong! Lhagang!"

We get about half full and now he starts to prowl up and down the main road, doing a mobile version of the same routine. We finally get the van packed to the gills, luggage and humanity intertwined like a tapestry, with overflow baggage piled high on the roof rack. We are a total of eleven persons for a six-person combi van, plus enough baggage to open a Marrakesh bazaar. Having silver hair and letting everyone know I'm a professor is a wonderful passport of convenience during my travels, and often affords me *most favored seating status*, but my hopes of getting to ride shotgun are dashed, since one of the passengers is a crumpled up, crippled old Tibetan woman older than Mrs. Methuselah. She looks tired beyond her centuries, confused and ready to pack it in. She is using a pair of crutches you would swear were brought here on the Silk Road, back when Alexander the Great was slaughtering Persians, like so many soulless Myrmidons. I just can't compete against a wizened, withered woman on crutches who looks like she kept a diary during the Qing occupation of Kham. I of course offer her the front seat and pile in with the rest of her brood in the back. One big happy family. In the back seat are three Tibetan adults and two small children, all scions of Granny Tibet up front, and all resplendently dressed in Tibetan attire, with crimson tunics, multicolored smocks and head scarves. There is a quiet young man crouched on the floor between Zhaxi and Granny T and sitting next to me are a mother and her four year old boy. As we get started, I learn from the Tibetans that they are farmers out of Tagong and went to Kangding for the day to run errands. They are extremely nice and utterly fascinated to be in contact with a foreigner. It is not impossible that I'm the first one they've ever talked to directly. The first one to get off is the young man, as we pull up to a military compound at a small hamlet called Danzixiang. Composed entirely of big camouflaged tents, it looks to be about battalion sized, to house five hundred or so soldiers. This taciturn, proud young recruit has his PLA issued backpack, day pack and two big red duffle bags; his whole life is wrapped up in these belongings. A couple of his crew cut army buddies come out from behind the high, hog wire fence, smiling warmly to greet and help him with his gear. The Tiananmen Tank Man aside, whose life was spared, I shiver knowing that given the order, these teenagers would unfeelingly kill every one of us on this bus. *Vive la revolution.* One thing is for sure, being in western Sichuan, they are not here to protect the Tibetans from Punjabi Indians. The whole place looks brand spanking new, so I have to ask myself if any outbreak or protest took place around here recently. I'm not about to ask anyone for fear of getting an errant citizen of China in trouble with omnipresent Baba Beijing, but it's a very plausible hypothesis. As I get back in the now slightly less compressed combi, I look at the five Tibetans in the back seat and ponder what is going through their minds, as they gaze out across this show of Han military might right in their back yard.

The lady and her pre-school age son next to me are from Hunan, celebrated for being Mr. Mao Zedong's birthplace and renowned for some of the spiciest, flame throwing food on the face of the Earth. They must be from the southern part of that province, since their accent is very much in the mold of Guangdongese (Cantonese). They moved to Tagong three years ago and Ms. Ke and her husband work for the state electric company. They install power lines in the area, anchoring poles, constructing pylons, climbing up and installing roll after roll of high tension cables. Ms. Ke tells me they love living here, the air and environment are pristine and the work is steady. I ask about her son's education and she proudly beams that he is learning both Mandarin and Tibetan, but she and her husband have only learned a few words of the local language at best and speak Mandarin with everyone. They are coming back from Hunan, where she took her son for a vacation to see the grandparents and their *laojia* (老家= ancestral home). I'm sitting here between two cultures, two opposing philosophies and outlooks on what it means to be happy. The five traditional Tibetans and Granny T speak broken Mandarin and climbing up on high tension power pylons is not their cup of tea. Their idea of success is not material and money, but spiritual and metaphysical. They are farmers, raising their Alpine barley, potatoes, yaks and sheep, go to the temple, spin the prayer, or Mani wheels, working their rosaries and chanting their mantras - and this is a good life, enough of a life, a fulfilling life for them. They are listening to me talking to this Han woman and I can't help but think, yes Ms. Ke and all the Han coming here to seek their fortune are highland carpetbaggers, but I suspect the vast majority of the local Tibetans don't see the benefit of working for the electric company. Han Chinese are all about the material and money: buy-buy-buy, acquiring *Stuff* and living the good life, their Americanesque version of success via ownership and possessions. But, if it weren't for these lowland opportunists, the hostel I am going to stay in tonight probably wouldn't have electricity and the restaurant would be without heat. This cognitive dissonance about our human existence gives me pause, as China hurtles at breakneck speed into the 21st century.

Much like many other cultural and economic clashes throughout history, with the European settlers vs. Native Americans at the tip of my tongue, life will go on here. More and more Han will keep moving onto the Tibetan Plateau and Baba Beijing will continue to pump billions into Tibet's betterment, to the tune of 93% of Tibet's revenue, which is fueling a provincial GDP growth that is even outstripping the country's white hot rate - 12.8% since 1994, compared to 10% for the country as a whole. Infrastructure will be modernized and the quality of life as measured by international and Chinese agencies will improve.[4] Children will be educated, diseases will diminish and illnesses will be cured. And the Tibetans, who have survived here for ages in the harshest and humblest of conditions, mostly alone, will adapt and seethe with frustration and rage at what they surely perceive as a sacrilege to their spirituality, even though they are materially benefitting from it all.

The Tibetans can count themselves lucky. Unlike countless other cultures and peoples throughout history, at least the Chinese have not exterminated them and simply stolen their land. We can go back to the Old Testament for starters. If the tribe was not unceremoniously decimated, about the best that could be hoped for, for many peoples was to have the men folk all killed, the women kept as concubines and the children forced into slavery. Such is humanity through much of world history. European colonialism is at the top of the list and the US slaughter of Native Americans together complete my ancestral gallery of shame. For better or for worse, the Han have controlled all of Tibet for half the time the Mongols lasted in the 13th century, and I see them breaking that long standing record in another 60 years. They are never leaving the Land of Snow and they are trying to make their paradigm of progress and development be of help to the local people here, howls of sanctimonious Western protest and an exiled Dalai Lama aside. One way or another, the Tibetans are going to have to reconcile themselves with this 21st century certainty. And the Han will also learn a bitter lesson from the Tibetans, as they race to the top of the world's economic slag pile: all those cars, cameras, clothes, computers, gadgets, gear, games, jewelry, junk, junk and more junk to heap in their houses will bring their culture and country to the same state of social psychosis and spiritual vacuousness that many mega-materialist Americans find themselves in. A life of Stuff has no future, no fulfillment and is the antithesis of freedom. The Han will learn, as Mother Earth's planetary ecosystem collapses on top of them later this century, that Stuff is in fact a life of slavery and bondage, and the truly liberated people in China are the Tibetans, bathed in a sea of transcendental timelessness. It is one of the great conundrums of the human condition: we want it *all*. We want our cake, *baby*, and to eat it too. Yet we waste so much valuable energy futilely trying to ram this square peg of self-indulgence into the round hole of reality. Remember Reinhold Niebuhr's Serenity Prayer?

God, grant me the serenity to accept the things I cannot change,
The courage to change the things I can,
And the wisdom to know the difference.

Tibetans have much to teach their lowland brethren about the emptiness of Stuff, the loneliness of endless acquisition and the naked, pure joy of just *being*. Tibetans and Han, with their titanic clashing of cultures and spiritual vs. material ways of life, would both be wise to memorize and apply Niebuhr's most elegant of sage advice.

1- Genghis Khan and the Making of the Modern World *(2004), by Jack Weatherford, is must reading for anyone interested in Asian, European and Chinese history.*

2- *Muslim militias continued to fight the Communists and Xinjiang was not fully secured until 1955, at which time Baba Beijing named it an autonomous region of China.*

3- *If all of the US's water surface areas are added (mainly the Great Lakes), America just beats out China for 3rd place.*

4- *english.people.com.cn/90001/90776/90785/6613303.html*

Chapter 28: Tagong

Hanging out with Tagong Sally, Basan, Sanglou and Mama Ala on the Tibetan Plateau at 100m higher than Lhasa – the pitfalls of blended families, fighting with a pack of feral canines on Mad Dog Hill, inching my way up the precipitous, sacred Mount Jinire and crossing an ocean of wind horses, while laughing at death in the face.

Granny T and her brood were dropped off at their farm 20km or so outside Tagong, so Ms. Ke, her son and I pile out of Zhaxi's combi, where he stops at Tagong Town's main central square. I get Zhaxi's phone number for the return trip to Kangding the day after tomorrow. My hostel is nestled right next to the Tagong Monastery, which imposingly occupies the whole north side of the square. Sally, the public face of the Snowland Guesthouse, gives me a gracious and friendly welcome. She knew I was coming, as we have been in contact by Chinese text messages. She shows me a single room on top of the roof looking out the back, towards an impressive, Buddhist festooned mountain, a huge precipitous hill actually. It will play a central role in my visit here, before all is said and done. Sally mulls over how much to charge me, hums, rolls her beautiful Tibetan brown eyes behind her professorial looking, black framed glasses, and comes up with the princely sum of 30 kuai (€3.80/$4.80) a night. Gotta play my part. I feign fiscal consternation and reluctantly accept. Secretly, I think I can live with that. It has been a long day on the road, so I decide to just hang out at the hostel, reconnoiter and plan out my time in Tagong. Snowland has a nice Tibetan flavored restaurant on the ground floor that functions as its grand central station for guests to hang out, in traditional youth hostel fashion. When I sit down, a very majestic and regal looking older woman, in her everyday Tibetan garb, comes out to greet me from behind the large curtain that serves as the kitchen's saloon door. Ala beams a surprised and very humanitarian smile when I start speaking in Mandarin and for an older Tibetan, I am equally pleased at how good and Beijing accented is hers. Needless to say, we make friends on the spot and Mama Ala takes very good care of me over the next two days. The restaurant is classic backpacker. The walls are garlanded with amateur drawn menus and notices, multitudes of scribbled trekker notes, suggestions for local outings, dusty and fly specked maps, faded photos of clients in triumphant poses during memorable hikes and small trinkets and souvenirs to enchant, tempt and leaven the imaginations and fantasies of us future trekkers around Tagong.

I order a Tibetan style bowl of noodles, with veggies and yak meat, am still hungry and get the local version of a *what's left in the kitchen* crêpe, with scrambled eggs. Very tasty. Then like out of a mirage, rarely seen foreigners start to trickle in for dinner. I have been mostly all alone in the *dabizi* department on this journey, so it is strange to be this far out in the countryside in this small restaurant with westerners. The last time I saw this many *waiguoren* was at Charley Johng's hostel in Dunhuang, Gansu. True to the new China, there is a big table of Han who are staying at Snowland, and all together, with another smaller group of Chinese, they outnumber us. There is one solo American guy, a group of three South Africans, two (unrelated) Dutch families and a blended US-Singapore family with their young son in tow, as well as their American in-laws. Along with the impressive Chinese delegation, it is making for a really nice cosmopolitan feel. I visit with all of the *laowai* except the solo Yankee, who is preoccupied with his guidebook. As is often the case in situations like this, the restaurant informally divides along linguistic lines, with the large Chinese contingency on one side and the English speakers on the other.

It is impressive to learn that the two Dutch families are visiting Tagong for a *second* time. They just love it here, the tranquility, and the sparsely populated, surreal Tibetan Plateau, with its crystal cerulean dome that kisses your soul every step of the way. They could go anywhere in this continent sized country of over 50 cultures and four millennia of history, and they choose to come back to Sally's quaint little hostel and chillax for a couple of weeks. That is saying something about the visceral, spiritual pull that Tibet's 3km high plateau offers, in contrast to the hectic, *consume more stuff* culture that westerners want to escape, at least for a little while, to put life and their existence on this Pale Blue Dot in proper perspective. You can juxtapose this place against the mightiest skyline, the most sophisticated architectural and engineering wonders humankind has ever concocted, and words like *majestic, sublime, transcendent* and *unparalleled* grace the Tibetan Plateau, its people and culture over the former. There seems to be an infinite nothingness, as I travel across the cavernous countryside of this cosmic-high plateau, with its Spartan ascetics, humble hospitality and galactic sky. But alas, everything *is* here.

Tomorrow morning I look forward to joining in the spiritual fray of the plateau's fulfilling nothingness. Everybody in the Snowland restaurant seems in fine spirits after a gratifying day of hiking and exploring Tagong. Except the blended Singaporean-American family. Maybe they are all just having a bad day, but I doubt it - it's all so visceral. Their handycam reality TV show is just too, well, *real.* As a husband and a father, my heart goes out to them, as they seem truly miserable, down to their bone marrow. The husband speaks good Mandarin, is trying to keep things patched up and the pressure of having U.S. mom and dad tagging along must be excruciating, what with all the pretenses and face saving needed in this public setting. All of the anguish is suppurating out of their relationship, probably a marriage of regretful remorse, and is being poured into their young child. It sure shows. Being a grade school teacher, I can see right off that he is a first class mess. As the evening winds down, I have a chance to visit with the husband, who explains that their child has separation anxiety with his mom. This may explain why she keeps disappearing from the restaurant, either to try to break him of his condition or simply to have a few minutes of sanity and respite. The in-laws carefully keep to script, acting the roles of meddling temple Mandarins in their own real life tragedy, which is being played out on this sky high Tibetan stage. They stiffly extol the virtues of their son's marriage, the heavenly sainthood of their daughter-in-law and the fine future that beholds the pride of their son's loins. Coming from upper crust Connecticut, these New England blueblood patricians play their stoic parts to perfection. Where's Oscar when you need him? I indulgently bow, curtsy, wryly smile and extend my plebian hand to shake, all the while keeping a corner of my eye on their stage mates, as they silently destroy each other.

As a partner in a culturally blended marriage, I understand the added challenges this couple is facing. It sounds easy, but you do not just marry the person, you marry the culture, history and society of your spouse too. It has its award winning synergies, the sashimi goulashes and chocolate barbeques of daily life and love, but also its obvious pitfalls. Two cultural ships passing in the night or as is often the case, a pair of titanic expectations colliding in societal flames of misunderstanding and acrimony. A blended marriage can also be especially rewarding and very tetchy, when it comes to raising children - centuries of inculcated, parental memes just waiting to be passed onto the next generation, and often in direct conflict with your partner's preconceived ambitions. When the two teachings meld or co-exist, it opens up horizons that are the envy of their peers. But when the opposite happens, and the parents are willing to go to the mat to assure that their national pedagogy prevails, then the children can quickly become caught in the grizzly familial middle. So, that could be a big part of the problem for this mixed couple. They may be crashing down the abyss of a cultural chasm.

The next morning, I meet brothers Basan and Sanglou, along with Ala at breakfast, and quickly learn that Ala really is the mother of this operation. Sally and these two strapping men are her three children. All of them are gems, well adapted to their jobs of running this hostel in the middle of nowhere and taking good care of their guests. Sally is the big sis, which in Chinese culture has added significance. Dating back to the writings of Confucius, *dagege* (大哥哥- big brother) and *dajiejie* (大姐姐- big sister) are expected to assure that the male line's family name is passed onto the next generation, loyally supporting the parents in every way and helping assure that the younger siblings do their part to maintain harmony and balance in the nuclear family.[1] Big bro and sis are expected to play the role of family majordomos, as it were, keeping the brood together through thick and thin. With Confucian culture permeating across Asian peoples, this is true in other regional cultures, including Tibetan society.[2]

The Snowland gang all speak excellent Mandarin and good hostel English. Their place is nice and comfy. They try hard to cater to foreigners' needs. On the menu it clearly states they take requests for no/low hot pepper, MSG and salt, dishes flavored to your tastes, etc. Before leaving, I can see why people come back, even halfway around the world, and choose to stay here. Snowland does have competition. Right next door is an American woman and her Tibetan husband with a big hostel and there is another one across the main square catering to international tourists. Around Tagong, there are many more *zhaodaisuo* that scout more economy and locally minded clients, although how much cheaper they can get than ¥30 per night is beyond me. Tagong is getting more popular: Sally's American neighbor is adding a wing to her hostel, which unfortunately partially blocks the view of Snowland, when looking from Tagong's main town square. Ditto the Tibetan shopkeepers and restaurant owners, who for the most part, speak good Mandarin, whereas many other highlanders, especially rural people don't, or at least choose not to. But one thing I've learned in all my years of traveling around the world: commerce is commerce and customers are customers. Local traditions can fade to gray when it comes to getting clients' money, especially visiting ones.

After a nice breakfast of scrambled eggs and a decent cup of strong black coffee, Ala recommends that I go see Zhoumogongban, off to the northeast, on the road towards Qinghai. She tells me this place is several kilometers away and excellent for hiking. I cannot find it on Google maps, in Pinyin nor in Chinese; named geographical landmarks is one of this wonderful application's biggest deficiencies. With only a four character name to go on, I step outside and take off for the day to explore Tagong. Wow, what an initial rush… The sky is so limpid, I can see all the way back to the Big Bang. I swear, if I looked in the right direction, I could see the Andromeda Galaxy in broad daylight. However, as Tibetan towns go, outside of its monastery, Tagong is not terribly interesting: its dirty, poorly maintained streets are lined with repetitious shops, restaurants and silversmiths. No, people come here to hike all over kingdom come. I venture north up the two lane road that brought me here yesterday. After about 1.5km, there is a huge, sterile looking new temple with high walls obscuring the view of everything inside. It does not appear to be open to the public. Its name is *Muyajin* (木雅金= Wood Elegant Gold). Outside, a good one hundred real live, yak herding Tibetan cowboys, cowgirls and all their horses are having a hootenanny of some kind; they are all milling around or standing in small groups, talking and enjoying the beautiful summer day. One big group of about twenty is sitting in a circle, having a picnic, with sacks and pots full of food in the center, all being passed around among the gabfest. They are having a grand old time and it is a lot of fun to watch. They seem to be taking my *laowai* presence in stride by totally ignoring me. This is impressive, since in similar situations, a lone foreigner in a crowd in China can cause a commotion, especially in more isolated and rural areas. I will notice this nonchalance towards me is the norm during the rest of my journey deep on the Tibetan Plateau, compared to other areas of China. I can't help but think it is due to Tibetans' prioritizing the spiritual over the material in all aspects of their lives, and I don't think my big white nose counts in the metaphysical department. I ask several of them how to get to Ala's Zhoumogongban, even approaching a couple of Han Chinese to be sure of the Mandarin characters, and nobody has ever heard of it. All I can figure is it must be the range of tall, grass covered mountains further on, about 5km away. Pretty they are indeed, but given all the uncertainty, I am not going to go off on a wild *vulture* chase. Instead, Mt. Jinire towering imposingly above Tagong, the one I can see from my hostel window and festooned with Buddhist regalia, definitely looks enchanting, so I decide to head back towards town.[3] On the way, I run into a group of ten Austrians for a quick chat. I keep smiling at the thought that I am in a virtual *end of the line* locale, yet I'm seeing more *waiguoren* here than any other place on my journey. Bizarre…

On the east side of Tagong, opposite to Mt. Jinire, is a low and elongated hill perched right above the center of town, so I decide to take in the view from there first. It will help me put Mt. Jinire in perspective and give me a chance to see what I am about to tackle. There is a small hand painted sign asking to pay 10 RMB (€1.30/$1.60) for the pleasure, but no one is there to take my money, so I keep climbing up the path. Up on top is one anchored end of a very impressive multicolored banner that stretches low, maybe 50m over Tagong and runs across the river valley to the west side, sagging down from its weight right above the town square. The total length must be a good 300m. It is about 1.5m tall and stretched between the two very thick, parallel steel cables are swaths of vertically vented, colored silk cloth: red, yellow, green, blue, white and orange. These colors, with Tibetans prayers and images of the mythical flying wind horse (like in Langmusi) or lotus-sitting Buddha, continually adorn Tibet wherever I go.[4]

Wind horse flags depict a usually winged horse in the center surrounded by written mantras and prayers, with an animal in each corner to represent the cardinal points: a mythical Tiger, Snow Lion, Garuda and Dragon. The wind horse is to carry these prayers and mantras to the four corners of the firmament. These texts ask for health, longevity, wealth, wisdom and power. And true to their name, with the wind, the vents shimmer hypnotically the full length of the valley wide banner. It is really mesmerizing to watch and hear the breeze coursing through its whole length, fluttering with the sound of birds' wings, and its the variegated colors flickering like tropical feathers in the bright Tibetan sky light.

Where this extended banner is attached over on the Mt. Jinire side, there are two large collections of vertical poles haphazardly planted into the ground and draped with larger versions of the same kaleidoscopic, tantric wind horses. These two bunches of poles are shaped like nearly equilateral triangles. Using my binoculars, I scan the valley and see other, thinner and lighter versions of this massive, cabled wind horse display. They too stretch across the river, all with the same variegated color scheme. It is almost as if Tibetans can't fly their own national or provincial flag, so these rainbow wind horses serve as an admirable and subversive substitute in the face of political censorship. On the side of Mt. Jinire itself is another huge triangle shaped forest of tall banner wind horses, with two smaller ones sitting above its apex, left and right. In between the two smaller triangles and perched on the point of the big triangle's peak is a large phrase in Tibetan, laid out on the ground, made with broad sheets of white silk cloth.[5] Above it all is the outline of a barely visible triangular wind horse forest. This is the newest addition to Mt. Jinire being installed by Tagong's faithful. Together, these four triangles take up most of Mt. Jinire's east face, nobly gazing down on Tagong's citizens below. Encircling this quartet of bannered forests is a low lying contiguous, rectangular fence, which appears to be made out of long rolls of the same colored silk material. Inside this silk fence, I can even see some other faint, inchoate, smaller triangle forests that have been started at the summit, disappearing over the mountaintop crest. Spotting the small silhouettes of several pilgrims high up, busily walking around on the face of Mt. Jinire, I confidently tell myself that it should be a cinch to climb to the top, since the mountain's vertical height is only about 300m up from Tagong and its river below. Wow, that would be right at 4,000m above sea-level Beijing. While scanning the valley, I fail to trace out my path to get from here, across Tagong and the river, to the base of Mt. Jinire. This omission comes back to bite me a little later in the morning.

Out of the corner of my eye, I suddenly notice a very old Tibetan monk, blazing in his vermillion tunic and shiny, bald head. We wave to each other and trade friendly hellos. He is right under the big concrete rampart that is holding up this side of the overhead town banner. Sitting in the full lotus position, fingers clacking away on his wood rosary and meditating, I err on the side of cultural sensitivity and opt not to bother him with questions and chit chat. But who needs cross cultural, human interaction right about now? I suddenly have to prepare myself for a more visceral, atavistic sport. It's called survival, so let the games begin. Three feral dogs come charging over the rise of the hill from the opposite side straight for me, viciously barking and snarling, with menacing canines exposed and mal intent. I have been in this situation many times in my life's journeys, so I instinctively go into my standard *surviving-a-dog-attack* pose, by not backing down, arms stretched above my head and moving them slowly in an up and down fanning motion.[6] Never taking my eyes off of them, I scream and yell at the top of my lungs and keep my mouth open, imitating a growl as much as possible. I am now an antediluvian animal, an Australopithecine, and for the next few minutes my instinctive reptile brain, the medulla and cerebellum take control of my being: fight or flight? I know from experience that *fight* is the only recourse. Only 15,000 years ago, these domesticated carnivores were *Canis lupis* - wild wolves, so in order to survive an attack like this, you have to think like one. Out of the corner of my eye, I see a one meter long stick broken off from a tree branch. It is thin and scrawny, but will have to do. I slowly squat down, screaming, grimacing and waving my hands all the time, and then quickly pick up the stick. Three ill-humored dogs to one of me and this is all I need to equalize the battle. Now insensate and armed like a crazed caveman making his last stand, I hold the stick high above my head, charging at these canine miscreants, swinging my stick at them in musketeer sword fashion, and screaming like a bloodlust banshee all the way. They back off five meters and regroup. While they communicate to make their next move, I see some small rocks, snatch one and throw it at them. I miss hitting them, but they get the idea. I have an opposable thumb and they don't. The game's up and they slowly run back over the hilltop from whence they came, saving face with a pitiful, final barking retort. Victory. Survival has never tasted so sweet, at least as far as this trip is concerned. As my lizard brain rapidly gives way to its more evolved parts, I pause to catch my breath and senses. You would have thought the lotus monk would have reacted in some way, or at least enjoyed the show, but nooooo. Deep in meditation, rosary and chants, he never turns around and keeps laser focused on his saintly ritual, overlooking Tagong's public plaza below.

The hair is still instinctively raised all over my body. I reflexively put two nice sized rocks in my back pockets and keep my joke of a dog killer stick, just in case I come across any rear guard action, as I go back down the hill.[7] I take one last look from the east side of Tagong, before heading across the river to Mt. Jinire. It is a spectacular vista. Tagong sits in a narrowing of this broad plateau valley that is graced with sparsely tree-, grass- and rock-covered mountains. They jut 200-500m above the wide, shallow, fast moving river that cuts through here and runs the length of Tagong. The crown jewel of it all is Mt. Jinire, silently welcoming me from across town. On my way to Mt. Jinire, I cross the main square where Snowland is situated right outside the big Tagong Monastery. Behind the monastery is a large, enclosed sanctuary area, about 150 meters long, in an oblique, rectangular shape. Facing out from the long east-west sanctuary walls are tens of Buddhist brass Mani wheels, which are housed in open sided sheds their entire length. They spin on vertical wood, metal or stone spindles and are mounted on both ends in leather, bone or coarse cotton. These Mani wheels can be as tall and round as an oil barrel, or small enough to sit atop a carved handle, no bigger than a small soup can. Mani wheels are often embossed on their metallic exterior with the mantra *Om Mani Padme Hum*. In its general sense, it means *jewel of the lotus flower*, which is the sacred plant of Buddha. Broken down into its six individual syllables though, and the mantra's meaning becomes much more profound and sacred. As the faithful walk past each wheel and spin it with their hand, their spoken mantra is doubly amplified and means,

Syllable	Six Perfections	Purifies
Om	Generosity	Pride / Ego
Ma	Ethics	Jealousy / Lust for entertainment
Ni	Patience	Passion / Desire
Pad	Diligence	Ignorance / Prejudice
Me	Renunciation	Poverty / Possessiveness
Hum	Wisdom	Aggression / Hatred

This ubiquitous liturgy says worlds about Tibetans' outlook on their life and place on Earth. Clearly for Tibetans, the material is out, the spiritual is in and their way of life reflects this profound, peaceful philosophy. Now that my brain is normally functioning again, after the canine attack on what I now call *Mad Dog Hill*, I recall seeing about a hundred small stupas haphazardly and randomly built inside this hidden inner garden. The central one towers over the level of the sanctuary walls and is gold crested and regal. What were once in pre-Buddhist times tomb markers, have evolved over the centuries into highly stylized symbols of the Buddha himself. The white pentagonal stupas that dot China's spiritual landscape represent the great prophet sitting in meditation. His crown is the top of the (often gilded) spire, his head is the square underneath the spire's base, the vase shape is his body, the lower terrace's four steps represent his legs and the base is his lionesque throne.[8]

On the exterior of the north end of the sanctuary garden is a coarse, slate rock stele with many slabs of engraved stones, vertically piled high beside it. Each one is etched with Tibetan sayings from their sacred texts, like the 8th century *Book of the Dead*. This worldwide classic is a guidebook for believers on how to prepare for death, the act of dying, the rituals to go with it, and what consciousness to expect during the forty-nine days between leaving this material word and then rebirth, or reincarnation into the next cycle of life. Also known by its Tibetan name, *Bardo Thodol*, it is divided into three sections, each one dedicated to the various stages of transcendence. It offers comfort and reassurance to many millions of Buddhists around the planet and has even made it into popular western culture: The Beatles' *Tomorrow Never Knows*, the *final* song (get it?) on the *Revolver* album, is inspired by the Bardo Thodol. John Lennon couldn't find any Buddhists monks in 1966 London to chant on the song. So their producer, George Martin, piped John's voice through a Leslie Box to give it a warbling effect, and added some sitar licks, in hopes of mimicking a Tibetan temple's ambiance. Close enough of a sound for the uninitiated and a great song indeed. Maybe I'll have the best of both worlds, western and eastern, and play this tune on my death bed.

Solo, in pairs, groups of four and more, Tagong's citizens are doing the circuit of walking along this walled sanctuary, spinning the huge, brass Mani wheels by hand, all the while chanting, singing and meditating. There are benches along the stretch for worshipers to stop, rest and meditate. And who do I see, but Mama Ala. We both beam warm, friendly smiles at each other at this unexpected encounter. She is with a waifish, wrinkled old woman who is sitting on a bench, catching her ancient breath. Ala is actually doing taichi stretches to keep her aging body nimble. She proudly claims me and explains in Tibetan our association to her ancient friend, who is totally nonplussed. After moving on, I realize this older woman may be Ala's mother and thus Sally's grandmother.

Following the Mani wheel circuit, I make my way back to the town square, peering between the rows of houses towards the river and Mt. Jinire, which is imposingly planted right on the other side of the water, looking for a way across. I was careless when I was on Mad Dog Hill and didn't think to look for a crossing. Then again, maybe I did and am in a fever of adrenaline infused, canine attack amnesia. The river is not deep but fast moving and wide, and I'm not wild about trying to wade across its glacial, freezing waters. Where does everybody cross? I ask every 100m or so and keep getting shunted to the south, past the town plaza and onto the main street where all the shops are. At this point, I walk back to the banks of the river and notice for the first time it has a pretty sharp bend towards the west, as it wraps itself around the base of Mt. Jinire. I follow the river's contours and off in the distance, see a low lying bridge that traverses its waters. I make my way through the residential neighborhood that lines the river, with huge two-story Tibetan style stone homes, low perimeter walls and all in a state of continual architectural birth, destruction and rebirth, just like in Xiahe and Langmusi.

The walk up Mt. Jinire starts off innocently enough and after my mighty hikes in Langmusi, this place seems like a bunny slope. I foolishly jettisoned my dog killer stick back in town, a careless act of chutzpah that I will come to rue very shortly. I enter Jinire's huge triangular forest of tall wind horse poles. Even though I am blessed with superannuated lung capacity, Tagong still sits 100m higher than Lhasa, the Tibetan capital and I'm adding to this altitude every step of the way. Stops become more frequent as I work my way up. Today I wish I hadn't brought along my usual 6kg backpack. The climb quickly becomes so steep, it is like angling up the side of a pyramid. There are no switchbacks really, just one long, tortuous path. I find myself having to bend forward, walking like a broken backed old slave. In this position, I can really feel the vertical pull of gravity on top of me. The sacred mountain's hundreds and hundreds of multicolored poles stand two to three meters in height. Coursing through this dense thicket are countless, long, horizontal strings of smaller tantric banners woven between the silk trees, serving as vines to complete this metaphysical rainforest. Some of the poles stand erect, but many are leaning or falling over, which makes it seem even more like some lost, primeval land.[9] Multitudes of tiny foot trails are etched between the silk trees and vines, chaotically wending their way up and down the breathtaking grade. The ground is very wet and slippery from recent seasonal rains, so I am just focusing on the main trail that keeps aimlessly making its way ever upward.

I get to a low lying shoebox shaped edifice, all made out of slate colored stone, with Tibetan tablets piled up alongside its exposed face, which is protruding out of the mountainside. Its roof is also made of slate rock and has inscribed slabs haphazardly tossed about, to help secure the roof. It is less than 1m tall, about 5m long and 2m deep, so it must surely be a sarcophage of some kind.[10] I pause to sit, catch my breath and scan the stupendously beautiful vista before me. Tagong sits below with its centerpiece walled-in white stupa sanctuary, the two long lines of sheltered Mani wheels on each side, the rustic rock stupa on its north end and the large monastery facing the town square to the south. Mad Dog Hill sits innocently across the town. Off in the distance, I can easily see where I first hiked north this morning up the road. There, I spot the massive walled temple and indeed, there is a large gilded stupa in its center courtyard, shining like gold ingots piled high.

Now I know why all the yak herding Tibetan cowboys are there: off to the side is a big stage I never really noticed and a Han master of ceremonies is on it, testing out the public address system. He starts going through his scripted routine for some pending show. The sound system is Woodstock impressive and for the next quarter of an hour, the huge towers of speakers incongruously and ingloriously fill this infinite valley with his echoing cacophony. As the MC maestro finishes his long distance amplified barrage, I can hear someone inside the Tagong monastery below me randomly and badly learning how to play a Tibetan long horn, giving out loud, languorous and squeaky blasts. This goes on in a very spasmodic fashion for the next couple of hours. It is so loud that it almost seems to rival the arena rock speaker towers across the way, as each extended blow echoes across Tagong. I can just imagine a group of young monks sitting around taking turns on the monstrously big *fahao* (法号), challenging and daring each other to see which one can let off the longest, cleanest note. From the sounds of it, they all have a long way to go to pass the test to join the band.

Lines and groups of the fervent are continuing to make their circular routine around the Mani wheels, going on past the front of the monastery and crossing the town square to repeat the loop. Many are spinning handheld Mani wheels, as well as spinning the big ones, as they walk. Like Ala, many appear to be local town folk and their numbers indicate just how much spiritual practices permeate their daily lives. Some of them are also surely shepherd and farming families, coming into town from the infinite, pastured hills and mountains all up and down this valley, to run errands and sooth their spiritual souls. Most of them are older and retired, so while the material world may be eschewed by the Tibetan faithful, children and adolescents still have to go to school, crops have to be tended to, animal flocks must be herded and shops and businesses must open. Life goes on. On top of a monastery wing that is surely the dorm rooms and offices, is a group of about fifteen young monks practicing their dance routine. It is total chaos. They are laughing raucously, clapping, cheering and rough housing with each other, flying around in helter skelter fashion, playing out-of-control highland dervishes. Evidently, their elder monk is not there and this is their chance to cut loose and let their proverbial hair hang down, if only their heads weren't as smooth as cue balls.

My Zeiss binoculars are bulky and take up space in my backpack, but using them on Mad Dog Hill and Mt. Jinire today makes me realize just how much they add to my journey's impressions and memories. I have a real love-hate relationship with them. First, they cost a small fortune, so I'm always on pins and needles about not losing them, remembering my bone headed maneuver during the White Dragon River hike in Langmusi. There are those days when I find no reason to get them out, so I curse them for their weight and volume in my backpack, whose space is preciously prioritized on these long journeys, and I start to wonder why I even brought them. Depending on the setting and conditions, I may not get them out for two to three days at a time. But when I do, all bets are off. They add such a dynamic and informative dimension to my travels and observations that I cannot imagine taking a trip like this without them. Their focal length is only 5.2 meters, so they can bring a whole new view of the world around me from very nearby - insects, flowers and birds - to galaxies in the Cosmos.

Time to keep climbing. A large, walled-in garden with a house, maybe a small monastery, greets me further up Mt. Jinire. Its gate is standing wide open, so I stick my head in. A middle aged monk is on his hands and knees, measuring out lines with a meter stick and cutting with big pinking shears a large yak skin, tanned side up, laid out on the grass. Feeling invasive, I try to justify my intrusion by greeting him and calling out if it is OK for me to continue climbing up Mt. Jinire. He never answers out loud, nor lifts his head to stop working and just slowly and sagely nods in silent affirmation. From here on out, the ascent is starting to get hoary-scary. While we all tend to exaggerate just how many degrees is an incline, I am not far off the mark by saying this mountain face is close to 45°. I start to instinctively lean into the mountain, hugging its surface. To keep from toppling over, I use my arms in a crossing relay fashion, keeping at least one hand on the mountain side at all times. One thing is for sure: if I slip and fall down this rocky roller coaster ride, I'm a dead man, or at best in a wheelchair for the rest of my life, and that is one physics experiment in gravity and motion I care not to participate in.

Against my better judgment, I keep pushing myself, spiritually spurred on by the Tibetan long horn and Mani wheel procession below. I decide to go all the way over to the north side of the silk perimeter fence, thinking I can use it to pull myself up and brake my way down from the top. Inching my way up and over, scared out of my wits, I finally make it. I fall back to sit down for a few minutes, taking in the sublime vista and checking my altimeter. From the town level below, I have vertically ascended 100m, about a 30-story building, and am at 3,856 MASL. I crane my neck back and look up the long woven and twisted lengths of color-faded silk that serve as the Mt. Jinire's Wind Horse Forest perimeter fence, as it disappears over the summit. These long bolts of silk cloth are haphazardly woven on a mish mash of sticks and branches stuck in the ground, which serve to hold it all up. About 100m above me, prancing around like Gene Kelly singing in the sunshine, is a Tibetan enjoying his solitude. A woman and a child are further up, working on the newest triangular forest of flags, and seem unfazed by the precipitous incline. I flash back to the Tibetan shepherdess at White Dragon River in

Langmusi, scaling up and down ravine walls like a Spiderwoman mountain goat. These people have been walking these precipices since they could crawl. It is second nature to them to hike and climb them with ease, no matter how severe the gradient.

That is definitely not my case and I assess my situation: alone, heavy with backpack and I cannot even see the apex from here, so it's at least twice as high as I've come so far. Time to make like Nixon and Obama, or the Chinese in Vietnam in 1979, pull out all the troops and declare symbolic victory. We all learn the hard way as children that it is much easier to climb a tree than descend it, and my current situation is no different. I'd like to tell the traveler's war story of gallantly making my way up to 4,000m to the top of a sacred Tibetan mountain, but today, I'm going to come up about 150m short. Quite frankly, I'm scared to death, as I gaze down at model train sized Tagong below. From here the climb back down looks like a free fall it's so steep, but descend I must. It reminds me of my youthful, reckless days, when as a novice snow skier I'd get to the top of an advanced black slope, gape drop jawed at the pitch below me, and knew I was cruisin' for a bruisin'. Before starting down Mt. Jinire, I take a few photos of this unforgettable, unparalleled panorama, while I buck up my courage. I am clearly way beyond my comfort zone. I slowly scale my way back down, body towards the mountain face, and using all fours for safety. Then, like Darrin Stephens in the TV show and movie *Bewitched*, who has gotten himself into an intractable mess and is in dire need of Samantha's twitching witch's nose, there laying before me is the perfect walking stick. Just what the doctor ordered. Who needs a scrawny, ersatz dog killer stick when a stout 1.5m long staff will do? It is obviously a piece of an old, broken wind horse banner pole, which just lends to its significance. Now I can walk down facing forward, leaning sideways into the mountain and using my newfound wonder wood on my left to brace against falling. This magic stick cuts my time back down in half on these slippery trails. I tell myself that for future trips, a really solid, telescoping, anodized aluminum walking stick will be at the top of my packing list.

Back in the main triangular wind horse forest, I wearily sit down in a tangle of silk and cannot resist the temptation to take a wind horse, as a well-deserved keepsake of Tagong's sacred mountain. I find an orange wind horse, my alma mater's school color, about 20cm x 30cm. I cut it off with my utility knife, furtively wad it inside my backpack and relish my absconded booty. A few meters on and I see some sun streaked, weathered wood and stone rosaries hanging in a tangle of some brambles that can somehow survive at this altitude, one of the few copses of bushes that dot this otherwise mostly barren, grass covered mountainside. Hypoxic and drunk with plundering, I quickly extricate three of them, when suddenly, the solo American I did not talk to last night at Sally's walks up on me. We are both caught a little off guard, surprised to find each other up here and start to make conversation. I tell him my experiences about the lay of the land and he seems not to believe me, and I can see why. I too was fooled by Mt. Jinire's deceptively steep pitch. The fact that you can see the entire, compact mountain from top to bottom, when gazing up from Tagong, makes it look much more diminutive than it really is. Then again, maybe I'm just a rank amateur and this guy's dad is a full blooded Indian Gurkha. He must be close to half my age, so he has in his favor youth and the sense of immortality that comes with it. Before going our separate ways, I feel the contrition of the highwayman's code of thievery: *three for me and one for you…* I point to the last string of rosary beads visible in the bramble and offer it to him, which he excitedly accepts. Three is all I need in any case, one each for my wife and two daughters.

I joyously get back down to Tagong Town's flat ground and make my way back to the main square. The Tagong monastery has an interesting story to tell, going all the way back to the 7th century. According to legend, Princess Wencheng, the bride to be of Tibet's king Songtsen Gampo, was making her way to their marriage in Lhasa. Among her belongings was a priceless statue of the Jowo Sakyamuni Buddha. It fell off its horse drawn wagon and to compensate for this logistical faux pas, a brand new facsimile was carved right here on this spot, whence this temple was built to house it. The sturdy, unharmed original was hoisted back into the princess's royal entourage and is today the most iconic and revered graven image of Buddha on the Plateau, where it is housed in Tibet's granddaddy temple of them all, the Jokhang. As temples go, in reality Tagong's is nothing spectacular, outside of the celebrated Buddha and the great folkloric story backing it up. Labrang in Xiahe, Gansu, is a hard act to follow. Well, well, well, as I walk through the large temple atrium area, who do I see but the young rooftop dervishes, who are officially performing their circular Tibetan reel dance. I furtively go sit down in a dark corner and watch their performance for a while, taking some photos. Now inside the temple confines, all the chaotic frenzy they displayed earlier has disappeared. Here in the monastery temple, it's back to ritual and routine. Their steps are energetic and youthful, but timed and choreographed. I hang out in the temple area until dinnertime, soaking up all the culture and history of the place and its inhabitants.

What a day. What an adventure. I savor another great meal at Snowland, chit chat with a slightly changed group of dinner mates and zap off a text message to my main man Tibetan chauffeur, Zhaxi, to pick me up tomorrow morning at 07:00. As the Sun is setting, I gaze out of my hostel room window overlooking Tagong's sacred Mount Jinire. From this distance, it looks like a cake walk, a mere frolic - proof positive that looks can be deceiving, very deceiving. I scan what was left to scale to get to the summit and silently nod that I made the right decision to turn back when I did. In fact, as I trace my entire trajectory, I realize I should have stopped at the monk's house and not tried to make it to the silk fence line. What was I thinking? I'm knackered. It has been an amazing, unforgettable day on this sky high plateau, with all its nothingness that really *is* everything. The evolutionary animal that was me most of the day - fight, flight, fear and survival, is still pulsating in my being, thanks to an overextended pituitary gland. My rooftop abode is now pitch black and in total silence. It takes a while, but ensconced in a thick Tibetan quilt and breathing in the Top of the World's cool, pristine, summer night air, I slowly wind down for a restful, meditative sleep.

1- For an excellent window into the inner workings of traditional Chinese families and simply a great historical read on China during the Republican era (first half of the 20th century), check out Sterling Seagrave's The Soong Dynasty, *1986, Harper Perennial. The three Soong sisters actively and powerfully influenced the course of Chinese, and therefore, world history.*

2- This Asian obsession for carrying on the male family name is so strong that in traditional Japanese culture, a younger brother who marries into a family without a male heir can even be legally adopted as a son and take his newlywed's family name.

3- I have Tagong Sally to thank for giving me the name of this mountain, which cannot be found on any map or in any guide. Jinire is one of the many names attributed to Buddha, a lot like the 100 names accorded Allah in Islam.

4- A Tibetan's definition of wealth and power differs with that of materialistic Westerners and Han. For an expert explanation of this Tibetan symbology, read The Arrow and the Spindle: Studies in History, Myths, Rituals and Beliefs in Tibet, *1998, by Samten G. Karmay, Mandala Publishing; pgs. 413-422.*

5- I later learn from a Western professor of Tibetan studies, who prefers to remain anonymous, that this mountain banner is the celebrated mantra Om Mani Padme Hum. *This is recited or chanted to the Bodhisattva of Compassion, and can be seen all over the Tibetan Plateau.*

6- Before my knees gave out in the early 80s, I calculated that I jogged and ran more than the circumference of the Earth – 40,000km. Through all that long distance training, I got routinely attacked by loose dogs, including German Shepherds, Dobermans, Rottweilers and the like. Using these techniques, I have never had blood drawn, but have had many frightening confrontations over the years.

7- As soon as you turn your back, they will often come charging back. Back turned, evolution has primed them that I am in flight mode and therefore to be hunted down. That is why you can never *back down or flee in the heat of the moment.*

8- Read the brief but informative article, www.stupa.org.nz/stupa/intro.htm for a nice introduction to stupas, or chortens, *as they are sometimes called. For the truly fascinated, there is Robert Beer's* The Encyclopedia of Tibetan Symbols and Motifs *(2004) Serindia Publications Inc. ISBN 1-932476-10-5. Thanks again to my mysterious professor of Tibetan studies in Footnote #5, for providing me valuable resources on this subject.*

9- According to Sally, this panoply of silk flags serves a very important spiritual function. If there is a death in the family or something unfortunate happens, a believer takes one of these silk banners, large or small, to a monk, who is considered to be a living Buddha. The monk incants and prays over it and then it is taken by the believer up to Mt. Jinire to be planted on a pole or strung out along the ground.

10- Tagong Sally later confirms that it is a Mani stone and is not a tomb of any kind. It is just a rectangular (or square) pile of rocks that brings good fortune to believers. Maybe this Mani stone helped me make it down Mt. Jinire.

Chapter 29: Liqi River Valley - Jiulong

A wild, end-of-the-planet Tibetan enclave with earthquakes, landslides, a blocked-at-every-turn road and the Chinese staking a claim on it all – Han style.

Zhaxi, my Tibetan taxi driver who drove me from Kangding to Tagong two days ago, meets me at Snowland promptly at 07:00. He lives near here, outside of town, with his stay-at-home wife and young children, a boy and a girl. Time to say my goodbyes to Tagong, its magical, mystical Jinire Mountain and Mad Dog Hill. However, until I get near Lugu Lake, on the border with Yunnan, I am still flying high on Top of the World, 3km above Beijing, where they are sweating like galley slaves in nectar thick humidity and choking on windless, rain drenched summer air. As much as I love my adopted Chinese hometown, I deliciously give it a big fat seasonal raspberry, as we take off for Tibetan points unknown. Zhaxi has a tough time getting a quorum of passengers this morning to go to Kangding. We finally take off with a Tibetan man in the back seat, who is decked out in a beautiful, color blazing vest and traditional bloomer pants, with a wide, Santa Claus belt; a Chinese bicycler who straps his two-wheeler on top, three local women in their rainbow of Tibetan smocks, dresses and head scarves, and myself. Next to these four wonderfully attired highlanders, the Chinese bicycler and I look like sartorial sissies. Wow, six people for a six passenger van. What a luxury. I'm the oldest in the car, so I get to ride shotgun this morning. I am reminded of how nice it is to be in the front seat on these raucous, rolling roads, as we pass back by the farm of old Mrs. Methuselah and her paleontological crutches, when she claimed riding shotgun, coming to Tagong. Even on a good day of travel in one of these cheapo local brand combi vans, the suspension feels like riding on a bareback, stiff legged old mare from dawn to dusk. In any case, up front is the only place in most Chinese vehicles where there is half a chance to find a seat belt.

I've noticed it since being on the Tibetan Plateau, but the isolation of this narrow, two lane road makes it more manifest. Goats, sheep and yaks use every strip of badly maintained asphalt and concrete as wall-less barns and open air paddocks. They are in obvious search of heat radiation. The powerful Sun beats down on this thin air, highland plateau, penetrating the concrete and asphalt all day long, turning the roads into thermal nighttime heating pads during the cool to cold summer nights. It chills down quickly as soon as the Sun sets and summer nights on the Plateau have average low temperatures around 10°C and can drop as low as 4°C at night. I have seen this all over the world, where fences are rare or when stock animals are kept communally. This especially includes reptiles, amphibians and insects, exothermes all, in desperate search for warmth, which is why road kill can be so high when the temperatures start dropping. Hundreds of ruminant animals dot our routes, in singles, small groups and herds, standing, walking or sleeping soundly. Zhaxi cajoles them with his revving motor, tooting horn and even gently nudges them with the front of his van, to get them to get up and move out of the way. The funniest ones are the wise guys who are sound asleep, *deep* REM asleep. A couple of them are so conked out that Zhaxi has to almost drive up on top of them, blasting his klaxophone full throttle. They groggily wake up, hungover from deep slumber and *sheepishly* straggle off the road.

We get to the east-west highway that runs from Kangding, which is perched on the plateau edge to the east 30km away, and in the opposite cardinal direction is Lhasa, Tibet's capital, 1,500km further on. This is the G318 highway, continuing down towards Chengdu, the capital of Sichuan. Off in the distance next to Kangding sits the mighty Paoma Mountain (跑马山= Running Horse Mountain). It rises 2.5km off the plateau, to 5,500m. In Tibetan, its name means Fairy Mountain (仙女山= Xiannvshan) and is considered sacred. Paoma Peak has even entered popular Chinese culture: a 1990s smash hit song swept the country's radio stations and karaoke clubs. Celebrating Kangding and its spectacular peak, this love song is still heard on the equivalent of Classic Pop FM radio and badly belted out in bars full of inebriated karaoke glory seekers. Paoma is an impressive road marker on this historical trade route. It is nestled in one of the series of ranges that run up and down the eastern edge of the Tibetan Plateau. Similar to the perma-snow Qilian Range I saw in Gansu, the Gongga Mountains (贡嘎= Tribute Cake), or sometimes known as the Daxue Range (大雪山= Great Snow), are about 20km to the west of Tagong and Kangding. It is hard to imagine that in western China, 6,000m peaks are mundane: there are twenty of them within a 60km radius of Kangding. It is like being in a land where there is one Mt. McKinley after another (McKinley in Alaska, North America's biggest, tops out at 6,194m). The beast of them all, Gongga Peak towers to 7,590m and is the third tallest peak in the world outside the Himalayas. This north-south column of mountain ranges collides perpendicularly with the even more massive east-west line of the Himalayan Range to the south. This mother of all geological intersections happens where the southeast corner of Tibet meets with the common border of southern Sichuan and northern Yunnan. All of these Tibetan mountains are being created by the Indian subcontinent tectonic plate crashing into the Asian continental plate from the south, at a rate of five centimeters a year, or five meters a century. This helps explain why this area is prone to so many earthquakes – big ones – that are so common in this part of the country, alongside some of China's most densely populated areas, rendering their predictably grizzly aftermaths.

Much to my surprise, once we get to this ancient lowland-highland trade route, connecting Sichuan to Tibet, everybody else in Zhaxi's combi gets out and starts looking for other rides to points beyond. Now I have to wait for him to rustle up another carload of passengers. It's looking pretty grim. He is running around smoking like crazy and commiserating with his fellow drivers, who are in the same boat. They are all circulating among the waiting passengers, barking like circus hustlers on the midway, all trying to get out of this Tibetan version of Dodge City. Zhaxi starts talking it over with a group of eight hard looking Tibetan men, in their 20s. They've been approached by other drivers, so in this microcosm of a supply side market, Zhaxi has apparently come down to a price that both parties are willing to accept. They start heading towards the combi with all their massive nylon bags. Alright, it won't be long till I get to Kangding and catch a bus on the modern G5 toll road highway towards Lugu Lake, situated on the Sichuan/Yunnan border, which is my next destination. Well, not exactly. Zhaxi tells me that these guys are going to *Jiulong*, due south of here 166 klicks, and now he's going with *them*, and not to Kangding. Hmm, OK… Can't say that I blame him. He's got a family to feed, is not making any money sitting here smoking cigarettes and watching me keep his shotgun seat warm. So it's nut cutting time Brown, time to make an executive decision. Do I get out and find another ride to Kangding in order to stick to my original planned route? Or do I hang with my Tagong buddy Zhaxi and this merry band of Tibetan ruffians, to points unknown?

I confer with Zhaxi about his route, to make sure I can get to Lugu Lake. This provincial highway he is taking to go to Jiulong is the S215, which runs roughly parallel to the G5, which I would take from Kangding south anyway, and the S215 feeds back into the G5 north of the turnoff going to Lugu Lake. So far, so good. The S215 starts here at Xinduqiao (新都桥) and the main stopping points are Shade (沙德) to Jiulongxian (九龙县) to Liangshan/Xichang (凉山/西昌) and then onto to Luguhu (泸沽湖= Lugu Lake= Lu Commercial Lake)emer. The map looks really beautiful, going through one long continuous narrow valley all the way there. The G5 hugs the Plateau, is in a broader, more navigable river plain and is fast four-laner. The S215 may take longer, Zhaxi tells me, since the road is not very good and that there could be some rock slides that slow us down. Also as an aside, *he's not sure if the road from Jiulong onto Liangshan is open*, where I would pick back up the G5. Not paying attention amongst all the goings-on, I will come to learn later he's either suckering me into a paid seat to make up for a bad commercial start of the day, or is truly misinformed beyond a reasonable doubt. But in the heat of the moment, why the heck not? I'm sticking with my pal Zhaxi. Off we go to Jiulong (九龙= Nine Dragons). Turns out Zhaxi sure knows what he is talking about concerning the condition of the road. The first part we already experienced coming to Tagong. It's a stretch of transportation inferno just a few klicks long and is a perfect movie set for an area that was carpet bombed by American B-52s in Southeast Asia during the Vietnam War. All that's missing is the Agent Orange, napalm and burning babies. Hundreds of intrepid bicyclists and drivers are snaking, weaving and bobbing à la Mohammed Ali butterflies, dodging lethal vehicles in all this mess. Some of the craters boggle the mind and with the recent rains, it is not only a ride across the surface of Jupiter's hypervolcanic Io, but a slippery, treacherous slide as well. Luckily, this stretch is not very long.

We turn south onto the S215 and begin a long and I mean *long* day navigating over, around and under road work project after massive land slide. The conifer and deciduous covered mountainsides have non-stop, huge fantailed swaths where the forests have been completely obliterated by sliding scree, all caused by localized earthquakes of varying magnitude. These constant geological scars were not caused by a one-time occurrence. Each fantail of sliding scree tells you when it happened, by looking at how much of the plant life has come back. You can estimate how long ago a rockslide happened, from fully mature, lush alpine forest to decimated rubble and back again. I see all these phases during this drive. A local rumbler first causes total destruction of the valley wall, starting out at a point high up with a growing, triangular, fantailed swath decimating everything in its path towards the river below. Years pass and enough erosion soil from above slowly fills in rocky crevices for grasses to take root. Then come small flowering plants. Animals and birds then move in to help spread their seeds. Next in its ecological recovery are brambles and bushes, which over years slowly connect into thickets. It is sort of a virtuous circle, as more and more runoff soil is trapped and slowly starts to cover the exposed rock surface with patches, then larger and larger blankets of undergrowth. This finally allows the establishment of sapling trees, which then take generations to get the affected area back to its original glory. Based on today's Liqi Valley drive, I estimate the whole cycle from landslide back to healthy Alpine forest must take one to two hundred years. Over the course of the S215, I see just about every stage of Mother Earth's remarkable self-healing, via the processes of geology, evolution and natural selection. Clearly, there is a lot of earthquake activity around here. I later learn that there were serious 6.9-7.9 Richter quakes in this area in 1923, 1948, 1955, 1973 and 1981. The 1973 7.9'er ranks as one of the world's biggest in the 20th century. Then on February 23rd, 2001, a mere 6.0 rumbler tore up Kangding, killing only a few people and wounding a few hundred, but 20,000 Tibetan houses collapsed. The only thing that spared more carnage and deaths is that it hit at 08:09, so everybody was out and about going to the fields and walking to school. An hour or two earlier and the deaths would have skyrocketed inside all those flattened residences. As a souvenir, the Kangding earthquake left a huge crack in the Earth's crust - five kilometers long. The incredible frequency of earthquakes in this area means it is getting hit with a page one, headline grabbing rumbler about every twenty years.

The scale and frequency of just this rainy season's wanton destruction is a sight to behold. Massive mud and rubble slides block our passage every 15-30 minutes. So we just line up with all the other vehicles going in our direction and wait for the road crews to alternatively signal it's our lane's turn to go, while the opposing line stops to let us by. But in numerous cases today, we stop and go nowhere. Everybody on both sides of the landslide pour out of their cars, buses, trucks, semis, bicyclists included, to smoke, eat, drink tea, talk, while sitting outside to enjoy the stunning beauty, wilderness and timeless feel of the Liqi River Valley (立启河沟= Immediate Awakening). Today's bus ride is sort of an all-natural, moving Tibetan rave party up the S215, as it were. The river and its valley are truly one of the most photogenic places I get to see on this journey and it reminds me of the bus ride from Lanzhou to Xiahe, in Gansu. On that ride though, I was on a big interurban bus flying at high speed the whole way. Thanks to the awesome power of Planet Earth, today I get to spend a lot of quality time in the valley wilderness walking around to see everything.

Earthquakes and localized tremblers causing massive scree and rockslides over generations I can understand. But I am scratching my head at all these fresh rock- and mudslides afflicting us today. I spend some time at each long-haul stop to explore the geology of the rock formations in this valley to see if I can learn more. Surprise, I come to discover there *aren't* any geological rock strata. And that's the problem. This area of Sichuan gets so shaken and violently joggled so often, that these mountains have been turned into huge piles of small rocks, gravel and soil, all being precariously held together by their sheer mass and the pull of Earth's gravity. All of these constant earthquakes, big and small, keep this part of Sichuan's crust as fragile as geological Jell-O. In some places I can see faint remnants of what used to be clearly defined strata. But at most stops today, I can pick up handfuls of mountain, as if I'm grabbing mixed grain out of a burlap sack. All those millions of years, eras and eons in the layers of strata, one on top of the other, that normally paint a clear timeline of evolution and geological activity, have been disintegrated into dust and chaos in this ancient, earthquake inclined valley. No strata, no structure. This is what sets the stage for all these seasonal rock- and mudslides: the summer downpours come. As a result, Liqi Valley's walls, as well as many others near the Longmenshan (龙门山= Dragon Gate Mountain) fault line that is the geological boundary between the eastern border of the Tibetan Plateau and the Sichuan Plain below, coming roaring down the mountainsides, obliterating everything in their paths. Come to think of it, given all the geological confusion in this area, this would be the perfect place for ersatz experts to come and tout it as geological proof that the Earth was created on Sunday, October 23rd, 4004 BC,[1]

Hey Bubba, get over here and take a look at this rock formation.

What is it Buford?

Praise the Lord, why that's a rabbit skeleton right underneath *a dinosaur bone, see? I told you that EVIL-lewww-shun is godless humanism!*

CUT! Wait right there gentlemen. That's enough of you buffoons. Where can I sign in permanent ink, no, make that with my blood, that I am firmly in the ranks of evolutionary humanists? It's time we get back on the road to Kangding. Keeping digging for your version of the truth and hasta la vista, boys…

There are other geological processes that keep this part of Sichuan in a nonstop, precarious situation. Over the winter, there is limited snowfall in these plateau valleys, but temperatures routinely drop below -10°C, freezing the surface rock solid.[2] At ground level, the snow turns into ice, which expands 9% more than water. All that expansion during the winter happens in the soil, cracks and crevices, creates microfissures in the rocks, which weakens what little surface cohesion there is in these earthquake shaken surfaces. Thus, this Jell-O like consistency of the Earth's surface is further weakened each year. And up above, in the towering peaks, there is a lot of snowfall and at least for now, many glaciers that stock up huge quantities of snow water over the winter.[3] When spring comes, earth-moving equipment better be ready, as all that high altitude snow melts, the surface ice turns to water and it all comes crashing down the valley faces, carrying millions and millions of tons of surface rock and rubble along the way. No wonder landslides and mudslides here are almost banal, if they weren't so impressively numerous and Herculean in scale. Add all this to centuries of earthquake-induced, mountain sized scree and boulder slides crashing down the length and breadth of these valleys and well, you get the idea, it's quite a sight. At each slide zone, there are American Caterpillar D-6s and, D-8s, Korean road graters, Japanese heavy duty front loaders, and massive German backhoes. To help break up the rubble into manageable chunks, monstrous looking Chinese needle nosed jack hammers, with big articulated spikes at the ends of their long necks move in for the stony kill. This cosmopolitan armada of Earth shapers could be a wild scene in the movie *Transformers* - robotic insects working in clusters, busy clots of mechanical colonies probing, moving and hauling Earth up and down the S215. All the falloff has to go somewhere, so large mining sized dump trucks cue up in both directions to get filled up with rubble and taken to points beyond. With the impressive Liqi Valley towering over us on both sides of an outsized river right out of a Jules Verne science fiction novel, as well as standing beside these interplanetary sized excavation machines, it is easy to feel very small and otherworldly about right now.

This valley is timeless, its villages and houses equally so. The Liqi River is another one of China's patented kayaker suicide courses. Trying to cross it or navigate it in any way, shape or form would mean instant, bloody and bludgeoned death. Outside of the hamlets that hug both sides of the raging waters, are large farms with sea green Alpine barley, fields of white flowering potatoes, multihued vegetable gardens and gorgeous fruit orchards that work their way up towards the mountain crests, until the soil can give no more. Above all this, ruminant animals graze and at river-village level their flocks and herds intermingle in the lives of these hardy, courageous Tibetans. I am pondering all that I see and am in sincere admiration for these people. In this geologically fragile, climatically cruel valley, road or no road, they have lived, survived and meditated here for centuries on end. And the Tibetan Plateau is full of tens, if not hundreds of valleys just like this.

Zhaxi is smiling, rolling his eyes and chain smoking at the vicissitudes that this unwieldy, should-never-have-been-built road is throwing up in his face. When you are a long distance taxi driver in these parts, you know everybody and he is making the rounds at each stop. He could play to perfection the role of a glib diplomat, glad handing all the guests at a reception. As we gaze out at these spectacular multipurpose farms, I see nothing but incredible wealth, yet Zhaxi is lamenting how poor all these people are. I point to the big two to three story homes and he tells me they only cost 200,000 RMB (€25,000/$32,000) to build, which I find hard to believe. But then I remember reading in *Tibet, the Last Cry*, where

Eric Meyer discusses a government program to provide low/no interest loans to Tibetans to build these homes and mentions a similar cost.[4] And Eric's right, they all do have an almost identical floor plan and size. Each story is about $100m^2$, so the houses are $200\text{-}300m^2$, which are French aristocrats' chateaus by middle class Chinese standards. These Tibetans have land, food, meat, abundant water and it must be said, a life threatening earthquake every generation, but still. I can only conclude that Zhaxi and I have conflicting paradigms of exactly how wealth is quantified. Maybe he has been watching too many reruns of *Dallas* on TV.

About halfway through the valley to Jiulong, we arrive in a nice sized town, Shade. Zhaxi suddenly stops his combi, while he explains to our Tibetan posse of eight young men what's going on. Waiting to get it in Mandarin, my rugged mountain men companions start piling out of the combi and Zhaxi explains he is turning around from here and his older brother Ge, believe it or not, is going to take us the rest of the way to Jiulong.[5] So, it's a family affair. We eat at a restaurant in Shade before leaving and while doing so, Zhaxi explains that he cannot take passengers all the way to Jiulong. If he does, he'll go to jail. Well, OK, if you put it that way. I'm not sure what the rationale is for the interdiction, but he says his Tagong plates are forbidden. Is it an attempt to compartmentalize potential unrest through here, maybe a division of the taxi spoils, or both? I give Zhaxi a warm goodbye and off we head ever southward.

One immediate advantage of the change is Ge's van is really a small bus and more comfortable. He is also a much better, saner driver and does not have half his face buried in his mobile phone while passing over hillcrests. His Mandarin leaves a lot to be desired, but at least he has in his vocabulary words like *yield* and *speed limit*, so the rest of the trip is more relaxed. His bus also has a TV screen showing cheesy Tibetan karaoke videos. Some are just as syrupy and ingratiating as the plethora of pop songs that saturate Chinese music culture in the lowlands. Others however seem remarkably political in nature, expressing wishes of intellectual freedom and spiritual liberty. They show scenes of armies of monks and nuns around temples, head priests leading them in chants and martial maneuvers. Other songs depict throngs of Tibetan children reading their native language out of books, while others have vignettes that fade in and out on temple scenes, with walls of yak butter candles, giving legions of monks and nuns the light they need to read their sacred Tibetan texts. All the subtitles are in Tibetan, so I cannot be sure. But they look manifestly subversive and anti-colonialist to me. Does Ge play these DVDs when there are Han passengers aboard? My gang of Tibetans accompanying me seems to confirm my suspicions. They sing and hum these songs out loud over and over again as we finish our drive to Jiulong, and they sound like they are belting out La Marseillaise or the Star Spangled Banner. I can only assume the DVDs were smuggled in from Nepal or India. Producing these in China would surely result in very long prison terms.

We suddenly start climbing out of the Liqi Valley and begin to switch back and forth up one side of a huge mountain, wrap around and continue climbing up its steep connecting shoulder to make it to a high altitude pass. This is the source of the magical Liqi River below. The views through here are simply stupendous; I cannot believe my eyes and want to pinch myself that I am even here. Clearly, Jiulong is in another valley on the other side of this mountain range. The pass sits at 4,454m, so we have climbed 1.5 klicks today. We stop briefly. The pass has the obligatory monster-sized stone stele with its name carved and painted in Chinese and Tibetan: Nine Dragon Pass (九龙沟= Jiulonggou). It is actually very cold and windy in this rare mountain air and everybody temporarily closes all the bus windows. Thinking today's drive cannot get any better, on the other side of this pass, we go through an amazing primeval forest. The flora changes dramatically and for 15km it looks like we are driving through a Triassic Period diorama, with strange looking spruce and cypress trees towering into the air. These arrow thin tall stands are showing off long flowing fronds of tree moss, which are hanging from their sad, droopy branches. These pendulous tresses could be interpreted as the mythological beards of mountain spirits. Given the colorful iconography that I've learned about Tibetan Buddhism, this would not be an outlandish mythology story on the Plateau. The ground is covered in huge, dinosauresque ferns, brackens and other strange looking plants, grasses and flowers that are unfamiliar to me. This is clearly a localized biome and probably very unique. It's almost eerie and other-worldly as we wend and wind our way now, ever downward through this section on the west side of the Jiulong Pass. I just hope they can protect it from speculation and commercial depredation, because it is really special.

Further on, we abruptly stop and the Tibetan delegation disgorges itself in the middle of nowhere. Ge pulls down their overstuffed baggage that was strapped on the roof up till now, and strategically hides it inside the now empty bus, so that it is out of sight from the road. Each of the Tibetan men takes a smaller hand bag to carry or toss onto their shoulders. What the heck is going on? Something is going on further up the road and I'm trying to figure out what it is. All I can see around us are half a dozen waterfall driven, Buddhist Mani wheels, that spin non-stop, as their bottom side paddles are worked by the cascading water tumbling ever downward from the mountains above. In typical Tibetan fashion, a couple are being built, a couple work and a couple are completely broken down. Birth, life and death. According to believers, every time a Mani wheel is spun, it helps a person make it safely across the 49 days between material death on Earth and their eventual reincarnation on the other side. However, much like imponderable questions such as the Gordian knot and how many angels can dance on the head of a pin, great philosophical debates rage in the halls of monasteries: if a believer is not themselves spinning the Mani wheels with their faithful hands, does it really count if a non-human force is doing the same thing, like these water paddles? Or, what about some Mani wheels I will see during *44 Days* that are driven by the wind? Only Buddha knows.

As soon as my Tibetan buddies get out, Ge and I start to take off alone, leaving them behind. I am asking him what's going on, but his Mandarin is a big step or two down from Zhaxi's and I struggle to figure out what he is telling me. As we pull up to an armed police check point, with a barrier blocking the road to get in and out of the Tibetan Liqi valley behind us, I start to catch on. Ge gets out, signs a log in the guard house and points to me to explain his reason for being here. We go just far enough around a couple of bends to be completely hidden from the guard house's view and wait. I now understand Ge that it is illegal for him to take these guys to Jiulong and if he gets caught, he too could go to jail. Jeesh, long distance taxi drivers face a lot of draconian and punitive restrictions on the Tibetan Plateau. And the boys took handbags to make it look like they are traveling on foot. Clever and obviously not being done the first time. This is a well-practiced deception. I am reminded of the Qiqing village in Gansu that has similar, armed, military security to get in and out of that Tibetan enclave. Have the Liqi people lashed out at what they consider to be spiritual persecution and economic exploitation by the lowland Han? And what about my Tibetan posse? Is it their numbers? Too many young Tibetans being transported in a group, hoping to start a protest in Jiulong town? Did they cut through the forest or register at the guard station? The way Tibetans can effortlessly scale near-vertical inclines, it would be a summer saunter for them to go off trail. That being the case, then why the hand bags? As a cover if they are discovered in the woods – *uh, sorry, we got lost*? With Ge's limited Mandarin and in any case his certain reticence if I really started to pose a bunch of pointed questions, I can only speculate. While waiting for them to get here, I scan a series of 2m x 1m road signs in Chinese and Tibetan exhorting the road repair crews to do quality work, use only the best materials and to build roads that will last a hundred years. Haha. Mother Earth will humble their most earnest of efforts and reduce their toil to dust, if not every twenty years or so with a major earthquake, then every spring when the snows thaw and the seasonal rains come flooding down off these mountains made of mud Jell-O… About a half an hour later, our buddies lollygag up to the bus, chain smoking all, and not even winded from carrying their big handbags with them. Ge quickly reloads the hidden luggage back on top and off we go.

We are still about 30km from Jiulong and now outside the security barrier, we suddenly start seeing the red flag of China flying everywhere, on houses, offices and businesses. It is as if we left one country and entered another. Being this close to the Tibetan Liqi Valley border, it's all overkill and obviously a statement. Are these Chinese who have set up a colony outside the castle moat and are just biding their time, waiting for the most propitious moment to make their move? Or are they Tibetans who have cashed in and are being plied with all of the material wealth and benefits bestowed on those who sell their very souls for filthy lucre? It is now dinner time and the streets are almost vacant of people, so the dress of the citizens is not much of a clue. But all the signs are in Chinese, with almost no Tibetan script alongside, so I suspect the truth is probably the first scenario. I wonder if that guard station is discretely moved further up the Liqi River every year a few hundred meters, so that this Han enclave can surreptitiously encroach on the Tibetans' valley?

We arrive to Jiulong and it is getting dark. I am told the long distance taxis hang out at the main square to look for passengers, so head in that direction. I ask several of them about going further south tonight, to Lugu Lake, and not only can I not go tonight, I can't go tomorrow, or the day after that. They explain to me that the road has so many landslides that it is *completely* shut off. Great. I get to go back to Kangding tomorrow, from whence I came today. After all, I have no other choice, I'm in a geological cul-de-sac. And how long has it been blocked? Two months. I let that sink in for a few seconds.

Two months. And Zhaxi and big brother Ge didn't know that? At this point, I'm finding it harder and harder to believe, but what can I do? Today's little ten hour foray into the Liqi Valley and back up tomorrow will add two days to my journey. I am two days ahead of schedule, so it's a wash at this point. But still, as an act of protest, I refuse to go back to the parking lot where Ge dropped us off and parked for the night. Tomorrow, I'm going upscale. I go to the long distance bus station, buy a ticket for Kangding tomorrow at 06:00 and get a room at a Spartan Chinese *zhaodaisuo* right across the street. The owner has a couple of hundred egg mushrooms spread out all over the floor behind his shop counter. They grow up in the mountains and really do look like something out of one of the *Alien* movies: big, purple, black and green, fist sized pods with shanks growing out of one end, where they are anchored into the forest floor. Inside the outer shell, which opens up like some sci-fi tulip flower, is a delicious, succulent, ovoid shaped mushroom. As I go out to eat a big bowl of spicy red noodles and stir fried cabbage for dinner, the hotel owner is earnestly trimming and prepping the egg pods with a paring knife. What is he going to do with all these oversized fungi? The next morning I find out. While I get on the bus, he is there to send two big Styrofoam boxes full of them to be delivered to a buyer who meets us when we arrive in Kangding.

I could spend a worse day than getting to see the amazing Liqi Valley from its opposite direction. Yesterday in the combis, I was sitting low to the ground on the mountain (shotgun) side of the road and was observing the Liqi River crashing towards me. Today, I am seated high up on the river side and am watching its waters flow in the same direction we are traveling - downstream. The change in perspective is so dramatic, it is as if I am driving on a completely new road. The villages have ancient looking, dark stone towers in the shape of tall, thin pyramids, with the tips squared off on the top, where sentries can stand guard. They have the feel of medieval lookouts, and maybe that is what they are. One of the strangest differences is the look of the raging river waters. It is very violent when it crashes into its countless submerged boulders. The force of the speeding water is so powerful that the water curls up and back when it hits them, almost like backwards surfer tunnel waves. It is a hypnotic and fascinating visual deception, what magicians call a *trompe l'oeil*, as sections of the river appear to be flowing forwards *and* backwards simultaneously, like M.C. Escher's early tessellation drawings of fish and fowl.

We go back through the primeval forest before the rising Sun can beat down on top of it. It is now a real live pixie story, a *Lord of the Rings* fantasy land. The air is barely moving and there is a blanket of fog slowly breaking up on the forest floor, with all the ferns and brackens poking through the veils of mist. The towering, bearded cypress and spruce trees are adorned with tufts, puffs and little pillows of clouds hanging chaotically in their branches. Up above the tree line, small clouds still float down inside the valley and cling to the mountainsides. Not only in long chains and suspended in the breathless air, but on many trees thick moss is growing in billowing loops hanging down from the branches, giving the appearance of huge pale green, flaxen necklaces. It is easy to see why Tibetans call so many of their landmarks *Fairy*, because much of the Plateau is truly enchanted. One downside to this moss: it is killing a good number of the trees. The ones that are heavily festooned are manifestly dying and some are even dead. It may be like Spanish moss, which is not parasitic, but can block enough sunlight to limit photosynthesis, killing the tree. Or this variety could be like mistletoe which is a true parasite, tapping into the tree's nutrients. It looks similar to Spanish moss, so I'm inclined to think this Tibetan variety is of the first kind. Countless little babbling brooks pour forth and larger waterfalls cascade down from the valley walls above, crashing into the roiling river beside us. This forest is devoid of human occupation, which lends me to believe it must be some kind of nature reserve, thank goodness. The lack of human impact makes this whole section seem a dreamy drive in H.G. Wells' *Time Machine*, set at 225,000,000 B.C. or landing on some utopian exoplanet. One thing is for sure: I will never, ever forget this incredibly vivid and memorable last half-hour bus ride here on present day Earth. We drive right past yesterday's guard station without stopping and then it occurs to me, on these official bus lines, every citizen must show their *shenfenzheng* (national ID) and the computer knows how far they are going. If there are any disturbances, the local Han authorities can pretty well know who's in the valley, other than those who come overland on foot.

As we make our way further up and out of the forest, this surreal idyll is soon shattered by a stab wound of human progress. The mountain face is being gouged and gutted by a big gravel pit that is feeding a ravenous cement plant next to it, which in turn is supplying a hungry concrete mixer, which hence is being used to try to keep the S215 operational. Ugh. And it's barely working at keeping the road open. Today, the road crews and their titanic Transformer toys that block the traffic, while they excavate and haul off the landslide rubble, take our big commercial bus more seriously, so we do not seem to wait as long to get the all clear. Instead of the ten hour, 166km haul with the Tibetan brothers yesterday, we make the 196km return trip all the way to Kangding in a breezy seven, which is a breakneck average speed of 28kph.

During this trip back, I also have a lot of time to ponder the Liqi Valley, its people, their history and the role that the Han Chinese have played here, since the Communist Party took control of the unified People's Republic, after independence in 1949. These rugged, hard living Tibetans have done just fine for centuries, thank you, without a paved road. I imagine this S215 is as slick as frozen goose diarrhea during the long subzero winter months. Just a sprinkling of snow or sleet would do it. And it is barely navigable the rest of the year, as layers of mountain face sheer off and come crashing down to the Liqi River below. Then throw in a devastating, world class earthquake every 20 years or so, just to up the ante. The local Liqi Tibetans seem to be able to live without the S215, its use is sporadic and problematic at best, and the cost to keep pushing these Sisyphean mountains out of the way, day after day, season after season must be astronomical. It took a round trip up and down this unforgettable valley to understand why. It is not Tibetans who work infatigueably on this *Mission Impossible* road repair. It is Han carpetbaggers who own these engineering companies and who operate their metallic monsters. Yes, they do it for progress, but also for more allegorical reasons. This wreck of a road, this transportation joke is all about symbolism. It is a long, concrete & asphalt victory banner running the length of this valley, to remind the Tibetans that they may work the land and graze their livestock here, as they have for an eternity, but this place is Han controlled and the locals have masters to heed, be it rain, snow, earthquakes or landslides. The Chinese will not let the Tibetans fly their national flag, so they substitute it with myriad colored wind horse banners all over the place. I see nary a flag of China, even on the government buildings in this valley, apparently to not enflame local sentiments. So for the Han, the S215 will serve as an enduring asphalt and concrete substitute just the same, thank you, since this Kabuki highway is the only flag Baba Beijing can fly. This laughable road is a powerful reminder that Baba Beijing will never leave the proud, independent people of Liqi Valley alone. Never. To do so would be to renounce all claims to its governance. From Baba Beijing's perspective, it is also about maintaining legitimacy in the eyes of these hard scrabble Tibetans: look at what we are doing to make your lives better. See how hard we are working for you. The irony of this dichotomy is that the Han are right, they really are doing just that. With the Heavenly Mandate bearing down on their historically minded souls, ever paternal Baba Beijing sincerely wants to improve these people's lives: hospitals, schools, telecommunications – and roads. But, the Tibetans' point of view is equally valid. Like America's natives once were, before being exterminated and assimilated, they are fiercely proud, independent, conservative and devout. So, are the people of Liqi Valley snickering at the Han's folly, or are they seething at their bullheaded insistence? Only the 21st century knows.

1- *Check your watches: for the fundamentalist Christian, the universe was created the day before, on October 22n, 4004 BC - at 18:00, to be exact. James Ussher (1581–1656), an Anglican Archbishop counted all the* begats *in Genesis to arrive at this specious pseudoscientific claptrap. To this day, this spot on the calendar is still bandied about by millions of believers around the world, especially in the US, where Gallup polls since 1982 consistently show 40-50% of Americans believe that God created humans in their present form within the last 10,000 years. Ever onward into the 21st century. The Chinese have no such delusions, as has been seen in the museums I visit.*

2- *The annual precipitation on the Tibetan Plateau is only 100-300mm. The low end of this range is what deserts routinely get each year and the upper end of this scale is classified as arid to semiarid. Like in Beijing, almost all of it falls during the summer season. So, all the* wetland *look of the Plateau I have been seeing is mostly due to snow pack and glacier melt from the peaks above.*

3- *The Tibetan Plateau contains the world's third-largest store of ice, after the Antarctic and Greenland. Times are good right now for agriculture and tourism. The lakes and rivers are full, the lands bountiful and the temperatures more moderate. But this is because human induced climate change is causing Tibet's temperatures to rise* four times faster *than the rest of China. Thus Tibetan glaciers are melting and retreating quicker than anywhere else in the world, releasing all those thousands of cubic kilometers of prehistoric fresh water to flow to the lowlands below. Once the glaciers are gone though, all bets are off. The lifelines of many major Asian rivers, including the Indus, Ganges, Mekong and Yangtze will be greatly diminished, and will impact a huge percentage of the world's seven billion human inhabitants.*

4- Tibet, the Last Cry, *by Eric Meyer and Laurent Zylberman, 2013, www.blacksmithbooks.com or www.amazon.com*
5- Ge (哥) *is a common honorific accorded to older brothers and among close older friends.*

Chapter 30: Kangding - Xichang/Liangshan

Saying goodbye to the Top of the World, a cruise along one of the planet's most ambitious, boggle-the-mind superhighways, while being accompanied by the white light of madness and bus driver bravado; Wild West towns, a beaudaciously beautimous Tex Avery hooker and unfortunately, humankind's proclivity for Orwellian nostalgia and holocaust amnesia, past and present.

I took the 06:00 bus from Jiulong, up through Liqi Valley and on to Kangding this morning. So, it is still early afternoon and I have plenty of time to catch a fast moving, interurban coach from Kangding to Liangshan/Xichang, the gateway to get to Lugu Lake, my next destination on the Sichuan-Yunnan border. The drive from Kangding to Liangshan on the G5 is similar to the ride from Chengdu to Tagong: flying on the G5 again defies engineering limits: a four-lane superhighway as tall as skyscrapers built across mountain canyons, long distance tunnels, bridges crossing more Herculean rivers and breathtaking valleys, with great roadside food at lunch and interesting people to talk to on the bus. Ho-hum, I'm getting spoiled. How spectacular is this 244km long section of the G5 highway, from Ya'an (雅安) to Xichang? Just opened a few months ago at a trifling cost of €2,400,000,000/$3,000,000,000 (financing thanks to Baba Beijing), 54% of its length is either built suspended above ground or drilled through mountains via tunnels. *Gargantuan* doesn't even begin to describe it. Just like a huge number such as sextillion or quintillion, the G5 is almost out of the realm of human perspective.

Two bizarre events happen on this jaunt down the edge of the Tibetan Plateau. In one of the long tunnels, a mad man is dancing and pirouetting in the middle of the high speed traffic, a crazed leprechaun in his own fantasy world. Everybody slows down to a crawl and politely navigates around him. Probably a schizophrenic. Where is his bottle of meds? It reminds me of a story my dad told me about a young woman, who was managing the Dairy Queen, a drive-through restaurant in town, in Oklahoma, where I grew up. One day, answering to the Siren call of schizophrenia, she took the mop she was using, walked out into the middle of the main highway and started dancing, as if she had an invisible waltzing partner, to the tune of the Blue Danube. She was unceremoniously taken off to the local Bellevue, never to be seen again. Back then the drug of choice was Thorazine, along with electroshock therapy. Wipes the slates clean, right? We all remember *One Flew over the Cuckoo's Nest*. This book cum movie is not an inaccurate depiction of modern mental health care back in the day. Like the Chinese, Europeans have a tolerance for crazies to be a part of their daily lives. When we lived in Normandy, France, everybody in the neighborhood knew Jean's name, said hello and gave their coins and cigarettes to this enlightened man who spent his days at a couple of habitual spots, in search of the warm Sun. Nobody minded. He of course had universal health care and he actually saw the same family doctor as we did. On several occasions, we were in the waiting room together. At night, I suspect he went and stayed at the local shelter. This is Looney Tunes madness for many Americans,

"That's not fair. Hey, that's not right. Why should my taxes pay for him? *Why doesn't the bum get a job- I hold down three of them. There ought to be a law!"*

Life goes on. Where we live in Beijing, a man stays on the streets who is in much worse shape than his French homologue. This guy never bathes, lives in rags, looks like warmed over Hades and I've never seen him in *my* doctor's office. I've said hello to him a few times, and he always replies back, *buliang*. (不良= not bad). Once I tried to offer him some food and he told me no, he goes home every day for dinner. I asked some local friends about him and apparently it's true. He was married and has two kids. One day, he walked into the blinding light of schizophrenia, never to return, as can happen to the afflicted when they are young adults, just like the waltz-in-the-road woman in our town. Apparently he insists on living on the street, but his family keeps him fed. Between his rambling mutterings to himself, answering to the all too real voices in his head, people treat him nicely, chat and offer him cigarettes.[1] Americans are much less tolerant of the harmless mentally ill in their midst and public daily lives. These touched souls tend to get apprehended and sent some place, sight unseen. I've seen many a crazy person in public places in countries around the world, as part of the fabric of daily life. They are accepted members of humanity's panoply. Can't say that I have seen this in the U.S. However, America does warmly embrace the physically and mentally handicapped, and may be tops the world in this category, to make a better life for these citizens. But the Sun seeking crazies? Not so much. I'm not sure why Americans go to such extremes to embrace two groups of afflicted, yet erase another from their routines. Denial? Collective shame? After all, just like the physically and mentally handicapped, they were born as such, but maybe that is forgotten or not well understood.

The other strange happening on this leg is how the bus driver handled what could have been a dangerous accident. We are flying along on the G5, about 50km north of Xichang, when all of a sudden there starts a loud, rapid thumping racket with each turn of the bus' fast spinning tires. It is also really vibrating and shaking everyone in their seats, so like uncomfortable turbulence on an airplane, all the passengers sit up and take notice, as seat mates begin worriedly jabbering to each other. The drive calmly pulls over onto the nice modern shoulder and I can't resist getting off to see what the heck is going on, along with a few other onboard rubberneckers. A chunk of tread on the back right inside tire is coming off. Apparently, these are retreads or really lousy quality original ones. I'm thinking, darn, it's going to take the rest of the day to call a bus repair truck, remove both tires off the axle, replace the shredded one and put them both back. The lug nuts on the outer tire are the size of walnuts and there are about thirty of them. But nooooo. Our chauffeur, Mr. *Groundhog Day* has been here before. He calmly goes behind the bus, unlocks the tool kit box, brandishes a hunting knife and proceeds to calmly cut off the big loose piece of tread separating from the tire, which is about 40cm long. Grinning from ear to ear with joyful self-pride, he holds it up inside the bus, waving it over his head like a prized trophy in the winner's circle. There is a round of applause for his heroic, and what is really on everybody's mind, super time saving maneuver. The rest of the way into town, he doesn't even bother to slow down and we have this loud, whistling, whirring sound humming inside the bus. But hey, he gets us to our destination safely.

Liangshan/Xichang (凉山/西昌= Cold Mountain/Western Prosperity) is one of those urban areas that gives any place a less than stellar reputation. It is a sprawling, uninspired, cluttered mess that has grown haphazardly and aimlessly where it can. It is about halfway between Chengdu, the capital of Sichuan, and Kunming, the capital of Yunnan. You would think this would be an area with not many people, but when you harbor 20% of our Planet's souls within your boundaries, cities are bound to swell. That is why this place has two names. It is two medium sized cities that grew and melded into one big muddled metropolis. China became a majority urban population in 2010-11 and a few million compatriots planted their flags here to help assure this benchmark was attained. My local hotel would indicate that it's a pretty rough place too. Closed circuit cameras are on every floor and all the employees are walkie-talkie equipped. There is a sentry employee on every floor, making their presence known. As I walk up the stairs to my third floor room, a drop dead gorgeous, beautifully made up woman, with waist long hair, a canary yellow miniskirt barely covering those parts of her body that most societies would consider to be of prurient interest, a voluptuous breast-baring white silk blouse and jet-black knee-high leather stiletto boots, is sauntering past me. She is so striking and so Tex Avery *real* that it is impossible to keep my eyes off her. I think it is safe to assume she is not here to sell Girl Scout Cookies door to door. Once in my room, the tools of the trade confirm her noblest of endeavors. A tray with Dream Sea brand condoms is on offer, price list included. How thoughtful. The normal rubber is ¥10 (€1.30/$1.60) and the vibe-ring model costs a handsome 30 kuai (€3.75/$4.75). Dream Sea also sells a hand towel with a disposable razor for ¥12. Where is Gideon's Bible or the Quran when you need it most? I flash back and recall how totally poised Ms. Yellow Fanny was, sauntering her way down the stairs, walking just like she was on a fashion runway. Who knows, maybe she moonlights on her back for the income she desires to fund her more lavish modeling lifestyle. She sure is good looking and long legged enough to be on the cover of *Cosmo*.

This experience reminds me of Shenzhen, right on the border with Hong Kong, back in the early 90s, when it was just being opened up as a *Special Economic Zone* (SEZ). Deng Xiaoping, the feisty, flinty, Sichuanese revolutionary warrior turned

Premier, who was always good for a pithy, all-knowing parable or axiom, made the call. This was Deng's first real market test tube, with Chinese characteristics. It was the early days, the buckaroo times of China and Shenzhen in particular, was a real Wild West, or Wild South frontier town as it were. *Seedy* only scratches the surface of what Shenzhen was like back then. There were scores of country girl prostitutes on every city block, all freshly emigrated from the hinterlands to seek their fortune. Tackily and kitschily dressed with Chinese opera thick make-up and RMB signs in their pupils, they would cat call you every step of the way. The western financial press ejaculated in their Brooks Brothers pleated pants and gyrated in their Gucci's at this marvel of unchained jungle capitalism - the China Miracle, with Shenzhen as its crown jewel. The mythological dogs of Lust, Greed, Envy, Pride and Gluttony, venal beasts all, were unleashed upon the land by the Gods of FIRE. The pavement of Shenzhen was crawling with hungry, avaricious Fast Freddys and Easy Eddys: pimps, loan sharks, fencers, drug dealers, counterfeit merchandise sellers and black market money changers. Obnoxious whorehouse, nightclub and restaurant touts pullulated on every street corner, harping and hawking the passers-by, like a sleazy circus midway. It was an exhausting obstacle course in depravity, a twisted Fellini street scene, cartoonish and buffoonish, but all too real, just to get from the hotel to the restaurant and back. The prostitutes slept during the day, so it calmed down a little bit when the Sun was up, but not by much. Back in those crazy days of soul survivor free trade (in truth, it never has been free markets in China - Baba Beijing heavily steers the markets towards long term goals set out in each Five Year Plan), all over China I would get phone calls to my hotel rooms, with a young woman breathlessly asking me if I needed any company or a *special massage*. Of course the hotel was in on it, playing the part of the money skimming King Pimp Sino-Superfly. It was always a hoot when my wife traveled with me and the phone would ring,

"Honey, there's a nice young lady on the phone who would like to give me a *private* massage. Are you OK with that?"

This even happened at big name, international hotels, with the on-duty managers raking in some extra filthy lucre on the side. Since being back in China fourteen years later, I was handed a business card as I was walking into a Beijing Holiday Inn Express. The tout was offering the usual massage. Just call and give them your room number, he tells me. Googling *massage+escort* on the Internet here will pull up pages of multi-talented masseuses. Price lists are posted. They will come to your place and for ¥800 (€100/$127), give you that ninety minute *special massage* you've always fantasized about. Don't forget your Dream Sea vibe-ring condoms. Yee-hah Cowboys of Maroussi.

Baba Beijing's and the provincial governments' preoccupation with prostitution waxes and wanes, an oscillating socio-political sine wave that undulates across the national zeitgeist in fits and starts. Officially, prostitution is a scourge that like opium, was proudly eradicated by the revolution after independence in '49. But it never really goes away does it? For the 1% and the politically privileged, those phone calls and calling cards never stop flowing, even in the most draconian of societies. It is no secret now that Mao would routinely organize one man orgies, where a dozen virgin teenage peasant girls, all freshly plucked off the farms, would be at his carnal beck and call; he deflowered over a thousand of them during his rule of China.[2] Talk about rank hypocrisy, but it's no better in the West. It's called SOP, standard operating procedures. Heck, in the Middle East, why rent when you can pay top dollar to buy young concubines like so many bagatelles? Prostitution is a funny business. For most johns and *service providers*, it's just a coldly calculated transaction: an orgasm for cash on the barrelhead. But the problem lies elsewhere on both sides of the ledger, where the bottom line sinks into the mucky, murky algorithms of control, humiliation, domination, manipulation and too often, violence. It works in the two directions. At the end of the day for the john, what could be more manipulative and humiliating than to pay good money for what in essence is glorified masturbation? My Tex Avery hooker is giving me all this food for thought as I am walking around town, but my stomach needs more than philosophical ruminations. I luckily stumble across an atypical restaurant this evening, so dinner in Xichang is memorable. It is not the first Communist China nostalgia place I've ever been to, but this one may be the most hip and camp. The Communist Food Party (社会食党= shehui shidang) restaurant's exterior and interior décor are done up in a collective kitchen and canteen motif, much like the real zombiefied, mining company one where I ate in Jingtieshan, Gansu, except here of course it is not authentic, with its Disneyworld ambiance.

Revolutionary posters from the ersatz glory days of the Great Leap Forward extol the inevitable domination of China's proletarian industrialization over the corrupt U.S.A. (中上美底!= *zhongshang meidi!* = China Up - America Down!). Nothing like a little nostalgia for the perfection of revolutionary ardor and the people's crusade against the perfidy of Western hedonism. Forty million kindred Chinese souls perished with empty stomachs and shattered dreams during those three short years of mass delusion, but what the heck, the leaders' hearts were in the right place. Give'em an A for effort! Cultural Revolution posters are also displayed, which after the Great Leap Forward, abandoned all pretenses for ineluctable world domination, to instead obsess on ideological purity and expunging the landscape of counterrevolutionary rats and riffraff. And they did, oh man did they, big time. Cute metal camping cups and collective rice bowls, with simple, jungle style bamboo stools and tables help fill out the place. The walls are done up with split bamboo, to give the impression that we are in a tropical hut someplace, like Guangxi or Hunan, two of the historical cauldrons of Chinese Communism. There are also historical photographs and newspaper front pages with pictures of Mao, Zhou Enlai and Chinese citizens performing to perfection Lei Feng feats of bravery and heroism. I especially like the portrait banners that show the busts of Marx, Engels, Lenin, Stalin and Mao, their heads all lined up neatly in an oblique row, looking very erudite and sage – men on a sacred mission. Ah, those were the days of cross border, fraternal love.

Being in a retro-restaurant like this is an uncanny look into humankind's amazing ability to expunge and eclipse the most horrific of demented follies. This limitless capacity for collective amnesia can be seen all over the world, not just here in Xichang, China. Western pundits love to round on the Chinese for conveniently glossing over their post-independence generation of madness. It is easy to throw brickbats at China's artful omissions and jaundiced justifications. But not so fast: we Westerners have a whole heap of misery swept under our communal rug of shame. The United States' history books and many public venues don't just whitewash, but glorify the extermination of ten to fifteen million natives and the brazen theft of a continent. For all of the New World, European colonialists slaughtered and infected, like so much as vermin - by some estimates - upwards of 100,000,000 original Americans.[2,3] Let's be really honest: sanitized Western notions of progress are exalted on the bones, blood and plundering of the world's dark skinned peoples and their natural resources. Aye aye Capitan Ahab, all in a day's work. The case book is thick of these mass, collective bouts of amnesia, real life tragedies unceremoniously flushed down Orwell's Memory Hole. For starters, during the day you read this book, over 20,000 of our fellow humans, ages 0-5 will die like dogs in the gutter, for the simple lack of food, potable water and preventable diseases. And tomorrow and the day after, 7,500,000 per year, not even counting those over five years of age. That's over six September 11ths *a day*. It's perversely called progress, and we are all guilty of compartmentalizing it, shutting it out, denying it,

"The headlines are wall to wall about those four tourist skiers killed in an avalanche in France today. Did you see that? Wow, what a tragedy! Honey, please pass me the salt and pepper..."

A few Westerners die inopportunely and their demise saturates the 24-hour news cycle. At the same time, Muslims are being droned and bombed by the village full around the world, while 20,000 helpless children, almost all dark skinned, die during every one of these daily news spins. Clearly and repugnantly for most of us, a Caucasian, Western, Judeo-Christian life is worth much, much more than a dark skinned, Eastern, Muslim/Hindu/Buddhist soul. Protestations aside, this is sad but true for the Washington/London/Paris consensus. Listen to what they say, watch what they do – and most importantly, watch what they don't do.

More specifically, if you are an American, French, Brit, Russian or Chinese, all members of the UN Security Council, countries that could have screamed bloody murder, there is the trifling little matter of sanctions against Iraq, which are in part, still in effect. At their height, 1990-2003, the terms were so onerous as to make the post-WWI Weimar Republic feel grateful. Those humiliating Western sanctions were the calling card for Hilter and the Nazis, as a nationalist cry to stand up and save the German people. Sixty years later in Iraq, sanction results were nothing less than genocide and war crimes: 100,000-1,000,000 young children, depending on your sources, were starved to death like desert rats. Madeline Albright, Bill Clinton's handpicked UN Ambassador and sanctions fanatic, infamously said on *60 Minutes* in 1996, that for the death of half a million (Iraqi) children,

"We think the price is worth it."

Really? *We* being of course Clinton and his administration, representing the American people.[5] The Chinese people can be rightfully accused of collective amnesia for their post-independence history, but it must be kept in perspective with this and so many other similar, shameful bouts in the West and around the world.

The Orwellian Newspeak and Perpetual *War on Terror* is only the latest, disturbing permutation of humanity's never ending trajectory of victimizing the Other. Muslims know all too well that this latest, deadly pogrom firmly plants them in the role of the West's newest bogeyman, and they are suffering dearly the bloodiest of consequences. Muslims don't hate Americans' and Europeans' freedoms. They hate the slaughter and destruction of the lives of millions of Muslim innocents in the name of said freedom and the West's support of despotic governments who oppress them, and that it is tolerated by Western people, if not welcomed by many, especially among the Princes of Power and their political elite. Manically keen observers of deep history, Baba Beijing understands all this perfectly well and with crystal clear foresight. China is patiently biding its time to use this criminal chapter in human history to their tactical and strategic advantage. Afterall, there are as many Muslims on Earth as there are people in China. And when the time comes, they will hit pay dirt without much effort. All Baba will be doing is showing up on the right side of justice and decency. Ka-ching baby… Banco.

For too many, it is much more visceral and in their face – the ones we so conveniently compartmentalize. For Westerners' short memories, there's the West's then ally, Iraq, instigating the 1980-88 Iran-Iraq War. Europe's and America's sale of large quantities of weapons of mass destruction (nerve gas) was sent in desperation, since our BFF (best friend forever) Saddam Hussein and his army were losing on the battlefield to those evil Iranians and their just-won Islamic Revolution, helping to push the war casualty total toward one million. These container loads of Western nerve gas, in contradiction to all accepted international conventions and simple decency, could be described as the opening salvo of the West's Perpetual War on Muslims. But in fact, the West's demonization of Muslims goes further back, almost a hundred years. Israel was carved out of the ethnic holocaust of 750,000 Palestinians (including ironically, thousands of Christians), who were chased, murdered, robbed and extorted out of their ancestral lands. This shameful factoid of human suffering, the 1948 Al-Nakba (The Catastrophe), has been conveniently sponged clean from the world's collective conscience, like it never happened[6,7]. In fact, Al-Nakba started in 1917, when the British had their post WWI self-appointed colonial Mandate over the area, with the United States and Europe giving them a big pat on the back for their bloody efforts. Back in those days, in many Westerners' eyes, Palestinians were no better than bothersome riffraff to be eliminated from the streets of Jerusalem. Tragically, not much has changed since then and the ethnic genocide continues with a vengeance, under the cynical eyes of the Western powers, who nostalgically admire the cruelest forms of colonialism and apartheid when they see them.[8] And like America's parks and museums, Israel has its own icons and heroes vaunting the annihilation of their *other* people, in what was once Palestine only two short generations ago. What is being perpetrated on the Palestinians is accepted as the bitter truth across the planet, outside the West's official narrative. Even among Jewish Israelis, a sizeable plurality are against their country's regional hegemony and destruction of the Palestinian people. What I am stating is only heretical in the halls of Western and Israeli influence. This sidebar into understanding the plight of the Palestinians is absolutely essential, as China and the West grapple on the world's stage for 21st century influence, allies, resources and power. The fact is, many, if not most international political turf wars happening before our eyes are colored by Jerusalem's prism. The gates of this holy city have changed hands no fewer than 44 times during its +5,000 year existence and will undoubtedly change again. China's views of the past, present and future are just as long winded as this this city's violent history and Baba Beijing is keenly preoccupied with events in the region. As China's international influence grows, their participation in Middle Eastern affairs will surely multiply. After all, alongside North Korea, what happens in Jerusalem could determine whether we have the launch of nuclear weapons and the start of World War III. This is not just about the Palestinian-Israeli *conflict*. As Lord Arnold Toynbee, the cebrated British historian summed it up succinctly,

"*The tragedy in Palestine is not just a local one; it is a tragedy for the world, because it is an injustice that is a menace to the world's peace.*"

Jerusalem and Al-Nakba are the crucible, the hub on which turns the world's titanic clashes between West and East, North contra South, rich versus poor, white against black. To leave it out of so many international sociopolitical discussion spanning the globe, China included, is to ignore that it is the ultimate cipher to understanding so many of humanity's rivalries. Bluntly stated, any accommodation between the West and 21st century China will, by the force of history, pass through the gates of Jerusalem.

A full set of Encyclopedias Britannica could be filled with these and thousands of other cases, going back through the annals of human history. It must be said though, that the big numbers, in the hundreds of millions who were and are still being exterminated or destroyed, happened in the last five hundred years of Euro-American colonization of the New World, Africa and Asia, along with the febrile sociopolitical madness of the 20th -21st centuries. Stalin's USSR and Mao's China top this second category, while mentioning Hitler's WWII blood fest, but there are too many others to even begin counting, large and small, on every one of the world's inhabited continents. We can touch wood that China is keeping to its historical pattern of obsessing over their Heavenly Mandate and taking care of business at home. Except for buying fair and square as much of Africa and resource rich corporations around the world as possible, it is not mimicking, at least for now, Western military and expansionist delusions of grandeur.

It's funny how a place like the Communist Food Party restaurant can trigger such a protean tangent of ruminations on the state of human affairs. After traveling, living and working much of my life in many parts of the world, I have learned to look at these many goings-on from the perspective of all the parties involved, especially the viewpoint of *The Dreaded Other*. What I have learned over the decades has long ago pushed me way beyond my comfort zone of accepted truisms, myths, conventions and perceptions of reality. As a result, I have changed and grown so much since leaving the United States in 1980. When I moved back to America in 2001, it was to a shockingly differently country, I could barely recognize it, but I too had been transformed over that last twenty-one years. For those who have not gone through all these horizon-expanding experiences and the philosophical renaissance that comes with them, it can be very upsetting for some people to accept who I am now, especially if they've known me for a long time, friends, colleagues and family included. I make no apologies for the arc of my personal and moral growth, understanding that the Other has just as compelling and all too real story to recount. After all, I represent *their* Other. I am merely speaking truth to the Princes of Power, but it does take courage, is always risky, and as millennia of headlines demonstrate, can turn deadly for many - the official narrative is controlled and enforced with an iron fist. Speaking out can mean being shunned by family and friends, losing one's job, making hard choices and worse. At the end of the day though, as a result of my spiritual metamorphosis, I feel a real sense of inner peace and harmony with my existence and purpose during my brief life on our Pale Blue Dot. Conversely, over the years, I have also grown very empathetic and completely uncritical of anybody who has experienced a similar path of inner and spiritual growth, in whatever direction it takes them, even if it is contrary to my own, but due to the heavy weight of conformity, that official narrative, they are compelled to hew their consciences to this onerous, inside-the-beltway status quo. They've got a job to keep, a family to feed. They cannot express themselves openly, even though freedom of speech is enshrined in their countries' constitutions. I am speaking from personal experience, as I lived it for the better part of twenty-eight years. It's hard, I know, and oftentimes it is downright dishonest: don't make waves, stick to the program, just go with the flow – and like Damocles, that iron fist of official narrative is hovering just over your head. You feel compelled to lie to yourself, friends and colleagues, which is unhealthy and very stressful for the soul. Psychologists call it *cognitive dissonance* and it can eat away on a person's spirit like cancer. It also helps explain why the more things change, the more they stay the same. Upton Sinclair, the late, great and courageous American journalist famously observed,

"*It is difficult to get a man to understand something when his salary depends upon his not understanding it.*"

Amen brother... Walking leisurely back to my urban jungle hotel, it is easy to see that even though Xichang ranks as a smaller provincial city, there are a lot people flowing through here. Eight bus stations are marked on the city map, between two of which I transferred, and the first one is humongous. As would be expected, these multiple bus and train stations in Chinese cities are strategically located and frequently named after the cardinal points of a compass. My third floor hotel window overlooks a bus station parking lot and it has over fifty interurban coaches that will all be lined up, ready to take off every which way, first thing tomorrow morning. Chinese bus stations resemble small airports in their organization, size and activity, ditto the bigger train stations. China: the world's people mover. We pull out of the station early the next morning to head to Lugu Lake. It is still not yet light and Venus and Jupiter are resplendent, hanging majestically above the eastern horizon. Not so long ago, humanity moved across the face of the globe with the help of these and other bright, blinking beacons in the sky. As we make our way out of town towards the road to Lugu, these two planets desperately fight being obliterated by the swelling light of the rising Sun. They will inflame our imaginations, when they return every morning for the next several weeks, putting on their amazing show. Well, it had to end eventually. Time to say goodbye to the Tibetan Plateau and come back down to Earth, which to be told, has already happened. I check my Galaxy's altimeter as we leave and see Xichang sits at 1,500m. Without even realizing it, we descended over a kilometer from the Land of Snow yesterday. Yikes, I am in denial. But *I'll be back*, as all good traveling Terminators say. I sit and reminisce about my first twenty-five days on the road in China. What an amazing journey *44 Days* has been so far. Saying goodbye to the Tibetan Plateau, it does not take me long to buck up and get excited about exploring Yunnan and its minority peoples. Ever onward Jeff. Tally ho.

1- *Recently reissued in the US, Paul Ableman's* I Hear Voices *is a fascinating look into the perceptions a schizophrenic experiences every waking hour. Ableman is reportedly a schizophrenic himself. I guard my first edition 1958 Olympia Press copy jealously.*

2- The Private Life of Chairman Mao, *1996, by Li Zhisui. Dr. Li was Mao's personal physician for 22 years, up till the Helmsman's death in 1976. This is gripping and at times, lurid reading for anybody who has an interest in Mao Zedong. The details of Mao's private life are unbelievable.*

3- American Indian Holocaust and Survival: A Population History Since 1492, *by Russell Thornton (1990). University of Oklahoma Press. pp. 26–32. ISBN 0-8061-2220-X.*

4- *Alan Taylor (2002). American Colonies; Volume 1 of The Penguin History of the United States, History of the United States Series. Penguin. p. 40. ISBN [Special: Book Sources/780142002100|780142002100].*

5-. *Wikipedia does a nice job of summarizing the whole criminal affair, including Albright's infamous interview: .*

6- *As long as you are robbing their land, you might as well go ahead and steal their cultural heritage while you're at it:* Israel's 'Great Book Robbery' Unraveled;
www.aljazeera.com/indepth/features/2013/01/201312114556875749.html .
Israelis learned well from their Nazi tormenters. For the whole history of Al-Nakba, watch the riveting and soberting documentary: www.aljazeera.com/programmes/specialseries/2013/05/20135612348774619.html

7- The suffering of Sderot: how its true inhabitants were wiped from Israel's maps and memories; *www.independent.co.uk/voices/co suffering-of-sderot-how-its-true-inhabitants-were-wiped-from-israels-maps-and-memories-8348734.html*

8- *Israeli historian Dr. Ilan Pappé and British journalist Robert Fisk are essential reading to fully understand what is going on in the Muslim and Arab Worlds. I keep expecting to read a headline any day that one or both have been assassinated by Zionist extremists and Mr. Fisk infuriates everybody on all sides, including Muslims. They are both very courageous people, who have really opened my eyes and given me an education about where World War III could easily start. en.wikipedia.org/wiki/Ilan_Pappé and www.independent.co.uk/biography/robert-fisk.*

CHAPTER 31: XICHANG/LIANGSHAN - LUGU LAKE (LUGUHU)

An amazing look at why half of China's territory is deserted. Bitter green walnuts, China's minorities, mountain climbing agriculture, an atypically bad roadside lunch, Daniel Boone architecture and hanging in there at 2,700 MASL.

The bus ride from Xichang to Luguhu is geographically notable. After leaving the Land of Snow and its 3,000 MASL, we descended to 1,500m in Xichang yesterday. Today, we quickly get back up over 2,000m and stay above this altitude until I get on the train and start heading back to Beijing next month. What this means is that from the first stop in Yinchuan, Ningxia, until I am well out of Guizhou Province at the end of this journey, I am never less than 1,100 MASL. This is a powerful, empirical statement about how elevated Western China really is.

What this demonstrates is that China is topographically divided in two parts. One is the narrow strip of coastal plain that starts in Heilongjiang in Manchuria, in the northeast of the country, down through Beijing, Shandong, Shanghai, Fujian and on south to Guangdong and Hong Kong, in the shape of a big letter J. A staggering 94% of the Republic's citizens live on only 46% of the land, and a huge chunk of those are found on this coastal plain. These are the highly successful *Blue Provinces*, named because of their proximity to the Pacific Ocean, as opposed to the interior *Yellow Provinces*, aptly named for the color of the soil frequently seen in these parts. The North China Plain (including Beijing) and the Shandong Peninsula together have more people than the *entire* United States, but this area is only the size of *France*. The Sichuan basin is the size of Michigan and touts over one hundred million souls. A third major population center in China is the Yangtze River basin (including Chongqing), which houses another 150,000,000. Let these numbers sink in for a moment. They are staggering. So far on this journey I have been in the western deserts and highlands that make up over 54% of the Republic's surface area, yet have only 6% of the total population. This explains why it is not hard to travel in Western China and sometimes feel like you are the last remaining survivor of the human race, acting out the final scene in the book/movie, *On the Beach*.

Changes are not only a question of altitude, but one of latitude also. Xichang already has a very semitropical feel about it, with huge Bougainvillea stands, banana trees and lush tropical greenery. Leaving there and heading southwest on the S307 towards Lugu Lake, we climb back up 1,200m, to 2,700 MASL over the course of this leg, and the lush landscape would make you think you are in Southeast Asia. There are towering bamboo forests, thick Tarzan jungle vines crawling everywhere, laterally and vertically, with flowering trees dotting the mountainsides. Stately magnolia trees are in resplendent bloom, tropical acacias, whose leaves are more blue than green, pomegranate groves are seen and what look like thick leaved jojoba trees. There are also venerable old eucalyptuses towering over it all, playing the role of emergents overlooking this verdant canopy. The big surprise is seeing walnut trees and freshly harvested nuts for sale. They are evidently well adapted to the mild, sub-tropical latitude and cool high elevation. The trees are smaller but the fruit looks just like the same in Europe and North America, so I buy a half a kilo during one of our stops. I crack one open and find out very quickly that they are still soft and green and as a result, taste bitter and make your mouth pucker up, like eating green persimmons. I keep them for a few days and realize they are going to take weeks to really dry out and be edible, so I just leave them in a hostel room as a parting gift. Buying these walnuts is also a wakeup call that the cultural landscape is changing too. The women vendors are members of the Yi Tribe (彝族), or sometimes known as Lolo or Nuosu in the West, since those can also be the name of their language. One of the fifty-five minority peoples in China, they number 8.7 million and mostly reside on the border between Sichuan and Yunnan, as well as Northwest Guizhou. Here in Yi country, no matter how steep the valley face, tessellated terraces, which don't know the meaning of erosion and gravity, staircase right up the precipitous walls, scaling hundreds of meters towards the morning slate grey, tropical sky. Above that, they tend ruminant animals on the grassy areas among the peaks, tiny black and white dots almost imperceptibly moving along. It is not dissimilar to other sections of this trip, except here the terracing is incline-defying. When you realize the farmers carry seed, water, fertilizer and chemicals up and down these plots, and then harvest and bring down all the grain and produce to the river bottom below, it makes these ancient agriculture systems and the Yi people who farm them all the more impressive. Above all this, the mountains top out at 3,000m, the crests are covered in deciduous and pine forests, with patches of scrub trees in between. Along the way, we go over several 2,200 to 2,500m mountain passes to get from one incredible valley to another.

The Yi have their own Lolo alphabet, which starting in Xichang and until I leave Luguhu, I see on many of the public signs, along with Chinese and Pinyin or English. It's really cool looking, like some funky script in a *Jetsons* cartoon. Jokes aside, it is much like Native American scripts and symbols, which again gives me pause at how we are all so interrelated, thanks to Homo sapien meanderings out of Africa 50,000 or more years ago.[1] Like Chinese, Lolo was originally logosyllabic (a tactful way of saying hieroglyphic) but after independence, the Communists unified all the various competing versions into a syllabic alphabet. It is the largest in the world, with about 1,400 letters. This is to allow for a unique consonant plus vowel sound for each of their three tones, instead of using accents. I'd still rather learn this many letters (a bit like the Japanese alphabet hiragana), than several thousand Chinese ideograms. Too bad Mao didn't finish his visionary dream to do the same with Chinese and Pinyin. The traditional, formal dress of the Yi women is to wear brightly colored pants and blouses of the same hue, but with a rainbow of different shawls, vests and scarves. These days, Scot plaid and African batik motifs have made their way to China, and all these patterns frequently clash together on the same Yi woman in a cacophony of colors. They each carry a beautifully needlepointed, mosaic satchel bag hanging around their necks, which has very long, usually red or yellow tassels hanging along the bottom. As is so true around the world, the headgear sets them off with distinction. They sport perfectly round, horizontally color-banded hats, flat on the top and with two rows of large cream colored beads along the top and bottom edges. I know they would not appreciate the comparison, but their headdresses look like very ornate, Gilded Age hat boxes worn upside down, like oversized, rimless bowlers. I later see a number of younger Yi women formally dressed like this in tourist areas. However taking the Xichang-Luguhu bus today on the S318, up in rural mountains, there is not time for such colorful niceties. Here, sinewy, strong-backed, rugged looking, work-a-day mountain Yi women are selling their apples and walnuts and can't be bothered with this level of sartorial allure. They surely dressed up just as regally for their marriages and probably do so for seasonal festivals and the like. But today, they are sporting banal Mao britches with mismatched shirts and sweaters, along with tufted jackets to fight the high altitude, nighttime cold. For headwear, they have each taken a shawl or big scarf, folded it flat and worked it like a square turban to cover their hair. Seeing them and reflecting back on the other minorities I have talked to on this trip, it is a worthwhile observation that we never see the hair on a vast number of traditionally dressed women, especially the older they get. There are a number of reasons women wear scarves to cover their hair and heads, whether Buddhist, Muslim or Christian: modesty, a sense of centeredness about one's faith, it identifies the woman as to her religion or minority race - to the mundane: they are fashionable, sexy, something fun to wear and offer a style or trend to follow. So far on this journey, I have visited with Hui (10.5 million) in Ningxia, Uighurs (10 million) in Ningxia and Gansu and Tibetans of course in Gansu and Western Sichuan (6.2 million). Along with the Yi, I will have a chance to run into a few more minorities before this trip is out. In every case, the women have distinctive head gear.

I flash back to the 90s as I observe my fellow bus passengers. After-lunch snacks like diced, pickled chicken feet and walnuts (I guess they like them raw - I pass) are the favorites, along with farm fresh apples, as well as open fire roasted corn on the cob. Twenty years ago, the floor of the bus would be littered with the refuse of inedible chicken gristle, walnut shells, apple cores and chewed up corn cobs, all glued together with copious quantities of sputum. Now, all the passengers collect their leftovers in little plastic sacks and ceremoniously place them in trash cans spaced up and down the aisle on both sides. Not only is their infrastructure developing, but I continue to confirm that the Chinese are also evolving as a people too. These long distance buses haul more than humans. Every once in a while, the driver slows down in the most unlikely of places and honks his horn. Playing the part of a stealthy road pirate, somebody who is expecting us is waiting on the shady roadside, jogs out onto the highway and runs obliquely up to the window next to the driver. The chauffeur then hangs out a thick envelop or small package to grab, with the bus still slowly rolling. Very well executed and sort of a specialized courier service. At one place the driver stops and honks for quite some time at a totally inert construction site along the road. Two hard hatted workers come stumbling and swerving towards us, either drunk, just awakened or both, and grab a bag with three big ball bearings in it. They start prancing, shouting with joy and holding the machine parts up above their heads like some World Cup trophy. I suspect this broken part has brought the entire operation to a grinding halt, maybe for a concrete mixer, compressor or pump.

I almost always enjoy and finish my meals in China, but today's lunch is a bust. I get something called *wangdaping* (王大坪= royal big flat). It is pork, about half fat, probably off the belly, like bacon. This chef puts in so much fresh ginger (which can be very pungent) and *huajiao* that I cannot even begin to finish it and almost all of it ends up as pig slop, from whence it came. I buy my favorite Chinese dry snack, Haochidian, which with a cup of tea from my thermos, tides me over till dinner, by expanding in my stomach, making me feel full. It is also through here that for the first time, I discover orchard after orchard of a crop I have never seen before. They are 2m tall trees with thin, scaly, bark-covered branches that all radiate from a central root stock in the ground. They have little dark green leaves growing close, all up and down the length of the narrow branches, making them look like some spindly cactus or succulent. In between the leaf rows, little red berries run up and down the top half of the tree branches, growing right on the surface of the bark. It almost reminds me of coffee plants I have seen around the world, but I know it's not that. This mystery tree continues to perplex me and it isn't until I'm in Lijiang later in the week to discover that these are actually *huajiao* trees. Yes, that infamous, numbing spice that puts your mouth to sleep and made renowned by Sichuan chefs, grows right on the branches of trees, not on bushes or plants. During the drive, I can see that the farmers double crop all these *huajiao* orchards, along with many apple farms, by planting potatoes underneath the tree stands. Very efficient, as long as there is the water and nutrients to sustain it all. The farmers slice and dehydrate the apples to sell to all the passersby. I buy a bag for ¥10 (€1.30/$1.60) and they are out of this world, naturally sweet with no sugar added. The other double crop system is corn and hot red peppers, similar to jalapeno, but smaller and more deadly. To get two crops per year off the land, the corn is seeded in ground-level plastic tents, to maximize the high altitude sunlight against the chilly nights up here. I even see a few maniac farmers triple farm: orchard/*huajiao* trees with corn *and* hot peppers. It obviously is not terribly successful, as these triple crop fields seem to be struggling. There is only so much water and fertilizer that the ground can absorb.

Along the way, there are a number of roadside apiculturists owning a dozen hives each, selling fresh honey with and without the comb. Going back a decade, the Chinese have had their honey exports blocked by the US and EU, for antibiotic use, to counteract the mysterious *colony collapse disorder* that has thrown the world bee industry into seizures.[2,3] It is hard to tell whether these WTO sanctions have any merit, or if it is one of the school boy tit-for-tat shoving matches countries routinely go through, to support or protect a national industry, or punish a country for perceived trade misdeeds. I will not let this health issue onto my radar; I eat Chinese honey. It's not like I drink 5kg of honey a day and the quantities found are measured in micrograms per kilogram. I haven't taken an antibiotic for infections in over a decade (other than to get rid of the waterborne amoeba, Giardiasis), so I'm not worried about building up a resistance.

On our way to Lugu Lake we drive across a broad, flat, plain at 2,500m and as we get closer to the lake, the architecture of the houses changes dramatically. We transition through villages of white stucco homes that have painted on them big, bright motifs of garlanded hot red peppers and three loose, red apples in a triangular arrangement – which does a nice visual job of summarizing this area's claim to fame. Then, as we leave this plain and start climbing up into the mountains, many of the homes are good old fashioned log cabins, with eucalyptus and pine trunks serving as the exterior. These log houses are painted white, mustard yellow or are varnished a natural wood color. Are we in Kentucky or Sichuan? Some days it's hard to say, but the telltale dragon-curved tips on the clay roof gables give away our cultural coordinates.

There is also a huge change in the geology. Gone are the earthquake weakened mountains of the Liqi Valley. Here, there are just a few minimal rockslides and the exposed faces along the road show clearly defined and layered strata. Geological ages and evolutionary development are intact here, Sorry Ken Ham, founder of the Creation Museum in Kentucky, no saddled triceratops being ridden by Adam and Eve to be found along this stretch.[4] This solid substrata helps explain how the farmers here can push terraced crop production to such vertiginous levels up the valley walls. As we approach the lake, the valley really narrows and the river we are paralleling and which feeds into Lugu Lake is the color of creamed coffee. For the first time on this journey, I see a small, local hydroelectric dam running across it, to provide power to the villages in the area. Given the hundreds of rivers I have crossed over the last month, I am perplexed not to see more of these generators at the village/town level. Somewhere between paddle driven Buddhist Mani wheels and Three Gorges Dam, the scale of efficiencies in hydropower reaches its point of diminishing marginal returns.

The bus finally stops in a tourist village, Luguxian (泸沽县= Lugu County) and everybody gets off. No famous lake in sight, not even a puddle of water. A big billboard-sized map shows that the place I want to go, Wuzhiluo (五支罗) and then onto Luowa (洛瓦), which is about ten klicks away. I am choosing the Sichuan side of Lugu Lake today, since this side is much less traveled, compared to the Yunnan side. The Sichuan side is also interesting, since these villages are situated on an ever narrowing peninsula, that juts out to the southwest like a long, pointed isosceles triangle, with its apex marking the center of the lake. Thanks to this needle like peninsula, Lugu Lake is remarkably shaped like Cyprus. Tomorrow, I can boat over to the tourist-thronged Yunnan side. I quickly learn the local taxi drivers abuse the privilege of this drop off point, being far away from the hot spots, by charging ridiculous rates to get around the lakeshore They start out at 400 kuai (€50/$63) and drop to a *mere* 200 (€25/$32). Out of curiosity, I check my altimeter. I am stunned to see that we are perched at 2,700m, 100m higher than Kangding. We're talking close to Tibetan Plateau elevations. Oh yeah. Back in the high altitude biz, baby, right where I want to be. To heck with these ravenous ripoff drivers. The road looks excellent, the sky has burned off most of its clouds and is a startling deep cerulean. My rolling backpack still has its wheels intact, I am inured to my omnipresent 6kg backpack and the pure, mountain air is so anti-Beijing, so wild and so invigorating, as to feel liberating. Get a leg up, Brown… Time to get in character and explore. I am going to walk the whole distance to the tip of the peninsula, and stand at the center of the lake. What a way to get to know Luguhu: ground level, slow and easy. Little do I know that I'm about to come across one of the biggest illicit agricultural industries on the Pale Blue Dot.

1- *Google the* Lolo, Creek, Cherokee *and* Inuit *alphabets, as well as Native American symbols to compare. It's uncanny.*

2- *www.itmonline.org/arts/bees.htm and articles.latimes.com/2007/may/03/business/fi-chinahoney3.*

3- *blogs.reuters.com/great-debate/2012/04/09/mystery-of-the-disappearing-bees-solved/*

4- *sensuouscurmudgeon.wordpress.com/2012/11/11/ken-hams-creationist-empire-is-foundering/*

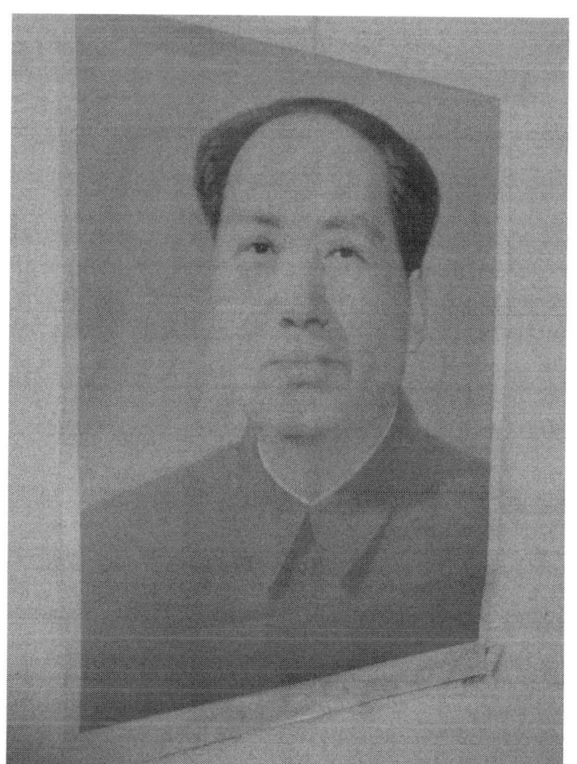

Figure 51: Langmusi: Mao Zedong, greeting us to our hostel. He still exemplifies a tremendous nostalgia among the Chinese for what they see as lacking in society – sacrifice, hard work, the common good, patriotism and brotherhood.

Figure 52: The eternal cycle of birth, life and death is on display in Tibetans' spiritual and architectural lives. Nonstop construction next to decaying buildings is the order of the day. Two young Langmusi monks sift sand to mix concrete.

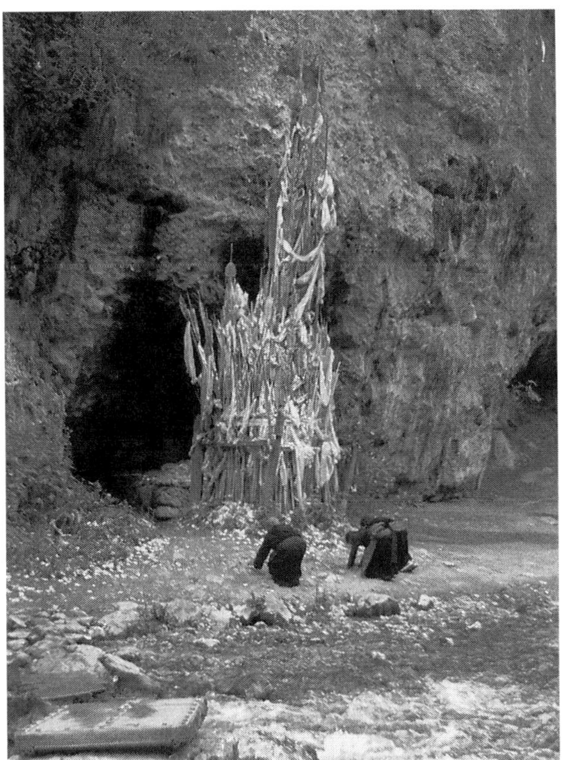

Figure 53: Langmusi: Three of the many Tibetan faithful outside the Great Namo Gorge Fairy Cave entrance, praying around its shrine. The white debris on the ground is paper wind horse votives that can be burned or offered as a form of supplication.

Figure 54: Langmusi's residential area, with heavy rocks set on top of roofing material to keep it from blowing away.

Figure 55: Langmusi: The incredibly beautiful Great Namo Gorge valley, with the creek at my feet. Hikers and explorers will find themselves alone.

Figure 56: Langmusi: the Great Namo Gorge valley. A Tibetan Buddhist monk shepherds his sheep and yaks grazing on the rising mountain face behind.

Figure 57: Langmusi – Songpan: The Tibetan rosary that the very faithful grandmother is using on her bus ride. The blurriness of the photo is testament to just how rough these secondary bus rides in China's hinterland can get.

Figure 58: Songpan: Tasty air dried yak testicles for your pleasure. Bon appétit!

Figure 59: Mirror Lake at UNESCO's Jiuzhaigou World Heritage Nature Park after closing time. Mummified tree trunks can be seen below the multihued, translucent waters.

Figure 60: The resplendent Pearl Falls at Jiuzhaigou Nature Park, after closing hours. There isn't a soul for kilometers. What an incredible day – and night!

Figure 61: Colorful Lake at Jiuzhaigou Nature Park. Chinese tourists like to have their picture taken next to a stele or marker, showing the name of the place. Animal motif hats, gloves, and masks are quite popular with Chinese women.

Figure 62: Another amazingly beautiful Chinese valley between Songpan and Chengdu. Two bridges are being built is this section, very near where the murderous Wenchuan earthquake turned this part of Sichuan upside down in 2008.

Figure 63: Chengdu – Tagong: riding on the multimillion dollar G5 highway and looking out over another multimillion dollar highway stretching off elsewhere. There are so many of these colossal transportation infrastructure projects in China that they become banal.

Figure 64: Chengdu – Tagong: the Qingyi River, one of many spectacular, wild river valleys that I traverse up. In these truly remote valleys, it is easy to feel like you are traveling in a Lost World or on Avatar's Pandora. Simply stupendous.

Figure 65: Chengdu – Tagong: one of the many roadside, open air restaurants one encounters on interurban bus travel. I only have one bad meal during the whole trip. Usually delicious and always freshly cooked.

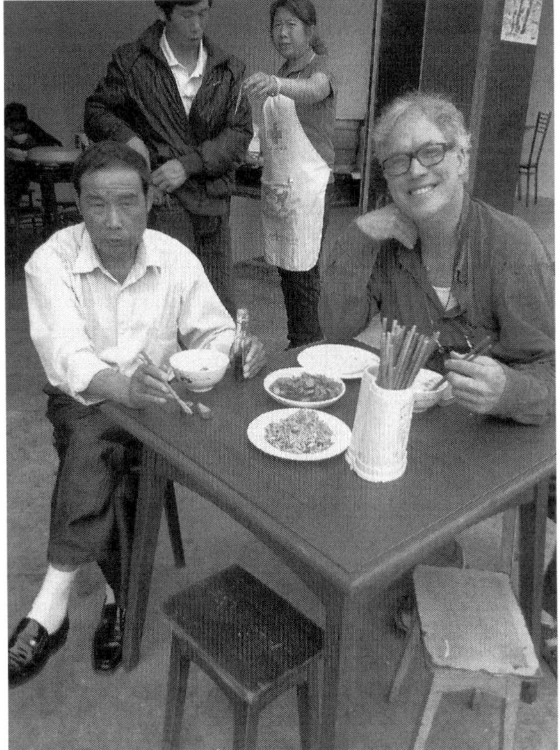

Figure 66: Chengdu - Tagong: roadside lunches are a great place to get to know the salt of the earth Chinese, like Mr. Jiang enjoying his whiskey lunch.

Figure 67: Tagong: Zhaxi, my taxi driver, helping a young Tibetan girl out of his packed and cramped combi. The girl's pink ears headband is a popular fashion style for girls and even young women.

Figure 68: Tagong: outside the Muyajin Temple, a large group of Tibetan cowboys and cowgirls are enjoying a picnic lunch.

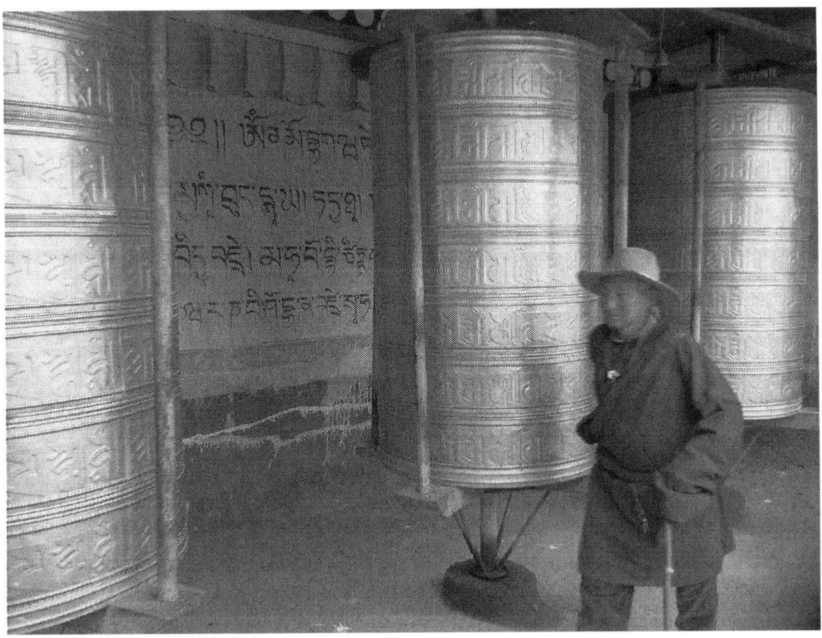

Figure 69: Tagong: a Tibetan Buddhist spinning the two long rows of brass prayer drums of the town's celebrated monastery.

Figure 70: Tagong: Modern China slowly encroaching upon traditional beliefs. Tibetan Buddhist faithful circuit the Tagong Monastery spinning hand held prayer, or Mani wheels and answering the odd phone call.

Figure 71: From Mad Dog Hill, a view of the Tagong Monastery garden sanctuary with its many stupas, and outside a long line of prayer drums, with the ambulatory faithful. On the mountainside is part of the Kerti Gompa Monastery and below it, the Tagong River.

Figure 72: Tagong: next to the large, colorful temple stele is a collection of hand carved, stone tablets, with passages of Buddhist texts, prayers and supplications.

Figure 73: The Tibetan stele at the north end of the prayer drum circuit of the Tagong Monastery. In the background, the tough climb up Mt. Jinire.

Figure 74: The long, suspended wind horse banner that runs across the valley can be seen stretching from Mad Dog Hill over Tagong. In the foreground is the upper right triangular wind horse forest overlooking Tagong. Looking down to the lower left gives a good impression of just how steep this climb is.

Figure 75: Tagong: my furtively absconded souvenir from the Wind Horse Forest on Mt. Jinire. It is made of fine silk and is a faded sherbet orange color, 20cm x 30cm in size.

Figure 76: A tessellated collection of wind horse votive papers. The ground around Tibetan temples and shrines is often littered with these little pieces of paper.

Figure 77: Tagong Monastery: after frolicking like dervishes on the rooftop earlier in the day, these young monks settle down and put on quite a choreographed dance routine, in the temple's atrium.

Figure 78: Liqi River Valley – Jiulong: six of the eight Tibetans riding with me, my cultural posse during the wild ride that day.

Figure 79: Liqi River Valley – Jiulong: the incomparable Tibetan Liqi River Valley. The villages along the barely passable road are one breathtaking National Geographic postcard after another.

Figure 80: Liqi River Valley – Jiulong: like giant Transformer robots, huge earth-moving equipment keeps us company at almost every bend along the river, thanks to massive land- and mudslides from the region's earthquake-weakened upper crust.

Figure 81: Liqi River Valley – Jiulong: My Tibetan posse and I have to get out and help push Zhaxi's combi forward. He finally gets a head of steam, takes off and we have to catch up at the top of the hill, on foot.

Figure 82: Liqi River Valley – Jiulong: mountain cascade powered Tibetan prayer, or Mani wheels, where Zhaxi and I wait for the Tibetan posse to catch up with us after going through the heavily guarded check point.

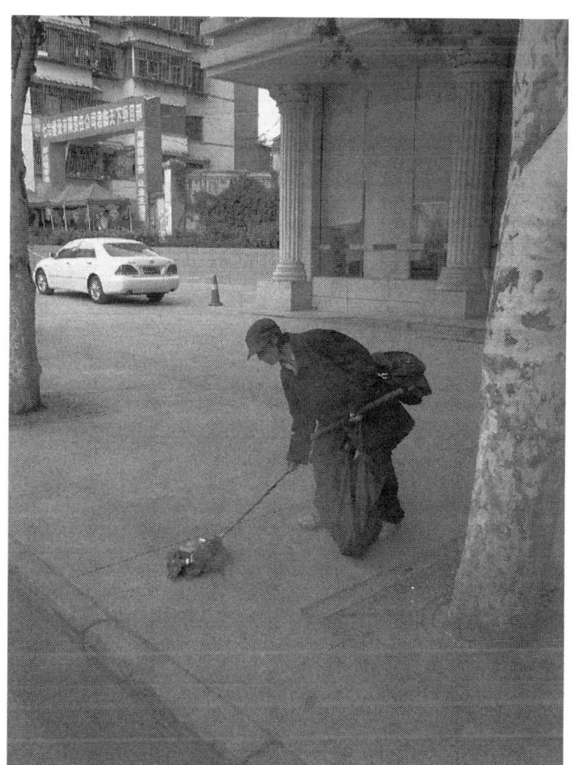

Figure 83: Xichang/Liangshan: A wandering Tibetan pilgrim nun on the streets of Xichang, burning an offering of fake money bills on the sidewalk. Wearing mourning black, she is offering this tribute to a loved one who has died, to provide them with all the necessities for their transcendence, and onto a new, reincarnated life.

Figure 84: Xichang/Liangshan: The parking lot overlooking the bus station, taken from my condom-furnished hotel room. China's ability to move many millions of people from city to town to remote village and back on a daily basis is impressive.

Figure 85: Xichang/Liangshan bus terminal. They are lined up like this, one after another, leaving for every compass point, eighteen to twenty hours a day, seven days a week, nonstop.

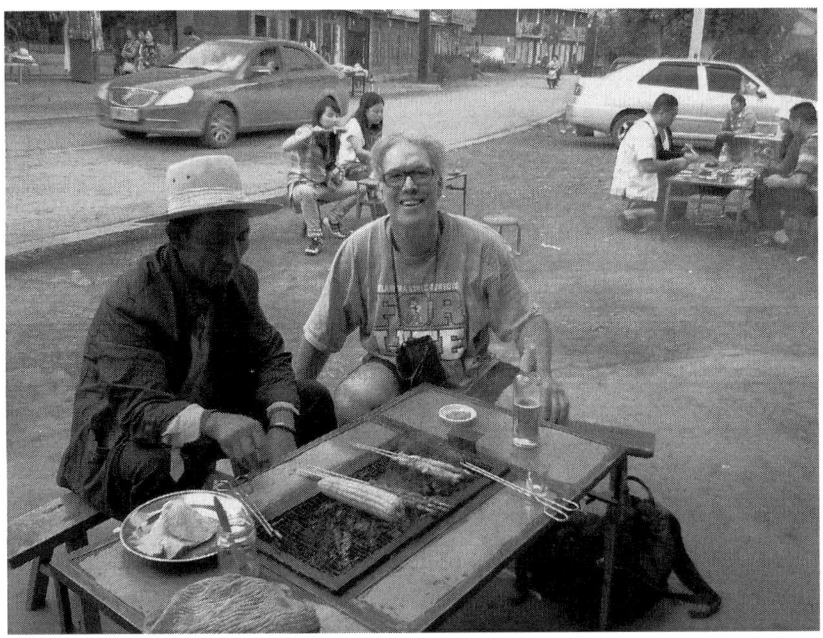

Figure 86: Luguhu – Luowa: Mr. Bin and I having a tasty outdoor Mosuo barbeque. You can see the massive, pure copper bracelet on his left wrist

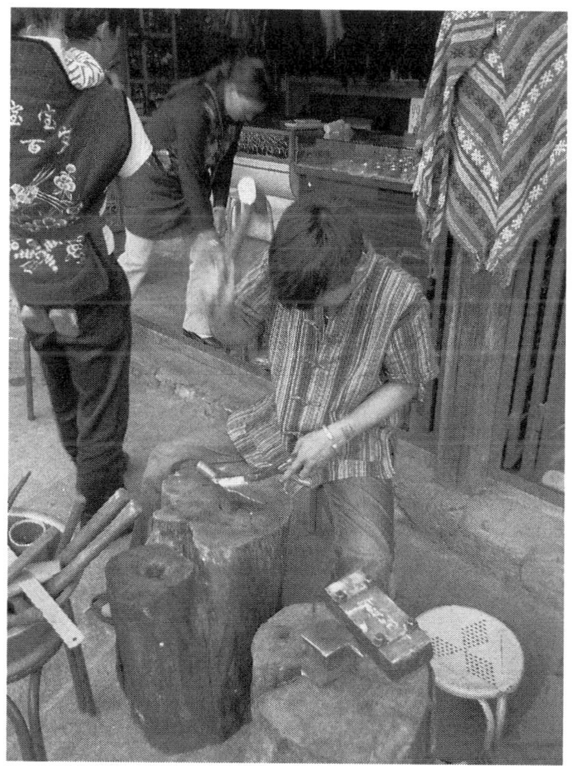

Figure 87: Luguhu – Luowa: silver- and goldsmiths are a popular profession in Western China and jewelry is very popular among its citizens. Some smiths just plop their tree trunk anvils and tools on a busy sidewalk and get to work.

PART VI

YUNNAN

Rules of the Road: Tolerance

"He who cannot agree with his enemies is controlled by them."
Chinese proverb

"The price of hating other human beings is loving oneself less."
Eldridge Cleaver

"Live and let others live!"
Italian proverb

Chapter 32: Lugu Lake (Luguhu)

The good, the bad and the ugly of Lugu Lake - marijuana free for the stealing, more floral species than a fancy Kew Gardens, a tasty outdoor BBQ, the amazing Mosuo people, their way of life that could save the planet and skiff riding sex maniacs. And sad to say, endangered wild cat skins are being sold like so much as tourist trash.

Leaving the Lugu Lake bus drop off area on foot and I have not even seen water yet. This area is very hilly at ground level and mountainous all across the horizon. Up to now, the lake is hidden from my very localized view. As I walk towards the road leading out to the lake peninsula, I see a very old Bai minority (who dominate the Dali area) gentleman sitting peacefully in the shade of a stand of trees, dressed in his full, ceremonial red and gold regalia, looking primed for a psychedelic Shriner's convention. I shamelessly check him out in my Zeiss. I also see an ancient looking Tibetan woman walking past, and am reminded that Tibetans populate the countryside this far south too, although in diminishing numbers. Many of the log houses are big two story affairs, ski resort classy and very impressive. I later learn that this architectural style is built by the Mosuo people.

I turn towards the center of the lake and slowly start to see water. South of the peninsula is a huge wetland area, known as Caohai (草海= Grass Sea). It is all part of Lugu Lake, but so shallow that it becomes a dense growth of marsh plants. The flora around Lugu is so prolific and different than any other place on this trip, that I find myself taking tens of pictures. The lakeside and hillsides are equally resplendent, with a panoply of colorful flowers, strange fruit, seeds, pods, leaves and buds. And one plant *really* sticks out. There are farmhouses on both sides of the road and as is typical around the world, each family is growing all kinds of vegetables and flowers on their properties, as well as several varieties of bamboo. At first, I don't believe it, but then I keep seeing it again and again - nice young marijuana plants mixed in with the veggies and colorful flowers. Beautiful smoking buds are poking out the tops of these pot plants and they look very handsome as I walk by the farms. Officially, marijuana use is illegal in China. These Lugu plants are way too small to be used for hemp, so it is safe to assume they are used for medicinal and recreational purposes by the farmers. However, Baba Beijing treads very lightly on the needs and customs of their many minority citizens, so I suspect its use here is just part and parcel of the local culture. And why shouldn't it? If there were not so many worldwide hundreds of billions of dollars to be made off all the profit centers of interdiction – growing, trafficking, eradication, law enforcement, legal fees, bail, incarceration and money laundering - then cannabis would be legalized. But the Princes of Power have too much invested and such high profits standing on its interdiction for legalization to happen any time soon. Compared to the West, especially the United States, China is little concerned about the financial advantages of illegality, since law enforcement and incarceration are still the bailiwick of Baba Beijing, and have not been privatized into market sectors. Now dear readers, for those who partake, before you storm Lugu Lake with chainsaws and stadium sized trash bags, please do me a favor and leave these gentle rural folk alone. You don't need to go to Yi/Mosuo Country to get Mother Nature gift dope anyway. In the first place, these plants are on people's property, so it is stealing. And secondly, marijuana grows wild all around Beijing in the mountains, along the roadsides, where it is free for the asking. During my other travels around China, I have also seen it growing wild on the roadsides. Have I ever harvested any and how good is it? Only my book publisher knows.

I continue walking on out towards the middle of the lake on this ever narrowing peninsula. Small, flat bottom skiffs are out in Caohai harvesting piles of a long, dark green reed grass. I later see mounds of it piled outside the roadside farms being fed to cattle and horses. A lot of it is being brought in off the lake. As the local population grows, you have to ask if this is a sustainable practice, before they start to deplete the wetland. My binocs show there is a meager selection of bird life, definitely not at the level you would expect for summertime in such an ideal location for wildfowl to flourish. That's the problem when you have so many of the planet's citizens. The blood and money lust for fauna and fowl and the difficulty in controlling their illegal harvest in a continent scaled country, on top of laissez-faire or mutually beneficial corruption, is a big reason I see very few birds and wild animals in all my travels around China. Luckily, the demand for flowers and ornamental trees is not as voracious, so I concentrate on admiring the flora instead, which is absolutely throbbing and teeming in a riot of rainbow colors on this whole journey, especially here. One of the most photogenic moments of the trip is talking with an old Mosuo woman, as we walk along beside each other. She has a cane stick and is herding a massive, white lactating sow in the middle of the peninsula road. Her amiable old pig is enjoying this slow summer saunter on such a beautiful day. Over her lifetime, I suspect this 200kg hog has provided many a pork carcass for the old matriarch and her extended female family. Given the moderate summer temperatures here, the Mosuo like to air cure their pig carcasses whole (gutted and dressed of course) and then store them flattened, one on top of the other in their basement larders.

I get to Luowa late in the afternoon. This is high season on the lake and a popular place to visit. The first two *zhaodaisuo* I check out are pricey and I settle on a big hostel. The room has three beds. The owner, young Mr. Qiong, a Han, tells me a huge group is on its way, and he is right. Before I take off after checking in, about thirty Chinese from Shanghai take over the place, but it does not fill up to the point where I have roommates. Very nice of Mr. Qiong to give me some privacy. At the end of the peninsula is a nature park, with a nice walking trail going out to the very tip. I go about 2km, almost to Goddess Bay (*Nvshenwan* = 女神湾) and can see that there is not enough time to get all the way out and back before dark. In any case the views here are breathtaking and I'll be boating across the water tomorrow. In front of me is tiny Princess House Island (王妃岛= *Wangfeidao*), which has a palace of a place on it, in modern, multi-storied log cabin motif. Further out at the tip of the peninsula is another bigger island, Liwubi (里务比岛), which sits just across the border on the Yunnan side, where the lake is administratively cut in two, north and south. Even further beyond that, behind the popular tourist town if Lise (里色), rises the 3,754m Gemu Goddess Mountain (格姆女神山) peak that towers over the lake. Elsewhere around this almost 50km^2 lake are cascading mountain peaks fading into the horizon. The lake's waters look well protected. Along the shoreline below me, it is transparent down to the shallow lake bottom, before plunging to depths of up to 90m. A spectacular sight in anybody's travel book and I can add this memorable view to Lakes Como, Tahoe, Crater, Geneva, Finger, and countless others in Africa, North and South America, China, Europe and elsewhere. As I come back to the trailhead, tens of shutterbug-loving Han are on the little pebble beach taking the normal assortment and permutations of *I have been here* photos. Many of them have taken off their shoes and are wading in the cool lake waters. That is about as exciting as it gets here tonight, in this end-of-the-peninsula, comparatively laid back village of Luowa.

I eat dinner outside of a Mosuo restaurant, seated at a low, open air BBQ grill. The man of the operation, Mr. Bin, is nice enough to cook my food for me, while we have a chance to talk. Mr. Bin is wearing a thick pure copper bracelet on his left wrist. It is a hunk of extruded copper cable over 1cm in diameter. It has a millimeter slit in it to get it on and off. Mr. Bin says he never takes it off, as it enhances his vital energy (气= Qi). Silversmiths are on the streets here with their anvils and hammers, making silver and copper jewelry. I am tempted to buy one, but pass. Mr. Bin's wife and their daughter take the orders, money and bring all the drinks and ingredients to be grilled. To get started, I first choose my meal from a long table with a smorgasbord of raw delectables spread out like a banquet. I choose freshly sliced eggplant, some strange looking forest mushrooms harvested locally up in the mountains, lean air cured, Mosuo pork slices, some yak meat shish kebabs and a tall, cold bottle of beer. A feast fit for Marco Polo. My new Mosuo buddy is charming and much attuned to his business as welcoming host. While the matrilineal Mosuo people are sensationalized by their tradition of the *walking marriage* (*zouhun* = 走婚), Bin, who is about my age, is proud to tell me he is married to his wife monogamously. They live right across the street in an apartment, below which is another restaurant, and which their two older children manage. He tells me that he and his wife, who stays busy taking care of the other tables with guests, have been together twenty-eight years. He does not act defensive about the reputation the Mosuo have for their matrilineal, women-wear-the-pants customs, just very matter of fact.

Being in the midst of a matrilineal culture and talking with a real live Mosuo man offers much for a Westerner to mull over. Since men typically strut around with their brains in their pants, the idea of a walking, or open marriages brings to mind hopelessly horny Austin Powers and his over the top shagadelic, shagalicious exploits, chasing after an endless supply of equally amorous females. But once the Mosuo woman picks her man, the rate of fidelity is similar to traditional western marriages. Promiscuity is not a byword in Mosuo couples. Also, their *premarital* freedom is not much different from a typically modern Western couple, where before a woman decides on Mr. or Mrs. Right, they may have more than one intimate partner or live with someone before tying the knot. Same goes for men too. It is true that once a young Mosuo woman reaches estrus, she traditionally is given her own private bedroom to prepare finding a suitable partner to eventually be the father of her children. If the house is too small, the child bearing members that do not have their own rooms share what's known as the Flower Room. This would help explain the very large log cabin homes needing several bedrooms, with the paramount mother as the head of the household and all the daughters, sisters and aunts living communally, where they take care of all the child rearing, education and wellbeing of their children. The chosen men who come to sleep with their appointing partners, live elsewhere, and work for the benefit of their children's household, making a living, fishing and farming. In other words, bringing home the bacon. Sounds awfully familiar, doesn't it? It is also true that the woman makes all the decisions about with whom she beds. She can make her desires known to her chosen man, or the menfolk are free to come calling at a matrilineal communal home, knock on the bedroom door of the woman he likes and talk across the divide to plead his worthiness. If she accepts, he hangs his hat on the outside handle so that everybody in the household knows a liaison is happening. If by chance another beau comes calling the same evening, they can see the hat and try elsewhere, or go home and lick their jealous wounds.

Let's also categorically dispel a claim made in the Lonely Planet, that,

The Mosu are the last practicing matriarchal society in the world...

It reminds me of that worldwide Cold War urban myth that,

The Great Wall is the only human made object which can be seen from the Moon.

Go on, admit it, we've all believed in canards like this at one time or another. Who needs the Internet, when I can just simply talk to someone who is the child of a matrilineal society - in India. Donald Lyngdoh set the record straight for me that his tribe, the Khasi, is matrilineal. This usually means all or part of the children taking the mother's family name, hereditary wealth passing down to the daughters and the man moving in with the woman's family (matrilocality). Donald has studied this subject and he's right. In some ancient cultures, membership in their groups was (and still is if in **bold**) inherited matrilineally. Example cultures or societies include the Cherokee, Choctaw, **Gitksan**, Haida, Hopi, Iroquois, Lenape, Navajo, and Tlingit of North America; the **Minangkabau** people of West Sumatra, Indonesia and Negeri Sembilan, Malaysia; the Nairs of Kerala and the Bunts of Karnataka in south India; the **Khasi**, **Jaintia** and **Garo** of Meghalaya in northeast India; the **Mosuo** of China; the Basques of Spain and France; the **Akan** including the **Ashanti** of West Africa; the **Tuaregs** of West and North Africa; and the **Serer** of Senegal, the Gambia and Mauritania. Not to mention Jews, who are very much a part of Western culture. Matrilineal societies exist across the four corners of the Earth, vestigial pockets of what was once surely standard operating procedures for humankind.[1]

I have read Barbara Walker's two majestic encyclopedias more than once from cover to cover, as well as a number of other related history reference books.[2] Based on Walker's work and everything else I've researched, before men came to control most societies and cultures across the world, before cities and agricultural production 10,000 years ago, humankind was predominately matriarchal (not just families, but society run by women) and matrilineal in social organization in the first place.[3] The arrangements were certainly very similar to the Mosuo: women took care of assuring the prosperity of the tribe from one generation to the next, educating and taking care of the children, until the boys reached puberty to join the menfolk; men helped on the outside of the households to bring home the vittles, be it meat, fish or fowl, grow food and provide protection from aggressive outsiders. Men could burn off all their excess testosterone playing manly war games and sports competitions, amongst themselves and with rival neighboring tribes. In 21st century parlance, we guys would play poker, golf, go huntng, drink beer, arm wrestle, belch, scratch our testicles a lot, and shower and shave less frequently. Back in the day, men were called and came to the temples and women's homes as suitors to be chosen, just like the Mosuo today. Once men put two and two together and figured out their participation was necessary for procreation, women's mystical, magical and goddess inspired ability to create children became just half the equation, and shattered their perceived holiness and uniqueness. Now, all that was necessary was for men to use their aggressive, sexually motivated, violent behavior to bring women into servile submission. The tables did not turn overnight, but happened over many centuries, in a predictable power struggle across most of the world's cultures. The list above is the vestiges of what once was commonplace across the planet. The women's religions' Great Goddess Maia/Gaia, got cleaved and expunged from her heavenly consort, leaving angry, bellicose, macho gods in her place. Temple priestesses and their ladies in waiting became palace harlots who were eventually degraded by patriarchs to three typecast: virgins, marital property or whores. With patriarchy firmly in control since then, written history is, alongside technological advancement, mostly one long soliloquy of wars, genocides, exterminations, conquests and environmental annihilations. The group of people who really lost out are one-half of humanity – women, and to this day are treated as second class citizens in the best of times and more commonly around the world, as domestic slaves and concubines for men's s leisure and sexual control, respectively. It's been a long, long fall, temporally and socio-politically for females over the last 15-20,000 years and the human race has paid dearly for their loss, as it has been equally disastrous for all of us. It has all culminated in the human race now standing on the precipice of global environmental meltdown. From the standpoint of humanity's ability to survive into the 22nd century, its chances would greatly increase if we all lived in a matriarchal system, or at least adopted its tenants and foundations of mutual and communal prosperity. But that's not going to happen within my lifetime. It probably will not until the Earth's ecosystem collapses, there is a resulting reduction/stabilization in the human population and new, no-growth, sustainable models for humanity that are adopted. When we soon reach this ecological tipping point, the traditional Mosuo way of life, with an inclusive, holistic, helpful, healing mother, in place of an all-powerful, vindictive, jealous warrior patriarch, has much to teach us about how to endure on this Pale Blue Dot for future generations.

Early the next morning, the lake all along the shorelines is blanketed with small white and yellow surface flowers called *shuixing yanghua* (水性杨花). The aquatic plants that produce these beautiful beds of floating flowers look like a mass of stringy vines under the shallow waters. This Mandarin name also refers to an unfaithful woman, which is very symbolic, since this flower shows its face in the morning (blooms during daylight), and then disappears during the night. Its name has even entered popular Chinese culture. The title of the 2008 Canadian romantic comedy movie, Noel Coward's *Easy Virtue*, was accorded this flower's name when it was distributed in Asia. The flower's Chinese name is a backhanded way of condemning the Mosuo way of matrilineality, especially coming from uber-patriarchal, Confucian Han culture.

Near all the hotels and restaurants at the tip of the Luowa peninsula, flat bottomed skiffs are lined up along the pebble beach looking for customers to transport across the lake. The waters are translucent and cool. Further out on the lake, the windless, calm surface of the water under the cloudy grey skies takes on the color and texture of obsidian. On the left is the shallow Grass Sea, Caohai. On our right are Princess Island and the trade routes to the Yunnan side of the lake. The ride all the way to Lige, in the far southwest corner of the lake in Yunnan is 200 kuai (€25/$32) per person and no boatswains want to go there unless they have at least six passengers. Right now, there are just not that many travelers looking for a ride there. However, for 90 RMB (€11/$14) each, they will take three or four of us to go the shorter trajectory across from the tip of the peninsula to a village called Luoshui (洛水), where I want to go today. Total strangers start to rub shoulders to see who wants to team up. I find a young Han couple. They are so in love it is fun to watch. I sure don't want to bother them and don't ask, but I suspect they are on their honeymoon. Not that I would get an answer. They can't keep their hands off each other and are oblivious to the outside world. I guess tonguing and fondling each other in a small lake skiff with a *dabizi* looking on will add some spice to their stories in future years. Our boatswains are a Mosuo couple. The man, Mr. Den is sitting face-forward on the stern and his woman partner is sitting on the bow, facing back, with *all we want to do is screw* and yours truly seated in succession, from back to front. The couple coyly try to hide their escapades under a small pink parasol, but to little avail. Den has a handheld oar to power us, like in a canoe, except the handle and the whole shaft are about as big around as my forearm. I don't see the advantage of not being able to fully grip the thing, but they've been going back and forth across this Lu Commercial Lake for hundreds, if not thousands of years. His partner has a narrow, metal tubed oar held in an oarlock on the bulwarks of the boat. As she gets tired, she moves the oar to the other side's oarlock and Den adjusts his paddling accordingly.

Like the Yi roadside fruit and walnut sellers yesterday, there are sartorial considerations for this boating couple to work today. Den is wearing a round brimmed, beige felt hat, with a tall bowl over his crown and a cream colored band decorating its base. Mr. Bin last night at the BBQ was wearing a similar hat, although Bin's attire was very run of the mill. Yang's long sleeve shirt is beautiful red silk with a wonderful Gothic pattern of gold and green vine flowers all over it. It has a button hook at the shoulder, much like a medic's smock, and a wide, open, white Nehru collar. His pants are again standard issue Mao blue. They are hard to beat for working class people. His face looks hard lived and if we were not in China, I would swear I am talking to a Native American. Bin also was the spitting image of a New World Indian. Again, the apparent deep historical connection between minority peoples in China with Native Americans is striking. Were the nascent Han people too dominating? Did some of these minority tribes make it across the Bering Straits as a result? His female partner is not in formal Mosuo attire, but can still be identified as one. She has on non-descript brown pants and a thick, long white apron to cover her lower body while she rows, since she's splay legged a lot of the time as she is pulling on her oar and wants to be discrete. Her blouse is identical in style to Yang's, but is solid red with white cuffs and she is wearing a funky looking dark, sleeveless Haight-Ashbury biker vest covered with semispherical, chrome, reflecting brads all over it. Janis Joplin my dear, you would have killed to wear this Mosuo woman's hippy vest, I tell you. Her headdress is actually a long, 40cm wide horizontally striped scarf that she has folded up like a towel and draped over a beaded crown frame on top of her head. It does offer her some protection from the thin atmosphere's sunlight. Formal Mosuo hats are similar, just much more ornate and turban looking. The one piece of clothing that really sets off Mosuo people is their belts. They are very broad, 15cm wide, multicolored, woven sashes that are wrapped tightly around and high up on their waists. Mosuo women are known for their weaving of shawls, scarves, sashes and the like. Many of the Mosuo men and women also sport western style cowboy hats, which makes them look all the more New World, but I suspect this is something recently imported, along with cowboy TV shows and western movies. The Marlboro Mosuo Man.

Much of the lake is shallow enough that the bottom can be seen ten meters down, which really adds to the charm of the boat ride. The water temperatures are warmer than I would have thought at this altitude, around 15°C. It is after all, cold and snowed-in up here during the winter. As we pass the Princess House Island, I get a close look at the impressive residence that sits on it. It would make a great set for a James Bond movie. Den tells me it's all mine - for only ¥28,000 (€3,500/$4,400) per night. He tells me rich people rent it or companies for employee retreats. We pass the tip of the peninsula and go by the Liwubi Island. Den offers for us to get off and see a temple there, where there are another ten skiffs already docked along the shoreline. My boat mates have their tongues deep in each other's ears and mouths and couldn't be bothered, I'm enjoying the thousands of *shuixing yanghua* flowers everywhere and the solitary calm of the skiff gliding over the deep blue waters of Lugu. We three wave Den on, passing the island and get out into the deep open waters of Lugu, where a flotilla of skiffs can be seen coming from Lige, as well as twenty more heading towards us from Luoshui. There are not many skiffs to go from Luowa to Lige, but the teeming numbers of tourists in Lige obviously want to make their way over on the Sichuan side to spend the morning, eat lunch and then head back. We finally make it to the Yunnan side. At Luoshui, there must be close to a fifty skiffs docked along the shore, which gives a good indication of just how much Lugu has become a tourist haven. Luoshui is full of tour buses, new construction of hotels and stores going up, all very smart looking. I remember my horny skiff mates and hope they can find a hotel room sooner than later. While walking along the shore and deciding what to do, I see the skin and desiccated skeleton of an impressively big, long serpent hanging on a fence wire by the lake. Snakes just don't stand a chance with humanity, especially here in China. I talk with a few people and confirm that the buses to Lijiang, Yunnan, my next stop, take off from Lige, about 10km away on foot. After my smashingly successful walk yesterday to Luowa and wanting to not give the ripoff taxi drivers here the satisfaction, I decide to make it a day walk.

Outside of Luoshui is a tiny village, Xiaoyuba (小鱼坝= Little Fish Dam). The place is all set up for tourism, but is totally dead. As I pass all the deserted stores selling Yi and Mosuo traditional handicrafts and jewelry, I start to feel a little sorry for them not heeding the three most important tenants of real estate: location, location, location - when I am stopped in my tracks by some impressive looking wild animal skins hanging in the stores. For only ¥600 (€75/$95) you can buy the skin of a Caobao (草豹= Grass Leopard). The lady tells me they are hunted up in the surrounding mountains. I ask her to write the names of the three differently marked animals and I get this name and the Chinese words for *unprecedented* and *mountain hunting*. A wise China hand friend, Bernard Terminet Schuppon, tracked down their identity based on the photos I sent him, for which I am eternally grateful. The skins being sold are from a family of wild cats called *Felis silvestris*, or Forest Cat in Latin. They populate much of Africa, as well as a large band of territory stretching from Scotland, all the way across Eurasia and hooking down into China's, Sichuan and Yunnan, which are the furthest eastern and southern limits of its inhabited territory. Like most cats, they prefer to live a solitary life, except for when they mate, and the mother nurses one to seven babies for 3 to 4 months, after giving birth in April to May. Their body length is 80cm and they weigh a streamlined five to 8kg. While most of the subspecies are not rated as endangered, the two in China are: *F. silvestris beili* and *F. silvestris ornata*, the striped and spotted skins, respectively, that are being sold in Yunnan. They are both rated as *vulnerable*, which is one grade below *endangered*, but based on what I see today, it is only a matter of time before they move up the scale of risk towards the dreaded *extinct* level, Another issue is their interbreedability. Like ligers and tigons being the offspring of captured lions and tigers mating together, or wolves and domesticated dogs, these wild mountain cats can and do breed with feral house cats, thus diluting their gene pool. It floods me with a rush of despondency to see the beautiful remains of what are endangered species for sale, and in such a tacky and cheapened fashion. There are about ten of them in the stores here, proudly displayed on the interior walls or hanging outside. China can be such a frustrating place sometimes, and seeing these precious animals skins being sold like cheap tourist trinkets is one of those days. It reminds me of the store at the tightly controlled UNESCO World Heritage Site, the Mogao Caves in Gansu, selling tons of ivory. It's just lunacy and such a feeling of helplessness when confronted with this ugly and ignorant face of human behavior. Before leaving these wild cat skin festooned stores, I do buy three handmade silver bracelets for my wife and two daughters.

The rest of the 10km walk is quite hilly, thus, oxygen starved bicyclists dot the route, standing hunched over their handlebars gasping for air and pushing their two wheelers on foot up the many inclines. For tourists, a popular pastime at Lugu Lake is to rent bikes, solo or tandem and ride on as much of the 53km circumference road as possible. But at almost 3km above sea level, with many of the visitors being recent arrivals from the lowlands, most riders end up walking with their bikes as much as they actually ride. Everybody wants to do the complete circuit. Few have the high altitude adaptation or lung capacity to realize it. The slow paced views of Lugu's often calm, royal blue waters, islands and peninsula are humbling. The fast moving, broken, misty-grey clouds that shroud the mountains surrounding the lake give it an even more enchanted, mythical feel. I wear my finger out taking pictures of bizarre trees, plants, grasses and flowers. Along the way are posted narrow, two meter tall *dazibao*, the long, red propaganda banners, glued to power and telephone poles. They exhort the people to conserve precious bird life. I think they are about 50 years too late on this point. Other than seeing a few ducks and coots on the lake and magpies in the forests, the wildfowl here is just as destitute as every other place I've been on this journey. Other *dazibao* plead to keep the environment clean, which the Chinese have improved upon immensely during the last generation; others exhort us not to urinate and defecate outside of designated restrooms and not to spit on the ground. These foul habits have been drastically reduced since being here in the 90s. The Chinese continue to raise expectations of themselves.

All in all a very satisfying hike. My body, lungs, spirit, binoculars and sense of place in the Universe get a good workout this morning. I finally hike down into the tourist town of Lige. Too bad about Lige. It's a mini-Jiuzhaigou on crack, which is a real insult and meant to be. Just like China's crown jewel ecotourism mecca that I visited in northern Sichuan, Lige is ridiculously commercial, crawling with tour buses and throngs of swaggering and self-important humanity setting the scene. Americans are known around the world for being loud and obnoxious travelers. Han Chinese tourists are carrying that baton to new national levels here. It's no better on the other side of the commercial equation, with brusque, can't-give-a-hoot hostel attendants (no rooms pal - bye!) and nonchalant, putting-on-airs vendors (you want to buy *what*?) round out the scene. But Lige is just getting into character. Three Han guys are stumbling down the street, liquored up, carrying bottles of cheap local Maotai and one of them blows lunch all over the sidewalk. Niiiice. Chinese men are known to come here in search of Mosuo women, in hopes of capitalizing on the walking marriage traditions. Looks like these yeah-hoos are striking out big time. I find a room in a crappy hotel that is straight out of the 90s. The Han husband and wife owners run around the place, perfectly playing their roles as Marcus Crassus and the Queen of Hearts. The service at a nearby, uncaring restaurant is, well, uncaring. The food is equally forgettable. I cannot wait to blow this place off. But I'm not going to let it skew what has otherwise been an outstanding, culturally enriching and fascinating trip to Luguhu. Tourist traps are just that, all over the world.

Even trying to get a bus out the next morning is a hassle. All the hostels tell me there are no seats to Lijiang and I am sure that I will be hitchhiking for the first time tomorrow. I slowly figure out there are 18-passenger buses bringing in groups from Lijiang. I meet a woman Han driver, Ms. Yu, who is halfway sympathetic, tells me to be standing in front of her bus at 07:00 tomorrow and she'll take me. She doesn't want to sell me a ticket until then, but assures me she is spending the night here and will be leaving in the morning. I'm not taking any chances, hang around to see her check into a *zhaodaisuo*, wake up the next day and am out there right after six. She comes out shortly thereafter, unlocks her vehicle, I quickly toss my gear inside and jump in the shotgun seat. To heck with breakfast. I ain't movin' and you can pry this front seat out of my cold, dead hands, pal. I just cannot stand the thought of another day in Lige. Blech. When Yu finally fills up with passengers, puts her fully depreciated bus into grinding first gear and takes off, I mark another milestone on this trip. Ningxia, Gansu, Sichuan and now the amazing province of Yunnan awaits me.

1- en.wikipedia.org/wiki/List_of_matrilineal_or_matrilocal_societies.

2- The Woman's Encyclopedia of Myths and Secrets *(1983) ISBN 0-06-250925-X and* The Woman's Dictionary of Symbols and Sacred Objects *(1988), Castle Books, ISBN 0-06-250923-3 are magisterial in their depth, research and importance. She portrays thousands of everyday symbols, myths, objects and based on years of careful study, explains their history and matrilineal origins. I can almost guarantee you that Dan Brown has these page-turning, erudite tomes gracing the shelves of his private library.*

3- The Great Cosmic Mother: Rediscovering the Religion of the Earth, *by Monica Sjöö and Barbara Mor*; When God Was a Woman, *by Merlin Stone*; The Chalice and the Blade: Our History, Our Future, *by Riane Eisler; and* The Living Goddesses, *by Marija Gimbutas, are all a great place to start to learn about humanity's pre-patriarchal world.*

Chapter 33: Lijiang

Lijiang Old Town is a metastasizing, out of control tourist tumor and a canker sore on UNESCO's good name - do the right thing and pull its charter. Shuhe Old Town and the Naxi people save the cultural day. The wild hike up and down the side of Jade Dragon Snow Mountains is unbelievable and will be a Grandpa story for me to tell in my doting old age.

Lijiang was *officially* opened to tourism by Baba Beijing around 1986. It is hard to understand why, but even back in the early 90s, there was a lot of administrative hassle for foreigners to go to Lijiang. I remember us wanting to go and the best we could get was,

"*Take the two-day train to Kunming and see if you can go to Lijiang from there.*"

The Kunming airport didn't even open until 1995. I recall there needing to be travel permits in Kunming, just like Tibet today. So, getting to Kunming meant maybe not even going to Lijiang, not to mention Dali, along the way. You could get to Kunming and neither could be in the cards, nor Zhongdian (Shangri-La) for sure, which didn't open up till later?[1] Unless you had a ton a time on your hands, those kinds of nebulous odds seemed about as winnable as the Chinese lottery. We passed on the gamble. At that time, my wife and I had our six-month old daughter, Maia, who was nursing her mother, and when traveling, she was strapped on my back. So to travel at that time, we wanted reasonable assurances we could get where we wanted to go, never mind all the discomfort and usual daily hassles. For that particular journey, we ended up going to the lazy, hazy, portrait perfect sugar loaf mountains of the Li River in Guangxi, a trip from those wild, 1990s Wild West days that we still reminisce about. Slowly during the 90s, areas outside Kunming in Yunnan began to open up. Then Lijiang got international attention in 1996 with a 7.0 earthquake that proffered its predictable results: hundreds dead, hundreds of thousands of homes collapsed and equal numbers whose houses were so weakened as to be uninhabitable. The upstart of the aftermath is the World Bank financed much of the rebuilding and restoration, which was instrumental in getting Lijiang Old Town (丽江古城) certified as a UNESCO World Heritage Site a year later. That first year, 1997, 200,000 tourists visited Lijiang. Ah, those were the halcyon days, let me tell you. I remember hearing about Lijiang finally opening up, as we were preparing to leave China that same year, after seven years here, to seek our fortune in France.

Much has transpired in the last 15 years. Today, the Old Town it is so shockingly depraved, so Sodom and Gomorrah as to be an embarrassment to the whole country and especially to UNESCO. You might as well film *Debbie Does Dallas II* on the altar of Notre Dame during Easter communion. Any culturally significant place to visit within its confines is totally lost in a cynical sea of crass, cheap, craven and crapulous commercial excess. The rabid hounds of venal lust have been unchained on this little divot of land and have even had their neck collars removed, free to feast on the metastasizing, out of control commercial carcass at their feet. How bad is it? Imagine Disney World with 10,000 cruddy stores flogging all the same tourist trinkets at Zimbabwe dollar inflated prices, with 10,000 restaurants between them, all offering lousy fast food at Weimar Republic paper Mark prices, and another 10,000 street stalls regurgitating both of the above at the same usurious levels - all to flatter and fleece the 100,000 people who are squished inside like a can of Spam in a cannibal supermarket, well, that is what it feels like. I last less than an hour and leave in total disgust. On your honor, you are supposed to buy an ¥80 (€10/$13) *site protection* (*sic*) ticket and there are signs pleading with you to do so, as well as canned admonitions on the PA system. I do the right thing, but these ticket windows are deserted of people performing this meaningless *beau geste*, making me look like a *dabizi* chump. Apparently though, UNESCO swallows this fatuous fig leaf, hook, line and sinker.

Thus, in reality, there are *no* controls whatsoever to limit the number of people who come, with predictably hedonistic, inane results. While I joke that there are 100,000 people packed into Old Town today, I may not be exaggerating, especially given the peak season. Disney World averages about 44,000 visitors a day, covers 117.5km^2, and we all know how crammed their parks can feel on any given day. Lijiang Old Town covers a miniscule 3.8km^2, or only 3% of Disney World's surface area. In 2005, 4,000,000 tourists were already visiting Lijiang and currently 8,000,000 are flooding here every year, which is 22,000 visitors per day, half the rate of Disney World, on only 3% of the land.[2] Lijiang is now being touted as China's most visited tourist spot for its own citizens. This is a scary thought. China has the fastest growing middle class on Earth, one of the world's highest savings rates, and these 300,000,000 plus, whose feet are firmly planted in the rapidly growing Chinese middle class have money to burn, including on travel.

There is a second big difference. Disney World empties out at night. Lijiang Old Town has thousands of people who call this place home. So before the first tourist steps foot in the place, it is already crowded. This is China after all. And this trend is only going to get worse. With its moderate year-round climate, high altitude mountains and clean air, Lijiang is now a highly sought after place for the Chinese to come live, *hukou* or not.[3] According to some references, Lijiang has been and is projected to continue increasing its population 18% per year until 2020. These are numbers that put El Dorado gold rush towns and Las Vegas to shame. I am not an urban planner, but this twin headed Hydra of geometric growth in both tourism and city population is clearly unsustainable madness. And where is UNESCO, playing the part of cultural Nero in this Chinese version of a burning Rome? The UNESCO World Heritage designation is not something to be taken lightly; it is a very prestigious and coveted cachet. Based on their cultural criteria, Lijiang Old Town initially deserved the UNESCO moniker, with its priceless 800 year-old Song/Yuan Dynasty and Naxi cultural roots. However, what the local, provincial and national governments have allowed to happen to the place should not be tolerated. There is precedence. Oman and Germany have each had a site delisted. Obviously, this is not something UNESCO is elated to do. But, unless there is serious, long-term remediation of this cancerous canker sore, Lijiang Old Town should quickly be the third site added to this hall of shame. I see only one solution. Jiuzhaigou is bad enough with its ¥310 one day ticket and a 15,000 visitor-a-day entry limit. But Jiuzhaigou has no choice and neither does Lijiang Old Town. It's the only option to save its insatiable, slutty, swinish soul. Put up turnstiles and shut them down when X number of tourists pass through each day. The money changers in the temple, the philistine pilgrims coming in droves and the Mandarin Pontius Pilates in the stately halls of government will quickly adjust to the new sustainable model.

Shuhe Old Town (東河古城) is the current release valve for all this madness and is situated about 6km from Lijiang Old Town. I walked there just to get a flavor of Lijiang in general and take in the spectacular 2,400 MASL, 27° latitude (Algeria and Florida) weather. Lijiang is like other high altitude subtropical areas, where the annual temperature range is narrow and moderate. The average daytime temperature is 23°C and at night, 12.9°C. Summer temperatures only average 28°C and the lowest nighttime temperatures in winter are 3°C, which all means that your typical daily attire is going to include a long sleeve shirt, sweater and for the coldest days in December-January a light coat. No wonder people are thronging to come here to live, *hukou* in hand or not. Right now, Shuhe is busy, pleasant and comfortable, with a kind of Euro-cool, hippy dippy, early days Mallorca, Spain feel to it. Clear water, stone lined canals and water pools course through the town, crossed over on quaint, arched bridges, which really accentuate its charms. But if Shuhe is not careful, it will quickly become the second out-of-control Old Town in Lijiang, losing its chic Balearic mojo in the process. Just the background population growth of 18% per year is eyebrow-raising, not to mention the overflow crowds from the Fat Trollop down the road. At least you have to buy a cheap ticket to get in. But it too is wall-to-wall restaurants, shops, hostels and local hotels. The fact that this was once a celebrated stopping point on the ancient and treacherous Tea-Horse trading route, sometimes called the Southern Silk Road, that connected India and Burma to Sichuan, is pretty much lost, once you get past the little signboard out front.

Shuhe is an atypical visit for me, in that I spend the day with Beijing work friends, Ian and Mona Bayly, who quite coincidentally are here at the same time. Normally when I travel, I answer to yours truly and make all the decisions based on what the Traveling Oracles' entrails offer me. I love the open ended sense of adventure, the surprising permutations of tourist chaos theory that are thrown at me, so this is a power I only grant to other people very reluctantly. As it turns out, it was a great choice to spend the day together and could not have turned out better. Once inside Shuhe, I find a public bench and wait for Ian to come get me. The bench overlooks one of the limpid water canals and is right next to a little arched Chinese bridge. The main drag is bustling with people making their way around. A nice intro to the place. I start to chat with an older Naxi woman sitting next to me, whose Mandarin is good enough for us to exchange the twenty questions. She is in Naxi traditional dress, which is magnificent attire, but this is a hard working farmer and her clothes show it. She is selling some spices out of several small wooden boxes, including dried red pepper, anise, sesame and as usual, a few that mystify me. But *one* really catches my eye. What do I see, but those little red fruit that I saw on the wiry orchard trees during my drive to Lugu Lake from Xichang. And what are they mixed up with in their various stages of dehydration, because I recognize the dried ones. After all, I've fished out a few in my days from many a Chinese dish. Drum roll please… Ta-da! They are *huajiao*, or *majiao*, those mouth paralyzing peppercorns. Son of a numb gun, I finally figured it out. *Huajiao* grows on trees. Who would have thought?

The Naxi (or Nakhi) people make up a large percentage of the population in Lijiang; this is their unofficial capital. They are related to the Mosuo of Lugu Lake, the Yi of Xichang and their language is part of the Yi/Lolo group. While once fully matrilineal, patriarchal Han influences have largely relegated this way of life to the history books. Early in the 20th century, they were made known to the outside world by a Russian and an Austrian-American: writer Peter Goullart and botanist Joseph Rock, respectively. Traditional Naxi dress is the spitting image of something you would see on a Native American from the Great Plains or Desert West, again, incredibly uncanny and thought provoking about the origin of America's original people.

Ian's and Mona's contact here, Jerry, is a young American from the West Coast, who came here for a work study program and fell in love with a local Naxi woman; they have a child and are now based here. He teaches English at the branch campus of Yunnan University. He helps me find a nice hostel that one of his extended local family runs. With my Beijing friends, we all have a lovely Naxi inspired family style lunch. I get to eat and visit with his local family, which is a real pleasure. Jerry is very engaging and helpful with suggestions about what to do here. He is very high on the Jade Dragon Snow Mountain Park and I decide to make it my activity tomorrow. We say our goodbyes and I explore Shuhe till time to go to bed. Most of the restaurants, bars and shops are on the main drag. The hostels are off on the residential streets where it is quieter. After three to five kuai per big bottle of beer, I brace at its cost here in the night clubs and bars, ¥35-80 (€4.40-10.00/$5.50-12.70). As a result, my 1.2 liter thermos full of hot tea is getting a good workout and my evening of abstinence saves me a chunk of change.[4]

Early next morning, I take a local bus to the interurban bus station, buy my Dali ticket for tomorrow and check into a next door Chinese hotel. Then I continue by local bus to the city center to find a private hire combi to go to Jade Dragon Snow Mountain (玉龙雪山= Yulong Xueshan). Downtown, there is a groovy square that is a paean to The Great Helmsman, replete with his towering, stately statue, flags, revolutionary plaques and red *dazibao*, the propaganda signs. Mao's statue is completely ghost white, except for two Chinese flags, one on each side of his Mao jacket's collar. Far out, Mao! It's a bit mysterious in Lijiang to find the right spot to look for your desired taxi destination, but about 100m away on the statue side of the street, I find an informal bus station, where a number of drivers and passengers congregate. Clots of other combis are also lined up in nooks and crannies up and down the street, so it is a little like a supply and demand, open air commodities market for transportation.

The drive out to the park is about 35km due north. City slickers and college students stop and ride horses at various spots on the ever climbing, straight section of road to the park gate. Some are even trying to bike there. Good luck with that. The vertical climb from Lijiang to the park valley is 600m. I wince a little at the 180 RMB (€23/$29) entry ticket, knowing that in common Chinese fashion, the front gate ticket is just the first bloodletting, and it can be death by a thousand cuts to see everything, once inside. Our combi continues on inside the park and we get dropped off in the middle of nothingness, where there are massive parking lots with tens of buses. I talk to one of the police officers, who are always charming and helpful, as long as you are not being arrested, and he explains it to me. This is just the staging place to buy more bus tickets to go to points further into the park, especially to several mountain meadows, with colorful Chinese mythology names like Dry Sea and Cloud Fir. Another one goes up to a chair lift, which takes you to a glacier up in the Jade Dragon Snow

Mountains. I try to go stand in line for a couple of the buses and find it as absurd as the line-waiting crowds at Jiuzhaigou. To heck with this lunacy. I cannot see the 5,500m mountain peaks, nor the glaciers, as clouds cling to the mountain range above the tree line level. This series of mountains, which runs due north-south, is several klicks long and even below the tree line, the wilderness looks magnificent. The Sirens of Mother Nature are calling me and I am not going to let these ridiculous lines ruin my day. I again ask a police officer which road goes up to the glacier chair lift and he points down the road not far, on the opposite side of the madness. I walk up to the gate where all the buses and private cars are going in and the guy runs me off. No ticket, no entry, even on foot. We'll see about that buddy boy… There are no fences anywhere blocking me from climbing up. I go about 200m behind the guard house (to the north) and start walking due west up the mountainside. Eerily, there develops a straight lane in the low pine forest, like the story of the Red Sea being split in two, and I smile as I walk unimpeded in a perpendicular direction towards the range. The ground is wall to wall ferns on the floor of this pine tree forest. I am greeted by grass foraging cows, the usual bounty of flora and paucity of fauna and fowl. Like everywhere on this trip, I wear my camera out taking pictures of beautiful, and for me, never-before-seen plants, bushes, flowers and trees. I come on to a ranger's house which looks abandoned, circumnavigate it and keep climbing straight up. My private walking lane starts to peter out, as I get closer to the sheer rocky cliffs that shoot into cloudy oblivion above the tree line. I get to a well house, where I can hear glacier melt water loudly rushing through it, being piped down below. On my way up, I can see cars off in the distance, down below me, and from this high up, they look like little mechanical ants. I can also see that the glacier chair lift is still well to the north. I get as high up as I can in the now random meadows and at 3,270m take off laterally along the side of the mountain range to the north. I pick up a good trail and keep pushing forward. It does not take long for me to be in a fully shaded, primeval forest of indescribable beauty. Towering trees, some a meter across at their girth and many in the 50-100cm size gaze down on me benevolently. This ancient forest is the real McCoy, with emergents, the canopy, understory and forest floor.

In the pale, almost translucent light of the forest canopy, the floor is covered with huge swaths of many different and multihued lichens, mosses, crazy colored and bizarrely shaped mushrooms, prehistoric fungi, Pleistocene plants, fairytale flowers, Flintstone ferns, brackens and vines, all growing on the thick bed of hundreds of years of rotting trees and trunks. Even though there is not much sunlight penetrating through the high canopy, the forest is a riot of colors, thanks to all the various stages of decomposition and the amazingly adapted flora and fungi. Multi-colored flowers are sprinkled ahead of my view. The massive trees are adorned with long beards of many different species of moss and lichen. Each rotting trunk becomes a natural statue, piled high with the same, as well as teeming fungi shooting out of them. Huge, fallen trees the size of whales, lay beached on the forest floor, providing nourishment for all the decomposer species for the next thousand years. The iridescent colors, shapes and sizes of the mushroom toadstools leave me speechless, evoking images of Wonderland fantasy forests and mescaline dreams. In fact, I have a name for this place now, Mushroom Mountain. And it just keeps *going and going*. Utterly peaceful, totally alone, humbled and emotionally drained by this experience; it is all just mind bogglingly beautiful. I feel so lucky, so serendipitous for my day on Jade Dragon Snow Mountain to be unfolding this way. Lijiang Old Town, that great Mad Money Machine, now seems a forgotten memory. The nice, rarely used trail finally fades out and I have to get creative. The forest floor is so thick with an eon of detritus and so entangled, that I really have to slow down and watch what I'm doing. I'm not scared because I'm not lost and unlike Mt. Jinire in Tagong and White Dragon River in Langmusi, this lateral hike is fairly level and sane. I keep working my way northward through this natural obstacle course, when down through the trees, I can see some asphalt and for the first time begin to hear vehicles again. This is the road up to the chair lift, whose guardhouse below told me to bugger off for not having a ticket.. At this point, I figure I can't be more than a 1-2km from there, so I opt to stay on the road and suffer through the noise of the passing cars and buses, as well as their black cloud, diesel fumes. My time in the Mushroom Mountain Forest was a sublime one and a half hours.

The chair lift station sits at 3,363 MASL, so my total vertical climb today is 327m. This is the equivalent of climbing the steps of a one hundred story sky scraper, or one Empire State Building. The workers milling about at the lift station see me come up the steep road on foot and cock their heads in curious amazement. I don't think they believe it when I tell them I walked the whole way up, as it is just not done, not in 21st century China. The chair lift is the expected swarm of humanity, as droves of locals rent snow boots, insulated outerwear and the like. I could be at any ski station in the world: overpriced food and beverages, post cards and the banal selection of tourist souvenirs. In the store, four large glass jar displays catch my eye. One is full of the cordyceps fungus, which is a natural source of steroids and only found in Tibet and the Himalayas.[5] The other three are full of desiccated frogs, dried lizards and small dead snakes. *Real ones*, not plastic toys. Each one in Chinese folkloric medicine cures some perceived physical or mental frailty. Here is all the wild life I didn't see on the mountain hike today, not to mention during the rest of my journey in Western China. Unfortunately, traditional Chinese beliefs are rapidly denuding Mother Earth. Too many of them, even those educated and having lived overseas, truly believe that if you eat a snake, it will make a man's sex organs more powerful, a bear's paw will turn your hands into Superman steel, gorilla brains rend more smarts, rhino horn will cure everything from cancer to diabetes, etc., and the list of products and their cures is endless. Sad but true, this country is the world's biggest consumer driver of endangered animals, birds, fish, plants and their parts, helping empty our oceans and precious living resources on land and in the air. The Chinese have made great strides, incredible gains in bringing their society forward in the last thirty years, complimenting their soon to be world's number one economy bragging rights. But this horrific aspect of their traditional customs is for me the deal breaker, the litmus test. I will know that China and its citizens will have really come of 21st century age, when these kinds of devastating, antediluvian superstitions are a thing of the past.

Lonely Planet says you will not get out of this park without spending at least 450 kuai (€56/$71) and I am getting the picture loud and clear. The chair lift ride is 240 RMB (€30/$38) and I joke with the ticket taker that we foreigners don't have that kind of money, only the Chinese do, and she gets a good guffaw out of it. I mean heck, that is US or EU prices, yet they are lined up for fifty meters to get up there. Plus, they each spend another ¥100 (€13/$16) on rented footwear and outerwear. Why go up to the glacier right now anyway? The tops of the mountain range are completely ensconced in thick clouds and I doubt the glacier is something you can reach out and touch. The chair lift disappears into grey-white opaqueness 100m up after taking off. Even if there is a trail to the glacier, how comfortable would it be walking on a strange mountain path with near zero visibility? I like excitement and adventure, but come on. These people have too much money on their hands. Use some common sense.

I snack, refill my thermos with hot tea and start to head back down. Descending affords me a completely different point of view, because I can see the serpentining road switchbacks below, getting smaller and smaller in perspective. I walk in between the switchbacks to stay in the forest as much as possible and off the asphalt. A few people are parked along the way and walking around to hunt for edible mushrooms. In one isolated area of the forest I run into a woman with a bucket full of mushrooms and a hand trowel. In her forties, with short, unattractive hair and a burdened, overwrought demeanor, like she has lived a hard life, she has the side of her forlorn face smashed into her mobile phone, which she keeps cradled on her shoulder. She totally freaks out when she sees me, this *laowai* from out of nowhere, maybe a white forest ghoul. She literally runs away, describing every frightening moment to her telephone interlocutor. Sorry about that. I tire of the switchbacks and decide to take off over totally wild terrain towards where I started, to the southeast. And then the strangest thing happens. It just never stops. I keep pushing ahead, convinced the road is just behind the next copse of trees, but no. How far can it be? I run out of tea and start to fatigue. Today has been quite a jaunt, more than I care to admit, and now I'm beginning to wonder if I am biting off more than I can chew. I look behind me at the mountain range above me to the sky, to my two sides, desperately searching for something to find a reference point, but completely draw a blank. I get out my Galaxy and turn on my compass to confirm I'm heading in the right direction, but frankly, I'm really starting to get scared that I'm disoriented, dehydrated and much more hypoxic than I realize. What if I *think* I'm going in the right direction, but in fact it is the *opposite* one, like going in circles when lost in the desert? There is no sign of civilization anywhere and I start pondering wandering out here, lost until dark, and then trying to figure out what the Hades to do. The stars aren't going to help much, since my compass confirms my direction. That is if I'm not muddle headed. At this point I can't even think straight, adding to the panic. It starts to flatten out, almost like a sloping, tree speckled savannah. Finally, *finally*, I come upon a guy walking out here, just enjoying the total solitude, so I know I can't be far from the main road back. I don't know why I don't ask him anything. He is about 100m away and in this most serene of places under the Jade Dragon Snow Mountains, I feel compelled to leave him in his spiritual peace. Just seeing him reassures me though, and boosts my confidence. Since we are going in oblique angles, he quickly disappears. About another klick more and I see vehicles zipping along off in the distance and I walk towards this main park road whence I started. I get on the opposite side of the road, go off about 100m, to get away from the traffic and head due south to the parking area. And then it happens. The clouds begin to unchain themselves from the mountain peaks, breaking free and the splendor and grace of the entire range on the western horizon, greets me in its majesty. The glaciers are there and I can clearly see the chair lift operation making its way up to the observation platform. Do I get out my Zeiss? You know the answer to that question by now. They show that in fact, the glacier is facing the platform across a broad deep crevice in the mountainside. I'll take my 240 kuai-less, binocular fueled view from here, thank you. More than satisfactory. The Jade Dragon Snow Mountains live up to their name on this east face, as they are jagged as broken glass and uneven in altitude, rising up in an arc-like fashion. This is why its name is so apropos, since the peaks really do look like the ridgeback of a charging dragon.

No tea tonight. I deserve a tall cold beer, no let's make that three or four of them. I am going to be so sore tomorrow. Near the bus station, away from the Old Cities of Lijiang and Shuhe, the prices are back down to China levels. I have a wonderful Yunnan dish called fragrant mushrooms and stir fried meat (香菇炒肉 = *xianggu chaorou*). While the basic ingredients are not different than the typical Chinese dish, the spices and seasoning are really unique. I flash back to the people who were mushroom hunting in the mountains. The uniquely delicious flavors could also be due to the aroma or taste of the local mushrooms. The Naxi Hotel ranks as one of the best I stay in the whole trip. For all of ¥100 (€13/$16), I have a big clean room, double bed, toiletries, towels, hot water, tea bags, hot water thermos, electric mosquito wafers, toilet paper, screens on the windows - and that is not all. When I wake up at dawn, I open my window curtains and I am delighted to see the entire range of Jade Dragon Snow Mountains off on the horizon. It really does have the shape of a rodeo dragon trying to throw off its rider. How nice of them to give me this fourth floor, rooftop room. What a splendid mental postcard to leave here. Lijiang Old Town? Never heard of it.

1- *Since independence, Zhongdian was the Chinese name for this Tibetan region in far northwestern Yunnan. But in 2001, some really cheeky promoters renamed it Shangri-La, in a bid to boost the tourist industry. I am not sure the estate of James Hilton approves of them using this name from his 1933 fiction novel,* Lost Horizon, *but it has caught on really quickly in the tourist trade. Unless you are speaking Mandarin, everybody now calls it Shangri-La. It was a brilliant, gutsy marketing ploy that has worked like a charm.*

2- *Of course everybody is not visiting the Old City simultaneously. But my walk through Lijiang town and out to Shuhe definitely indicates that the vast, vast majority of them are right here, worshipping at the feet of the Great Harlot.*

3- Hukou *(户口) is the birth certificate of every citizen and has a long history here, as well as in other Asian countries, adopted from the Chinese over the centuries. It is attached to the location where their parents' ancestral home is based, even if they are born somewhere else in China. It is really part of a family registry, much like France's* Livret de Famille, *as well as in many other locales around the world. Before the economy was opened up back in the 90s, it was very difficult for any Chinese person to live anywhere outside their hukou designated* laojia *(老家) or hometown. Internal travel was strictly controlled, with official passes and permits required to leave their area. Now, hundreds of millions of Chinese have moved around the country, principally to the larger cities. There, they can work, buy and rent property, but without a local hukou, they lose many advantages for medical care, children's education and other social services. Not having a local* hukou *does make someone second among equals, which is why it is so disliked by the Chinese and criticized by Westerners. But foreigners don't have to maintain the social stability of 1.3 billion citizens, 56 culture groups (including the Han) and a long history of hatred between the north & south, east & west. Beijing's city government is offering* hukou *to anyone who files income taxes for six consecutive years.*

4- *Customer or not, you can walk into any business, office, hotel, restaurant, etc., in China and if they have hot water (开水=* kaishui*) handy, you will get it for free. Drinking tea in China is a human right. If some joker ever gets the idea of trying to charge for boiled water, there will be riots in the streets.*

5- *Eric Meyer's* Tibet the Last Cry *has a great section on the economics and politics of this vociferously fought over fungus. Criminal gangs are now moving in on the business, as it is just as profitable as running heroin or cocaine.*

Chapter 34: Dali

To quote Sinatra, Doin' Dali My Way, baby - I tour Dali Old Town, its pagodas, temples and pavilions, from 700m above it all in the Cangshan Mountains, overlooking the entire expanse of the Erhai Lake basin below. Oh, and all it took was a Herculean mountain climb up a slippery, horse manure covered, pyramid-steep trail to get there.

Lonely Planet talks about the Highlander Hostel that sits 2,950 MASL in the Cangshan Mountains (苍山), overlooking Dali and the Erhai Lake (洱海湖) region below, and I'm fascinated at the thought of going up there. Shan actually means mountain in Chinese, so Cangshan is a transliterated tautology. I guess it just sounds better in European languages to say Cangshan Mountains and not just Cang Mountains. Lijiang Old Town was a sobering experience of tourism run amok and I hear that Dali is just as popular, especially with the Chinese these days. Not that I'm getting misanthropic, which is an emotional suicide pill in a place like densely populated China, but it is more that the highlight reels of this trip are happening more and more in the bosom embrace of Mother Nature, and less so at all the factual, historical and cultural icons that are so meticulously detailed in tourist and travel books. It is also a question of accessibility. I can hop onto a city bus or subway in Beijing and within minutes, be transported to some of China's greatest historical and culture sites. Getting to see picture book natural wonders is not so simple, especially since I do not have a car in Beijing. In Europe, there is the common refrain of *ABC*, Another Boring Church, which is cynical, but there is an element of truth to it. After a while, they all start to blur together and their magnificence, architectural genius and history begin to dilute themselves. Here in China, I call it *TOY*, *Temples out the Yazoo*, and the repetitive, inured effects are no different.

Once we get into the Erhai basin from Lugu Lake on the S221 Lijiang-Dali highway, the bus starts making several stops along the way, but the highway is at lake level and just far enough away, so spotting water en route as a reference point is hopeless. Using GPS, I decide to get off at a no-name place called Qiliqiaoxiang (七里桥乡), which appears to be below where the Highlander Hostel is in the mountains. There is a lot of confusion about the name Dali. There is the new, modern Dali, which sits at the southwest corner of Lake Erhai. It is either called Dali City or Xiaguan (大理城-下关= Lower Connection), and then there is the old Dali, called Dali Zhen in Chinese (大理镇= Dali Town), which is where most of the cultural sites are found. I am getting off at about the midpoint between them. There is absolutely nothing here except a restaurant, so I go inside, explain my situation, am told to sit down and wait over a nice cup of green tea. The manager/owner of the place is quite a character, someone who I will long remember. The poor thing has terrible acne. She is wearing her hair in a pushed up bouffant, Lucille Ball style; has on a skin tight, low cut knit shirt with her breasts protruding out of her push-up bra, strutting in thigh hugging, reflecting Lycra leopard print tights and balancing all this in tall, stiletto black pumps. To accentuate her very narrow waist, she is wearing a 10cm tall, shiny, black patent leather, buckled belt. If she is trying to divert my attention from her pimply face, I think it almost works. She carries herself like Princess Grace of Monaco and has incredible poise and style. I had bad acne during my adolescence and sure did not have all the weapons she possesses to overcome my self-consciousness. She has a *femme fatale* body to kill for. In any case, I can tell she runs a tight ship. The place is neat and clean and the employees jump at her every request. I call the Highlander Hostel to let them know I'm coming and ask if there are any rooms. No problem, take your time. Be very careful coming up, etc. A private taxi pulls up and this is the restaurant owner's connection. I thank her for her kindness, the cup of good tea (she refuses my money) and I silently salute the amazing chutzpah of her garish, 50s moll girl outfit and regal demeanor.

We start driving through town. Because Dali Old City is a major tourist hot spot, a number of vendors and others in the service sector are dressed up in traditional Bai people's attire. Bai (白) means *white* in Mandarin and is a revered color for this tribe of two million, most of whom live in the Erhai Lake area. They claim settlement of this area going back 3,000 years, which rivals Chinese historical connections to the Yellow and Yangtze Rivers. That may have something to do with them supposedly being the most assimilated of China's fifty-five minorities, which like Oklahoma's Five Civilized Tribes, may or may not be a good thing, depending on your point of view. Over eight hundred years ago, they created their own language with remarkable similarities to Japanese. Since independence, the language has been Latinized and is in common use by the Bai. The women have a formal costume that looks almost Thai. It sports a red smock with gold embroidery, worn over white pants and a blouse with lavish, gold embroidered cuffs and hems. The hat with this costume is really cool, with red bands wrapped around their foreheads and every larger concentric rings of knitted, woven and embroidered materials piled on and behind the head, much like an Egyptian pharaoh's obtuse crown. It is just one of several outfits they wear. I tell the taxi driver where I want to go and that I want to take the chairlift up to stay at the Highlander Hostel. He's outwardly dissing my plans, telling me the chairlift no longer works and nobody in their right mind would even think about trying to hike up that far with two bags like I have, blah, blah, blah, and what I need to do is go up on a *horse*. Yeah, sure wise guy. I don't believe a word he's telling me and start to smell a ripoff rat right away. But he's at the wheel and I'm not, so we end up in front of a horse rental place. At this point, he's on my radar big time and just on principle, we squabble over every yuan of the taxi fare, for 30 kuai (€3.80/$4.80). He waits within earshot of the horse rental open stall venue, which has a big graphic map of all the different routes they offer up into the Cangshan range. I have zero curiosity in riding a horse, since I grew up on one during my adolescence and all the way through high school. While it is a highlight for many city slickers to say they rode a horse on their vacation, for me it is a flying NBD – no big deal. Plus, trail horses are usually snarky, misanthropic bores. So already, this slick salesman doesn't realize his deck of cards is missing all four aces. He starts out at an absurd 400 RMB (€50/$63) and seeing I'm a poor prospect, quickly drops it down to two hundred. But still, I find that is a lot of money to climb up a short, but admittedly steep trail. Much to everybody's surprise, I insist on hiking. I still find their story that the chairlift is closed hard to swallow, but it is definitely a possibility. Thus, my two stout legs are what I decide to count on. My demonic driver tisk-tisks under his breath as we get back in. He's naturally bummed at not getting a tip for bringing home the horse bacon, but you know what the Russians say, right? Tough poopsky. Please take me to the park entrance. He only goes about 100m to the north and turns into a desolate parking lot, with a ranger station and ticket office.

They confirm the chairlift is closed down. I ask about the trail robbers I read about in the Lonely Planet and the two rangers tell me that is old news and has been cleaned up for a long time. I ask two or three times, since I am carrying a pair of $4,000 Zeiss binoculars, and they continue to insist it is not a problem. They reassure me there is mobile phone service all the way up and if anything happens, just call the equivalent of 911 and they will be there in a jiffy. What else can I say? To be safe, I call the hostel again to let them know I'm coming. The woman is surprised when I tell her I'm coming on foot. Take your time, it is a very steep climb, she tells me. With much bravado and an air of insolence on my part, I say goodbye to my driver. Nice try pal. No sooner do I take off and get onto the mountainside that I see a Chinese father and his young child coming down from. That is reassuring. How difficult can this hike really be?

By the time I get to the top, I think my driver almost gets the best of me. I check the altitude before starting out and it is 2,030 MASL. According to Lonely Planet, the hostel is at 2,950m, which makes for a 900m ascent. This is the equivalent of climbing three high-altitude Empire State Buildings back to back. It would be one thing making this almost 1km climb without any added weight, but I've got a 6kg backpack *and* a 12kg rolling backpack. I lull myself into complacency from the nice paved roads around Lugu Lake and the walk to Shuhe in Lijiang. Not to mention the White Dragon River's mudslide hike is a faded memory about right now. Big mistake. This isn't even a walking trail, it's a chopped up, slick as snot, greasy as goose runs, mucked up, mess of a horse manure covered path, and with the seasonal rains we are having here, it is extremely hard to get any footing at all. I try to pull my rolling backpack on the steep incline, but it is just impossible. The total horizontal length of this hike is only 1,700m, but it is easily one of the steepest I have ever attempted. I put my small backpack on my chest and hoist the big one on my back, pulling out its normally hidden shoulder straps. It is also unfortunately one of the hottest days of the trip and still early enough that the Sun is beating down directly overhead on this eastern mountain face. As a result, my tea water is gone before I know it. I'm taking two steps up and sliding one back, hanging on to exposed roots and rocks to guard my progress. Luckily, I am wearing a long sleeve shirt to protect me from the blistering, high altitude Sun and it and my pants are quickly soaked to the point of saturation from sweat. As if to rub it in, two teams of horseback riders pass me and in both cases, nobody has any water to offer. I am seriously dehydrated and can feel it. My head starts spinning and pounding and my joints start to stiffen up. I know I am hypoxic too, since I'm no longer breathing, but heaving for air. Every spot of shade, I stop and gasp for oxygen. At every stretch of sun soaked pathway, I cheer myself up,

"Come on Brown, you can DO *this!"*

Then I walk as fast as I can to the next shady area to rest, collapsing in the welcoming shade. I am cursing my bags every step of the way. A klick of ascent with 18kg of dead weight bearing down on my torso? What in Hades was I thinking? I obsessively keep checking my altimeter, 2,100, 2,200, 2,300, 2,400, 2,500, 2,600m. Another 350m to go? Rest time is now much more significant than climbing time. My organs are screaming for fluids and my mouth is Atacama Desert dry. I honestly start to think I am not going to make it and will have to ask for help when the horses come back down. This is kind of how I felt at the end of the hike at Jade Dragon Snow Mountain yesterday, but there, it was probably more psychological, with some panic setting in. Here, it is just out and out acute physical stress, pushing body and determination to way beyond my expectations. I collapse into a cool, shady muddy spot and tear off my backpacks, lungs heaving for survival. I look down on the ground, but what do I see? One of the horseback city slickers dropped about fifteen Chinese salt brine peanuts-in-the-shell on their way up, the kind served as a cold appetizer at Chinese meals (水煮花生= *shuizhu huasheng*). And the even better news? They are sitting daintily on top of the mire, no horse managed to step on them and they are amazingly unscathed and edible. I ravenously tear into them, as I have not eaten since the early lunch during the bus ride this morning. The salt soothes my parched mouth and brings succor to my electrolyte starved body. The peanuts rapidly get absorbed in my stomach and I suck on all the soft, brine soaked shells to get all of the moisture and salt that I can. This little tidy packet of flotsam may just save the day. At about 2,650m I start to see some small Buddhist temples, open sided chapels really, for a couple of people to pray at the icons and statues inside. I delude myself into saying,

"Just 300 meters more to go straight up, Jeff, one more Empire State Building..."

These creations of human civilization give my delirious mind and throbbing body a faint sense of hope. A little further on, I see several horses tied up outside a red wall sticking out of the mountainside. What could this be? I thought the hostel was another 300m higher. I go through the passageway and walk into the courtyard of a very dilapidated, unkempt Buddhist temple. The horseback riders are nowhere to be found. An older man and woman come out of one of the out buildings and I quickly size up they have a little business going here: a small store and restaurant. I enquire about the hostel and they tell me it is straight up, about ten minutes from here. My head is spinning like a wavy top and I hear in an echo,

"Why don't you sit and rest, get something to drink and eat, before heading up, since they do not have any food or beverage service?"

"Just what the doctor ordered!"

There are a woman and three kids eating a late lunch and they gasp and laugh when they see me. It is no exaggeration to say that I look like I just got out of a swimming pool, I am so drenched with sweat. We takes pictures with each other's cameras and I get a good souvenir photo with her three children in tow, who are just ecstatic at having their picture taken with a *laowai*. I savor the big bottle of cold beer that is brought out to me. This is one of those times when saying a beer has *never* tasted so good is actually a pitiful understatement. Ten kuai? What a bargain, knowing it was brought up here on mule or horse pack. For being 2,650 MASL on the edge of the Cangshan Mountains, overlooking Old Dali Town, the food is excellent. After I eat and rehydrate, my head stops spinning and my body quits trembling from fatigue, I walk around the temple area and take in the spectacular view of the Erhai Lake basin below. Except for the very southern end of the lake, this temple, called Zhonghesi (中和寺= Central Peace Temple), affords a spectacular, panoramic vista of the entire lake and its surroundings. Below us, 700m down, I can see the Old City, with the Chongsheng Temple (崇圣寺) and its Three Pagodas (三塔寺), the emblematic postcard of this town and its Bai people. My binoculars pull it all in very nicely. The towering 70m central pagoda is unmistakable, along with its twin 42m tall sisters, forming a spiritually significant triangle.

The triangle in Buddhism is used to represent the Eye of Providence. Never seen one? Just look at the back of a US one dollar bill. That is a Buddhist appropriated symbol. There is a Catholic Church built in 1927 down there somewhere, but its spire does not stick up far enough above the city buildings to be identified.

Time to head to the Highlander. Something is wrong here. The restaurant owners say it is only ten minutes up the mountain and the Lonely Planet says it sits at 2,950 MASL. No way anybody, even a horse, is going to go up a sheer 300 meter Slip 'n' Slide trail in that time. Luckily, it is the restaurant owners who are correct, since quite honestly, my stomach for another serious stretch of vertical ascent has evaporated. The hostel sits at 2,700m exactly, only 50m higher than the temple. This daunting climb ranks as one of my career toughest, so I just have to run the numbers. I climbed 670m over 1,700m (1,823m on the hypotenuse) in two and a half hours, with 18kg of dead weight. That is a nearly 40cm of ascent for every one meter of sloped trail. Those are risers that make the steps of Mexico City's Teotihuacan pyramid envious. That works out to a vertical rise of 22°, which doesn't sound like a lot, but angle of ascent is very deceiving for the human brain. Remember this when you climb or descend a road that is marked with only 8-10% of pitch. It feels like hanging on to a seat-of-your-pants roller coaster ride.

No problem about a room at the Highlander. I'm the only person here. Over the next two nights, I get the whole story about the chairlift and this hostel. Ms. Bao is the lady tending the place. She is in her early 30s and lives here with two dogs. Born in Qinghai of Han parents, she came here a few years back to visit friends, fell in love with the place, got a job and never left. This time frame would make it very possible that her parents were exiled to Qinghai, a favorite human dumping grounds during the Cultural Revolution and decided to stay. A lot marriages were destroyed in the chaos and violence, with spouses split up for years in different places, for re-education, often hundreds or thousands of kilometers apart. At the same time, many couples found solace, companionship, hope and love with new partners in this cruel crucible of daily humiliation and gut-wrenching insanity.

Painfully shy, wiry, nervous and at peace with herself, Bao's dark glasses frames enhance her introspective, philosophical mein. She is a classic hermit, just loves living up here in virtual isolation, with her wood burning stove, books, music, cigarettes, two big mutts, and most of the time, in deafening silence. If she wasn't here, she would probably be in a monastery on a mountaintop someplace. Bao has been living as such for a year, after the other manager left when the chairlift was closed just before. She receives no pay, but lives here for free and has all her necessities paid for. She is here to make sure the place stays safe, while she does get two to three clients a *month*. The reason the chairlift was shut down is pure local politics. This lift's ticket costs ¥75 (€9/$12) and drops everybody at the temple level, less than a klick from here. But there is another, competing chairlift about 10km south of here, charging ¥240 (€30/$38). The owners of the other one are better connected and got this one shut down. The other lift belongs to Dali natives. The owner of the Highlander lives in Dali, but is a carpetbagger and doesn't have any political clout. Anyway, business is great for the horse rental guys, but not so good for Bao, since 99% ride up and back down the same day. Bao cannot tell me who the owner is of this chairlift, but it may be owned by the Dali government and they are happy to not mess with the maintenance and operation of it. She calls the owner and orders her food and necessities, which are brought up by mule pack. Or if it is a small delivery, she has a couple of friends who live in Old Dali City and hike up to bring her a backpack full of stuff. Water is piped in from the 4,000m mountain peaks above. Electricity is very expensive and is only turned on in the evening before bedtime. After that, lights out, literally. This evening, I ask for special permission to charge up my Galaxy and external power pack and she agrees. There is a nice, big kitchen with the capacity to feed all the people who can fill the six rooms. But since Bao only gets a few customers per month at most, she cannot stock any food above what she eats. So, anyone who stays here must now eat at the temple below.

Nothing like a crystal clear mountain sky and a nearly full Moon hanging in Capricorn to wish you goodnight. With the bright moon, the sky is a little bleached out, but I offer to give Bao a stargazing lesson, putting my 3km green light laser to work to point out major constellations and bright stars. We also check out the Moon. My Zeiss 8 x 56 are designed for wildlife watching, but they are unparalleled when used for astronomy, the main reason I bought them back in '88. She tells me no one has ever shown her the night sky before, she has never used such nice binocs and just keeps saying,

"WA! WA! WA!"

Which means *Wow* in Chinese… We have a nice strong coffee together for breakfast and she invites me to take a long walk with her pooches. The centerpiece of the Cangshan Park is an impressive walking trail that runs parallel to Lake Erhai below. Between the levels of the Zhonghe Temple and the hostel, it is an incredibly well built, level, wide, granite stone walking lane, carved into the side of the mountain. It looks like designers and builders put as much thought into it as the Chinese have done for their multibillion yuan skyscraper tall super highways. The trail's total length is about 15km and at the far southern end is where the expensive chairlift is. Today, we go in the opposite direction until it ends. We go about 4km and the walk is incredibly scenic, as we hug the sheer mountain face, weaving into steep canyons and turning onto lookouts that drop off hundreds of meters straight down, to the level of Lake Erhai below. Safety was planned, as there are solid, steel balustrades in most of the right places. This long walkway cost a small fortune in materials and labor to install. The Erhai Lake Basin is very transparent this morning, before the heat of day can kick up the clouds. With the Zeiss, we can clearly see the range of mountains behind the opposite shoreline to the east. At the north end of the lake is a large wind turbine farm, which is surprising, given that I would not consider this to be a terribly windy area. But prevailing north-south winds probably get a good draw over the 40km long, 250km^2 lake. It is dead calm at this early hour of the morning and all the turbines are just as tranquil.

It is mind boggling to see several little stone lookouts built into the side of the mountain, well above us. How does anybody get into them? Is it monks who go there to pray, fast and meditate? My binocs cannot tease out any trails that even come close to them. I suspect they get there the same way I did yesterday, straight up. Above them, near the tops of the 4,000m crests are wild, tall waterfalls dropping straight down into the forest covered mountains. We walk across a couple of impressive streams cascading out the canyons, pleasing us with small waterfalls along the way. Bao climbs down into one to give her dogs a chance to swim and she takes the opportunity to give them a soapless bath. After Jade Dragon Snow Mountain and yesterday's monstrous climb, I tiredly watch from this impressively well built, level stone path and wave. Bao tells me now there is way too much water during the rainy season, but that in the winter, before the spring melt, the waterfalls and cascades almost dry up and it is really spectacular to hike up into them to the source. I can only imagine, thinking about how I tried to do so in Langmusi, in the Great Namo Gorge, with its Fairy Cave, solitary Tibetan monk shepherd and my faceoff with a hard charging mountain marmot.

Suddenly, this royal route just stops and there are signs expressly warning people to not continue on the old trail. I can see why. It is pure Jules Verne science fiction times Indiana Jones movie set bravado. Bao says it actually goes on at this level for several klicks, before descending into the lake basin to the north of Dali Old City, where a regular bus can take you back to town. Completely overrun with vines, plants and washed out at irregular intervals for lack of maintenance, it would appear the budget dried up to finish it, like the 15km of luxurious stone walkway behind us. How treacherous is it, you might ask? A few people actually died falling off the narrow, rocky ledge, so the signs went up and a token chain blocks the path, but there is nothing stopping some professional rock climber from taking it on. This slender strip is a daring unicycle, tight wire act, as it rapidly dwindles down to 50cm or less in anus clenching width. I'll pass.

I am actually so knackered from the last two days of (at least for me) formidable treks and decide to take advantage of the hostel's monastery-calm atmosphere to relax, write *44 Days* and take a nice, much deserved, long mountain kip. To reciprocate for her hospitality this morning, I invite Bao for dinner at the Zhonghe Temple *down under*. She seems to really appreciate the gesture. After dinner, Bao has a nice, warm fire stoked in her wood stove, in what serves as the hostel's now ghostly hangout room. It is cold in my bedroom, since there is no electricity. She invites me to share the fire with her, lights several candles, we chat, listen to western music, which she likes and I take written notes for *44 Days* as we do so. Then a second night of hibernation in the fading moonlight and total silence.

Next morning, it's time to leave. I pay the princely sum of 60 RMB (€8/$10) for my two-night stay, including getting to do my laundry in this pristine, lost and laconic world. Bao is a different kettle of fish and obviously very happy to be living out her dream of a secular, intellectual, monastic life. She explains to me that I should have never come up the horse trail and did not know that was where I was, when I called yesterday. She tells me to go about 8km to the south on the good stone lane, look for a small temple roof below it and there I will find a granite staircase all the way back down to the park entrance. Really? You don't say? As I leave, I put my little backpack on my chest and the big one on my back and until I get all the way down to the second park entrance, I never take them off and I never sit. On the whole route down, I run into only one local woman taking in a morning hike and one young man who is doing the same. I ask him to take a picture of me with my two backpacks and pick up a walking stick to ham it up; unfortunately, it is blurred, but I do have the memory.

The staircase is just as good as the walking path above, wide and in excellent condition. I could be walking down the steps of a 670m tall open air skyscraper, just this one switches back and forth instead of spiraling. By the time I get to the bottom, I am calling it the Stairway to Heaven (thanks Led Zeppelin) and have to ask myself what happened the day before yesterday, as to why I was not taken to this proper walkway up and down the mountain, and only offered the mudslide, horse manure heave-ho: 1) my driver doesn't know about this correct way to get up and down Cangshan - but being a local taxi driver, I seriously doubt it, 2) he knows about it, but just forgot and went to the closest entrance - this correct entrance is about 400m south from the horse trail, which we were right next to, or 3) he knows about it, remembered the good entrance and wanted to teach me a lesson for refusing the horse ride up, and therefore, a loss of finder's fee for him. Just knowing humanity's proclivity for revenge and spite, I give minimum odds of two-thirds for scenario number 3 and could easily argue for odds of three-fourths in favor of the driver's dishonor. In any case, over the last two days, I got a great workout, pushing my body's physical capacity to some serious limits and renewing my humbling respect for the awesome grace of Mother Earth. Going up the stairs or holding onto the neck of a tired old trail hag would just not be the same. The Cangshan Mountains, the Hideaway Hostel and Dali were made extra special - I did it my way.

Chapter 35: Dali - Kunming - Caohai

Yunnan's capital, Kunming, gets very short shrift on this leg, an old pickpocket on the prowl, Guizhou's attempt at world class wildlife protection is a miserable failure: Caohai Lake is one of the low points of this journey. Also, proof positive just how easy it is to get from one isolated place to another in 21st century China, all in synchronized fashion.

Kunming, Yunnan's bustling capital unfortunately gets the extreme short end of the stick on this trip. It gets the same treatment Chengdu got on this journey: I arrive in the evening, walk across the street to stay in a very Spartan *zhaodaisuo*, get up the next morning to go to the station and leave the place. Wham, bam, thank you Mao. Being ahead of schedule two days is also nice. I cut short stays in Jiuzhaigou and Lijiang for all the right reasons: crass Las Vegas style commercialism. This gained me two days. But, I spent an extra day doubling back up the Liqi Valley and gained it back today with unexpected, precision connections between destinations. So, I'm still two days ahead of schedule. While I take whatever the cards deal me every step of the way, I just don't stumble into a station and throw a dart on the timetable to see where I'm going to land next. I spend days and weeks planning a trip like this, with a detailed itinerary extending into the schedule as far as possible, and I expect to stick to it. Based on my research, I have a good feel for how much time is needed to see and do what I want at each stopover. This trip has worked like a charm, beyond my wildest expectations. Will I extend a stay someplace if something pleasing and unexpected pops up, even if it means getting behind schedule a day or two? Of course. But on this journey, that has not happened. Nor am I a hostel hound. I don't like hanging out at hostels, as hippy cool and groovy as they may be, to chat with other expats, or more accurately these days here, with Chinese tourists. One of my ulterior goals on this journey is to give my Mandarin language the Iron Man triathlon challenge, which is not going to happen inside hostels and which I'd much rather do face to face with China's salt of the Earth - which brings us back to Kunming…

Not that I would have wanted to spend a lot of time in Kunming. Half the size of Beijing, with ten million citizens, it is in essence a scaled down version of where I live, as is Chengdu, with its fourteen million souls: all are big, sprawling, teeming, growing-like-weeds metropolises. That is definitely not a criterion I am seeking out when I travel around China. I live in a big, sprawling, teeming, growing-like-weeds megalopolis and there are just simply too many faraway and adventurous places in China to see and experience. Why spend time in the busy cities? Lanzhou (3.6 million) was more than enough on this trip and when I wrap up this trek in Guiyang (4.3 million) that will be another big city visit. Enough is enough. Kunming has gone through its typical developmental growing pains. Back in the 90s, its huge 40km long, 300km^2 city lake, Dianchi (滇池), was the local version of Cleveland's Cuyahoga River back in the 60s-70s. I don't know if Dianchi could catch on fire, but it got national and international press as being one of the most polluted metro area bodies of water on the planet, with the stench of sewage and chemicals filling up the city streets for days on end. Since then, the Cuyahoga has gotten largely cleaned up, but the Dianchi is proving to be much more recalcitrant.[1] In spite of billions of dollars having been spent since 1990, when 90% of Kunming's raw sewage was being pumped directly into the lake (as were Beijing and every other city in China at the time), the lake's water today is still undrinkable and has the worst quality assessment possible, a Grade V. Kunming seems decent enough and Lonely Planet raves it up. They are installing an underground metro and the public buses and bikes get reserved lanes everywhere, which the cars seem to be respecting. Bossy, bullying Beijing drivers, please take notice. The public buses have English recordings along with Mandarin, to identify each stop, which is very cosmopolitan. I see there is the Secam International Hospital. I understand there is a very active expat community here, especially college students, as like Lijiang, the low latitude (25°) and high altitude (1,900m) weather is like eternal springtime here most of the year. Kunming is notable for one date: August 1st is when I arrive here. I am into my second month of travel. From here on out, the rest of the trip is marked by my amazing ability to get from one obscure, off the beaten path place to another, either by train or bus or a combination of the two, with very little waiting time. It is a testament to China's incredible gains in infrastructure and development that I get everywhere I want, in some of the most undeveloped areas still left in the Republic.

My destination from Kunming is Caohai (草海= Grass Sea), Guizhou, a bird reserve in the middle of nowhere on the Yunnan border.[2] At the very civilized Kunming train station, I see for the first time ever, ticket windows allowing purchases forty days out and not the usual ten. It is too bad they don't do that in the rest of the country. It would sure take some of the frenzied pressure off when buying train tickets. Bravo Kunming! Over the next twenty-four hours, I will make synchronized connections from Kunming to Qujing (曲靖), Xuanwei (宣威), Liupanshui (六盘水), Weining (威宁) and Caohai: train-bus-train-train-taxi, all without so much as a hiccup. This would have been beyond the realm of drug fueled imagination back in the 90s.

The bus ride to Xuanwei is really fascinating. As we leave Qujing, we could be in the western half of the Red River Valley in Oklahoma. It is arid, with white limestone rock formations, scrub covered buttes and deserty outcroppings. Then we turn into another valley and it is like Central France or Kentucky, sporting rolling hills covered with thick forests of trees. It is one fascinating geological and geographical wonder after another. By the end of my stay in this province, I can see that Guizhou is rough and rugged, wild and wooly, hoary and scary, and just being here and traveling around all this wilderness makes it worth the visit, not to mention the wonderful sites I see too. Getting off the bus in Xuanwei is a real treat. I am standing right outside the bus asking several locals about the best way to get to Caohai, when I feel a tug, like a fishhook caught on my right front pocket, being pulled on from a distance. Two or three slow, purposeful tugs and I look down, turn around and don't see anything, so I continue my conversation with these people. But now, my BS antenna is at full mast and as soon as I feel it again, I quickly turn around and there is this stately old, genteel Chinese man, in a black suit, white collared shirt and dress shoes, trying to pickpocket me. What a great cover, with his advance age and fancy get-up. I start screaming,

"Pickpocket, pickpocket!" (扒手, 扒手!= *pashou, pashou!*)

With this very public alert, he quickly slinks away and melts into the crowd. The people I'm talking to act as if he's a regular part of the social fabric here, and the way things played out, I wouldn't be surprised. The best thieves work in teams. Luckily, the cargo pants I am wearing have Velcro strips on the inside of the pocket openings and this pocket was partially sealed without me even trying, as Velcro is wont to do. Also, the pockets are quite deep. Not to mention the old codger was not very good at this low percentage shot. About the only way he could have pulled it off would have been with a partner to start a fight or tussle with me and get me completely distracted. Still, it is a wakeup call to get in the habit of sealing the Velcro shut on that pocket, when I'm in bus and train stations. This makes the second time my family has been pickpocketed since returning to China in August, 2010. It happened to others we knew when we lived here from 1990-1997, but we were not personally robbed or pickpocketed then. In any case, it would have been superfluous, since we were fighting off commercial pickpockets every which way we turned - in the market, paying for anything or visiting anyplace. Since returning though, in the summer of 2011, my family and I traveled to Shanxi and in the chaos of a strikingly impressive flash flood in Taiyuan, my 14-year old daughter had 30 RMB taken from her little money purse she had clipped to her belt buckle. It doesn't sting so badly when the amount is small, which is why I don't carry much cash in my billfold when I travel. I keep the big boodle in a passport/currency tote hanging on my neck every waking hour, and if the hotel lacks confidence, I'll sleep with it on, as well as with my Zeiss under my pillow. Even that, I never carry my billfold in my back pocket, since the day I got pickpocketed in Tunisia when I was in the Peace Corps. I had *just* gone to the bank and gotten my meager monthly pay in cash. Being my only source of money, it was a huge hit and the next month was edifyingly different and difficult, compared to all the others. It taught me a valuable lesson: never carry a billfold in your back pocket. Since that day, in spite of traveling across 85 countries in some pretty intense places and situations, my front pocket protected billfold has never been successfully stolen, including today.

Leaving Kunming and heading into Guizhou is an accelerated trip on a time machine – in reverse. Guizhou has the dubious distinction of claiming to be China's poorest province, although Gansu, which I visited earlier on this trip, likes to point out its humble status also. As a result, traveling in Guizhou is like being in China a generation ago. The infrastructure is really dated, including the architecture, cities, towns, villages and roads. For someone like me who lived in China more than twenty years ago, it is a fascinating glimpse into the days that were. I get to Liupanshui on the last train in, about 23:00 and I step off into a world unto its own. I immediately flash to Cormac McCarthy's post-apocalyptic, dystopian novel, *The Road*, which in 2010, was adapted to a wonderfully grim and frightening, yet ultimately hopeful movie. So what's it going to be for me tonight: grim or hopeful? The beginning is not very inspiring. The whole place has a dreary, fatalistic, Great Leap Forward feel to it. There is almost no use of electricity and the air is heavy with dank, dirty fog. The waning gibbous Moon is almost invisible through the thick, atmospheric blanket covering us. A small market with guys selling food and beverages under hanging lanterns can offer me no advice about where I might find a room tonight. I keep getting pointed around the corner, where it is pitch black, but I do see a police station door in amongst scads of scaffolding on the outside of the buildings, and knock on it. They point me straight upstairs, but with my flashlight, I can see it is nothing but a construction site. Do they expect me to sleep on the bare concrete floor? Anyway, the staircase only extends from upstairs to my head level. The bottom half of the stairs is missing and I'm in no mood for any midnight scaling, police or no police. I walk back to the train station and it is now haunted in total darkness and completely deserted. Where did all the passengers who got off go? They melted into the heavy haze like so many doppelgangers. I'm the last man standing here and to be honest, this place is downright creepy. I wish I could say I am feeling relaxed and comfortable. I head across a funky looking bridge heading out of the area, thinking there might be a town down the road. I swear they shot the movie, *The Road* here. All that is missing are the crazed cannibals, and who knows at this point? As soon as I get across this bridge, a woman approaches me, speaking Mandarin a little bit better than I speak Spanish, and like Spaniards, her mouth is going a klick a minute. I understand she has a room to offer me and to follow her. It is almost midnight and Liupanshui is looking more and more desperate, as I gather in my options: I don't really have any – she is it. I agree and she starts leading me on a wild goose chase overland, with no trail in slate black darkness and we suddenly start climbing a big hill. I'm thinking, this is a robbery set up, right? Well, at least I know where the police station is. We finally get to a series of crudely made concrete shells for buildings and she takes me upstairs to a big cubicle shell and says, all excited and beaming proudly,

"Here it is!"

Other than needing to sleep on the sidewalk, this is the roughest place I will stay on this journey. My room, as it were, is one big naked concrete shell that looks like a first grade class did the stucco work with their bare hands. One naked light bulb, one electrical outlet, one really crappy bed with Mao era bedding and of course, a thermos of boiled water. Never fails. There is one big window to the outside and no curtains, so I'm on display for the whole world to observe me. Nor is there a key for the outside door. There is one other interior door, which I have no idea opens onto what, but at this hour, I just close the latch on it. I pay her 20 kuai (€2.50/$3.20) and I don't know if I should feel thankful or ripped off. At least it is a roof over my head. Since anybody can come in during the night, I move the bed across the empty room and set it in a defensive position, with all my belongings behind it in a corner and where the electrical plug is close enough to the bed so I can charge my Galaxy and keep it within reach. I mean, it's not like I have a roomful of furniture to move around. When I move the bed, I discover a standard issue wash pan found in almost every Chinese room. I use the boiled water to clean up a little and brush my teeth. This place makes the zombieland Jingtieshan Mining Company hotel look like a penthouse suite at the Savoy. When I say concrete shell, I mean it. All I can do is toss the leftover water and spit in the corner of the bare room. This is one of those places where the passport/money tote, Zeiss, flashlight and utility knife sleep with me. It is hard to get any sleep at all in these conditions and then at dawn, I hear knocking on the door. What the hey? I open the door and no one is there. Then I hear the knocking coming from the *interior* door right next to me, unlatch and open it and there is *another* concrete shell with two Chinese men, a woman and her baby staring at me in disbelief. The baby starts crying of course. This is a scene right out of the 90s: let's build a hotel or office building without plans or blueprints and just *wing it*. One big happy family. Classic.

In the daylight, I can now see what's going on. This lady and her family have built their version of a rural, end of the line Guizhou hostel to serve the train station crowd. I start to understand her Mandarin patois a little better this morning. She is beaming with pride at what they have done and given the generational leap back in time this far out in the Guizhou hinterland, for her origins, she probably has every reason to be satisfied. What seemed like an eternity getting here last night in the total darkness is only about 300m to the train station, which is easy to see from this little hillock looking down. Before leaving, I chat with this proud, entrepreneurial landlady and her kiddos for a few minutes. She is prima facie Display Number One why China is creating the fastest growing and largest middle class in human history. She and her brood are all smiling ear to ear, pinching themselves, giggling and gawking at me like I'm some Capitan Kangaroo alien visiting Planet Earth. The children's Mandarin is better than their Mamma's, since that is what they are studying at school. It must be these pups who did all the brick and stucco work here. I sure hope they are not inside when an earthquake strikes this area… We say our goodbyes. Next to her place is a funky looking concrete mosque, so she could be Hui or Ouigher, which would help explain her barely passable pigeon Chinese. One thing is for sure: Lonely Planet says almost no foreigners come to Guizhou and I believe they are right. And to think this is what Beijing, Shanghai and Guangzhou were like only one generation ago. The big wheel keeps on turning. Another punctual train gets me to Weining, which, with its nearby Caohai Wildlife Reserve, is trying to make itself into a big ecotourism destination. I wish them luck, because it is really getting off to a bad, unhealthy start. The taxi from the train station goes through town and it looks very 90s, with construction for construction's sake: chaotic, haphazard and poorly built. He drops me off in the weirdest, most unlikely place, points and says,

"There it is!"

He's right. Off in the distance, I can see a little lake that is supposed to be a huge repository of bird species from around China. All there is between me and the lake is nonstop construction, crop and vegetable plots. Peak migratory bird populations are here during the winter, when tens of species roost here during the cold months, but I should still have plenty of wildfowl to see, as the guide brags it is home to one hundred and eighty species. Unfortunately, the saving grace of Zhou Enlai and one of his desperate telegrams to the local Communist cadres did not reach here and Southwest China's largest and most important wetland was drained dry during both the Great Leap Forward and the Cultural Revolution, so the land could be cultivated, for desperately needed food. It was originally a massive 4,666km^2, but because of these twin induced human catastrophes, as well as climate change, it is now a microscopic 5km^2. That is a microscopic 0.1% of its original size. On the upside, it sits at 2,200 MASL and just 3° north of the Tropic of Cancer, so the conditions are excellent for both humans and wildlife. Agriculture needs won the first two big sociopolitical duels and even though the people have stolen 4,661km^2 of lake surface, it's still never enough. They are growing corn, melons, other crops and applying Chinese levels of chemicals, right up to the lakeshore. As a result, the shoreline I see today stinks of oxygen starved, fertilizer stench. Not good. The shallow waters are stagnant and poisoned, and I sure do not see any wildlife amongst the noxious fumes. I try to walk out to the edge of the lake for a hike and even put on the rubber boots I used to hike up to White Dragon River in Langmusi, but it is impossible to get anywhere. There are about fifty or so small skiffs, smaller than the ones at Lugu Lake that can be rented. There is one price per skiff and each skiff can carry up to six passengers. The two ladies at the ticket window are very nice and ask all the Chinese who don't have a full load, if they will take me. Three people who settle on the middle priced route (halfway out) invite me, so I throw in my 60 kuai (€8/$10) share. One of my new boat mates is a young male college grad and the others are a retired teacher from Xishuangbanna, Yunnan, near the border with Myanmar, and his daughter, who is also a teacher. Our boatswain is a rough-hewn Yi woman who looks like she's been around the block a number of times and sings us bawdy songs in Mandarin, much to the joy of my fellow passengers. She loves the attention and getting a laugh out of us.

The whole trip is barely interesting. At least once we get away from the shore, the pollution dissipates and the 2m deep lake water is clear, with a thick undergrowth of different water grasses on the bottom. But for how long will this place stay relatively clean? The retired teacher smokes several cigarettes and tosses the butts into the water. The boatswain says nothing to that, so neither do I. The student on board, who has a camera set up that would make anybody blush with material envy, tosses a wrapper overboard. Through my binocs, I see many other boats and people are tossing plastic water bottles and the like. What can I say? We go about 1km out to the middle of the diminutive lake and start to turn around.

Here, the water is over 5m deep. OK, I see some interesting birds, but as long as the shoreline is dead, the web of life is going to be severely crippled. One hundred eighty species? Mainly what I see are cormorants, coots, snowy egrets and mallard ducks, all of which I can spot on almost any body of fresh water around the world. The whole visit just depresses me. My boat mates complain about the lack of birds, as they should, and our Yi guide tells us that if we each add 10 RMB (€1.30/$1.60), she'll take us on a *really good* route back to see *lots of birds*. Everybody agrees, so I passively join in. What am I going to do, as the invited *waiguoren* - say no? It would be so beyond the pale to consider it, under the circumstances. As a result, we see absolutely no more birds than we did earlier, and the bawdy boatswain pockets an easy 40 yuan (€5/$6). The environment here is just too distressed. The only thing that saves it for me is my Zeiss. At least with their power and clarity, I am able to see pretty much everything within sight. Like I said, I see a few unusual birds, but to make a special trip to come here? Never. Highly unrecommended. It might be better during the winter residence of northern migratory species, but I'm not taking the chance of coming back again. Oh well. So my first visit to Guizhou is a bust. That happens sometimes. I sure am not going to curl my tail under my haunches and throw in the towel. And luckily I don't. Because the rest of Guizhou ends up having some of the most amazing and beautiful natural sites I see on the entire trip, highlight reel memories. What is that adage? Today is the first day of the rest of my life. Amen, brothers and sisters. Amen.

1- *The infamous Cuyahoga River catching fire was one of those rare arcs that burn brightly across the zeitgeist, searing and steeling people into action. Rivers catching on fire were almost a daily occurrence in the US before Cuyahoga. It took the leadership of Cleveland's outstanding mayor of the day, Carl Stokes, to use it as a cudgel on the bully pulpit, to effect change. Soon after, Earth Day was born, and American citizens were breathing, bathing and living superior lives with the new Environmental Protection Agency and Clean Water Act. The Cuyahoga River fire, along with Rachel Carson's* Silent Spring, *are often cited as helping spawn the modern US environmental movement. These revolutionary arcs are funny things. History is full of them: Rosa Parks, Stonewall, Watergate, the Paris May '68 protests, etc.*

2- *Not the same Caohai I saw at Lugu Lake. This* grass sea *moniker is common in Chinese to describe any wetland or march area.*

Author's note: perceptive readers will notice that Caohai is in Guizhou and not Yunnan. However, the flow of *44 Days* is such that the leg from Kunming to Caohai is best kept together in the same chapter.

Figure 88: An Yi minority log cabin on the drive from Xichang/Liangshan to Lugu Lake (Luguhu), complete with a pig in the yard.

Figure 89: Luguhu: a huge matrilineal Mosuo log cabin house. The exterior is painted a bright mustard yellow color, with pinkish red doors and windows.

Figure 90: Luguhu: an old Mosuo women walking her huge sow along the peninsula road to Luowa.

Figure 91: Luguhu: a look back towards Luowa village, with the transport skiffs and behind all this, Caohai, or Grass Sea, a huge wetland area.

Figure 92: Luguhu: Mr. Den our boatswain canoes the lusty couple and me across the lake. The resemblance of China's minorities to Native American Indians is uncanny and hard to deny.

Figure 93: Luguhu: Noel Coward's Easy Virtue lake flowers, shuixing yanghua, give this mountain lake a fairytale, enchanted ambiance.

Figure 94: Luguhu: the striped skins are Felis silvestris beiti and the spotted one is F. s. ornata. These magnificent wild cats are rated as vulnerable species, one grade below the endangered classification.

Figure 95: Lijiang: the Jade Dragon Snow Mountain primeval forest is an amazing ninety minute stretch of ancient Tolkienesque wonderland to walk through. I call it Mushroom Forest.

Figure 96: Dali: inside the country kitchen where from Lijiang to Dali, I have lunch. These roadside restaurants do a lot of business, as can be seen by the huge quantities of ingredients.

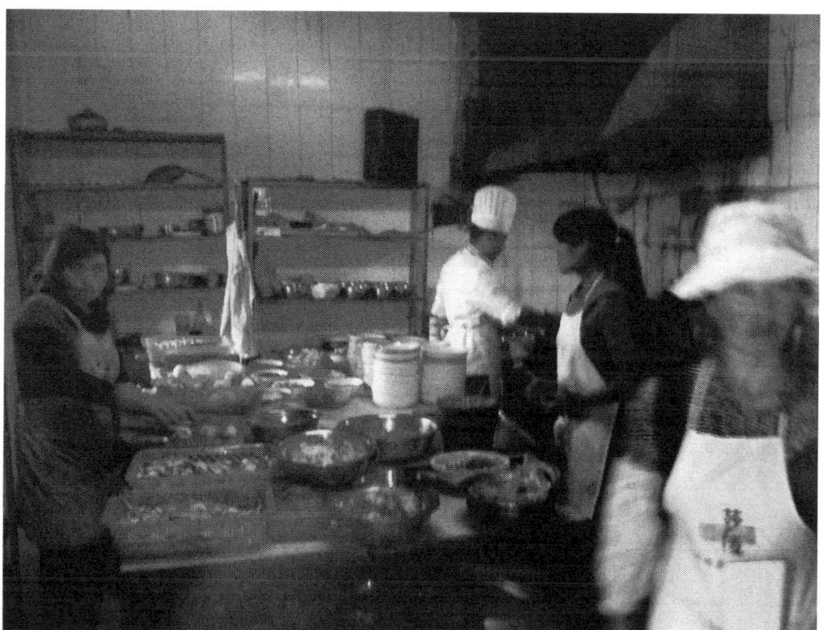

Figure 97: Dali: country kitchen. The chef has three sous chefs, plus the table help and cashier for the public.

Figure 98: Yunnan: the China traveler's breakfast, lunch and dinner of champions. Great nutrition, delicious, available everywhere, anytime of day, and cheap!

Figure 99: Dali: the Lake Erhai basin from 700 meters up, in the Cangshan Mountains, shot from the Zhonghe Temple. Ten minutes further up the extremely steep mountain is the deserted Highlander Hostel.

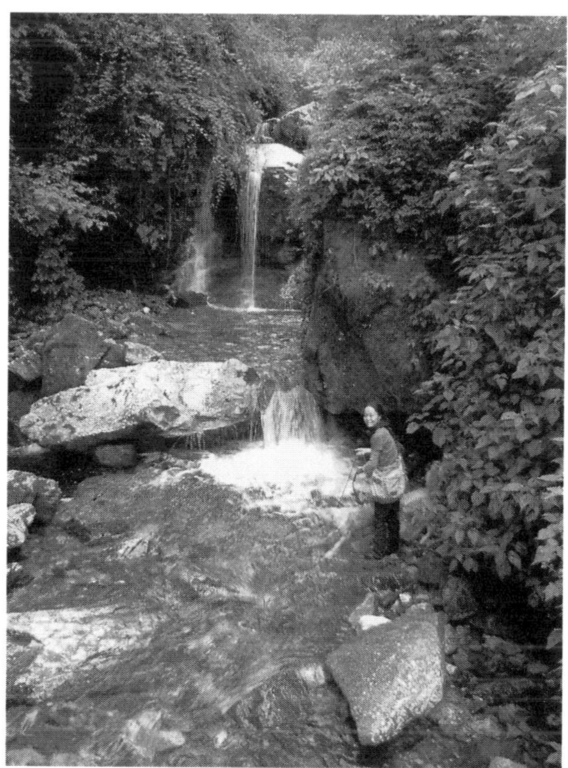

Figure 100: My Dali Cangshan Mountains walk with Ms. Bao, who is giving her two dogs a bath in a beautiful cascade.

Figure 101: Dali Cangshan Mountains: With so many people in China, remains of the dead are everywhere. These moss and fern covered Buddhist tombs are still being tended to. National policy now requires cremation for the nine million Chinese who die each year, minority Tibetan sky funerals excepted.

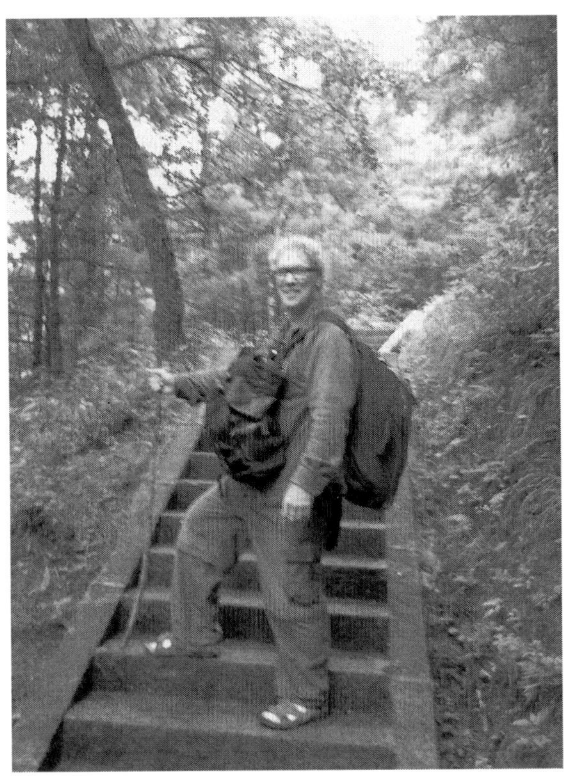

Figure 102: Dali: hiking leisurely down the well-built granite staircase from atop the Cangshan Mountains to Dali below.

PART VII

GUIZHOU

Rules of the Road: Governments

"Government is an association of men who do violence to the rest of us."
Leo Tolstoy

"When an emperor makes a mistake, all the people suffer."
Chinese proverb

"Experience hath shown that even under the best forms of government, those entrusted with power have, in time, and by slow operations, perverted it into tyranny."
Thomas Jefferson

Chapter 36: Zhijin

China's biggest grotto is also one of the world's best. Definitely worth the effort to get here. The routes are tortuous, but blazingly beautiful. This part of 21st century China is still the end of the world - I just can't tell my new Communist Party cadre friend that!

Lonely Planet has many nice things to say about Zhijin Cave. As an amateur geologist and all around science hound, I have been through some spectacular grottos in all my travels around the world, so today the bar is set pretty high. Going to Zhijin today has me fondly reminiscing about one great cave adventure I lived to tell about. Two of my Oklahoma State University college buddies and I, Ken Fraley and Terry Bresin, visited Mammoth Cave National Park, Kentucky, in the summer of '73. Being young and reckless, we jumped over several *Do Not Enter* barriers and took off exploring forbidden areas. One led us to a staircase that worked its way up in jointed, shambolic fashion about 100m above the main cave level and landed us on an incredible overlook of the biggest chamber in the cave. It was frighteningly dangerous and we could have been a post-mortem flash on the national news the next day, but when you are 19, you're bulletproof, right? The rickety staircase had bridges that went over deep, echoing crevices and Edgar Allen Poe black pits, where if we fell, it would have surely meant death. The staircase was made out of wood and most of the risers and steps were rotted out, not to mention the joists and laterals holding it all together. Pieces of this wood were breaking off each step of the way. We tried not count the seconds it took to hear them finally hitting the bottom of the blackness below us, with faint, muffled echoes. Were we scared? *Terrified* wouldn't begin to describe it. We were lucky to make it back down alive. When we reentered the main path, a park ranger was waiting for us, arms crossed in paternal consternation, half upset, half relieved and smiling admiringly. He had spotted us up on the lookout and explained this celebrated route is called The Corkscrew. It was one of the area's early Great Depression WPA projects, when Mammoth got an upgrade. Unfortunately, with the cave's high humidity and mold, it deteriorated rapidly, remained open only a few years and was deemed way too dangerous for public use thereafter. And there we were, 40 years after it was built, risking life and limb for the best panoramic view of Mammoth. Come to think of it, maybe I was bulletproof back then. With this experience in my back pocket, how will Zhijin compare today?

While only 200 kilometers straight as crow flies, today's trip leg ends up being a three segment endurance test. I have to get from the southwestern border of Guizhou where the ecotourism disaster, Weining/Caohai, is located and which I visited yesterday, to south central Guizhou and Zhijin Town, and its celebrated namesake Zhijin Cave. I ask a number of people, to get the traveler's consensus, and discover the best route. From Weining/Caohai, I head back to Liupanshui and from there continue to Nayong (纳雍), with the third leg being onto Zhijin (织金). Liupanshui is the transportation nexus to get in and out of Weining/Caohai and there are a number of trains that shuttle between the two towns. Today, just for a change, I take the bus back to Liupanshui. Now I see why there are so many trains. The S102 from Caohai to Liupanshui is gawd awful and atypically of Chinese valley routes, the drive is not especially interesting. Through here, the evidence of human stress on the land is manifest. There is coal and limestone mining, intense production of corn and rice and it all just looks very tired and run down. Since leaving Lugu Lake and coursing through Lijiang, Dali, Kunming and now here, corn and rice are the king and queen of food production, dominating the lowlands, with the usual terracing of every available valley, up its slopes and rises.

The bus ride on S307 from Liupanshui to Nayong, further east is unforgettable for two reasons. First, it is easily *the* worst road I travel on during this trip, which is saying something. Actually, the worst road taken on this trip *was* the Weining-Liupanshui leg I just took, but that record sure was ephemeral. Most of the time in China, there are bad road sections that are interspersed between decent to good stretches. Today's route takes off out of the Gates of Hades, rapidly descends into the morass of Oblivion and we get thrown all over the vehicle the entire way, ragamuffin dolls in a mobile, four-wheeled clothes dryer. By the end of the day, my insides feel like a case of broken eggs, my joints rheumatic and my muscles contused. Who needs an arduous, uphill scrape on the side of a mountain? Today's workout of hanging on for dear life is just as strenuous, and almost as scary. I have never seen so many vomit bags handed out as fast as today. Unfortunately, several don't ask for them in time, which adds to the raucous atmosphere. Hats off to the drivers of today's fifteen-passenger buses. They ought to get an honorary degree from America's Terry Don West Rodeo School. A bull ride only lasts eight seconds. This ride from Weining to Nayong lasts for several hours. The second reason the S307 is unforgettable is a positive one: most of the drive is like cruising through the spectacular Luberon Mountains, north of Marseilles, only these are much more rugged and uninviting, and without the wild French lavender. This whole magnificent stretch of natural and rural beauty more than makes up for all the bumps and bruises.

By the time we get to Nayong, it is after dark. Right in front of the bus station is a big street performance taking place and there is a huge crowd of people standing, gawking and milling about. A traveling gypsy show is taking place and hundreds of locals, young and old alike, three generations of families, are enjoying the cool, high altitude summer night. Out of the side of a cargo truck is a small stage. It's big enough for four people, as they stand in front of a little red velour and gold embroidered curtain, disappearing and reappearing in various costumes and masks. It is quite the variety show. They sing, have oriental Punch and Judy puppets, do dance routines, as well as performing funny skits that get the whole audience guffawing. Everybody can hear, since the actors are all wirelessly mic'd up with the as-usual-in-China, too loud sound system. The whole crowd is having a grand old time and I'm enjoying watching this very social and cultural of scenes. Millions of hamlets, villages, towns and cities use public funds to bring in traveling acts like this in China, including opera, comedy, magic, dance and puppets. These traveling troupes can also do their shows independently and pass the hat for payment, or find a walled in area where they can charge an entry ticket. Just like around the world, posters and flyers can be seen glued all over a town to announce their arrival, and later, they become faded souvenirs of their long ago departure. This kind of social and cultural interaction has been going on at least since the times of ancient China, Rome and Greece and it is fun to see this old madrigal style of art still being practiced.

Next morning, the S307 section from Nayong to Zhijin is Part II of the same rodeo bull ride cum wild, desolate, rugged mountain roads. The whole trip from Liupanshui to Zhijin gets an A for undeveloped beauty and an F for comfort. My seat buddy on the Nayong-Zhijin leg is Mr. Liang, a youngish Communist Party cadre working for the Zhijin County Ministry of Agriculture. Even without the CCP lapel pin, Party members just have that *look:* nerdy, cloistered, punctilious, obsequious and self-conscious in behavior; conservative and outdated in their style and dress – and like evangelicals, they always seem to be scheming and planning their next move to save humanity from the shackles of what they see as depravity and sinfulness everywhere they turn. Jocks, suits, babes, geeks and Chinese Communists - you can see them coming all the way down the street. Being with Liang is just like back in the 90s, when Chinese government employees were solicitous and unctuous to a fault, because they were so insecure about China's ever-rising standing with the West. Being incredibly insecure about their status means having to constantly make comparisons with the rest of the world, and today is no different: food, clothing, housing and the like. After covering these topics, Liang starts asking me how the roads and infrastructure compare to the US or France. Well… I'm in a real pickle here. This last thing I want to do is dis this guy's home base, which would be pointlessly unnecessary and for him to even ask me this question while we are being thrown about on a Journey to the Center-of the Earth-black hole of a road, is evidence enough of his lack of knowledge of the world at large. At the same time, I don't want to blow pixie dust up his backside either and leave him with the impression that the S307 is standard road fare around the world. I explain that in general, the roads in France and America are very good, avoiding the comparative *better*, but that there are off road mountain and desert tracks that can be very rough, which is true. I also suggest that it depends on where you are in China and the West. Beijing's public transportation network runs circles around almost any US city, with its rapidly expanding, 442km subway system, 1,000 bus routes, 67,000 taxis and hundreds of daily regional bullet and standard trains. But Paris's subway and RER (Réseau Express Régional = Regional Express Network) rapid transit system are the envy of the world and something that places like Shanghai will have to work long and hard to attain.

Upon arriving to Zhijin Town, Liang shows me where to find the combis going to the cave. Liang stays in touch via text messages during the rest of my trip and occasionally, out of the blue, even months later, I am getting SMS messages from him. I keep telling him if he ever makes it up to Beijing, that I would like to see him, and I sincerely mean it. Maybe one of these days our paths will cross again. To plan my day, I first get a room, eat a quick lunch and then take off. There are a number of combis going out to Zhijin Cave, about 22km away. It is really strange, they stop about 1km from the entrance. Why can't they go into the cave parking area? Like so many places around the world, all these drivers need to earn a living, and this is the way they make it happen. Still, I decide to walk up the long, sloping hill to get there, instead of paying 10 kuai (€1.30/$1.60) for a motorbike/small taxi ride up. At first, I take off down into a beautiful valley to the left, then get the directions correct from a shopkeeper: at the fork in the road, go straight up. Today is hot and the Sun at this 2,000m elevation is pounding down. Getting into the cave will be a relief.

The outside of the main entrance has the usual phalanx of restaurants and souvenir shops. The parking lot even has a nice sized waterfall crashing down from above. The entrance and waiting room area are very nicely done. I worry about depredations inside the cave, when I see polished natural rock formation statues being sold for thousands to tens of thousands of RMB each. I must admit they are spectacular. Unfortunately, a tropical hardwood forest also died in small part to make all the wooden pedestals. As soon as we get a quorum of visitors to make a group, a guide takes us into the cave. As usual, I'm the only white boy. We are supposed to stay together, but that does not last long. I elatedly spend my entire time in the cave alone, and being well lit and laid out, I can see I am not going to be repeating my 1973 Mammoth Cave Corkscrew adventure here. I take my sweet time and spend three hours inside, getting out after 17:00. From the cave's concert hall sized, open air atrium entrance to the 6km of climbing, spiraling, twisting, turning, overhead-looking, rubbernecking, crane-gawking, sitting and smiling in true admiration, I can say that Zhijin Cave ranks as one of the best places I've visited in the eighty-five countries I have traveled to on this planet. Any worries about depredations to the cave interior evaporate immediately, which is a relief, as I have seen a lot of damage in caves around the world, including China – theft of rock formations and visitors destroying others by touching and trampling on them – but the Zhijin Cave is in pristine condition. Also, looking back on China's modern history, I guess the local Cultural Revolution Red Guards were too busy desecrating priceless Buddhist treasures, torturing and killing perceived counterrevolutionaries, to be bothered to come out to such an isolated place to smash up a cave. Tisk-tisk, so little time for a decade of mayhem and destruction.

During my visit, there is one football-field-long chamber after basketball-arena-big-and-tall cavern after another, and they are all full of some of the most massive and beautifully preserved stalactites, stalagmites, rock formations, water pools and cave streams, that I have ever seen. There are also some small sized formations that are extremely rare and found in only a handful of caves around Earth and they are all in immaculate condition. The whole place is beyond description. From a Western aesthetic, one weakness the Chinese have for caves, ice shows and the like is to go way overboard on the kitschy lighting effects. Here, it is on display, but they do reign in their most ghastly impulses. Some of the lighting they do is quite nice in fact, and in harmony with the backdrops. In one of the biggest chambers, they have installed a large floor light show that appears to start up with sound or motion detection from the passing groups of visitors. Once it starts, it slowly mutates and unfolds into a moving graphic cartoon of a solar system, with cartoonish comets flying by. Kitschy but cool actually. Today's well laid out tour is just part of the cave's complex. When my initial group was going into the Zhijin Cave, the guide presented a big 3D model of the whole system, that shows a parallel series of chambers just as impressive, but not ready for the public. Even with only half the cave system open, Zhijin is one of the most spectacular caves in the world, in scope, scale and level of geological preservation. I could easily plan a whole trip to Guizhou, with Zhijin Cave as a main attraction. And Mr. Liang, you have every reason to be proud of this place. Your roads are antediluvian, but Zhijin Cave is world class.

One thing I would do differently, as I did not get here until the afternoon. When I got out, it was already pretty late. The cave exit is actually on the backside of this mountain dome and to get back to the entrance, there are big golf caddies to take you, for a fee of course. This return route is about 10km and it would make a terrific hike. The views off the mountainside are precipitous, spectacular wilderness vistas, with the Liuchong River (六冲河= Liuchonghe) in the valley bottom. In one far off valley can be seen the construction of a suspension bridge, part of another massive highway project, and it as big as the Golden Gate in San Francisco. To walk this 10km return back to the entrance and take in these beautiful views would be a great way to top off the cave visit. I just needed to start earlier in the day to make it happen.

Chapter 37: Zhijin - Guiyang - Zunyi

A provincial Chinese O'Hare-Heathrow sized bus station, Chinese Communist Party and Long March history and myth, plus the less than flattering virtues of China's white lightening: Maotai.

I guess it is possible to get from Zhijin overland to Chishui (赤水= Naked/Bare Water), where I want to go next, which LP touts as one of the last great undeveloped scenic areas in China. From Kunming up till now, I didn't have much of choice in transportation options, crossing some of the poorest, most infrastructually challenged parts of China. But after the raucous, bruising rides over provincial roads to get this far into Guizhou, I take everybody's suggestions, hands down. The best way to get to Chishui from Zhijin is going east to Guiyang (贵阳), Guizhou's provincial capital and then north to Zunyi (遵义), catching a bus from there to Chishui. What this means is driving the base and leg of a triangle, instead of shooting across the countryside on its hypotenuse, but so be it. This base and leg is shaped like a backwards L. I will start at the lower left in Zhijin, go east to Guiyang at the vertex, turn north and continue through Zunyi and on to Chishui at the top.

The road from Zhijin to Guiyang is a continuation of the infamous S307, which starts in Liupanshui and roller coasters its way across southwestern Guizhou, through Nayong, where I saw the nighttime traveling gypsy show and then over to Zhijin and its wonderful, world class cave. This continued section of the S307 does not want to disappoint its preceding parts. It is once more a rock and road show of Mother Nature and rural culture eye candy. It's getting to the point where if the drive is not stupendously, unforgettably beautiful, I'm really disappointed. All this magnificent scenery is the compensation I've come to expect for getting pummeled over the medieval, Marco Polo ruts being traversed. The S307 terminates at the ring road encircling Guiyang. Our bus terminates at the Jinyang (金阳) station about 10km outside of downtown Guiyang, just inside the ring road. It is massively impressive, as big as a small airport and run like one. There are hundreds of buses in the drop off zone and it is so huge, the walk to the station is like going across a big aerodrome tarmac. Airport scenes from great movies like *Casablanca*, *Bullitt* and *Heat* flash through my head, as we all amble several hundred meters to the front of the bus station. The hangar sized station is incredibly civil, given that thousands of people are lined up at nearly forty ticket windows and then chatting, standing, sitting, eating, sleeping and milling about in a dozen large waiting areas. Amazingly, not one person is smoking. I flash back at what would have been *Soylent Green* street riot scenes in a place like this twenty years ago, replete with choking smoke, garbage, spit, urine and leftover food all over the place. I just smile at the Chinese people's progress. Outside the waiting areas, fifty buses are prepped and filling up for points in every cardinal direction. And this goes on almost 24 hours a day.

From this mega big Jinyang terminal, a local bus goes downtown to get to the bus station that serves Zunyi, the transit town I need to go through to ultimately get to Chishui further north. From Guiyang to Zunyi, the modern G75 toll road is a nostalgic traveling pleasure. After the last few days of cage fight roller coaster rides, Zunyi's big interurban bus seems like stepping into a futuristic dreamland of century-later modernity, a zany contraption that today's people can only fantasize about. All this luxury is downright *boring*. I get to Zunyi mid-afternoon and need to spend the night to catch a bus to Chishui first thing in the morning. Anyway, my bus beaten, bone broken, body bruised self needs a little rest. I can see on Google maps that tomorrow's all day, buckboard bronco ride is going to be another anus clenching adventure. As usual, it is easy to find a decent and cheap Chinese *zhaodaisuo* room near the bus station and I get my ticket to Chishui to lock everything up. I pay ¥10 (€1.30/$1.60) extra and get a computer in the room with an internet connection, so I can check my bank accounts, purge my home email of unwanted messages and the like. I really do Zunyi a great disservice, partly due to my arrival time and partly by choice. I could rush out and try to see a place or two before dinnertime, but am just wanting to chillax, sit on my beleaguered bee-hind in a decent local restaurant, eat some great southern food, drink ice cold beer, people watch, chat with strangers, write this book and collect my thoughts about what is rapidly becoming the end of an amazing six-week journey.

Zunyi does not register at the non-Chinese international level, but in Sinoland around the planet it is very famous for two reasons. First, this town has a rich and colorful place in the history and mythology of the Chinese Communist Party. I don't use the word mythology disparagingly here. George Washington and the apple tree? France and her Marianne? Every nation state, culture and religion is chocker block full of myths and symbols. They nurture the creed, sustain the cause and reinforce absolutes and certitudes from one generation to the next. Zunyi is famous for being the site of the January, 1935 meeting that pitted the two factions of the Communist Party at that time – Mr. Bo Gu with his German aide-de-camp Otto Braun, versus Mao Zedong. Braun was there at the behest of the Soviets to offer counsel to the young and green CCP. His Chinese nom de guerre was Li De (李德), which means *Li the German*. At that time, it was the beginning of the Long March, which started in Guangdong, or Canton. As the Communists were moving north from Guangdong into neighboring Hunan province, they had to traverse the Xiang River. In a bloody span of forty-eight hours, the Red Army lost 40,000 men to Chiang Kai-Shek's KMT army at this crossing. Talk about a bad day on the battlefield. All the loss of men and materiel caused a huge drop in troop morale and the party faithful started to desert. Licking their wounds, the two rival Communist factions decided to meet and decide what to do. Zunyi had just been taken over and secured by Red Army troops, so its name was pegged to enter the annals of CCP lore.

Bizarrely, the Zunyi Conference was not even acknowledged to have taken place until the 1950s, well after Chinese reunification. No details of the meeting and who attended were divulged until the 50th anniversary in 1985, nine years after Mao's death. Whichever story version you choose to side with, and a meeting of such importance and so shrouded in mystery is still debated and argued to this day, but one thing is clear: Mao walked away from Zunyi as the paramount military leader of the Chinese Communists. He now had the arduous task of saving and pulling together all the remnants of the Red Army, who were scattered and exposed across China's southeastern flank. Let the hagiography begin, or the demonization, if you are at the other end of the ideological spectrum. To the victors goes the prose that fills the history books, at least China's editions in this case. Mao, who was infinitely charismatic, visionary, driven and politically savvy, brought the CCP back from near extinction and finished the 12,500km Long March. It lasted 370 days and was essentially a long, drawn out retreat on foot to recoup, rearm and rebuild his forces. Mao's reunited group ended the Long March in the mountains of Shaanxi, outside of its capital, Xi'an. Eventually, the Red Army drove the KMT troops and its Mafiosi to Taiwan, as well as helping force the WWII Japanese invaders out the eastern door. Their *pièce de résistance* of course, was taking control of the country on October 1st, 1949, to lead and govern a newly independent and reunified China after one hundred years of humiliation and chaos. Thanks to all this Communist Party history and Zunyi's celebrated namesake conference, there are a number of places in town that have been restored and preserved for visiting: the conference sites, participants' homes and secret meeting places of the attendees and grandees. But I'm just going to have to pass this time. To do it correctly, a good one to two full days would be ideal and I've got less than half of one.

Besides the Conference, Zunyi is renowned as the birthplace of Maotai (茅台酒), China's contribution to the world of strong spirits. This water clear, slightly syrupy, 53% alcohol beverage and I go way back. During the 90s in China, I was the director of a trade association that represents about one hundred agribusiness corporations and I later oversaw the installation and managed the first dedicated modern bakery in China, to produce hamburger buns for McDonald's. Much more than in the West, banqueting with vendors, customers and government officials is an almost non-stop affair in China. It was quite an honor to have the foreign Big Boss (大头= datou, or Big Head) attend a banquet, whether I was the guest or the host. And the most prestigious drink to offer was Maotai. Of course, like Parmesan cheese and French champagne, innumerable imitators were and are on the market, of varying to disgusting degrees of quality, and it was these cheap imitations that we were often plied with during banquets. So, like a good trooper marching my steps, I would drink whatever clear liquor was served (白酒= *baijiu*, white liquor). As bad as it could get, it got even worse for me, since every

Ding, Dong and Deng attending, and there were frequently half a dozen tables of ten guests each, insisted on the honor of approaching me, filling our shot glasses, waxing eloquently about eternal friendship and international cooperation and then shouting out,

"BOTTOMS UP!" (干杯! = GANBEI!)

Upon which I would dutifully do so. If I was the host, I had to go around and do the same thing with the most important person sitting at each table. The problem was after several rounds of these macho Kabuki challenges, I was pie-faced. And to make matters worse, my body never adjusted to whatever the distillation process leaves in Maotai, especially the cheap, rock gut versions. I would be horribly hung over, head and body aching, sick to my stomach and belching for days what tasted like unfiltered kerosene. And since I had two or more of these reciprocating banquets each week, and when traveling on business, almost daily, I was on a collision course to a shortened life span, and an unhealthy one at that. After six months of literally imitating Malcolm Lowery, Jack London and Ernest Hemingway in the besotted drunkenness department, I finally said,

"No more!"

However, I was in a delicate situation, in that I had to represent my role as the Big Boss, since I was conducting business, negotiating contracts, etc. And I already did not smoke, which is another great social binder in China, as well as in many other cultures. So, I had to come up with a compromise and I found it. I saved face by replacing the Maotai with *beer*. I am much bigger physically than most Chinese, the alcohol content of beer is a fraction of white lightening's and I could down many jiggers of suds, drink the whole banquet under the table *and* not get very drunk. Brilliant. Not to mention not burping up the La Brea Tar Pits for days on end. It was a clever move, since almost every larger city and if not, every Chinese province has its own brand of blond. So, I could flatter my hosts by extolling the quality virtues of their local beer and still fulfill my social business obligations. Let's be honest, some brews are much better than most others, but 90% of the world's suds are quite drinkable, for better or for worse, warm or ice cold, from the bottle/can or out of a glass and with or without food, thank you. The art of brewing is a pride filled, time honored craft and very competitive. To make the point, I love the Aussie joke,

*Why is drinking American beer like making love in a canoe? Because it's f***ing close to water.*

Every country, every region and city I have visited around the world is convinced their local brew is the best on Earth… Just writing this chapter, I can still taste that Maotai, motor oil refinery festering in my gut and gullet, like the Three Weird Sisters' wicked brew,

Double, double toil and trouble;
Fire burn, and cauldron bubble.[1]

Hey, that's my stomach we're talking about! Blech. Time to move on.

1- Macbeth, Act 4, Scene 1. These are some great thespian lines that have influenced many a medium form, including Harry Potter.

Chapter 38: Zunyi - Chishui

A fascinating drive through the White Horse Mountains, which are steeped in Long March lore; another multi-billion RMB super mountain highway, which gets me to thinking about China-US-EU relations, currencies and how the US will be beaten by China militarily, without the PLA having to fire a shot.

This Zunyi-Chishui leg is like several other routes during this voyage, but with really cool historical and cultural twists. First, we are again driving on Guizhou Greco-Roman wrestling, hide bound provincial roads, in today's case, the S302, S208 and X380. Secondly, overhead for kilometers on end is a new skyscraper-tall, suspended in mid-air, multibillion yuan super highway, being built to connect Chishui to the outside world. No matter having seen others that are similar, you just cannot take your eyes off their grandiosity and breathless engineering. Thirdly, the big valley we drive up celebrates its support of the 1st Front Red Army's passage through here during the 1934-35 Long March. At the start of the Long March, the 1st Army started out with 86,000 troops. How suicidal was this desperate escape? Only 7,000 were left of this group when it joined up in Shaanxi with the other two fleeing Red Armies, the 2nd and 4th. Out of a total of over 200,000 followers at the start of the Long March, Mao only had left 30,000 trek hardened, revolutionary zealots to move forward and change world history forever. Zhou Enlai and Deng Xiaoping were also members of this Long March, paying their dues for further leadership roles after independence.

Of historical interest is that Lin Biao (林彪) was one of the marshals leading this army. After later heroically heading the fight against the Japanese when they invaded China in 1937, he died in a plane crash in 1971 in Mongolia, fleeing to Russia, apparently after having failed in an attempted coup against Mao. This in spite of the fact that Mao had appointed Lin in 1966, at the start of the Cultural Revolution, to be his heir apparent. It would appear that Lin was fed up with all the mass psychosis and social cannibalism destroying his beloved republic. Ironically, Lin was instrumental in building up the Cult of Mao and the Great Helmsman's pharaonic, almost psychopathic hagiography after independence. Sycophantic Lin created the Little Red Book of Quotations of Chairman Mao, which is still a bestseller here and a popular souvenir for foreign tourists to take back home, being available in several languages. But, he seems to have realized his errors and tried to rectify them for the good of the country, failed, fled and went down in flames. As is true for a lot of China's modern Communist history, what happened during the coup, who was involved, how it failed and how Lin's plane went down, are all shrouded in a political haze as dense as London fog. One theory is that Lin tried to keep Mao under house arrest and then wanted to govern in his name. All we know is that Lin conveniently became one of the two biggest scapegoats of the Cultural Revolution's massive failure. Along with Mao's wife, Jiang Qing (江青), they were and still are branded as being fully responsible for the revolution's excesses, thus whitewashing Mao's manifest involvement. Again, words like *massive failure* and *excesses* cannot even begin to scratch the surface of just how bad it was for China's people during that darkest, most demonic and deepest dungeon of decades.

As we snake our way out of Zunyi on a small bus, my appreciation of the Long March's challenges is really brought into focus while driving up this valley, where the 1st Red Army was trying to move northwest. Strangely, they could not find a passage out of the Chishui River Valley and ended up circling back to Zunyi, finding an escape route there to the southwest, then moving north. It is a testament to just how rugged and unforgiving the topography is in northern Guizhou, that Mao and the Red Army had to double back at great risk of being trapped by the KMT. It is the narrow, sinuous, county level road, the X380, that runs the length of the Chishui River, forking off the S302 to the northwest at Tuchengzhen (土城镇),

with the White Horse Mountains (白马山= Baimashan) towering overhead. Here in the 21st century, the X380 is already an inhospitably rugged asphalt road, in a relatively comfortable 15-seat bus. So, it is sobering thinking about 86,000 hungry, battle shocked, retreating soldiers marching on foot at the bottom of this spectacular river valley, exposed to the elements and living off the handouts and aid provided by the hardy people who live here. How degraded and destitute were the people living here in pre-independence China? This area is a Miao minority stronghold and in the 1930s they did not get preferential treatment, like Baba Beijing so assiduously applies to its fifty-five minorities today. When the Red Army marched through this valley, the Miao women had to hide in their houses, naked for a lack of clothing. Children, even post pubescent teenagers had to tend the fields without much to hide their bare boned bodies. It was not uncommon that several men in a family would have only one pair of pants to wear. The two crops were opium and corn. Opium deadened the suffering and killed the hunger pangs of starvation. Only one out of two infants born survived. Many of those who did make it to childhood were sold into slavery and prostitution, in order to keep the rest of the family alive. Yet, with this Dante-esque infernal Hades on Earth, these miserable wretches offered what little they had to the 1st Army, whose members were not much better off at the time. Is it no wonder that in horrific, animalistic conditions such as these, and which were commonplace over much of rural China at the time, that charismatic and inspirational Mao and his ragtag bunch of revolutionaries were able to lift up and rouse the masses to defeat Chiang Kai-Shek and his mafia thugs in the KMT, as well as help remove the Japanese from mainland China?

The incredible support and succor these desperate people gave to the Red Army was not forgotten. It is easily one of the neatest, most attractive looking valleys I see on this journey. Even though it is narrow and serpentine, the X308 is actually in much better shape than the other provincial roads I take in Guizhou. It is obviously well maintained. The houses are all beautifully kept and have the same matching, eye catching architecture, giving the villages through here an almost movie set look. The houses are two-story, with white stucco walls. All the windows, exterior trim and garage doors are painted kidney red, giving them an Alps chalet look. On the front of each house are two possible logos. One is a red pentagram star with a black hammer and sickle in the middle. The other is a round Buddhist, ochre and black mandala with a gold star above and *Red Army* (红军= *hongjun*) written below. In most cases, on either side of these logos are the two characters that make up the words for Long March (长征= *Changzheng*) written in a very stylized fashion. On the side walls of many of the houses are painted big frescoes lauding the Communist revolution, proletarian victories, bountiful communal production and harmony of the masses.

And then there is the super highway going up in the White Horse Mountains above. Depending on your point of view, Baba Beijing's commitment to infrastructure development, on a continental scale never really seen before in modern history, is either narcissistic megalomania or prescient Five-Year planning for the 21st century. This consensus driven, heavily subsidized, long term infrastructure and production planning is brazen control of the economy's levers. It is the antithesis of the libertarian disease the United States is experiencing, which is totally infecting the UK like malarial fever and slowly rubbing off on the Old Continent. Just imagine how world history and development would have been different if post-war America was saddled with today's Republican extremists doing everything they can to destroy the commonwealth of the nation for their corporate overlords. The national interstate highway system would have never been built for starters. At best, there would be a hit and miss scattershot of private toll roads. All the billions of dollars in grants to cities and states that turned the United States into the post-war infrastructural envy of the world, would have never been funded and built. Now, these ideological nut jobs, just as deluded and fanatical as Mao and Stalin at the other political extreme, are doing everything they can to privatize it all, to sell it to Firemen for pennies on the dollar, as it crumbles to pieces. On the other side of the aisle, imagine the United States with the current sold-out Democratic water boys for Wall Street, if they were in power after WWII. I see no men on the Moon, no Pell grants, food stamps, unemployment insurance, no Medicare, no Medicaid, no improved Social Security programs, no Clean Air, no Clean Water, no EPA, no OSHA workplace safety rules - just an Ayn Randian capitalist jungle to be feasted upon by the 1%. This mentality is overwhelming the EU too, much to the West's peril and ruin. Firemen are calling the shots on both sides of the Atlantic now. As Napoleon Bonaparte said, he who is owed the money owns the process and calls the shots.

So, how long can China hold off these Western dogs of doom? For now, Baba Beijing has a huge layer of insulation in the fact that the RMB is not yet fully convertible. When that happens, it will be the most cataclysmic shift in international banking and finance since the Bretton Woods Agreement in 1944, which helped establish the US dollar as the preeminent reserve currency for the entire planet. When Bretton Woods was signed, the United States had almost half of the world's GNP, was the world's largest trading partner and until the 1980s, was the largest creditor nation on Planet Earth.[1] Now the US's share of world GNP is less than 25% and falling, as China and the other BRICS countries are soaking up the world's wealth like a sponge, while forging their own paths outside of America's orbit.[2] In the meantime, the American and Euro central banks allow reserve banks to print their money and then must borrow that money and pay interest to the private banks, sucking their treasuries dry.[3] The Chinese have no federal interest to pay, since Baba Beijing prints the nation's money and can send it to its national bank, interest free.

You don't have to have a degree in economics to see the obvious. China already has the world's largest foreign exchange reserves and is the world's second largest creditor nation. For the record, Japan is the number one creditor nation and the US became the world's biggest *debtor* nation in 1985. China is also the world's largest trading partner, has the world's largest manufacturing base and a thirty plus year history of prudent, interventionist, rapid response, FIRE go-take-a-hike economic policies that continue to irritate and confound the Washington consensus. And in just a few years, China will be the world's largest economy. Looking at all this, which country do you think will have the world's preeminent reserve currency when it becomes fully convertible? Hmm… Let me guess… The BRICS countries are not waiting in the bandstands. Nor are Japan, the EU, OPEC and a whole host of other international trading partners. They are all quietly starting to do cross border business in RMB and their national currencies, circumventing the US dollar as the world's trade settlement currency. This is very bad news for Americans and the value of their dollar. Countries having to stockpile trillions of US dollars to settle bilateral trade is a huge buffer against high inflation in the US and allows America to finance (print money for) its multi-trillion dollar worldwide war machine. Little of this non-dollar trading is being reported by the countries involved, so no one knows how much is involved, but given the impressive list of known bilateral agreements, it is surely already in the many billions of currency units and growing rapidly.

Baba Beijing is not stupid. They know as soon as the US dollar loses its historical domination as the world's trade and reserve currency, that America's 700 plus military installations circling the globe, with their 250,000 plus soldiers in 130 countries will be conquered - brought to their knees - broke and unfunded, all without firing a shot.[4, 5] They only have to use bank accounts to bring about total victory. China's leaders are employing the Thirty-Six Stratagems (三十六计= *sanshiliu ji*), which have been refined over the last 2,000 years, to help fulfill their Heavenly Mandate. One they are using to great effect right now is,

Wait at leisure while the enemy labors (以逸待劳= yiyi dailao).

In the boxing ring, Mohammed Ali called it *Rope a Dope* and he won 1974's *Rumble in the Jungle* against George Foreman, doing just that. Baba Beijing will subtly and surreptitiously keep the United States fearful and militarily overextended around the planet, while feigning concern for America's priorities. They will tacitly encourage FIRE's Orwellian Newspeak perpetual *War on Terror* to be expanded in Africa, so the US borrows more money to protect China's already sizeable investments there - anything to weaken America's overly indebted economy and flat broke citizens of the 99%. It is the ultimate war game plan to take over the world, without so much as firing a shot. When China makes the RMB fully convertible, watch out Western world. It will be lock and load time, Yankee brothers and sisters.

China's advantage is huge for another reason. While America is myopically looking as far as the next monthly government statistics and quarterly stock reports, China is gazing across the rest of the 21st century; slowly and deliberatively, like a thoughtful old tortoise. Tortoises figure very prominently in Chinese culture and are depicted in temples everywhere, carrying huge steles or tablets on their backs, bringing revealing and historical information, to educate their readers. You remember Aesop's fable, the *Tortoise and the Hare*, don't you? The tortoise won.

1- Paul Craig Roberts, a high ranking member of Reagan's treasury team is excellent at explaining these economic forces: www.paulcraigroberts.org/. He very bitterly explains that the federal debt built up under Reagan, which was necessary to pull the country out of the 70s' stagflation, could have been paid down if Wall Street had not moved America's manufacturing sector overseas, mainly to China. With it went much of the country's corporate, individual and payroll taxes to fund good government and the commonwealth. True conservatives in the Reagan administration overestimated Firemen's patriotism and post-war taking care of the local community *corporate attitude that died signature by signature with GATT, NAFTA, WTO and every law dismantling 50 years of regulation, oversight and control.*

2- *There are many articles to be found discussing one of the primary reasons the US attacked Iraq, one of the world's largest petroleum exporters, is that they had started selling all their oil in euros, not dollars: www.thirdworldtraveler.com/Iraq/Iraq_-dollar_vs_euro.html_*

3- *Based on my research, the BRICS countries and many others do not give their private banks the power to lend money back and receive interest from their governments. But this is true of the US, the Euro Zone and Canada, among others. The rational is that by having to borrow and pay interest on their debt, governments won't just print money to finance their needs. But that is exactly what Western countries have been and are doing right now in spades anyway. America's quantitative easing is Orwellian Newspeak for printing one trillion dollars a year and giving it to the world's too-big-to-fail banks to invest in stocks and bonds. There is precedence in the West: Canada did not change over to government borrowing until 1974. Maybe all these extremely broke OECD countries should take a look at going back to a central-bank-as-mint system of government financing. While each system has its good points and its flaws, it surely seems to be working comparatively better for Brazil, Russia, India, China and South Africa.*

4- *www.globalresearch.ca/the-worldwide-network-of-us-military-bases/5564. Many websites discuss these facts.*

5- *www.politifact.com/truth-o-meter/statements/2011/sep/14/ron-paul/ron-paul-says-us-has-military-personnel-130-nation/. This is routinely covered on a number of websites.*

CHAPTER 39: CHISHUI

Zhongdian in Yunnan stole the Shangri-La name, but Chishui, Guizhou is the place that really deserves it, hands down. It's a natural paradise on Earth, with three nature parks that I will never forget visiting. Hurry and go before the super highway there is finished.

Hurry up and visit Chishui, before the multi-billion RMB superhighway connects it to Chongqing and Guiyang, and in whose shadow I drive to get here. Once this monster is opened, there will be an influx of humanity that will forever overwhelm this amazing area, its unpopulated charms and absolute wilderness. An excellent test tube comparison of what Chishui has to look forward to is Zhongdian, Yunnan, otherwise named by its promoters as Shangri-La. Once the influx reaches critical mass, the uniqueness and charms of the place get buried by an avalanche of tour groups. The bottomless greed that possesses the locals metastasizes to satisfy every visitor's need, and the place's cultural soul, the genesis of all this overkill in the first place, ends up being sucked dry, like a mummy.[1] Chishui really does have a time machine, lost world feel about it. Deep, scarred valleys with powerful, coffee and cream to red ochre colored tropical rivers fill their floors. There are estimated to be over 4,000 waterfalls, some are world class in height. Bamboo forests teem up the valley walls and underneath them are huge stretches of gargantuan ferns, including the encyclopedic *Alsophila* and *Cyathea* varieties. These have evolved little over the last 200 million years, were the staple diet of brontosauri, stegosauri and all the other herbivore dinosaurs, and which later became a huge component of Mother Earth's petroleum, coal and gas, buried deep underground. So to call Chishui Jurassic is not inaccurate. I keep expecting to see Rachel Welch come walking around a cliff corner in her lusty, *One Million Years B.C.* animal skin costume. Yabba Dabba Doo!

While not plentiful, I am able to see a few lizards, frogs and birds, as well as lots of butterflies and many insects. Still, other than here, at Jiuzhaigou afterhours and a little in Langmusi, the country's fauna and fowl are tragically devastated. In spite of this zoological disappointment in China, Chishui has rainbows of flowers and densely lush vegetation pullulating everywhere you turn. With all the waterfalls seemingly every few meters, liquid soaked cliff faces are garlanded with exotic, multihued brackens, lichens, mosses and liverworts at every level. Red, purple, yellow and brown sandstone cliff faces tower hundreds of meters from the valley floors. On many of these gorge-high cliffs are falling cascades of varying height. Some start dropping right off the tops of the mountains, while others come gushing like jets right out of the rock faces, from fissures and large crevices, dispersing into a fine mist as they crash down below. While relatively empty of tourists, except some coming from Chongqing, Zunyi and Guiyang, the local governments have spared no expense in developing their nature parks. After my teeth gritting climbing adventures in Gansu and Sichuan, the trails here are beautifully laid out in sandstone and wood boardwalk, well-marked and well maintained. Not only that, but the entrance ticket prices are all around 30 kuai (€3.80/$4.80), which is 1990s prices, even for foreigners. All this being said, what are you waiting for? Chishui easily ranks as one of my top visits during *44 Days*, and that's in the face of some amazing competition.

Chishui Town literally sits on the border of Sichuan. Like Langmusi, the town is cut in half by a river, in this case, its namesake. Go across a bridge and the other town in Sichuan is called Jiuzhi (九支). People here are wonderfully warm and inviting. A foreigner like me is akin to a UFO sighting, so it's got that 90s feel to it, with people coming up to me to ask all kinds of questions and are just exhilarated to have a chance to rub shoulders with a *laowai*. A few of them even can't resist touching the hair on my forearms and making a big deal out of me being left handed, two traits that are not often seen among the Chinese.[2] It started in Yunnan and has gotten to be progressively more challenging, but the Mandarin accents in this part of China are thicker than sod turf and just about as hard to digest. Like in Tibetan Sichuan, some of the older people don't even bother, or can't speak Mandarin, and try to speak to me in their local dialect, one of thousands of mutually incomprehensible argots that dot the Chinese linguistic landscape. The only common cipher that holds it all together is the Chinese written language. In some cases, I find myself in the funny situation of needing a third person to communicate: the extra interlocutor translates from the local dialect into Mandarin for me.

Even though this is the middle of the week, Chishui's central market is one of the best I go to on this trip. Vendors and shop keepers are flattered when I approach them and if I wanted, I could not pay for any food in Chishui and just live off all the samples being handed to me at each stand, replete with smiling faces and inquisitive banter. Anything and everything to eat is for sale here, under this mostly covered, open air market, so I end up spending quite a bit of time visiting with the vendors, customers and admiring all the eye popping products smartly presented on display. There are tens of brands of rice, all kinds of different white, tan, brown and caramel colored tofus that look and taste like cheese; bread roll bakers, piles of once buried one hundred year-old eggs, roasted ducks like in Beijing, all kinds of exotic, tropical tubers and vegetables that I have never or only occasionally seen, young bamboo shoots and tender bamboo hearts, big fresh chains of ginger root that look like yellow and pink fingers amputated off of deformed, extraterrestrial monsters; twenty different kinds of dried noodles to choose from, vinegar and locally made moonshine shops selling their years-to-decades old elixirs at ever increasing prices, according to their age. It is easy to spend a couple of hours in this joyful, laid back and welcoming market, just taking it all in. A couple of the stands *really* stick out. They are two competing dentists offering their services to anyone who wants to sit down for what orally ails them, getting drilled on in front of a thousand passersby and gawkers. Nobody seems to give them any mind. They are very much a part of the daily market fabric here. They make dentures, clean, polish and pull teeth, lance mouth boils, pack abscesses with Novocain and antibiotics, work on gingivitis, you name it. Customers walk up, explain their problems or some are obviously old patients, so the dentist asks how it has been since the last visit and then says,

"Open wide!"

One of the dentists is quite diffident about my curiosity, but the more accessible of the two and his clients and I have a grand old time laughing and joking. I get some great pictures of the whole operation. The dentist is relaxed in a t-shirt and before getting to work with his full arsenal of solution-sanitized hand instruments and electric drills, he puts on a spelunker's head light to see what's going on, as well as a gauze face mask. No latex gloves though…

Time to leave the society of local markets and embrace Mother Nature in all her splendor. I visit three of the four popular nature parks in Chishui, each unique and well worth the time and effort. Due to scheduling constraints, I skip going to Sidonggou (四洞沟= Four Caves Canyon) the park closest to Chishui, which is the most frequented. I catch Red Rock Canyon (红石野谷= Hongshi Yegu) on a great day. It's fairly hot today and the place is almost empty. The ambiance is striking and serene. There are various shades and hues of contrasting sunlight coursing through the bamboo trees, giant ferns, steep walled sandstone canyons, nonstop waterfalls and cascades, making it all very intoxicating. The park trail is essentially a big rectangular hike. You enter and walk along the valley floor towards the back of the park. From there, it is a nice climb up along a series of falls to the top of the mountain. Once on top, there is a really wonderful, sunny, level hike along the mountainside back towards the entrance. Then there is a climb back down another series of ravines with more spectacular waterfalls and mini-canyons.

At the top of first gorge is a great little shaded canteen, with beverages and food. There is only one group of four Chinese and myself to enjoy it. During the whole park visit, I can count all the visitors I see on two hands. Along the climb down, I pass through a picturesque overhanding cliff, tall and wide It looks like locals have been coming here for thousands of years to live, practice religious ceremonies and bury their dead, and it's from where the park gets its name: Red Rock Canyon. It's beyond fabulous and we could be in some national park in the United States out in Colorado or Arizona, with cliff hugging pueblos and ancient anthropological ruins everywhere. The whole semi-shaded, pottery bowl-shaped overhang has about every hue and color the Earth has to offer: yellows, reds, browns, purples and oranges. The Sun's oblique, afternoon rays shoot down into bowl cutting the whole scene into two halves, one illuminated, the other in semishade. The entire idyllic setting is set off by long vines hanging from the overhang above. A finely misted waterfall, about 2m wide drops a cascade into the middle of the bowl, seeming to be falling from the sky, since it is easy to walk 360° around it down under the rim of hollowed out canyon. You can stand underneath it, to get cooled off by its chilly, misty waters, which evaporatively cool off during their descent. Am I on our Pale Blue Dot, or some utopian exoplanet that has yet to be colonized? It's just mind bogglingly beautiful.

My next stop is a park called the Bamboo Sea (竹海= Zhuhai), which is isolated and more difficult to get to. It is part of a bigger park complex called Jinshagou (金沙沟= Gold Sand Canyon). The combi from Chishui drops us off in the town with the same name as the park. Once there, you either walk the 11km up to the top of the mountain, where the park is, or haggle for a taxi. I really want to hike up to the park, but it took longer to get here than anticipated, so I pay the 50 RMB (€6/$8) for a taxi up. As it turns out, it was a very wise move. The drive up is incessant and precipitous for an everyday road. It would take time to get to the top on foot. The only possible way to walk up and down in one day would be to spend the night in Jinshagou Town and take off early in the morning, which is time I do not have today. The road winds up the 800m tall mountain like an uninterrupted counterclockwise apple peel, 11km long.

The Bamboo Sea is another well-of-course-it's-to-be-expected great visit in a spectacular nature park, replete with towering bamboo forests, armies of giant ferns, multi-colored flowers and trees, dancing butterflies, rainbow hued insects, glorious waterfalls and cascades. Even though it is around noontime, it quickly becomes apparent that the Bamboo Sea's mosquitos are a superbreed in a class of their own. At first, I spray my head, hands and neck with DEET, thinking that this will do the trick. But not more than a minute later, they are bombarding my face, ears and head worse than ever. It's almost as if I put on anti-DEET full of pheromones that attract these blood suckers. They have evolved to be DEET resistant and it is simply a waste of time putting it on. My Arabian *shamagh*, the red and white checkered cotton square that is folded into a triangle and worn on men's heads in the Middle East, saves the day again. It is so useful for any number of situations and these marauding high noon skeeters in the Bamboo Sea are just such an occasion. I put it on correctly, like Arabs do and then use it to completely cover my face, leaving only my glasses exposed. I pull my floppy fisherman's hat down low to seal off the top. They continue to bombard my now protected face and really do not even mess with my exposed hands, so they have really evolved to be attracted to carbon dioxide from my exhalations. They are evil looking little buggers, pitch black with white stripes like the knee high socks worn by some rugby or soccer teams. Thank goodness for my shamagh, I can enjoy my time in this incredibly tall bamboo forest, which was turned into a nature park to preserve the ancient, treelike, dinosaur Alsophila ferns.

They spent a fortune on the walking path here. While not very long, much of it is a raised steel frame with a wood boardwalk to saunter on. Other than a party of about ten from Zhejiang, the place is deserted. As I continue on, it is really bizarre. There is an exact elevation where the mosquitos pounce on you en masse and continue to do so above that altitude and then a few steps below, they stop. I have no idea what they are feeding on to be in such large numbers. I don't even see any livestock. It could be they go down to where people and animals live when it gets dark. Either that, or it is a duel to the death between these wisebugs and a million insect bats that may live in caves nearby. I run into a really strange looking wasp nest. It is hanging off the end of a pine tree branch. It is long and narrow, having the color of and looking like a stretched out loofah sponge, covered with hundreds of humming, caramel colored wasps. They are all hanging onto the outside of the nest and beating their wings furiously. Needless to say, I don't mess with them and after getting as close as comfortable can be to observe, I step back a few meters and check them out with my Zeiss.

I decide to walk the 11km down the mountain and am sure glad I did, although the last two klicks are a little more than I bargained for. On this nice, downward sloped trek, my eyes gorge on plants, flowers, forests, critters, butterflies and other insects and even a few birds. One place I see what I think is an animal stretched out in the distance, on a side road. I go check and in fact, it is a swarm of black and gold butterflies clustered together, drinking water percolating out of the cool, shaded sandstone. A really beautiful, natural sight. I walk through some Miao farmhouse properties and get to study their mud on bamboo lattice frames. The fine mud is spread on the lattice and then smoothed out with a trowel. Then, it is painted white, and all the window frames and door trim are bordered with the Miao red ochre paint I saw in the White Horse Mountain valley on the way to Chishui from Zunyi, where Mao's Red Army passed through during their Long March. Corn and hot peppers are being harvested, laid out on the road to dry. Rivulets seem to be running everywhere and there is enough water for quite a few stands of wetland rice production, even high up here in the mountains. The terraced valley sides along the way are immaculate. About two klicks away from Jinshagou Town, still further down the mountain road, I stop at a really cool restaurant, which has its own private waterfall that feeds a big pond to raise fish. Impressive and idyllic. I stay for a good hour, talking to the three people who run the place while rehydrating. Unfortunately, they hurt their business by not having any rooms to rent for the night, so you can only stop and eat. They agree with my suggestion, but a quick survey of the place shows that they really have no possibility to build or convert space into bedrooms.

No sooner do I take off to finish the trek down into town, that it starts raining. Afternoon showers during this rainy season have been a common occurrence, starting in Langmusi, but until now, like in many subtropical to tropical zones, these afternoon showers only last a few minutes and then stop. Not today. I find myself in the middle of real, long lasting, live, flash tropical storm. It quickly gets very violent, with lots of overhead thunder, lightning and thrashing, gusting, high-speed winds. I am totally unprepared for this and only have my rain poncho to protect me *and* my full backpack. Try as I might, I cannot get the poncho over the pack on my back by myself. I always find somebody nearby to help me. Not today. The stand of bamboo trees that was blocking the sheets of rain a little, is now water soaked and of no use. It's time to bite the bullet. It's either me or my backpack and I opt to protect my pack, Zeiss and everything else I'm carrying. I fashion the poncho over the backpack and step out into the flooded road, whose water is moving very fast, given the deep pitch of the mountain. Water is rushing as deep as my ankles in some places. There is nothing I can do, I am soaked and shivering cold within seconds, as I am buffeted and blown about by the powerful gusts of tropical storm winds. Luckily, the lightning has moved a few klicks away, so I feel less threatened about getting struck. As timing would have it, I get back down to Jinshagou Town just as the flash storm passes. The townsfolk get a real guffawing hoot at seeing me, as my drenched-as-a-street-cur look is quite a sight. As luck would have it, I run into the taxi driver who took me up to the top this morning, and he really lets out a roar, heavy on the mocking side, hounding me that I should have called him. I blurt out,

"We foreigners are not like *you* - we like adventure!"

This is totally unnecessary and such a gross generalization as to be off color. I sincerely regret saying it. To get back at me, he tells me the 16:00 bus has already left and there are no more. I'll have to go back with him. I sit down in front of a store to let the water drain off my clothes and body. The nice shop lady and her daughter tell me to be patient, that a 17:00 bus from Zunyi will stop here briefly. Luckily they are right. I can't help being human and smile like the Cheshire cat at the taxi driver, as I get on board. Hey you! See!

The following day, as if the first two parks weren't spectacular and unforgettable enough, the third one proves to be Chishui's culminating event. The Shizhangdong Waterfall (十丈洞瀑布= 33 Meter Cave Waterfall) is a world class nature park, with one of the best series of big time waterfalls I've ever seen. I'm not talking Victoria tall or Niagara wide. But the whole ambiance is full of lost world Jurassic forests that are tumbling down precipitous valley walls. Jutting out of the tree canopy are skyscraper high sandstone cliffs, with vines and multiple waterfalls shooting out, up and down their heights, crashing into the Fengxi River (风溪河) and Danxia (丹霞) valley below, all in an ambiance of total isolation and wilderness. It is really special. The village at the bottom of the cascades is photogenic in itself, with three and four story Miao style buildings right on the waterline, like Venice on the canals.

I hike up to the biggest falls, which is the namesake of the park. It is 76m tall and only 1m shorter than Guizhou's tour group tourist trap, Huangguoshu Falls (黄果树大瀑布) in the province's southwest. It is about a 6km walk up the Danxia valley to the Shizhangdong Waterfall, as the road goes. I make a day of it, taking trails that go down to the river level and back up. Each track leads to nice hikes in and around the huge boulders that dot the valley floor and adorn the Fengxi River. The view of the scaling, color banded sandstone cliffs and the mountains above them are something to behold. Several of the trips down to water level lead to beautiful, postcard quality, river wide water falls. The Shizhangdong Waterfall is actually 25m taller than Niagara Falls, but is only about as wide as it is tall. Niagara is about one kilometer wide, so this Fengxi River fall is very tall and compact. I approach the falls from the right side via a secondary path. The main path comes straight down from the road, walking into the charging waters. It creates a continual roar and a mist-soaked wind that is blasting away from the crashing waters, nonstop, at about 30kph. Some visitors have umbrellas, which are futilely ripped out of shape by the powerful water wind. It's really impressive to stand there and face it. It feels like standing on an ocean dike somewhere, with a storm roaring in off the water.

Vendors are selling cheap plastic ponchos that people are using for five minutes and then dumping on the ground in a pile. Yuck. I'm enjoying chilling down with all the evaporative cooling coursing over my sweat soaked clothes and body, and opt to spend my money on a fresh cucumber for lunch instead. I've never eaten a whole, big, fat, yellowish, raw cucumber like this before. Quite refreshing, although a little salt would be nice. Shizhangdong is one of the nicest and most impressive nature parks I've ever been in. What I see today just scratches the surface of the whole park, as a huge billboard sized map shows there are many hiking trails in the mountains above. Definitely a place to revisit, especially before that monster highway in the air pulls up here.

My Chinese landlady in Chishui, Ms. Guo and I become good buddies during my stay, as she adopts me like I have been several times on this journey. She shares the food out of her refrigerator with me and I reciprocate by bringing her fresh fruit from the market. She invites me to eat dinner with her, her friends and son, lets me use her clothes washer and does not charge me. The TV in the front room is going non-stop, except for sleep time and is the focal point of her *zhaodaisuo*. A very beautiful woman in her late thirties, I never see Ms. Guo's husband and can't help but inquire,

"Oh, he doesn't stay here, he has job someplace else."

That could surely be the reason, as it is not uncommon for Chinese couples to live in different cities because of their two jobs. I met the couple in Shapotou, Ningxia, who adopted me for the day, Mr. Wu and Ms. Yang. They live far away from each other for their two jobs. I know many other Chinese couples in the same situation. But there may be more to her story than just work. This is because Ms. Guo is a mahjong (麻将= *majiang*) addict, as are her three female friends. This celebrated Chinese game is a cross between dominoes and cards on steroids, with its 144 (or 152 or 160) thick, colorful tiles, chock block full of numbers and suits. It is not dissimilar to gin rummy, but local permutations and rules abound, from region to region and table to table. This four-player game is not ancient like Chinese chess or Go, purportedly having been invented in the 19th century by bored soldiers with time to kill, sitting around in their barracks. But its popularity and addictiveness are renowned, including being the most popular table game in Japan, and played by millions of overseas Chinese across the planet. It is also an excellent game for gambling and was actually banned by Baba Beijing after independence in 1949, being vilified as a capitalist weakness to be shunned. After the PTSD (posttraumatic stress disorder) hangover of the Cultural Revolution, the Chinese needed healing and entertainment. Many found succor in playing mahjong together and Baba Beijing wisely looked the other way. In any case, Communist ideology had ironed out the gambling aspects that were so central to its pre-independence play. Its prohibition was officially lifted in 1985, where thereafter, mahjong joined cards and chess on the sidewalks, and under the shade trees of hot sultry summer evenings. Mahjong has even entered international popular culture. Eddie Cantor, the WWII American jazz crooner, sang a song called, *Since Ma Is Playing Mah Jong*.

And mahjong is all these four Chishui Mas do, during their waking hours. When she is not there, I ask her son where she is and he tells me she's at her friend's, you guessed it, playing mahjong. From the moment she wakes up and has breakfast, there they are, playing mahjong in the front room. She has one of those really nice mechanical, casino parlor quality tables. It is equipped with four trap doors on the green felt surface that open up with the push of a button to drop in all the previous game's tiles into a mixer below the tabletop. To start a new game, they are all shuffled underneath and out of sight, then each person gets a fresh hand through the same trap door for the next round. A crystal ball with cheesy neon lights in the middle rolls the dice for them too. I am surprised when she tells me this high tech toy only costs about 2,000 RMB (€250/$320). I wouldn't be surprised if Ms. Guo's husband is a mahjong widower. They are a part of Chinese social lore, especially in the southern part of the country where mahjong is especially popular. Practice the Twelve Steps of Mahjong Anonymous, Ms. Guo, twelve steps.

Saying goodbye to Chishui, the bus ride back to Zunyi takes me back along the X308, so I get the see the magnificent Miao/Red Army valley in the White Horse Mountains again. Like doubling back up the Liqi Valley in Sichuan, the different light and perspective make it a completely new trip. Zunyi gets even shorter shrift this second go around. I don't even spend the night and opt to take an evening train to Guiyang. I could stay one more day in Zunyi or could have done so in Chishui for that matter, but absolutely do not want to take the risk of missing my August 11th train back home to Beijing. Sad to say, but the end of this amazing *44 Days* is starting to rear its ugly head.

1- For a fascinating look at what is happening in Zhongdian and what Chishui has to look forward to, once the superhighway is finished, this three-part series is a must-read: www.globalpost.com/dispatch/news/regions/asia-pacific/china/130213/china-shangri-la-global-economy-tourism-part-1

2- Like all of humanity, China's people have the same, consistent percent of the population of lefthanders, about 15%. The difference here is once they go to kindergarten, all bets are off: they are forced to write with their right hands, no matter how difficult or stressful. But you can still spot them out. They use chopsticks with their left hands, playing ping pong, badminton, kicking and throwing a ball, etc.

Chapter 40: Guiyang - Beijing

Guiyang gets more of my time than expected, walking 21km around town checking the place out. Why Chinese toilets are so un-Western; one final jerk to cap off this amazing journey; the long train ride back home to Beijing is as expected: lots of mixed emotions reflecting on the meaning of 44 Days Backpacking in China.

My initial welcome to Guiyang does not fit in the rubric of *friendship and international cooperation*. Arriving by train from Zunyi about 22:00, I have to go to four *zhaodaisuo* before one will let me stay there. They all tell me gruffly,

"Go to the tourist hotel!"

The place I find doesn't even want my ID, just my money, ¥50 (€6/$8). Even then the next day, when I tell them I want to stay a second night, they try to get me to leave. I convince them to call their neighborhood Gongan to explain I have a Gongan stamped Chinese residence permit. Like everywhere else on this trip when it has gotten to this DEFCON 5 level, I get the go ahead to stay. This *zhaodaisuo* ranks right at the bottom, in terms of amenities and cleanliness on this journey, and the toilets are especially redolent and ripe. I have given a lot of thought to China's toilets on this trip and think I have the answer as to why, by Western standards, they are so *crappy*. In one short generation, here is a country that now has the largest bullet train system in the world, the number two and number three longest metropolitan subway systems, Beijing and Shanghai (Seoul gets the world's gold Tube prize for total length), has sent astronauts into space, has built a continent sized wireless communication system for more than a billion mobile phones, built some of the world's most daring and innovate architecture, splashed Shanghai's super sexy skyline onto the world scene, and on and on. But you go into 99% of China's restrooms and it's like a turn of the 20th century outhouse, even in many modern buildings. Do they not know what a P-trap is, that simplest of elbow shaped drain pipes seen on sinks everywhere, that blocks the stench of the sewers from welling up? What's going on? It is just a question of expectations. For the Chinese, toilets are *supposed* to be smelly and less than hygienic, so that is how they are. If and when spiffy, laboratory clean restrooms become a priority for the Chinese, then that is the way they will become. But for right now, they just can't be bothered.

Guiyang is about as close to a new, frontier city, as they can get in China. When Mao & Co. met in Zunyi for their big Commie powwow in January, 1935, it's hard to believe that it was Guizhou's largest city. A lot has happened since then, as Guiyang was officially named Guizhou's post-independence provincial capital, and it has exploded in growth since then. It also has geographical advantages. It is situated at the crossroads connecting Kunming to the West, Chongqing to the North, Changsha in Hunan to the East and Nanning in Guangxi, southbound. Now Guiyang has over four million souls, four times as many as Zunyi. Zunyi gets the Communist Party chops and China's white lightning, Maotai, but Guiyang is getting the lion's share of the regional metro development.

I've got some time on my hands here, so I do some exploring. The provincial museum is a hodgepodge of you-name-it artifacts, objects and displays. A huge section of the ground floor has been turned over to a curio and souvenir store. I get my fill of hand painted silk umbrellas and famous local flora painters in what's left of this level's floor space. Upstairs pays tribute to Guiyang's place in the geological history of Planet Earth, its dinosaurs and like the other museums visited on this trip, matter of fact Darwinian evolution. There is one cool section where room-tall, full color photo, backlit panels display all of the minorities living in the province. Very striking and well done. Most of the museum displays have English, so it is definitely worth a walk through for us *laowai*. As I walk to Guiyang's big city park, several food vendors offer me gratis their wares: nuts, fruit and candy. And not just a piece. They are happy to keep me standing there stuffing my face if

I choose to, talking with them. When I decline the gift of a bottled drink and tell one lady I have a tea thermos, she steps inside her stand, comes back out and fills it up with fresh *kaishui*, piping hot boiled water.

Qingling Park (黔灵公园) is in the northern part of town, down the street and catty corner to the museum, up a completely sycamore tree-shaded boulevard. The place is huge. Over five hundred hectares in area, Qingling is an obvious pole of attraction for Guiyang's citizens, so much so, that it is apparently open twenty-four hours per day. Given its size and the number of people thronging inside, it is remarkably well kept. There is enough construction and renovation going on to show that the municipal government understands its importance to the cityscape. It has a 700m long pedestrian tunnel piercing through a big hill, which is a real trip to walk through and the equally tall, eponymously named mountain, with a 17th century temple up top, so there are all kinds of mountain trails to hike. Down below is a series of lakes, which I opt to hike along. I keep seeing people with big jerry cans on luggage rollers and bicycles, coming into the park empty and leaving full of water. I track down the source and there is a mountain spring with water pushing up out of the ground like an artesian well. The people tell me this water is especially healthy in mineral content. I ask if they drink it as is, or do they boil it first and they all tell me they boil it. Is it because there are really dangerous microbes in it, or is it due to millennia of inculcated habit? I suspect the latter. A man in a pickup truck, with new tires piled in the back, sees me coming up the road, gets out and acts like we have not seen each other in years. He is the owner of a Michelin tire dealership in a town near here and is taking a rest in the lakeside shade with his girlfriend, before heading back. He just can't get over my hairy forearms and keeps rubbing them in amazement while we talk. He calls his girlfriend out of the truck and at his insistence, she shyly brushes her hand on my forearm, giggling embarrassingly. Funny stuff sometimes in China... He is not bisexual, just enthusiastically curious. This has happened to me countless times over the years, but less and less so with China's increasing exposure to outsiders. Nor am I offended in any way. It's just that we Westerners are very hirsute compare to their usually very light beards and almost total absence of visual body hair.

While banal compared to the Tibetan Torquemada I dealt with in Xiahe, I get my second real jerk of the trip at the Guiyang train station. I stand in the Change Ticket line and manage to get my train ticket changed to a twelve-hour earlier departure, just assuming it would get to Beijing that much sooner. But as soon as I get back to my *zhaodaisuo* and check online, I see that it arrives at about the same time, it just takes twelve hours longer to get there. Lemme see... a half a day longer on a train with a hard seat ticket, or do I spend that time chillaxing in a restaurant and enjoying the beautiful summer weather outside? Hmm... So I go back to the station, get right back in the Change Ticket line and the same attendant is there. When I explain what happened, I get taken aback, because she gets really jazzed and starts whinging on me hard, complaining vociferously through the thick glass via the dual microphone-speaker, that I can only change a train ticket one time. This trip has been so universally pleasant with all the hundreds of everyday Chinese whom I have met, that she really catches me off guard, so I stop for a second, take a deep breath and bite my tongue, refusing to end *44 Days* on a sour note,

"It is my fault. I am just a *waiguoren*. I did not know about the 'change only one time' rule for train tickets. I am sorry I made such a huge mistake. Please forgive me and please, please change my ticket back to the later departure."

Of course by now, all nearby necks are in full rubber mode and craned in our direction, and as Chinese train stations go, that's a lot of necks. It's like playing a part in an impromptu reality television show. The attendant senses this, as she peers through the thick glass outside behind me, seeing all the pairs of eyes drilled on her next move. She does her own hurried, deep-breathing routine and to cap it off, barks at me,

"OK, but you have to pay a five yuan service fee!"

Well, if you insist, ma'am, whatever you say. Also, just to prove her point, she refuses my residence permit this time and makes me dig out my passport. OK, OK, uncle, uncle, I understand who's in charge here. In any case, I end up not torturing myself unnecessarily for twelve extra hours on the train back to Beijing. Time to pull the plug on Guiyang and get ready for my train ride home tomorrow. I'm shocked to see on my Galaxy that I end up walking 21km today and 250m in vertical ascent, an 80-story skyscraper's worth of steps. Yikes. What a nice urban hike to end the trip, not at all what I expected. And all I did was walk all over kingdom come in this fair city, as well as trekking around the city park.

I can hardly even remember returning to Beijing. The ride back is not at all relaxing. I only have a hard seat ticket and the train is of course standing-room-only packed to the gills. I make the obligatory pass through Car #13 to get the attendant's numerical scrawl on the back of my ticket, for a hopeful sleeper berth, sooner than later. It does not look promising at all: I am number 23 this go around. Like the teeming mass of working class, rural people surrounding me, I fitfully close my eyes, while lying curled up on the bare floor of this hard seat car, with my Zeiss-filled backpack serving as a very boxy, hard pillow. The whole place looks like an overcrowded, rolling flop house. This 2,228km leg on the cross country T88 train is a hard-nosed way to return home after *44 Days* on the trail, but I'm going to make it back home, somehow, some way. I finally get the Car #13 call for a hard sleeper berth six hours outside of Beijing, and gladly take it, a grace of luxury to finish out the train ride.

After twenty something hours, I'm back in the magnificent Stalinist architecture of the Beijing Train Station. On my way out, I peer into Waiting Room #4, where *44 Days* all started. It is sultry hot in Beijing, without a fly's fart of a breeze. Getting off the train is like stepping into a sticky honey bath of nearly 100% humidity. Ugh. Goodbye freedom of the road, hello the workaday responsibilities of holding down a job and being a member of my family back at the house. As I exit the BTS and make my way to the metro stop across the street, I immediately feel a sense of pride, relief and resignation. Wonderment, sadness, elation. Memories and nostalgia. Above all, I harbor sincere feelings of accomplishment. I not only survived, but thrived.

Forty-four days is a long time to be on the road and I readily admit I really pushed myself to the limits physically. However, I am subconsciously fighting the confession that I'm also mentally drained, and in my case doubly so, with all the total immersion in speaking and reading Chinese from sunup to sundown for weeks on end. Foreign languages can really be like burning the proverbial mental candle at both ends. There was a certain amount of scheduling pressure too. I have a planned itinerary and want to follow it, yet not dogmatically cutting off my journeyman's nose in spite of my traveler's face, in order to stick to it. The fact that I stayed on schedule says as much about China's marvelous transportation network, as it does Lady Luck and making a few wise, empirical decisions along the way. I envy Steve Evans, the gadabout Englishman I met in Ningxia, who takes six month voyages around the world, resting up one month back in the UK and then heading out for another half year jaunt. During his adventures, he can throw a mercurial dart onto the map in the general direction he is heading, and has the time to kick back at various points in his itinerary, relax, sleep in for a day or two to vegetate and recharge his body and brain synapses. With my six weeks of vacation a year to do some seriously fun traveling, there is no other way to describe it: my days are *intense*. Thus, the power meter on my batteries was admittedly starting to hit the red zone by the time I got to Chishui and Guiyang.

But I did it: 12,000 kilometers of road and rail, hundreds of klicks walking and trekking, and a few more climbing up many Empire State Buildings, usually starting out two to three thousand meters above China's coastal plain. I am humbled at meeting and talking with hundreds of Chinese, on their streets, in their homes and places of business, getting to know them and finding empathy and humanity in our exchanges. My understanding and appreciation of China - for its unparalleled three millennia of continuous history, the mind numbing madness of its post-independence revolutions and its vertiginous, meteoric rise to the top of Planet Earth's economic food chain – are deeper, fuller and more meaningful than ever before. And so is my respect and admiration for the peoples of China; they have accrued an amazing social and cultural transformation in just one short generation. I witnessed hands-on their creation of the fastest growing and largest middle class in human history. I got to see at street level, eye to eye with China's salt of the Earth, the vision its leaders have for their country and their citizens, and how they are realizing these goals in a very un-occidental fashion. Baba Beijing, ever aware of their Heavenly Mandate and its historical millstone that weighs so heavily on their shoulders, will continue to confound, frustrate and infuriate the West, particularly the United States and Europe. The view the Chinese have of themselves and the rest of the world reflects in a looking glass that transcends 3,000 years of retrospection, in often bitter, intractable circumstances. As a result, their world perspective is for the most part totally alien to western conventions and assumptions. But no matter, this is their century, the twenty-first, and they are making the most of their time on the world's stage, molding and shifting humanity's script, for better and for worse.

一路平安!

(*Yilu ping'an* = May your road be flat and peaceful!)

Figure 103: Caohai - Zhijin: Wild mountain wilderness is everywhere you turn in Western China. Where is everybody?

Figure 104: Nayong: the late night street crowd enjoying the traveling gypsy troupe's Chinese version of a madrigal variety show.

Figure 105: Zhijin – Guiyang: terraced mountainside farming up to the sky. It is ubiquitous all over China and always impressive. Like the house at the bottom, many homes in this area cleverly use their flat roofs as water cisterns, to catch and store rain water.

Figure 106: Guiyang: another day in paradise. The airport sized Jinyang bus station on the outskirts of town. Forty ticket windows are open up to 24 hours a day, seven days a week - and Guiyang has several more bus stations.

Figure 107: Zunyi – Chishui: A great sampling of the many fresh ingredients that keep a Chinese roadside, country kitchen serving delicious vittles. A huge assortment of spices are creatively added as each dish is individually prepared. Voilà!

Figure 108: Zunyi – Chishui: the White Horse Mountain valley, whose Miao minority helped Mao Zedong's 1st Red Army at the beginning of the Long March. The old woman tending corn grain has the Long March circular mandala painted on the front of her home, and behind it, the super highway being built between Guiyang and Chongqing.

Figure 109: Chishui: a dentist working in the huge, open air, covered market, drilling on the teeth of a patient. Dentures and tools of the trade are on display.

Figure 110: Chishui market, a display of rice. The Chinese are great connoisseurs of an infinite variety of rice, plus they have just as many different types of noodles as the Italians have pasta.

Figure 111: Chishui market: the Chinese have a whole panoply of condiments: cooking and seasoning oils, vinegars, soy, fish, hot pepper and many other kinds of sauces and myriad spices – these are the secret mixtures that go into each chef's unique cooking mojo.

Figure 112: Chishui: next to the huge market is a large tea parlor area. Hundreds of imbibers of the green, black and red leaf are enjoying each other's company, tea and cigarettes.

Figure 113: Chishui street vendors, all lined up in a row, selling vegetables. Unlike in the West, mutual competitors will congregate right next to each other, one after the other, be it cars, hardware, computers or TVs.

Figure 114: Chishui: this is a Maotai store, China's renowned, high alcohol, clear liquor. Customers come with their own empty bottles and it gets ladled right in with a funnel.

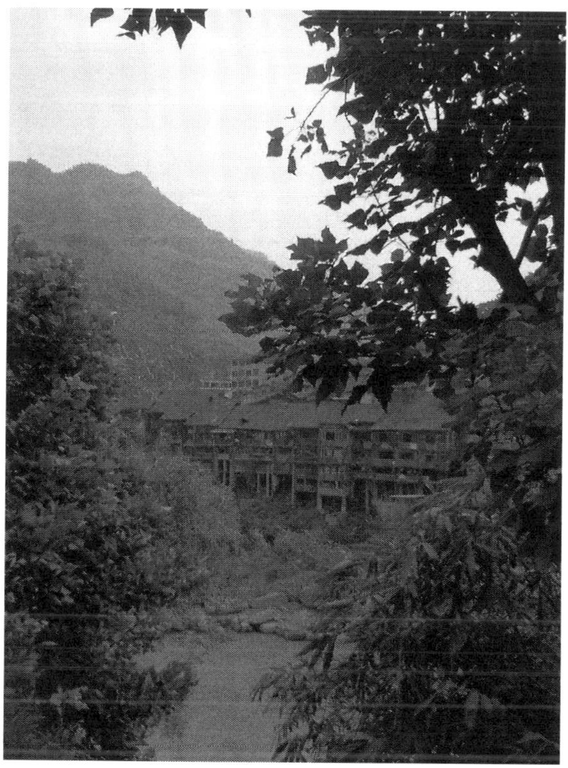

Figure 115: Chishui: a Miao village on flood resistant stilts, hugging the shoreline of a bamboo ensconced mountain river.

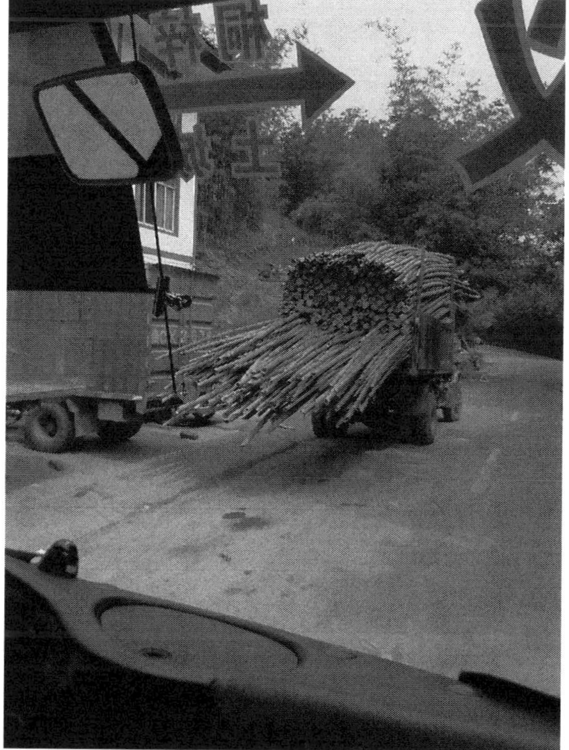

Figure 116: Chishui: bamboo is a big industry in southern China, for chopsticks, scaffolding and construction.

Figure 117: Chishui: the magnificent, bowled Red Canyon site. Below are the ruins of ancient pueblos and religious shrines and above is a waterfall gracing the whole scene. Idyllic and surreal.

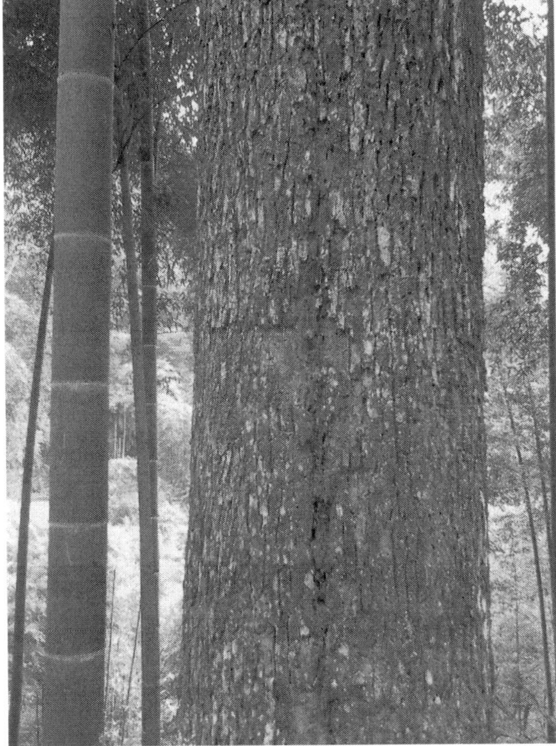

Figure 118: Chishui: Bamboo Sea Park juxtaposition of a big tropical tree trunk next to a bamboo plant. The tree trunk is 60cm in diameter, making the bamboo shoot 10cm thick.

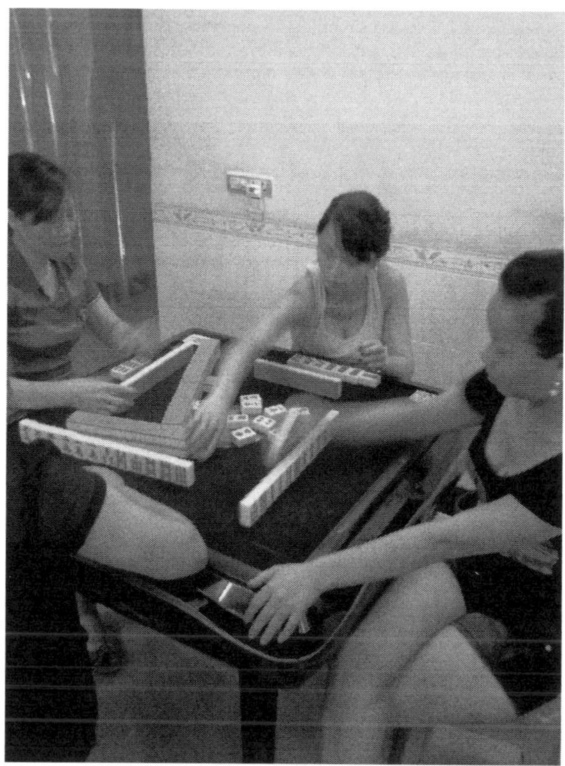

Figure 119: Chishui: Ms. Guo with three friends in her hostel reception area, satisfying her mahjong addiction. She is seated on the left, in the striped shirt.

Figure 120: Chishui: the incomparable 76 meter tall Shizhangdong Waterfall in the wonderful, eponymously named park. While not wide, Shizhangdong is over 3.5 times the height of Niagara Falls.

Figure 121: Guiyang: a very kitschy, long table style restaurant with fluorescent colored food, mauve chairs, rainbow colored beverages on the wall, all lit with colored and UV lights. A lot of effort went into its design. The Chinese like their kitsch.

Figure 122: Guiyang: Lei Feng, the 1950s super patriot turned into modern day myth is still everywhere, beseeching the masses to good citizenship, honor, duty and personal sacrifice.

Figure 123: Guiyang: inside the huge Qingling City Park, one of the favorite popular pastimes of the Chinese is playing cards, Western chess, Chinese chess or Go outdoors, with friends, family and neighbors. It is perfectly OK to stand up close and gawk. In fact, they enjoy the celebrity.

Figure 124: Guiyang: inside the huge Qingling City Park, another favorite popular pastime is to convene with fellow musicians and create an ad hoc orchestra and perform songs together. Nostalgic, patriotic and fervent Communist songs are favorites.

Part VIII

Epilogue

RULES OF THE ROAD: THE PAST

"Do not dwell in the past, do not dream of the future,
concentrate the mind on the present moment."
Buddha

"May the saddest day of your future be no worse than the happiest day of your past."
Irish proverb

"The past should be a springboard, not a hammock."
Ivern Ball

EPILOGUE

A look back with a definite eye to the future...

Reflecting back on this amazing and unforgettable journey into the heart and soul of the Middle Kingdom, my most lasting memory of *44 Days* is the civility of the Chinese people, in crowded and cramped conditions that would try even the most indulgent and people-loving of Westerners. Over and over again, day after day, eyeballs to elbows, their behavior is beyond my greatest expectations. Twenty years ago, just buying a kilo of veggies, getting across the street or ordering a meal was often a knock down drag out verbal and psychological battle, and sometimes with some pushing and shoving for good measure. Hats off to the Chinese for their amazing social, cultural and public evolution as a people, which is paralleling their meteoric economic rise.

The other refreshing aspect of Chinese society is how much the attitude of the Chinese has radically changed vis-à-vis foreigners. Of course we are still targets for higher prices to get this or that. Sticking it to foreigners has been a time honored business model since the dawn of civilization and intertribal trading and bartering. On the contrary, I was blessed with numerous acts of generosity and kindness, both material and spiritual. It is not like the 90s, when there was an openly expressed, frequently hostile attitude towards *dabizi* and the genuflecting expectation that we should pay more for everything, *lots more*. The Chinese's self-perpetuating *century of shame* will never go away and will always be present in the national collective thought, when dealing with the outside world and other peoples. After all, Christian Serbian Slobodan Milosevic helped inspire his people to commit war crime atrocities against Bosnian Muslims in the 1990s, with the (paraphrased) cry of, *Never forget the Battle of Kosovo!*[1] This Christian defeat was the beginning of Islam's onslaught of former Yugoslavia - *600 years ago - in 1389*. For humans, it's never too late to set things right and avenge a perceived wrong, even centuries later. Still, it would appear that the Chinese are learning to put their long standing one hundred years of humiliation into more proper perspective, when working with foreigners on a daily basis.

The third very pleasant observation of *44 Days* is how easy it is to travel to even the remotest areas of China nowadays. When you are responsible for moving 20% of the world's people around a continent scaled country, the Chinese have to be humanity's best logistical experts. It is now possible to seamlessly move from bus to train and train to bus almost anywhere, in a timely and coordinated fashion. I'm not suggesting that Chinese public transportation is up to Louis Vuitton and Michelin Guide standards, but if you have sense of adventure, understand the situation and can rein in your most misanthropic of impulses, getting around China is now a breeze.

These three aforementioned plusses to Chinese society are fueling an incredible number of local tourists, who are mobilizing by the millions around their huge land, and it is something to be seen. Currently, the number of internal tourist trips is estimated to be an eye popping 1.93 billion, and this number is increasing 10% per year. The Chinese have an income savings rate of 40% and China already has the largest and fastest growing middle class on the planet, so these travel numbers will continue to explode. Chinese tourists going abroad already rank their country internationally as the world's number three. Their rapidly growing impact on tourism is going to change the industry around the world. More importantly, the perspectives and observations these globetrotting Chinese bring back home are going to transform the impressions they have of themselves and their co-citizens. This in turn will fuel their rising expectations of Baba Beijing and their country's ongoing potential, what is and what could be. Yet, the paucity of foreign tourists is shocking. Where are they? I guess they just see Beijing, Shanghai, Guangzhou, Guilin, Xi'an, and then go home. China may be the world's number three international tourist destination, but I spent days by myself as the honorary *laowai* of wherever I was, a white head bobbing above an undulating sea of locals. If I add up the total number of foreigners I saw in *44 Days* of travel across five provinces, it equals less than a hundred. That's crazy. For the adventurous, there is so much more to see in this amazing country than just the big five tourist stops, but truth be told, this tendency of hitting the hot spots is not uncommon around the world.

On a positive ecological note, the richness and variety of the flora that I saw was staggering. Calling all botanists, flower bugs, green thumbs and plant lovers. I came home with a wonderful collection of photos (and lasting memories) of all the grasses, plants, flowers, bushes, trees, mosses, ferns and forests that I saw. The floral scenery is simply jaw dropping, be it the mountains, plains, plateaus or deserts. Conversely, the catastrophic destruction of all things fauna is downright depressing. Whether it is insects, birds, amphibians, reptiles or mammals, the tragic absence of wildlife in some of the remotest regions of China, during the lushest season of the year, is shockingly manifest. After thirty years of post-independence lawlessness and now thirty more years of unhinged wealth accumulation and gluttonous consumption, coupled with prehistoric notions about the curative powers of consuming body parts from the most fragile and endangered of species, means the prognosis is not good for China's denuded animal kingdom. Seeing ivory for sale at UNESCO's Mogao Caves and wildcat skins being flogged like baubles at Lugu Lake, just underlines how far China has to go to confront its demons of animal ecology disaster.

On the economic front, China has overtaken the US as the world's biggest trading country. The only other prize left to dominate all the world's economic categories, is to stand atop the GDP podium. That is not going to happen in the next year or two, but it will be critical to see how the West reacts to the reality of its approaching inferior economic status. As this new world order approaches, will Baba Beijing let its growing clout go to its head? I tend to think not so, but any number of internal and external dynamics could all too easily incite the Chinese to drink deeply from the poisonous waters of nationalism, tit-for-tat politics and one-upmanship. China will not be making the RMB fully convertible for a few more years, but the multiplying factor of bilateral currency trade agreements between the BRICS block, Japan, OPEC and the Euro Zone will continue to cut the US dollar more and more out of its post-war historical role as the world's trade settlement currency, further weakening the US's increasingly precarious, international economic standing. Until recently, these settlement deals used to be backroom affairs, away from the harsh consternations of Washington. Now, they are front page news. I predict China will probably use its pending status as the world's largest economy, as a convenient moment to make the official announcement that the RMB is fully convertible. When that happens, enter stage East the world's new, preeminent reserve and trade currency, with the concomitant and inevitable decline of the American Empire and its pan global military machine.

The US is *pivoting* the majority of its naval fleet from the Middle East to the waters off China and Russia. The US is also aggressively trying to expand its physical presence in China's first sphere of influence, by negotiating for military bases in Vietnam, Australia, Singapore and the Philippines, while maintaining its strong arms presence in South Korea and Japan. This is ostensibly to keep an eye on North Korea, but China and Russia are not fooled. They clearly understand it is an attempt to intimidate them and for America to flex its worldwide *Wehrmacht* up close and personal. As a result, the US is almost guaranteeing a second marriage between China and Russia, reigniting the brotherly love from their post WWII halcyon days of international Communism. Historians wearily call this *unintended consequences* and have filled annals of them going back for millennia; unintended consequences have changed humanity's trajectory at least as much as their preceding events... How China responds to all this American military braggadocio on their front porch, and Russia being threatened on its eastern flank, is critically important for Earth's wellbeing. FIRE's bogus, Orwellian Perpetual War on Terror has moved to Africa, a continent as big in land area as the United States, China, India, Japan, and much of Europe *together*, and with some of the world's greatest abundance of natural and energy sources.[2] France is playing its role of nostalgia fueled ex-colonial plunderer, world dominator and American proxy army, by invading Mali - while next door, the US already has troops in Niger.[3] Like an obedient lap dog, the UK pedantically follows America's every call, which is very disappointing. The Brits I know are much better than this, but I understand that the London narrative is equally as oppressive and onerous as the Washington consensus, not to mention the subconscious, national, collective desire to relive the glory days of world domination, to be a player on the world's stage. Thus, since 1980, America's and England's *special relationship* has been very pernicious for the world. With Iraq's and Afghanistan's trillion dollar pipelines drying up for the Fortune 500, Africa is the next military boondoggle on their quarterly marketing lists. The problem is, China is pouring billions into Africa, has hundreds of capital development and investment projects and over a million nationals living there. China already has investments and citizens in Mali. Libya has been given the West's Shock Doctrine Disaster Capitalism makeover, during which Baba Beijing saw $20bn of its investments go up in US-UK-French bombing smoke, and had to evacuate 35,680 nationals working there.[4,5] How many more of these reckless, destructive Western invasions is China going to stomach in Africa?

It's a two-edged sword. Baba Beijing is more than happy for the United States to borrow money from them, further increasing America's colossal indebtedness, only to turn around and watch as the US pays for protecting the Chinese's African investments. It's an incredibly virtuous circle for China. But what happens when America's military or its British and French proxy armies kill a serious number of Chinese nationals in Africa? It is very possible this could cause an anti-Western texting tidal wave on China's one billion mobile phones. Baba Beijing would have to respond to their citizens' calls, one way or the other. Or conversely, Baba needs to shore up public support for the Communist Party and they fan nationalist flames into a feeding frenzy, with only one option to respond accordingly. It's one thing for the West to be militarily colonizing and *liberating* millions of Muslims around the world, starting with the 1990 Gulf War. Unlike the Islamic World though, China will likely do more than just complain diplomatically at the United Nations. I think we can also discount the Chinese going on a suicide bomber tear. They have no such feelings of weakness and hopelessness in the face of relentless Western hegemony. Africa is a flashpoint that could easily blow up in the world's face at any time.

UNESCO needs to start the formal process of delisting Lijiang as a World Heritage Site. Its Old Town was the low point of the whole trip and deeply disappointing, with its crass, Las Vegas commercialism. Lijiang no longer deserves this internationally honored moniker. Likewise, UNESCO needs to come down like a ton of bricks on the Mogao Caves in Dunhuang and pull all the ivory for sale in the museum store there. What a travesty that this is happening in the name of the United Nations.

Lonely Planet needs to get up from their computers and telephones, hit the pavement and make corrections to numerous errors in their May, 2011 *China* guide. They are resting on their corporate laurels a little too much these days. BBC Worldwide paid a dear £130.2 million for LP in 2007-2011, is now a bean counter's haven, and management seems to be cutting corners to lower costs. Next time for a change, I will try the *Rough Guide*.

As for road gear, a telescoping, lightweight aluminum walking stick was sorely missed, for increased hiking efficiency, climbing safety and as protection from attacking dogs. That omission will not happen again. Nor will I take off without a good quality +1-liter stainless steel thermos, with a top that serves as a cup. This is absolutely vital in tea-crazy China, whose water fountains function via boiled water available everywhere you turn. A waterproof backpack cover would be indispensable for getting caught in the rain. The folding tripod stool I was expecting to use waiting around stations and in packed trains, and which took up so much space in my backpack, barely saw the light of day.

What an amazing time in world events to be living and working in the People's Republic of China. Riding on the back of this colossal, historical and cultural dragon is the thrill ride of a lifetime. Baba Beijing has its Mandarin hands more than occupied, fulfilling its Heavenly Mandate for 1,300,000,000 brethren, among fifty-six peoples across thirty-three provinces, while racing through civilization's largest and fastest economic and social transformation.[6] There are so many variables and potential surprises to consider, not only internally, but from outside its borders as well. They are all harbingers for China's accelerating push into the 21st century. Any one of them could be that crazy chaos theory *mote of sociopolitical dust* that lands on China's great gyroscope of stability (稳定= *wending*), quickly pulling it spiraling out of control.

I'm hanging on for this wild adventure in the bowels of the new century China beast. You may not sense it, but wherever you are on Planet Earth, no matter how far away, no matter how out of sight or out of mind, so are you.

1- en.wikipedia.org/wiki/Gazimestan_speech - history of Milosevic's speech and references to the Battle of Kosovo.

2- africabusinessreview.net/how-big-is-africa-really - wonderful map of Africa with other continents superimposed on top.

3- rt.com/usa/us-troops-deployment-niger-299/ - This is how the US got started in Vietnam, with a few advisors.

4- www.brookings.edu/research/opinions/2013/01/23-china-france-intervention-mali-sun. Sure didn't hear much about this in the Western press.

5- news.xinhuanet.com/english2010/china/2011-03/03/c_13759456.htm. I mentioned the Chinese are really good at the logistics of moving people. This again barely made waves in the Western media.

6- More precisely, 22 provinces, four municipalities, five autonomous regions, and two special administrative regions (Hong Kong and Macao); plus Taiwan (eventually) equals 34.

Part IX

Maps and Charts

RULES OF THE ROAD: MONEY

"When a government is dependent upon bankers for money, they and not the leaders of the government control the situation, since the hand that gives is above the hand that takes… Money has no motherland; financiers are without patriotism and without decency; their sole object is gain."
Napoleon Bonaparte

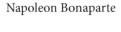

"I believe that banking institutions are more dangerous to our liberties than standing armies."
Thomas Jefferson

"A greedy person is like a snake that tries to swallow an elephant."
Chinese proverb

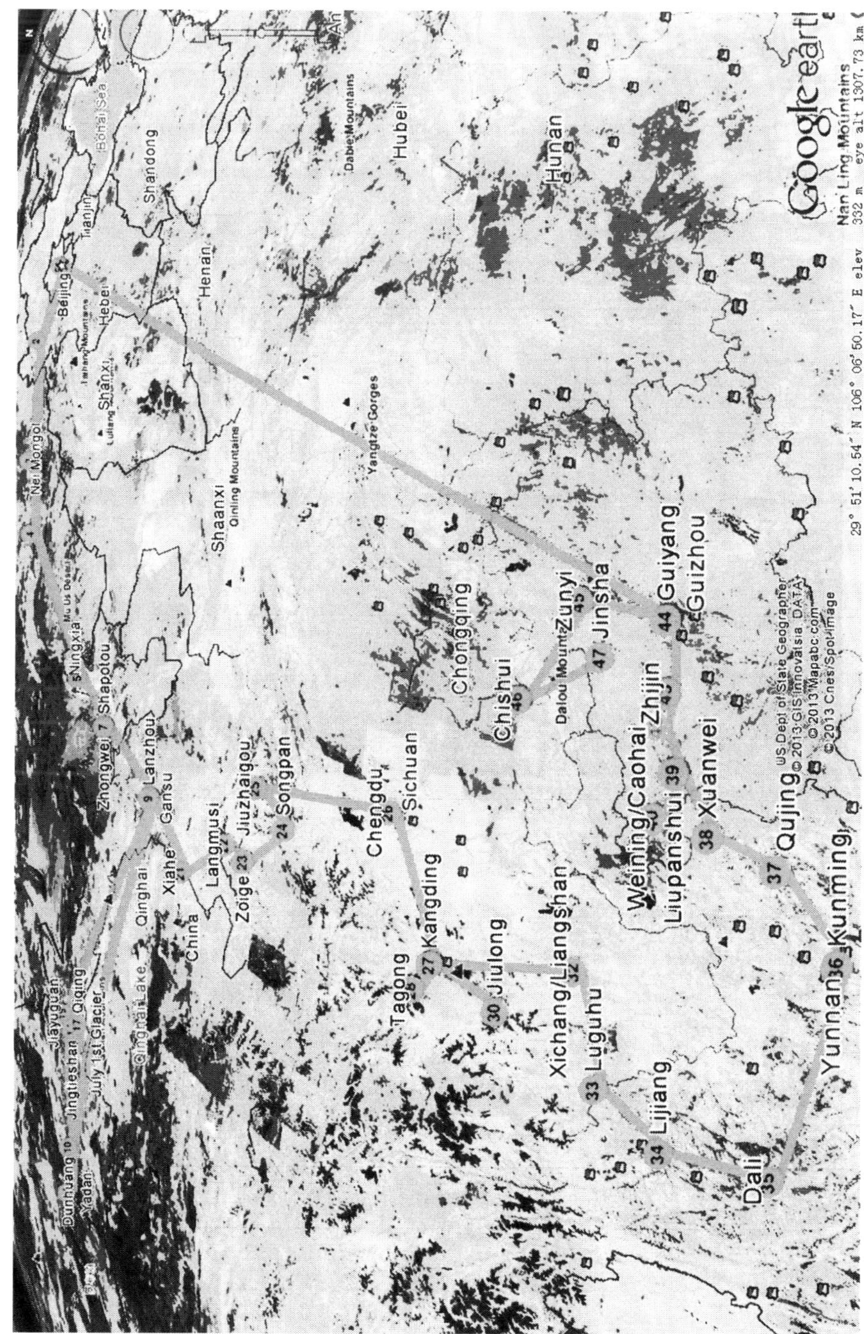

Figure 125: Starting and finishing in Beijing, I make a 12,000km, counterclockwise circuit, with a big extension to the western edge of Gansu, in Dunhuang, Yumenguan and Yadan, on the border with Xinjiang. The route looks like a corn cob pipe with a very short stem. Created with Google Maps, using www.tripline.net to plot the itinerary.

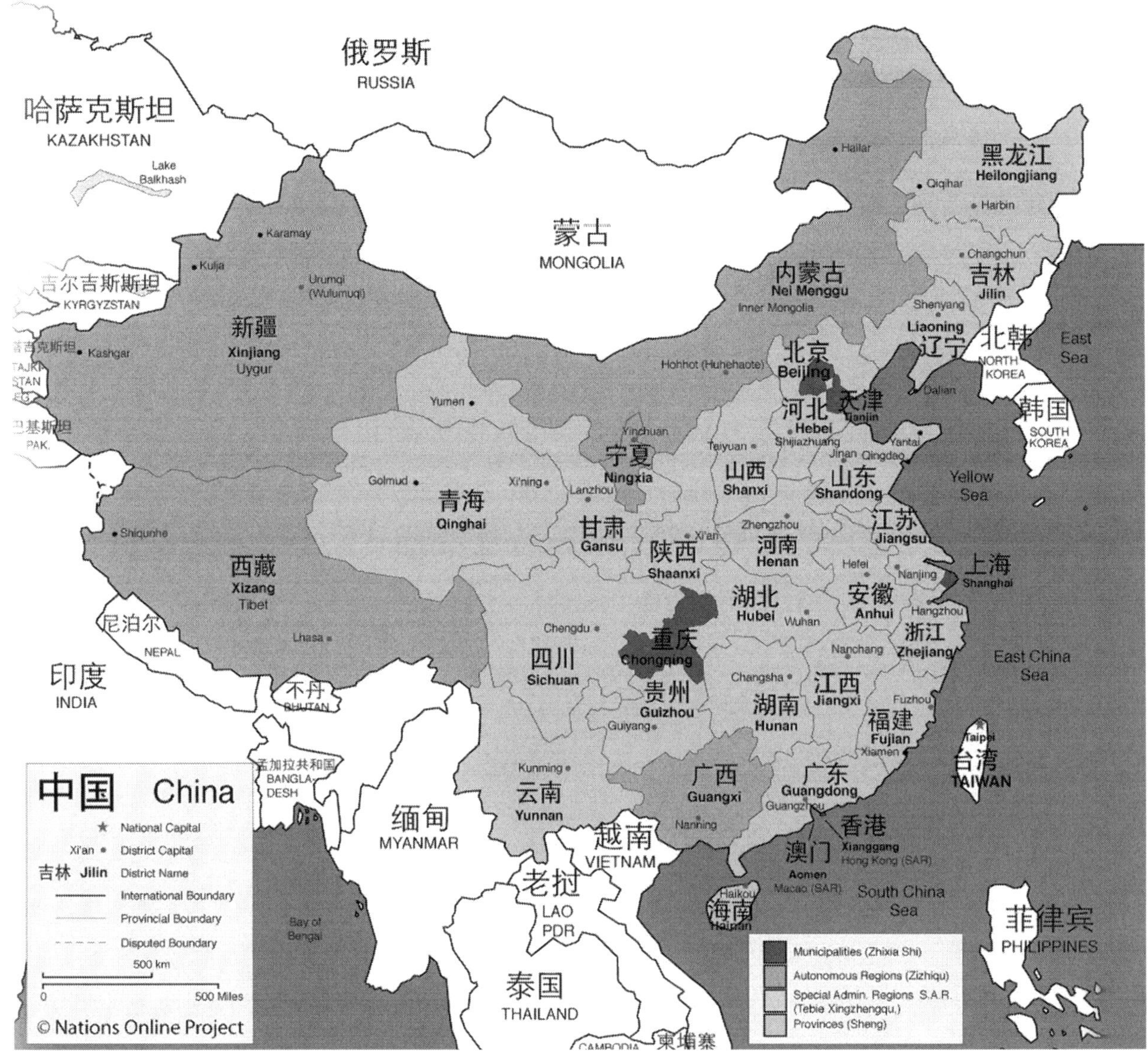

Figure 126: Political and provincial map of the People's Republic of China, by the Nations Online Project.

All the dates, trains, buses and distances traveled during 44 Days are presented below. In the notes column, approximate departures are italicized. Distances are calculated with www.distancesfrom.com.

44 Days Itinerary	Leg #	Km	Mode	Date	Note
Beijing-Tianjin	-	139	Train	2012.6.30	Not used in book
Tianjin-Beijing	-	139	Train	2012.7.3	Not used in book
Beijng-Yinchuan	1	888	Train	2012.7.4-5	K1177- 13:20
Yinchuan-Zhongwei	2	208	Train	2012.7.7	K1295- 12:07
Zhongwei-Shapotou	3	20	Bus	2012.7.8	Dist. Estimated
Shapotou-Zhongwei	4	20	Bus	2012.7.8	Dist. Estimated

Zhongwei-Lanzhou	5	326	Train	2012.7.9	T175- 01:19
Lanzhou-Dunhuang	6	1,099	Train	2012.7.9	K9667- 17:50
Dunhuang-Yadan	7	200	Bus	2012.7.11	Dist. Estimated
Yadan-Dunhuang	8	200	Bus	2012.7.11	Dist. Estimated
Dunhuang-Jiayuguan	9	371	Bus	2012.7.12	8:00
Jiayuguan-Jingtieshan	10	223	Train	2012.7.13	#7529- 07:00
Jingtieshan-July 1st Glacier	11	50	Bus	2012.7.13	Dist. Estimated
July 1st Glacier-Jingtieshan	12	50	Bus	2012.7.13	Dist. Estimated
Jingtieshan-Qiqing	13	50	Bus	2012.7.14	Dist. Estimated
Qiqing-Jingtieshan	14	50	Bus	2012.7.14	Dist. Estimated
Jingtieshan-Jiayuguan	15	223	Train	2012.7.14	#7530- 17:03
Jiayuguan-Lanzhou	16	731	Train	2012.7.14	K9662- 21:00
Lanzhou-Xiahe	17	236	Bus	2012.7.15	8:30
Xiahe-Langmusi	18	397	Bus	2012.7.16	7:40
Langmusi-Zoige	19	85	Bus	2012.7.18	6:00
Zoige-Songpan	20	156	Bus	2012.7.18	10:00
Songpan-Jiuzhaigou	21	101	Bus	2012.7.19	9:10
Jiuzhaigou-Chengdu	22	101	Bus	2012.7.20	7:20
Chengdu-Kangding	23	337	Bus	2012.7.21	7:15
Kangding-Tagong	24	212	Bus	2012.7.21	15:00
Tagong-Kangding	25	212	Bus	2012.7.23	7:00
Kangding-Jiulong	26	235	Bus	2012.7.23	9:00
Jiulong-Kangding	27	235	Bus	2012.7.24	7:00
Kangding-Xichang/Liangshan	28	341	Bus	2012.7.25	6:00
Xichang-Lugu Lake	29	284	Bus	2012.7.26	8:10
Lugu Lake-Lijiang	30	203	Bus	2012.7.28	7:00
Lijiang-Dali	31	183	Bus	2012.7.30	8:00
Dali/Xiaguan-Kunming	32	337	Bus	2012.8.1	13:05
Kunming-Qujing	33	153	Train	2012.8.2	K854- 09:40
Qujing-Xuanwei	34	101	Bus	2012.8.2	14:00
Xuanwei-Liupanshui	35	236	Train	2012.8.2	K156- 19:36
Liupanshui-Weining/Caohai	36	74	Train	2012.8.3	K1140- 01:12
Weining-Liupanshui	37	74	Bus	2012.8.3	13:40
Liupanshui-Nayong	38	97	Bus	2012.8.3	17:00
Nayong-Zhijin	39	86	Bus	2012.8.4	7:00
Zhijin-Guiyang	40	145	Bus	2012.8.5	7:00
Guiyang-Zunyi	41	143	Bus	2012.8.5	12:40
Zunyi-Chishui	42	262	Bus	2012.8.6	9:50
Chishui Parks	43	100	Bus	2012.8.7-8	Dist. Estimated
Chishui-Zunyi	44	262	Bus	2012.8.9	14:10
Zunyi-Guiyang	45	143	Train	2012.8.9	K831- 22:02
Guiyang-Beijing	46	2,228	Train	2012.8.11-12	T88- 08:00
TOTAL/AVERAGE	290	12,746	13/08/2012	30/06/2012	44

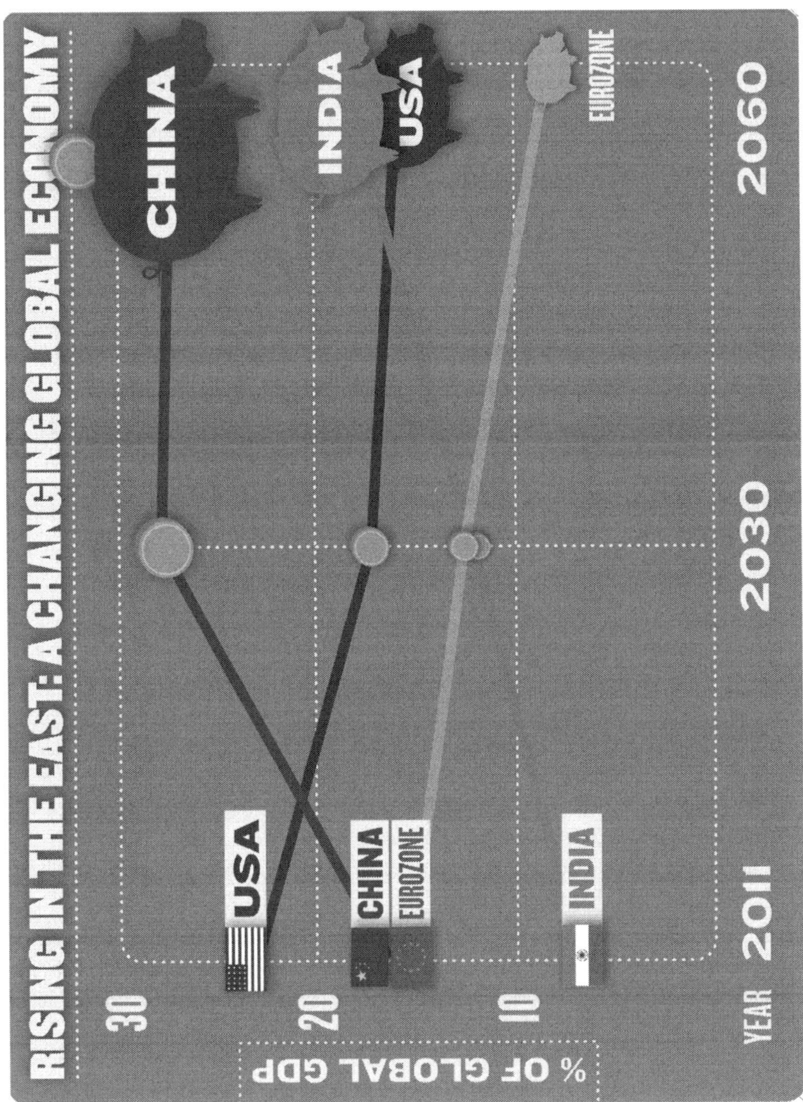

Figure 127: Trading places: America's and Europe's 21st century conundrum - how they and China respond and adapt to this new world order will largely determine whether humanity survives and if we do, how we will live our lives for decades to come. Notice by 2050, that other Asian colossus, India, relegates the United States and Europe to fading third and fourth places. By Tutu at www.theday.co.uk.

Part X

Reference Guide and Abbreviations

Rules of the Road: Relaxation

"For fast-acting relief, try slowing down."
Lily Tomlin

"Tension is who you think you should be. Relaxation is who you are."
Chinese Proverb

"Every now and then go away, have a little relaxation, for when you come back to your work, your judgment will be surer. Go some distance away because then the work appears smaller and more of it can be taken in at a glance, and a lack of harmony and proportion is more readily seen."
Leonardo da Vinci

Reference Guide, Abbreviations and a Chinese Pronunciation and Name Guide

$: US dollar. The exchange rate is RMB6.3/$, rounded up or down for simplicity.
¥: Official symbol for China's currency. It stands for *yuan*. Also used in Japan (yen) and Korea (won).
€: Euro. The exchange rate is RMB8.0/€, rounded up or down for simplicity.
°C: Degrees Celsius. A rough conversion is Fahrenheit divided by 2, or Celsius times 2 for Fahrenheit. -°C is below freezing, water freezes at 0°C, room temperature is 20°C, 30°C is a warm day, body temperature is 37°C and blazing hot is 40°C.
1G: Early generation mobile phones that cannot send attachments, emails, etc.
1st Army: Red Army's biggest group during the 1930s' Long March, along with 2nd and 4th Armies. The Third never materialized.
1.3 billion = 1,300,000,000 citizens: Number of Chinese citizens, in round numbers.
20%: China's percent of the world's total population.
3G: Newer generation mobile phone technology that can send attachments, emails, access the internet, etc.
8 x 56: Binocular magnification x aperture diameter, in mm.
Acacia: Type of tree, especially famous on the African savannahs.
Adam: Biblical character in the Book of Genesis, believed by the faithful to be the first man created by God.
Aesop: 7th century BC Greek author, famous for his fables involving talking animals.
Agate: Semiprecious stone highly revered by Tibetans for its medicinal and spiritual properties.
Air Force One: American president's jet.
Akan: Matrilineal people in West Africa.
Alan Taylor: 20th-21st century American historian and author specializing in early American history.
Alexander the Great: 4th century BC Macedonian king and military genius.
Alexis de Tocqueville: 19th century French historian who wrote extensively on American society
Alice in Wonderland: 1865 book by British author Lewis Carroll, about a fantastic, dream world, with amazing characters and properties.
Alice's Restaurant: Antiestablishment song by American folk rocker, Arlo Guthrie.
Alien: 1979-97 American science fiction horror movie franchise, with frequent settings on distant planets.
All that Jazz: 1979 American movie, with lots of choreographed dancing.
Al-Nakba: Palestinian ethnic genocide caused by the creation of Israel, forcing 760,000 people to be dispossessed of their ancestral homes, and whose diaspora now counts about 11 million people, or about ¼ of all the world's refugees.
Alps: The largest mountain chain in Europe.
Alsophila: Huge, treelike and ancient species of fern; it prospered back during the age of the dinosaurs, and can still be found around Chishui, Guizhou.
Ambrose Bierce: Late 19th-early 20th century American editor, journalist and satirical writer of *The Devil's Dictionary.*
Amdo: Region of the former Kingdom of Tibet. See map at .
American Midwest: Large, rich, agricultural area between the northern Mississippi and Ohio Rivers.
Amylopectin: Long chained wheat sugar.
An Inconvenient Truth: 2006 double Academy Award winning movie produced by Al Gore, underscoring the world threat of global warming.
Arbuckle Mountains: Geologically famous mountains in south central Oklahoma, US, for their age and the way the rock strata are so dramatically exposed, compared to the Helan Mountains in Yinchuan, Ningxia.
Arlo Guthrie: Antiestablishment American folk rock musician and son of Woody Guthrie.
Arrow of Time: A law of physics that time can only go forward, cannot be stopped or turned back.
Art Deco: French 1920-40s architectural style with traditional craft motifs, Machine Age imagery, rich colors, bold geometric shapes and lavish ornamentation.
Ashanti: matrilineal people in Ghana.

Atacama Desert: Located in Chile, Bolivia and Peru, it is the world's driest desert.
Auriel Stein: Early 20th century British anthropologist who went the Mogao Caves, Dunhuang, Gansu.
Austin Powers: 1997-2002 American movies, whose main character is a hilariously oversexed British spy.
Avatar: 2009 American movie, with a utopian moon called Pandora, whose people practice a form of Communism, and who fight off invading Princes of Powers and their armies.
Ayn Rand: American-Russian libertarian writer whose books extoled the virtues of greed and total self-interest, at the expense of everyone else. Playbooks for jungle capitalism.
Baba Beijing (爸爸北京): Baba mean father in Chinese, so this is my affectionate name for the very paternalistic, Confucius driven central government and leaders of China.
Bai (白): A minority based around Erhai Lake and Dali, in Yunnan.
Baidu: The Chinese version of Google. There are also the search engines Soho and Youdao.
Baisikou Twin Pagodas: Outside Yinchuan, Ningxia, are rare examples of Xixia architecture, built 1038-1227 AD.
Bamboo Sea (竹海): The beautiful mountain park outside of Chishui, Guizhou, above Jinshagou, where DEET mosquito repellent is absolutely worthless.
Bang Kao (帮考): Strange Tibetan man offering advice on the White Dragon River hike, Langmusi, Gansu.
Bank of China: One of the top 10 largest banks in world and where I bank in China.
Bankster: A modern day libertarian banker, coined from the word *gangster*.
Baotou (包头): Inner Mongolian town, passed through from Beijing to Yinchuan, Ningxia.
Baozi (包子): Steamed dumplings, a staple breakfast dish in China.
Barak Obama: 44th US president, 2009-2017.
Barbara Mor: 20th century American matriarchy historian and author.
Barbara Walker: 20th century American matriarchy historian and author, who wrote two definitive encyclopedias.
Bardo Thodol: The Tibetan Book of the Dead, to guide people before, during and after death.
Barnum & Bailey Circus: Famous American 3-ring traveling circus.
Basan: One of the siblings managing the Snowland Hostel in Tagong, Sichuan.
Basques: Matrilineal people in Spain and France.
Battle of Kosovo: Muslim victory over Christian forces in the Balkans, Europe, in 1329.
Bayou State: Nickname for Louisiana, American southern Gulf Coast state with New Orleans and its Depression era, populist governor and US senator, Huey "Kingfish" Long.
Beatles: Seminal rock/pop group that changed the world in the 60s-70s.
Beijing (北京): Political capital of China.
Beijing Train Station: Famous for its classic Stalinist architecture.
Bellevue: A euphemism for a mental hospital.
Bellum Americana: American policy of Orwellian Perpetual War, in order to maintain world hegemony.
Bernard Terminet Schuppon: French friend who doggedly researched and found the identity of the wild cat skins being sold at Lugu Lake, Yunnan.
Bewitched: Popular American TV show, 1964-72; the main character is a good witch who is constantly using her magic to get her husband, Darrin Stephens, out of numerous problems.
Bharal: An endangered mountain goat found in the Helan Mountains, outside Yinchuan, Ningxia.
Bibliotèque Nationale: the National Library of France, in Paris. See *Mogao Caves*.
Billion: 9 zeros = 1,000 million = 1,000,000,000.
Billy Crystal: Comic American actor in the movie *City Slickers*, whom I remember while hiking White Dragon River, Langmusi, Gansu.
Bin Laden: See Osama Bin Laden.
Blankfein (Lloyd): CEO of Goldman Sachs, a Wall Street bank.
Blue Danube: A classic waltzing song.

Blue provinces: See *coastal provinces.*
Bo Gu: 1930s Red Army senior leader, who faced off against Mao Zedong and lost control of the Communist movement.
Bo Xilai (薄熙来): 21st century Chongqing politician whose career was destroyed by Baba Beijing for his overly populist sentiments. He has been arrested and disappeared.
Bodhisattvas: Buddhist icons exemplifying various states of enlightenment.
Bohai Sea: The seas just east of Beijing and Tianjin.
Book of the Dead: See *Bardo Thodol.*
Bookends: Early Simon and Garfunkel album, 1968, with happy go lucky, celebratory song, *Feeling Groovy.*
Bosnia: European site of Muslim genocide during the 1990s Yugoslav Wars.
Boxing Day: British holiday, the day after Christmas, when employers and superiors are supposed to give boxes of gifts for their employees. It has now been largely reduced to a bank holiday.
Brackens: An ancient kind of fern plant.
Break on through (to the Other Side): Great traveling song by the rock band, the Doors and sung by Jim Morrison.
Bretton Woods Agreement: The post-WWII accord making the US dollar the world's reserve and trade settlement currency.
BRICS: Brazil, Russia, India, China and South Africa, all considered to be future leaders of the 21st century.
Broadway: Street in New York City famous for musical shows.
Bronx: Famous New York City, working class neighborhood.
Brooks Brothers: Men's business clothing company, popular for up and coming Firemen.
Buck: Slang for one dollar.
Buddhism: Major world religion started in India, but developed further east in Asia, and is the biggest religion in China and most other Asian countries.
Bullet train: High speed train, which in China cruises at 300kph.
Bullitt: 1968 American movie, with a famous airport scene.
Bunts: A matrilineal people in India.
Bushobamavilles: Modern day Hoovervilles, tent and shantytowns for the homeless and unemployed, cropping up around the US during the W. Bush and Obama presidencies.
Cameron Diaz: American movie actress, active 1990s-2010s, whose career was launched in *The Mask.*
Cangshan Mountains (苍山): Overlooking Erhai Lake and which I climbed, to stay at the Highland Hostel, Dali, Yunnan.
Canton (Cantonese): A popular name for the region comprising Hong Kong and Guangdong Provinces.
Caobao (草豹= Grass Leopard): Local name for the endangered wild cat skins I see for sale at Lugu Lake, Yunnan.
Caohai (草海= Grass Sea): Lugu Lake wetland marsh, on the Sichuan side.
Caohai Wildlife Reserve (Guizhou): The very disappointing failure-as-bird-sanctuary that I visited, also called Caohai (草海= Grass Sea), which is a common name for any wetland.
Capitan Ahab: Capitalism and naked greed are personified in the allegorical American classic, *Moby Dick*, by Herman Melville. Ahab's ship is named after an exterminated Native American tribe, the Pequod, and he venally offers a gold doubloon to the first crew member (of whom there were 30, to represent the 30 US States at the time) who sights the great white whale – piggish lust for the doomed crew, as they inexorably plunge ever onwards to their collective death. Wow. One of America's greatest contributions to English literature and a must read.
Capitan Kangaroo: Immensely popular American TV show for young children, 1955-84.
Capricorn: Constellation in the southern sky.
Capsicum: The chemical molecule that gives pepper its spiciness.
Carl Stokes: First black American mayor of a major city, Cleveland, 1968-71, whose burning Cuyahoga River helped him start the environmental movement.
Carpetbagger: Any outsider who comes to a new area, for the expressed purpose of making money, usually at the expense of the local people.
Casablanca: Famous 1942 American movie, with an unforgettable airport scene.

Catastrophe, The: See *Al-Nakba*.
CCP: Chinese Communist Party.
Century of humiliation: The 1840s-1940s, when an impotent China was force fed British opium, while Western powers and Japan colonized much of the coastal territory and bigger cities.
Chairman (Mao Zedong): See Mao Zedong.
Chamdo: A region of the former Kingdom of Tibet. See map at .
Changsha: Capital of Hunan province, a deeply historical city, it is where Mao Zedong became a believer in Communism.
Charles Darwin: World changing 19th century British scientist who explained to the world the irrefutable life processes of evolution and natural selection. Frequently ranked as one of the ten most important people who ever lived.
Charleston Heston: 20th century American actor, who played many gritty, macho roles, including *Planet of the Apes* and *Soylent Green*.
Charley Johng's: Groovy, hippy dippy hostel, where I stayed in Dunhuang, Gansu.
Chengdu: The provincial capital of Sichuan, known for its ancient tea houses, Sichuan cuisine, bevy of famous Chinese writers, Giant Pandas, and I almost forgot, zero degree, ice cold beer!
Cherokee: Native American minority.
Cheshire cat: Alice in Wonderland character with one of the most famous smiles in the world.
Chiang Kai-Shek (蔣介石= Jiang Jiashi or 蔣中正= Jiang Zhongzheng): Leader of the Kuomintang (KMT), who lost to the Communists and fled to Taiwan to create the Republic of Taiwan; known for his rapacious greed and close cooperation with criminals and Mafiosi.
China Unicom: A major mobile phone company.
Chinese Dream: Playing off the concept of the American Dream, the Chinese version is more and more being bandied about by foreigners and Baba Beijing.
Chinese Google: See *Baidu*.
Chinese Twitter: See *Weibo*.
Chinglish: Badly and often hilariously translated Chinese into English.
Chishui (赤水= Naked/Bare Water): Far Northwestern Guizhou paradise of waterfalls, canyons and ancient greenery.
Choctaw: Native American minority.
Choekyi Gyaltsen: 20th Century Tibetan 10th Panchen Lama, who is greatly admired by both exiled Tibetans and Baba Beijing.
Chongqing (重庆): City-state hived off the Province of Sichuan in 1997, formerly known as Chung King, famous for straddling the Yangtze River and being one of the biggest megalopolises in the world, with a humble 32 million souls.
Chongsheng Temple (崇圣寺): Famous temple in Dali, Yunnan, with its iconic Three Pagodas.
Cicero: 1st century BC Roman philosopher, statesman, lawyer, orator, political theorist, consul and constitutionalist.
Cidu: The hyperactive Tibetan I meet on the Great Namo Gorge hike, Langmusi, Sichuan.
Cimarron Turnpike: Oklahoma, US, where I saw construction corruption taking place.
CITES: Convention on International Trade in Endangered Species of Wild Fauna and Flora, the governing body that allows the sale of ivory.
City Slickers, 1991 American movie, about inexperienced city people who go on a guided, horseback riding trip, starring Billy Crystal and Jack Palance, with hilarious results. Very much on my mind while climbing to the source of the White Dragon River, Langmusi, Gansu.
Clash: 80s British rock band, with a seminal punk rock sound and anthemic song, *Should I Stay or Should I Go?*
Clean Air Act: American law started in the 1960s to regulate for clean air.
Clean Water Act: American law started in 1972 to regulate for clean water.
Cloud Fir: Name of one of Jade Dragon Snow Mountains' high altitude plains, Lijiang, Yunnan.
cm: Centimeter. 2.5cm/inch. 30cm/foot. 90cm/yard.
Coastal provinces: In China, the coastal, or blue provinces, which are richer and more developed.

Cold War: In a nutshell, the post WWII struggle between Capitalism vs. Communism.
Colonel Francis Younghusband: Early 20th century British officer whose army invaded Tibet, and who was able to force a trade treaty for his efforts.
Colonel Muammar Gaddafi: late 20th-21st century leader of Libya, until assassinated in 2011, during the West's Disaster Capitalism Libyan Civil War.
Columbus (Christopher): 15th century Italian explorer who sailed to North America.
Colza: A vegetable oil seed also called rapeseed. Its flowers are an unforgettable deep yellow color.
Comanche: Native American minority.
Combi: African term I picked up over the years, for small buses used in public transportation.
Communist Food Party (社会食党= *shehui shidang*): Bizarre retro restaurant in Xichang/Liangshan, Sichuan that precipitated an avalanche of thoughts on the human condition, world history and George Orwell, while eating dinner there.
Como (Lake): Italy.
Confucius: Foundational 5th-6th century BC Chinese teacher, editor, politician, and philosopher, who emphasized personal and governmental morality, correctness of social relationships, justice and sincerity, while harmonizing the interrelationships of leaders, family and the individual. His impact on humanity is at least as important as that of Jesus Christ.
Consommé: A clear broth, made from vegetables or meat.
Coq au vin: French chicken dish prepared with wine.
Cordyceps: Steroid filled fungus growing wild in the Himalayas, which is as valuable as cocaine and heroin.
Corkscrew, The: Harrowing Mammoth Cave National Park trail I took with friends Ken Fraley and Terry Bresin, in 1973, Kentucky, US.
Cormac McCarthy: 20th-21st century American novelist and playwright, who wrote the novel, *The Road*.
Cosmo: Short for *Cosmopolitan*, a trendy women's fashion magazine.
Cowboys of Maroussi: A tongue in check reference to one of the greatest travel books of all time, *The Colossus of Maroussi*, by Henry Miller. Henry loved sex as much or more than his amazing insights to life on Earth, and the people who make it happen.
Crater (Lake): Oregon, US.
Creation Museum: Kentucky, US, depicts the science of astrophysics and cosmology as the biblical book of Genesis. It has dioramas showing Adam and Eve riding saddled and bridled Triceratops - and you know why T. Rexes had such large canine teeth, don't you? Why, it was God's plan for people to have something sharp enough to break open coconuts! Yabba Dabba Do!
Cree: Native American minority.
Cult of Mao: The pedantic, unquestioning worship of Mao Zedong, after independence, which was carefully orchestrated and exploited by Baba Beijing's leaders, such as Lin Bao. One of humanity's greatest, Orwellian success stories.
Cultural Revolution: The 1966-76 political campaign launched by Mao Zedong, to shore up his credentials after the disastrous Great Leap Forward, when 30 million citizens died of starvation. OK, time to move on. The whole thing quickly spun out of Baba Beijing's control (oops!), and China's 800 billion people turned on themselves, in a psychotic frenzy of social cannibalism. Only Mao's death in 1976 put a stop to the madness. One of humanity's greatest Orwellian experiments in population control.
Cyathea: A kind of ancient fern, which prospered back during the age of dinosaurs, and which can still be found around Chishui, Guizhou.
Dabizi (大鼻子= big nose): An affectionate term for non-Asian foreigners, since Orientals typically have smaller, flatter noses.
Daduhe (大渡河= Big Ferry River): Famous Sichuan spot on the Dadu River, where Emperor Kangxi built a bridge in 1706, linking Tibet to China, and which is still used to support Han historic claims to sovereignty over Tibet.
Dahuaxiyou (大话西游): Popular Chinese horror flick, shot at Western Film Studios, Yinchuan, Ningxia.
Daiichi nuclear reactor: The badly leaking Japanese power plant damaged as a result of the 2011 Fukishima earthquake and

tsunami.
Dairy Queen: Iconic southern US drive-in restaurant chain, where customers dine in their cars by pulling up in parking spaces equipped with electronic menu boards to place orders, and have them delivered by a waitress.
Dalai Lama: Tibetan Buddhism's paramount leader, the 14th is currently Tenzin Gyatso.
Dali (大理): Yunnan city along the Erhai River, stronghold of the Bai minority and which above, are the Cangshan Mountains.
Dallas: Incredibly popular American soap opera TV show, 1978-91, glorifying an Ayn Randian world of greed, lust and naked self-interest.
Damocles: Greek myth about having a sword hanging over your head by a thread, symbolizing being in a very precarious or threatening situation.
Daniel Boone: 17th-18th century American pioneer, who was famous for building log cabins to live in.
Danxia (丹霞): The beautiful gorge graced by the 76m Shizhangdong Waterfall, outside of Chishui, Guizhou.
Danzixiang: Small Tibetan hamlet near Kangding, Sichuan, where I saw a newly installed PLA garrison.
Daoxiao noodles (刀削): Famous Shanxi noodles, which are made by the chef cutting them off a hunk of fresh dough, with a knife.
Darrin Stephens: The husband character in the American TV show *Bewitched*, who is always getting into binds.
David Lee Roth: American rock musician in the band Van Halen, known for being flamboyant and outrageous.
Daxia River (夏河= Big Summer River): One of the incredibly beautiful valleys I drive up, in between Lanzhou and Xiahe, in Gansu.
Day the Earth Stood Still: Highly ranked 1951 American sci-fi flick about two aliens, Klaatu and his ray gun robot, Gort, who land next to the White House, warning humanity about its violent tendencies, this, at the height of the nuclear Cold War. Please come back Klaatu. We still need you now, more than ever.
Dazibao (大字报= big word report): Large propaganda, social and cultural banners seen all over China. Read an informative article about them at .
Debbie Does Dallas: A well know 1985 American porn movie, with several sequels. She's a hard working woman, that Debbie.
DEET: A popular ingredient in mosquito repellent, that is usually very effective.
DEFCON 5: On a scale of 1-5, it is the highest level of alert about a pending (nuclear) attack.
Democratic: One of two American political parties, which during the 1930s-1970s, generally supported poor, working and middle class citizens.
Deng Xiaoping: China's Sichuanese, paramount leader from 1978 to the early 90s and who spearheaded his country on a market economy path, at the end of the Cultural Revolution.
Desert West: A name accorded to the Southwest United States, typically West Texas, New Mexico, Arizona, Nevada, Utah and Southeastern California
Dharma: One of Buddhism's Three Jewels, this one being the path to righteousness; the other two being *sangha* (community) and Buddha himself.
Dianchi (滇池): Kunming's large city lake, which is still terribly polluted, even after billions spent to fix the problem.
Dickens (Charles): 19th century British author famed for his portrayal of libertarian England, pitting the 99%, at the mercy of the 1% Princes of Power.
Disaster Capitalism: Libertarian (jungle) capitalism practiced in places after they have been ravaged by war, natural or manmade disasters. See *Shock Doctrine.*
Discovery: Well-known popular science TV program.
Dodge City: Kansas, US frontier town famous for its lawlessness back in the 19th century. *Get out of Dodge* means making a quick exit from a dangerous situation, or fleeing punishment for a wrongdoing.
Donald Lyngdoh: a friend and member of the matrilineal Khasi people in India, who helped explain to me matrilineal cultures.

Doors: Iconic 60s-70s, American sex-drugs-n-rock-n-roll rock band, fronted by bad boy Jim Morrison.
Doris Day: American actress and singer, 1940s-60s, who projected a pure, saintly image, frequently sporting headscarves.
Dream Sea: The Chinese brand of condoms offered in my hotel room in Xichang/Liangshan, Sichuan.
Drum Tower: Many Chinese cities and towns have a drum tower. This one is in Zhongwei, Ningxia.
Dry Sea: High altitude meadow in the Jade Dragon Snow Mountains, Lijiang, Yunnan.
Dunhuang (敦煌= Sincere Brilliance): the quiet desert oasis town in far Western Gansu, with Charley Johng's Hostel, sand dunes at sunset, a camel town and two distant national parks..
Dunhuang Desert Park: The pricey sand dune park in Dunhuang, Gansu, that my Chinese friends and I avoided paying for, by hiking out past the park boundary.
Dzi: The Tibetan name of the 108 beads found on a Buddhist rosary.
Eastern Empire: The part of the Roman Empire that lasted from 330–1453AD.
Easy Virtue: A play/movie, written by Noel Coward, and which the movie's Chinese name is the Lugu Lake flower, *shuixing yanghua* (水性杨花).
Eddie Cantor: Popular 20th century American jazz singer, famous for rolling his eyes when he sang.
Edgar Allen Poe: One of the greats - 19th century American author who popularized the horror genre and is credited with writing the first detective story, *The Murders in the Rue Morgue*.
El Dorado: Name given to any place like a gold rush town, symbolizing greed, naked self-interest and living the high life. The name means *The Golden* in Spanish.
Eldridge Cleaver: 20th century American author and civil rights activist, who was an early leader of the Black Panthers.
Elizabeth Gilbert: 20th-21 century American author, most famous for writing *Eat, Pray, Love*.
Emeishan: In Sichuan, with its famous Buddhist mountain, one of the four holiest in China.
Emma's Kitchen: Hostel where I stayed with Rafal Cebulko and Marta in Songpan, Sichuan.
Emperor Kangxi: 17th-18th century Qing Dynasty ruler who built the Daduhe Bridge, physically connecting Han China to Tibet. The rest is history.
Emperor Qin Shihuang (秦始皇): First Emperor to unify China, in 221BC, establishing one of the key tenants of the Heavenly Mandate: keep the country whole.
Empire State Building: 100 stories tall, a unit of measurement for vertical ascent I use when climbing during hikes.
Engels (Friedrich): 19th century German philosopher and co-founder of Communism, with Karl Marx.
EPA: American Environmental Protection Agency, established in 1970 to help enforce the Clean Air Act, etc.
Erhai Lake (洱海湖): The big and beautiful body of water graced with Dali Town and the Cangshan Mountains.
Erhu (二胡): 2-stringed musical instrument, looking like a skinny banjo and played upright with a bow.
Eric Meyer: French 20th-21st century author who has written a number of books on China, including *Tibet, the Last Cry*.
Ernest Hemingway: Nobel Prize winning, 20th century American author and renowned alcoholic, who blew his brains out before the ravages of dipsomania could take their toll.
EU: The European Union, currently 28 countries comprising the bulk Western and Eastern European countries, except Switzerland and Norway.
Euro: See €.
Eve: Biblical character believed by the faithful to be the first woman on Earth, created from Adam's rib.
Eye of Providence: Buddhist icon seen on the back of US $1 bill, atop the truncated pyramid.
F. silvestris bieti: The striped endangered wildcat skin I saw for sale at Lugu Lake, Yunnan.
F. silvestris ornata: The spotted endangered wildcat skin I saw for sale at Lugu Lake, Yunnan.
Fahao (法号): The celebrated Tibetan long horn, which has a very loud and deep sound.
Fairy Cave: Tibetan enchanted cave on the Namo Creek, where I see pilgrims praying, chanting and singing, Langmusi, Sichuan.
Fan Zhongyan: 10th-11th century Chinese poet, who uncharacteristically spoke out for civil disobedience in the face of centuries of Confucian conformism and respect for social hierarchy.

Fantastic Voyage: 1966 American movie, with the lovely Rachel Welch & Co. coursing through a human body inside a microscopic, miniaturized submarine.
Federal Emergency Management Agency (FEMA): Government office set up to handle disasters, such as floods, tornadoes and hurricanes, and which was such a resounding failure after Hurricane Katrina, as it deferred to Disaster Capitalist Firemen to do their job.
Feeling Groovy: Wonderfully dreamy, happy-go-lucky Simon and Garfunkel song, off their 1968 *Bookends* album.
Fellini (Frederico): 20th century Italian movie director, known for his absurd, surrealistic, canvas art scenes.
Fen (分): 1/100th of an RMB, like a penny or cent. No longer minted, but they are still in circulation.
Fengshui (风水= wind water): Also known as geomancy, it is the Chinese philosophy that use the laws of both Heaven (Chinese astronomy) and Earth to help one improve life, by receiving positive *qi*, or energy. This includes how a house is laid out, as well as all the furniture inside it.
Fengxi River (风溪河): The spectacular river in the Daxia Valley, where is located Shizhangdong Park and its namesake 76m tall waterfall, outside Chishui, Guizhou.
Fidel Castro: 20th-21st century Cuban leader who led his country to independence and throwing off the shackles of FIRE, much to the chagrin of Firemen around the world. Sixty years on, they are still licking their chops, waiting for the next big El Dorado Shock Doctrine play.
Finger (Lakes): New York.
FIRE: the finance, insurance and real estate sectors, collectively, the Princes of Power, the 1%, the world's owners and their political elite who pass and enforce their laws. Their agents are Firemen.
Firemen, as in FIRE.
Five Civilized Tribes: Southern Native American minorities who were exterminated and those who survived, were ethnically cleansed via forced marches to live in Oklahoma, called The Trail of Tears.
Five Flower (Colorful) Lake: One of many in Jiuzhaigou Park.
Five Year Plan: Baba Beijing's budget and state plan for the country's economy and development.
Flintstones: 1960-66 American TV cartoon show about cavemen living in the dinosaur age, and whose main character, Fred, is fond of saying *Yabba Dabba Do*, when he is excited. It's Ken Ham's favorite science program.
Floating population (*liudong renkou*): The hundreds of millions of migrant Chinese who travel the country sweeping streets, selling trinkets and working as unskilled laborers, all to make a living.
Florence Nightingale: 19th century British nurse who is credited with founding the Red Cross.
Flower Room: The love nest in the homes of the Mosuo matrilineal minority, where women can sleep with their walking marriage partners, around Lugu Lake, Sichuan/Yunnan.
Forbidden City: The massive, Imperial Palace of Beijing, which overlooks Tiananmen Square.
Forest Cat: See *Felis*.
Fortune 500: The world's largest corporations, collectively the Princes of Power, the 1%, the world's owners and their political elite who pass and enforce their laws.
Français: The word in French that means *French*.
Frankenstein: The 1818 British novel by Mary Shelley, which is considered one of the first examples of science fiction literature, as it questions humankind's incessant drive towards progress and manipulation of nature.
Free market: libertarian (jungle) capitalist concept that businesses should be able to make money with little or no interference, rules or regulations established by governments, to protect their citizens and the environment from exploitation.
Fujian: A Chinese province, south of Shanghai and which is due west of Taiwan.
Fukishima: The site of the devastating 2011 tsunami in Japan, which wrecked the Daiichi nuclear power plant.
g= gram: 30g/ounce and about 450g/pound.
Gaia: During the Age of Matriarchy, a name for the Great Goddess. Also *Maia*.
Galaxy: A popular Samsung Android mobile phone, the one I use.
Gallup: Respected American public opinion polling company, with offices around the world.

Ganges (River): Major river system in India with its headwaters in the Himalayan glaciers.
Ganhaizi Wetlands: They sit atop Jiuzhaigou Valley, Sichuan, and whose waters violently cascade down into the valley below.
Gansu (甘肃= Sweet Su): Large desert province in Western China and which figures prominently in *44 Days*.
Gao Park: One of the packed public parks where I am with Xiao Gao and her two friends, in Zhongwei, Ningxia.
Garo: Matrilineal people in India and Bangladesh.
Garuda: Buddhist and Hindu icon depicting a bird that resembles a phoenix.
GATT: General Agreement on Tariffs and Trade, was signed in 1947 and lasted until 1994, when it was replaced by the World Trade Organization (WTO) in 1995; established to reduce import tariffs and trade barriers.
GDP: The gross domestic product of a country or state, the sum total of the value of its economic activity.
Gedhun Choekyi: Tibetan 11th Panchen Lama who, at the tender age of six, was and still is disappeared by Baba Beijing.
Gelugpa: The Tibetan Buddhist sect known for its ecclesiastically shaped yellow hats.
Genesis: The first book of the Bible, depicting the Christian creation story, as the first seven days after the start of the universe.
Geneva (Lake): In France and Switzerland.
Genghis Khan: Mongolian, 12th-13th century leader, who reigned over the largest contiguous empire in human history, including much of China.
George Carlin: 20th-21st century American comedian famed for his irreverent, antiestablishment humor.
George Foreman: Retired American boxer, former two-time World Heavyweight Champion, Olympic gold medalist, ordained Baptist minister, author, and entrepreneur. He made millions selling his George Foreman Grill.
George Martin: 20th century British music producer famed for his work with Beatles. His collaboration was so important that he is often called the Fifth Beatle.
George Orwell: 20th century British author who famously wrote the all too prescient, life imitating art, dystopian political novels, *1984* and *Animal Farm*
George W. Bush: 43rd US president, 2001-09.
George Washington: First US president, 1789-97.
Giardia= giardiasis: Intestinal amoebic parasite which can cause severe cyclic diarrhea and go undetected for months. It is treated with tinidazole.
Gideon's Bible: Famed bibles left by Christian proselytizers in hotels and other public places.
Gilded Age: 19th-20th century period in America, where libertarian (jungle) capitalism reigned, culminating in the Great Depression, in 1929.
Gin rummy: Very popular and easily learned card game played in the West.
Girl Scout Cookies: Cookies sold door to door by Girl Scouts to raise money for their troops.
Gitksan: A matrilineal people in Canada.
Gluten: Protein found in wheat but not in rice, which is stretchy and sinewy, like chewing gum; thus giving wheat based noodles much more tensile strength and less friability. Having no gluten, rice noodles are the exact opposite.
Gobi desert: The huge desert covering much of Western and Northern China, as well as Mongolia
Goddess Bay (Nvshenwan = 女神湾): On the Luowa peninsula, Lugu Lake, Sichuan, looking out across the lake.
Golden Bell Lake: Colorful lake in Jiuzhaigou Park, Sichuan.
Golden Gate Bridge: Symbol of San Francisco, California, and the Western United States.
Goldman Sachs: One of the largest Wall Street banks.
Golmud: Provincial city in Qinghai, known for salt lakes and being in the middle of nowhere.
Gongan (公安): China's local security police, found in almost every decent sized town.
Gordian knot: Metaphor for any intractable problem. According to legend, Alexander the Great cut to the chase by simply slicing the knot in half, instead of trying to unwind it by hand. Often associated with Occam's razor.
GPS: global positioning service, which in a mobile phone, has changed the way travel can happen.

Great Depression: The economic and social meltdown of the United States, starting in 1929, following 50 years of Ayn Randian, libertarian (jungle) capitalism.
Great Helmsman: An honorific title given to Mao Zedong, for his *guiding* leadership after independence in 1949. Many would debate his guidance, given the massive failures of the Great Leap Forward and the Cultural Revolution.
Great Namo Gorge: Fabulous, isolated valley on the Sichuan side of Langmusi, Gansu, where I run into the hyperactive Tibetan shepherd, Cidu.
Great Plains: The large grassland area between the Rocky Mountains and the Mississippi Valley, stretching from Canada to Texas, in the US.
Great Wall: Thousands of kilometers worth, stretching across much of Northern China, and built over many centuries, as a defensive barrier from invaders. I saw sections of it in Jiayuguan and Yumen, Gansu.
Gu Kailai (谷开来): 21st century Chinese politician and wife of Bo Xilai, she was convicted of murdering Neil Heywood.
Guangxi: Province in Southern China famous for its picturesque Li River in Guilin.
Guangzhou: Capital of Guangdong Province, known for its rich Cantonese culture, cooking and nonstop work ethic.
Guantanamo: Enclave American prison in Cuba, with a well-deserved reputation for torture, illegal detention and unlawful rendition of Muslims. It is known outside the United States as "the gulag of our times".
Gucci's: Status symbol and very expensive Italian shoes worn by those who can afford them.
Guilin: Guangxi provincial city famous for its beautiful Li River Valley.
Guiyang (贵阳): Capital of Guizhou Province, known for its huge Qingling Park.
Guizhou: Southern province in China that figures prominently in *44 Days*, highlighted by Zhijin Cave and Chishui.
Gulf War: 1991 American led invasion of Kuwait, to liberate it from Iraq, which had invaded and annexed it. Afterwards, Western sanctions that would make the Weimar Republic feel lucky, directly caused the death of 500,000 Iraqi children, by starvation. Madeline Albright, Bill Clinton's ambassador to the UN said, "It was worth it." Really?
Gurkhas: Nepalese people who briefly invaded Tibet and sacked the Tashilhunpo Monastery in 1791.
Gyaltsen Norbu: The other 11th Panchen Lama recognized by Baba Beijing, but rejected by the rest of the world.
G5, G6, G75, G213 and G318: National toll expressways, each costing billions of dollars and together contain hundreds of bridges and as many long tunnels.
H.G. Wells: 19th-20th century British author who wrote science fiction masterpieces such as *Time Machine*, *Invisible Man*, *Island of Doctor Moreau* and *War of the Worlds*.
ha: Hectare, one of which equals 2.5 acres. A hectare is 100m square, or 10,000m^2
Hades: synonym for hell.
Haida: A matrilineal people in British Columbia, Canada.
Haight-Ashbury: San Francisco neighborhood famous as ground central for the sex-drugs-and-rock-n-roll, hippy counterculture of the 1960s.
Halal: Food that is prepared according to Muslim edicts.
Han Dynasty: 206 BC – 220 AD, noted as a golden period of reunification and economic prosperity.
Han: The majority race in China, making up about 92% of the country's citizens. The other 8% are spread out over 55 minorities.
Hangzhou: Zhejiang Province's capital, just south of Shanghai and known for its West Lake and beautiful natural surroundings.
Haochidian (好吃点= Good Eating Snacks): My favorite Chinese brand of lightly sweetened crackers.
Hard seat: The cheapest train ticket you can buy, guaranteed to be packed to the gills with SRO passengers.
Hard sleeper: cheapest train ticket with a bed, each open compartment consisting of three pairs of beds, top, middle and lower.
Harrison Ford: American film actor, active 1967-2010s, who gained fame starring in the swashbuckling, action packed, adventure filled *Indiana Jones* movies.
Harry Potter: British book and movie franchise, 1997-2007, with many elements of witchcraft, inspiration which was drawn

in small part from the Three Sisters, in Shakespeare's play *Macbeth*.
Heat: 1995 American movie, with a climactic airport duel between Robert de Niro and Al Pacino.
Heathrow: London's main airport and one of the busiest in the world.
Heavenly Mandate (天命= *tianming*): The unwritten protocol of all Chinese leaders to keep the country whole, protect the people and provide for their economic prosperity.
Hebei (河北): Mountainous province surrounding Beijing like a big, backward *C*.
Heilongjiang Province: The most northeasterly province in China, with a long border alongside Russia.
Helan Range (贺兰山= Helanshan): Young, desert mountain range outside Yinchuan, Ningxia.
Helanshan Rock Carvings: UNESCO World Heritage Site with 6,000 year old rock carvings, Yinchuan, Ningxia.
Helmsman: See *Great Helmsman*.
Helmud: Afghanistan city occupied by the American military.
Helter Skelter: A Beatles song with frenetic, harrowing guitar riffs, haunting lyrics, and which inspired Charles Manson and his gang during their murderous, 1969 California rampage.
Hexi Corridor (河西走廊= Hexi Zoulang): Famous Silk Road passage through the Qilian Mountains, connecting Dunhuang and Lanzhou, in Gansu.
Hezuo: Grimy industrial town on the drive from Lanzhou to Xiahe, Gansu. White Dragon River's Hong Bei's children go to trade school here.
Highlander Hostel: Deserted hostel where I stayed in the Cangshan Mountains, Dali, Yunnan.
Himalayas: Tallest mountain range in the world, running east from Pakistan to India, China, Nepal and Bhutan, including Mt. Everest in Nepal, the world's tallest peak, at 8,848 meters.
Hinduism: A major world religion, concentrated in India.
Hiragana: One of the Japanese alphabets, which resembles the Lolo minority alphabet in China.
Hitler (Adolf): Austro-German fascist, 1930s-40s, and prime instigator of WWII.
Hobbesian: A dog eat dog world, from Thomas Hobbes, 16th-17th century British philosopher.
Hohot (呼和浩特): Capital of Inner Mongolia and a transit town between Beijing and Yinchuan, Ningxia.
Holiday Inn: Medium priced American hotel chain.
Hollywood: American movie capital, located in Los Angeles, California.
Homo sapiens: The human species.
Hong Bei (红北= Red North): Tibetan tent host at White Dragon River, Langmusi, Gansu.
Hong Kong: Special Administrative Region of China, once a colony of Britain.
Hoovervilles: Great Depression shantytowns for homeless and unemployed people, now replaced with Bushobamavilles.
Hopi: matrilineal people in Western United States.
Houdini: American stunt performer, active 1891-1926, and famous for his escape acts.
Howard Zinn: 20th-21st century American historian and author of the best-selling and influential *A People's History of the United States*.
Huajiao (花椒= flower pepper): Numbing pepper, which puts your mouth to sleep. Very popular in Sichuan inspired dishes and terribly overused these days, in general. All called *majiao*.
Huanglong: Isolated Sichuan airport built solely to serve Jiuzhaigou Park.
Huckleberry Finn: 1884 book by American author, Mark Twain, whose character is very mischievous and playing pranks all the time.
Huey "Kingfish" Long: Left wing Louisiana governor and US senator during the Great Depression, who was gunned down on the steps of the state capitol. His *Share the Wealth* program, scared the bejeezuz out of the Princes of Power and they were overjoyed at his assassination. They of course had nothing to do with it.
Hui: Muslim minority with a big presence in Ningxia Province.
Hukou (户口): Internal passport-like family birth certificate that ties a Chinese where they were born, or even going back to where their parents and grandparents came from.

Hunan: Province in Southern China, home of Mao Zedong and a cradle of Chinese Communism.
Hurricane Katrina: American Gulf Coast monster, which in 2005, largely destroyed New Orleans. Ranked as one of history's 10 most destructive hurricane's ever.
Hydra: A mythological water snake monster.
Hydropower: Electricity generated by turbines, turned by flowing water, and usually built into dams.
Ian and Mona Bayly: Friends with whom I work in Beijing.
Ibiza Rhapsody: The 32GB MP3 player I use to listen to music.
Ice Age: Periods where the Earth largely ices over, especially during last 500 million years.
ID: Any piece of identification, usually with a photo.
Ilan Pappé: 20th-21st century Israeli "new" historian and author, who has shattered all the myths of Israel's founding and ongoing ethnic genocide of the Palestinian people, known as Al-Nakba.
Imelda Marcos: Filipino politician from 1965-2010s and wife of the former president, Ferdinand Marcos. She is known for her flamboyant extravagance and suffered much public ridicule for her collection of 2,700 pairs of shoes.
Inception: American sci-fi movie, 2010, with fabulous concepts of people entering others' dreams and creating dreams within their dreams.
Indiana Jones: Swashbuckling, adventure movie franchise, 1981-2008, starring Harrison Ford.
Indus (River): Flows through Pakistan, with its headwaters coming from the Himalayan glaciers.
Inner Mongolia (内蒙): Huge Autonomous Region in China, comprised of the Gobi Desert and much wide open pastureland, full of cattle, sheep and horses.
Inspector Clouseau: Farcical, French satirical movie character from the Pink Panther movies.
Intelligence agencies: Spy agencies that typically work in other countries, like the CIA (US), MI6 (UK), SVR/GRU (Russia) and the DGSE (France). The US has no fewer than 16 intelligence agencies at home and around the world.
Intercontinental: Worldwide, higher end hotel chain.
Interior Provinces: Chinese provinces that are poorer and less developed, compared to the Blue, or coastal provinces.
International Arabian Horse Association: place where Michael D. "Brownie" Brown worked before heading W. Bush's FEMA.
Inuit: Native American minority, used to be called Eskimos.
Iron Man: A very challenging sporting event of endurance usually involving running, swimming and biking.
Iroquois: Matrilineal people in North America.
Islam: Major world religion concentrated in Northern Africa, the Middle East and the southern half of Asia.
Ivern Ball: Mysterious American poet who has a number of great quotes on the internet.
Ivy League: Elite New England universities, such as Harvard, Princeton, Brown, Dartmouth and Yale.
J.R.R. Tolkien: 20th century British author of the hugely popular *Lord of the Rings* trilogy.
Jack London: Late 19th-early 20th century author of great and gritty outdoors adventure stories, who was an infamous alcoholic.
Jack Palance: American TV-movie actor, active 1947-2004, who won the Academy Award for his role as the trail boss, Curly, in *City Slickers* and whom I remember while hiking White Dragon River, Langmusi, Gansu.
Jade Dragon Snow Mountain (玉龙雪山= Yulong Xueshan): The magnificent mountain range north of Lijiang, Yunnan, where I hiked through the primeval Mushroom Forest.
Jaintia: A matrilineal people in India.
Jalapeno: Spicy hot pepper from Latin America.
James Bond: British MI6 superspy and gadget master, whose book/movie character almost single handedly helped shape a highly romanticized and glorified superman version of espionage around the world.
James Hilton: Early 20th century British author of Shangri-La's *Lost Horizon*.
James Ussher: Irish Catholic Archbishop, 16th-17th century, who counted all the begats in the Book of Genesis, to determine the beginning of creation in 4004 BC – October 22nd at 18:00, to be exact.

Janis Joplin: 60s-70s American Haight-Ashbury diva and rock/blues singer, famous for her hippy clothing or lack thereof; Janis overdosed on heroin at the tender age of 27.
Jared Diamond: 20th-21st century American scientist, historian and author, who wrote *Guns, Germs and Steel* and *Collapse: How Societies Choose to Fail or Succeed*, the former winning the Pulitzer Prize.
Jell-O: Famous, sugary gelatin dessert that wiggles and shakes in the pan, when moved.
Jethro Tull: 1960s-2010s British rock band, who cultivated an old time, woodsy, madrigal theme.
Jetsons: Funny, futuristic American TV cartoon, 1962-87, with zany architecture and technology.
Jews: matrilineal people with origins in the Ancient Near East.
Jiabo Ancient City: Strange tourist center above Jiuzhaigou Park, in Sichuan.
Jialing River: One of the mighty tributaries feeding into the Yangtze River, stretching across Gansu, Sichuan and Chongqing; this last city straddling where these two great rivers meet.
Jiang Qing (江青): Mao's wife, who was set up to take the blame for all the excesses and failures of the Cultural Revolution, along with the then dead Lin Bao.
Jiao (角): 1/10 of an RMB, like a dime. Synonymous with *mao*.
Jiayuguan (嘉峪关= Glorious Valley Pass): Gansu town with its famous eponymous fort.
Jim Morrison: Frank Sinatra-voiced singer of the Doors, famous for exuding a raw, shamanic sexuality. Drank himself to death at the virile age of 27.
Jimmy Stewart: American movie actor, active 1932-91, who played in countless movies, teamed up with Hollywood's best actresses.
Jingtieshan (镜铁山= Mirror Iron Mountain) = Jingtieshan Iron Ore Mine = Jingtieshan Mining Company: The eerie, Twilight Zone town, where I hang out with Communist zombies.
Jinshagou (金沙沟= Gold Sand Canyon): Town outside Chishui, Guizhou, at the foot of Bamboo Sea.
Jinyang Station (金阳): Massively huge bus terminal on the outskirts of Guiyang, Guizhou.
Jiulong (九龙= Nine Dragons) = Jiulongxian (九龙⊠= Jiulongxian): Sichuan town where I got blocked by rockslides and had to turn back up Liqi Valley, to make my way to Lugu Lake, Sichuan/Yunnan.
Jiuzhaigou (九寨沟= Nine Camp Gulley) = Jiuzhaigou World Heritage Nature Park: Crassly commercial Sichuan town and UNESCO World Heritage Site, where I hide out and have the place all to myself for hours.
Jiuzhi (九支): Sichuan's twin city to Chishui, Guizhou.
John Lennon: Beatles member and British rock musician, active 1957-80, until he was gunned down on a New York City sidewalk.
John Pomfret: 20th-21st century American journalist and author of *Chinese Lessons*.
Johnny Appleseed: 19th century American pioneer nurseryman, who planted apple trees in Eastern US.
Jonathan Spence: 20th-21st century British historian and author, who wrote *In Search for Modern China*.
Joseph Rock: Early 20th century Austrian-American explorer and botanist, who traveled in Yunnan.
Joseph Tainter: 20th-21st century American anthropologist, historian and author of *Collapse of Complex Societies*.
Journey to the Center of the Earth: Exciting, by-the-seat-of-your-pants sci-fi adventure book/movie, by Jules Verne.
Jowo Sakyamuni Buddha: Famous 7th century statue at Jokhang Temple, Lhasa, Tibet, which fell out of a wagon in Tagong, Sichuan, whereupon Princess Wencheng ordered a duplicate to be built there on the spot, as well as the town's temple, to protect it.
Jules Verne: Latter 19th-early 20th century French author who wrote great sci-fi/adventure classics such as, *Five Weeks in a Balloon*, *Journey to the Center of the Earth*, *20,000 Leagues Under the Sea* and *Around the World in 80 Days*.
July First Glacier (七一冰川= Qiyi Bingquan): Where I climbed up to at 4,300m, in the Qilian Mountains, Gansu.
Jurassic Age: Primetime era of the dinosaurs, 201-145 million years ago.
Kabul: Afghanistan's capital, which the US military occupies.
Kaishui (开水): In Chinese, this is boiled water, a fixture of daily life for the people here, as they drink tea by the ocean full every day.

Kangding (康定): Important crossroad town on my way to and from Tagong, Sichuan.
Karnataka: Matrilineal people in India.
Kayak: 1-2 person canoe using two bladed paddles and which originated from the Inuit in northern Canada and Greenland.
Ken Fraley: Longtime high school and university friend who, along with Terry Bresin, we climbed up the harrowing Corkscrew at Mammoth Cave.
Ken Ham: Fundamentalist Christian founder of the Creation Museum in Kentucky, US.
Kerala: A matrilineal people in India.
Kerti Gompa monastery: Located in Langmusi, Sichuan.
Kew Gardens: Located in London, one of the world's greatest botanical collections.
kg: Kilogram. 1kg is about 2 pounds.
Kham: Region of the former Kingdom of Tibet. See the map on .
Khasi: A matrilineal people in India.
King Charles XII: Swedish, war mongering 18th century ruler who lost it all invading Russia.
Klick: Slang for a kilometer.
km: Kilometer. 1.6km per mile or 1km is about 0.6 of a mile.
km^2: $1km^2$ is about 0.4 square miles.
KMT: See *Kuomintang*.
kph: Kilometers per hour. 100kph is about 60mph.
Kuai (块): An everyday term for China's currency unit, the RMB.
Kunming: Yunnan's capital, known for its universities, Dianchi Lake and wonderful climate.
Kuomintang: Chiang Kai-Shek's political, military and criminal machine, and later political party in post-independence Taiwan. It means Guomindang (国民党= National Party) in Mandarin.
Kyoto Treaty: 1997 international environmental treaty, ignored by most of the 192 signatories.
La Brea Tar Pits: Dinosaur fossil pit in Los Angeles, full of thick, black, liquid asphalt and tar.
Labrang Tibetan Temples: Located in Xiahe, Gansu, and the most important Tibetan temple complex outside of the Autonomous Region of Tibet.
Land of Snow: A descriptive name for Tibet.
Langmusi (郎木寺= Bright Wood Temple): Tibetan town in Gansu where I take two unbelievable hikes: Great Namo Gorge and White Dragon River.
Lanzhou: The capital of Gansu, known for its Yellow River and Silk Road history.
Lao Pu: Ancient Tibetan woman in whose home I am able to visit, in Qiqing, Gansu.
Laowai (老外= old outsider): Affectionate term for any foreigner.
Lascaux Caves: UNESCO World Heritage Site in France, famous for its Paleolithic paintings; they are compared to the Helan Rock Carvings, Yinchuan, Ningxia.
Laurent Zylberman: 20th-21st century French photographer, photojournalist and co-author of *Tibet, the Last Cry*.
Lawrence Stratton: 21st century American historian, political scientist and co-author of *The Tyranny of Good Intentions*, with Paul Craig Roberts.
Led Zeppelin: 1960s-1980 British rock band, with their iconic ballad, *Stairway to Heaven*.
Lei Feng: Chinese super patriot turned mythical Communist hero and who is still popular today.
Lenape: A matrilineal people from North America.
Lenin (Vladimir): Russian politician and leader of 1917 Bolshevik Revolution.
Leo Tolstoy: Latter 19th-early 20th century Russian author who wrote classics, such as *War and Peace*, *Anna Karenina* and *Death of Ivan Ilych*.
Leona Hemsley: 20th century American businesswoman, famous for being flamboyant, tyrannical and greedy.
Leonardo da Vinci: 15th-16th century Italian Renaissance polymath, writer, inventor and artist.
Leprosy: Mycobacteria skin disease known since biblical times, and unnecessarily but greatly feared in popular culture.

Leshan: Sichuan site of huge Buddha statue, built on the banks of the Min River, during the Tang Dynasty, 618–907AD.
Leslie Box: Music studio speaker that spins, giving a warbling or oscillating sound and used by the Beatles on their Tibetan inspired song, *Tomorrow Never Knows*.
Lhasa: Tibet's ancient and modern capital.
Li De (李德)= Li the German: Otto Braun, German Communist who helped the Red Army in 1930s.
Li River: In Guangxi Province, famous for its sugarloaf mountains.
Li Zhisui: 20th century Chinese historian and author, who was Mao's personal physician for years and wrote *The Private Life of Chairman Mao*.
Liangshan (凉山= Cold Mountain): Sister Sichuan city to Xichang.
Libertarian: Capitalist philosophy that there should be no laws, regulations or government interference in making money, i.e., jungle capitalism.
Lichens: Symbiotic organisms combining fungus and algae, getting their energy from photosynthesis.
Lige: Lugu Lake village where I spend a disappointing evening, Yunnan.
Lijiang Old Town: Song/Tang Dynasty UNESCO World Heritage Site turned into a commercial Sodom and Gomorrah.
Lily Tomlin: 1965-2010s American TV/movie actress and comedian.
Lin Biao (林彪): Red Army general, then in 1966 was appointed successor to Mao Zedong; later failed attempted coup in 1971, where after he died in a mysterious plane crash trying to escape.
Linxia River (临夏= Lookout over Summer): One of the spectacular valleys I drive through on my way to Xiahe, from Lanzhou, Gansu.
Liqi River Valley (立启河沟= Immediate Awakening): Stunningly beautiful Sichuan Tibetan valley I drive up and back down, due to being blocked by rockslides.
Little Red Book of Quotations of Chairman Mao: Handbook edited by Lin Bao and originally published 1964-76. Still a big seller today.
Liuchong River (六冲河= Liuchonghe): Scenic valley outside Zhijin Cave in Guizhou, where I see a bridge being built which is as big as San Francisco's Golden Gate.
Liupanshui (六盘水): Guizhou town where I spend the night on the movie set of *The Road*.
Liverworts: Small, ancient fern-like plants.
Liwubi (里务比岛): Lugu Lake island that is half in Sichuan, half in Yunnan.
Loess (黄土= *huangtu* = yellow soil): Fantastically eroded mesa topped farm land found in Western China.
Lolo: Minority language in China, centered around Northern Yunnan and Southern Sichuan.
Lonely Planet (LP): Celebrated travelers' guide for the budget minded.
Long March (长征= Changzheng): Red Army's 12,500km retreat from Southern China to Shaanxi, in 1934-35, in order to regroup, recoup and rearm.
Longmenshan (龙门山= Dragon Gate Mountain): The 300km long geological fault line in Sichuan and the source of so many devastating earthquakes. I drive across it going up to Kangding/Tagong and back.
Looney Tunes: 1930-60s American TV cartoons, with Bugs Bunny, Daffy Duck, Porky Pig, Foghorn Leghorn and Yosemite Sam, to name a few.
Lord Arnold Toynbee: Acclaimed 20th century British historian and author of *A Study of History*.
Lord of the Rings: Towering science fiction trilogy and movie franchise, written J.R.R. Tolkien.
Lost Horizon: 1933 book, written by British James Hilton, with its fictional, utopian locale, Shangri-La.
Lost World: 1960 American movie, which frequently comes to my mind, as I travel in deserted Western China.
Louis Vuitton: A high end French travel guide and luxury goods merchant.
Louisbourg: Canadian historical theme park in Nova Scotia, which I think of while at Western Film Studios in Yinchuan, Gansu.
LP: See *Lonely Planet*.
Luding (泸定): Sichuan town I pass through on wild ride from Chengdu to Tagong.

Luguhu (泸沽湖= Lugu Lake): Magnificent mountain lake that straddles the Sichuan-Yunnan border.
Luguxian (泸沽县= Lugu County): Village on the Sichuan side of Lugu Lake.
Luhua (绿化= Green Change) Train Station: The second train station in Jiayuguan, mentioned in Lonely Planet, and which almost causes me to miss my train.
Luoshui (洛水): Lugu Lake village on the Yunnan side.
Luowa (洛瓦): Lugu Lake village on the Sichuan side.
Luqu County: Isolated town I drive through from Xiahe to Langmusi, notable for the big glass greenhouse structures the locals install outside their houses, for heat and to dry clothes.
Lvhua: See *Luhua* and *Figure 31*.
m: Meter. 1m equals about 1 yard.
m^2: $1m^2$ is about 10 square feet.
Ma Jian: 20th-21st century Chinese author, whose wonderful travel book, *Red Dust*, helped me formulate 44 Days' concept.
Macbeth: Shakespeare play, where witches, the Three Sisters, figure prominently in the story.
Mad Dog Hill: Name I give to the place where I am attacked by feral dogs, in Tagong, Sichuan.
Mad Max: 1979-85 Australian movies, about a futuristic, post-nuclear, ecosystem-collapsed dystopia.
Mahjong (麻将= *majiang*): Very popular parlor game, with domino like tiles, but played similarly to card games like gin rummy, and which is notorious for being addictive.
Maia: During the Age of Matriarchy, a name for the Great Goddess. Also *Gaia*.
Majiao (麻椒): Numbing pepper, which puts your mouth to sleep. Very popular in Sichuan inspired dishes and terribly overused these days, in general. Also called *huajiao*.
Mala: The Tibetan name for a Buddhist rosary.
Malcolm Lowery: 20th century British author who spent his life writing the towering *Under the Volcano,* while drinking himself to death.
Mama Ala: Tagong Snowland Hostel mother of her three children, who all run the place.
Mammoth Cave National Park: World's longest cave system, in Kentucky, US, and which I recklessly explored by climbing the closed down Corkscrew.
Manchuria: Another name for Northeastern Asia.
Mandarin: Another name for the Chinese language, the national standard version taught throughout the educational system and the *lingua franca* for Chinese speakers all over the world.
Mani stones: Cubed or rectangular prism Buddhist icons built to ask for good fortune and a virtuous life.
Mani wheels: Buddhist drums spun to help those who have died to make it safely to their new reincarnated life.
Mao (毛): 1/10 of an RMB, like a dime. Synonymous with *jiao*.
Mao Zedong: Chinese leader of the Red Army, who unified China to independence in 1949, and was the country's chairman, until his death in 1976. His post-independence track record was mixed at best.
Maotai (茅台酒): China's high alcohol clear spirit, originated in Zunyi, Guizhou.
Marco Polo: 13th-14th century Italian merchant, explorer and author, whose book, *Travels of Marco Polo*, regaled the world for centuries.
Marcus Crassus: 1st century BC Roman general and politician known for his rapacious lust of material wealth and money. Poster boy for the Princes of Power and their political elite.
Marija Gimbutas: 20th century Lithuanian-American matriarchy historian and author.
Mark: The German currency before the creation of the euro. At the end of the Weimar Republic, due to impossibly onerous economic sanctions forced on Germany by the Allied powers after WWI, the Germans were forced to crank up the printing presses to pay all their war debts, resulting in hyperinflation, to the point where it took a wheel barrow full of marks just to buy a loaf of bread.
Marseillaise: The French national anthem.
Martin Jacques: 20th-21st century British author and editor who wrote *When China Rules the World*.

Marx (Karl): 19th century German philosopher and economist, who co-founded Communism with Frederic Engels.
MASL: meters above sea level.
Matriarchy: Societies led or ruled by women.
Matrilineal: Societies where the family lineage follows the mother's name.
Matrilocality: Societies where the groom moves into the bride's family or tribe.
May '68 protests: Widespread, antiestablishment youth protests that transformed national, even European politics.
Maya Angelou: 20th-21st century American poet and civil rights activist.
Medicaid: American social program to provide medical care for the least fortunate.
Medicare: American social program to provide medical care for the elderly.
Medieval 5th-15th centuries.
Meghalaya: A matrilineal people in India.
Mekong (River): Starting in the Himalayan glaciers, it flows through Yunnan, Laos, Cambodia and Vietnam.
Melamine: A chemical that can be added to foodstuffs to give false, higher protein levels when tested, and which was used by unscrupulous players in the Chinese milk business in 2008, causing a number of deaths and thousands of ill people.
MEMC: American company making silicon wafers for solar panels.
Memory Hole: From George Orwell's book, *1984*, a figurative place where any past or present information harmful to the Princes of Power is put, to be expunged from the public's conscious and forgotten forever. Works every time.
Mengniu Dairy Company (蒙牛): Inner Mongolian outfit caught up in melamine-tainted milk scandal.
Merlin Stone: 20th century American matriarchy historian and author.
Mesoamerica: Academic name for Central America.
Methuselah: Biblical character believed by the faithful to have lived for 969 years
Metro: a French synonym for subway; also the British tube.
MI6: British foreign intelligence or spy agency.
Miao: Minority based in Yunnan and Guizhou.
Michael D. "Brownie" Brown: Hapless, unqualified head of FEMA in George W. Bush's administration, who totally bungled the government's response to Hurricane Katrina.
Michelin Guide: High end travel and restaurant guide.
Middle Ages: 5th-15th centuries.
Middle Kingdom: A quaint name for China, translated from its Chinese name.
Milk scandal: See *melamine*.
Min River: Major river in Sichuan and on whose banks is carved the massive Leshan Buddha.
Minangkabau: A matrilineal people in Western Sumatra.
Ming dynasty chronicle (明史= *mingshi*): The official government document that recounts the travels of Zheng He to Africa and the Middle East.
Ming Dynasty: 1368–1644AD, known as "one of the greatest eras of orderly government and social stability in human history."
Mirror Lake: In Jiuzhaigou Park, Sichuan, where I make my getaway to be all alone in the park the rest of the day.
Mission Impossible: 60s-70s American TV show, then movies, 1996-2010s, full of exciting, action packed spy thriller scenes.
ml: Milliliter. About 30ml to an ounce, 250ml/cup and 950ml to a quart.
mm: Millimeter. About 25mm to an inch and 300mm to a foot.
Mogao Caves: UNESCO World Heritage Site in Dunhuang, Gansu, where ivory statues and jewelry are being sold.
Mohammed Ali: World champion American boxer and antiwar activist, active 1960s-70s.
Monica Sjöö: 20th century Swedish matriarchy historian and author.
Moon Gate (月门= Yuemen): A movie set at Western Studios, Yinchuan, Ningxia.
Moss: Small, ancient plants that generally cover the ground or live on trees.
Mosuo: Minority centered around Lugu Lake, Yunnan, and still a practicing matrilineal culture.

Mount Jinire: Sacred Tibetan mountain overlooking Tagong, Sichuan, and upon which I have a harrow climb up.
Mr. Bean: 20th-21st century British comedic TV & movie character, played by Rowan Atkinson, portraying a child-like, self-centered, totally hapless man, whose only friend is his stuffed animal, Teddy.
Mr. Bin: With whom I eat BBQ, while discussing Mosuo matrilineal culture, at Lugu Lake, Sichuan.
Ms. Bao: My Highlander Hostel hostess in the Cangshan Mountains, above Dali, Yunnan.
Ms. Guo: My Chishui hostel owner who is a mahjong addict.
MSG: monosodium glutamate, another kind of salt condiment used a lot in Chinese cooking.
Mt. Olympus: The mythical home of the major Olympian gods and goddesses. The real mountain is located in Greece.
Musée Guimet: Located in Paris, France, it houses one of the world's largest collections of Asian art outside the region. See *Mogao Caves.*
Mushroom Mountain: Name of the primeval forest I hike through on Jade Dragon Snow Mountain, due to the amazing variety of colorful fungus growing everywhere, Lijiang, Yunnan.
Muslim: An adherent of Islam.
Mussolini (Benito): Italian fascist leader from 1922, till his ousting in 1943, during which time he allied Italy to Germany and Japan during WWII, in what was known as the Axis Powers.
Muyajin Temple (木雅金= Wood Elegant Gold): New looking temple outside of town, where I see many Tibetan cowboys and cowgirls hanging out and picnicking, Tagong, Sichuan.
My Way: Jazz vocal song made famous by Frank Sinatra.
Myanmar: Another name for Burma.
Myrmidons: Mythical Greek soldiers created from ants, who blindly and bravely followed their heroic leader, Achilles, into battle.
NAFTA: 1994 North American Free Trade Agreement, which reduced tariffs and trade barriers between Canada, the United States and Canada, and which caused tremendous social and economic dislocation, as a result.
Nairs: A matrilineal people in India.
Nakhi: A synonym, see *Naxi.*
Namo Creek: See *Great Namo Creek.*
Nanjing, Jiangsu Province's capital, known for its rich Chinese history, occasionally being the country's capital and for the Rape of Nanjing during WWII, at the hands of the Japanese military.
Nanning: Guangxi Province's capital, known for its lush, green tropical vegetation.
Napoleon Bonaparte: 18th-19th century French politician, general and leader, who knew a thing or two about bankers and being in debt. His observations still hold true today.
National Geographic: American based magazine covering all living things, culture and geography. Famous for its outstanding photography and maps.
National People's Congress: China's legislative body, like the House of Representatives in the US or House of Commons in the UK.
Native American: Also known as Indians.
Navajo: A matrilineal people in Western United States.
Naxi Hotel: Probably the nicest hotel I stay in during the whole trip, with an unforgettable view of the Jade Dragon Snow Mountains from my window, Lijiang, Yunnan.
Naxi: A minority concentrated around Lijiang, Yunnan, that used to be matrilineal.
Nayong (纳雍): Isolated Guizhou town, where I see a late night madrigal gypsy traveling show.
Nazi: 20th century fascist movement headed by Adolph Hitler.
Negeri: A matrilineal people in Malaysia.
Nehru: Political family dynasty in India, whose men wore celebrated, open, collarless shirts.
Neil Heywood: British businessman who got caught up in Chongqing intrigue and was poisoned to death by Gu Kailai, wife of Bo Xilai.

Neil Shubin: American paleontologist, who in 2004 discovered the evolutionary, sea-land connecting fossil, Tiktaalik, much to the chagrin of creationists.
Nembutal: A powerful, fast acting narcotic.
Nero: 1st century Roman emperor, who orchestrated arson of a city quarter to make room for his new palace, and thus making no efforts to extinguish it. Using it as a black flag operation, he skillfully blamed the Christians for it, thus giving a pretext to persecute them.
New England: Northeast US corridor, stretching from Maine in the north to Massachusetts in the south, but popularly includes New York, New Jersey and Pennsylvania.
New Orleans: Large Gulf Coast port city on Mississippi River in Louisiana, US, which was largely destroyed by Hurricane Katrina in 2004.
New World: Name given by Euro-American colonialists for North, Central and South America.
Newspeak: From George Orwell's book, *1984*, to describe language used by the Princes of Power to negate the truth, like calling nuclear missiles *Peacekeepers*, torture as *enhanced interrogation* and the slaughter of innocents in war *collateral damage*.
Niagara Falls: Wide but not tall falls on the border between the US and Canada, famous for honeymooners.
Ningxia (宁夏= Peaceful Summer): First province I visit during *44 Days*, with Yinchuan and Shapotou.
Nixon Richard, 37th US president, 1969-74, resigned from office to avoid impeachment for perjury and corruption.
Noam Chomsky: 20th-21st century American, MIT professor, author, linguist, philosopher, cognitive scientist, logician, political critic, activist, and a major thorn in the side of the Princes of Power.
Noel Coward: 20th century British playwright, composer, director, actor and singer, who wrote the play, *Easy Virtue*.
Normandy: A region in Northern France, where I lived for five years.
Notre Dame: A celebrated medieval, gothic cathedral in Paris, France.
Novocain: a local painkiller, often used in dentistry.
Number 9: A bizarre, psychedelic Beatles song, composed of almost nothing but sound effects and recordings of everyday life, all connected and mixed together.
Nuorilang (诺日朗): The big connecting point in the middle of Jiuzhaigou Park, Sichuan.
Nuosu: Synonym for Lolo, see *Lolo*.
O'Hare Airport: In Chicago, Illinois and one of the world's biggest and busiest, which I think about at Guiyang, Guizhou's massive bus station, Jinyang.
Obi Wan Kenobi: The heroic *Stars Wars* Jedi Knight movie character.
Occam's razor: The concept that the simplest solution to difficult problems is usually the best one.
OECD (Organization for Economic Co-operation and Development): Essentially, Europe, North America, Australia and New Zealand, with Japan, South Korea, Chile, Mexico and Israel added for good measure.
Official narrative: Synonym for the Washington/London/Paris consensus, i.e., what the Princes of Power and their political elite want the public to accept as the truth, with the help of Newspeak and the Memory Hole.
Oklahoma State University Stillwater, Oklahoma, where I got my Bachelor's Degree.
Oklahoma: In West South Central United States, the state where I grew up.
Old Continent: Another, somewhat disparaging name for Europe.
Old Testament: The first half of the Bible, based on the Jewish Pentateuch.
Olympia Press: French book publisher famous for printing Vladimir Nabokov's *Lolita* and William S. Burroughs's controversial novel, *Naked Lunch*, as well as Paul Ableman's *I Hear Voices*.
Om Mani Padme Hum: Universal Buddhist chant of supplication.
On the Beach: 1957 British-Australian post-nuclear war, end of the world story, by Nevil Shute; made into a movie in 1959. The final beach scene is of the last human survivors left on the Planet.
One Flew over the Cuckoo's Nest: 1975 American movie, based on the eponymous 1962 book by Ken Kesey, which takes place in a mental asylum, back in the day of lobotomies, shock therapy and tons of Thorazine.

One Million Years B.C.: See *Raquel Welch.*
One-fifth: China has this proportion of the world's people.
Orson Welles: 20th century American movie actor, director, writer and producer, most famous for his film, *Citizen Kane.*
Orwellian: From the book *1984*, written by George Orwell, means anything depicting a fascist/communist totalitarian dystopia.
Osama Bin Laden: Purportedly, the mastermind of the 2001 9/11 attack on the United States.
Oscar: Statue given for the Academy Awards, during this big annual Hollywood extravaganza.
OSHA (Occupational Safety and Health Administration): US, federal agency established in 1970 to regulate the safety, health and wellbeing of employees, laborers and workers.
Other, the = The Dreaded Other: Outsiders, foreigners and any groups of people that your tribe decides should be feared, persecuted, ethnically cleansed or exterminated.
Otto Braun: See *Li De.*
Ouigher (魏格): Turkic speaking Muslim minority concentrated in Western China, especially in Xinjiang.
Overseas Tibetan Hotel: A place that tried to rip me off when I tried to check in, Xiahe, Gansu.
Paichusuo (派出所): The local police station.
Pale Blue Dot: A name for Earth, from the book by the same name, written by astrophysicist Carl Sagan.
Palestine: Near East territory surrounding Jerusalem, that was ethnically cleansed to create Israel in 1948.
Panchen Lama: A Tibetan religious leader, second only to the Dalai Lama.
Pandora: See *Avatar.*
Party: When capitalized, it means the Chinese Communist Party.
Paul Ableman: 20th century British playwright and novelist, wrote *I Hear Voices*, a day in the life of a schizophrenic.
Paul Craig Roberts: Economist, columnist, co-founder of Reaganomics; former editor for the Wall Street Journal and Business Week, and who co-wrote *Tyranny of Good Intentions.*
Paul Pelliot: Early 20th century French anthropologist and adventurer, who went to Mogao Caves, Dunhuang, Gansu.
Peace Corps: 2-year American volunteer program, to work overseas with local partners in development projects.
Peacock River: One of the colorful rivers in Jiuzhaigou Park, Sichuan.
Pearl Shoals and Pearl Waterfall: The huge expanse of shallow cascades that finish as the roaring Pearl Waterfall in Jiuzhaigou Park, Sichuan.
Pell grants: Federal American program to subsidize university expenses for those with limited income.
Penguin Books: Highly regarded British publisher.
People's Liberation Army (PLA): The largest standing army in the world and protector of the Heavenly Mandate. It is the third rail of China's Communist political hierarchy, along with the State Council and the National People's Congress.
People's Republic of China: The official name of China.
Perpetual War: From George Orwell's novel, *1984*, the Princes of Power never stop engaging in war in order to maintain fear among the people, hatred of the Other and profits from its conduct for the 1% and their political elite.
Persia: Ancient civilization in what is now modern Iran.
Peter Goullart: Russian-born traveler, explorer and author; during the latter half of the 20th century, he traveled to Yunnan.
Pink Floyd: 60s-90s British rock band; the iconic cover of their *Animals* album depicts London's Battersea Power Station, with a pig floating above it.
Pink Panther: 1964-2010s American-British movies, with bumbling spoof investigator, Inspector Clouseau making a mess of everything he touches or tries.
Pinyin: The Latin alphabet transliteration of written Chinese characters. It is what I use to input and write in Mandarin on computers and mobile phones.
Pivot: The US's not so subtle shift of the majority of its naval fleet from the Arab Gulf to the coast of China and Russia's eastern flank, in an effort to enforce its Bellum Americana.
PLA: See *People's Liberation Army.*

Planet of the Apes: 1968 American futuristic, sci-fi movie, whose final post-apocalyptic scene shows astronaut Charleston Heston walking up to the Statue of Liberty, which is sticking halfway up out of a shallow, deserted ocean beach. It was filmed near Malibu, California.
Plateau: When capitalized, it means the Tibetan Plateau.
Pleistocene: Age of early Homo sapiens and repeated Ice Ages, 2,588,000 to 11,700 years ago.
Posttraumatic stress disorder (PTSD): A state of psychosis that develops in people who see or live through shocking or traumatic events, such as combat, war, rape, torture, extreme violence or severe bodily injury. As a result, the victim can have serious psychological problems, resulting in violent outbursts against others or oneself, abusive behavior, substance abuse and suicidal tendencies. Studies since the Vietnam War, up to today's Iraq and Afghanistan, show that 10-30% of US combat veterans return home with varying degrees of PTSD, even if they were not physically injured.
Prayer wheel: See *Mani wheel.*
Pre-Columbian: Means the time before Columbus arrived to the New World, in 1492.
Princes of Power: The world's owners, the 1% and their political elite who pass their laws and enforce them.
Princess Grace of Monaco: Former Academy Award winning American actress turned married royal, whose stunning beauty was outdone by her incredible poise, presence and sangfroid in public settings. I think of her when I meet the acne faced restaurant owner in Qiliqiaoxiang, Dali, Yunnan.
Princess House Island (王妃岛= Wangfeidao): Tiny island on the Sichuan side of Lugu Lake, where I see a huge, luxurious, *James Bond* chateau for rent.
Princess Wencheng: 7th century princess who had the monastery built in Tagong, to protect a newly built statue of Buddha. She was traveling to Lhasa to marry the Tibetan King, Songtsen Gampo. See: *Jowo Sakyamuni Buddha.*
Pueblos: ancient Native American stone or brick houses built into or against the side of cliff faces in the Western US, as well as in Red Rock Canyon Park, Chishui, Guizhou.
Punch and Judy: Puppet show dating back to 16th century, Italian, traveling madrigal shows, like what I experience in Nayong, Guizhou.
Punjabi: A tribal and language group in modern Pakistan, which was part of colonialized British India, and during the Sino-Sikh War, they briefly and miserably invaded Tibet.
Qiang: A minority people found in the Y-shaped Jiuzhaigou Valleys, Sichuan.
Qilian Mountains: The 5,500m range that figures so prominently in my travels in Gansu.
Qiliqiaoxiang (七里桥乡): Deserted stop where I get off to start my adventure in Dali, Yunnan, and where I meet the acne faced Princess Grace of Monaco.
Qing Dynasty: 1644 to 1912AD, considered a huge failure for not maintaining the Heavenly Mandate, with the century of humiliation happening on their watch. The fact that they were Manchu and not Han, just makes it worse.
Qingdao: Shandong city famous for its German inspired beer.
Qinghai (青海): Neighboring province next to Gansu, known for the source of the Yellow and Yangtze Rivers, vast isolation and being Amdo in the former Kingdom of Tibet.
Qingke (青稞): Alpine barley, which grows above 3,000 MASL, where other grains will not. Thus, it is widely grown on the Tibetan Plateau.
Qingling Park (黔灵公园): The huge city park where a total stranger and his girlfriend amuse themselves in wonder, as they stroke the hair on my forearms, Guiyang, Guizhou.
Qingyi River (青衣江): The amazing Lost World cum Pandora valley I climb up, from Chengdu to Tagong, Sichuan.
Qiqing (祁清= Vast Clear): The strange new town where I explore a deserted Tibetan mud hut village and get invited inside the home of Lao Pu, Gansu.
QQ: This is the equivalent of Chinese email. It is also a text messaging service.
Quantitative easing: Newspeak for the US government printing one trillion dollars a year of paper money to keep the too big to fail banks solvent and Wall Street's stock market afloat.
Queen of Hearts: From the book *Alice in Wonderland*, the cruel and blood thirsty monarch who loves cutting off heads.

Qujing (曲靖), Guizhou town I drive through on the Kunming-Caohai leg.
Quran: Islam's holy book. Also spelled Koran.
R&D: research and development.
Rachel Carson: American marine biologist, conservationist and author, whose 1962 book, *Silent Spring*, helped launch the worldwide environmental movement.
Rachel Welch: American TV/movie actress and sex symbol, active 1964-present, whose animal skin bikini in the UK movie, *One Million Years B.C.*, helped launch her to stardom. The poster sold in the millions.
Rafal Cebulko: Polish friend I traveled with from Xiahe, Gansu to Songpan, Sichuan, whose last name means *onion.*
Rapeseed: See *colza.*
Reagan Ronald, 40th US president, 1981-89.
Red Army (红军= *hongjun)*: Mao Zedong's Communist soldiers who liberated China from the Japanese and the KMT, 1930s-49, and became the People's Liberation Army after independence.
Red Guards: Millions of Cultural Revolution youth, who for years went on murderous, bloody, terrifying rampages, mass vandalism and destruction, all ostensibly to purify China and its people of counterrevolution.
Red River Valley: Very scenic river running between Oklahoma and Texas, US.
Red Rock Canyon (红石野谷= Hongshi Yegu): Chishui, Guizhou park where I see ancient pueblos, like those found in the Western US.
Red Rock Hostel: Where the innkeeper told me they had no beds to let, and where I was probably set up by the Tara Tibetan Torquemada, Xiahe, Gansu.
Red Sorghum: 1987 film by Zhang Yimou, which helped put Chinese cinema on the Western map.
Reed Lake: One of the colorful lakes at Jiuzhaigou Park, Sichuan.
Reinhold Niebuhr: 20th century American theologian, ethicist and author, whose Serenity Prayer has been adopted in many languages around the world.
Renewable energy: Wind, solar, wood, ethanol and hydropower.
Renmin Street: The very long street making up the town of Xiahe, Gansu.
Republican: One of two US political parties, known for giving priority to the 1%, the Princes of Power.
RER (Réseau Express Régional = Regional Express Network): The magnificent French train system around Paris.
Reserve currency: The currency countries save up in order to import goods and services; since WWII, this has been the US dollar.
Revolver: 1966 Beatles album, with the Tibetan Book of the Dead inspired song, *Tomorrow Never Knows.*
Rhinoceros Lake: A colorful lake in Jiuzhaigou Park, Sichuan.
Riane Eisler: 20th century Austrian-born American matriarchy historian and author.
Richter: Logarithmic earthquake scale. A 7.0 quake is 10 times more powerful than a 6.0 and an 8.0 is 100 times stronger than a 6.0.
Rizegou Valley (日则沟): One of the three valleys in Jiuzhaigou Park, Sichuan.
RMB (人民币= people's money): China's official currency. For *44 Days*, the exchange rate is about RMB 6.3/$ or RMB 8.0/€.
Road, The: 2009 American movie, based on the post-apocalyptic nightmare world of Cormac McCarthy's 2006 novel of the same name.
Robert Fisk: 20th-21st century writer, journalist and Middle East correspondent of The Independent; holds more British and international journalism awards than any other foreign correspondent.
Rock Hudson: American TV/movie actor, active 1948-84, whose dashing good looks put him teamed up with all the top actresses of his day.
Rod Serling: American TV producer and writer of the wildly popular sci-fi show, *The Twilight Zone*, 1959-64. I imagined his bobble head in Jingtieshan, Gansu. He was also a fearlessly outspoken liberal activist, at a time when it was dangerous to do so in the United States.

Ron Paul: American libertarian politician from Texas, who gets plaudits from the left for his principled stand against America's war machine and hegemony around the world.
Ron Unz: 20th-21st century American author, political activist and editor of the American Conservative magazine.
Roof of the World: A colorful name for Tibet.
Rope a Dope: Technique whereby a boxer lies against the ring's ropes, clammed up in a defensive position, while letting their opponent wear themselves out pummeling them, without really sustaining any injury.
Rosa Parks: African-American activist who, by refusing to sit in the back of a public bus, helped ignite the civil rights movement.
Route 66: Iconic 2-lane highway from Chicago, Illinois to Los Angeles, California, symbolizing America's post WWII freedom of the road consumer ethic.
Rumble in the Jungle: Historic 1974 boxing event in Kinshasa, Zaire. It pitted the undefeated world heavyweight champion, George Foreman against former world champion and challenger Muhammad Ali. Ali won by knocking out Foreman in the eighth round. It has been called, "arguably the greatest sporting event of the 20th century".
Rumbler: a synonym for earthquake.
Rumi: 13th century Persian poet, jurist and theologian.
Russell Thornton: 20th century American historian and author about Native Americans.
Sangha: One of Buddhism's Three Jewels, this one being community; the other two being *dharma* (the path to righteousness) and Buddha himself.
Sanglou: Member of the Tibetan family who owns Snowland Hostel, Tagong, Sichuan.
Sanlu Dairy Company (三鹿): Inner Mongolian infant formula provider caught up in the melamine tainted milk scandal.
Savoy: High end hotel in London, with a long historical list of the rich and famous who stayed there.
Sderot: Town in Palestine/Israel.
Sembilan: A matrilineal people in Malaysia.
Serenity Prayer: Famous aphorism about wisdom, written by Reinhold Niebuhr.
Serer: A matrilineal people in Senegal and Gambia.
Serti Gompa Temple: Where I watched a sermon given to monks, by a beautifully decked out chief priest, Langmusi, Gansu.
Seventeen Point Agreement: Sino-Tibetan accord signing away Tibet's independence, after China's invasion in 1950.
SEZ: See *special economic zone*.
Shaanxi Sculpture Design Institute: Made the 39m tall, steel, abstract, revolutionary statue in Jiayuguan, Gansu.
Shade (沙德): Liqi Valley town where Zhaxi handed my Tibetan posse and me off to his brother, Ge.
Shamagh: Red and white checked Arab headdress that has a thousand uses when traveling.
Shandong Province: Large northern coastal province known for its agricultural production and Qingdao beer.
Shanghai: City-province, one of five designated by Baba Beijing: Beijing, Tianjin, Shanghai, Guangzhou and Chongqing. It is the financial capital of China and has one of the sexiest skylines in the world.
Shangri-La: Zhongdian's adopted name to increase tourism, and it has worked brilliantly, Yunnan.
Shanxi (山西): Northern province known for the Yungang Caves, Xuankongsi, Pingyao and Wutaishan, among many interesting sites.
Shapotou (沙坡头= Sandy Hilltop): Town that sports the Disneyland-in-the-sand park on the Yellow River, and where I stay on Xiao Gao's peaceful farm, Ningxia.
Sharengang (杀人岗= Murderer's Ridge): An historical location on the ride from Chengdu to Tagong, Sichuan.
Shenfenzheng: Chinese national ID card.
Shenzhen: China's first Special Economic Zone, just north of Hong Kong.
Shigatse: 2nd largest city in Tibet, after Lhasa, known for the Tashilhunpo Monastery
Shijiazhuang (石家庄), Hebei Province's capital and largest city, known for its numerous military schools and some of the world's worse air pollution.
Shizhangdong Waterfall (十丈洞瀑布= Meter Cave Waterfall): The resplendent 76m tall waterfall that is 3.5 times

taller than Niagara Falls, in Chishui, Guizhou.
Shock Doctrine: Libertarian (jungle) capitalism ploy where formerly protected economies are opened up with minimal or ignored rules, regulations and controls, for the Princes of Power, both local and foreign to exploit. Excellent examples of this include the USSR, Libya, Iraq, Afghanistan, Poland, South Africa, Chile and the tiger economies during the 1997 Asian financial crisis.
Shriners: An ancient Arab order with very colorful, Ottoman inspired costumes.
Shuanglong Falls: One of the many beautiful falls in Jiuzhaigou Park, Sichuan.
Shuhe Old Town: The release valve for people to seek refuge from the Las Vegas, harlot madness of Lijiang Old Town, Yunnan.
Shuixing yanghua (水性杨花): Lugu Lake flower and Chinese name of Noel Coward's 2008 inspired movie, *Easy Virtue.*
Shuzheng Falls (树正沟) and Lake: Beautifully combined lake and falls in Jiuzhaigou Park, Sichuan.
Sichuan Province: the belly of the Han beast and the heart of the Yangtze River, it sits on one of the most earthquake prone fault lines in the world, Longmenshan.
Sidonggou (四洞沟= Four Caves Canyon): The most popular and one park I did not visit in Chishui, Guizhou.
Siheyuan (四合院= four enclosed court): classic Chinese home with an open air, square courtyard and three sides of rooms for living quarters, with the front wall facing the street with its main entrance.
Silent Spring: See *Rachel Carson.*
Silk Road: Land and sea trade routes that connected Asia, Africa and Europe, from the 3rd century BC till the 15th century AD.
Simon and Garfunkel: 50s-2010s American folk and rock duo, who sang *Feeling Groovy*, on their *Bookends* album.
Sinatra (Frank): Very popular American jazz vocalist, active 1935-1995, who sang *My Way.*
Since Ma Is Playing Mah Jong: Song about mahjong, made famous by singer Eddie Cantor.
Sinoland: Synonym for all the Chinese people around the world.
Sino-Sikh War: One of the few times Tibet has ever been invaded, this time in 1841.
Sirens: Mythical Greek enchantresses, whose hypnotic singing would lure sailors towards them, so their boats would crash ashore.
Skeleton Coast: In Namibia, Africa, where hundreds of boats have crashed ashore over the centuries, even in modern times.
Skiff: A flat bottomed boat.
Slip 'n' Slide: Children's water game.
Slobodan Milosevic: Serbian politician and leader convicted of war crimes and genocide against Muslims, for his involvement in the 1990s Yugoslav Wars.
SMS: A text message.
Snow Lion: Mythical Tibetan icon.
Snowland Guesthouse: Where I stayed in Tagong, Sichuan.
Social Security: Federal American program to provide Old-Age, Survivors, and Disability Insurance (OASDI), as well as social welfare and social insurance programs.
Socrates: Heavyweight 5th century BC Greek philosopher, who famously would answer his students' questions with more questions.
Sodom and Gomorrah: Biblical place of carnal sin, from which comes the word *sodomy.*
Soft seat: On Chinese trains, slightly wider and more comfortable version of the hard seat.
Soft sleeper: On Chinese trains, luxurious, private cabins with four big beds, whose train tickets are very difficult to get.
Song Dynasty: 960-1279AD. Considered successful in honoring its Heavenly Mandate, as it was the first government in world history to nationally issue banknotes or true paper money, and the first Chinese government to establish a permanent standing navy. This dynasty also saw the first known use of gunpowder, as well as the first discernment of true north using a compass. Most importantly for the Heavenly Mandate, the empire doubled its population, through expanded and improved rice production.

Songpan (松潘): Staging town to get to Jiuzhaigou Park and where I unwittingly buy a maggot infested hunk of dried yak meat, Sichuan.
Songtsen Gampo: See *Princess Wencheng*.
Sophia Loren: Italian movie actress, active 1950-present, of exceptional womanly beauty.
Sotheby's: British brokers of fine and decorative art, jewelry, real estate, and collectibles.
Southern Silk Road: See *Tea-Horse Road*.
Soylent Green: 1973 American sci-fi movie, depicting futuristic, Malthusian nightmare America, with people teeming like rats and secretly being fed human meat, via a product being sold as vegetarian Soylent Green. Starring Charleston Heston and Edward G. Robinson in his last acting role before dying, and whose character ironically commits suicide.
Special Economic Zone: Zones set up by Baba Beijing, offering tax and duty concessions, along with favorable investment subsidies, starting with Shenzhen in the 80s; now they are everywhere in China.
Special relationship: UK's decision to faithfully follow the US's lead on most world economic, diplomatic and military matters, as the British Empire began to weaken, starting in the 1890s. Since WWII, Britain's obedience has unfortunately been slavish.
Spiderman: 2002 American movie, depicting the wall climbing, skyscraper leaping superhero from Marvel Comics.
Spiderwoman: Less well known wall climbing, skyscraper leaping Marvel comic book heroine.
Spielberg Steven: 20th-21st century American film director, screenwriter and producer, including many science fiction and adventure themes.
Spinal Tap: Fictional British parody heavy metal band, who made the spoof movie, *This Is Spinal Tap*. In one scene, a band member shows the audience how on *their* amplifiers, the volume knob doesn't go to 10, but to *11*, just like at Jiayuguan Fort, Gansu.
SRO: See *standing room only*.
St. Elsewhere: A metaphor for someplace better.
Stairway to Heaven: Anthemic Led Zeppelin ballad song.
Stalin (Joseph): Early Russian Communist revolutionary, then political leader of the Soviet Union, active 1910s-50s. Knew how to beat Hitler and the Nazis and not somebody you wanted to mess with. He killed millions of people.
Stand Up: Jethro Tull album depicting the band members as wildly hirsute, bearded gnomes.
Standing room only: Any public venue, like a train or concert, where all the seats are taken, and everybody else is forced to stand.
Star Spangled Banner: American national anthem.
Star Trek: American TV/movie science fiction franchise, 1966-2010s, depicting interstellar space travel.
Star Wars: American TV/movie science fiction franchise, 1978-2010s, depicting interstellar space travel.
State Council: China's main governing body and most authoritative leadership group, akin to a president's/prime minister's cabinet in the US/UK, but much more powerful.
State Grid: China's national electric company, playing a big role in electric car use, Yinchuan, Ningxia.
Statue of Liberty: Famous statue in New York City, a gift from the French government, symbolizing freedom.
Stele: Any geometric shaped structure often with religious or spiritual significance, usually made of stone or rocks.
Sterling Seagrave: 20th century American historian and author, specializing in China and Asia. He wrote the *Soong Dynasty*.
Steve Evans: World traveling friend I meet during *44 Days*, Yinchuan, Ningxia and Dunhuang, Gansu.
Stonewall: 1969 New York City riots protesting harassment and arrest of gays. It was later recognized as the start of the gay liberation movement.
Studs Terkel: 20th century American author, historian, actor and broadcaster. Won the Pulitzer Prize in 1985 for his book, *The Good War*, an oral history of WWII.
Stuff: Capitalized, it is accumulated belongings, mostly superfluous and short lived.
Stupa: Also called a chorten, a statue-like figure that abstractly represents a sitting Buddha in meditation.
Sumac: Large bush with big heads of red berries that make an excellent herbal tea, high in vitamin C.

Sumeri: Part of a Buddhist rosary, where it is held together and contains a counter.
Sun Yat-Sen: 20th century Chinese politician and founder of the modern Chinese republic, started in 1912.
Suyukou National Park (苏峪口公园): Beautiful, forested mountain park, outside Yinchuan, Ningxia.
Swan Lake (天鹅湖= Tian'e Hu): Mysterious Tibetan village advertised in Lonely Planet, but never found, Qiqing, Gansu.
S2, S102, S208, S213, S215, S302, S307 and S312 highways: Provincial, 2-lane highways of varying quality, most of them anus clenching roller coaster rides.
T: Metric ton equals 1,000kg, or about two US tons.
Tagong (塔公= pagoda public): Isolated Tibetan town visited in Sichuan.
Tagong Sally: Tagong Snowland Hostel owning family member, who helps run the place.
Tahoe (Lake): On the border between California and Nevada, US.
Taiwan: Independent island republic created by the KMT when fleeing Mainland China after WWII, and according to the Heavenly Mandate, is considered by Baba Beijing to be part and parcel of the Grand Chinese Republic: it has just temporarily lost its way for the time being.
Taiyuan: Shanxi's province capital, known for the Yungang Caves and the nearby Muta pagoda and Hanging Temple, Xuankongsi.
Tang Dynasty: 618–907AD, had a very mixed bag of good and bad for the honoring the Heavenly Mandate.
Tangshan: Massive 1976 earthquake, Hebei Province, killing hundreds of thousands of people
Tao River (洮河= Cleansing River): One of the beautiful valleys I drive through from Lanzhou to Xiahe, Gansu.
Tara Guesthouse: Where I meet the Tara Tibetan Torquemada, Xiahe, Gansu.
Tarzan: American Edgar Rice Burroughs' early 20th century books about a feral child raised by great apes in the African jungle.
Tashilhunpo Monastery Tibet, built in 1447 by the Gelugpa Yellow Hat sect, and sacked by invading Gurkhas in 1791.
Tassili Plateau, Algeria: Magnificent high altitude desert plateau along the southeastern border of the country; they are compared to the Helan Rock Carvings, Yinchuan, Ningxia.
Tea-Horse Road: Also called the Southern Silk Road, it connected China and the more famous Silk Road to Burma, Tibet, Sichuan and Yunnan, and went right through Lijiang and Dali.
Tenzin Gyatso: The current Dalai Lama, exiled in India.
Teotihuacan pyramid: In Mexico, whose precipitous incline I compare to my ascent up the Cangshan Mountains in Dali, Yunnan.
Terminator: 1984 sci-fi movie classic, directed by James Cameron, whose cyborg character, played by Arnold Schwartzenegger, tells a police station receptionist, "I'll be back", when refused entry. He proceeds to go outside and drive a car at high speed in the reception area, tearing down the wall, to gain entry inside.
Terry Bresin: Old university friend who, along with Ken Fraley, we climbed up the harrowing Corkscrew at Mammoth Cave.
Terry Don West Rodeo School: Famous place to learn how to ride bulls, broncos, etc., in the US of course.
Tex Avery: 20th century American animator, cartoonist, voice actor and director, who created Bugs Bunny, Daffy Duck and Droopy, among others, and whose voluptuous cartoon hooker I meet at Xichang/Liangshan, Sichuan.
Third millennium: Means the 22nd century.
Thirty-Six Stratagems (三十六计= *sanshiliu ji*): A set of aphorisms to strategize how to defeat one's enemy.
Thomas Jefferson: 3rd US president, 1801–1809.
Thorazine: powerful psychoactive drug used extensively among mental patients, starting in 1950s
Three Gorges Dam: On the Yangtze River in Sichuan, it's the world's largest power station in terms of installed capacity, 22,500 MW.
Three Pagodas (三塔寺): Dali, Yunnan's iconic postcard image and tourist site.
Three Weird Sisters: Witches from the play *Macbeth*, by Shakespeare.
Tiananmen Square: Ground central in Beijing, where Mao Zedong is buried and has a huge portrait of himself overlooking

the square.
Tianjin: City-province, one of five designated by Baba Beijing: Beijing, Tianjin, Shanghai, Guangzhou and Chongqing. It is an important deep water port and sister city to Beijing.
Tianquan (天全): Sichuan town I pass through from Chengdu to Tagong.
Tibet, the Last Cry: Book by Eric Meyer and Laurent Zylberman.
Tibet: Autonomous Region of China, whose religion and history play a big part in *44 Days*.
Tibetan antelopes (*Pantholops hodgsonii*): Endangered species protected by building raised train tracks and highways, so they can roam the Plateau. Also called Chiru, or *Zanglingyang* (藏羚羊).
Tibetan Book of the Dead: See *Bardo Thodol*.
Tibetan Plateau: The tallest plateau in the world, perched at 3,000 MASL.
Tibet-Pueblo Connection: Credible theory that Tibetans migrated across the Bering Straits over the last 20-30,000 years, helping populate and become Native Americans.
Tiger Lake: One of the splendid lakes at Jiuzhaigou Park, Sichuan.
Tiktaalik: Evolutionary crossover fossil discovered by Neil Shubin and conveniently overlooked by creationists.
Time Machine: 1895 sci-fi thriller by British H.G. Wells, later made into two big screen movies and two for TV.
Tinidazole: Medicine to get rid of giardiasis, actually an anaerobic antibiotic.
Tlingit: A matrilineal people in Alaska.
Tofu: The amazing food product which can be made to look and taste like anything, made by fermenting soybeans.
Tofu-dregs schoolhouses (豆腐渣校舍= *doufuzha jiaoshe*): A derisive term that went viral in China to describe the thousands of poorly constructed schools in Sichuan that collapsed during the 2008 Wenchuan earthquake, slaughtering many thousands of young innocents.
Tom Sawyer: 1876 novel by American Mark Twain, whose character is very mischievous and always playing pranks.
Tomorrow Never Knows: Beatles song on the *Revolver* album that was inspired by the Tibetan Book of the Dead.
Top of the World: A colorful name for Tibet.
Trade settlement: The process of two countries or businesses paying and getting paid across international borders. Right now, the US dollar is still the dominant currency for these transactions, but it is slowly losing its advantage.
Transformers: Japanese-American TV/movie/toy franchise, 1984-2010s, with huge, fantastic robotic machines that can collapse and metamorphosize into everyday objects. I am reminded of them on the wild ride up and down the Liqi River Valley, Sichuan.
Trembler: Synonym for earthquake.
Triassic: Early age of the dinosaurs, 250 to 200 million years ago.
Trillion: 12 zeros = one million million = 1,000,000,000,000.
Tropic of Cancer: 23.5°N of the equator.
Tuaregs: A matrilineal people in Western Africa.
Tube: A British name for subways, along with the French metro.
Tuchengzhen (土城镇): Guizhou town I drive through in the White Horse Mountains, between Zunyi and Chishui.
Turim Basin: Huge desert basin occupying much of Xinjiang Province.
Turkic: A language widely spoken from Turkey across southern Asia, into Xinjiang, China.
Twilight Zone: Famous American TV show, 1959-64, with tales of fantastic science fiction, surrealism, dreams, the bizarre and the macabre; created by Rod Serling and which paralleled my time in Jingtieshan, Gansu.
UFO: unidentified flying object, aliens.
Ulanchaab (乌兰察市): Transit town in Inner Mongolia, on the train ride from Beijing to Yinchuan, Ningxia.
UNESCO: United Nations Educational, Scientific and Cultural Organization.
Unintended consequences: Unexpected, secondary, usually unrelated and often bad things that happen, because of a prior decision or action.
Universal Studios: Hollywood, US, theme park based on famous films, with some similarities to Western Film Studios in

Yinchuan, Yunnan.
University of Oklahoma Press: An American publishing house with many books printed concerning Native Americans.
Upton Sinclair: Early 20th century American investigative journalist, author and political activist, who still has a lot to say about current events and world affairs. He knew exploitation, greed and abuse when he saw it.
Urumuqi: Capital of Xinjiang known for Heavenly Lake (Tianchi) and Glacier No. 1.
US exceptionalism: Concept, started by Alexis de Tocqueville in 1835 and evolving with George W. Bush and Barak Obama claiming that America's unique role in the world affords it the freedom to invade, attack and occupy other countries at its own discretion, for the purposes of maintaining its pre-imminent position as the Planet's sole military and economic superpower.
USSR: Union of Soviet Socialist Republics; see *Soviet Union.*
U-Tsang: Region of the former Kingdom of Tibet.
Van Halen: American rock band, active 1970s-2010s, with flamboyant front man, David Lee Roth.
Vespa: Famous Italian brand motor scooter.
Victor Hugo: 19th century French author who wrote *Les Misérables*, *Hunchback of Notre-Dame*, *Ninety-Three* and countless others. He is actually most admired in France for his poetry.
Victoria Falls: One of the world's greatest natural wonders, along the border between Zimbabwe and Zambia.
Vioxx: American anti-inflammatory drug that killed up to 500,000 victims, and it was all sucked into the Memory Hole by the Princes of Powers, with the active non-participation of a vassal press. Compare this to what happened to the perpetrators in the *melamine* scandal in China.
Votive: Anything offered to seek help from gods and spirits, such as candles, money, food, etc.
Waiguoren (外国人= outside country person): Affectionate term for any foreigner.
Walking marriage (*zouhun* = 走婚): Matrilineal arrangement of the Mosuo people.
Wall Street: Collectively, America's corporate class.
Wang Yuanlu: Early 20th century custodian, who sold away the treasures of Mogao Caves, in Dunhuang, Gansu.
War on Terror: America's campaign of Orwellian Perpetual War on the Muslim World. It started as early as the West providing Saddam Hussein with tons of chemical weapons to attack Iran in the Iraq-Iran War, 1980-88, and in 1990-91 during the Gulf War, with its genocidal economic sanctions thereafter.
Washington consensus: The version of history and current events dictated by the Princes of Power, using Orwellian propaganda methods such as Newspeak and the Memory Hole.
Water Wheel Park: A place in Lanzhou, Gansu, that takes me on a wild goose chase, because of a big error in the Lonely Planet Guide.
Watergate: Scandal that brought down Richard Nixon's presidency in 1974.
Wehrmacht: German for *war force*.
Weibo (微波): Chinese Twitter.
Weijin Tombs: In Gansu.
Weimar Republic: German government succeeded by Hitler's National Socialist German Workers' Party in the 30s.
Weining (威宁): Guizhou town right next to the miserable Caohai Bird Sanctuary.
Wenchuan (汶川): Epicenter of the horrific 2008.5.12 earthquake, in Sichuan.
West Coast: In the US, the states of California, Oregon and Washington State.
Western Empire: This part of the Roman Empire lasted 27 BC–AD 476, then collapsed.
Western Film Studios: Famous movie studio in Yinchuan, Ningxia, where *Red Sorghum* was made. It has some similarities to Universal Studios, in Hollywood.
White Album: 1968 Beatles album that originally showed John Lennon and his wife, Yoko Ono, standing naked on the front cover. It was quickly censored and Capitol Records took to repackaging them with plain white covers, hence, it stayed the *White Album*.
White Dragon River (白龙河): Amazing 24km hike I take to find its source, while having lunch in the Tibetan tent of Hong

Bei, Langmusi, Gansu.
White Horse Mountains (白马山= Baimashan): Miao minority valley between Zunyi and Chishui, Guizhou, which figures largely in Long March lore.
White Temple: Not so great temple, but I do get to have a nice conversation with a Buddhist nun and ride a zip line, Lanzhou. Gansu.
Wild South: A name I give to the lawless early days of 80s-90s China, especially Shenzhen.
Wild West: The lawless 19th century, west of the Mississippi River, US.
Wild yaks (*Bos grunniens*): Endangered species for which Baba Beijing is building raised train tracks and highways, so these animals can continue to roam the Tibetan Plateau.
Williamsburg, Virginia: American historical theme park, which I think of while at Western Film Studios in Yinchuan, Gansu.
Wind horse: Tibetan prayer banners that function as a national flag, and which I learn much about in Tagong, Sichuan.
Winston Churchill: 20th century British politician and leader, who was the UK's prime minister during WWII.
Wolong Falls: A beautiful cascade in Jiuzhaigou Park, Sichuan.
Wonderland: As in, *Alice in*
Woodstock: 1969 New York outdoor rock concert, which was loud and proud.
World Heritage Culture Site: Natural, cultural and historical places registered by UNESCO.
World Trade Organization: Body that arbitrates and lobbies for minimal tariffs and subsidies to help stimulate international trade.
WPA: 1930s Great Depression era Works Progress Administration in the US.
WTO: See World Trade Organization.
Wuhai (乌海): Inner Mongolian town I pass through on the train ride from Beijing to Yinchuan, Ningxia.
Wuzhiluo (五支罗): Lugu Lake village on the Sichuan side.
WWII: World War II, 1939-45. Over 60 million people were killed, which was over 2.5% of the world population.
WWIII: World War III, my prediction is it will start in the Middle East, with Israel and its 200+ undeclared nuclear warheads starting the fire. Lord Arnold Toynbee knew what he was talking about.
Xi'an (西安): Capital of Shaanxi province, famous for the Terra Cota Soldiers.
Xiaguan (大理城-下关= Lower Connection): One of the names for Dali, Yunnan.
Xiahe (夏河= Summer River): Gansu town with the Tibetan Labrang Temples.
Xiang River: In Hunan Province, where the Red Army lost 40,000 men at the start of the Long March.
Xiaowutai Mountain (小五台), Hebei Province's tallest peak.
Xiaoyuba (小鱼坝= Little Fish Dam), Lugu Lake village on the Yunnan side, where I see the *Felis* skins for sale.
Xichang (西昌= Western Prosperity): Sichuan city with the Communist Food Party restaurant, Dream Sea condoms and a Tex Avery hooker.
Xinduqiao (新都桥): A town near Kangding, in Sichuan.
Xinhua Meiri Dianxun (新华每日电讯) and Xinhuawang (新华网): Chinese press agencies I learn about at the Yinchuan Provincial Museum, Ningxia.
Xining (西宁): Capital of Qinghai Province, known for the Sun and Moon Mountain, Qinghai Lake and Bird Island.
Xinjiang (新疆): Large Muslim Autonomous Region in Northwest China, famous for the Silk Road town of Kashgar and the 7,000m Tianshan Mountains, among countless natural wonders.
Xishuangbanna: Yunnan town near Myanmar border.
Xixia Tombs: First place visited during *44 Days*,Yinchuan. Gotta start someplace.
Xuanwei (宣威), Guizhou town I pass through and where a dapper old man tries to pickpocket me.
Xuehua (雪花= Snow Flower Beer Company): Very popular beer brand and whose CEO I meet on a Yellow River raft at Shapotou, Ningxia.
X : A 2-lane highway on the wild ride between Zunyi and Chishui, Guizhou.

Ya'an (雅安= elegant peace): Town passed through driving from Chengdu to Tagong, Sichuan.
Yabba Dabba Doo: Flintstones TV cartoon shout given out by Fred Flintstone when he is happy or excited.
Yadan National Park (雅丹= Elegant Red): Outside of Dunhuang, Gansu, the site of a huge extraterrestrial desert topography.
Yaks: Bovine animals a bit of a cross between cattle and bisons, which are indigenous to Tibet.
Yangtze River: Asia's longest river dividing China north and south, with its headwaters in Qinghai.
Yanshan (燕山= Swallow Mountains), Mountains surrounding Beijing, in Hebei Province.
Yarlung Tsangpo River: The highest major river in the world, descending from 4,500m to 3,000m across Tibet.
Ye Zhihua: Artist friend I meet at the July 1st Glacier, Gansu.
Yellow Hat: Tibetan Gelugpa sect.
Yellow Provinces: See *interior provinces*.
Yellow River (黄河= Huanghe), Second longest river in Asia, with its headwaters in Qinghai, this ancient river runs across northern China.
Yellowstone Park: Famous national park in Wyoming, US.
Yen: Japan's currency.
Yes: British rock band, active 1960s-2010s, with celebrated album covers depicting fantastic exoplanet landscapes and floating rocks, like in the movie *Avatar*.
Yi (彝族): Minority concentrated in Yunnan, southern Sichuan and Northwestern Guizhou.
Yili Dairy Company (伊利): Inner Mongolian group caught up in the melamine-tainted milk scandal.
Yinchuan (银川= Silver River): Ningxia's capital, famous for the Xixia Tombs, Western Film Studios and the Helan Rock Carvings.
Yosemite National Park: Famous park in California, US.
Yuan (元): Everyday term for China's currency unit, the RMB.
Yuan Dynasty: 1271–1368AD, led by the family of Genghis Khan. It was run with all the efficiency and statecraft expected of the Khans, thus honoring the Heavenly Mandate, but finally fell apart with famine and popular dissatisfaction.
Yumenguan National Park (玉门关= Jade Gate Pass): Outside of Dunhuang and where I see the 2,100 year old, mud and thatch, Song Dynasty Great Wall, that is little taller than me and not as wide.
Yungang Caves (云冈石窟): Near Taiyuan, Shanxi Province, and which can be compared to Mogao Caves, Dunhuang, Gansu.
Yunnan Province (云南): The amazingly beautiful, subtropical Chinese province, which figures large in *44 Days*, including Lugu Lake, Dali, Lijiang and Kunming.
Zeiss: High quality binoculars, sought after by bird watchers and astronomers, and whose top line is still made in Germany.
Zhangjiakou (张家口): City in northern Hebei Province I pass through on the train from Beijing to Yinchuan, Ningxia.
Zhaodaisuo (招待所): A cheap Chinese hotel that is officially off limits to foreigners.
Zhaxi: Tibetan taxi driver who takes me around Tagong, Sichuan.
Zhejiang: South of Shanghai, this historically important province has as its capital, Hangzhou and Taishan, a Zen Buddhist mountain.
Zheng He (郑和): Early 15th century Chinese explorer whose armadas traveled to Africa and the Middle East, two generations before Columbus and infinitely superior in technology.
Zhijin (织金): Guizhou town, with its namesake, world class cave.
Zhijin Cave: Near Zhijin Guizhou, it is China's largest grotto and one of the best in the world to visit.
Zhongdian: Far northern Yunnan town, adopted name of Shangri-La with great commercial success.
Zhonghesi (中和寺= Central Peace Temple): Lonely, rundown temple atop the Cangshan Mountains, Dali, Yunnan.
Zhongshan (Bridge): First bridge built across the Yellow River in 1909, in Lanzhou, Gansu.
Zhongwei (中卫): Nice town near Shapotou, and which I visit with Xiao Gao, in Ningxia.
Zhou Enlai (周恩来): Mao Zedong's right hand man, who saved many priceless sites from Cultural Revolution Red Guards.

Zhoumogongban: Never found place recommended by Mama Ala in Tagong, Sichuan.
Zhu "Meng" Biying: Teacher friend met at Dunhuang, Gansu, and with whom I climbed a massive sand dune.
Zip line (飞行挂索= *feixing guasuo*): A cable used to ride sitting in a harness and slowly descending over a river or rugged expanse of land, in Shapotou, Ningxia and Lanzhou, Gansu.
Zoige (若尔盖= Ruo'ergai): Sichuan town full of line cutting Tibetan monks, on the way from Langmusi to Songpan, Sichuan.
Zunghar: From Xinjiang, invaded Tibet in 18th century.
Zunyi (遵义): Guiyang city famous as the site of the Communist Zunyi Conference in 1935, which put Mao Zedong at the head of Communist Red Army.

Part XI

Chinese Pronunciation and Name Guide

Rules of the Road: Work

"Choose a job you love, and you will never have to work a day in your life."
Confucius

"Nothing will work unless you do."
Maya Angelou

"The French work to live and Americans (or Swiss) live to work."
French proverb

Chinese Pronunciation and Name Guide

Pinyin	English Equivalent
Baba Beijing	Bah-bah Bay-jeeng
Bai	Bay
Baidu	Bay-doo
Baifan	Bay-fan
Baijiu	Bay-jee-you
Baisikou Twin Pagodas	Bay-sih-kow shuh-wang tay
Bamboo Sea	Jzu-hay
Bang Kao	Bahng Kaow
Baoche	Bow-chuh
Baotou	Bow-toe
Baozi	Bow-zuh
Beijing	Bay-jeeng
Bo Gu	Bow Goo
Bo Xilai	Bow Shee-lay
Cairen Zhuoma	Tsay-jzen Jhew-ooh-ma
Cangshan	Tsaang-shaan
Caobao	Tsaow-baow
Caohai	Tsaow-khey
Changzheng	Chaang-Jhung
Chaocuoyu	Chow-tswoo-oh-you
Chaofan	Chow-fan
Chayedan	Chaa-yeh-dan
Chengdu	Chung-dew
Chiku	Chuh-koo
Chishui	Chuh-shwee
Chongqing	Chohng-cheeng
Chongsheng Temple	Chong-shung-sih
Dabizi	Dah-bee-zuh
Daduhe	Dah-doo-khuh
Dagege	Dah-guh-guh
Dahuaxiyou	Dah-khwah-shee-yow
Dajiejie	Dah-jee-yeah-jee-yeah
Dali	Dah-lee
Dali City	Dah-lee-chung
Danxia	Dan-shee-ya
Daoxiao	Dow-shee-aow
Daxia River	Dah-shee-ya Khuh
Daxue	Dah-Shuh-way
Dazibao	Dah-zuh-baow
Dazixiang	Dah-zuh-shee-yang
Deng Xiaoping	Dung Shee-ow-ping
Dianchi	Dee-an-chuh
Doufuzha jiaoshe	Doe-foo-jha jee-aow shih

Dunhuang	Dwenn-khuh-wang
Erhai Lake	Urr-khay Khoo
Erhu	Urr-khoo
Fahao	Fah-khaow
Fanqie chaodan	Fan-chee-ay chaow-dan
Feixing guasuo	Fay-sheeng gwah-swoah
Feng	Fung
Fengxi River	Fung-shee Khuh
Ganbanmian	Gaan-baan-mee-an
Ganbei	Gaan-bay
Ganhaizi	Gaan-khay-zuh
Gansu	Gaan-sue
Ge	Guh
Gemu	Guh-moo
Gongga	Gong-gah
Gongquhu	Gawng-choo-khoo
Gu Kailai	Goo Kay-lay
Guangdong	Gwaang-dawng
Guanguan jiaozi	Gwaan-gwaan jee-aow-zuh
Guangxi	Gwaang-shee
Guiyang	Gwee-yang
Guizhou	Gwee-joe
Haochidian	Khaow-chuh-dee-an
Hebei	Khuh-bay
Helanshang Rock Carvings	Khuh-lan-shaan Yaan-khwaah
Hexi Zoulang	Khuh-shee Zow-lang
Hohot	Khoo-khuh-khow-tuh
Hong Bei	Khong-bay
Hongjun	khongjun
Hongkao qiezi	Khong-kaow chee-ay-zuh
Hongshao shucai	Khong-shaow shoo-tsay
Hongshi Yegu	Khong-shuh Yeah-goo
Huajiao	Khuh-wah Jee-yaow
Huangguoshu	Khuh-wang goo-ow-shoo
Huanghe	Khuh-wang-khuh
Huanglong	Khwaang-laawng
Huangmian	Khuh-wang mee-an
Huangtu	Khuh-wang-too
Hui	Khuh-wee
Hukou	Khoo-kow
Hunan	Khoo-naan
Jiabo	Gee-ah-bow
Jialing	Gee-ah-leeng
Jiang Jiashi	Jee-yang Jee-yah-shuh
Jiang Qing	Jee-yang Cheeng

Jiang Zhongzheng	Jee-yang Jong-jung
Jianzhi	Jee-an-juh
Jiao	Jee-aow
Jiayou Jiefu	Jee-yah-yow Jee-ay-foo
Jiayuguan	Gee-ah-you-gwaan
Jingtieshan	Jeeng-tee-ay-shaan
Jinshagou	Jeean-shah-goh
Jinyang	Jean-yang
Jiulonggou	Jee-you-long-goh
Jiuzhaigou	Jee-you-jay-goh
Jiuzhi	Jee-ew-jzuh
Kaishui	Kay-shwee
Kangding	Kang-ding
Kuai	Kuh-why
KUAI YI DI'ER	KWAY-EEE-DEE-ER
Kunming	Kwin-meeng
Labrang Temple	Lah-boo-lang Sih
Laduzi	La-doo-zuh
Langmusi	Lahng-moo-suh
Lanzhou	Lan-joe
Lao Pu	Lao-poo
Laojia	Laow-jee-ya
Laowai	Lao-way
Li De	Lee Duh
Liang	Lee-ang
Liangmian	Lee-yang mee-an
Liangshan	Lee-yang-shan
Lijiang	Lee-jee-yang
Lin Biao	Lean Bee-ow
Linxia	Lean-shee-ya
Liqi	Lee-chee
Lise	Lee-sih
Liuchong	Lee-you-chong
Liudong renkou	Lee-yew-dong jen-kow
Liupanshui	Lee-you-pan-shuh-wee
Liwubi	Lee-woo-bee
Luding	Loo-ding
Luguhu	Loo-goo-khoo
Luguxian	Loo-goo-shee-an
Luoshui	Lew-oh-shuh-wee
Luowa	Loo-oh-wah
Mahjong	Ma-joong
Majiao	Ma-jee-ow
Mao	Maow
Mao Zedong	Maow Zuh-dong
Maotai	Maow-tie

Meili	May-lee
Meiyou	May-yo
Meiyou banfa	May-yo ban-fah
Meng	Mung
Mengniu	Mung-nee-ooo
Mianpian	Mee-an pee-an
Min	Mean
Min Mountains	Mean-shaan
Mingshi	Ming-shuh
Mingtian jian	Ming-tee-an jee-an
Mosuo	Mow-sue-oh
Muyajin	Moo-yah-jean
Nayong	Nah-yoong
Neimeng	Nay-meng
Ni bu qu le	Nee boo choo luh
Ni shi jiu hao ma	Nee shuh jee-yew khaow ma
Nin	Neen
Ningxia	Neeng-shee-ah
Nuorilang	New-oh jzi-lang
Nvshenwan	New-shin-waan
Old Town	Goo-chung
Ouigher	Wee-gurr
Paichusuo	Pay-choo-swoo-oh
Paoma Mountain	Paow-ma-shaan
Pashou	Pah-show
Peichang	Pay-chang
Peng Zhaozhi	Pung Jaow-juh
Pinche	Peen-chuh
Qie	Chee-ay
Qiezi	Chee-aye-zuh
Qiliqiaoxiang	Chee-lee-chee-aow-shee-yang
Qin Shihuang	Cheen Shuh-khuh-wang
Qing ting che zher	Ching-ting-chuh-jurr
Qinghai	Cheeng-khay
Qingke	Cheeng-kuh
Qingling Park	Cheeng-leeng Gong-you-wan
Qingyi River	Cheeng-eee Jee-yang
Qiqing	Chee-cheeng
Qiyi Bingquan	Chee-eee Bing-tchwaan
Qujing	Choo-jeeng
Ren Xiaode	Jzen Shee-aow-duh
Renminbi	Jzen-men-bee
Rizegou	Jzi-zuh-go
Sanlu	Saan-loo
Shaanxi	Shuh-an-shee
Shade	Shah-duh

Shaguo tuji	Shah-gwow too-jee
Shapotou	Shah-pow-toe
Sharengang	Shah-jzen-gaang
Shenfenzhen	Shin-fin-gin
Shijiazhuang	Shuh-jee-yah-jew-wang
Shizhangdong	Shuh-jzang-dong
Shuhe	Shoo-khuh
Shuixing Yanghua	Shuh-wee-sheeng Yang-khwah
Shuizhu huasheng	Shwee-jhew khwa-shung
Si	Sih
Sichuan	Sih-chwan
Siheyuan	Suh-khuh-yew-wahn
Song	Sawng
Songpan	Song-pan
Suyukou	Sue-you-kow
Tagong	Tah-gong
Tang	Taahng
Tao River	Taow Khuh
Tian'e Hu	Tee-an-uh Khoo
Tianming	Tee-an-ming
Tianquan	Tee-an-choo-wan
Tonghao	Tawng-khaow
Tongshi	Tawng-shuh
Tuchengzhen	Two cheng jen
Ulanchaab	Ooo-lahn-cha-shh
Waiguoren	Way-gwow-jen
Wan'an	Wuh-an ahn
Wang Yuanlu	Waang You-an-loo
Wangdaping	Waang-dah-ping
Wangfeidao	Waang Fay-dow
Wansui	Won-swee
Wei Hongwei	Way Khong-way
Weibo	Way-bow
Weijin	Way-jean
Weining	Way-ning
Wencheng	Win-chung
Wenchuan	Win-chew-wahn
Wending	Win-ding
Western Film Studios	Jen-bay-bow Shee-boo-chung
White Dragon River	Bay-long-khuh
White Horse Mountains	Bay-ma-shaan
Wo bu hui chang ger, xiexie	Woah boo khwee chaang gher, shee-ay shee-ay
Wo bu neng xiangxin ni zenme zisi zili	Woah boo nung shee-yang-sheen nee zen-mah zuh-suh zuh-lee
Wo ZHEN bu zhidao	Woah JEN boo juh-dow
Wu	Woo

Wu zuowei	Woo-zuh-woah way
Wuhai	Woo-khay
Wuzhiluo	Woo-jzhuh-loo-oh
Xiaguan	Shee-ah-gwaan
Xiahe	Shee-ah-khuh
Xi'an	Shee-an
Xiang	Shee-yaang
Xianggu chaorou	Shee-yang-goo chaow-jzoe
Xiangsuanjiang	Shee-yang-suh-won-jee-yang
Xiannvshan	Shee-an-new-shaan
Xiao Gao	Shee-ow Gow
Xiao Wei	Shee-ow Way
Xiaowutai	Shee-aow-woo-tay
Xiaoyuba	Shee-aow-you-bah
Xichang	Shee-chang
Xihongshi jidan banmian	Shee-khong-shuh gee-dan ban-mee-an
Xinduqiao	Sheen-doo-chee-yao
Xinhua Meiri Dianxun	Sheen-khwah Mayjuh Dee-an-schwin
Xinhuawang	Sheen-khuh-wah-wang
Xining	Shee-neeng
Xishuangbanna	Shee-schwaang-bah-nah
Xixia Tombs	Shee-shee-yah Wang-leeng
Xuanwei	Shu-wan-wai
Xuehua	Shew-ay-khuh-wah
Ya'an	Yah-an
Yadan	Yah-dan
Yancaisi	Yaan-tsay-sih
Yang	Yaang
Yanshan	Yaan-shaan
Yi tribe	Eee-zoo
YI! ER! SAN! SI	EEE-URR-SAAN-SUH
Yili	Eee-lee
Yilu ping'an	Eee-loo peeng-an
Yinchuan	Yeen-chew-wan
You	Yow
Youcai	Yoah-tsay
Youjian	Yow-jee-an
Yuan	You-waan
Yulong Xueshan	You-long Shuh-way-shaan
Yulu	Yew-loo
Yumen	You-men
Yumenguan	You-men-gwaan
Yungang Caves	Yew-when-gaang Shuh-koo
Yunnan	Yew-win-nan
Yuxiang rousi	Yew-shee-yang jzew-oh-suh
Zanglingyang	Zaang-leeng-yang

Zhang	Djaang
Zhangjiakou	Jang-gee-ah-kow
Zhaodaisuo	Jaow-day-swoo-oh
Zhende	Jen-duh
Zheng He	Jung Khuh
Zhijin	Djuh-jean
Zhonghesi	Jong-khuh-sih
Zhongwei	Jong-way
Zhou	Joe
Zhou Enlai	Joe In-lye
Zhouyi Xiuxi	Joe-eee Shee-yoo-shee
Zoige	Jzew-oh-urr-gay
Zouba	Zoow-bah
Zouhun	Zow-khwin
Zunyi	Zwin-eee

Part XII

Acknowledgements

Rules of the Road: History

"To remain ignorant of things that happened before you were born is to remain a child."
Cicero

"An account mostly false, of events mostly unimportant, which are brought about by rulers, mostly knaves, and soldiers, mostly fools."
Ambrose Bierce

"To forget one's ancestors is to be a brook without a source, a tree without a root."
Chinese proverb

Acknowledgements

I would first like to thank my father's inspiration. He has written four excellent novels, but because he is not in a position to jump through all the corporate hoops demanded now by the bottom line, bean counting book industry, he can't get any takers.

My wife, Florence and younger daughter, Chara were indulgent enough to let me go tearing off across the Chinese countryside alone for six weeks and encouraged me upon my return, as an inchoate, very rough draft of a blog slowly coalesced into *44 Days*.

Annette Oevermann, Dirk Meyers, Florence Langlois and Chara Brown in Beijing, and Howard Helmer and Tom Arsenault in NYC were all nice enough to read early version chapters of *44 Days*, and offered very helpful, critical advice. They all inspired me to go back and seriously revamp the book in a constructive fashion. Dirk and another friend, Chad Bryant critiqued the book cover.

Eric Meyer, whose success and knowledge as a journalist and writer about China, has been an inspiration for years.

John Pomfret, with the Washington Post, has been very kind in offering me professional advice about the realities of today's book publishing industry and putting me into contact with people in the business. His book, *Chinese Lessons*, was also an informative inspiration while writing *44 Days*.

Pete Spurrier at Blacksmith Publishing in Hong Kong, has been very encouraging, reading some chapters and also helped me with publishing contacts.

Gail Ross, of Ross Yoon literary agency, had very nice words about a (very) rough draft chapter she read, helping me realize I had more than just a blog on my hands.

Steven Evans for his worldwide traveling inspiration. He is surely on the road, as I write.

Ma Jian, the author of *Red Dust*, whose amazing and gripping account of backpacking across China, while putting it all in sociopolitical and historical context, helped me envisage the unique format of 44 Days: report on China, but turn the tables and also put my ancestral homes, the United States and Europe, in parallel perspective.

I read Alexis de Tocqueville's socio-political masterpiece, *Democracy in America*, when I was an impressionable teenager, and it continues to influence my thinking. The way he observed and commented on American society in 1835 had a huge impact on developing the style and format of *44 Days*.

Dr. Paul Craig Roberts, who read through a chapter dealing with currencies and central banks, to make sure it was not totally inaccurate.

Sally in Tagong for helping me decipher Tibetan symbols and explaining the lay of the land in Tagong.

An anonymous Tibetan Culture professor who educated me about the symbols and language on Top of the World.

Bernard Terminet Schuppon was a tireless researcher and discovered the identity of the *Felis silvestris* animal skins being sold at Lugu Lake.

Donald Lyngdoh, whose real life education growing up in a matrilineal culture, made my visit with Lugu Lake's Mosuo people that much more meaningful.

Chara Brown and Roland Chen for creating their and my first book cover. Ah…The enthusiasm of youth.

Joanna Zhou, who saved me a ton of time and effort by translating the statue sign plaque in Jiayuguan and the signs at the Western Film Studio's Cultural Revolution screen set.

And last but not least, my book editor, John Chan, who, when presented with what I thought was the finished book, guided me from the first page to the last, wearing me out with many hundreds of insightful comments, observations and blunt criticisms from the viewpoint of the reading public. He confirmed Ernest Hemingway's great empirical observation that, *The first draft of anything is s**t.* So true. I could not imagine publishing *44 Days* without John's eagle eyes and detached judgment.
johnchanaway@yahoo.co.uk.

PART XIII

ABOUT THE AUTHOR

Rules of the Road: Culture

"As one digs deeper into the national character of the Americans, one sees that they have sought the value of everything in this world only in the answer to this single question:
how much money will it bring in?"
Alexis de Tocqueville (1835)

"Going into a country the first time, ask what is forbidden; on entering a village, ask what the customs are; on entering a private house, ask what should not be mentioned."
Chinese proverb

"I am not an Athenian or a Greek, but a citizen of the world."
Socrates

About the Author

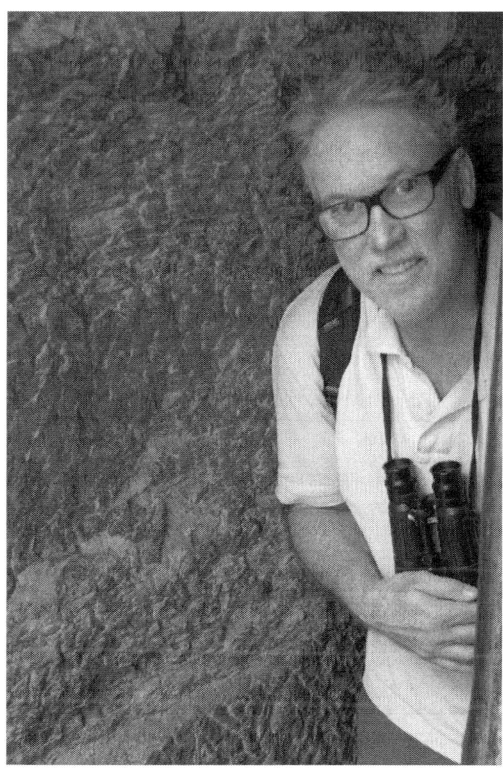

Jeff grew up in the heartland of the United States, Oklahoma, and went to Brazil while in graduate school to seek his fortune, which whet his appetite for traveling the globe. This helped inspire him to be a Peace Corps Volunteer in Tunisia in 1980 and he lived and worked in Africa, the Middle East, China and Europe for the next 21 years. He then returned to the America for nine years, whereupon he moved back to China in 2010. He currently lives in Beijing with his wife and younger daughter, where he is an elementary school teacher in an international school.

PART XIV

INDEX

Rules of the Road: Food

"Ask not what you can do for your country. Ask what's for lunch."
Orson Welles

"Everything you see I owe to spaghetti."
Sophia Loren

"Sour, sweet, bitter, pungent, all must be tasted."
Chinese proverb

Index

Made in the USA
Middletown, DE
15 February 2015